A Cruising Guide to the
NORTHEAST'S

THE HUDSON RIVER,

INLAND

NEW YORK STATE CANALS, LAKE ONTARIO,

WATERWAYS

ST. LAWRENCE SEAWAY, LAKE CHAMPLAIN

Marian, Thomas W., and W. J. Rumsey

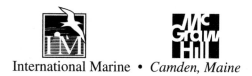

International Marine • *Camden, Maine*

Published by International Marine®

10   9   8   7   6   5   4   3   2   1

Library of Congress Cataloging-in-Publication Data
Rumsey, Marian
      A cruising guide to the northeast's inland waterways : the Hudson
River, New York State canals, Lake Ontario, St. Lawrence Seaway, Lake
Champlain / Marian, Thomas W., and W.J. Rumsey.
            p.   cm.
    Includes index.
    ISBN 0-07-158011-5
    1. Inland navigation—Northeastern States—Guidebooks.
2. Marinas—Northeastern States—Guidebooks. 3. Northeastern
States—Guidebooks. 4. Inland navigation—Canada, Eastern—
Guidebooks. 5. Marinas—Canada, Eastern—Guidebooks. 6. Canada,
Eastern—Guidebooks. I. Rumsey, Thomas W. II. Rumsey, W. J.
III. Title.
GV776.N75R86   1995
797.1'0974—dc20   94-27926
                                         CIP

Questions regarding the content of this book should be addressed to:
International Marine
P.O. Box 220
Camden, ME 04843

Questions regarding the ordering of this book should be addressed to:
McGraw-Hill, Inc.
Customer Service Department
P.O. Box 547
Blacklick, OH 43004
Retail customers: 1-800-822-8158
Bookstores: 1-800-722-4726

 A Cruising Guide to the Northeast's Inland Waterways is printed on 60-pound Renew Opaque Vellum, an acid-free paper that contains 50 percent recycled waste paper (preconsumer) and 10 percent postconsumer waste paper.

Printed by R.R. Donnelley, Harrisonburg, VA
Design by John Reinhardt
Production by Molly Mulhern and Dan Kirchoff
Edited by James R. Babb, Dorathy Chocensky, and Pamela Benner

*This book is dedicated to the States of New York and Vermont
and the Provinces of Ontario and Quebec.*

They made these cruising areas enjoyable.

Contents

Region 1
THE HUDSON RIVER

Region 2
THE ERIE, OSWEGO, AND CAYUGA AND SENECA CANALS, AND CAYUGA AND SENECA LAKES

Region 3
THE UPPER NIAGARA RIVER, EAST END LAKE ERIE, AND THE WELLAND CANAL

Region 6
RIVIERE RICHELIEU, THE CHAMBLY CANAL,
LAKE CHAMPLAIN, AND THE CHAMPLAIN CANAL

Preface

This guide presents one of our favorite cruising areas in the Northeast: the Hudson River, the New York State Barge Canal System, Lake Ontario, the Thousand Islands, the St. Lawrence Seaway, a portion of the St. Lawrence River east of Montreal, the Richelieu River, the Chambly Canal, and Lake Champlain. It includes open water, protected inland river cruising, and canalling. There are outstanding cities, historical canal ports, rocky islands with quiet coves, charming waterfront villages, and unspoiled wooded lowlands.

We provide tidbits of each region's history and point out what to see and do along the way. We try to tempt everyone to venture into the next system to enjoy new horizons.

We want to make cruising this area pleasant for a family. Our clear instructions and accompanying sketch maps will help you locate more than 90 safe, proven anchorages and over 200 marinas and nonmarina dockage areas with a comfortable average distance between ports of about 15 to 25 miles.

We answer the questions that we asked our first time in these areas: "What am I going to see?" "What is the most enjoyable time of year and when will the weather be best?" "What restrictions govern navigation?" "What are the best routes of travel?" "How do I find lock and bridge statistics?" "What charts do I need and where do I buy them?"

This guide encompasses an area that still retains an easy attitude toward the boating public, unlike many East Coast areas. When you cruise here, you feel welcome.

How to Use This Book

Cruising canals and rivers differs from cruising coastal or offshore ocean or lake waters. In "Enjoying the Area" (pages 6–19) and the Appendixes (pages 412–416) we discuss river and canal knowledge, currents, height and depth restrictions, locks, bridges, water levels, adjusting charted depths, and regional topics on navigation, weather, communications, customs, transit fees, anchoring, and getting help, supplies, and services. We suggest you read these sections before you set off on your journey.

FINDING YOUR WAY

This book is divided into six regions (see map on page 2), each preceded by a regional map. The regions are subdivided into smaller geographical sections, each with a locating map. Some sections are divided into parts; most of these, too, have a locating map. All are listed in the Contents.

Each region has its own mile numbering system bearing a prefix of the region or section. Some regions and sections have offshoot systems; these are numbered separately.

Each numbering system has a starting point. We have endeavored to follow the mileage system generally used in a particular region by commercial vessels and found on government charts and in *Coast Pilots, Sailing Directions,* and associated publications. Not all numbering systems in this guide read in the usual manner of heading upstream.

In each region or section we note which mileage scale—**Nautical Mileage (NM)** or **Statute Mileage (SM)**—is in use. In the past, Statute Mileage was the standard throughout this guide area. Some sections have begun the Nautical Mile–scale conversion process; this has resulted in a confusing and conflicting combination of both. Eventually the conversion to Nautical Miles will be complete; meanwhile, we use the mile measurement most commonly found in the area.

Mileage markers appear in bold type, like this: **Mile AONT-16.2 (NM).** (AONT stands for American Shore of Lake Ontario.) They may also include a bank side (**E,**

W, N, S) for quick reference. A (+) symbol [**Mile AONT-32.7 + (NM)**] means the additional distance to the anchorage is approximate and determined from the middle of the navigational channel. Magnetic compass directions are approximate and intended only to point you in a general direction. Once you have located your destination, plot a compass course.

ANCHORAGES, MARINAS, AND NONMARINA DOCKAGE

Every anchorage, marina, or nonmarina dockage area has a mileage number as well as a name. To find a particular place to stop, check Appendixes 6 and 7 for anchorages, marinas, and nonmarina dockage, listed by mile and alphabetically. To find a layover in a particular area, consult that region's section map and look for a suitable stop. You'll find detailed information and a sketch map for your choice in the section's anchorage text.

Read anchorage, marina, or nonmarina dockage information as if you are traveling in that particular region as described in the text. If you are heading in the opposite direction, make appropriate adjustments.

Often the number of marinas available in a small area is astounding. We have listed only those that expressed interest in accepting vacationing and traveling sail and power vessels for overnight accommodations. We have visited each one and have included only those with friendly dock staff who offered courteous treatment to visitors.

Occasionally our selection of a place to stay is based on its convenience to town and local attractions.

We have not included the cost of dockage, as it's perishable information that often varies even during the season. Highest rates are from June 1 to September 1; higher rates may be charged on holidays. Canadian and American dockage rates are usually about the same. Due to its tax system, the average Ontario dockage rate is slightly higher than in New York, Quebec, and Vermont.

We do not note admission fees for shoreside special activities. These vary annually. Most have a modest fee.

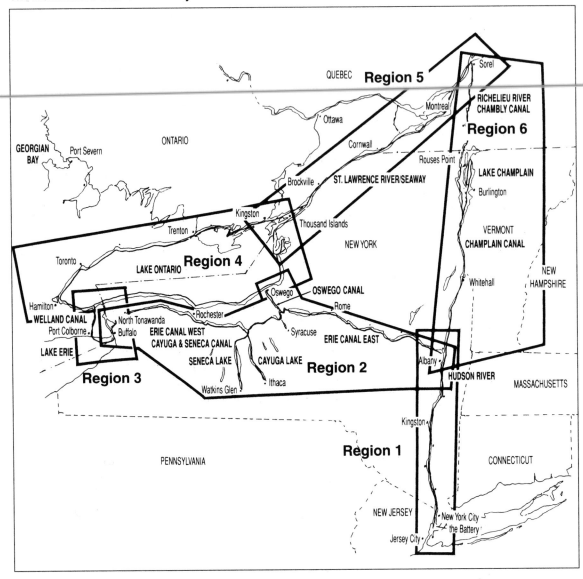

During the popular cruising season dockage space in certain areas can be difficult to find. If slips are in great demand, a seasonal dockage time limit usually is in effect. Reservations at Canadian and American parks generally are on a first-come first-served basis. Private marinas in popular areas are also very busy, but most accept reservations.

The New York State Barge Canal System has many commercial terminals rarely used by commerce; they are available for free dockage. Some commercial terminals have been improved by canalside towns; a few of

them charge a small fee for overnight.

Canadian Public Docks almost always charge an overnight fee.

Ratings

Anchorages, marinas, and nonmarina dockage are rated for Beauty and Interest, Protection, and Facilities. Beauty and Interest for the marinas and nonmarina dockage facilities are rated for the surrounding areas; they are not suggestive of the stop's quality, facilities, or services offered. A rundown marina or tie-up in a jewel-like setting with nearby attractions is thus rated higher than a modern, everything-at-the-docks marina situated in pedestrian surroundings.

Beauty and Interest

★★★★★ Extremely beautiful or interesting. Not to be missed.

★★★★ Very pretty or interesting. Worth going out of your way.

★★★ Attractive or interesting.

★★ Nothing special but still pleasant.

★ Not very attractive.

Protection

5 Best protection available. Excellent anchorage.

4 Well protected in most wind conditions. Very good anchorage.

3 Well protected for most regional prevailing winds. Good protection.

2 Reasonably protected under most conditions except violent thunderstorms or severe frontal passage. Fair anchorage.

1 Exposed in two or more directions with a good chance a vessel must move in severe weather. Poor anchorage.

✕ Open anchorage; no protection. Possible lunch stop only.

Facilities

Note: If an anchorage has slips and/or moorings, fuel, repairs, ice, and groceries, we have not listed facilities symbols but have designated that anchorage as having "All facilities."

 Slip (may include mooring)

 Fuel (gas, diesel, or both)

 Repairs

 Pumpout

 Laundromat

 Shower

 Ice (block, cube, or both)

Groceries within 0.5 mile

Restaurant and/or snacks within 0.5 mile

NO FACILITIES

CHARTS

Use this book as a supplement to official United States National Oceanic and Atmospheric Administration (NOAA), National Ocean Service (NOS), and Canadian Hydrographic Service (CHS) charts, and their assorted publications.

For convenience we list chart numbers as if a person plans to travel only one region's section. If you plan to cruise more than one area, be certain to double-check your list so as not to purchase similar charts.

In many instances when Canadian and American charts overlap, we list both. If we feel one of these charts has more detail than the other, we tell you in the chart list and the text.

Note: **N** = NOS; **C** = CHS; **m** = metric chart; **c** = Loran C chart.

Region 1

The Hudson River South
    N 12335
    N 12341
    N 12343
    N 12347

The Hudson River North
    N 12347
    N 12348
    N 14786 (booklet)

Region 2

The Erie Canal East, the Oswego Canal, the Erie Canal West*, the Cayuga and Seneca Canal, Cayuga Lake, and Seneca Lake
    N 14786 (booklet)
    *Chart unavailable Lyons, **Mile E-219.7 (SM),** to North Tonawanda, **Mile E-330.2 (SM)**

Region 3

Tonawanda to Port Colborne
    N 14832
    N 14833
    N 14822

The Welland Canal
    C 2042 **(m)**

Region 4

Lake Ontario, American Shore
    N 14815
    N 14806 **(c)**
    N 14805 **(c)**
    N 14804 **(c)**
    N 14811
    N 14814
    N 14803 **(c)**
    N 14802 **(c)**
    N 14800 **(c)**/C 2000
    N 14768/C 2017
    N 14816
    N 14813 (included in N 14786 [booklet], page 0-1)

Lake Ontario, Canadian Shore
    C 2031
    C 2077 **(cm)**
    C 2070
    C 2085 **(m)**
    N 14816/C 2043
    N 14800 **(c)**/C 2000
    C 2050 **(m)**
    C 2064
    C 2069
    C 2011 **(m)**
    C 2054 **(m)**
    C 2006
    C 2007

    C 2058
    C 2067 **(m)**
    C 2048
    C 2086
    C 2061

Region 5

The Thousand Islands
NOS charts are recommended for best detail.
    N 14768
    N 14767
    N 14773
    N 14772
    N 14770
    N 14774
    N 14771
    C 1439 **(m)**
    C 1438 **(m)**
    C 1420
    C 1400
    C 1419
    C 1418
    C 1417

The St. Lawrence Seaway and the Upper St. Lawrence River
NOS charts are available for only part of this section (Morristown to Cornwall). CHS charts also cover this distance, and are also good.

Morristown to Cornwall
    N 14763
    N 14762
    N 14761

Morristown to Sorel
    C 1417
    C 1414
    C 1412
    C 1411
    C 1400
    C 1416
    C 1413
    C 1409
    C 1340
    C 1415
    C 1410
    C 1339
    C 1338

Region 6

Riviere Richelieu and the Chambly Canal
    C 1350 **(m)**
    C 1351 **(m)**

Lake Champlain
    N 14781
    N 14782
    N 14783
    N 14784

The Champlain Canal
    N 14786 (booklet)

PUBLICATIONS

Navigation

U.S.A. (NOS): *U.S. Coast Pilot #6*
Canada (CHS): *Sailing Directions, Great Lakes, Volume 1*

Locking

"St. Lawrence Seaway Pleasure Craft Guide"

Weather

U.S.A. (NOS): "MSC-12, Marine Weather Services Chart, Great Lakes: Huron, Erie and Ontario"
Canada (CHS): *Marine Weather Services 94*

Where to Purchase Publications by Mail

Charts, Weather, Pilots (U.S.A.): National Ocean Service Distribution Branch (N/CG33), National Ocean Service, Riverdale, MD 20737-1199; (301) 436-6990
Charts, Sailing Directions (Canada): Hydrographic Chart Distribution Office, Department of Fisheries and Oceans, 1675 Russel Road, Box 8080, Ottawa, Ontario K1G 3H6; (613) 998-4931, -4932, -4933; FAX (613) 998-1217
Locking (Canada/U.S.A.): Transport Canada, Place de Ville, Ottawa, Ontario K1A 0N5
Weather (Canada): The Port Meteorological Offices, 25 St. Clair Avenue East, 3rd Floor, Toronto, Ontario M4T 1M2

SKETCH MAPS

Every anchorage, marina, or nonmarina docking facility has a sketch map located in the regional section's anchorage text. Each also is noted on its section map by mile number with either a ⚓ or a ▲. The purpose of a sketch map is to help you identify the anchorage, marina, or tie-up and to navigate an entry, identify the preferred place in the harbor to stop, and locate some shoreside services. All have been chosen to accommodate a vessel with a 6.5-foot draft at a normal summer water level. For convenience, all sketch map depths are recorded at a normal summer canal pool, lake, or river water level. You can find a plane of reference table for each area preceding each section's anchorage text. For more information about chart datum and water level see page 8.

Sketch maps are **NOT TO SCALE** and **NOT FOR NAVIGATION.** We do not note all topographical features, only those we feel will assist you in locating your position. Sketch map information is intended only to supplement official American and Canadian Hydrographic Service navigational charts and their associated publications.

Though guide anchorage and dockage approach depths are generally stable, many are unlike those found in coastal cruising. River systems not constructed for flood control can be seasonally affected by the currents of a rapidly rising river or an unusual flood condition. After water level returns to normal, the rise may have permanently changed depths and channels.

OUR INTENT

We have made every effort to provide correct and up-to-date information in this guide, but it's impossible to guarantee complete accuracy. By their nature, river and canal systems are susceptible to change due to high water conditions. Lake harbors at the mouth of a river or creek are often seasonably unstable. Always use prudent seamanship and sound carefully whenever leaving a maintained channel.

Marinas frequently change ownership, which often results in a reduction of facilities offered. Sadly, many marinas available today may be closed tomorrow.

The authors and publishers disclaim any liability for loss or damage to persons or property that may occur as a result of the use or interpretation of any information in this book.

Enjoying the Area

WHEN TO COME

Severe winter conditions completely close most waterways in this area for a few months of the year. The first of May is usually the earliest you can be certain the most southerly canals are open for the season and ice is clear in rivers and lakes. Weather is pleasant from about June 1 until the middle of September. May and October can be cold; cabins will need supplemental heat.

See Appendix 1, "Approximate Seasonal Opening and Closing Schedules," for more specific information.

WHERE TO GO

This guide covers about 1,400 nautical miles including eight canals, three major rivers, an abundance of lesser rivers and deepwater creeks, all or parts of five large lakes, and thousands of islands. Although it's possible to travel any region in any direction, we put this book together keeping in mind seasonal limitations, current, and locking ease. In normal water levels, you seldom face unfavorable currents exceeding 0.25 mph, except for 8 miles on the Upper Niagara River. The Welland Canal and the St. Lawrence Seaway locks, for example, are very difficult for pleasure craft to ascend, but descents are easy to negotiate.

It's helpful to your purse, speed, and comfort to travel in the direction with least opposition. For the popular circle trip beginning and ending at New York City, our chosen route for a low-powered vessel having a top speed of 6.0 mph or less is to enter the Hudson River in the spring at New York City. The Hudson's ice season extends from early January to mid-March; in more northerly systems freezing begins earlier and ends later. To make certain you aren't delayed by winter leftovers, plan to leave the Battery, **Mile H-0.0 (NM),** about May 1 to May 15.

The Erie Canal West, one of the eight canals covered in this guide.

The Hudson River (Region 1) is the navigable route from the Battery in New York City to Waterford, and for part of the Champlain Canal. The river flows through Hudson Valley forests with a background of the Catskills, the Berkshires, and the Green Mountains.

The 333-mile-long historic Erie Canal (Region 2) has entrances at Waterford on the Hudson and at North Tonawanda on the Upper Niagara River.

The Oswego Canal (Region 2) is a 24-mile downstream route off the Erie Canal to Lake Ontario's eastern end.

The Cayuga and Seneca Canal (Region 2) branches off the Erie into the famous wine country of two Finger Lakes, Cayuga and Seneca (Region 2).

At the Erie Canal's western entrance you enter Region 3, which takes you from North Tonawanda to Buffalo and from there to the Port Colborne entrance at Lake Erie's northeastern end. The Welland Canal takes you downstream into western Lake Ontario. In Lake Ontario you can cruise the 157-mile American shore or the 212-mile Canadian shore (Region 4).

Region 5 begins at Wolfe Island in far northeastern Lake Ontario where the St. Lawrence Seaway threads through the Thousand Islands. East of the islands is the lower St. Lawrence Seaway and a part of the Upper River that takes you as far as Sorel, just east of Montreal.

Here you turn south and travel the Richelieu River, the Chambly Canal, Lake Champlain, and finally the Champlain Canal (Region 6).

Now you are back to the Hudson River, the only area repeated on this circle route. You started with blossoming spring flowers and returned with fall foliage.

PREPARATIONS

Traveling rivers and canals is pleasant cruising. One requires only a well-found vessel and the skill to safely pass another vessel, steer a buoyed channel, and not careen into a narrow canal's towpath. The water is calm and you are within a few feet of the bank; you can sit back, sip iced tea, munch on cookies, and enjoy the ever-changing scenery.

In the larger lakes, however, land is often out of sight. Someone aboard must understand offshore navigation, and you must carry proper offshore lake charts, parallel rules, dividers, a deviation card, and a compensated compass. In addition, **loran** (main chains are 8970 and 9960), **GPS,** and **radar** are helpful in low visibility,

especially with the frequent dense fog of Lake Erie and Lake Ontario. Canals and rivers are often misty in early mornings.

A **fathometer** is indispensable for sounding out of the maintained channel and for following an offshore fathom curve. Have a **lead line** aboard in case something goes amiss with the fathometer. For very shoal draft vessels, a **sounding pole** helps when wandering about in very shallow water. Have **binoculars** for picking up distant buoys and daymarks. Delays occur, and you may get caught out after dark; nearly all unlighted buoys and daymarks have reflector tape that can easily be picked up by a strong **spotlight.**

An **autopilot** makes long lake runs much more appealing because you don't have to manually steer the vessel continuously.

Be sure to have plenty of **extra line** in long lengths to aid in docking and locking.

To make life more enjoyable, take along a **dinghy** and an **outboard motor;** hot-weather provisions, including awning, wind scoop, and fans; screens and bug repellent; fishing equipment; swimming paraphernalia; a French-English dictionary; and binoculars and wildlife guidebooks.

Waterfront improvements and the repair and rebuilding of locks, dams, and river and canal embankments are undertaken during canal close-down. The early onset or dawdling departure of winter affects the work's completion; delays may lead to changes in opening and closing schedules. Temporary in-season closures often result from high water conditions with subsequent dangerous currents, damage to navigational aids, or flood drift jamming lock valves and gates.

CANAL, RIVER, AND LAKE KNOWLEDGE
Dams

You encounter several types of dams in this area. An *open-crested* or *fixed-crested spillway* has water flowing over it at nearly all stages; there's little visible structure. This is a dangerous dam to approach heading downstream. It's almost impossible to see until you are practically on its crest—which may be only inches deep or more than your draft.

An open dam often is accompanied by a *gated spillway* or *movable dam*. These dams have individually operated gates that can be opened or closed to control a river or help regulate pool levels. They are common on the New York Barge Canal System's canalized rivers. At a distance, the dam resembles a bridge; it has concrete piers and abutments and arched steel spans. Here the resemblance ends, for on the dam's downstream side there are steel uprights hung by a hingelike apparatus with one end of the uprights sitting on a river-bottom sill. Machines alongside lower and raise the gates. If the lock crew closes all the gates (lowers them to the bottom), the structure becomes a total dam. If more water is needed downstream than flows over the closed gate crest, gates are raised sufficiently to release the specified amount. In the event of floods the crew can remove the gates completely by swinging them up under the bridge floor, leaving a clear passage for water. A downbound small boat could slip through an open gate and topple over a dam, but since the dam structure is large and conspicuous, that's unlikely to happen.

Taintor gates open with a cantilever appearance. They are often found singly or accompanying a small open-crested dam. Similar to gated spillways, they open or close to control water level. Downbound, they resemble a vertically hinged gate. If waiting upstream of a lock with an accompanying dam, do not navigate between the ever-present "Danger Dam" buoys and the dam. If spillway gates are open, the current increases dramatically at the dam crest. Many dams have hydroelectric power plants that are automatically controlled; currents above and below the intake tubes may increase unexpectedly and violently.

A dam's *tailwaters,* or *tailrace,* is the flow immediately below the dam or spillway gates.

Water Levels

Water level, pool level, and *lake level* refer to the water stage. Many systems are designed specifically for irrigation, flood control, or navigation. Many stable systems maintain water levels with movable dams and locks but can be temporarily affected by heavy area downpours, extended irrigation, heavy power generation, severe droughts, and floods. If the water is neither rising nor falling, it's often called the *normal water level* or the *pool level* (a *pool* is the water held upstream of a dam).

Depths, clearances, and land heights in the Great Lakes and in the St. Lawrence Seaway, the St. Lawrence River, and their tributaries are all measured from chart datum for the *particular* body of water. All the Great Lakes are subject to short periods of increased or reduced water levels due to wind tides that can range up to 2 feet.

The Hudson River—132 miles of it—is the only region in this book whose water level is affected by tidal flow.

Charted Depths and Clearances

Always remember that depths and overhead clearances are recorded on government charts at their particular chart datum. They must be adjusted to your daily water level, since they may be off 4 feet or more.

Boats drawing 6.6 feet should have no problems in the navigational channel on rivers and canals except during unusually low water conditions. The most shoal area is the Chambly Canal (Region 6), with 6.6 feet over the lock sills, but with forehand knowledge of your draft, lockmasters can raise this level slightly. For our draft of 6 feet 2 inches we usually are given a depth of 8 feet. Chambly channel depths average from 7 to 8 feet, depending on seasonal water level. Depths in all other guide areas often greatly exceed maintained depths, yet there can be unexpected pockets of shoaling in rivers and canals not heavily used by commercial vessels.

For your convenience, sketch map depths are recorded at normal summer water canal pool, lake, or river water level. Venturing off the main channel at any time can be an enjoyable adventure, but do so with extreme care, feeling your way with fathometer or lead line. This area's canal, river, and lake charts are unlike coastal charts, which have convenient soundings that need only be adjusted to tidal flow; here you must adjust charted depths with the system's daily water level.

See Appendix 5, "Maintained Depth and Overhead Clearance Limitations," for more information.

How to determine water depth for rivers, canals, lakes, and the St. Lawrence Seaway, the St. Lawrence River, and their tributaries. All the areas we cover have charted depths, but they are not necessarily going to be your daily area depth. Since each system has its own plane of reference at which the depths are recorded (chart datum or low water datum), and since conditions are seldom normal, you must adjust charted depths for the system you are cruising.

For convenience when traveling outside the confines of the sketch maps, we list a system's chart datum preceding each region's anchorage text. You can find individual systems' chart datum on charts, in *Coast Pilots,* and in *Sailing Directions.* With this you need to know your daily water level, which you can get from U.S. or

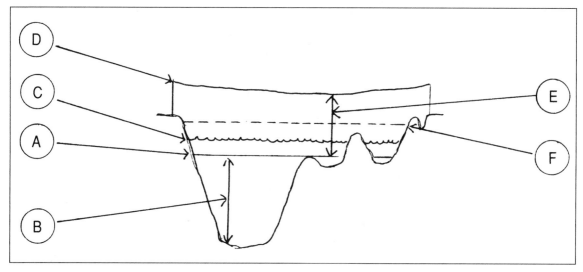

The relationship between chart datum and other levels and clearances:
A. Chart datum is a chosen value for a specific area so the water surface will seldom fall below it.
B. Charted Depths are given at chart datum.
C. Water Level refers to the status of the water surface at your position at a given time.
D. Overhead Obstruction that is recorded on charts.
E. Charted Clearance of an overhead obstruction is given above chart datum.
F. High Water Line is a level above which the water will seldom rise.

Canadian Coast Guard officials, some bridge tenders, all lockmasters, and many waterside businesses in the Great Lakes/St. Lawrence River area. Marine weather stations often note monthly lake levels in their broadcasts for shipping.

The water level (or pool level) in a canal or canalized river controlled (or partially controlled) by movable dams seldom varies more than a few inches from the normal water level. In a severe drought, water levels change very slowly over a matter of months. In severe flooding conditions, however, levels can rise a foot or more in a matter of hours.

In the Great Lakes, lake level change is very gradual, often taking a month to register a few inches. In Lake Erie and Lake Ontario the lowest levels generally occur in January and February; the highest levels occur in June. If this is your first trip into the Great Lakes and conditions are normal, you might glance at a lake chart and automatically eliminate many harbors simply because charted depths are less than your draft. This is not always true, since each lake's charted depths are recorded at their chart datum.

Once you have your daily water level or lake level and the chart datum, you can calculate your daily depths and clearances easily.

Example: On May 24, 1995, I plan to anchor at Fort Hunter on Schoharie Creek in the Erie Canal East, **Mile E-43.4 S (SM),** but a regional drought has me concerned that I might not have depth for my 5.4-foot draft. Since the chart datum for the Erie Canal East is at normal pool level, I know the charted depths where I want to anchor are accurate at that water stage. As I came upbound through Lock E #12, the lockmaster told me Lock E #13's pool level was down 1.3 feet. What is the depth of water I can depend on in the anchorage?

Charted depths in Lock E #13 at normal pool:	8.0 feet
5/24/95 Lock E #13 pool level:	–(down) 1.3 feet
5/24/95 real depth at anchor:	6.7 feet
My draft:	–5.4 feet
Water under my keel:	1.3 feet

Though I have water, I would need to sound carefully for swinging-room depth.

Example: I am in Lake Ontario on September 5, 1995, and the current lake level is at 244.8 feet. My boat has a height of 22 feet and I want to know if I can clear the low steel of the Stutson Street bascule bridge in Rochester without it opening. It has a charted closed clearance of 24 feet.

9/5/95 Lake level of Lake Ontario:	244.8 feet
Lake Ontario chart datum:	−242.8 feet
Lake Ontario is up:	2.0 feet
Stutson Street Bridge low steel charted at chart datum:	24.0 feet
9/5/95 Lake Ontario is up:	−2.0 feet
9/5/95 real height of Stutson Street Bridge low steel:	22.0 feet
My height:	22.0 feet
Clearance under the bridge:	0.0 feet

I'd better have the bridge raised, or I'll lose my pilot-house.

High Water

Flooding can occur any time, but is most common on the New York State Barge Canal System and the Hudson River. The first indication is an increase in current. If you are unsure of upcoming conditions, call a lockmaster on VHF and find out what's happening and what to expect for the next few days.

Should a flood be in the making, seek a safe off-river anchorage immediately. During floods excessive current and drift become dangerous. Lock crews open dams with movable gates to relieve upstream runoff; current immediately downstream of gates can be more than 10 mph in the tailrace, which in many instances is directly alongside the main channel.

Choose your waiting-out position with care. Find an off-river anchorage if possible and wait until excessive current and drift subside. Be sure you are well upstream of a dam, at least a quarter of the distance to the next upstream dam.

A rising river affects depth when you leave the main channel. More importantly, it affects your ability to return to the main channel if the river drops before you return. If you enter an anchorage during high water conditions, be sure to put out some sort of gauge on a fixed point ashore. A good choice is a fluorescent ribbon that can be seen easily during the day and picked up quickly by spotlight after dark. Check your gauge periodically to ensure that you have enough depth to regain the channel once the water level begins to return to normal.

Rising water can dangerously reduce overhead clearances. Carefully calculate chart datum with daily water level before traveling under bridges and power lines.

Shoaling

Any system used primarily by pleasure craft can be subject to shoaling; commercial traffic warrants much more care with depth maintenance. Keep in mind that an aid marking a dredged channel does not always mark the channel's edge. Going aground at cruising speed is the most common problem encountered by pleasure craft traveling narrow waterways. It's normally the result of helmsman inattention, passing too close to aids, or cutting corners. These mishaps can be nearly eliminated if a pleasure craft operator views his vessel as the same size as a towboat with a wide barge tow and allows for this width when passing any aid.

Never travel along the edge of a channel in a canal or river system primarily intended for pleasure boating. Stay in the middle until you are required to pass or to be passed. Wind and current greatly affect vessel set. A helmsman who does not monitor his wake astern to see the direction of this set can quickly be set over shoals.

Be aware of the type of canal or river channel you are traveling, as sections have various bottom widths that regulate the distance from the bank you can travel safely. This is most evident in the New York State Barge Canal System.

River and canal channels are often narrow and winding and have many navigational aids. Mind the chart; do not mistake one set of markers for another and make into shoal water. Avoid cutting corners in narrow waterways; shoals often extend well out from inner bends. Rivers and canals often have persistent shoaling at tributary junctions due to silt deposits left during flood conditions.

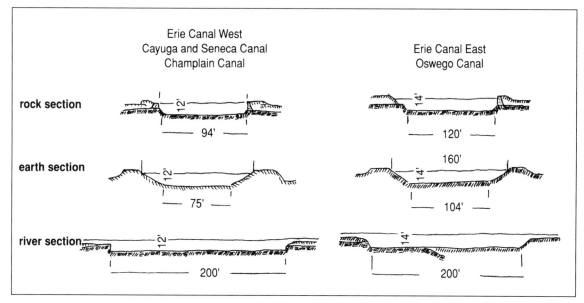

Canal sections, New York State Barge Canal System

Drift

There's very little drift in the lakes, but all river and canal systems have some of nature's flotsam floating free. There's minimal debris in the rivers and canals in normal water level; it tends to collect just down-current of a sharp bend or at upstream lock gates. A rising river washes drift off banks where it was left when the river rose and then fell at some other time. Amount and size of drift increases as the water continues to rise. Hitting drift is the major cause of propeller damage when traveling rivers and canals, so if drift is excessive, don't travel.

Current

There's almost always current when traveling rivers and canals. Every system has its own individual bottom profile that determines its amount of fall in elevation and therefore its amount of flow. Current partially depends on how the river or canal is dammed in the greatest bottom contour fall line and whether the system is designed for flood control. It also depends on daily water levels and the distance a vessel is located from the upstream dam. Each region includes a Current Direction and Speed table (except Region 4, where current information is in the text on page 189).

Areas with increased current during normal conditions can occur below dams and on the outside of riverbends, even if a dam powerhouse is not generating. Increased current can be a useful tool when downbound on a fast flowing river; it increases speed. When upbound, avoid it. Remember: Always monitor the depth if traveling near channel edges.

Commercial Traffic

Too many pleasure boats sound the wrong horn signal to pass another vessel. Memorize passing signals before leaving the dock. If you have trouble remembering them, post a diagram of horn signals beside the ship's wheel.

Ships nearly always travel in areas sufficiently wide for two to pass, but use caution and common sense if traveling with ships in narrow channels with adverse currents. Most large commercial traffic is found on the Hudson River, the Welland Canal, the St. Lawrence Seaway, the St. Lawrence River, Lake Ontario, and Lake Erie. There's very little towboat and barge tow traffic in the canals and smaller river systems.

Locks

There are 74 locks in the area covered by this guide. All use the same general method of water exchange.

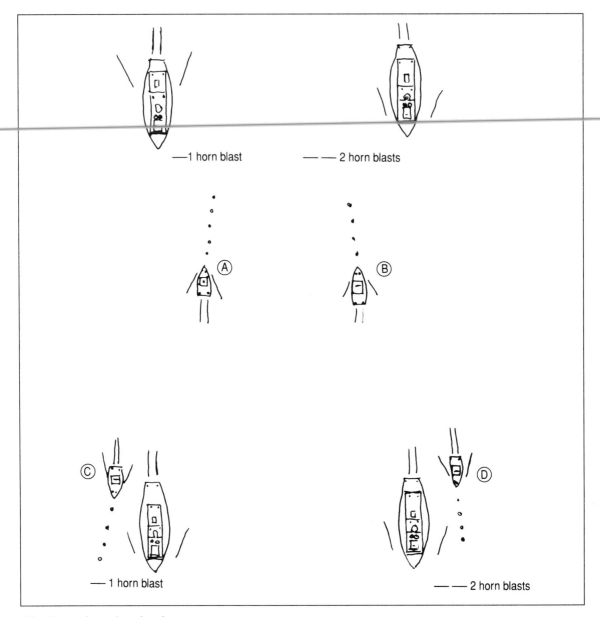

Meeting and passing situations
A. A pleasure craft meeting an oncoming vessel passing port to port gives one horn blast.
B. A pleasure craft meeting an oncoming vessel passing starboard to starboard gives two horn blasts.
C. A pleasure craft overtaking and passing on the starboard side of the vessel that is being overtaken gives one horn blast.
D. A pleasure craft overtaking and passing on the port side of the vessel that is being overtaken gives two horn blasts.

The systems differ slightly in regard to lock size and method of securing inside the chamber.

The lock tables in the text usually include mile number, lift, signals, method of securing in the chamber, VHF and land line phone numbers, preferred or required placement, and schedule.

Lock Approach*

A. A mile before the lock, call the lockmaster on VHF and inform him of your position, the direction in which you are traveling, and your intention to lock. Ask when you are to lock, where you should tie in the chamber (if he doesn't care and you are upbound, ask him to suggest a chamber position with the least turbulence), and which VHF channel he monitors during lockage. If you are to lock with a commercial craft or raft, get clear instructions on chamber placement and when to enter and exit in regard to the other traffic.

Prepare fenders and lines on both sides of the boat.

B. Waiting to lock, pull to the side of the channel about 400 feet from the approach wall. If a long wait is anticipated, long approach walls can be used for dockage. Most short approach walls have poor dockage, as they are too close to lock gates. The Welland Canal and the St. Lawrence Seaway have specific pleasure craft reporting-in docks with a direct telephone connection with the lockmaster.

C. Downbound it is difficult to see the crest of an open dam.

D. Currents can be strong below a dam during periods of high water or when dam power plants are generating.

E. A green light means that it is time to enter the chamber, slowly and in the order of arrival; a red or a yellow light means wait for the green. An entry horn signal of one blast may or may not be given at small-system locks.

F. Watch for debris near gates.

G. If upbound, a waiting area opposite a dam occasionally has a reverse current.

H. When upbound and spillway gates are open near the lock wall, the dam-side approach wall can have a severe current flush and a consequential hard set away from the dam.

I. Watch for turbulent water near the lock if the drain valve is located just outside the gates.

J. After lockage, remain secured until receiving the exit horn signal or the lockmaster's hand signal.

K. Leave the chamber in the order of entry at a slow speed.

*The St. Lawrence Seaway System has strict regulations regarding pleasure craft transit. These differ considerably from all other systems. Consult the "St. Lawrence Seaway Pleasure Craft Guide."

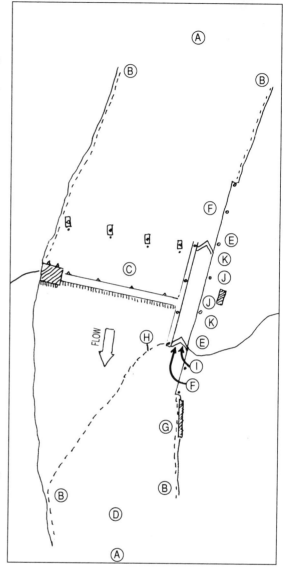

A specific number of crew aboard is not required for locking except in the Welland Canal and the St. Lawrence Seaway. Here you must have three aboard when ascending; you usually are allowed to descend with two aboard. In some systems, lockmasters require line handlers and deck crew to wear life jackets. Keep children and pets below or secured with a safety harness or a short leash during lockage.

In the New York State Barge Canal System, the Richelieu River, and the Chambly Canal locks, two standard, cylindrical, inflatable fenders are adequate when descending; four or more are necessary when ascending. Regular fender boards or vertical fender planks are acceptable, as are large bags filled with hay.

(These are often for sale at marinas near systems with locks.) Automobile tires are not allowed. If **ascending** the very turbulent and difficult-to-negotiate large locks on the Welland Canal or the St. Lawrence Seaway, you need additional protection in order not to suffer damage.

Fit each line handler with a pair of work gloves to keep hands clean and unbruised. A 3- or 4-foot pole (a mop handle works well) will help you push off a chamber wall; longer poles are awkward to manipulate in restricted areas.

If a lockmaster does not care where you tie in his lock when ascending, for least turbulence choose a chamber position at the lock's far forward end. When descending, any convenient place is suitable. Never secure a line inside the chamber to anything **unless** it has one free end or is secured with a hitch that can be removed instantly.

A towed dinghy is a nuisance in a turbulent lock ascent. Secure it fore and aft alongside, away from the chamber wall. In midsummer on the Chambly Canal, a dinghy has to be aboard or tied hard against the transom due to the small locks and the large number of transiting boats.

If drift has collected inside the lock, watch it carefully during ascending turbulence. This debris can squeeze between the hull and chamber wall and scar topsides. Protruding underwater branches can foul rudders and propellers.

There's little apparent turbulence during a descending lockage, but ascending produces significant turbulence that increases with the lock lift. Large, hard-to-handle vessels can use their engines to help maintain position.

Rafting in locks is usually confined to systems with small locks. A lockmaster normally directs rafting positions with the largest vessel on the chamber wall. Rafting vessels usually supply their own lines.

In an emergency in a lock, blow the danger signal and contact the lockmaster on VHF. Unless it's a life-and-death situation, do not climb the dangerously slick lock ladders.

There are various ways to secure in a lock, depending on what the system offers inside the chamber, how many vessels are locking together, and whether you are ascending or descending. Methods include the following:

Lines furnished. Some locks may not have a lot of lines, so if traffic is heavy prepare for another method

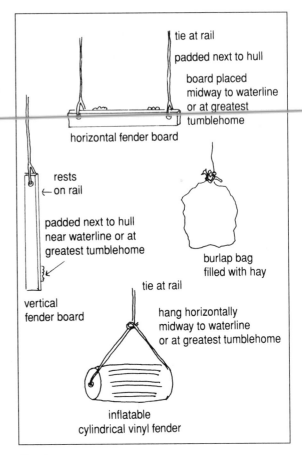

Fenders

of securing. Usually two lines—one for the bow, one for the stern—are either handed to you by the locking crew when descending or lowered to you when ascending. If systems are short of staff, the lines permanently hang in the water, weighted so as not to threaten propellers. Always choose a line for the bow and one for the stern. Once you have these in hand, center the boat midway between them and keep the lines snug during the transit. When ready to exit, drop the lines and go.

Chamber poles or fixed cables. Both are permanently attached at the chamber rim and the lock bottom. Poles are recessed in the chamber wall; cables are directly on the wall. Here you are required to furnish a line for your bow and one for your stern, with both attached to the boat at their respective cleats. As you enter the lock to ascend or descend, choose two poles or cables fairly close together. As you approach the first pole or cable—the one for the stern—slip the end of your stern line behind the cable or pole. Pay it out while slowly powering ahead until the line handler at the bow can slip the bow line's end behind the cable or pole you have chosen for the bow. Re-center the boat so lines are about even and keep them snug as you ascend or descend. The lines slip up or down the pole or cable without further attention. When ready to exit, remove your line by pulling it in from the secured end.

Ladders. A ladder requires an amidships securing position when ascending or descending. You must furnish one lock line of sufficient length to attach at the bow cleat and reach amidships with 10 to 12 feet to spare. Another line must be of sufficient length to attach at the stern cleat and reach amidships, with an additional 10 to 12 feet. A line handler positions himself amidships on the chamber wall side of the boat, holding in his hand a loop in the loose ends of the bow and stern lines. The captain enters the chamber, positions the boat with the ladder or pole directly amidships, and comes to a dead stop. The line handler loops the bow and stern line through ladder rungs at about the same level as the sheer strake. The lines are not tied, but are taken up tightly to hold the vessel straight in the lock. During lockage and as the vessel begins to ascend (or descend), one line loop is removed from its rung and looped upward (or

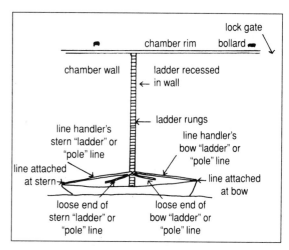

Ladder method for ascending and descending locks

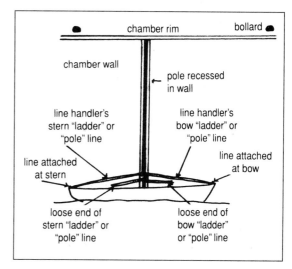

Pole method for ascending and descending locks

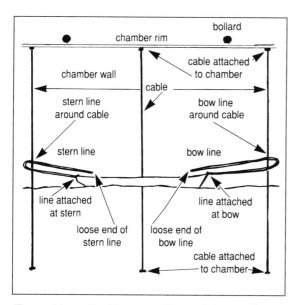

Two-cable method for ascending and descending locks

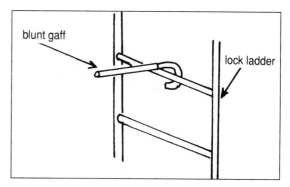

Hooking a ladder for ascending and descending locks

downward) through the next rung. Then the other line loop is removed and placed upward (or downward) through the next rung. During this "walking" up (or down) procedure, one line handler is able to handle both lines amidships or two handlers can each take a line. When lockage is completed, the looped lines are removed from the ladder and the vessel exits.

Very small boats and runabouts can use a **lock hook** as an adequate ladder lockage method. One person must hook a ladder rung and manually hold the boat against the ladder. Take care "walking" up (or down), and do not lose hold of the ladder completely.

Floating bollards. Floating bollards are large—steamship size—and recessed into a well in the chamber wall. Secure amidships with your own lines, similar to the ladder method. Remember that the bollard is floating and ascends (or descends) with the vessel during lockage.

Bridges

There are hundreds of bridges in this area. Most are fixed. They, and the overhead power cables, are the main restrictions for traveling the canals and rivers used primarily by pleasure craft. Height varies by region. There are also a great number of lift, bascule, and swing bridges. A movable lift bridge also has a fixed open height and, when open, its clearance is usually no higher than the system's restricted navigational fixed height. When closed, many movable bridges are often inches off the water's surface and require opening for passage of all vessels, even rowboats. For each region that has movable bridges across most-used waterways, we provide bridge information in tabular form.

Navigation Aids

Nearly all United States aids to navigation are the same standard shapes and sizes as those in coastal waters. There are channel, midchannel, and junction buoys; daymarks; solid and wire towers; piles; lighthouses; and ranges. Colors are standard red and green. They may have lights, whistles, bells, horns, and radar reflectors, and most are numbered, with the exception of some buoys and daymarks in lesser canals. In the Great Lakes, fog signals are on a seasonal basis, with many maintained only from April 1 to November 1.

Canadian navigation aids in steamship channels are similar in type and size to American aids. Usually, day-marks, lighted towers, and lighted buoys are numbered. Areas outside the main channels in the lesser rivers, in bays, and around island throughways usually have large daymarks and towers that are lighted, but quite a few buoys generally are not. The latter are spars, which are thin and tall and often difficult to pick up. The differentiating small cone on a red buoy and the flat top on a can are not obvious at any great distance; by the time you approach closely enough to distinguish them, color and number are also more apparent. It is imperative to know exactly at which buoy you are located in areas of rocky islands and extensive shoals.

Inland navigation generally follows the normal procedure of red aids to starboard coming from the sea. In some areas the sea's placement in relationship to the river or canal is not easily apparent.

PUBLIC AND PRIVATE PROPERTY

When you want to go ashore but are uncertain if it's okay to do so, follow these general rules of thumb.

1. Check available literature to see if the land is privately owned. If you believe it may be, yet there's no evidence of habitation and no signs warning you to keep out, you usually can go ashore for a walk or to get to the nearest village.
2. Public land, parks, wildlife refuges, and bird sanctuaries nearly always have signs posted; follow their instructions.
3. If the land is obviously built up and inhabited, even though there are a few vacant lots with access ashore, never land. Residents of most densely populated American waterfront areas are extremely nervous about strangers abroad and are likely to call the police.
4. Never land at an island where there's a cottage, house, or dock that is obviously privately owned. Such islands may not be posted with No Trespassing signs, but **do not trespass.** Most are summer cottages on private islands; the land and dock are only for the owner's use, even if he is not currently in residence.

ENVIRONMENT

When visiting this cruising area, make every effort to leave it as you see it. Simple environmental practices will enable other visitors to enjoy these regions as you do. Here are some tips:

Human waste. You must have a functioning holding tank in all regions covered in this guide. Violators are not tolerated; inspections are frequent and thorough. Pumpout stations are at nearly every marina and nearly all charge a very substantial fee no matter the tank's size. All recreation and park facilities in both countries have shoreside rest rooms.

Gray water. Watch for updated government reports from the Ontario Ministry of the Environment restricting "gray water" (from sinks and showers) overboard discharge. This will apply to boating visitors as well as Canadians.

Trash. Bag all your garbage and dispose of it properly. Ramp areas, parks, visitor centers, recreation areas, and marinas all have disposal facilities. Ask permission or pay a fee before you dump. Go out of your way to pick trash from the water and dispose of it properly. Carry a plastic bag in your dinghy; make an effort to retrieve trash from along the shoreline or fish it off the bottom when in shallow, clear water.

Camping. All regions have camping areas that are usually maintained by state or provincial governments. Boat-in camping by runabout is especially popular in the Canadian islands. Nearly all camping is restricted to particular areas. There is a facility use fee. If you plan to camp ashore overnight, use of park docks for your boat may be included with the camping fee. In isolated areas or islands, many nonboating campers are brought in and out by water taxi.

Whenever you leave a campsite or picnic area, thoroughly saturate with water all campfires and grill coals to be certain they can't be fanned alive by the wind. And pack out all trash if garbage facilities are not provided.

Fire. If there's fire danger due to an especially dry year, never build a fire or light a grill. Keep in touch with the outside world. Fire danger warnings are usually broadcast on radio, TV, and often on the continuous NOAA and Canadian weather broadcasts.

Wildlife. An enjoyable part of cruising some of these areas is the abundance of birds and animals. Birds, squirrels, and raccoons are common scavengers and often visit dockside park areas. Don't disturb these wild creatures; frightened parents often do not return to nests or dens.

Speed regulations. Most narrow canals or canalized rivers have posted speed limits to minimize bank erosion and destruction of shoreside structures. Speed limits are seldom obeyed, especially in Quebec. The wake damage caused in this province is extraordinary, and dockage and anchorages are often made untenable.

Canal speed limits for upcoming river and canal sections normally are posted on lock gates. A lockmaster knows the time a vessel leaves his lock and calls the next lockmaster to warn him of its upcoming arrival. If a vessel appears too soon, it has surpassed the speed limit. This can result in a severe lecture or fine.

WEATHER

Weatherwise, the time to cruise is late spring, summer, and early fall. Earlier and later there's more chance of cold weather, windy conditions, and a risk of severe storms. The season's first warm weather stairsteps north from the Lower Hudson Valley to the New York Barge Canal System and then to Lake Erie. The northerly areas of Lake Ontario, the St. Lawrence River, the Richelieu River, and Lake Champlain are the last to warm up and the first to experience the fall changeover.

The guide area has a mid-continental climate and lies at the convergence of diverse air masses from the Arctic, the Pacific, western North America, the Gulf of Mexico, and the Atlantic. The cruising season is usually under the influence of the back side of the Bermuda High. Clear skies associated with this high are broken every few days by the passage of low-pressure systems. During the summer these lows are often very weak, yet they bring about a weather change that includes overcast skies, occasional rain, and cool temperatures.

Southern Ontario, northern New York, the St. Lawrence and Richelieu rivers, and Lake Champlain are also in the circulation path of the cyclonic lows. These dangerous storms are most common in late spring and early fall; occasionally one passes through in summer. These lows can bring gale-force winds and high seas. Summer has thunderstorms with accompanying violent winds and severe lightning, though the storms are neither as frequent nor as severe as those found in America's heartland or along the mid-Atlantic coast. Lake Champlain is prone to thunderstorms that are especially unpleasant because dense summertime haze makes them invisible until the final minutes of their approach.

Cruising-season winds are generally light. The strongest winds are those that precede a front and those that occur after the frontal passage along with its building high. Prevailing winds in summer are usually southwest. The strongest prevailing winds are in eastern Lake Ontario and the Upper St. Lawrence River. They range from near calm to 15 to 20 knots. Winds decrease near sundown to a light breeze or calms that continue until late the next morning, when the cycle begins again.

A warm front generally has the wind back first to south and then to southwest. During a cold front's approach, wind from the southwest strengthens; the amount depends on the front's severity and the line of delineation between the high and the low. After a cold front, wind normally swings northwest and may increase to 20 to 25 knots. In time it will swing back southwest and decrease. Strong northeast, north, and northwest winds more than 25 knots are most common in early spring and late fall; they accompany fronts and storms.

Fog during the cruising season is most common on Lake Erie and Lake Ontario and is primarily due to the water-temperature lag that occurs in spring and early summer. Burnoff may occur as soon as the sun rises sufficiently to warm the air, or the fog can last all day and more. Rivers and canals often have early-morning fog; its burnoff is rapid once the sun is up.

See Appendix 3, "Continuous Weather Reports," for information on American and Canadian weather broadcasts.

SUPPLIES AND SERVICES

You are almost always within a few miles of some sort of facility that can provide you with basic marine supplies and advice. Small towns and cities abound, and their dockage is nearly always within short walking distance of grocery stores, pharmacies, hardware stores, assorted shops, laundromats, post offices, libraries, doctors and dentists, hospitals, police, and fire stations. Fuel, ice, and a pumpout can be found at nearly every large marina.

Canada and the United States use different systems of measurement. If you cannot make instantaneous metric/English conversions, bring along a pocket-size conversion calculator. You will need it when reading charts, filling tanks, using engine additives and oils, purchasing material by length and weight, and grocery shopping. See Appendix 2, "Metric Conversions," for metric/English equivalents.

When traveling in Quebec, remember that the population is often not bilingual. Government employees of Quebec are no longer required to speak English, so dealings concerning locks, depths, overhead clearances, and use of government dockage may be conducted in French.

General repairs, engine work, or maintenance usually can be contracted at marinas or boatyards. Marine stores carry the popular paints and supplies of that country. A Travelift for drafts more than 4.5 feet is often found at the larger marina complexes, boatyards, or yacht clubs; small shoal-draft sailboats and powerboats often are handled by crane.

Canadian and American marinas normally accept each other's major credit cards. Each nation accepts the

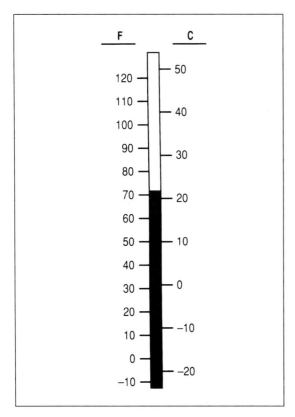

Temperature conversion

others traveler's checks. Do all money changing at banks to ensure a correct rate of exchange.

Mail pickup from general delivery is the rule when traveling in either nation. If you expect but do not receive a package or a large, fat manila envelope mailed from one country to the other, it probably was sent to the Customs office after it was received by the post office. It will remain there until you pick it up and declare the contents. Ask the postmaster where the Customs office is located; it might be miles away in another town.

Region 1
THE HUDSON RIVER

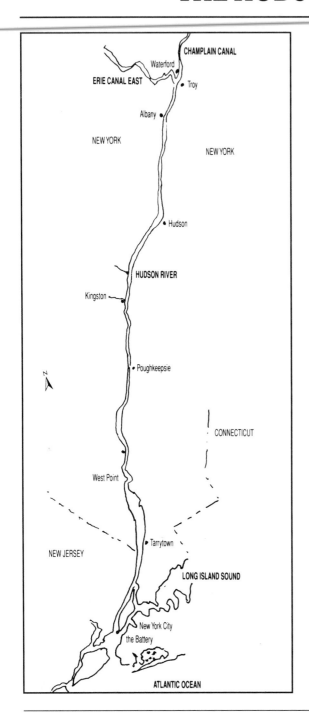

Mile H-0.0 (NM) to Mile H-134.3 (NM)

NORMAL TIDAL VARIATIONS AND CURRENT VELOCITIES
THE BATTERY TO FEDERAL LOCK

Place	Mile	Mean Tidal Range	Current Velocity (knots)	
			Ebb	Flood
The Battery	H-0.0 (NM)	4.5 feet	2.3	1.5
Yonkers	H-16.0 (NM)	3.7 feet	2.2	1.6
Newburgh	H-53.0 (NM)	2.8 feet	1.2	0.9
Poughkeepsie	H-66.0 (NM)	3.1 feet	1.2	1.1
Kingston	H-79.0 (NM)	3.7 feet	1.6	1.3
Albany	H-126.0 (NM)	4.6 feet	0.8	0.3
Federal Lock	H-132.0 (NM)	4.7 feet	0.7	no flood

CURRENT DIRECTION AND SPEED

The Hudson River flows south

	Place	Speed in mph*
Hudson River South*	H-0.0 (NM) to H-35.2 (NM)	About 1.8
	H-35.2 (NM) to H-79.0 (NM)	About 1.7
Hudson River North**	H-79.0 (NM) to H-132.0 (NM)	About 1.6
	H-132.0 (NM) to H-134.3 (NM)	About 1.5

*At normal water level

**Mile H-0.0 (NM) to Mile H-35.2 (NM) at Mean Low Water; Mile H-35.2 (NM) to Mile H-79.0 (NM) at Mean Low Water during lowest river stage

***Mile H-79.0 (NM) to Mile H-132.0 (NM) at Mean Low Water during lowest river stage

Mile H-132.0 (NM) to Mile H-134.3 (NM) at normal pool level

The Hudson River South
The Battery to Rondout Creek

Mile H-0.0 (NM) to Mile H-79.0 (NM)

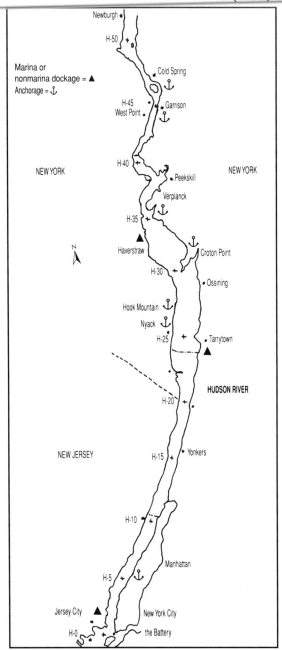

Marina or
nonmarina dockage = ▲
Anchorage = ⚓

NEW YORK

NEW YORK

Newburgh

H-50

Cold Spring

H-45
West Point   Garrison

H-40

Peekskill

Verplanck

H-35

Haverstraw   Croton Point

H-30

Ossining

Hook Mountain

Nyack

H-25   Tarrytown

HUDSON RIVER

H-20

NEW JERSEY

H-15   Yonkers

H-10

Manhattan

H-5

Jersey City   New York City

H-0   the Battery

Mile H-0.0 (NM) to Mile H-52.5 (NM)

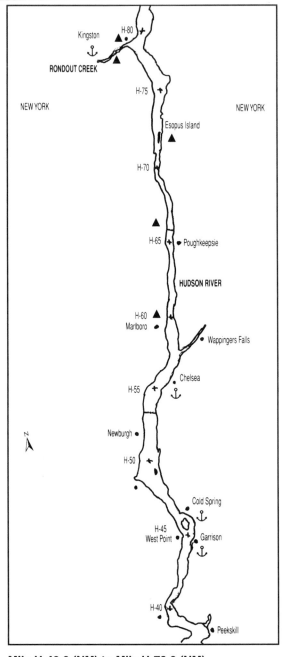

Kingston   H-80

RONDOUT CREEK

H-75

NEW YORK   NEW YORK

Esopus Island

H-70

H-65   Poughkeepsie

HUDSON RIVER

H-60
Marlboro

Wappingers Falls

Chelsea

H-55

Newburgh

H-50

Cold Spring

H-45
West Point   Garrison

H-40

Peekskill

Mile H-40.0 (NM) to Mile H-79.0 (NM)

> *Far to the northward of us we saw high hills. This is a very good land to fall with, and a pleasant land to see.*
>
> ROBERT JUET, First Mate of
> *Half Moon,* 1609

This region begins at the Battery, **Mile H-0.0 (NM),** at Manhattan Island's southern tip and the Hudson River's mouth. South across Diamond Reef, 173-acre Governor's Island sits in the middle of the East River, the deep-draft access route to Long Island Sound from the Upper Harbor. Southeast in the Jersey Flats is Liberty (Bedloe's) Island and the site of old Fort Wood's star-shaped ramparts; facing southeastward is the patina-clad Statue of Liberty.

Ballast dumped by sailing ships built up 27-acre Ellis Island, 3.5 miles north. For 62 years, beginning in 1892, it served as an immigrant station through which more than 12 million people passed. Refurbished to its 1918 to 1929 architectural flamboyance, it's now part of the Statue of Liberty National Monument.

In 1524 Giovanni da Verrazano, an Italian sailing for France, became the first European to enter New York Harbor and discover Manhattan, but the Hudson River takes its name from Henry Hudson, the English explorer who sailed for the Dutch East India Company. Hudson sailed *Half Moon* upriver as far as what is now Albany. His 1609 visit and his reports of the beautiful estuary

The Statue of Liberty and Bedloe's Island in the Jersey Flats.

and the "Beaver skinnes and Otters skinnes . . . which we bought for Beads, Knives, and Hatchets" attracted other Dutch traders eager to share in the loot.

The 275-mile-long Hudson River has a watershed of more than 13,000 square miles; its source is the Adirondack Mountains' Lake Tear-of-the-Clouds. The river flows southerly but is tidal for 132 miles; its current is affected by wind, droughts, and freshets. Sometimes called "the Rhine of America," the Hudson has scenic palisades and wooded landscapes and is bordered by mountains.

Commercial traffic is heaviest in the Upper Harbor around the Battery and the East River. It decreases dramatically a few miles north and becomes slight by the time you reach the George Washington Bridge.

For the first 10 miles on the river it's enjoyable to travel the eastern shoreline alongside the commercial piers. Here you have a city view and pass nearly at the foot of the World Trade Center with its twin 120-story skyscrapers. Wharves also line this shoreline for nearly 5 miles—some for gaily bedecked passenger liners.

Built on the site of a 1650 trading post, the Jersey

Things to Do and See in New York

Trying to describe this city in a few paragraphs would be an insult, so we cheerfully refer you to the many guidebooks that are devoted to the task. The following are just some of our favorite destinations.

American Museum of Natural History, Central Park West at 79th Street; (212) 769-5100. Exhibits feature cultures of all continents, wildlife, dinosaurs, prehistoric man, and gems and minerals. There is also a natural history library. Take the highlights tour first, then explore on your own. Admission fee is a suggested donation. Open 9 to 5 daily, except Thanksgiving and Christmas.

Cathedral of Saint John the Divine, 1047 Amsterdam Avenue at 112th Street. A Gothic wonder—the largest church of its kind in the world, featuring neck-craning vaulted ceilings supported by eight 55-foot-tall granite columns; bronze front portals with intricate scenes from the Bible; and the 40-foot rose window. Open Monday through Saturday from 9 to 5, and on Sunday after last service. Tours Monday through Saturday at 11, and on Sunday after last service.

Central Park, 59th Street north to 110th Street, between Fifth Avenue and Eighth Avenue; (212) 397-3080. Suggested by William Cullen Bryant in 1844 as a planned refuge from urban sprawl, the first formally declared park in Manhattan still admirably serves that purpose. Row on the lake, stroll through the recently renovated 5-acre zoo, play miniature golf, ride the carousel, or just eat lunch.

Metropolitan Museum of Art, 5th Avenue at 82nd Street; (212) 535-7710. Set aside a couple of days for this one, if you can. The museum houses the largest collection in North America—over 3 million items, including European and American artworks, the Costume Institute, arms and armor, and special exhibitions. A recorded tour is available. Admission fee is a suggested donation. Open daily except Monday, 9:30 to 5:15.

New York Public Library, 5th Avenue at 42nd Street. Built in 1911, this is the Central Research division of the city's library system. There's the Gottesman Gallery; the map room (our favorite); exhibitions of rare books and art in the Berg Room; and much more. Guided and self-guided tours are available. Open Monday through Saturday, 9 to 6; later some evenings.

Statue of Liberty. You can't tie up here, but the ferry leaves from Battery Park. It operates daily from 9 to 4, every half hour during the summer and on the hour the rest of the year. The fare was $2 last time we went; the park is free. Walk the statue grounds and tour the Lady herself, and take in the Statue of Liberty Exhibit, the Immigration Exhibit, and the Ellis Island Immigration Museum, open year-round except Christmas.

City waterfront is a manufacturing area, major seaport, and shipping center for railroads and highways. Watch for its famous Colgate Clock.

At **Mile H-1.5 (NM)** you sail over the 1927 Holland Tunnel, which connects auto traffic between Jersey City and midtown Manhattan; watch for its high ventilator shafts on both shores. Hoboken—by the Maxwell House coffee cup—is another New Jersey railroad center and seaport. North 0.2 mile you sail over the three-tube vehicular Lincoln Tunnel, which routes traffic to lower Manhattan.

The retired aircraft carrier U.S.S. *Intrepid,* **Mile H-4.4 E (NM)**, is part of the city's Intrepid Sea-Air-Space Museum. Across the river is Weehawken, where Aaron Burr killed Alexander Hamilton in their 1804 duel, the climax of their bitter conflict in national and New York politics.

In 1873 New York City created Riverside Park, a 320-acre landscaped strip of land bordering the river; its southern limit begins at **Mile H-5.6 E (NM).** In early spring, watch for the park's blooming pink cherry trees.

About a mile north of 79th Street Marina, at **Mile H-6.2 (NM),** look east on the hill to see the white marble Sailors and Soldiers Monument, designed by Paul E. M. Duboy. This Civil War memorial sporting 12 Corinthian columns is fashioned after the statue to Lysicrates in Athens.

Nestled in the trees a bit farther north is the 21-story Gothic Revival Riverside Church. Built in the 1920s, it has a 215-foot nave, and the top-floor stairway winds upward alongside the 74 bells of the Laura Spelman Rockefeller Memorial Carillon, the world's largest.

Above the trees at **Mile H-7.7 E (NM)** is the 160-foot-tall, white-granite, Classic-style General Ulysses S. Grant National Memorial. Grant and his wife, Julia, lie in a circular vault below the marble floor in granite sarcophagi.

Continuing north, the New Jersey shoreline's piers give way to forested cliffs. On a 340-foot promontory at **Mile H-9.5 W (NM),** a flag flies over Fort Lee, named for General Charles Lee of the Continental Army. George Washington built the fort, along with Fort Washington across the river, to defend New York and the river from the British. Fort Lee fell when Cornwallis's 5,000-man army crossed the Hudson and scaled the Palisades. Today reconstructed batteries, parapets, and a firing step are part of Fort Lee Historic Park.

From 1907 through the 1920s the nearby town of Fort Lee was America's movie capital, with seven major movie studios and 21 companies producing silent films. The precipitous Palisades were where Pauline—of *Perils of Pauline* fame—struggled for her survival.

In early spring, watch for protruding ends of fish stakes just north of the George Washington Bridge, **Mile H-10.0 (NM);** they can extend from near midriver to the western bank.

Eastern shore Fort Washington was manned by more than 2,800 Americans during the Revolution but surrendered to the British under General William Howe in 1776 as Washington watched from across the river at Fort Lee. One Fort Washington bastion remains near the bridge.

The Cloisters, the Metropolitan Museum of Art's branch for medieval European art, is just south of Tubby Hook and at the highest point in Fort Tryon Park. John D. Rockefeller Jr. donated the 4-acre site and then bought more than 700 acres of the Palisades across the river to preserve the view. Parts of medieval monasteries and chapels were brought from Europe and rebuilt; you can see Bonnefont Cloister from the river.

The site of Fort Tryon, once an outpost of Fort Washington, is on a 250-foot hill south of the Cloisters; you can see its observation tower with flag flying.

On the New Jersey shore, Palisades Interstate Park extends north for about 12 miles to Piermont. Volcanic undersea eruptions produced the Hudson's Palisades between 600 million and one billion years ago. Conservationists are responsible for saving the cliffs, which were due to be blasted apart for New York City building stone.

At **Mile H-12.0 E (NM)** the railroad bridge and a two-level blue-arched highway span mark the entrance to Spuyten Duvil Creek—Dutch for "Spouting Devil." This is an entrance into the 7-mile-long Harlem River and a route to the East River. It's a narrow waterway busy with commercial traffic and tour boats circumnavigating Manhattan. The channel has swift current and many low-level—though movable—bridges. This combination does not recommend it for cruising to the East River and Long Island Sound; for a more relaxing trip, divert to the sound at the Battery at the East River's mouth.

Yonkers, **Mile H-16.0 E (NM),** was originally ceded to Adriaen Cornelissen Van der Donck, the first lawyer of New Netherlands. He held the courtesy name of *jonkheer,* hence the development of the name Yonkers.

About opposite the Hastings-on-Hudson's water tank, **Mile H-19.0 E (NM),** look across the river to see the marker that notes the New York–New Jersey border. For the remainder of the Hudson River–region cruise, you are in New York waters.

In 1698 Jeremiah Dobbs, a colonial boatman, began shuttling passengers across the Hudson in his log canoe, the first Dobbs Ferry. The eastern-shore town is just ahead by the brick chimney.

Piermont Pier is the mile-long finger extending into the river at **Mile H-22.2 W (NM).** Originally called Tappan Landing, it was the port for Tappan, about 4 miles inland, as well as a terminal for the Erie Railroad and a connection point for early river commerce.

For a time George Washington used the DeWint House in Tappan as his revolutionary army headquarters. It was there that he gave Benedict Arnold command of West Point; in turn Arnold and Major John André arranged to surrender the garrison to the British. Authorities captured André at Tarrytown on his way to deliver documents to the British; he was returned to Tappan and hanged on what is now André Hill. Arnold escaped to fight for England.

High on the eastern shore at Irvington is Sunnyside, author Washington Irving's home for the last 25 years of his life. The Dutch Colonial Revival–style house has Moorish towers, intricate chimneys, quaint gables, and ancient weathervanes. The area was the setting of his "Legend of Sleepy Hollow."

For the next 8 miles you are in Tappan Zee, a 2-mile-wide lakelike section of river where many early trading sloops and steamboats floundered. Be forewarned: Legend tells of a ghost ship, the Storm Ship, that sails across the rough seas of Tappan Zee and "...woe betide the vessel that fails to give her way."

At Piermont the main navigation channel begins to hold to the eastern shore, and at **Mile H-23.5 (NM)** you pass under the $60 million 1955 Tappan Zee Bridge. The span rests on eight watertight caissons—some the size of half a city block—sunk in the riverbed.

The eastern bank of Tarrytown is north of the bridge; on the prominent point is the 1883 Tarrytown Lighthouse, one of the first eight built on the river as navigational aids. North of the light at **Mile H-25.0 E (NM)** is Philipsburg Manor, originally a large working farm community and colonial trading post owned by Frederick Philipse.

Directly across the river is Nyack, once a busy riverboat landing. For a scenic shortcut at Nyack it's possible to cruise in depths of 9 to 12 feet near the western shoreline as far as **Rockland Lake Landing Light #7.** Hook Mountain, a 720-foot-high National Natural Landmark, looms over the area, with Rockland State Park bordering it along the river.

On the eastern shore at the southern end of Croton Bay is Ossining, Iroquois for "a stony place." Once part of the Philipsburg Manor lands, it was confiscated by the government after the Revolution. The first European settlement became known as Hunter's Landing; later settlers called it Sint Sings, then Sing Sing. In 1824 correctional authorities built a 55-acre prison of that name and put its inmates to work in the nearby marble quarries. In 1901 the village of Sing Sing decided their town should not have the same name as the penitentiary, whose modern counterpart is visible along the eastern shore's low hills.

Croton-on-Hudson, **Mile H-30.0 E (NM),** on Croton Point's northern side, was once part of Van Cortlandt Manor, an 86,000-acre Dutch-English estate and family home for more than 250 years. Italian and Irish laborers founded Croton in the 1840s; they came to build the first Croton Reservoir Dam and Aqueduct, one of the earliest American water systems. When completed in 1842, the 38-mile-long aqueduct carried fresh water from the Croton River to Manhattan.

North of Croton Point and Hook Mountain you are in Haverstraw Bay, and the channel favors the western shoreline. The Dutch settled eastern-shore Haverstraw in 1664. They called it Averstoo after the river meadows' waving straw. An early resident, James Wood, discovered the system of firing bricks that boosted the village's economy. Up to 40 brickyards operated there until lack of clay closed them down in 1909. The mountain behind the village is 820-foot High Tor.

Stony Point, **Mile H-35.0 W (NM),** is the rocky, heavily wooded, prominent peninsula at **Light SP.** Early settlers called it "Gibraltar of the Highlands." In the 1700s the Kings Ferry crossed to Verplanck Point. During the Revolution the ferry was a main link in the American armies' east-west line of communication. At one time the British had control of it, until Brigadier General "Mad Anthony" Wayne captured their 600-man Stony Point garrison in a daring night attack.

A hundred years ago Hudson River fishing was big business. One of the profitable catches was sturgeon, prized by epicures for its veal-like meat, known as "Albany Beef," and its eggs, which were sold for caviar. Heavily overfished, sturgeon nearly disappeared from the river. They are finally returning, and it's not uncommon in springtime to see commercial fisherman setting their sturgeon nets around the Verplanck area.

Near Indian Point, at **Mile H-37.2 E (NM),** are the single stack and domes of the $120 million Con-Ed Atomic

Power Plant. North of the power plant is shoal Peekskill Bay; the city of Peekskill is on the harborfront. The colonists kept their main army here during the Revolution; fortifications on the bay's northerly point allowed them to watch up and down the river for an invasion.

At Jones Point, **Mile H-38.0 W (NM),** the river narrows. To the northwest is 1,110-foot Dunderberg Mountain. Sailing vessels might heed a Dutch legend concerning this reach. It tells of a goblin sitting atop Dunderberg (Dutch for "thunder mountain") and using a speaking trumpet to bellow orders to the winds, which oblige by whooping down the mountain valleys to the river.

Ahead on the western shore is the deserted naval depot at Iona Island, called Salisbury Island in the 1700s. Forested 1,300-foot Bear Mountain—home of Bear Mountain State Park—is just ahead; the bridge, **Mile H-40.5 (NM),** crosses to towering Anthony's Nose on the east.

Just north of the bridge, Popolopen Creek flows from Bear Mountain's heights. Just south of the creek's mouth is the site of Revolutionary War Fort Clinton; north of the creek is the site of Fort Montgomery. In

Fishing in the Hudson River

The lower Hudson offers some good sportfishing, especially if pursuing your quarry is as attractive to you as consuming it. Unfortunately, between Troy and New York Harbor industrial pollutants are so widespread that eating your catch is inadvisable. Get a "New York State Fishing Regulations Guide" when you buy your license, and be forewarned.

You won't need a license for fishing from New York City north to Troy; above the dam at Troy you'll need one if you are over 16. Licenses can be purchased on a 5-day or seasonal basis and are available at most sporting goods stores, at the Department of Environmental Conservation (DEC), and from town and county clerks.

In addition to licensing requirements, there may be local seasonal restrictions in some areas. Check your regulations guide.

Some of the best gamefish:

Largemouth Bass. Try for these along marshy banks very early or in late evening. Largemouth like cooler, shallower waters with lots of weeds. Cast into the target area and draw your lure outward, away from the center; we get our best strikes along the edge. Spinners and plastic worms seem to work best.

Shad. Hudson area south; best between Poughkeepsie and Coxsackie. Catskill Creek and Roecliff–Jansen Kill areas are especially popular. Shad like deepwater channels where there's a current. Troll or cast with a spinner, but use a good 10-pound test—these fish hit hard.

Smallmouth Bass. Available most anywhere. They prefer cooler water; during summer, try deeper waters, between 10 and 30 feet. Smallmouth are bottom fish, usually lurking around big rocks, piers, or other shelter. Natural bait (crayfish, crickets, minnows)—or a lure that *looks* natural—works best. On cool evenings, smallmouth come to the surface and allegedly make for good fly fishing, although we haven't had much luck that way. A 6- to 10-pound test should be sufficient.

Striped Bass. These like shallower, moving waters, usually between 10 and 20 feet deep. Best target areas are around pilings, rocks, and highway riprap. A white bone jig or a silver spinner trolled above the bottom works best. We've never caught anything that would break a 10-pound test, although there may be bigger fish out there.

Walleye. Night, late evening, and early morning are the best times for walleye fishing. Minnow lures in shallow water work well. Walleye are a might slow on the take, so don't troll too fast. We often let the lure sink to the bottom for a few seconds before tugging it again. Try casting or trolling over a shallow bar. Average weight is 2 to 3 pounds, so light tackle will work fine.

the 1700s the Americans stretched a chain across the Hudson to Anthony's Nose in hopes of stopping British ships sailing upstream. However, the British came by land over Dunderberg Mountain in 1777. They attacked Fort Montgomery from the rear, captured it, destroyed the river chain and boom, then continued upstream in their raiding advance toward Kingston.

At **Mile H-45.0 W (NM)** is the United States Military Academy at West Point, originally the site of Revolutionary War military posts. As you make the sharp bend west around Gees Point, watch your fathometer drop to 175 feet at World's End, the river's deepest point. Here another immense chain was once stretched across the river to Fort Constitution to stop the British fleet from sailing upriver. It took six weeks for the army's chief ironmaster to make the 180-ton chain, since each link weighed more than 140 pounds and was more than 2 feet long and 2.5 inches thick. Huge block-and-tackles protected by cannon emplacements attached the chain to both shores. When in place the device was buoyed with 16-foot logs.

Around rocky Magazine Point on Constitution Island, remains of Fort Constitution face the river and Foundry Cove. For many years Susan and Anna Warner lived on the island and held bible classes for cadets. In 1908 the island was deeded to the nation.

A freshwater spring at Cold Spring, **Mile H-46.5 E (NM),** on Foundry Cove's northern shore made it a watering place for river sailing ships. The town was also the location of the West Point Foundry, which cast cannon, shells, and shot during the Civil War.

Look northeast of Cold Spring to see Boscobel in the hills facing the river and the Military Academy. It's a New York Federal-style mansion built in 1804 by States Morris Dyckman.

In this area most of the hills along the river have elevations of more than 1,300 feet. They include Crows Nest Mountain and Butter Hill in the Scunemunk Mountains across from Cold Spring. In the 1800s author Nathaniel Park Willis named impressive Storm King Mountain, **Mile H-49.5 (NM).** Opposite Storm King is Breakneck Mountain; railroad tunnels burrow under its southwestern point. The quarry at Little Stony Point is in the foothills of Bull Hill.

The Hudson has an unusual geological past. Sixty million years ago, during the Tertiary Period, the river wound across the Harrisburg Peneplain, an eroded undulating landscape. Then the crust of the earth pushed upward and the river began to scour a deep channel—up

to 860 feet—here at Storm King Gateway. As time passed, layers of boulders, gravel, and silt filled up most of the gorge to leave the channel as it is today.

North of the gateway the river straightens and widens. The next 7 miles upriver can be a choppy run if there are strong northerlies. Be cautious of the western shore at Moodna or Murderers Creek—silt deposits extend more than 0.3 mile toward the channel.

The ruin you see at Pollopel (or Bannerman's) Island, **Mile H-49.7 E (NM),** is the abandoned Bannerman Island Arsenal. Bannerman, a munitions dealer during the Civil War, built the turreted castle as a storehouse for his excess ammunition and guns.

Palatines (German expatriates) settled Newburgh, **Mile H-52.6 W (NM),** in 1708. It was George Washington's Continental Army headquarters from 1782 to 1783. After the war it was an important river port. Much of its early economy came from the whaling industry.

Across the river is 1,550-foot Beacon Mountain, topped with assorted relay towers. The Continental Army used the hill for signal fires to warn the colonists of British troop movements. There were originally two settlements at Beacon: Matteawan and Fishkill Village. During the Revolution New York's largest military depot was in Fishkill. For a short time it was also the location of the State Constitutional Convention, which the British had routed from White Plains. By 1913 the towns combined to form Beacon. You make a slight right-hand bend north of the Beacon-Newburgh Bridge; mind the buoy on the shoal eastern shore.

North of Chelsea, **Mile H-56.0 E (NM),** you pass Wappinger Creek; the town of Wappinger Falls is about 1.7 miles above the creek's mouth. This area was once home to the Wappinger Indians, a confederation of nearly 5,000 members of the Algonquian tribes. In the early 17th century they lived along the eastern riverbank from what is now Manhattan to Poughkeepsie; they scattered during the Dutch War of 1640 to 1645.

There have been few hazards on the river so far, but now Diamond Reef, **Mile H-58.2 (NM),** is in midriver; a midchannel buoy notes its 5-foot shoal.

The Indians called Poughkeepsie, **Mile H-65.5 E (NM),** "apo-keep-sinck"; the Dutch arrived in 1687 and pronounced it Pokeepsie. Ninety years later it became another temporary capital of New York. Thousand-acre Vassar College, founded in 1861 by Matthew Vassar, a Poughkeepsie brewer, is 2 miles east of the river.

Though tidal flow continues to above Albany, Poughkeepsie is usually the final limit of saltwater invasion; for the rest of this tour, you travel in fresh water.

At **Mile H-68.0 E (NM)**—just before you start the slight bend at Crum Elbow—look east on the bluff to see Roth Hall and the 83-acre Culinary Institute of America campus. It has four student-operated restaurants and 95 international faculty members. Over 4,000 meals are prepared daily in its 32 teaching kitchens and bakeshops.

Hyde Park, **Mile H-70.5 E (NM),** is the location of the home and burial site of President Franklin Delano Roosevelt. For further information, contact the Roosevelt-Vanderbilt National Historic Sites, 249 Albany Post Road, Hyde Park, New York 12538; (914) 229-9115.

Uninhabited Esopus Island, **Mile H-72.5 (NM),** is nearly in midriver. There's good water on either side, but if you choose the eastern channel, watch your wake passing the club docks.

Northeast of Esopus Island at Indian Kill is Margaret Lewis Norrie State Park. Just to the north be certain to mind **Cave Point Buoy #9** and **Middle Hudson River Light #11** at **Mile H-75.2 (NM).** The river widens to over a mile between these two areas. Don't try to save time by cruising the western shore—rocks, stumps, and shallows extend almost to Rondout Creek. They are visible at low water.

Abandoned Esopus Meadows Lighthouse (now called the Middle Hudson River Light), at **Daymark #11**, was one of the early manned river lighthouses. In 1958 a 15-foot-high ice jam bumped it askew.

Rondout Creek just ahead and Esopus and Catskill creeks farther north drain part of the Catskill Mountains. In early spring heavy runoff from the creeks may cause current increases on the main river. Flow depends on the previous winter's snowfall, length of its melt, and spring rains. If severe, drift can become a problem.

These navigable creeks are the harbors of old riverport towns. They are usually deep, narrow, steeply banked, shadowed by high hills, and convenient to the village waterfront, and they make excellent stopovers. Coming up is Rondout Creek, **Mile H-79.0 W (NM),** the harbor for Kingston.

Things to Do and See in Kingston

Kingston is a State Urban Cultural Park with a transportation theme. The city's architecture includes Early Dutch, Federal, Greek Revival, Italianate, and Victorian structures. The restored city center along the waterfront and the row of 19th-century buildings are the survivors of the old riverfront commercial center. There are hotels, restaurants, an old general store, galleries, antique shops, and boutiques. The mansion at the corner of Broadway was once a 100-room stage stop and hotel.

Beside the marina is one of Kingston's two visitor centers, where you can get information and directions. Especially helpful are the walking-tour maps for the Stockade, Rondout, and Broadway areas.

The Shad Festival is held at the end of May, and the Pumpkin Festival is in October.

Hudson River Maritime Center, Rondout Creek, at the foot of Broadway; (914) 338-0071. A living museum, with sailing arts exhibitions, restored buildings, and ship displays. Open daily from May 1 to October, 11 to 5. There is an admission fee.

Senate House and Museum, 269 Fair Street; (914) 338-2786. Site of the first official meeting of the New York State Senate. The museum houses works by John Vanderlyn, a Kingston artist who achieved nationwide prominence as a landscape artist in the early 1900s. Open from April to December, Wednesday through Saturday, 10 to 5; Sunday 1 to 5. January through March, open Saturday 10 to 5 and Sunday 1 to 5.

Stockade District Walking Tours, (914) 338-5100. Tours of the reconstructed stockade district leave from the Senate House with costumed guides.

The Old Dutch Church, Main and Wall streets; (914) 338-6759. The present structure was built in 1852 from designs by the noted architect Minard Lafever. A museum, a garden, and a graveyard with some *very* old tombstones. Open year-round, Monday through Friday, 9 to 2.

Trolley Museum, 1 Rondout Landing; (914) 331-9300. Exhibits and photographs of the trolley era, and rides along the Hudson River. Open May through September, Saturday and Sunday, 10 to 4. There is an admission fee.

NEWPORT YACHT CLUB AND MARINA

★★★★

5

Chart: N 12335

Mile H-1.2 W (NM)

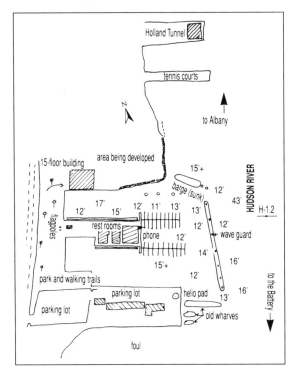

This 160-slip Jersey City marina is inside an old commercial slip north of the prominent Colgate Clock and south of the Holland Tunnel's western vent. It's protected by a 500-foot floating breakwater moored by pilings with white cone-shaped tops.

Entry is at the breakwater's southern end near a blue-and-white marina sign. Inside the basin are two floating piers of slips extending east. To their west is a solid bulkhead with more slips on each side—the Inner Basin South and Inner Basin North. Bulkhead docking is usually for very large pleasure craft.

Block or cube ice, 110-volt/30-amp and 220-volt/50-amp electric hookups, and engine repairs are available here.

Most facilities and the office are in the center bulkhead complex. There's 24-hour security, an on-site health club, a swimming pool, and tennis courts with passes issued to transients. For information, call (201) 626-5550.

The Newport Centre Mall—over 100 stores, a nine-screen theater, restaurants, and a supermarket—is across Washington Boulevard.

The marina is an excellent base for a visit to the World Trade Center, the Ellis Island Museum, the Statue of Liberty, and all the sights of New York City. The PATH subway station runs to the World Trade Center and West 33rd Street. A helicopter pad and ferry are nearby.

79TH STREET ANCHORAGES

★★★

1

NO FACILITIES

Chart: N 12341, *See sketch map, page 31*

Mile H-5.8 + 0.2 E (NM)

These anchorages are off 79th Street Marina's north or south mooring areas. Both are subject to severe tidal current, and when strong winds blow up- and down-river an unpleasant chop runs through the anchorages, especially when wind and tide oppose.

The river is deep, so you can approach at any angle,

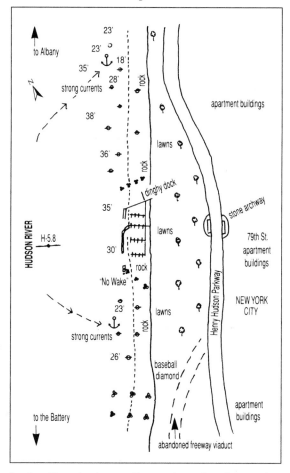

but head into the current. Bottom is mud, and you swing with the tide.

The marina has limited space. If you would like a slip, you can ask the dockmaster; he is usually somewhere near the old fuel dock area on the marina's outer north-south extending bulkhead. If you anchor and hope to land the dinghy at the marina—the only safe area to leave it—you must contact the dockmaster. Security is tight and docks patrolled; unidentified strangers are not always tolerated.

Bordering the river is Riverside Park, a popular jogging, bicycling, roller skating, and strolling area. If you plan to visit the city, taxis and transit systems are minutes away.

The view from this anchorage is magnificent; be sure to supper in the cockpit and watch the city lamplighting.

TARRYTOWN MARINA

★★★★

ALL FACILITIES

Chart: N 12343, *See A on sketch map, page 32*

Mile H-23.5 + 0.6 E (NM)

This seasonal marina—open March 15 to November 15—is in Tappan Zee in Tarrytown on the river's eastern shore. It's off the main channel in an enclosed basin.

Immediately north of the Tappan Zee Bridge, pick up the first pair of secondary channel buoys, **Buoy #1** and **Buoy #2,** at the main channel's edge. There's also a range to follow. The approach channel is wide, bears northeasterly, and is watched with two more pairs of buoys. At the most northeasterly pair, **Buoy #5** and **Buoy #6,** locate the basin to the east-southeast. The southerly side of the basin's western face is wood, and "Tarrytown Marina" is written on it in large yellow letters. A Sunoco fuel sign is also prominent. The northern side of this face is a barge. The marina entrance—marked with a tower with red and white circular stripes—is at the basin's northern corner around the barge's end. The entrance's northern side is partially bulkheaded for a picnic area and tennis courts.

The bulk of marina slips extend northerly from the basin's southern side. If no one answers on VHF 16, pull in to the fuel dock (gas and diesel) on the northern end of the most easterly of the four piers; you can recognize it in the distance by its high cupola.

Block and cube ice, electric hookups (110-volt/30-amp and 220-volt/50-amp), engine and hull repairs, and a 25-ton Travelift are available here. The land line number is (914) 631-1300.

The dock office has a few supplies, marine equipment, and local charts. The restaurant/bar, Dockside at Tarrytown, is at the basin's northeastern bight.

Tarrytown's Main Street is a few blocks away; there is a bank, a supermarket, restaurants, a pharmacy, a hardware store, a post office, and a library. Go out the gate, turn left, cross the road, and go up the steps over the railroad trestle. Across the tracks make another left; downtown is to the right at the light.

Car rentals and taxis are available. Tarrytown is about a half-hour train ride from New York; pick up

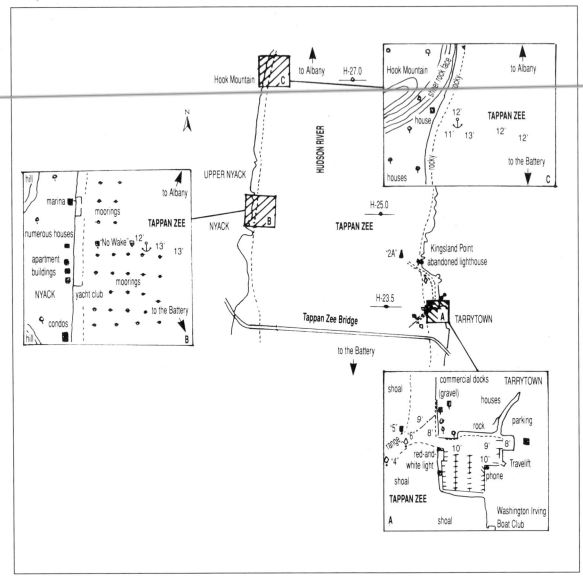

a schedule in the office.

There are some interesting historical sites to visit, though they are beyond walking distance. Gothic Revival Lyndhurst is on the main north-south highway, Route 9, about a mile south. They offer tours, an occasional summertime outdoor concert, and special events; call (914) 631-0046 for information.

North on the highway at College Avenue is the Captor's Monument commemorating the capture of Major John André by Tarrytown residents.

Philipsburg Manor—a mid-1700s Dutch Colonial stone house and gristmill once owned by Frederick Philipse—is north on Route 9.

Just north of Philipsburg Manor is the Old Dutch Church and Sleepy Hollow Cemetery. Philipse built the church in 1690; it became famous as the church and graveyard in Washington Irving's "Legend of Sleepy Hollow." Irving and many of Tarrytown's original settlers are buried in the cemetery.

The Historic Hudson Valley group owns Sunnyside, Irving's home, which is back south about 4 miles on Route 9. Call (914) 631-8200 for tour hours.

NYACK ANCHORAGE

★★★

Chart: N 12343, *See B on sketch map, page 32*

Mile H-25.0 + 1.4 NW (NM)

This western-shore anchorage is off the village of Nyack beside a large mooring area.

Leave the main channel on the river's eastern side about 1.2 miles north of the Tappan Zee Bridge. Bear northwesterly toward the moorings; they become more visible as you near shore. Preferred anchorage is at the northern end of the largest compact group of moorings and about midway between the outer line of moorings and shore. Approach heading into the current. Bottom is mud. Unless wind is strong you swing with the tide. This is an uncomfortable rolly anchorage in strong winds from the north and northeast—especially when wind and tide oppose.

Nearly all the shoreline is privately owned, so ask for permission to tie the dinghy if you go ashore. The mooring area belongs to a friendly yacht club located about midway in the main mooring area—spot it by the racks of stored dinghies. The club's steward is usually helpful and allows transients to use the dinghy dock.

Nyack is about four blocks southwesterly from the club. It has most supplies and services, though the only place within walking distance at which to buy groceries is a 7-Eleven.

HOOK MOUNTAIN ANCHORAGE

★★★★

NO FACILITIES

Chart: N 12343, *See C on sketch map, page 32*

Mile H-27.0 + 1.0 W (NM)

This attractive western-shore anchorage at the foot of Hook Mountain has a superb view.

Bear westerly from the main channel near **Light**

Buoy #5, Mile H-27.0 (NM). Depths decrease gradually as you near the mountain. Anchor close to shore in mud off a small stone shelter on the beach; you swing with the tide. In strong northeast and southwest winds the anchorage is choppy and rolly, especially if wind and tide oppose.

The shoreside stone shelter is a rest area for a park's jogging, bicycling, and hiking path, but the rocky waterfront makes dinghy access ashore difficult.

Occasionally on a summer Saturday evening fireworks are set off near the park pavilion just south of the anchorage; your view of this event is exceptional.

CROTON POINT ANCHORAGE

★★★

NO FACILITIES

Chart: N 12343

Mile H-31.2 + 1.7 E (NM)

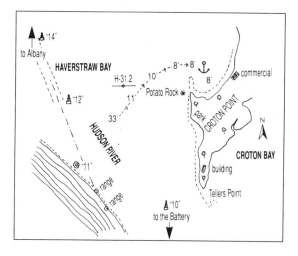

This popular weekend anchorage—open to the north and northwest—is on Haverstraw Bay's eastern shore on the northern side of 1.5-mile-long Croton Point, a long southwesterly reaching peninsula that ends at Tellers Point. Your destination is in a slight bight between Croton Point's Potato Rock and the river's eastern bank. Potato Rock is on the point about midway along its southwestern side.

Leave the main channel just south of **Light Buoy #12** and bear easterly to wooded Croton Point's northern side. Give the northern tip a wide berth; Potato Rock has a long northerly shoal. Once west of this shoal, anchor in mud as close to shore as depth allows. You normally swing with the wind.

During sultry summer days there's usually a cooling breeze. Unfortunately, this type of day often brings afternoon thunderstorms with brief but strong winds. Though this can build an uncomfortable chop from the northwest in a very short time, it usually is of short duration. The anchorage is not recommended if a severe frontal passage is forecast.

HAVERSTRAW MARINA

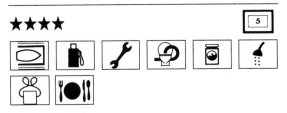

Chart: N 12343, *See A on sketch map*

Mile H-33.5 + 0.5 W (NM)

This western-shore marina's enclosed basin makes it a fairly secure stop if a hurricane threatens the southern Hudson area. If dockage is unavailable in normal conditions, check for an empty mooring, though if you take a mooring, buy supplies and take showers before picking it up. If a river chop is running, it's a rough dinghy ride back to the marina complex.

Leave the main channel just south of **Light Buoy #16**. Several landmarks will help you find the basin: It's north of a power plant with twin buildings and stacks; there is a large, white, roundish sculpture on a pedestal on the mole near the basin's southern entry point; just north of the basin's northern point is a large commercial facility with a crane whose prominent covered conveyor belt runs to the water; in the river off the basin's southern mole is the mooring area; and west of the mole is a collection of masts visible through the trees.

If no one answered on VHF 16, pull in to the fuel dock (gas and diesel) and office on the basin's northern side just inside the entrance. The ship's store has a selection of marine equipment, general supplies, gifts, and some nautical sportswear. The restaurant, Paulie's, overlooks the river.

Block and cube ice, electric hookups (110-volt and 220-volt), engine and hull repairs, and a 30-ton Travelift are available here.

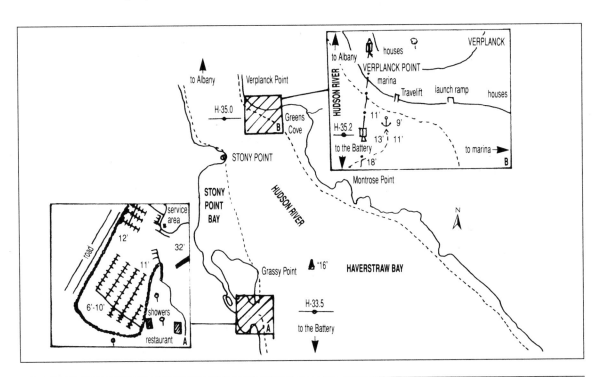

VERPLANCK ANCHORAGE

 ★★★

NO FACILITIES

Chart: N 12343, *See B on sketch map, page 34*

Mile H-35.2 + 0.3 E (NM)

This eastern-shore anchorage is south of Verplanck Point at the ship ranges **C1** and **C3.** Northbound, follow the range to its southern standard, then bear to its eastern side and anchor east of and between the ranges. There's good depth between the ranges for exiting or entering. The anchorage is close to a small shoreside marina with a pair of blue-painted Travelifts; don't block their access. There's a larger marina inside a bulkheaded basin a short distance east; don't anchor so far from the bank that you are in its approach.

The view across the river is of wooded Stony Point; south are valleys, mountains, and the wide river. In spring watch for large flocks of Canada geese and white swans.

GARRISON LANDING ANCHORAGE

★★★★

Chart: N 12343, *See A on sketch map*

Mile H-44.5 + 0.2 E (NM)

This eastern-shore anchorage is at Garrison about opposite West Point. It's south of a few moorings located just south of the bulkheaded Garrison Yacht Club basin. This is a deep anchorage and bottom is mud; you swing with the tide.

The yacht club is primarily for runabouts. Check at the grocery-deli by the railroad tracks if you want to tie up, make a phone call, or buy gas, basic groceries, or ice. You can land the dinghy on the beach at the basin's southern side.

If you plan to visit the military academy by dinghy, take care. The river is 0.4 mile wide and tidal flow is excessive. Another option is to rent a car when you get to Kingston, farther north, and return to West Point then.

Garrison Landing Anchorage, Cold Spring Anchorage

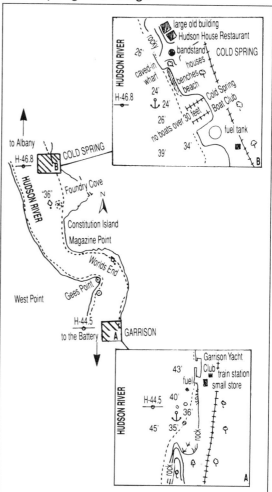

COLD SPRING ANCHORAGE

★★★★

NO FACILITIES

Chart: N 12343, *See B on sketch map*

Mile H-46.8 + 0.2 E (NM)

This eastern-shore anchorage is off Cold Spring just north of Foundry Cove. Northbound as you round Constitution Island, pick up **Buoy #36,** which marks a rock at Foundry Cove's southern end. Hold to the main channel until north of the cove and clear of the shoals, then bear easterly and head just north of the visible silver tank. As you close shore, you can pick up some remains of what at one time was a town dock and bulkhead—you usually can land the dinghy on the beach just south of the caved-in wharf. The Cold Spring Boat Club is in a shore indentation, so anchor in mud just to its north. If you don't feel like anchoring and are less than 30 feet long, you might try the boat club for a slip.

The Hudson House Restaurant is a walk up the road past the bandstand. After a repast you can have a look at the well-kept older homes or visit the Foundry School Museum, housed in a 150-year-old schoolhouse at 63 Chestnut Street—open Wednesday and Thursday, 1 to 4 and 7 to 9.

CHELSEA LOW POINT ANCHORAGE

★★★   3

NO FACILITIES

Chart: N 12343

Mile H-56.0 + 0.3 E (NM)

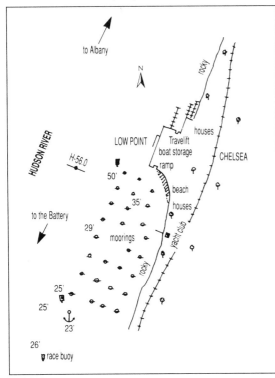

This eastern-shore anchorage is at Low Point at Chelsea. It's very visible; beside it is a large yacht club mooring area. There are two lighted buoys outside the moorings that set its limits. Preferred anchorage in mud is at the southern end of the moorings; at the northern section you could be in the way of the club docks and ramp area. It's very deep, and you swing with the tidal current.

Though permanent vessels usually occupy all moorings, the club will rent one if an owner is on holiday. For information contact the club's officer of the day.

WEST SHORE MARINE

★★★   2

Chart: N 12347, *See sketch map, page 37*

Mile H-59.6 + 0.3 W (NM)

This western-shore marina—open April 15 to October 15—is about 0.7 mile north of **Diamond Reef Light Buoy #44**. It's the first marina north of Danskammer Point and off the inland village of Marlboro. There are two facilities side by side: the marina, to the south, and Marlboro Yacht Club, to the north. Part of the marina sits at the southern end of a slight bight in the riverbank.

If no one answered on VHF 16, pull in to the floating fuel dock (gas and diesel) at 90 degrees to shore off an old terminal's face. A small dock office is on the bulkhead at the head of the ramp. Though there's a lot of current just offshore, the fuel dock is somewhat protected from the main flow. The main office is in the large building across the yard lot.

Most slips are on two floating piers that extend from the bight and parallel the shore. This gives them some protection from sweep and chop caused by northerly wind.

Block and cube ice, electric hookups (110-volt/30-amp and 50-amp), engine and hull repairs, and a 25-ton Travelift are available here. The ship's store has marine equipment and supplies and local charts. The land line number is (914) 236-4486.

Marlboro, which has a supermarket and a mall, is 0.1 mile down the road. If you don't want to walk, call a taxi. The restaurant, The "Other" Porch, is next door at the yacht club and is open to the public.

West Shore Marine

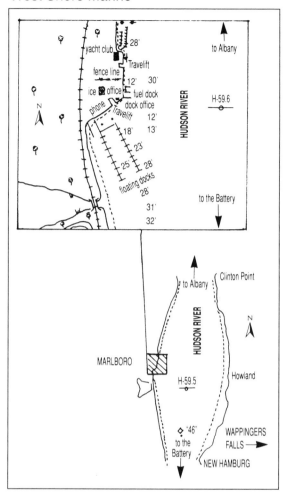

Mariner's Harbor

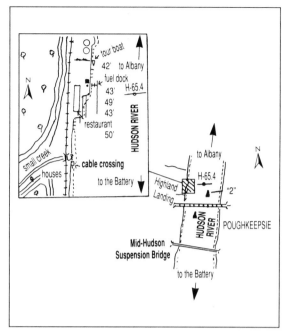

MARINER'S HARBOR

★★   2

Chart: N 12347

Mile H-65.4 + 0.2 W (NM)

This western-shore marina is immediately north of the Poughkeepsie Railroad Bridge. Once under the bridge you will see the docks in front of the Mariner's Harbor Restaurant, which has a reputation as the Hudson Valley's "#1 Seafood Restaurant."

The river is deep, so make an approach at any angle, but come in heading into the current. If wind is severe from the north or south, there can be an uncomfortable chop at the outer dock, especially when wind opposes the current.

Dockage is primarily for the restaurant, but if space is available, they gladly accept overnight travelers. The main floating pier parallels the bank with the fuel dock at its northern end. This is the place to pull in to ask about a slip, electric hookup (110-volt), or fuel (gas and diesel). Talk to the restaurant cashier for service, or call (914) 691-6011 for information. Most large-boat transient dockage is on this pier's eastern face but south of the fuel area.

POUGHKEEPSIE YACHT CLUB

★★★   3

Chart: N 12347, *See sketch map, page 38*

Mile H-72.4 E (NM)

This friendly eastern-shore club is the only complex with slips and moorings east of wooded Esopus Island. The club has three sets of piers with slips that extend off

Poughkeepsie Yacht Club

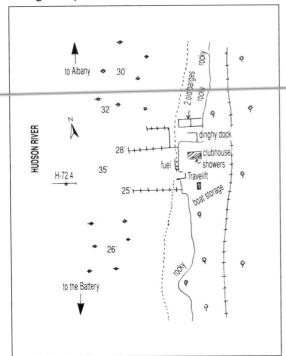

the shore. If no one answered on VHF, pull in to the fuel dock (gas and diesel) between the southern and middle piers. It is parallel to the bank and about in front of the clubhouse. Come in heading into the current.

The club has a Travelift for their winter boat storage yard behind the main grounds. Though intended for members, in an emergency contact the officer of the day about its use. If a slip is unavailable, ask about a vacant mooring.

Electric hookup (110-volt/30-amp) is available.

The clubhouse/bar is a place to meet the club's members, who can report on local cruising areas and river conditions. If you arrive on a weekend, you are usually included in club activities.

RONDOUT CREEK

Chart: N 12347, *See sketch map, page 39*

Mile H-79.0 (NM)

Rondout Creek, the harbor for Kingston, is on the Hudson's western shore. It is marked and navigable for 3 miles to the Eddyville–New Salem Bridge. It's used by pleasure and commercial craft. If you plan to transit the entire creek area, note the following bridge clearances: the fixed highway bridge 1 mile above the entrance, 56 feet; the next bridge, 86 feet; and the last bridge, 144 feet. This is a historical area and a popular destination; there are several marinas and an anchorage.

The creek entrance is watched by prominent, buff-colored Rondout Lighthouse on the northernmost dike. The dikes—visible at low water but underwater or awash at high water—are watched by four pairs of black and red daymarks. The dikes are best approached from the southeast as they make a left-hand bend around the natural creek contours. Hold to midchannel during entry for best depths.

After you make the first bend, favor the northern shore; debris and shoals reach up from the southern bank. Hold this course about a mile to the first upstream fixed bridge.

Kingston City Dock

★★★★

Chart: N 12347, *See A on sketch map, page 39*

Mile H-79.0 + 1.2 W (NM)

This is a convenient stop for visiting the city; you are at the hub of downtown's West Strand activity.

At the first upstream fixed bridge, the channel bears south of an island. Your destination is just west of the bridge, north of the island, along the Kingston waterfront. The marina extends into a cut north of the island that once was the tidewater terminal for the 1828 Delaware and Hudson Canal—in its heyday it was filled wall to wall with canalboats.

Most of the 2,000 feet of marina dockage is parallel parking. Pull in to the T-pier nearest the bridge to inquire for an overnight space. Availability changes continually; boats move in and out after owners visit town or have a meal ashore. It's usually well filled on summer weekends.

The docks border a city park with manicured lawns, park benches, flowers, clean garbage cans, and a bandstand. The Sunrise Deli and Grocery is about a block up from the water.

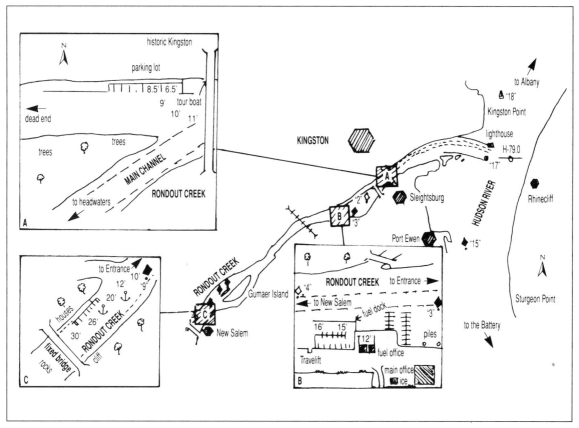

Rondout Yacht Basin

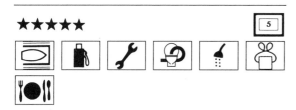

★★★★★

5

Chart: N 12347, *See B on sketch map*

Mile H-79.0 + 1.6 W (NM)

This marina is about 1.4 miles up Rondout Creek. Follow the entry instructions to the first upstream Kingston Bridge. In 1921 this bridge replaced an early chain ferry called "Skilleypot" (Dutch for tortoise).

The main channel continues west and is now on the island's southern side. James McEntee, a local engineer, built this 0.5-mile-long island in 1848 as a temporary storage area for coal shipped down the Delaware and Hudson Canal.

Almost immediately you come up to the Sleightsburg Bridge. The marina is about 0.3 mile farther west on the creek's southern side. Old-time visitors remember this area as the old Republic Shipyard.

If no one answered on VHF 16, pull in to the fuel dock (gas or diesel) in front of the dock office and small lunchroom patio. Come straight in from the buoyed channel. There are two easterly piers with fingers, an open dock next to the fuel pier, and more slips inside the western bight. The main office and most facilities are across the wide lawn and beyond the extensive winter cradle storage area. The ship's store stocks marine supplies, local charts, camera supplies, a book exchange library, and a few basic food items. The marina's land line number is (914) 331-7061.

Cube ice, electric hookups (110-volt/30-amp and 220-volt/50-amp), engine and hull repairs, and a 35-ton Travelift are available here. For canalling sailboats, the yard has a mobile mast-stepping crane. If the 56- or 86-foot clearance to the marina is a problem, the crane can be sent to other areas for mast work.

You are close enough to dinghy to downtown Kingston's village dock to visit the historical sights. You are actually in the hamlet of Connelly, whose post office is about three blocks south.

Eddyville Pond

★★★★

5

Chart: N 12347, *See C on sketch map, page 39*

Mile H-79.0 + 3.0 W (NM)

This anchorage is 3 miles upcreek at Eddyville. It's a protected, peaceful, scenic area if waiting out bad weather on the river.

Follow the approach instructions through the first bridges—remember their fixed heights (see page 38). At the Sleightsburg Bridge you approach impressive Kingston Gorge, which is spanned by a railroad bridge. Beyond this bridge there's an active sand, gravel, and crushed rock barge-loading terminal on the southern shore. On west about 0.6 mile, the creek is divided by Gumaer Island; the watched channel is on the island's northern side. The anchorage in a muddy bottom is just downstream of the low-level Eddyville–New Salem Bridge in a wide part of the creek. There's a small marina and picnic area on the northern bank; don't block their slip entry.

Make arrangements at the marina to leave the skiff when you go ashore. If you walk up the road about 100 yards, you can see the intricate stonework of an old Delaware and Hudson Canal lock. It's part of someone's front yard, so don't barge right on in; you can have a good look from the lane. This was a working lock for more than 70 years and the canal's eastern terminus.

The Hudson River North
Rondout Creek to Waterford

Mile H-79.0 (NM) to Mile H-134.3 (NM)

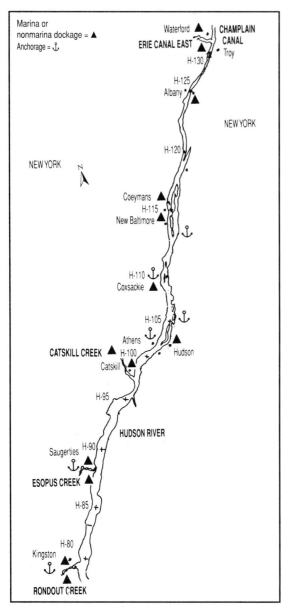

Marina or
nonmarina dockage = ▲
Anchorage = ⚓

Waterford ▲ CHAMPLAIN
ERIE CANAL EAST ▲ CANAL
H-130 Troy

H-125
Albany

NEW YORK

H-120

NEW YORK

Coeymans ▲
H-115
New Baltimore ▲

H-110 ⚓
Coxsackie ▲

H-105 ⚓

Athens ⚓
CATSKILL CREEK ▲ H-100 Hudson
Catskill

H-95

HUDSON RIVER

Saugerties H-90
⚓
ESOPUS CREEK ▲

H-85

H-80
Kingston ▲
⚓
RONDOUT CREEK

Mile H-79.0 (NM) to Mile H-134.3 (NM)

> *Whoever has made a voyage up the Hudson must remember the Kaatskill Mountains. They are a dismembered branch of the great Appalachian family, and are seen away to the west of the river, swelling up to a noble height, and lording it over the surrounding country. . . .*
>
> Washington Irving, "Rip Van Winkle"

MOVABLE BRIDGES, RONDOUT CREEK TO WATERFORD

Name	Mile	Clearance Closed*	Land Line
Albany-Conrail	H-125.7 (NM)	25 feet	
Troy–Green Island	H-131.1 (NM)	29 feet	(518) 271-8862
Troy–Cohoes 112th Street	H-133.5 (NM)	33 feet	(518) 235-2821

*At Mean Low Water

All bridges monitor VHF 13. Signals: Lights and Horn (1 long and 1 short blast)

Schedules:

Albany-Conrail Swing: Need not be opened for passage of vessels during the period December 16 to March 31 unless 24-hour advance notice is given.

Troy–Green Island Lift: April 1 through December 15, opens on signal from 0900 to 1600. Will not open from 1600 to 0700 unless notice is given before 1630. Does not open from 0700 to 0900 and 1600 to 1800.

Troy–Cohoes 112th Street Bascule: Opens on signal from 0900 to 1600 except from 0700 to 0900 and 1600 to 1800. Will not open from 1800 to 0700 unless notice is given before 1630. During periods when the Federal Lock does not operate the draw will not open.

North of Kingston Point the Hudson remains more than 0.5 mile wide, but now rocky shallow flats and extensive shoals appear in midriver or extend well off either shore. There are plentiful upper-river navigation aids—steamships navigate to Albany—but often they are far apart. Many mark entries into branch channels, and these could cause confusion since all aids are the same size. If you miss a marker and start a side channel, it may be impossible to get safely back into the main stream without backtracking for miles.

Surface-set shad nets are common on the river in springtime and are a propeller-fouling problem. The nets are set in unlikely places—often nearly bank to bank in the main channel. Don't cross between main net buoys, which tend to be marked by larger odd-colored buoys. A nearby fisherman—usually in a large outboard skiff—who waves frantically, blows a horn or whistle, or looks generally distraught is probably warning you away from a net.

North of Rondout Creek you cross and recross the river as you navigate around large river shoals and flats. In 1609 Henry Hudson's *Half Moon* spent five days in the area visiting and entertaining the local Indians—probably asking them how to find deep water.

In the 17th century the distinguished Livingston family bought a large eastern-shore land tract from the Indians. Philip Livingston was a Continental Congress representative and a signer of the Declaration of Independence. Harriet Livingston married Robert Fulton, who, with Robert Livingston, designed the

Henry Hudson

In September 1609 Henry Hudson's caravel-rigged *Half Moon* slipped through the narrows and anchored off Manhattan Island. Hudson was a determined searcher for the holy grail of European expansion: the elusive Northwest Passage to India. The mouth of the great river to his north seemed a promising course.

Traveling northward, Hudson paused near West Point long enough to visit an Indian village. There the aging, white-haired chief treated the Dutchman to some local delicacies: a brace of pigeons and "a fat dog skinned in great haste, with shells which they get out of the water."

At Albany, *Half Moon* ran into shoal waters. A small exploration team sent ahead confirmed Hudson's suspicions: his ship could go no farther. Disgustedly, he headed southward.

A peaceful retreat it was not. Near Stony Point, a canoe full of Indians silently pulled up to the becalmed *Half Moon*'s stern. One of the bolder natives climbed into a cabin and tried to make off with a pillow and some shirts. The first mate heard him and shot him dead as he tried to escape.

In retaliation, an Algonquian war party showered the *Half Moon* with arrows the next day. Hudson scattered the attackers with his bow cannon and a hail of lead from his musketry, and had no further problems on the remainder of the trip.

Hudson put to sea for home in late October. His unsuccessful venture opened the New York territories to a flood of explorers and immigrants, but Hudson himself never returned. Two years later, a mutinous crew set him and his officers adrift in a small boat in Hudson's Bay. Their remains were never found.

---

steam engine. Fulton's first steamboat, the *Clermont,* was named for the manor. It made its first voyage to Albany in 1807. At Turkey Point, **Mile H-84.8 W (NM),** look east over Skillpot Island. On the hill north of the chubby green standpipe is Montgomery Place, ancestral home of Janet Livingston Montgomery, widow of the Revolutionary War general.

Esopus Creek, **Mile H-88.0 W (NM),** is the harbor for Saugerties. The high land at the creek's mouth extends nearly 0.5 mile from the western bank. Buff-colored Saugerties Light, the Hudson's oldest existing lighthouse, watches a shoal delta at the creek's mouth.

The 1825 Barclays Dam, upcreek, confined a 3-mile mill pond; its tailrace—cut through rock east of the dam—diverted water for power to Saugerties factories, one of which produced the first machine-made paper in America.

Silas Brainard discovered the first bluestone (a type of building stone) in the Hoogebergs, a nearby chain of hills, and launched the town's multimillion-dollar bluestone industry, which continued into the 20th century.

North of Esopus Creek between midriver shoals, Green and Upper flats, is the Maelstrom, a whirlpool that is often active during flood conditions.

Asa Bigelow founded Malden-on-Hudson, **Mile H-89.7 W (NM),** in 1812 as a deepwater port for his racing-sloop shipyard and his trading fleet. For 70 years the port was another Saugerties bluestone shipping center.

You pass the Independent Cement Corporation plants at Cementon, **Mile H-93.5 W (NM),** and then clear wide and shoal Inbocht Bay. On the eastern shore are Germantown and North Germantown, where the British resettled German expatriates in the 18th century. The Palatines were given 40 acres of land in return for work in pitch-tar factories—tar was a vital product for the river's shipbuilding industry. Unenthusiastic about this work, they soon looked west for farmland along the Mohawk River.

Catskill Creek, **Mile H-97.2 W (NM),** the harbor for Catskill, was a prosperous Dutch riverboat port and shipbuilding center in 1790. If you look east as you pass the creek you will see Olana, a Persian-style villa, high on Church Hill. Frederic E. Church, a landscape painter of the Hudson River School, built Olana after noting the river views to be "most beautiful and wonderful."

Northbound the channel widens and for 2 miles holds to the western bank to clear the shoals south of Rogers Island. At **Mile H-98.7 (NM)** is the Rip Van Winkle Bridge—near here Rip took his 20-year nap.

Mount Merino, **Mile H-100.0 E (NM),** honors the Merino sheep that were imported and raised on the hill in the 19th century.

The mansard-roofed brick 1847 Hudson-Athens Lighthouse, **Mile H-100.8 W (NM),** watches 1.8-mile-long Middle Ground Flats, which separates the two towns. In early years a canoe ferry ran between Hudson and Athens; later a sailing scow replaced the canoe, and finally the more dependable power of six horses on a treadmill replaced the sails.

New England shipbuilders bought the Dutch farms on the eastern slopes in 1783—they wanted an inland port safe from British warships. Within four years Hudson became a bustling commercial city, a port of entry, and one of America's major whaling and sealing ports. In those days the town had two deepwater bays where sailing shipyards, warehouses, and wharves lined the waterfront. The discovery and use of petroleum sealed the fate of the sperm whale–oil trade, and Hudson turned to knitting and cotton mills, brickyards, and wheelworks.

For many years Hudson and Athens were transshipment ports; they were at the head of navigation for deep-draft sailing vessels. Upstream the treacherous shifting river shoals made traveling difficult even for the shoal-draft schooners and famous Hudson River sloops. In 1866 the Overslaugh Bar—just south of Albany—often had 30 to 40 vessels grounded at the same time.

The river narrows at **Mile H-104.4 (NM);** for the rest of the route to Albany it's often only 0.2 mile wide and dotted by wooded islands. The banks here are steep. Steamships can be disconcerting in this narrow section; they need plenty of room, so when passing hold as close to the bank as depth allows. Though their wake roll is seldom excessive in these northern reaches, their deep draft can displace water like an immense sponge. Depth can decrease up to a foot or more; in a matter of seconds it flushes back in again.

Coxsackie, **Mile H-107.3 E (NM),** is built along the waterfront hills. For nearly 200 years it was the exclusive Dutch settlement Kuxakee, meaning hoot-of-an-owl. Before modern refrigeration, the village was noted for harvesting river ice. Workmen shoveled snow off the ice, then horses pulling plows broke it into great chunks. These were hand-sawed into smaller blocks, stored in shoreside ice houses, and insulated with sawdust. The ice lasted till summer, when it was sent south by sailing ship to New York City.

Deepening the shoal upper river was imperative in the early days; Albany's economic development depended largely on water commerce. The Rivers and Harbors Act authorized the Deeper Hudson Project, which called for a 27-foot-deep, 400-foot-wide, 30-mile-long channel from Hudson to Albany. Dredges removed over 21 million cubic yards of rock and earth from the river's channel—most of which was deposited

at five small islands south of Castleton-on-Hudson. This made them one large peninsula that extended as far south as Stuyvesant; Houghtaling Island is the southern tip. Oceangoing-vessel depth became reality in 1931.

On the eastern mainland across from New Baltimore, **Mile H-113.1 (NM),** is "Children's Point," named by early Hudson River Sloop captains for the children that gathered on shore to watch the sailing ships. Kinderhook, a few miles east of the point, is the birthplace of Martin Van Buren, the eighth president of the United States.

Don't cut corners at Coeymans, **Mile H-114.5 (NM);** at high water a 0.5-mile-long rock breakwater protecting the waterfront may be awash or underwater.

By the time you reach **Mile H-121.0 (NM)** the skyline of downtown Albany is visible. Island Creek, **Mile H-122.8 W (NM),** marks the start of Albany's port and waterfront industry. The two eastern-bank turning basins are there to help steamships perform their about-face maneuver in the narrow river. Their terminals, **Mile H-123.8 W (NM),** mark the end of today's 32-foot maintained channel depths. North of the terminals the channel depths are maintained at 14 feet to Federal Lock.

Be prepared in this area for the New York State Marine Police and U.S. Customs to stop, board, and inspect pleasure boats; delays may be up to an hour.

In the mid-1500s there was no Albany, city or port, though fur traders had constructed a stone trading post about where the terminals are now located. In 1614, after Henry Hudson had cautiously navigated the shoal upper river, Dutch explorers Christiaensen and Block built Fort Van Nassau. It was not far from today's cloverleaf Highway 20 Bridge.

Albany had many names during its history. At first it was Pempopowwupqt-muhhcanneuw, or Fireplace of the Mahicans, and in turn became Fort Nassau, Fort Orange, Rensselaerswyck, Beverwyck, Willemstadt, and finally Albany. Midway in its growth Isaac Jogues wrote, "There is two things in this settlement. A miserable little Fort Orange built of logs and four or five pieces of cannon maintained by the West India Company. . . . "

In its early years Albany's port was also its downtown, lined with docks, wharves, and warehouses. Hundreds of shoal-draft Hudson River Sloops and schooners lay along the riverbank as far north as the Erie Canal and the settlement's famous Lumber District; none had drafts greater than 9 feet. Shoal-draft steamboat transportation arrived in 1808 and shortened sailing time to New York City to 20 hours.

The Dutch settled Rensselaer—east opposite Albany—in 1630. It was formed by joining several villages in the land grant of diamond merchant Kiliaen Van Rensselaer.

Over the eastern revetment is Crailo, the 1642 brick house at 700,000-acre Van Rensselaer manor. It has green shutters and a red roof, and a flag usually flies at the second floor. Located in what was formerly called Greenen Bosch (Dutch for pine forest), it resembles a comfortable two-story home, but lower-floor rifle loopholes serve as reminders that the owners built it for defense against Indian attack. It was at Crailo that Dr. Richard Shuckburgh composed "Yankee Doodle," which became an American Revolutionary War marching song.

The web of the South Mall Expressway Bridge, **Mile H-125.0 (NM)**, is about where Henry Hudson's *Half Moon* anchored; it was the end of his ship's river journey, though his shoal-draft longboats explored upriver a few more miles.

Once you pass Albany's expressway bridge, look west. Albany's downtown historical district extends along three nearby streets—State, Pearl, and Broadway—and includes the oldest settled city area. The impressively ornate, castlelike stone waterfront structure is the old Flemish Gothic Delaware and Hudson Railroad Building and the Albany Evening Journal Building. This 1914-to-1918 masterpiece is the work of Albany architect Marcus T. Reynolds. Today it's the State University of New York Administration Building. Farther inland is the spherical Performing Arts Center that residents fondly called "The Egg." Surrounding The Egg are the Empire State Plaza's skyscrapers.

Just north of the Albany Conrail Swing Bridge, about **Mile H-125.7 W (NM)**, is the site of the old Erie Canal's eastern terminus. It ran just inland of the Hudson as far north as Cohoes, where it turned northwest to follow along the Mohawk River's southern shore to bypass Cohoes Falls.

In the days of the old Erie Canal, Albany had a 4,300-foot-long, 80-foot-wide waterfront mound that was open at its upper end to allow scouring but could be closed against winter ice. Warehouses lined the mound where canalboats unloaded and loaded cargoes. By 1831, 15,000 canalboats tied at city wharves and 500 sailing ships in the coastal and West India trade were cleared from Albany.

In the early 1800s the city was a major lumber center. Log drives came in from the upper Hudson with an annual intake of 680,000,000 feet of timber. The lumber district, with 4,000 operating sawmills, extended for 1.75 miles along the canal north of the city. Destruction of the forests, demand for conservation, and duty on Canadian imports slowed the lumber industry; it came to an end in the early 1900s.

Watervaliet, meaning flats by the water, **Mile H-130.5 W (NM),** originally was part of Kiliaen Van Rensselaer's land tract. The active Watervaliet Arsenal is about opposite the winking King Fuels tank. The arsenal produced army munitions for the War of 1812 and built its first 16-inch seacoast gun in 1902 and first atomic cannon in 1953.

On the eastern bank is Troy, named for the ancient city. It became the early seat of the iron and steel industry on the upper Hudson; in the 19th century it produced half the horseshoes made in North America. After the invention of the sewing machine, the clothing industry dominated the 1800s economy. The manufacture of men's shirts established the city's fame and increased after a local woman invented the detachable collar.

There is a large island in midriver in this area. The navigation channel is to its east where you continue to pass Troy's waterfront and the unusual arched Troy–Green Island Lift Bridge, **Mile H-131.1 (NM).** The Troy City Dock, located on the eastern bank on both sides of the bridge at an old river terminal wall, offers floating docks, gas and diesel fuel, and accommodations while you tour ashore or spend the night.

In midriver north of the Green Island Bridge is Adams Island, **Mile H-131.5 (NM);** the watched navigation channel is to its west. Current may increase—you are now in the Federal Lock and Dam approach. It can be especially strong during spring runoff and can be affected by the dam's power plant. At the northern end of Adams Island, hold to the eastern shore; the dam waterfall area is shoal and filled with rocks.

The lower waiting area—technically between the northern tip of Adams Island and **Can #83**—always has some easterly current flow due to the tailwaters' proximity. There's almost nowhere for pleasure craft to secure on the lower approach bulkhead; waiting for lockage is a mill-about procedure.

Above the lock the Hudson joins with the New York State Barge Canal System. Keep to the watched channel that holds to the eastern shore to avoid midriver shoals. You can also switch to Chart N 14786 for more navigation detail.

The Federal Lock

The Federal Lock, which has a lift of 17.3 feet at Mean Low Water, operates 24 hours a day. To signal, use horn (1 long and 1 short blast to transit).

When you contact the lockmaster on VHF 13 to request lockage, he will give you a pole position; use the pole method of locking. (Poles are provided.) If you are alone in the lock, you probably will be assigned a western chamber position in midlock. Be prepared to answer a few questions: home port, destination, number of persons aboard, draft, and vessel registration.

The lock's land line number is (518) 272-6442, and the canal superintendent for **Mile H-132.0 (NM)** to **Mile H-134.5 (NM)** can be reached at (518) 237-0613.

The U.S. Army Corps of Engineers built, maintains, and operates the lock and dam; it's the head of tidewater. Once in the upper pool, don't venture west for a close-up dam view; the open-crested sills are difficult to see heading downstream.

At **Mile H-132.6 W (NM)** is one Mohawk River mouth between Van Schaick and Green islands. The former is part of Cohoes, whose main business district is across the Mohawk River. Gassen Van Schaick settled Cohoes. It was here that General Schuyler took command of the Continental Army before the Battle of Saratoga. The 1735 home of Anthony Van Schaick is still on the island; it was an army headquarters during the French and Indian Wars and the Revolution.

Upstream of Cohoes on the Mohawk River is Cohoes Falls. Though dams upstream have reduced their size, during high water stage the falls are still an impressive sight.

A two-canal junction and two more Mohawk River mouths are coming up at **Mile H-134.3 (NM).** Here the Hudson is to the north-northeast. As far as Fort Edward it's a canalized river section of the Champlain Canal (Region 6). The Erie Canal's eastern entrance is to the north-northwest at Waterford's waterfront (Region 2).

Sketch Map Depths

Sketch map depths are given at normal low water. When you venture outside the sketch map confines, you must adjust NOAA charts to chart datum. For convenience in adjusting, use the following:

Mile H-79.0 (NM) to **Mile H-132.0 (NM):** Plane of reference, Hudson River Datum, Mean Low Water during lowest river stage

ESOPUS CREEK

Chart: N 12347, *See sketch map, page 48*

Mile H-88.0 W (NM)

Esopus Creek, the harbor for Saugerties, is on the river's western shore. It has two marinas and an anchorage.

You enter the creek through two breakwater dikes on the Hudson's western shore; Saugerties Lighthouse is on the northern dike's end. Because of a large shallow wetland and tidal habitat north and south of the entrance, hold to the Hudson's main channel until the creek opens fully before making your turn off the main river. Keep to midcreek during entry. Once clear of the breakwaters, you pass a U.S. Coast Guard Buoy Tender station on the northern bank. The inner harbor has a steep wooded shore lined with waterfront homes.

Downtown is on the northern shore across the bridge; it's a long, uphill, 1-mile walk. On the way you pass the site of the 1825 Barclay's Dam over the first falls on Esopus Creek; the raceway furnished power for Barclay's Mills.

The village has shady tree-lined streets and lovely Victorian homes. In town there's a laundromat, department stores, small shops, cafés, galleries, a theater, and Partitions Street Market and Deli.

The Mum Festival is held in October in Seamond Park—taxi recommended.

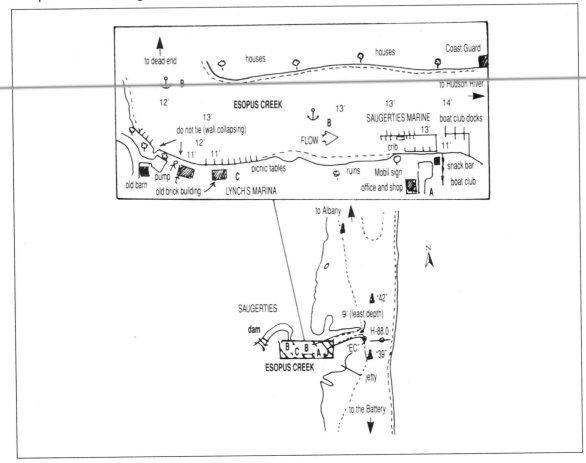

Saugerties Marine

★★★

Chart: N 12347, *See A on sketch map*

Mile H-88.0 W + 0.3 W (NM)

This southern-creek-shore marina is immediately up-stream of a boat club—members only—about 0.2 mile from the lighthouse. Landmarks are the marina's Mobil sign and the dock that parallels the creek. Though the marina is geared toward permanent runabouts, the owner will try to make room for a transient.

The office is in the large work building by the entrance road. Gasoline and 110-volt electric hookups

are available. The marina's land line number is (914) 246-7533.

Saugerties Anchorage

★★★

NO FACILITIES

Chart: N 12347, *See B on sketch map*

Mile H-88.0 W + 0.4 W (NM)

This is a narrow harbor. Best anchorage in mud is in midcreek west of Saugerties Marine. Except on week-ends there's not a lot of traffic, but don't block slip entry at the marinas. There's no public dinghy dock; make paying arrangements at a marina to leave the skiff.

Lynch's Marina

★★★

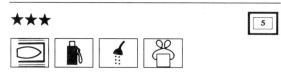

5

Chart: N 12347, *See C on sketch map, page 48*

Mile H-88.0 W + 0.7 W (NM)

This southern-shore marina is farthest upcreek at the first upper-right-hand bend; it has good depth. The slips are at 90 degrees to the bulkhead and face a manicured lawn. Gasoline and 110-volt electric hookups are available.

CATSKILL CREEK

Chart: N 12347

Mile H-97.1 W (NM)

Catskill Creek, the harbor for Catskill, has no room to anchor without restricting dockage. There are marinas, and one popular mast-stepping stop for canalling sailboats.

Leave the main river at **Light Buoy #67** about 0.2 mile south of Catskill Creek's prominent northern entrance point. Two cans guide you past extensive southerly shoals along the Hudson's western bank. Best creek depths usually favor the northern shore for the first 700 yards of entry as you pass the R.E. Smith Fuel Company.

If you plan to go way upcreek, approach the sharp bend at Hop-o-Nose Point, 0.5 mile upstream, favoring the northern bank, and do it carefully. An unwatched rock with only about 3.5 feet over it is about 55 feet off the southern creek bank just east of the bend. You have no warning of its approach; alongside the rock are depths of more than 40 feet. Once west of the bend, best water is on the southern shore for a few hundred yards; then the channel switches to the opposite side and shoals. Here you face a nonoperational bascule bridge.

Northern-shore Catskill is about 0.6 mile from the entrance point. It's a compact town within walking distance with post office, library, banks, pharmacies, restaurants, and hardware and sporting goods stores.

Catskill Creek: Riverview Marine Services, Catskill Marina

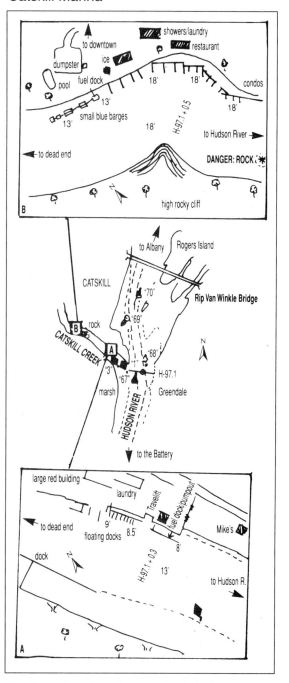

The Great American Supermarket is farthest away—over a mile—on the creek's western side. There's a convenience store with fresh meats on mid-downtown's western side. If walking is not appealing, call (518)

943-3606 for a taxi or (518) 943-4300 for a car rental.

For recreation there's a golf course in town, or you can go fishing in the creek. There are motels nearby, but bus and air terminals are not within easy reach.

Riverview Marine Services

Chart: N 12347, *See A on sketch map, page 49*

Mile H-97.1 + 0.3 W (NM)

This is the first northern-shore marina after you enter the creek. Landmarks are its prominent mast-stepping crane, Travelift well, and red two-story work shed. The docks are floating and divided by the 20-ton Travelift's well into two sections. If no one answered on VHF 16, pull in to the fuel dock (gas and diesel) at the slip's eastern section. The dock office is at the top of the ramp.

This is a small, busy marina and yard. Slips always appear filled to capacity, though the owner will try to make room for one more. There are usually traveling sailboats and trawlers waiting for mast stepping. If this happens to be on your agenda, call ahead to know your place in line.

Electric hookups (110-volt/30-amp) are available. The small ship's store in the dock office has marine equipment and supplies, local charts, snacks, and soda pop machines. The land line number is (518) 943-5311.

Mike's Catskill Point—a popular café—is about a block away. Walk out the marina gate and turn east toward the Hudson.

Catskill Marina

Chart: N 12347, *See B on sketch map, page 49*

Mile H-97.1 + 0.6 W (NM)

This marina—open May 1 to November 1—is on the creek's northern shore upstream at the sharp bend. Don't forget the submerged rock.

Most floating slips are at 90 degrees to the bank; you look across at wooded, prominent Hop-o-Nose Point. Pull in to the fuel dock; it's a string of metal barges with parallel parking in front of the Mobil sign and gazebo dock office. The main office is across the lawn, set back in the easterly trees.

Electric hookups (110-volt/30-amp and 220-volt/50-amp), gasoline and diesel fuel, and block and cube ice are available.

The ship's store offers a collection of marine equipment, nautical clothes, local charts, guides, a book exchange, a village walking-tour guide, and camera and picnic supplies. The marina's land line number is (518) 943-4170.

There's a heated swimming pool west of the gazebo; tall trees shade the whole area including the picnic tables and fieldstone fireplace. Cable-TV hookup is also available.

Though the supermarket is still more than a mile away, it's only a few blocks to downtown Catskill. Go out the gate, turn right on Green Street for a block and a half, then left on Main Street.

MIDDLE GROUND FLATS

Chart: N 12347, *See sketch map, page 51*

Mile H-100.6 (NM) to Mile H-103.0 W (NM)

Middle Ground Flats, a large wooded island in midriver, separates western bank Athens and eastern bank Hudson.

Athens Anchorage

Chart: N 12347, *See A on sketch map, page 51*

Mile H-100.6 + 0.5 W (NM)

Athens is on a wide back channel well off the main river; Middle Ground Flats is its barrier to the ship channel. Enter at either end of the island, but take reasonable care;

Middle Ground Flats: Athens Anchorage, Hudson Power Boat Club, Stockport Middle Ground Anchorage

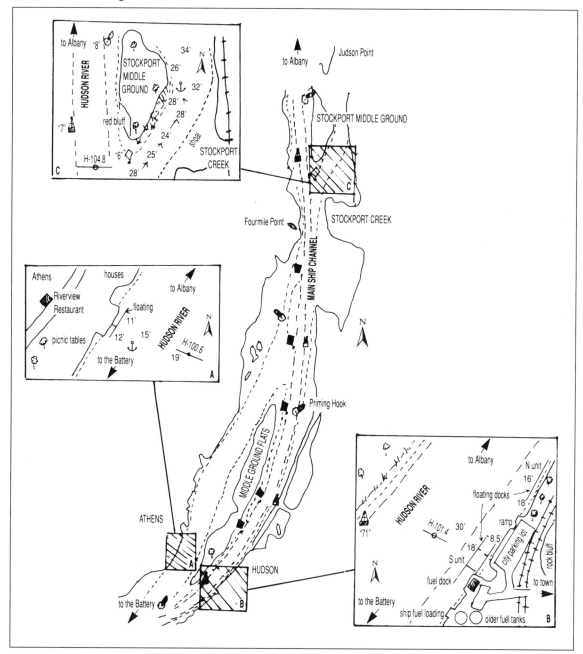

there's only one navigational aid off the main channel.

Preferred entrance is at the island's southern end about 0.2 mile north of the main channel's overhead power cables. Leave the channel between the power lines and Hudson-Athens Light, a combined brick lighthouse and dwelling high on a stone pedestal.

In the back channel, best depths favor the western shoreline. Bear toward a high terminal sea wall and a nearby launching ramp—Riverfront Park. There's usually a floating dock paralleling the terminal. Wake roll during daylight hours and a southwest wind chop make for rough dockage as wash ricochets off the terminal wall.

Anchorage is off the dock in about 16 feet with a muddy bottom; you swing with the tidal flow. If you plan a visit ashore, tie the dinghy behind the dock to be wake-safe.

Riverfront Park on Water Street has well-maintained lawns and landscaping, picnic tables, park benches, and garbage bins. Riverview Restaurant is across the street; they also sell ice.

A convenience store, post office, and library are about five blocks in town. On the way you pass a pretty fieldstone house with three gabled windows built by Albeertus Van Loon in 1724. The Athens Museum at #2 First Street has displays and memorabilia of Athens history, including its shipbuilding and ice industries.

You can safely return to the Hudson's main channel via the island's northern end. The riprapped tower **Light #2** is about midway up Middle Ground Flats' back channel. Keep to its west away from the island shoreline and follow the western riverbank to the northern end of the island's high ground. There's an extensive shoal making out north of the island, so continue slightly favoring the western shore and its three small islets. Hold this course until you begin to close the riprapped tower **Light #1**, 0.7 mile north of Middle Ground Flats high land. Hold west of main channel **Can #87** on this upper reach, and east of the yellow buoy marking Hudson Anchorage. When you are north of these, you have cleared the shoal and are once more in the ship channel.

Hudson Boat Launch Site and its parking lot. If assigned to a northern dock, you need a gate access key. Most passing river traffic is courteous, but bumper well for unexpected wakes.

Electric hookups (110-volt) are available at the club.

The clubhouse has a comfortable main lounge and bar and the hospitable members cheerfully answer your questions on river cruising and sights to see in town.

Picturesque Warren Street is Hudson's main street; it begins at the waterfront flagpole. Gallo's Grocery and Deli is at 1st and Warren; larger Sam's Supermarket is on the left at 3rd and Warren. There is a laundromat two doors from Sam's.

The center of town has shade trees, flying flags, and sidewalk sales. There's a hardware store, a pharmacy, banks, and various shops and stores.

Hudson's past is steeped in whaling and shipbuilding—note the whales on street signs. You might enjoy the Colonial Restoration and the Old Upper Hudson Walking Tours; tour maps are available at the chamber of commerce, (518) 828-4417. The Ezra Waterbury House is a three-and-a-half-story brick building with a cast iron front.

On the outskirts of town—about 2 miles away—is the American Museum of Firefighting on the grounds of the Firemen's Home. It has an excellent collection of fire apparatus dating from 1731.

Stockport Middle Ground Anchorage

★★★

NO FACILITIES

Chart: N 12348, *See C on sketch map, page 51*

Mile H-104.8 + 0.4 E (NM)

This eastern-shore anchorage is off the main channel in Stockport Middle Ground Island's lee. Leave the channel just south of **Buoy #6.** Bear east-northeasterly following the back channel's deepest charted bottom contour to the island's eastern side. Anchor in sandy mud fairly close to the island to avoid the mainline railroad noise. The anchorage is slightly exposed to the south but seldom untenable.

The island is part of Hudson River Islands State Park

Hudson Power Boat Club

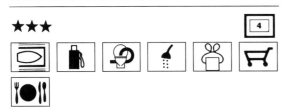

Chart: N 12347, *See B on sketch map, page 51*

Mile H-101.4 E (NM)

This private club welcomes all travelers. It's on the main channel immediately north of an eastern-bank tank farm. If no one answered on VHF 16, pull in to the fuel dock in front of the riverbank clubhouse.

There are two sections of club slips separated by the

and a popular summer camping area. If you plan a picnic, excursion, or swim off the island beaches, there's a shelter, rest rooms, and grills at the island's northern end.

Coxsackie Island: Coxsackie Anchorage, Coxsackie Yacht Club, and Houghtaling Island South Anchorage

COXSACKIE ISLAND

Chart: N 12348

Mile H-107.8 (NM) to Mile H-108.5 (NM)

There's no safe stopover on the river in downtown Coxsackie, **Mile H-107.3**; best anchorage and dockage are about 1 mile upstream, west of Coxsackie Island.

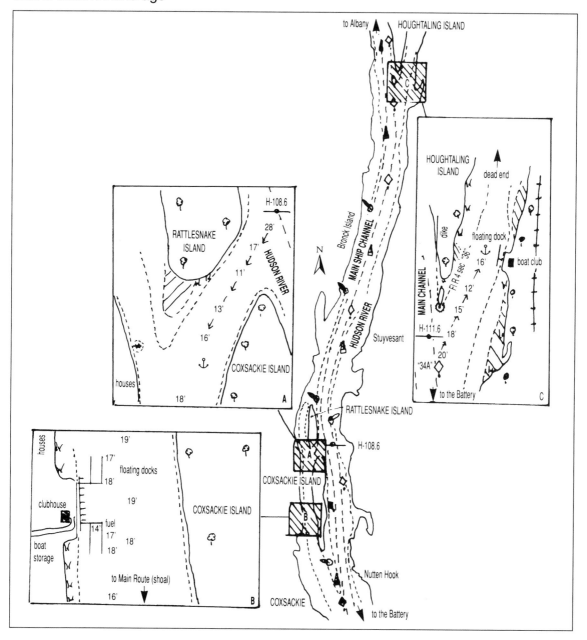

Both should be approached from Coxsackie Island's northern end; the southern entry is usually less than 5.5 feet—it varies seasonally.

Leave the river's main channel midway between Coxsackie Island and its northern neighbor, Rattlesnake Island. A long shoal makes out south-southwestward from Rattlesnake's southern end, so entering or exiting slightly favor Coxsackie Island's shoreline. An isolated rock is about 0.1 mile from Coxsackie Island's northern tip fairly close to the western mainland.

Coxsackie is a hilly mile back south and about a block from the river, but it's worth the walk to see the early architecture. There's a post office, a county clerk, a bank, a few shops, a small café, and an ice cream parlor. Though this was originally downtown, most businesses have left for distant suburbia—taxi needed.

Coxsackie Anchorage

★★★

NO FACILITIES

Chart: N 12348, *See A on sketch map, page 53*

Mile H-108.6 + 0.3 SW (NM)

Anchor about 0.2 mile south of Coxsackie Island's northern tip. Farther south, you are exposed to a main river southerly wind sweep and chop.

Do not anchor on top of the isolated rock. A Clorox-bottle buoy is occasionally in its vicinity, but do not depend on it to mark the rock—this type of bottle-buoy usually marks one end of a trot line.

If you plan to hike to town, make arrangements to leave the skiff at the nearby club.

Coxsackie Yacht Club

★★★

Chart: N 12348, *See B on sketch map, page 53*

Mile H-108.6 + 0.5 SW (NM)

This western-shore club—open May 15 to October 1—

is just south of Coxsackie Anchorage; it's the only back-channel marine facility with extensive dockage.

There are two dockage sections, with the clubhouse being the separation; each has its own access ramp. Dockage is parallel parking with a few 90-degree-to-the-bank runabout slips in front of the clubhouse. If no one answered on VHF 16, pull in to the fuel dock (gas only) at the southern slips' northern end and begin a search for the officer of the day. Transients usually dock on the southern outer dock.

Cube ice and 110-volt/30-amp electric hookups are available.

The club welcomes all visitors. Porch and lawn deck chairs are a good place to enjoy the island vista. If you arrive on a weekend, the club usually includes you in their cookouts and festivities. Call (518) 731-9819 for information.

Houghtaling Island South Anchorage

★★

NO FACILITIES

Chart: N 12348, *See C on sketch map, page 53*

Mile H-111.6 + 0.4 E (NM)

This anchorage is east of Houghtaling Island. The island is really a peninsula, the result of the Deeper Hudson Project's dredge disposal, which combined a group of islands. This is a pleasant stop in most conditions but not recommended in strong southerlies. No matter how far you go up the back channel, it's subject to chop and wind sweep. A better layover in these conditions is a few miles south and west of Coxsackie Island.

Leave the main channel with some caution near **Mile H-111.6 (NM)** about halfway between **Houghtaling Light #36** and **Buoy #34A**. The entry channel is nearly 0.5 mile wide, making it difficult to judge where shoaling begins on either shore. The light is not on the wooded southern peninsula tip but about 0.1 mile to its south on an old dike submerged at high water. Extensive shoals also make out from the eastern shore. If you come in on a rising tide, current is with you; approach very slowly and sound carefully. It's easier to arrive at dead low water—the shoals are visible.

Anchor far enough up the back channel to clear the eastern-bank boat club yet out of main tidal flow and traffic wake roll. Don't go so far that you are alongside the railroad tracks; trains that blow for a crossing right alongside sound suspiciously like a steamship that missed the turn. Bottom is mud; sound for swinging-room depth—there's about 4 feet of mean tidal range.

There's not a whole lot of back-channel traffic except on weekends when water-skiers arrive. If shad nets are strewn all over the channel entrance, look for the "in-charge" fisherman in his outboard to direct you through the maze.

The wooded island is the undeveloped Castleton Island State Park. You can dinghy up the back channel for nearly 5 miles past wooded and undeveloped Lower Schodack and Upper Schodack Islands—also part of the peninsula. Watch for debris and old wrecks.

SHADY HARBOR MARINA (NEW BALTIMORE)

★★★★

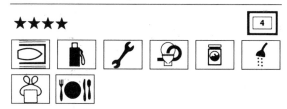

Chart: N 12348

Mile H-113.3 W (NM), *See A on sketch map*

This marina is along the western river channel. If riding the range northbound from Houghtaling Island's southern end, you are on target. Look for a large green shed roof that prominently says "Shady Harbor Marina."

This is a full-service marina divided into four major floating piers that run off at slight angles to shore. Each has its own access ramp. There's only one pier north of the 20-ton Travelift's well. If no one answered on VHF 16, pull in to the fuel dock in the marina's southern section on the long outer dock nearest the main channel. It extends south from a pier head with boats parallel parked. The pumps (gas and diesel) and a small dock office are on the eastern side at its northern end. Electric hookups (110-volt/30-amp) are available.

This is a well-kept marina with riverside lawns,

Shady Harbor Marina, Coeymans Landing

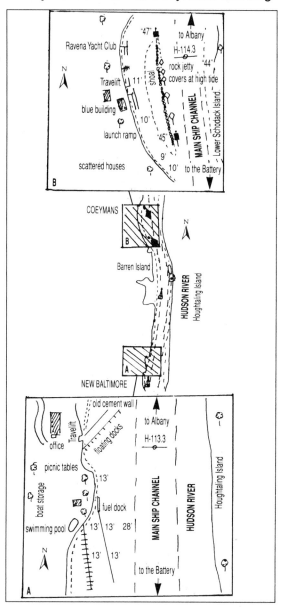

shade trees, picnic tables and grills, and a friendly staff. A swimming pool is near the southern pier section by the river; there's also volleyball and horseshoes. The large green building is the workshop; on its southern side is the main office.

The ship's store has marine supplies and equipment, a book exchange, local charts, nautical clothing, giftware, picnic supplies, basic groceries, fast foods, and ice cream. There's a microwave for customer use.

The marina's land line number is (518) 756-8001.

COEYMANS LANDING

★★

| 4 |

Chart: N 12348. *See B on sketch map, page 55*

Mile H-114.3 + 0.4 W (NM) or Mile H-115.0 + 0.2 W (NM)

This western-shore marina is protected by an offshore rock dike nearly submerged at high water. White-and-orange diamond "Danger" daymarks clearly mark the rocks. **Channel Light #45** watches the dike's southern end; **Light #47** watches the northern end.

Head into the tide when entering the back channel; it decreases entry speed and keeps you from being swept into the dike. The southern entry has about 9 feet, the northern about 8 feet. Keep clear of the dike's extensive western shoals. This leaves an extremely narrow deep-water back channel along the mainland's western bank. The marina on the mainland is about midway up the dike. Its two floating fingers of slips extend south off the access ramp in front of a two-story blue building. The Revena-Coeymans Yacht Club docks are to its north.

Block and cube ice, a 35-ton Travelift, and 110-volt electric hookups are available here.

You are about two blocks from Coeymans's main street and post office. Bruno's Grocery, at Westerloo and Main streets, is up from the Coeymans Landing Town Park. It's worth a walk to see Ariaantje Coeymans's two-story fieldstone house, built in 1675; it was once an Indian trading post.

ALBANY YACHT CLUB

★★★★

| 3 |

ALL FACILITIES

Chart: N 12348

Mile H-124.9 E (NM)

Albany Yacht Club—open May 1 to October 15—is on the western shore about 0.2 mile south of the South Mall

Albany Yacht Club

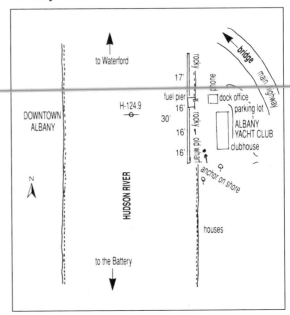

Expressway/Dunn Memorial Fixed Bridge. The club welcomes all visitors. It's the only pleasure-craft dockage facility near downtown Albany. A landmark is the hillside clubhouse with flags flying and an immense anchor in the front yard.

The main dock parallels shore and has parallel parking. If no one answered on VHF 16, pull in to the fuel dock (gas and diesel) in mid-dock by the Mobil sign—it's in front of the dock office at the head of the main access ramp.

Cube ice, electric hookups (110-volt/30-amp and 240-volt/50-amp), and a diver (check at the office) are available here. The land line number is (518) 445-9587.

The clubhouse has a front porch from which to enjoy the view of Albany across the river. This is a friendly club; if members are having a cookout, they usually invite visitors. The dockmaster, Ross McGowan, is extremely helpful and gives clear directions on how to reach the supermarket and restaurant. They are about a five-minute walk away.

Crailo Museum is a short walk along the riverfront. In September they host the Neighborhood Festival with craft exhibits, music, and other entertainment.

This is a good crew-change port. Taxis, car rentals, bus station, Albany County Airport, and Amtrak station are nearby. It's also a safe place to leave the boat while you tour Albany.

VAN SCHAICK ISLAND MARINA (COHOES)

★★★★   4

Chart: N 14786, page C-1

Mile H-132.4 + 0.3 W (NM) or Mile H-133.0 + 0.3 W (NM)

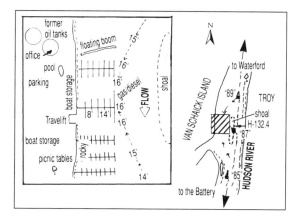

This western-shore marina—open May 15 to October 15—is upstream of Federal Lock near Van Schaick Island's southern end. This places it on the northern side of one Mohawk River mouth that flows into the Hudson between Green and Van Schaick islands. The marina is very visible; the main buildings are two large, colorful commercial storage tanks converted for marina use.

There's a well-watched midriver shoal off the marina; it extends north and south nearly 0.4 mile. The main channel holds to the eastern shore, so you must make your entry approach to the opposite bank from the shoal's north or south.

From the south: Northbound from the lock, the channel is on the eastern shore; 0.3 mile north you pass **Light Buoy #85.** If it's on station, it's well south of the

Mohawk River mouth that separates Green and Van Schaick islands. Do not approach **Light Buoy #87** closely; the shoal extends south from this buoy for more than 0.1 mile. Leave the channel when about opposite the very northerly tip of Green Island; you can see its bridge across this Mohawk mouth. Now bear slowly north-northwest. Keep clear of the Mohawk's mouth; there's a chance of seasonal silting.

From the north: Southbound from the Erie or Champlain canal you pass under the 112th Street Bridge about 1 mile from the canal junction. South of the bridge the main channel begins to bear to the eastern shore. Your marina departure point is just north of **Light Buoy #89,** located 0.6 mile south of the bridge. Now bear southwest for the marina.

This is a large facility with five floating main piers extending from a rocky bank; each has many slips. A log boom at 90 degrees to shore is at the docks' northern end; its intent is to block drift coming downstream during high water. If no one answered on VHF 16, pull in to the fuel dock (gas and diesel) on a long, channel-side end dock that extends north-south; it's just upstream of the 30-ton Travelift's well. Approach heading into the current. The dock office is up the fuel pier's ramp; the main office is in the multicolored storage tank with flags flying—the door is on the southern side. The blue tank is the workshop and service area.

Cube ice and electric hookups (110-volt; 220-volt/50-amp) are available here. The land line number is (518) 237-2681.

The marina grounds by the water have well-kept open lawns, picnic tables, and grills. Very welcome on hot summer days is their swimming pool just south of the tank. If you enjoy golf, the Golf and Country clubs are on Van Schaick Island's end.

It's too far to walk comfortably to Cohoes, but there's a taxi. If you want to stretch your legs, walk about one block west and you are on the old Algonquian and Mohawk Indian Trail; it was a 1690s colonial military route. General Ebenezer Learned and his troops used the road on their way to help Fort Stanwix when it was under British siege in 1777.

If you have transportation, the RiverSpark Park Visitor Center in Troy across the river has an audiovisual program, exhibits, and area history. It's open Wednesday through Saturday from 10 to 5, and Sunday from 1 to 5. Call (518) 270-8667 to check times for special programs. You can also pick up a walking-tour map for Troy's Hudson-Mohawk Cultural Park.

Region 2

THE ERIE, OSWEGO, AND CAYUGA AND SENECA

CANALS, AND CAYUGA AND SENECA LAKES

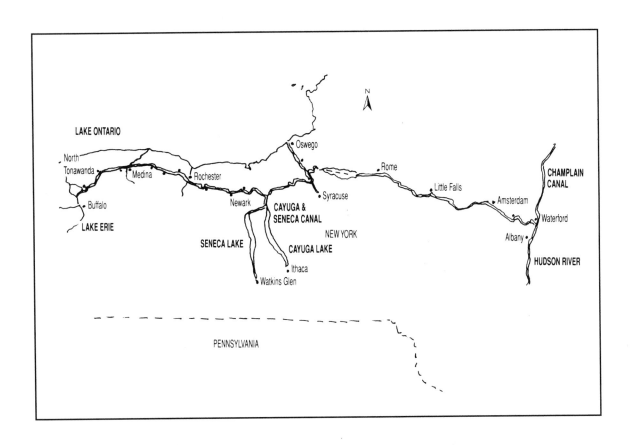

Mile E-0.0 (SM) to Mile E-333.2 (SM); Mile OS-0.0 (SM) to Mile OS-24.5 (SM); Mile LKCAY-0.0 (SM) to Mile LKCAY-36.1 (SM); and Mile LKSEN-0.0 (SM) to Mile LKSEN-32.5 (SM)

CURRENT DIRECTION AND SPEED

Place	Heading	Flow Direction	Speed in mph*
Erie Canal East	West	East**	About 0.25
Oswego Canal	North	North	About 0.25 to 1.1
Erie Canal West	West	East	About 0.2 to 0.0
Cayuga and Seneca Canal	South	North	About 0.25
Cayuga Lake	South	Wind-driven	Minimal
Seneca Lake	South	Wind-driven	Minimal

*In normal pool or normal lake stage
**Except from Mile E-123.1 (SM) to E-159.8 (SM), where flow is West about 0.25 mph

LOCK AND LIFT BRIDGE TRANSIT FEES FOR THE ERIE, OSWEGO, AND CAYUGA AND SENECA CANALS

Boat Length	Daily Pass	Unlimited Seasonal Pass
Under 16 feet	$5	$25
16 feet to under 26 feet	$10	$50
26 feet to under 39 feet	$15	$75
More than 39 feet	$20	$100

Fees may vary annually. Canal passes are available at locks and marinas along the system and at New York State Thruway offices across the state. For more information on where to purchase a seasonal pass, call (518) 436-3175. For commercial rates call (518) 471-5016.

The Erie Canal East
Waterford to Three Rivers

Mile E-0.0 (SM) to Mile E-159.8 (SM)

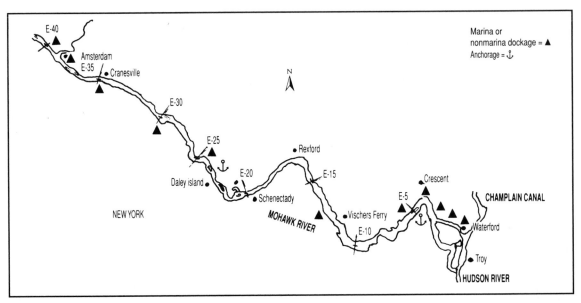

Waterford to Amsterdam, Mile E-0.0 (SM) to Mile E-40.0 (SM)

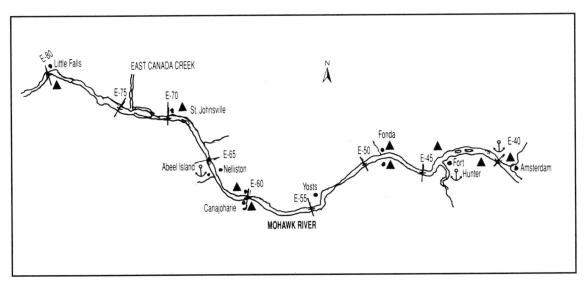

Amsterdam to Little Falls, Mile E-40.0 (SM) to Mile E-80.0 (SM)

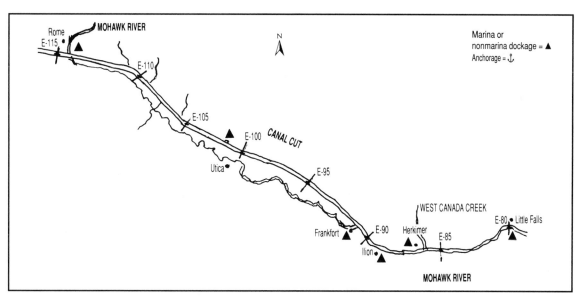

Little Falls to Rome, Mile E-80.0 (SM) to Mile E-115.0 (SM)

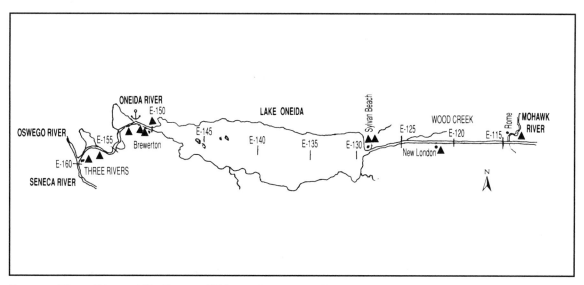

Rome to Three Rivers, Mile E-115.0 (SM) to Mile E-159.8 (SM)

LOCKAGE, WATERFORD TO THREE RIVERS

Lock	Mile	Land Line	Lift*	Tie-ups
Lock E #2	E-0.4 (SM)	(518) 237-0810	33.55 feet	Lines
Lock E #3	E-0.8 (SM)	(518) 237-0812	34.50 feet	Lines
Lock E #4	E-1.3 (SM)	(518) 237-0818	34.50 feet	Cables
Lock E #5	E-1.6 (SM)	(518) 237-0821	33.25 feet	Cables
Lock E #6	E-1.9 (SM)	(518) 237-4014	33.0 feet	Lines
Lock E #7	E-12.7 W (SM)	(518) 374-7912	27.0 feet	Lines
Lock E #8	E-23.7 W (SM)	(518) 346-3382	14.0 feet	Lines
Lock E #9	E-28.6 E (SM)	(518) 887-2401	15.0 feet	Lines
Lock E #10	E-34.5 S (SM)	(518) 887-5450	15.0 feet	Lines
Lock E #11	E-38.7 N (SM)	(518) 843-2120	12.0 feet	Lines
Lock E #12	E-43.0 N (SM)	(518) 829-7331	11.0 feet	Lines
Lock E #13	E-52.5 S (SM)	(518) 922-6173	8.0 feet	Poles
Lock E #14	E-60.3 N (SM)	(518) 673-3314	8.0 feet	Poles
Lock E #15	E-63.7 W (SM)	(518) 993-4161	8.0 feet	Poles
Lock E #16	E-70.5 N (SM)	(518) 568-2636	20.5 feet	Lines
Lock E #17	E-78.6 N (SM)	(315) 823-0650	40.5 feet	Lines
Lock E #18	E-82.7 (SM)	(315) 823-2419	20.0 feet	Lines
Lock E #19	E-94.4 E (SM)	(315) 733-5041	21.0 feet	Poles
Lock E #20	E-104.9 (SM)	(315) 736-4617	16.0 feet	Lines
Lock E #21	E-123.1 (SM)	(315) 336-8229	25.0 feet	Lines
Lock E #22	E-124.5 (SM)	(315) 336-4329	25.1 feet	Lines
Lock E #23	E-153.1 (SM)	(315) 676-4171	6.9 feet	Lines

*At normal pool level

All locks monitor VHF 13. Signals: If no answer, use 3 long horn blasts. Enter on green light only. Ladders are furnished (four per lock).

Daily operating hours for pleasure craft: 0700 to 2230 (may vary annually).

Exceptions to daily operating hours: the Flight, Locks E #2, E #3, E #4, E #5, E #6, and Guard Gate #2 operate from 0800 to 2000; Lock E #23 operates from 0700 to 2200.

Call (800) 422-1825 for updated canal information, including schedules and operation hours.

Canal superintendents:

    Mile E-0.0 (SM) to E-28.6 (SM): (518) 237-0613

    Mile E-29.0 (SM) to E-128.8 (SM): (518) 853-3823/(315) 793-2486

    Mile E-128.8 (SM) to E-159.8 (SM): (315) 428-4589

SPECIAL RULES AND CHAMBER POSITIONS

Lock	Period	Rule
Lock E #7	Weekends and holidays	Eastbound on hour; Westbound on quarter-hour
Lock E #8	Weekends and holidays	Eastbound on half-hour; Westbound on ¾-hour
Lock E #9	Weekends and holidays	Eastbound on half-hour; Westbound on ¾-hour
Lock E #17	Every day	Westbound use south chamber wall
Lock E #19	Every day	Westbound use south chamber wall
Lock E #23	Every day	Eastbound on quarter-hour; Westbound on hour

> *As an organ of communication between the Hudson, the Mississippi, the St. Lawrence, the Great Lakes of the north and west and their tributary rivers, it will create the greatest inland trade ever witnessed. . . .*
>
> GOVERNOR DE WITT CLINTON

The Erie Canal East begins between Peobles Island's northern end and Waterford's extending point. It's about 160 miles in length, with its western terminus at Three Rivers, **Mile E-159.8 (SM),** the historical dividing line of the entire 333-mile Erie Canal. It's part of the New York State Barge Canal System, which is under the jurisdiction of the New York State Canal Corporation. On the eastern Erie, you travel about 90 miles on the canalized Mohawk River, cover 70 miles of canal cuts, cross 20-mile-long Oneida Lake, and cruise 9 miles on the canalized Oneida River. Elevation increases through the

Mohawk Valley to a 420-foot summit level at Rome, **Mile E-114.5 (SM);** west of Rome you descend to Three Rivers. You have 22 locks to transit.

This is easy cruising, but on the wide, shoal Mohawk River keep to the well-watched navigation channel. Westbound, red aids are to starboard, green aids to port. A few white aids may be substituted for green in wide waters.

The Mohawk—the Hudson River's major tributary—drains 3,412 square miles. Its source is 148 miles northwest in Oneida County. The Mohawk River

Restricted overhead clearance on the New York State Barge Canal System requires sailing vessels to unstep masts.

Valley—the only natural passage through the Appalachian Mountains—was the early water route for Indians, fur traders, and westward-moving Europeans. The Falls of the Mohawk, an unnavigable river section with a 70-foot waterfall, extended from near today's Schenectady to Waterford; it was the major river obstacle. Waterford—at a ford across the Hudson—became the lower portage.

The same falls were a challenge to 1800s engineers when the first Erie Canal was under construction. The state built 27 locks to surmount the falls' elevation, with the eastern terminus at Albany. Today you do not begin to parallel the first canal until you reach Crescent, **Mile E-4.0 (SM).**

Early Waterford was not on the original Erie but on the first Champlain Canal and the Waterford Sidecut—a canal access into the Hudson. These were built at the same time as the first Erie. The Champlain Canal was destined to become the second most prosperous state canal system. During the 1800s, warehouses and docks lined Waterford's waterfront at the Battery—named for its New York City counterpart. Hundreds of canalboats collected at Waterford every spring, waiting for the seasonal opening.

In 1905 the state replaced the first Erie—and its two enlargements and improvements—with the Erie Division of the New York State Barge Canal System. It was at this time that the Waterford Flight became the canal's eastern terminus—the one you use today.

Westbound at Waterford, **Mile E-0.0 (SM),** the canalfront homes along the northern bank are typical of what to expect when canalling the Erie. Someone's yard is often within a few feet of the channel. Also typical is the Waterford terminal—about two blocks from downtown. Canal town terminals make excellent overnight stops and provisioning points.

The Waterford Flight, the world's largest series of high lift locks—five in 1.6 miles—is just ahead. A total lift of 169 feet—twice that of the Panama Canal—takes you from the Hudson to the Mohawk River. When you begin the Flight, passage is usually straight through, but don't be in a hurry.

If you arrive to transit and traffic is already in the system, the roving lockmasters' workload has doubled—they must handle two-way traffic. For minimum delay try to transit the Flight on a weekday as soon as the locks open.

The intricate Flight stonework is early-1900s vintage. Many of its stonemasons were descendants of Italian immigrants brought to this country to build the first Erie.

Upstream of Lock E #2 you cross a section of the first Champlain Canal. Just west of the lock is the old Waterford Sidecut, which operated for eight decades. It had a fall of 33 feet, with three limestone locks in succession, and shared four sets of wooden gates. Today the same locks serve as a Flight spillway.

In Lock E #6's upper pool, you are in a rocky cut that leads to Guard Gate #1 and Guard Gate #2. Don't be impatient if an immense steel door blocks the canal; one gate is kept closed and is usually manned by the roving lockmaster at Lock E #6. Guard gates are spaced throughout the system and are primarily used to close portions of a canal cut during rehabilitation work after the navigation season. A section has water pumped out so it can be cleaned and repaired. Guard gates also contain water in case of an embankment break—there have been nearly 20 over the years. Crews close gates on each side of a break so only minimal water escapes into the countryside. If water stage is high, crews may also close gates to control flooding—in which case through-navigation ceases. You are forewarned of gate closures as you transit locks nearest a closed gate. Except for the gate at the Waterford Flight, crews normally leave gates in the open position.

The first Erie was nothing more than an enclosed artificial ditch and not part of rivers, lakes, or streams; it used these only as water sources. During construction of the modern canal, the state canalized rivers to maintain a consistent depth. They built river dams and locks—the ones you see and use today. Despite these dams the eastern section was still vulnerable to summer water shortage—especially between Albany and Rome. To ensure a canal water supply for this area, the state built two offriver storage dams above summit levels.

West of Guard Gate #2 you enter the Mohawk River at **Mile E-2.6 (SM).** Once clear of **Daymark #5,** the main channel is on the eastern bank. Large, open-crested Crescent Dam is on the west; its sill is 39 feet above the river bottom.

The Dutch settled Crescent (named for the shape of the river bend), **Mile E-4.2 N (SM),** on the site of an Indian carry between the Mohawk and the Hudson. During the Erie's early days, the canal crossed the river at the carry on an arched aqueduct. It's here that the modern Erie begins to parallel the old. The state obliterated much of the old canal during the new system's construction, but if you keep watch along the riverbanks as you travel west you will see stonework remains of early walls, aqueducts, and locks.

Today's Crescent Bridge is another of more than 60 fixed, low-level bridges that cross the Erie Canal East. Be wary of pedestrians lingering on canal bridges, especially in summer during school break. A favorite pastime is to pepper passing pleasure craft with everything from ripe cherries to rocks. A good deterrent is to point a large camera or video camera at the culprits. The threat of identification usually makes them desist.

A nature and historic preserve at Vischer Ferry, **Mile E-11.7 N (SM),** has exhibits that include old Erie's double Lock E #19 and an early-era canal bridge. Farm bridges—used to connect a farmer's property with his fields and pasturelands—became part of the canal's construction, as did crossover bridges. Canallers used the latter when an obstruction blocked one side of the towpath or they needed a better towing angle around bends.

Canalboats were propelled by either horses or mules. Boat companies often paid orphan boys $30 a year to care for the teams and walk them on the towpath. One canal song exemplified a driver's pride in his team:

Attend all ye drivers, I sing of my team;
They're the fleetest and strongest that ever was
    seen. . . .
The three altogether in motion outdo
Any team of their age, the whole canal through.

When the "Great Horse Epizootic" disaster struck in 1872, the epidemic killed thousands of horses and mules; it nearly brought canal travel and the economy to a halt.

In Lock E #7's upper pool, **Mile E-12.7 (SM),** you are in the Schenectady reach. This pool submerged the first Erie, but at the bend at Rexford, **Mile E-16 E (SM),** the canal reappears along with old locks E #21 and E #22. The old canal crossed the Mohawk on the Rexford Aqueduct, then routed along the river's southern shore into Schenectady. Watch for a few remaining stone aqueduct arches and abutments at the Highway 146 Bridge (BR E-8).

Aal Plaats ("place of eels") was the original name for Alplaus, **Mile E-17.4 (SM).** French and Indian soldiers camped here on the eve of their 1690 attack on Schenectady.

Anrendt Van Curler and 14 Dutch families from Fort Orange (Albany) founded Schenectady in 1661 and named it after a nearby Mohawk settlement called Schanunactada, or "the other side of the pinelands." Within a year the farming settlers had a stockade enclosing an area of about four blocks, located at the angle of the Mohawk River and Binnie Kill, **Mile E-22.0 (SM).** Thirty years later Governor Louis Frontenac of Canada sent out a French and Indian raiding party. The resultant Schenectady Massacre destroyed the town, and all inhabitants were either killed or taken captive.

By the 1700s pioneers had built another fortified settlement. It became the prosperous terminus of the portage between the Mohawk and the Hudson. When the state built the first Erie, the canal ran through downtown. Immigrants and settlers poured in on canalboats; Schenectady became known as the Gateway to the West.

Thomas Edison opened his Electrical Machine Works during the late 1800s, then joined with other electrical firms to become the Schenectady Works of General Electric Company. Many of their modern buildings are on Van Slyck Island, between **Mile E-21 (SM)** and **Mile E-22 (SM).**

Movable dams are common on the Erie. Most are similar to the one at Lock E #8, **Mile E-23.7 (SM).** When you approach a movable dam, always note gate position next to the lock wall. If only a few need opening to control levels, the dam crew usually raises those farthest from the lock. If gates are open next to the lock, or even partially raised, it can mean lower-pool water flow along the damside lock approach wall; along that riverbank, this might be more than the normal river flow. It's visible as foamy or disturbed water. As you enter (or exit) the lock's lower pool in these conditions, allow for this momentary sweep of current that sets toward the adjacent bank. During flood conditions crews open many, or even all, the gates. At that time current set can be violent—the major reason for not traveling a river section during floods.

Above and below Lock E #9, **Mile E-28.6 N (SM),** watch for square cement bulkheads spaced along the northern bank. These are part of a World War I canal fleet. The government took control of the canals during the war and constructed 21 barges to add to the peacetime carriers; however, the war was over before the barges could be put into use. Eventually they were given to the state, but they were such poor towing vessels that they were soon out of service. The state sank five at Lock E #9 to serve as approach piers. During winter draw-down the barges are more visible, and it is possible to read their wartime numbers.

Lock E #9 is a canal park, one of many dotted throughout the system. Canal park sites are usually close to population centers, and most have extensive picnic facilities, playgrounds, rest rooms, and grandstands to view lockages. A few have floating docks and electric hookups for visiting boaters.

The southern outskirt of Amsterdam, **Mile E-37.5 N (SM),** is in sight by the time you reach Giordino Island. The settlement was founded in 1783 on the Mohawk Trail, the well-used land route first blazed through the valley by the Mohawk Indians. After the first Erie's completion, Amsterdam became an industrial center. Textile mills and the carpet industry started on North Chuctanunda Creek, a Mohawk tributary that still runs through downtown. Watch for it under the Key Bank building on the northern shore. By 1836 over a hundred industrial plants in Amsterdam produced buttons, carpets, brooms, clothing, and linseed oil; their intricate brickwork smokestacks still stand. The town reached its industrial peak in 1919, when factories manufactured goods valued at over $52 million and employed more than 11,000 workers.

Take note of the four gatehouses at each corner of Lock E #11, **Mile E-38.7 N (SM).** Typical of all Mohawk River locks, the state reinforced these gatehouses and rounded them on their upstream side to reduce damage from ice floes. They also placed the lock's electrical systems in the upper portion of each house, above flood level.

On this lock's upper-pool grounds is the Guy Park Historic Site. Sir William Johnson, the British Superintendent of Indian Affairs, built the house in 1766 for his daughter Mary and her Loyalist husband, Colonel Guy Johnson. (The colonel was Sir William's nephew as well as his son-in-law.) After a fire seven years later, Sir William rebuilt in stone the house you see today.

Sir William Johnson was an important figure in early area history and one of England's controlling powers in North America. One of his many exploits was the capture of the French fort at Niagara, which cut off France's communication with its southern settlements. As a reward for his service during the French and Indian Wars, Britain gave him large tracts of land throughout the area.

For the next 2 miles the channel holds to the southern shore to clear Robb Island, a cluster of islets, large

The old Erie Canal's Yankee Hill Locks.

Pepper Island, and Upper Pepper Island. Fort Johnson, **Mile E-40.5 N (SM),** built in 1749, is just west of the islets. It was Sir William Johnson's base and third valley home. Johnson and his son occupied Fort Johnson until the Americans confiscated it during the Revolutionary War. The Americans made good use of the lead sheeting on the hipped roof by melting it down for Patriot bullets.

Tribes Hill, about 0.4 mile inland of Lock E #12, **Mile E-43.0 N (SM),** was once a Mohawk Indian stronghold. The hills around the river and Schoharie Creek were historically bloody spots known as the Hills of Torture—where Mohawks tortured to death French and Indian captives.

Southern-shore Fort Hunter is just upstream on Schoharie Creek, **Mile E-43.4 S (SM).** The British built the fort in 1711 to help protect the Mohawk Indians; it was the site of the Lower Castle of the Mohawk Wolf clan, I-can-de-ro-ga. It was destined to become the last valley Mohawk village.

Schoharie Creek, a major Mohawk River tributary, drains part of the Catskill Mountains. Easily visible from the canal are the 7 remaining arches of the 14 that made up the 624-foot-long Schoharie Crossing Aqueduct.

Schoharie Creek is a difficult creek. The first Erie ran through Fort Hunter, and traffic crossed the creek directly. For this to work, the state built a dam to create a slack-water pond with the same level as the creek's canal section. To regulate the canal level regardless of the creek's level, they built a lock and the East Guard Lock. Canallers then manually dragged their canalboats across the pond by blocks and tackle—a difficult, time-consuming process. It was also dangerous, because the manmade pond's water level changed with the weather. Nevertheless, the lock and guard lock functioned for 70 years.

When the state built the Schoharie Crossing Aqueduct in 1845 to end the creek's traffic problems, the locks and dam remained in service and formed a feeder system for the improved canal. The state built old Locks E #29 and E #30 on the enlarged improvement. As a result they maintained one level from old Lock E #30 at Fort Hunter to old Lock E #31 at Sprakers, a distance of 10 miles.

As you round the westerly bend at **Mile E-44.0 (SM)** you will see trees planted in a cross shape on the southern bank's hill at the National Shrine of North American Martyrs at Auriesville. This is the site of Ossernenon, a Mohawk village whose inhabitants massacred Father Isaac Johues and five priests in the 1640s.

Fultonville, **Mile E-48.0 S (SM),** is at the Fonda-Fultonville Bridge. Northern-shore Fonda is named for Douw Fonda, its original settler. His home was just about in the center of what is now the Fonda Speedway. Indians killed and scalped Fonda, then burned his house after he refused to flee during a raid in 1780.

Johnstown—2 miles north of Fonda—is the site of the last Revolutionary War battle, fought six days after Cornwallis surrendered at Yorktown. Johnstown traces its lineage back to the time when Sir William Johnson built Fort Johnstown as a jail and Johnson Hall, a Georgian mansion, as another home and headquarters.

The Noses, distinctive bluffy landmarks at **Mile E-54.6 (SM),** formed when the Mohawk River cut through a ridge of Adirondack rock. Northern wooded Big Nose rises 800 feet and faces 600-foot Little Nose. The bluffs with their wide valley view were easily defended and became Mohawk village sites.

Canajoharie, **Mile E-59.9 S (SM),** along its namesake creek, faces Palatine Bridge across the river. It's home of the Beechnut Nutrition Corporation, which began in 1891 as the Imperial Packing Company, selling a home recipe for barrel-smoking Mohawk Valley hams. In 1779 General James Clinton made temporary headquarters in town while he arranged to haul his boats and supplies over the hills above the settlement. His army was bound for Otsego Lake to join General John Sullivan, where the Great Blue Snake—as the army was named by the Indians—was to rid the area of the Iroquois by laying waste to western New York.

Palatines migrating from the Schoharie and Hudson valleys settled Palatine Bridge in 1723. The governor expected the Germans to be the first attacked by the French and Indians and assumed they would do little more than slow down the invaders. However, many Palatines palisaded their stone houses along the river shores, turning them into forts. Pioneers considered Fort Plain, **Mile E-63.3 (SM),** on Otsquago Creek, one of the best valley fortifications. During the Revolutionary War it became Marinus Willet's headquarters and a gathering point for troops moving up the Schoharie Valley.

Abeel Island, **Mile E-64.4 S (SM),** is named for John Abeel, an Indian trader who married the daughter of a Seneca chief. Their son, Cornplanter, became a famous Seneca warrior.

Just upstream of Nelliston is the site of 1750 Fort Wagner, a stockaded home belonging to Lieutenant

Colonel Peter Wagner of the Palatine Regiment's Tryon County Militia. It was a refuge for the local farmers during Indian raids.

Johannis Klock built Fort Klock, **Mile E-67.8 N (SM),** another Palatine-fortified homestead. During the Revolution neighborhood families huddled in the fort while General Stephen Van Rensselaer and 1,500 militia fought 700 British raiders in the Battle of Klock's Field.

Immediately east of Lock E #16, **Mile E-70.5 (SM),** the Mohawk flows in from the north. During high water this intersection can have strong current and excessive drift, caused primarily by the flow of the East Canada Creek, a major Mohawk River tributary whose mouth is 2 miles upstream on the Mohawk.

The Upper Castle of the Mohawk clan is just east of Nowadaga Creek, **Mile E-74.2 (SM).** In 1756 Sir William Johnson built Fort Henrick on the creek near where he met his future wife, Molly Brant, sister of the famous Indian warrior Joseph Brant (Thayendanegea).

At **Mile E-77.7 (SM)** look south to see the Herkimer Monument, visible behind the red two-story home. This was the 1752 homestead of Nicholas Herkimer, whose lands included the Mohawk "carrying place," the old portage around Little Falls. Herkimer became the most prominent and the wealthiest member of the German-American community. He was a captain of militia during the French and Indian Wars; by the Revolution he was a general, famed for his role in defeating the British at the Battle of Oriskany.

The downstream end of historic Little Falls Gorge is to the north of Lock E #17's lower approach wall. In early days these rapids and falls made the river unnavigable. The Mohawks controlled the portage first; it gave them power in the Iroquois Confederacy. The town of Little Falls came into existence in 1725 when the Palatines moved in, developed a trading post, and collected tolls to haul bateaux over the rocks around the falls. The largest army to use their portage was General Amherst's. During the Revolution he transited with 10,000 men on the way to try to capture Montreal.

In 1795 the Western Inland Lock and Navigation Company, headed by General Philip Schuyler, built one of the first canals in North America around the gorge. The mile-long canal had five locks; it was 3 feet deep and 33 feet wide. It greatly increased Little Falls' commercial importance and economy, and by 1812 up to 300 boats—many of which transported military supplies—used the canal each day. Commodore Perry came through as a packet passenger in 1813 after his Lake Erie naval victory.

In the 1800s many local farmers began to specialize in cheese production. As a result, Little Falls was the country's largest cheese market for over 70 years. When the state built the first Erie on the southern bank, they also built a three-arched aqueduct across the gorge to access downtown Little Falls.

Modern Little Falls Lock, Lock E #17, has the canal's highest lift and a scenic westbound approach through rocky escarpments on both banks. It has a vertical-lift lower gate that resembles a giant slow-moving guillotine. Rock climbers often practice on the face of Moss Island's escarpment alongside the lock's western gates. The lock's western approach—a mile of canal—is impressive; it's through solid rock. Look north across Moss Island and the gorge to the rooftops and church steeples of Little Falls below you.

There are three dams in Little Falls Gorge. Two of them are visible as you exit the canal cut and reenter the river at **Mile E-79.6 (SM);** keep to the southern bank.

Fort Herkimer, **Mile E-84.6 S (SM),** was built in 1740 around the stone house of Johann Herchheimer. Here Nicholas Herkimer was born and spent his youth. On his way home from the Battle at Oriskany, Nicholas rested from his wounds at the settlement's steepleless stone church, which is still there today.

On the northern shore over the levee near **Daymark #509** is the mouth of West Canada Creek. About 25 miles upstream on the West Canada is the 4.5-square-mile Hinkley Dam and reservoir, a canal water supply.

Keep to the southern bank west of Guard Gate #5, **Mile E-86.8 (SM);** the collection of pilings across the river is just upstream of movable Dam #14.

Fort Dayton was the western outpost for valley settlers in 1781. Its site is in today's downtown Herkimer, north across the thruway. Early Herkimer and Mohawk—across the river—rivaled Little Falls as dairying and cheesemaking centers.

Remington Arms has manufactured firearms in Ilion, **Mile E-88.7 S (SM),** for more than 170 years. Eliphalet Remington made his first gun barrel at his father's forge. The company has made nearly every type of firearm, and also built the first successful commercial typewriter.

You leave the Mohawk River at **Mile E-91.1 (SM).** For the route to Oneida Lake you travel a 38.6-mile-long canal section. Frankfort is on the Mohawk just after it branches west. In 1843 William Gates founded the American match industry in Frankfort. He cut wooden matches by hand, dipped them in a sulfur solution, dried them, then sold them door to door along the canal. Later he invented a machine—built at the Remington plant in Ilion—to speed up his labor.

Another Frankfort industry was the development, in 1900, of hot-air balloons for research and adventure at the Balloon Farm, the home of inventor Carl Myers and his wife Carlotta, an early lady balloonist.

Immediately west of the mainline railroad bridge that angles across the canal is Lock E #19, **Mile E-94.4 (SM)**. This is a narrow approach that comes right after a fair northerly bend; the lock signal light is difficult to see until nearly under the bridge. Be cautious when you make the approach. There's little room to maneuver if you suddenly face the turbulence of a dumping lock; the outlet valves are immediately outside the lower gates.

Utica Lock, **Mile E-101.2 S (SM),** leads to the city's commercial harbor; the city center is about a mile south. Originally Utica had only a few inhabitants around Fort Schuyler, located at an Indian ford on the Genesee Trail. This was "the West" in the 1700s and sparsely settled until the first Erie Canal plunged it into settlement.

Oriskany, **Mile E-107.0 S (SM),** an early-era woolen mill town, is over the canal bank on the site of an Indian village, Oriska, on Oriskany Creek. At **Mile E-109.5 (SM)** look south; about a mile away is the 100-foot Oriskany monument at the site of the Revolution's bloody Oriskany Battlefield.

In 1777 the British initiated a three-pronged plan to invade and capture all the rebellious New York colonists and meet victorious in Albany. The main group intended to invade from Canada via Lake Champlain, while General Sir William Howe and his army planned to come up the Hudson River. The third contingent, commanded by Colonel Barry St. Leger, was an army made up mostly of Indians and Tories. St. Leger moved eastward from Oswego, planning to join the rest of the British Army after he had subjugated the river valley.

St. Leger faced his first major problem at Fort Stanwix (Rome). Unable to take the fort, he had to lay siege. The Americans managed to get word of their predicament to General Herkimer. He set out from Fort Dayton (Herkimer) with a force of 800 to come to Fort Stanwix's aid. A detachment of St. Leger's army ambushed the general at Oriskany on August 6, 1777, in a driving rain. After a six-hour battle in which 200 men

were lost, Herkimer's forces finally repulsed the British. Though they captured needed supplies and ammunition, the battle weakened the Americans so badly that they could not continue on to help Fort Stanwix. Their victory became a major turning point for the Revolution but was nearly catastrophic for the local population. The losses were extraordinary; in some families every male was killed.

The monument is itself historical; grateful valley residents erected it in 1883.

The terminal at Rome is next to a Mohawk River dam, the lower of two within 0.2 mile. This is the last you see of the Mohawk; from this point north to its source it's no longer navigable. About 6 miles upstream is Delta Dam and its 4.3-square-mile reservoir, another state storage facility for maintaining canal depth.

Old Fort Stanwix—named for General John Stanwix—is about 0.6 mile up the Mohawk on the western bank at the old portage over the divide between the Mohawk and Wood Creek. The Mohawks called it de-o-wain-sta, "The Great Carrying Place" on the "great bend of the Mohawk." For years it was on the main transportation route from the Atlantic to the Great Lakes; control of the portage was essential for the safety of the settlers' westward migration. Sir William Johnson used the fort after the close of the French and Indian Wars when the Iroquois signed the Treaty of the Five Nations and the Property Line Treaty of 1768. The latter still determines many land titles in New York and Pennsylvania.

The government rebuilt the fort at the start of the Revolution, and in 1777, when it was under siege by the British, the American flag flew for the first time in battle. Legend says the flag was stitched from a red petticoat, a captain's blue military cloak, and a soldier's white shirt.

By 1781 immigrants flocking into the region founded Rome around the fort. On July 4, 1817, it became the Erie Canal's construction site. Governor De Witt Clinton chose Rome as its starting point—east and west—because it was a canal summit level. For 80 miles there was no major impediment nor need of locks; it was easy digging. Canal sections went into operation as soon as they were finished and promptly made unprecedented amounts of money.

Near New London, **Mile E-121.0 S (SM),** the first Erie struck off southwest toward Oneida. There it turned westerly, passing the early canal ports of Wampsville, Chittenago, De Witt, and Syracuse. At the southern end of Onondago Lake it continued westerly another 30 miles, passing Weedsport and Port Byron. Today's canal once more intersects the first canal in the Montezuma Marsh.

Lock E #21, **Mile E-123.1 (SM)**, and Lock E #22 are 1.3 miles apart; westbound, both are descending locks. When exiting or entering these locks in the lower (western) pool, watch for strong current surges. Flow is now westward into Oneida Lake as Wood, Drum, Jenny, and Fish creeks drain into the canal.

The sandy shore of Oneida Lake has made Sylvan Beach a central New York summer spa for more than 100 years. The lake lies in an east-west direction and is 21 miles long and about 5.5 miles wide at its widest. Its deepest point is only about 50 feet, with best depth out of the main channel at the eastern end. Many shoals exist, but the channel through midlake is well watched. The lake's perimeter is low and dotted with small resort towns; few have adequate harbor protection or depth over 3.5 feet. Most offer ramps for the extensive bass-boat fleet.

The Sylvan Beach entrance into Oneida Lake is south of the harbor breakwater, whose outer end is usually awash. If eastbound on the lake, this entrance is difficult to distinguish from offshore. Its daymarks are neither large nor distinctive. The breakwater also makes a sharp jog just east of the entrance; it's not awash and very visible. Don't think this portion is the breakwater's western end.

The western lake entrance is easier to make out from offshore. It's straight forward, and the Highway 80 Bridge is visible from nearly 5 miles in the lake. Brewerton, **Mile E-150.1 (SM)**, the village at the lake's western end, is on the southern side of the two inner bridges. This was the 1616 site where Samuel de Champlain crossed the Oneida River and discovered its lake. The Indian village Techiroguen on the southern shore was visited by René-Robert Cavelier de La Salle in 1673. Eighty-six years later Sir William Johnson built Fort Brewerton on the northern shore. The fort bolstered the British western frontier and protected the well-traveled route between Albany and Fort Ontario at Oswego.

Oneida Lake is the Oneida River's source; westbound you travel downstream for the next 9.8 miles. Homes and summer cottages shaded with birches and weeping willows line both banks for 1.5 miles; then you bear southwest into a canal cut to Lock E #23. This is a "down" lock when traveling west, and the Erie Canal's busiest. Local pleasure boats use it regularly as they come and go to Oneida Lake, visit Lake Ontario 30 miles away, or go canalling west if the lakes are rough.

There's an asphalt tank farm terminal on the southern bank west of Bonsted Island. Towboats and their steaming barges once used this facility frequently. Commercial water traffic on the New York State Barge Canal System has dwindled to a trickle—a fate shared by many American canals. Some canals could not be maintained once commerce ceased, and they closed to all traffic. Today's water commerce is a far cry from the days of the first Erie—a year after it opened, 13,000 canalboats moved cargoes east and west.

West of the bridges at Three Rivers, **Mile E-159.8 (SM),** you have reached an elevation of about 363 feet. Here you must make a route decision. This is where the Oneida joins the Oswego and Seneca rivers. To the north is the Oswego Canal, a downstream, 24-mile run on the Oswego River to eastern Lake Ontario (see "The Oswego Canal," beginning on page 98). To the south on the winding Seneca River is the way toward Lake Erie and an access route into Lake Ontario's western end (see "The Erie Canal West," beginning on page 108). It's also the way to go to visit the Cayuga and Seneca Canal and the two Finger Lakes, Cayuga and Seneca (see "The Cayuga and Seneca Canal," beginning on page 138).

Sketch Map Depths

Sketch map depths are given at normal average summer canal pool level. When you venture outside the sketch map confines, you must adjust the NOAA chart to chart datum. For convenience in adjusting, use the following:

Mile E-0.0 (SM) to **Mile E-159.8 (SM):** Plane of reference, Normal Pool Level

WATERFORD AND THE FLIGHT

Chart: N 14786, page E-40, *See sketch map, page 71*

Mile E-0.0 N (SM) to Mile E-2.6 (SM)

Waterford Point, on the Hudson River's western bank at **Mile H-134.3 (SM),** is identified by a large green-and-white directional sign. The sign notes that the Champlain Canal is north-northeast, the Erie Canal

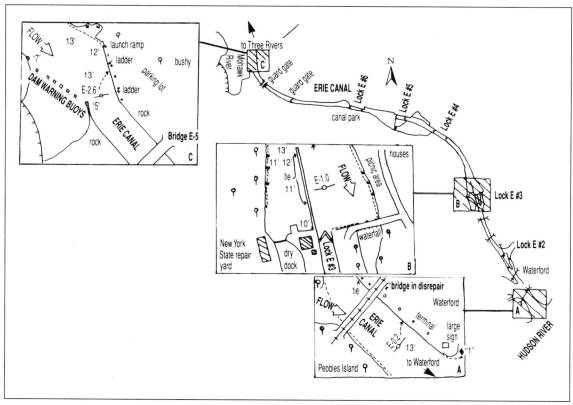

northwest. South of the point is Peobles Island; its northeastern shoals work their way eastward a little more each season. Make your turn westerly into the Erie Canal when looking straight in at the bridges and lock.

Button Park

★★★

4

Chart: N 14786, page E-40, *See A on sketch map*

Mile E-0.2 N (SM)

Button Park—immediately west of the northern-bank directional sign—extends east and west of the first canal bridge. It's a convenient place from which to make an early start upbound on the Flight.

The stop is not recommended during a fast-rising

river stage since the cut west of the railroad bridge has a dangerous current flow that ricochets against the terminal wall.

The terminal has an adjacent landscaped area with lawn, park benches, and a playground. If you dock at the foot of Third Street, you are near the site of the old Lysander Button Fire Engine and Manufactory, which built the famous Button Steamers and Pumpers in 1850.

If you walk about three blocks, you are on Waterford's main street; turn left, and you are about in the center of town. There's a Key Bank, a hardware store, a laundromat, a library, a collection of shops, and Pollocks Market.

On the way to town, on the northern side of the street, you pass the Samuel Stuart House, built in 1802 out of Dutch ballast brick. Stuart was a Hudson River Sloop owner, legislator, general, civic leader, and abolitionist—his house was a reported Underground Railroad stop.

There's no place to tie up above Lock E #2—you are in a narrow canal in the Flight transit—but a walk-in visit to its canal park is recommended. It has an excellent display on the 1823 Champlain Canal and Waterford Sidecut. Look for the ancient towline grooves left in the Sidecut's locks.

Waterford holds its Canalfest in May. Festivities include music, entertainment, boat rides, arts and crafts, food stands, and a parade.

Lock E #3 Upper Terminal

★★ | 5 |

Chart: N 14786, page E-40, *See B on sketch map, page 71*

Mile E-1.0 W (SM)

This terminal is above Lock E #3 at a state maintenance yard and dry dock. It's a current-free area and a recommended stop to wait out a Mohawk or Hudson River flood. For the time being the tie-up may be available only during high water conditions—the dry-dock lock and terminal are undergoing a major facelift.

If you plan to stop, tell the lockmasters—Lock E #2 when upbound, Lock E #6 when downbound—of your intentions. Roving personnel man the Flight locks; once a vessel is in the Flight, they prepare locks in advance of the boat's arrival to speed up transit. If you stop without telling them once you start, you will be extremely unpopular.

When you exit upbound into Lock E #3's upper pool, follow along the lock's western approach wall and make a left-hand wheel around its end. This brings you inside the wall away from traffic in a basin used by the yard and dry dock. Barges are stored inside the wall even when construction is not in progress, but normally there's room for pleasure boats. In fact, if a barge is clean and has a low freeboard, you can tie to it. You can use shorter dock lines, and the barge is the one to grind up and down the wall a foot or more with each lockage water displacement. If you don't care for barges, search about for a solid pier support on which to fender.

West is a wooded shoreline with a few stored ice booms. At the basin's southern end are the work buildings and the dry-dock lock.

You can walk down to the canal lock, chat with the lockmaster, and watch lockages. The way out is across the upper gates' walkway to a small parking lot, across a metal mesh access bridge over a gorge dense with greenery and ferns, then to the main road. If the lock is idle and its upper pool full, there's a waterfall under the bridge; it's the lock pool overflow. Crews lock the parking lot access gate after working hours, so if you are off for an evening stroll or a late dinner ashore, plan accordingly.

You have another chance to visit Lock #2's canal park and its historical displays. Though it's a little farther to walk from here than from Button Park, it's through a quiet residential area.

At the main road there's a small park with picnic tables and park benches. If you turn left, the road runs alongside the canal to Lock E #6 and the Mohawk River. This is a scenic hike. Originally called the Fonda Road, it was a colonial military route.

If you want to go to Lock E #2 or to town, turn right at the park. About a block down from the railroad track, Gola's Store has a selection of groceries, drinks, ice cream, deli items, ice, and a phone. If heading for Lock E #2, start bearing westerly; in two or three blocks you come to the canal park entrance. Town and Pollocks Market are a few blocks farther on.

Guard Gate #2 Terminal

★ | 3 |

Chart: N 14786, page E-40, *See C on sketch map, page 71*

Mile E-2.6 E (SM)

Guard Gate #2 is your last Flight upstream navigation obstruction. Once through its rocky gorge you are in the Mohawk River. West of the western approach wall is Crescent Dam. Don't wander off that way—its open-crested sill is extremely difficult to see.

The terminal is on the eastern bank. It has a dirt parking lot with a background of dusty trees. Come in with long dock lines, as bollards are far apart. The terminal's recommendation is for its pleasant view of the Mohawk River's midstream islands and rocky eastern bank. It's a good place to wait for an early-morning start down the Flight, or to stop if you don't want to travel the river at night. It is *not* a recommended stop during high water conditions. Though most current flows over the dam, much of it eddies around the terminal.

Unless your taste runs to frenetic activity, it's also not a recommended stop on summer weekends. Cars, vans, and pickups fill the lot day and night. Their doors and trunks are kept wide open so boom boxes can be appreciated as far as Schenectady. The river froths with speeding jet-skiers, fishing boats, water-skiers, and about everything else that makes wakes.

CRESCENT TERMINAL

★★   3

Chart: N 14786, page E-40, *See A on sketch map*

Mile E-4.2 + 0.1 N (SM)

This terminal is at the peak of the horseshoe bend at Crescent. Take your departure from midstream when

just east of the Crescent Bridge and bear northward toward the terminal. The tour boat *Nightingale II* may tie at the terminal's eastern end. If the boat is out on one of its three-hour cruises when you arrive in mid afternoon or early evening, leave room for its return.

Though this terminal is on the river, it's far enough from the main thoroughfare to be out of most wake roll. Of more concern is over a mile of deepwater wind chop fetch; if a southerly breeze pipes up, then it's rough.

There's a public parking lot at the terminal. The tour boat may have an office trailer at one side. From your boat you have a view of the lower river and the rather attractive Crescent Bridge. There's a Stewart's Convenience Store at the highway; across the street from it is the Deli House.

DIAMOND REEF AREA

Chart: N 14786, page E-40, *See B and C on sketch map*

Mile E-5.4 (SM) to Mile E-5.7 (SM)

This reef extends over a mile and has a wide, marshy shoreline. The main channel is between one large and

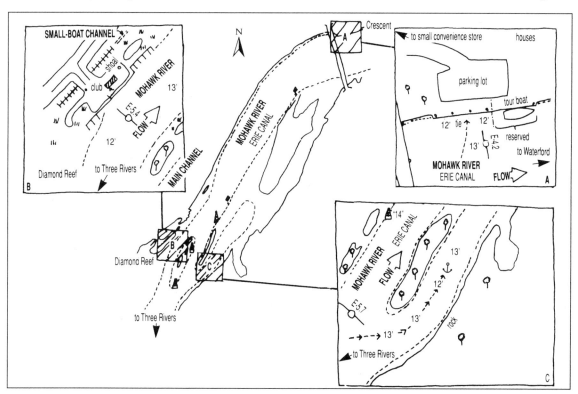

three small wooded islands. You have a choice of boat club dockage or an anchorage.

Crescent Boat Club

★★★   3

Chart: N 14786, page E-40, *See B on sketch map, page 73*

Mile E-5.4 + 0.2 W (SM)

This western-shore club is protected from the main channel by the three small islands. It welcomes all visitors.

Though it's possible to enter from either end of the island group, the route is more clearly defined if you come in from the northeast.

Leave the main channel at **Mile E-5.4 (SM)**; this should put you opposite **Buoy #17** if it's on station. Start bearing toward the western shore. Be aware that **Buoy #14** is more a leading mark for the main channel. It should be alongside the easternmost bushy small island; it does NOT mark the shoal that extends northeast of that island. Best depth to the club docks is favoring the northwestern mainland and not the offshore islands.

The club is built around a mole on which the club-house sits overlooking the floating fuel dock (gas only) that parallels the river. The rest of the slips in front of the club have finger piers. Behind the mole are more finger piers extending northeast-southwest of the approach road. This is a more shoal area; if assigned a slip back here, get clear directions for the entrance channel for each section.

Electric hookups (110-volt) are available here.

Diamond Reef Anchorage

★★★   4

NO FACILITIES

Chart: N 14786, page E-40, *See C on sketch map, page 73*

Mile E-5.7 + 0.2 E (SM)

This anchorage is east of the largest island on the eastern side of the Diamond Reef main channel. Make your

approach when at the large wooded island's southwestern end. At one time Daymark #19 was on its southwestern tip and made the departure point difficult to miss. For now the end of the big island is about midway between **Buoy #14** and **Buoy #16.** As you make your approach around the southeastern end, best depth is favoring the island. Anchor in mud midway along the island's eastern shore.

During the week this is a peaceful anchorage. Small-boat activity and wakes increase on warm summer days and weekends.

LOCK E #7 UPPER

★★★   5

Chart: N 14786, page E-39

Mile E-12.8 S (SM)

This well-protected tie-up is in Lock E #7's upper pool. There's a chance a state maintenance vessel may be coming in before closing and will need the space. If you

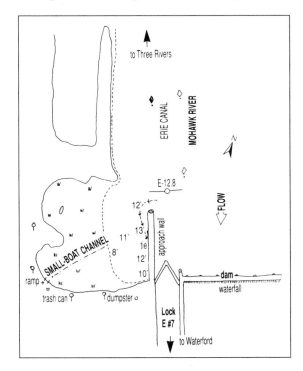

plan to stop for the night, get permission. If upbound, ask the lockmaster when you are in the lock if you can stay; if downbound, call ahead on VHF 13 but do it before he prepares his lock when he sees you coming up the long western river stretch.

If all systems are go, once you exit into the lock's upper pool follow the western approach wall to its end, round the corner, and tie on the inside wall. This puts you in a small lagoon protected from wind sweep, chop, and lock traffic. There's a beam protruding at a difficult angle low on the wall, so bumper properly.

Though weeds fill the lagoon—especially in the heat of summer—the inside wall is clear. There's one open channel into the lagoon's southwestern side launching ramp.

If you have a bicycle, this is an easy access point for a tour on an extensive paved bicycle path. You are also in a prime spot to watch lockages, lock traffic that passes within a few feet of you, and the dam's impressive tailwater waterfall. The ramp has a parking lot and occasionally a table and garbage bin. In late afternoon in the fall, using worms for bait, try fishing for perch in the weedy lagoon.

LOCK E #8 UPPER ISLAND ANCHORAGE

★★★

NO FACILITIES

Chart: N 14786, page E-37

Mile E-24.0 + 0.2 N (SM)

This anchorage is about 0.4 mile above Lock E #8. You have good holding in mud between the northern shore mainland and the unnamed large wooded island.

Your departure point from the river is immediately upstream of the main-channel overhead power cables located just downstream of the island's southern tip. Keep to the middle of the back channel as you enter.

Anchor fairly close to the island's southern end so you can watch passing river traffic, yet far enough to be protected from wake roll.

Lock E #8 Upper Island Anchorage

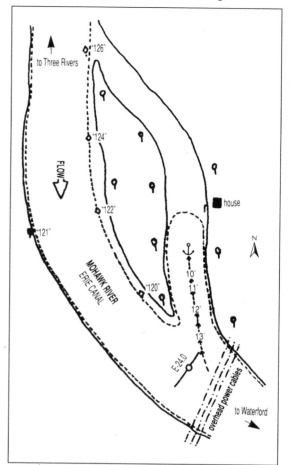

LOCK E #9 UPPER

★★★

Chart: N 14786, page E-36, *See sketch map, page 76*

Mile E-28.7 N (SM)

This canal park tie-up is immediately above Lock E #9. There are three places to tie, but ask the lockmaster's permission to stay at any of them.

The lockmaster may suggest you spend the night inside the upper southern approach wall. This puts your boat's bow practically sticking out over the dam, and though it's protected from toppling over the waterfall by the movable gate, this is not a tie-up for the faint of heart.

Lock E #9 Upper

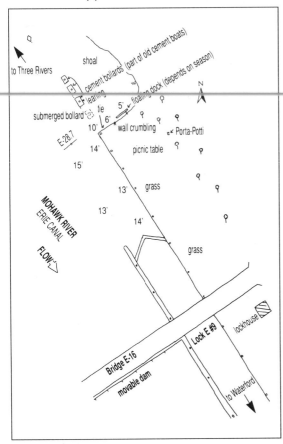

There is room for one boat of about 40 feet to tie on the northern approach wall's western end. Here you must round the approach wall's corner and put your boat at 90 degrees to the main channel. If you cannot tuck your stern completely off the channel, do not stay. When a towboat and barge come through—a rarity but very possible—they'll scrape along the approach wall and tickle your flagstaff. Be aware of the row of isolated approach standards west of the solid northern wall. These are the remains of the wartime concrete canal fleet. The downstream standard has submerged with age; this is the one you must miss when you swing the boat around the corner to park.

Occasionally there's a small canal park float north of this tie-up where you can spend the night, but depths are only 3.5 to 4.5 feet.

The lock grounds are well maintained. The western area is grassy, has a spot for picnicking, and is convenient for watching lockages. Bank fishing is fairly good off the lower-pool approach wall. There's a small pizza

parlor and ice cream shop at the highway bridge's southern end.

LOCK E #10 LOWER

Chart: N 14786, page 35 or 36

Mile E-34.5 S (SM)

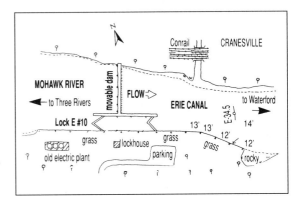

This southern-bank tie-up is below Lock E #10. You have a better stop at either Amsterdam, Lock E #11, or Fort Hunter. However, this is an adequate stop for overnight.

Though canal commercial traffic is extremely minimal, always expect it to appear any time. A towboat and barge approaching or leaving a lock need maneuvering room; don't be in the way.

Lock E #10's eastern approach is not completely straight; its eastern end angles south. Tie on, or near, the angle's end. A small creek flows into the river at the wall's end, and its runoff has caused some shoaling. To avoid bumbling into the shoals, come directly into mid-wall from midstream and then back up to your proper depth.

After you settle in, walk up, pass the time of day with the lockmaster, and tell him where you tied up. He can give you fair warning if a bargeload of tree stumps plans to come in to spend the night there, too.

Except for an occasional train rumbling past at night hooting for the Cranesville crossing across the river, this is a restful stop with lawn grounds. Early mornings and evenings large families of rabbits come out of the nearby forest, underbrush, and wildflowers to help with its mowing.

AMSTERDAM TERMINAL

3

Chart: N 14786, page E-35, *See A on sketch map*

Mile E-37.4 N (SM)

This northern-shore terminal is just downstream of Bridge 19A. Have long dock lines ready; the bollards are far apart.

Unlike most canal towns, Amsterdam has made no effort to improve its terminal. It's dusty and filled with weeds, mud ruts, and discarded beer bottles. This is a pity, since Amsterdam, just across the railroad tracks to the north, is a pretty town.

We recommend the terminal only as a fairly convenient supply stop. In the past the mall was only two blocks away; lately the area north of the terminal has been partially fenced, so you must cross the railroad tracks and walk about four blocks east to find the gate to the main road. At least this gives you an opportunity to look at the old cobblestone and brick streets and the fieldstone buildings with warehouse doors built to accommodate horse-drawn wagons. This was Amsterdam's bustling commercial shipping point during its early canal and railroad days.

Once you finally reach the main road, backtrack about five blocks west to reach the downtown mall near North Chuctanunda Creek. All the stores are within reach, including a Grand Union supermarket.

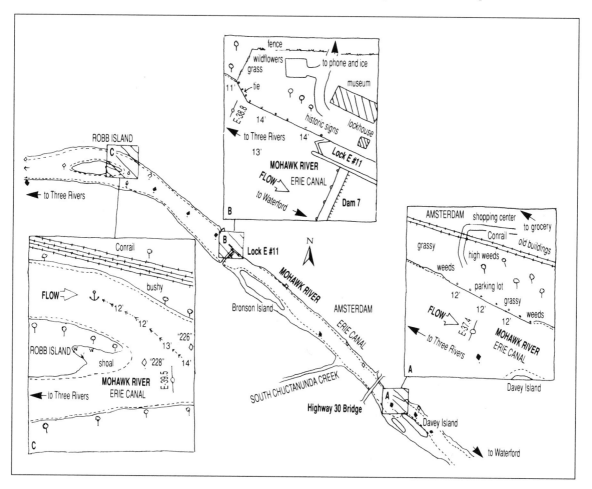

LOCK E #11 UPPER

★★★

Chart: N 14786, page E-35, *See B on sketch map, page 77*

Mile E-38.8 N (SM)

The preferred stop at Amsterdam is in Lock E #11's upper pool on the northern shore on the lock approach wall. Tie at the far western end—it juts off northerly—to keep clear of any commercial traffic.

Surrounding the compound are manicured lawns and wildflowers. Though the lock crew closes the grounds to the public after daily lock close-down, during the day Amsterdam residents come in to picnic, watch lockages, or chat with travelers.

After you identify the first of many hair-raising vibrations and earsplitting horn blasts of the mainline railroad just over the fence, you probably can sleep soundly the rest of the night.

On the grounds is Guy Park Historic Site. Sir William Johnson built and then rebuilt the fieldstone house in the 1700s. When the state finished Lock E #11 in 1917, it ended up in the mansion's front yard. The home is usually open during midweek May through October. You can browse through displays and exhibits of the Johnson family, who were prominent in the area's history. There's also information on the old Erie Canal on the lock lawn's information tablets.

If you follow the lock access road out and across the railroad tracks, you come to Main Street. A filling station across the road sells ice and has a pay phone. It's a good place to call for a taxi if you need supplies; Amsterdam's downtown mall and supermarket are now over a mile away.

ROBB ISLAND ANCHORAGE

★★★

NO FACILITIES

Chart: N 14786, page E-35, *See C on sketch map, page 77*

Mile E-39.5 + 0.2 N (SM)

This anchorage is upstream of Lock E #11 between wooded Robb Island and the northern shore. Leave the channel upstream of **Buoy #225** and **Buoy #226** and downstream of **Buoy #227** and **Buoy #228.** Hold to the middle of the back channel and go far enough inside to be behind the island's long easterly finger. This keeps you clear of passing river traffic wake roll. The railroad tracks run along the northern shore; expect periodic rumbles throughout the night.

YANKEE HILL BARGE

★★★★

Chart: N 14786, page E-34, *See A on sketch map, page 79*

Mile E-40.4 S (SM)

This southern-shore stop is highly recommended for its convenience to an interesting historical park: the old Erie Canal Yankee Hill Locks and their interpretive center are a few steps away.

The state has furnished a barge intended for boat-in park visitors. It nestles in the trees; watch for it on the southern bank between Robb and Pepper islands and about opposite Fort Johnson's charted northern-shore post office. Since canal buoys vary slightly with each season's placement, exact directional location from buoy position is never thoroughly dependable, but the barge is somewhere quite near **Buoy #229.**

Depth is about 8 feet on the barge's channel-side face, but this can vary since it depends on exactly where the state secures the barge for the season. If a strong wind blows up or down the river, it can be a bit bouncy, but it's easy to bumper against the barge's perpendicular topsides. The worst threat to your gelcoat and patience comes from pleasure boaters who cast vicious wakes.

This is part of Schoharie Crossing State Historic Site. There's a large, popular picnic area with tables and grills; the rest rooms are near the replica of Putnam's Store. The park closes at dusk. If you want to spend the night, get permission from the groundskeeper who appears late to close up. His office is on the site's approach road.

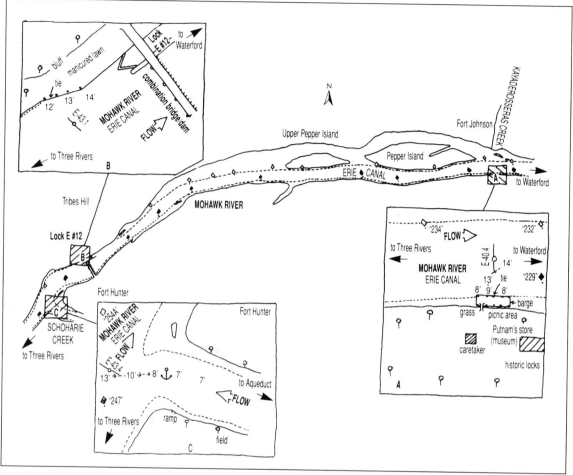

The Yankee Hill double locks were part of the 1835 enlargement of the old Erie Canal. At that time the state built 72 new locks, 57 of them doubles. The state built the 110-foot-by-18-foot locks side by side, then enlarged them again in 1889 to 220 feet in length. In 1917, after 70 years of use, the state abandoned the locks during construction of today's canal.

There's a replica of the real Putnam's Lock Grocery that stood on this site from 1850 to 1908. It was owned and operated by Garret Putnam and his sons.

If you tie to the barge, you are alongside old Erie Canal Culvert #33—better known in old Erie days as Putnam's Culvert. This is a 142-foot-by-6-foot-by-3-foot single-arch masonry culvert built over a hundred years ago to go under the old Erie bed. The state built more than 350 of these culverts; they averaged about one per mile. This one is still functioning; it drains the little creek flowing into the Mohawk.

LOCK E #12 UPPER

★★★

Chart: N 14786, page E-34, *See B on sketch map*

Mile E-43.1 N (SM)

The stop for overnight is in Lock E #12's upper pool. When you exit the lock upbound, follow the northern approach to its western end; tie on the angle section that is off the straightaway.

This is also known as the James Shanahan Lock. Shanahan was the Superintendent of New York Canals from 1878 to 1897. The lock grounds have lawns and flowers, and there are dense woods at the western end. There's public access day and night, but automobile traffic stops when they lock the gate at closing time.

If you want to visit the Schoharie Crossing State Historic Site at Fort Hunter but don't want to anchor there, this is a reasonable access point by dinghy. The entrance to Schoharie Creek is about 0.3 mile upstream, where you make a left and the old aqueduct is in sight.

SCHOHARIE CROSSING ANCHORAGE

★★★★

NO FACILITIES

Chart: N 14786, page E-34, *See C on sketch map, page 79*

Mile E-43.4 S + 0.1 S (SM)

This anchorage is in the mouth of Schoharie Creek on the canal's southern bank about 0.3 mile upstream of Lock E #12.

NEVER anchor in this creek if a river rise is occurring or forecast. Schoharie Creek is a major Mohawk tributary, and its runoff is the primary contributor to lower-river flooding. Throughout the old Erie Canal's history, Schoharie Creek caused more devastation to the canal system than anything else. It was the reason the state constructed the Schoharie Aqueduct.

Anchor only in fair weather when there has been no rain on the southern watershed. The creek still floods, with disastrous results. In May of 1987, a mile up creek, it caused a major highway bridge collapse that killed many people.

Be careful of the long unwatched shoal that makes out from Fort Hunter's northwestern point. Hold fairly close to **Buoy #254A** on the deep northern bank. After you have passed it, wide Schoharie Creek opens up. Don't become so goggle-eyed over the spectacular aqueduct remains that you cut the eastern corner turning into the creek—you'll end up stuck in the mud. Usually best water is about 150 feet off the creek's western shore, but don't count on it staying there. Approach

very cautiously despite the jet-skiers, racing runabouts, and water-skiers zipping by at 30 knots. Don't go very far up creek; you want a running start to safety if you hear thunder or a raindrop falls. Bottom is mud over well-scoured bedrock, and holding is not particularly good. Buoy the anchor; there's everything down there from tree stumps to bedsprings.

But it's worth it. Take the dinghy on up to Fort Hunter proper and land about opposite the end of the old aqueduct on the northeastern shore. Pack a lunch; there's a pretty park on the grounds with picnic tables, grills, and rest rooms.

This historic site has interesting remains of all phases of the old Erie Canal's development. The original canal, the 1825 to 1845 East Guard Lock, and old Lock E #20 are there; nearly everything was in service more than 70 years. You can see the Schoharie Creek dam sites that maintained the immediate area project depth throughout the canal era. Its location changed four times in the 1800s after it washed out seven times.

The visitor's center/museum is in the two-story yellow house beside the old locks. Hours are Wednesday through Saturday from 10 to 5 and Sunday from 1 to 5. From June to August there's a mule-drawn wagon train along the towpath, as well as guided walking tours.

FONDA AND FULTONVILLE

Chart: N 14786, page 33, *See sketch map, page 81*

Mile E-47.3 S (SM) to Mile E-48.1 N (SM)

There are two stops in this area, a marina and a terminal. If you plan to stop at either one, inform a lockmaster of your intentions. If westbound tell the lockmaster at Lock E #12; if eastbound tell the lockmaster at Lock E #13.

During rising river conditions the northern watershed runoff causes Cayadutta Creek, **Mile E-48.5 N (SM),** to be a threat at both these tie-ups due to its added current and excessive drift.

Fonda and Fultonville: The Poplars Inn and Marina, Fonda Terminal

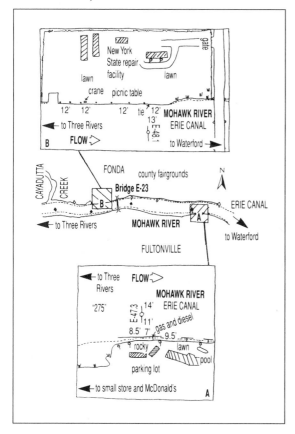

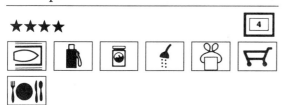

The Poplars Inn and Marina

★★★★

Chart: N 14786, page E-33, *See A on sketch map*

Mile E-47.3 S (SM)

This southern-bank resort complex is at the riverbend opposite **Buoy #274.** There are three sets of floating docks paralleling the bank. Pull in to the fuel dock (gas and diesel) on the westernmost pier's northern face. The dock office is at the head of the ramp. A large tour boat, the *Poplar Mist,* takes short cruises; if it's gone, don't leave your boat in its space. The marina also has a ramp,

boats for rent, and bait and tackle. Electric hookups (110-volt) are available.

If wind is strong up or down the river there's some chop, but it's not uncomfortable. Canallers are usually considerate, so wake roll is seldom excessive.

Lawns, large shade trees, flowers, a swimming pool, and festive umbrellas make this an attractive stop. The inn serves three meals a day and opens early. Call (518) 853-4511 for information.

Fultonville is about 0.8 mile away. Walk west to the bridge, then turn south for about two blocks. There's a post office, a hardware store, a Key Bank, a UPS shipping office, and Philbrooks Meats and Groceries. If you don't want to walk that far, The Switch, a small grocery and general store, is on the river road a tad west of McDonald's.

Fonda Terminal

★★★

Chart: N 14786, page E-33, *See B on sketch map*

Mile E-48.1 N (SM)

This northern-shore terminal just upstream of the Fonda-Fultonville Bridge has a long terminal wall surrounded by extensive lawns. The compound is a state work facility; its shops, parking lots, and service area are about 2 acres of lawn away. Occasionally a workboat or barge ties along the wall, but there's plenty of room. If you tie just east of the crane, the bollards are close together and there's usually a picnic table.

The crew locks the fenced compound after quitting time each afternoon. The night watchman may come down and have a chat at some point after closing. To save him the walk, after you tie up, wander up to the service area and tell someone you are spending the night. Remember, if you leave the grounds, you can't get back in after about 4 P.M.

The nearest grocery stores and post office are at Fultonville; the bridge has a safe walkway on its eastern side. If you go out to the main road and turn north, there's an ice cream parlor and fast food establishment about a half block away.

The Fonda Speedway—called the "Track of Champions" for stockcar racing—is across the bridge road at the Montgomery County Fairgrounds. If you tie at the terminal on a Saturday night April through August and make arrangements to get in the gate late, the races present an exciting evening's entertainment. If you want a restful sleep, however, you won't get it at the terminal until about midnight due to the roar of race cars shifting up and down.

The Montgomery County Fair is a late-summer attraction; its date varies annually. When it's in progress, dockage is limited. Pleasure craft from east and west arrive in large convoys and raft up to six deep. They always make room for a long-distance canaller somewhere, but you will be part of the all-night festivities whether you want to join in or not.

Do go to the county fair; you seldom find one so convenient. It's a wonderful opportunity to learn about country-oriented Montgomery County.

CANAJOHARIE

Chart: N 14786, page E-31

Mile E-59.9 (SM) to Mile E-60.5 (SM)

You have a choice of a downtown terminal with public access that is close to shopping, or a more attractive but isolated lock approach. Where you spend the night depends on your direction of travel, lock opening schedules, and need of supplies. If westbound, you can stop at Canajoharie Terminal, go shopping, then move on up to Lock E #14 Upper for a prettier setting and a head start on an early departure the next day. If eastbound, you can go down Lock E #14 and stay at the lower terminal, and can again depart early the next morning.

Canajoharie Terminal

★★

Chart: N 14786, page E-31, *See A on sketch map*

Mile E-59.9 S (SM)

Canajoharie: Canajoharie Terminal, Lock E #14 Upper

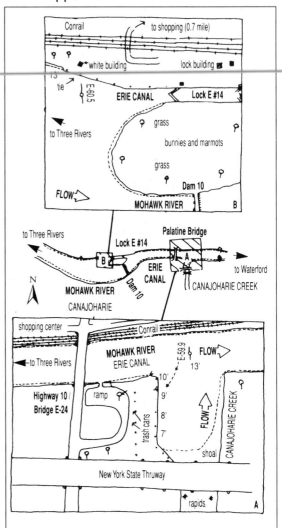

This terminal—the Canajoharie Fishing Access Site—is on the river's southern side and on the western side of Canajoharie Creek. The creek is another major Mohawk tributary. The stop is not recommended if the river or creek are on the rise.

The terminal is difficult to see from any distance; it's hidden by the creek's wooded eastern shore and the bridge. Leave the main river only when the creek opens fully. You'll need long lines for widely spaced bollards. There may be one or two small permanent pleasure boats tied at the southern end by the creek bridge, but if they aren't there, it's the most attractive spot—you have a grassy plot alongside the boat. Be cautious of depth as you close the bridge.

There's a ramp immediately east of the canal bridge. The adjoining parking lot has a phone. To exclude cars, wooden posts separate the large terminal park from the lot. Eventually, grass will cover the whole area, but for now most of it is dirt. There are plenty of picnic tables and garbage bins.

To reach Canajoharie go out the access drive and turn south. The library is a stone building about a block away on Church Street. Pop into its art galley and have a look at the full-size replica of Rembrandt's *Night Watch* and the collection of American paintings, which includes work by Winslow Homer. It's open Monday, Wednesday, and Friday, 9:30 to 8:30. Ask at the library for a village walking-tour map to help you with directions.

The post office is on Main Street—still only about a block from the terminal. In Wintergreen Park, a longer walk away, you can amble along the Canajoharie Gorge nature trails.

Dominating town is the Beechnut Nutrition Corporation; inquire about tours at its visitor center. The village has assorted shops, stores, pizza parlors, and cafés. The Great American supermarket is about 0.7 mile from the bridge. More convenient to the terminal is a shopping plaza at Palatine Bridge. Cross the canal bridge— it has safe walkways—then head for the big "M" of McDonald's, climb the little hill about a half block, and you are there. There's a post office, Stewart's convenience store, Pizza Hut, Radio Shack, Ames department store, a pharmacy, and a Grand Union supermarket.

Lock E #14 Upper

★★★

Chart: N 14786, page 31, *See B on sketch map, page 82*

Mile E-60.5 N (SM)

This northern-bank stop is in Lock E #14's upper pool. Tie at the approach wall's far western end on the portion that angles north. South is a large, landscaped, partially wooded island that separates the lock from its dam. In the early morning and on quiet late afternoons, watch

for grazing rabbits, groundhogs, and Canada geese— sometimes all side by side.

The Palatine Bridge plaza would be fairly close if you could fly. Since you can't, you have to use the lock access road to Highway 5, then take a right and hike a fair distance to town. This is not a convenient shopping point for a heavy carry home.

The terminal's major detriment is the mainline railroad track alongside the lock grounds—about 150 feet. The first few times trains blow for the access road crossing, it stands your hair on end. After that you settle back and try to ignore them.

ABEEL ISLAND ANCHORAGE

★★★★

NO FACILITIES

Chart: N 14786, page E-30

Mile E-64.4 S (SM)

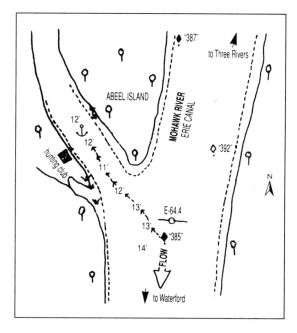

This southwestern-shore anchorage is between wooded Abeel Island and the river's western bank. The entrance is at the island's southern end; the northern entrance is shoal. Leave the river south of the island and just north of **Buoy #385,** which is usually on station. Hold to the middle of the back channel when you enter, then go upstream about 0.1 mile. Anchor in the middle in mud. There's no large-boat through-traffic in the cut because the northern exit is shoal. Most of the area is private; unless invited, don't go ashore.

ST. JOHNSVILLE MUNICIPAL MARINA

★★★★

ALL FACILITIES

Chart: N 14786, page E-29

Mile E-69.0 N (SM)

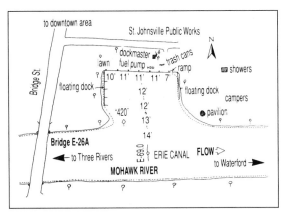

This northern-shore marina—open May 7 to November 1—is just east of the St. Johnsville Bridge. It's in a riverbank indentation just west of the sewer treatment plant. A gazebo with flag flying sits on the marina's eastern point. **Buoy #420** is close to the basin's western end; enter east of the buoy. If no one answered on VHF 13, pull in by the fuel pumps (gas and diesel); the dock office is at the foot of the hill by the road. If you need a diver or repairs, check at the office.

Electric hookups (110-volt/30-amp and 220-volt/50-amp) and block and cube ice are available.

Automobile traffic is restricted from the main marina, which can be reached at (518) 568-7406. There are lawns, tubs of blooming flowers, and picnic tables under the pine trees. On the rise west of the basin is a trailer park, the location of the marina showers, rest rooms, and laundromat.

St. Johnsville—a pretty, clean, compact town with flower baskets hanging from nearly every lamppost—is about a five-minute walk away. Go out the main gate, turn west to Bridge Street, and follow it north across the railroad trestle to Main Street. There's a post office, hardware stores, a pharmacy, restaurants, liquor stores, barber shops, assorted small shops, and a Big M super market that offers free delivery (call 568-7221).

Three blocks east of Main Street on Kingsbury Avenue is the Margaret Reaney Memorial Library and Museum. It's worth a visit to see its area historical displays and artifacts.

LITTLE FALLS UPPER

★★★

Chart: N 14786, page E-28

Mile E-79.7 S (SM)

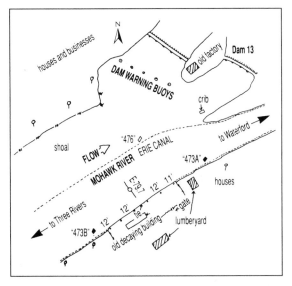

This southern-bank unimproved terminal is about 1 mile above Lock E #17 where the canal cut west of the lock rejoins the river. At about this same point there's a midriver mole and the site of a large commercial facility. Do not go down there. East and west of the mole, the river diverts downstream through Little Falls gorge and rapids.

At the western end of the terminal is a state canal warehouse stuffed with rusting canal buoys, so tie at the eastern end. Since the state does not usually mow, in midsummer you may have to stomp about in its hay field to find the bollards. Have long dock lines; the bollards are far apart.

This is a convenient stop if for some reason you are rebuilding your woodwork; the Little Falls Lumber Yard is next door. The state does mow a narrow path to the fence gate at the lot's eastern end so you can get out. If you need anything musical, the Music Supply is across the street.

The picturesque city center with its historical district is across the river bridge, too far away to walk to; however, there is a taxi in town.

Stop for a gorge view at the old Carrying Place, the falls and rapids that the Indians and first settlers had to portage around on their way east and west.

The Little Falls Historical Society Museum—a limestone Greek Revival building—is downtown on the corner of Ann and Albany streets. Its tour includes local history displays and area memorabilia. Close by for general shopping is a J. C. Penney, a little mall, a post office, hardware and auto parts stores, and banks.

In August the town has its Canal Celebration with art exhibits, parades, craft fairs, races, and hot-air-balloon rides. In July and August they have weekly concerts in the park and an occasional ice cream social. Well worth a walk is fieldstone Saint Mary's Church of Little Falls.

If you have rented a car, visit the Herkimer Home State Historic Site—you saw the monument from the river. It's back southeast about 3 miles on Highway 169 near the thruway's Exit 29A. This was the home of General Nicholas Herkimer, Battle of Oriskany hero. The visitor center has an audiovisual program on life in the late 18th century, as well as artifacts and memorabilia of the early area around Little Falls. The site is open Wednesday through Saturday from 10 to 5 and Sunday from 1 to 5. The Herkimer Home Volunteers group supports the historic site and presents several impressive programs on Sunday afternoons from March through October. Try to time your visit to coincide with one of these. Call (315) 823-0398 for more information.

HERKIMER, ILION, MOHAWK, AND FRANKFORT

Chart: N 14786, page E-25 and E-26

Mile E-87.0 (SM) to Mile E-91.1 (SM)

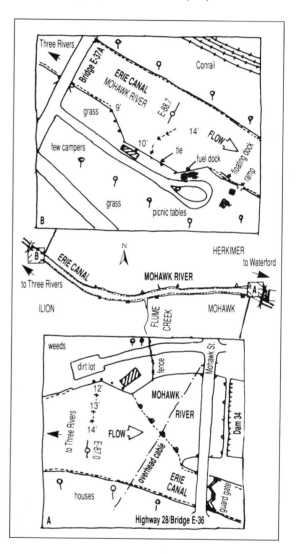

There are four villages in this area, with Herkimer on the northern shore and Mohawk, Ilion, and Frankfort on the southern shore. For overnight stays, two offer terminals and one a marina.

Herkimer Terminal

★★ 4

Chart: N 14786, page E-26, *See A on sketch map,* *page 85*

Mile E-87.0 N (SM)

This state work and storage terminal is on the northern shore. East of Herkimer is a canal section south of the river; at its western end you must clear Guard Gate #5 and Bridge E-36 to rejoin the river. Here the Mohawk is protected by a number of three-tiered pilings; immediately downstream of these is Mohawk Dam #14, with seven movable gates and an open crest. The cement terminal is clearly visible west of the pilings; it has a canal warehouse on its eastern end. You need long lines; bollards are far apart.

Space availability depends on canal work in progress. At times you tie with dredges, barges, floating dormitories, and workboats with stored equipment on the gravel lot; other times the workforce and equipment are absent. If no one is around but you see parked cars, tie at the terminal's western end; at quitting time in the afternoon, it's likely a state workboat and possibly a barge will come in so the crew can drive home for the night.

A high wire fence separates the grounds from the New York State Thruway. There's no gate on the access road that enters the terminal from the village street at the bridge. Local residents often come down to fish off the terminal or barges in the late afternoon and early evening.

This is a good stop to visit historic Herkimer. The center of town is north about 0.7 mile. Note the charted post office—that's about where you will be heading. Though general shopping is a bit more selective on the way into Herkimer, if you need a supermarket, you are closer if you hike off across the bridge to Mohawk. If walking is not your thing, Skinner Sales, at (315) 866-3530, has rental cars, usually with free pickup and delivery.

To get to either area, go out the terminal gate and get on Highway 5. To get to the Big M supermarket in Mohawk, turn south, cross the bridge, then stay on the main road as it bears west into the village; it's about five blocks. On the way you can stop for a repast at Burger King. At its western end is the site of Shoemaker Tavern, built before the Revolutionary War. In 1778 Indian scout Adam Helmer—nearing the end of a 44-mile run—stopped at the tavern to warn settlers that Joseph Brant and his warriors were hot on his heels. George Washington also ate dinner under the tavern tree.

To visit downtown Herkimer, turn north at the terminal gate. This takes you under the thruway and railroad underpasses. Just north of the railroad tracks on the street's western side is a Shell Bon Fare store; a block farther on is a Stewarts. These are typical convenience stores with ice and phones. Keep going north and you'll find a Friendly's restaurant; a little farther you have a Howard Johnson's motel and restaurant. As you move closer to downtown you have banks, shops, and hardware and automotive stores.

At Herkimer's historic Four Corners you can see the Reformed Church of 1835. The 1834 jailhouse has a museum, a gift shop, and the Leatherstocking Country Tourism Office, where you can pick up a wealth of information and brochures. The 1873 courthouse was the scene of the Chester Gillette murder trial that was the basis for Theodore Dreiser's bestseller *An American Tragedy*. To complete the Four Corners is the County Historical Society Museum—it's in the Victorian mansion with the beautifully carved front door. It's open Monday through Friday from 10 to 4. Since 1896 the historical society has been collecting, preserving, and publishing information on the county's past.

Ilion Marina

★★★★ 5

Chart: N 14786, page E-26, *See B on sketch map,* *page 85*

Mile E-88.7 S (SM)

This southern-shore marina is in a slight bank indentation just east of the Highway 5 Bridge (BR E-37). The fuel dock (gas and diesel) is toward the eastern end of the wall in front of a porched dock office.

Dockage parallels the wall. In the bankside trees at

the complex's eastern end is a launching ramp, a small floating dock, and a covered picnic area. There's a large building—an old canal warehouse—near the marina's western end. Across the driveway is a small travel-trailer park.

Electric hookups (110-volt) are available. The marina's land line number is (315) 894-9758.

Ilion is a fairly convenient supply point; everything is about 0.5 mile away. Go out the marina access lane to Central Street, the bridge road, and turn south. The Central Plaza might confuse you at first; the approach is from its rear and the mall stores are not visible. Cross Clark Street, turn west, and the mall opens up. There's a Great American supermarket, a bank, clothing and hardware stores, and small shops conveniently grouped.

The Remington Firearms Museum has a spectacular display of rifles, shotguns, and handguns dating from the first produced to those of today. To get there from Central Avenue, turn east on Highway 5 by the mall, go a long block to Catherine Street, then take a right for about a block. The large commercial sites are part of the Remington Arms complex. The museum is open Monday through Saturday from 9 to 4 and Sunday from 1 to 4:30.

Frankfort Terminal

★★★   5

Chart: N 14786, page E-25

Mile E-91.1 + 0.3 W (SM)

This terminal is well off the main channel in a Mohawk River section that's southwest of the improved canal. During high water the approach and terminal are not recommended; current and drift become excessive.

The river entrance is immediately northwest of the Frankfort Bridge (BR E-38); slow down or you will miss it in the trees. There's an overhead cable across the river entrance with more than standard canal clearance, since for many years the terminal was Frankfort's active commercial port. Wait until the cut opens fully, then hold to mid-Mohawk as you leave the canal.

This is a forested approach. About 0.25 mile inside

Frankfort Terminal

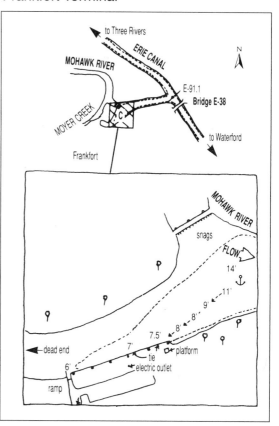

the cut you come to the tailwaters of a small dam on the northern bank. At this point begin to favor slightly the southern bank to the terminal. Between the dam and the terminal you might encounter a circular collection of buoys; keep to their east, where you have 14 feet of water.

The smooth-walled southern-bank terminal is nearly at the cut's end. Come in with long lines; the bollards are set back about 15 feet from the water and spaced for barges. Though Frankfort has made some terminal improvements, they aren't inclined to do a lot of mowing; you may have to beat the brush looking for the bollards. During this process you will arouse the grasshopper population, so if you are a fisherman, carry along a container and a fly swatter and try to capture them dead or alive. They are superb bait.

There are well-maintained picnic tables and garbage cans along the terminal wall. Bonfires or table grills are not recommended; the unmown terminal grounds are very combustible and the fire station is about six blocks away. At the terminal's eastern end is a raised platform intended as a dam pond overlook. There are several telephone poles on the grounds; the one with the spotlight has a collection of electric plugs for a hookup; the six black ones are 110-volt.

It's about two blocks to town. Go out the Fox Street access road gate—it's not kept closed or locked—pass a few homes, make a right at the first main street, and walk another block.

Frankfort is a compact small town that has about everything you might need within a few blocks. There's a pharmacy, an ice cream shop, a bank, a town hall, a liquor store, restaurants, a post office, and a library. If you turn east on Main Street, you have a Bon Fare convenience store and a large Foodland supermarket.

Frankfort was the 1900s home of Carlotta and Carl Myers's Balloon Farm, but the site is a long walk out Cemetery Road. In October the annual Autumn Balloon Festival is held at the fair grounds. Balloon Detail, Inc., (315) 894-9106, often offers hot-air-balloon rides during the rest of the year.

The Herkimer County Fair is held in early August at the 30-acre fairgrounds—another very long walk. It offers more than 100 exhibits, a demolition derby, fireworks, rides, contests, shows, a midway, and all the other adventures of a farming community fair.

Closer to home, take the dinghy back down to the dam tailwaters along with your grasshoppers and nod off catching catfish and perch for dinner.

MARCY MARINA

★★

Chart: N 14786, page E-22

Mile E-103.7 N (SM)

This northern-shore marina—open April through December—is in an enclosed lagoon. It's about 0.2 mile east of the Mohawk Street Bridge (BR E-47A) and about 0.5 mile east of the thruway bridge (BR E-47B).

Depths into the lagoon are about 4 feet. If your draft is obliging, stay in mid-entrance when you enter; once inside, depths range about 4.5 to 5 feet. The fuel dock (gas only) is on the lagoon's western shore.

Marcy Marina

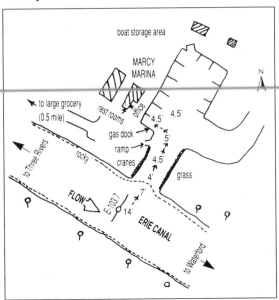

At the lagoon's northern end are two Travelifts, a pair of cranes, a workshop, and a repair yard. The ship's store has a collection of general marine supplies. Electric hookups (110-volt) are available. For more information call the marina at (315) 736-7617.

There's a large mall about 0.5 mile west, but it is not easily accessible.

LOCK E #20 UPPER

★★★★

Chart: N 14786, page E-22, *See sketch map, page 89*

Mile E-105.0 N/S (SM)

This canal park at Marcy is in Lock E #20's upper pool. It has immaculate grounds. On the northern shore are rest rooms, a playground, a lock viewing platform, and picnic tables and grills shaded by tall pines.

Immediately upstream of the north approach wall, on a slight angle to the channel, is a canal park floating dock with a 110-volt electric hookup. Depths here are only about 6 feet, and that decreases each time the lock dumps. It's a rocky bottom, so if grounding is a concern,

Lock E #20 Upper

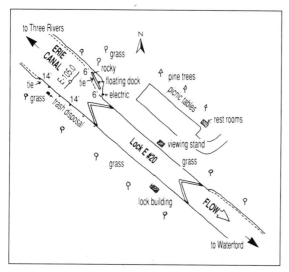

ask the lockmaster if you can spend the night at the southern approach wall's western end—it stretches to the bridge. Stay well west of the lock to keep clear of commercial traffic pulling in or out of the chamber. There is a grassy area along this wall, and there's a screened garbage disposal area nearby. To get to the picnic grounds go back across the upper lock gates' walkway to the northern shore.

This canal park is a summertime stop for *Betsy,* a spiffed-up canal work barge, and for the mobile Canal Museum, a large walk-through bus containing some interesting canal historical photographs. *Betsy* is decked out in bright paint and colorful flags, and has tubs of flowers around a stage used for live musical performances. When she visits a canal park, she parks alongside the bank; the audience sits on the grass. There's usually a weekly change of performers and an assortment of musical and singing groups, mimes, and juggling. *Betsy* also moves to canal villages during their particular Canal Days and Riverfest events.

ROME TERMINAL

★

Chart: N 14786, page E-20

Mile E-114.5 N (SM)

Rome Terminal

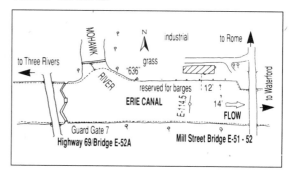

This is an unattractive stop for such a scenic city as Rome. It's on the northern shore in a heavily commercialized area in a rough part of town between Mill Street Bridge (BR E-51–52) and the Highway 69 Bridge (BR E-52A). Its only redeeming feature is its access to Rome.

Towboats and barges use the terminal. There may be a sign indicating that pleasure craft should tie on the cement terminal's eastern end by Bridge BR-51–52. This puts you in front of the weathered canal warehouse. At the terminal's western end, the Mohawk River flows in from its northern headwaters. There's a small dam here, rather attractive amidst the grubby industry.

Do not leave your boat unattended at this terminal, or wander off up the road looking for the city or a grocery store. Lock up at night if you plan to stay. The telephone on the building's eastern end toward the back has a large, very prominent sign on it giving you the phone number for the police. This, and being tied up amidst a pile of castoff beer bottles, is not conducive to a relaxed stay.

Fort Stanwix, a national monument, is tucked in a bevy of freeway approaches and off ramps about a mile away. Call a cab to get there, and be sure to tell the driver to take you to the main entrance. On our first visit we arrived at the fort's back side and found our entry thwarted by impregnable spike-tipped stockade and redoubts; the entrance was a half mile away.

This beautifully reconstructed 16-acre fort portrays its Revolutionary War history with costumed actors who simulate 1700s wilderness military outpost life. There are exhibits, films, and grounds to wander. It's open 9 to 5 daily, April through December.

The Rome Historical Society Museum and Library are at 200 Church Street in the 1936 Post Office Building behind the fort to the north. Here you have displays of early local paintings, prints, and photographs; examples of samplers and textiles; tools; and other artifacts. It's open Monday through Friday from 9 to 4 and Sunday from 1 to 4.

The Erie Canal Village—open May 15 to September 15 from 9:30 to 5—is about 3.5 miles west of the fort; off you go again in the taxi. This is a restoration of an 1840 village on the old Erie Canal. There are shops, homes, taverns, a church, museums, a schoolhouse, and a livery stable. They have a mule-drawn canal packet boat that takes you for a 45-minute ride on a refurbished old canal section. If your preference is for railroads, there's a 30-minute ride around the compound on a reconstructed steam train; catch it at the 19th-century railroad station.

terminal, though stored barges or old workboats are often dry-stored inside the lock. We have had up to four pleasure boats stay the night with us here; this pretty well fills up all available space.

If you want some exercise, there's a rutty access road at the northern terminal wall's end. Once away from the yard, have a look at the old Erie Canal beside the road—it's about the size of a storm drain. If you continue your outing, you'll pass two small farms and eventually arrive at a paved road. You can have a cold drink at Genuine Sachs Tavern before you turn around and head home. There's nothing else.

NEW LONDON TERMINAL

★★

Chart: N 14786, page E-19

Mile E-121.1 S (SM)

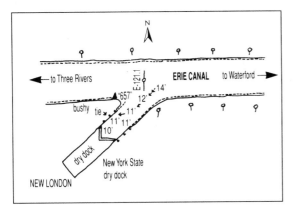

This southern-bank state terminal, dry dock, and maintenance area is in a short off-channel cut. **Daymark #657**—barely visible in the briar patch—is on the western entrance point. The best place to tie is on the smooth-walled terminal on the cut's western side, which puts you northeast of the dry-dock lock. There are a few state maintenance buildings on the lock's eastern shore and some unused cranes and pieces of heavy equipment stored on the grounds. Though not derelict, the place impresses you as being permanently out of service. We have never seen commercial activity at the

SYLVAN BEACH

Chart: N 14786, page E-17

Mile E-128.7 (SM) to E-129.0 (SM)

Skinners Harbour, Sylvan Beach Terminal

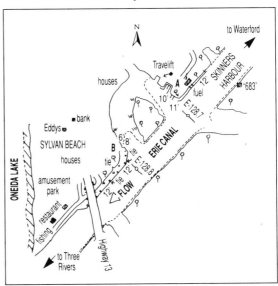

Oneida Lake is 19 miles across. During severe weather or prolonged winds out of the east or west, it produces an unpleasant chop. Calmest water for a crossing is usually in early morning and late afternoon. You have a marina and a terminal for a layover. From either stop you can walk to the beach or breakwater and have a look at weather conditions before you start across.

Sylvan Beach bursts with activity on warm summer weekends. Its main attraction is a small amusement park with a midway, arcades, and rides at the southern end of town just west of the bridge at the lake entrance. There's a popular miniature-golf course on the northern side of town.

The village is vacation and beach oriented, with many individually owned fast-food stands and beach-wear shops. There's a large park near the southern end of town; during the season, band concerts and various musical groups perform in the afternoon and early evening. If you enjoy browsing for white elephants, the bandstand usually has peripheral flea markets. The town has a touted 4-mile beach that is well populated in summer.

Eddys—a favorite canal restaurant—is by the park. Try to get there early for dinner or you'll wait in a long line. The restaurant also bakes and sells cream pies with up to 5-inch meringues. If you take one of these home, you will be very popular at coffee-down the following day.

The post office is about 10 blocks north of the bridge on Main Street; the Ship and Shore Market, a fair-size grocery, is about 2 blocks farther on in the Lake Shore Plaza.

Skinners Harbour

★★★★

ALL FACILITIES

Chart: N 14786, page E-17, *See A on sketch map, page 90*

Mile E-128.7 N (SM)

This northern-shore marina has part of its facilities in a small lagoon. It's west of **Daymark #683**—if it's on station in the trees—and about 0.3 mile east of Bridge BR E-63—the one just east of the lake entrance.

There is a Sunoco station with its fuel pumps (gas and diesel) on the main channel near the front of the dock office. The long dock paralleling the canal is usually the transient pier. More marina slips and the 20-ton Travelift's well are around the lagoon's eastern corner north of the launching ramp. Electric hookups (110-volt) and cube ice are available.

There's a ship's store in the office with a selection of marine equipment and supplies, charts, some nautical clothing, and basic groceries such as fresh bread, milk, eggs, meat, and frozen dinners. Its stock might save you

a long walk to the grocery store. Call (315) 762-0112 for information.

The center of Sylvan Beach is about five blocks away.

Sylvan Beach Terminal

★★★

Chart: N 14786, page 17, *See B on sketch map, page 90*

Mile E-128.8 N (SM)

This popular northern-bank terminal stretches from the Main Street Bridge at the lake entrance to the western end of the small north-shore lagoon with its offshore island. Though the terminal wall continues west of the bridge, it's not recommended for overnight. This section adjoins the amusement park, and noise level is high.

The terminal has a slight jog at its eastern end and hikes off north about 75 feet. This northern jog is the preferred stop. You are at right angles to and well off of the main channel. Depth gradually shoals off the terminal face, but the extreme northern end by a private home's fence still has about 6 feet. Bollards are far apart, but ingenious boaters use the state's heavy fence supports for intermediate cleats.

The terminal's top is wide and backed with the lawns and shade trees of well-kept residential front yards; across the canal are dense woods. The entire terminal is a town promenade. Visitors often bring their deck chairs and spend the day watching what seems to be an endless stream of small fishing boats and runabouts.

If you are a fan of small hometown amusement parks, this one is convenient; it's just west of the bridge. Since the bridge is Main Street, you are also within a stone's throw of downtown.

BREWERTON AND UPPER ONEIDA RIVER

Chart: N 14786, page E-15, *See sketch map, page 92*

Mile E-150.0 (SM) to Mile E-153.2 (SM)

Brewerton is Sylvan Beach's counterpart at the lake's

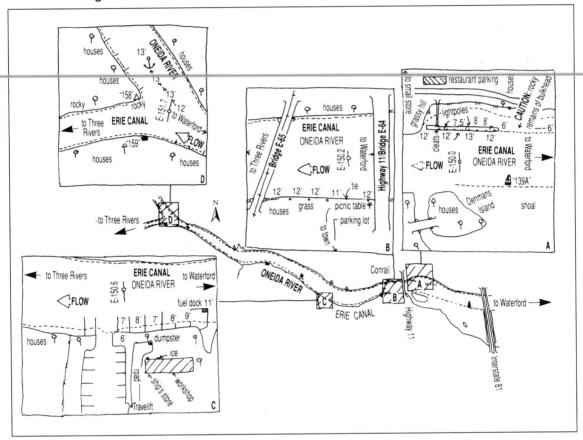

western end. It's geared more toward summer cottages and permanent residences than to boisterous beach bunnies. It's a good layover if eastbound and the lake is making up. You have two terminals, a marina, a quiet anchorage, or a pretty canal park all within a few miles of the lake entrance.

Distance from supplies and points of interest depends on where you stop. Some shopping is available just south of the Highway 11 Bridge. There's a bakery, a pharmacy, a liquor store that sells ice, a Family Dollar store, a laundromat, and a post office. The large shopping mall is about eight more long blocks south on Highway 11. Just keep walking until you reach McDonald's, then take a left. This large plaza overflows onto both sides of the highway, and offers just about everything: a True Value hardware, fast-food restaurants, banks, liquor stores, department stores, pharmacies, a pizza parlor, florists, restaurants, shops galore, and a very large supermarket.

If you stay at the North Terminal, the Waterfront restaurant, with festive umbrellas, pagodas, bar, and outside patio, is on the hill at the head of your access ramp. It's going to be a long walk to the mall and supermarket from North Terminal, but about a block north of the highway bridge is a Mobil gas and diesel station with a convenience store. Near it is a NAPA Auto Supply.

Just north of the bridge is the Fort Brewerton Site Reservation, where you can see the original fort earthworks. This was the western frontier in 1758 when Sir William Johnson built the fort to protect the settlers from the French and the Indians. The Oliver Stevens Blockhouse Museum is on the grounds.

If you arrive on a Friday from April through October, you can take in the Brewerton Speedway a block or so north of the fort. Races start at 7:45 P.M. It has a dirt track and features outlaw modifieds and pure stockcar and street-stock races. Even if you don't attend, you will hear the racing roar if you stay at North Terminal.

In mid-July the Brewerton Chamber of Commerce sets aside a busy weekend for the Blessing of the Fleet, accompanied by a downtown parade, parade of boats, and barbecues.

Brewerton Terminals

★

Chart: N 14786, page E-15

Mile E-150.0 (SM) to Mile E-150.2 (SM)

There are two terminals in Brewerton, neither of which is particularly inviting, but they are state terminals and you are free to stop.

North Terminal

See A on sketch map, page 92

This terminal is at **Mile E-150.0 (SM)** just east of the Highway 11 Bridge (BR E-64)—the second bridge west of the lake entrance. Tie up on the channel-side wall, though if your draft is under 5 feet, you might be able to tie inside the bulkhead for more protection. For many years this was an excellent stop because the wide terminal extended from the bridge eastward for over 1,000 feet, and you could tie on the inside of the terminal off the channel. Some catastrophic happening removed its eastern 600 feet; it's now submerged and a menace to navigation for deep-draft vessels.

There are terminal improvements, a paved surface, street lights, and yacht-spaced cleats. It remains a popular spot for walk-in fishermen; they line the outer wall and grumble audibly if you tie up.

South Terminal

See B on sketch map, page 92

This southern-bank terminal is between the Highway 11 Bridge (BR E-64) and the railroad bridge (BR E-65).

Tie on the section that has a low wall where bollards are set back from the rim about 6 feet; along the high wall they are back about 15 feet and you need long dock lines. You tie alongside a public parking lot with all-night access. Your view is of two hulking bridges; south across the lot is a residential area. You are slightly closer to village stores and the distant mall; you can eliminate your time spent crossing the bridge.

Ess-Kay Yards

★★★★★

ALL FACILITIES

Chart: N 14786, page E-15, *See C on sketch map, page 92*

Mile E-150.6 S (SM)

This southern-shore marina is about 0.4 mile west of the railroad bridge (BR E-65) and about opposite **Daymark #150**. It has riverside slips and more slips inside an enclosed lagoon. If no one answered on VHF 16, pull in to the fuel dock (gas and diesel) by a dock office at the far eastern end of a fixed pier on the canal.

This is a well-maintained marina with attractive lawns and flower beds, picnic tables and grills, even a hammock. The main office is across the lawn next to the river slips. There's a ship's store with marine equipment and supplies, nautical shoes, clothing, and rain gear. Highly recommended is the store's excellent supply of up-to-date, wide area coverage of American and Canadian charts, cruising guides, *Coast Pilots, Light Lists, Sailing Directions,* and other cruising publications. There's also a large bookstore with a fine selection of fiction, nonfiction, and children's literature.

Electric hookups (110-volt/15- and 30-amp and 220-volt/50-amp), a 14-ton Travelift, and cube ice are available. The marina's land line number is (315) 676-2711.

The collection of stores at the foot of the highway bridge is within walking distance, but the mall is a bit farther. If you do walk it, you can call the marina for a ride home. There are a few restaurants close by; some offer pickup and return service.

Oneida River East Anchorage

★★★

NO FACILITIES

Chart: N 14786, page E-15, *See D on sketch map, page 92*

Mile E-151.7 N (SM)

This anchorage is up the eastern end of an Oneida River oxbow on its northern shore. Lock E #23 at **Mile E-153.1 (SM)** has slightly different hours than most Erie locks and is one of the few that religiously maintains a timed schedule. This is a good anchorage when eastbound on the canal as you are east of the lock for an early morning start to cross the lake.

Since you exited the lake at Brewerton westbound, you have been traveling downstream on the Oneida River. At **Daymark #158** and **Daymark #159** the main channel diverts west into a canal cut to the lock about 1.5 miles away.

Leave the main channel just east of the daymarks and head northwesterly into the old river loop. Go downstream about 0.1 mile and anchor in soft mud. You have about 8 to 10 feet of depth in front of a collection of cottages along the wooded shoreline. If you go farther up the old river, be cautious of depths; the bottom contour is very uneven. Also be extremely careful of the overhead power cables downstream; their heights are unknown. Even if you have shoal draft and low clearance, you can't transit entirely through this old river loop. There is a movable taintor gate, a dam, and a guard gate 2.5 miles downstream at Caughdenoy.

Lock E #23 Lower

★★★★

Chart: N 14786, page E-15

Mile E-153.2 S (SM)

This southern-bank canal park is in Lock E #23's lower

Lock E #23 Lower

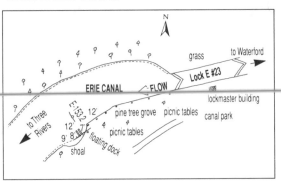

pool. It's a good stop when westbound if you like early starts, as you are west of the lock. It's 18.5 miles to the next lock on the Erie Canal West at Baldwinsville, and 8 miles to the timed lock on the Oswego Canal at Phoenix.

The park has a few pleasure-craft floating docks in the lower pool at the southern approach wall's far western end in a very slight indentation. The docks are at 90 degrees to the bank. If you plan to stay, get your entire boat off the channel; then double-check to make certain your stern is not protruding beyond the approach wall. A commercial vessel—though not a common sight nowadays—approaches closely or scrapes along the wall to line up a barge for lock entry.

This is a pretty park that is closed to automobile traffic at dark. Along the wall are manicured lawns under old pines that scatter cones everywhere. It's a cool and comfortable stop on hot summer days. The park has garbage bins, picnic tables, grills, rest rooms, and a lock viewing area. If seas are up on Oneida Lake or Lake Ontario, this becomes a local destination and is often full.

PIRATES COVE MARINA

★★★★

Chart: N 14786, page E-14 or O-6, *See A on sketch map, page 95*

Mile E-157.5 S (SM)

This popular marina—open May 16 to November 15—

Pirates Cove Marina, Big Bend Cut East Anchorage

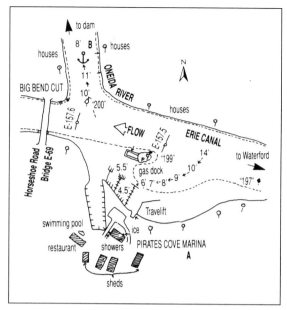

is close to Lakes Ontario and Oneida. Transient space is limited. It's on the Oneida River's southern shore just east of Big Bend Cut Off's eastern entrance. It's on a wide outer river bend, south of two grounded barges that serve as a breakwater.

If you draw more than 6 feet, make your approach very cautiously from the breakwater's eastern end at **Daymark #199.** Sound carefully; if water level is down, you may not have depth.

This is a large complex. Entering from the east you first see one long pier that jogs eastward; next is the 25-ton Travelift's well. The T-pier of the easternmost of the next three piers with numerous slips is the fuel dock (gas only). If no one answered on VHF 16, pull in here for slip assignment. There are also a few individual slips alongside the marina's northern mole bank, as well as a pretty inner basin with perimeter slips.

The ship's store is in the main office, which can be reached at (315) 695-3901. It has a fair collection of marine supplies, nautical clothing, and local charts.

Electric hookups (110-volt/30-amp) are available. If you need a diver, check at the office.

The grounds are attractive, with a lot of grass and flowers and a pleasant picnic area with tables and grills. About 100 feet from the office is a swimming pool in front of the marina restaurant.

Though you can hike off down the road to take a

walk, the mall and supermarket are more than 2 miles away. Far better to take the marina courtesy car.

BIG BEND CUT EAST ANCHORAGE

★★★   5

NO FACILITIES

Chart: N 14786, page E-14 or O-6, *See B on sketch map*

Mile E-157.6 N (SM)

This anchorage with wooded shorelines is in another old Oneida River loop east of Big Bend Cut Off. **Buoy #200** sits in the middle of the old river channel to prevent navigation from missing the Cut Off turn. When you leave the canal try to hold to midriver as you bear northerly. You may have to shave the buoy a tad close; it depends on exactly where it is seasonally placed. This is not a deep anchorage, so approach slowly and sound carefully. Anchor in mud in midstream not far from the canal. If you end up close to shore, sound for swinging-room depth.

THREE RIVERS TERMINAL

★   4

Chart: N 14786, page E-14 or OS-6, *See sketch map, page 96*

Mile E-159.8 S (SM)

Do not depend on this terminal being available; it's often used for barge storage. If one comes in when you are there, the towboat operator will probably ask you to get out and let him secure the barge, after which you are given permission to tie outside the barge. This is perfectly acceptable unless, as happened to us one time, the barge was carrying dredging sludge. Unfortunately, if a barge is already stored at the terminal, you should

Three Rivers Terminal

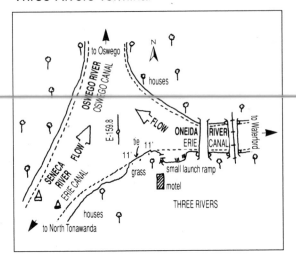

not tie alongside without permission.

Three Rivers is the point where the Oswego, the Seneca, and the Oneida rivers meet. The unimproved cement terminal is on the southern bank east of the last two Oneida bridges. Have long lines ready as bollards are far apart. Only the western terminal end is available; the eastern section has collapsed.

Your woodland basin shoreline vista is very pretty, but the terminal is unattractive. It's usually dusty unless grass has been planted recently, and if fishermen are there they grumble unpleasantly as you pull in and take up space. Although anchoring would be far more enjoyable here, don't do it. Never anchor in an area that carries deep water to riverbanks where commercial traffic is active; it's unsafe. Towboats often hug shores when there's good depth and offbank buoys do not exist. This applies to the large area of this three-river junction.

The Oswego Canal
Three Rivers to Oswego

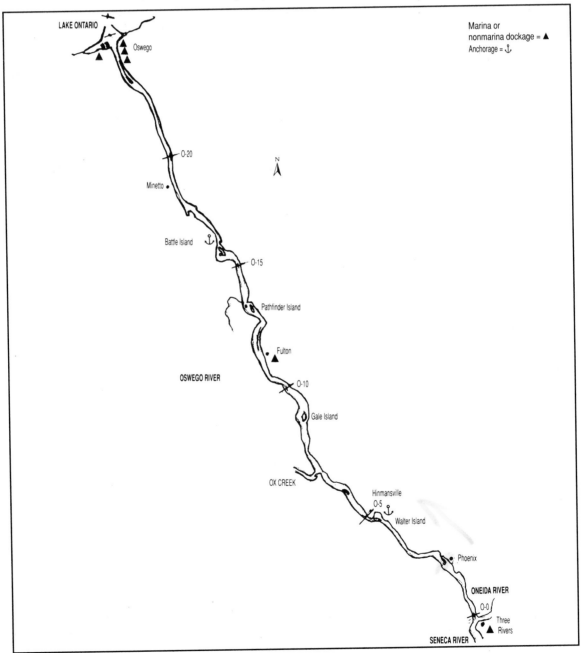

Mile OS-0.0 (SM) to Mile OS-24.5 (SM)

> *Heave Haw—It be down we go*
> *Ontario Bound, Ontario Bound*
> *Heave Haw—It be down we go.*
>
> 1848 Canalboat Song

LOCKAGE, THREE RIVERS TO OSWEGO

Lock	Mile	Land Line	Lift*
Lock OS #1	OS-2.2 E (SM)	(315) 695-2281	10.2 feet
Lock OS #2	OS-11.5 E (SM)	(315) 592-4155	17.8 feet
Lock OS #3	OS-12.0 E (SM)	(315) 592-5349	27.0 feet
Lock OS #5	OS-18.5 E (SM)	(315) 343-5232	18.0 feet
Lock OS #6	OS-21.9 E (SM)	(315) 343-9001	20.0 feet
Lock OS #7	OS-22.6 E (SM)	(315) 343-6304	14.7 feet
Lock OS #8	OS-23.1 E (SM)	(315) 343-0280	11.1 feet

*At normal pool level

All locks monitor VHF 13. Signals: Lights and Horn (3 long blasts to transit). Normally furnish lines; have ladders each chamber corner; may have cables.

Daily operating hours for pleasure craft: 0700 to 2230 (may vary annually).

Schedules: Locks are normally on the hour and half hour, but all are at the discretion of the lockmaster. Locks #6, #7, and #8 usually work as a series. Once you're in the series, lockage is straight through.

Call (800) 422-1825 for updated canal information, including schedules and operation hours.

Canal Superintendent: (315) 428-4589.

The first Oswego Canal, which opened for navigation in 1829, established a portage-free route from Lake Ontario to inland America and New York Harbor. When the New York State Barge Canal System began its four-canal improvement and updating in 1917, it included the Oswego Canal.

The modern canal is 23 miles long, winds through thick woodlands, and is primarily the wide, well-watched, canalized north-flowing Oswego River. It has very little commercial traffic. You descend 118 feet through seven locks to Lake Ontario's elevation. There are also seven fixed dams with vertical head gates at the power sluiceways—five have regulating taintor gates. Power plant operation greatly affects the amount of tailrace current. There's no canal summit level; the Erie and Cayuga and Seneca canals supply it with surplus water.

Stowell Island, **Mile OS-1.7 E (SM),** is known locally as Treasure Island. In 1658 a group of French colonists camped on the island hoping to escape the Onondaga Indians. Though nothing has been found, legend says the French lightened their load by leaving their cannons and gold on the island.

Once you pass Stowell Island hold to the northeastern-shore channel to keep clear of the large western-shore horseshoe dam and its protective cribs.

If you plan to stop over in the upper pool at the Phoenix Terminal, **Mile OS-2.0 (SM),** first tell the lockmaster via VHF. Though commercial traffic is slight, the terminal has very limited room for large craft to clear the approach wall; the lockmaster can tell you if anything large is coming through. If he expects nothing after evening close-down, you might even ask if you can spend the night. Phoenix makes an effort to make the terminal attractive with lawns and flowers, and an attendant is on duty during the day at the old bridge tender's house—it's now the Bridgehouse Interpretive Center, with crafts and information.

There's a phone by the lock and a pumpout behind the bridgehouse. The village, across the street from the terminal, has a collection of small shops, a Midland Bank, a laundromat, and a Red and White supermarket. The library is a block up on Main Street, and the post office is another two blocks away.

In June Phoenix hosts its Canal Days celebration. There are displays of 19th century art, more exhibits at the Bridgehouse, music and storytellers, and rides through the lock on a canalboat.

A lock island separates the river from Lock OS #1. Be aware that a low-level bascule bridge over the chamber accesses the lock island. The bridge is put in a raised position for downbound lockage—it has to be open to allow traffic into the lock. When southbound (upbound) make certain the bridge is in the up position if you are under it.

After you make the westerly bend around the lock island at **Mile OS-2.5 (SM),** you may have a sharp northerly current set if the upstream powerhouse is generating. Take time to glance back at the dam. This is the old river falls and rapids called the Rift; during the early canal days factories lined its shores.

Mind **Buoy #29** at **Mile OS-4.2 W (SM)** and **Buoy #31** at **Mile OS-4.6 W (SM);** they watch a dangerous 0.4-mile rock dike barely awash between them. The channel holds east of the large island at **Mile OS-6.1 W (SM).** The original Oswego Canal paralleled the river; portions are visible along the bend's northern bank.

The river widens as you approach Ox Creek, **Mile OS-7.5 W (SM),** a major Oswego tributary. Creek runoff has shoaled the area, so stay in the watched channel.

The channel is on wooded Gale Island's eastern side, **Mile OS-9.0 (SM).** You pass the Curtis Gale State Wildlife Management Area; in spring and fall it's a place to sight migrating Canada geese, snow geese, ducks, and loons.

In Fulton's approach, **Mile OS-11.0 (SM),** there's another barely submerged rock dike alongside the western channel edge. It's at the point where the channel narrows dramatically at the lock and dam approach. **Buoy #78** and **Buoy #79** guide you to the river's eastern side and east of the southernmost of three cement cribs that partially make up the upper-pool lock approach

wall. If you have shoal draft and are waiting for lockage, do not cross over these shoals for a look at the dam; there's a severe current increase near the crest.

Dutch settlers from the Mohawk and Hudson valleys established Fulton in the 1700s—it was at another river portage around the Falls of the Oswego and its downstream rapids. Waterborne cargoes were unloaded and hauled by oxcart around the two waterfalls. Before the state built the first canal, Onondaga Springs salt was one of the main products that came through downriver. With the opening of the first canal and locks, the village's economy increased; Fulton was on the shortest navigable water route from the Great Lakes to the Hudson.

On May 5, 1814, Fulton played a role in the War of 1812. England had decided it was time to take Oswego and Fort Ontario. Their goal was to capture the cannons and military supplies that Oswego was due to send to Sackets Harbor for the new American warship U.S.S. *Superior,* which was nearly ready for launching.

The Americans in Oswego realized the danger of occupation. At the start of the war Fort Ontario was in a state of deterioration. Gates were gone, buildings had fallen down, and earthworks were nearly useless. It was undependable protection. The Americans moved all the *Superior*'s supplies to safety in Fulton. The British succeeded in capturing Oswego and Fort Ontario but left the following morning when they found the cannons and military gear gone.

There are two locks at Fulton around the old falls; each has a dam. The power plant is on the western bank at the upper dam at **Mile OS-11.4 W (SM).** Downstream of Lock OS #3's dam, parts of the old Oswego Canal are visible on the western bank.

For the 0.5 mile between the two Fulton locks, the rocky, shoal main river flows directly alongside the navigation channel. After you exit the upper lock, stay in the channel along the eastern bank where there's almost no current even if the power plant is generating.

After descending Lock OS #3 you are inside a 0.7-mile-long, lower-pool land cut that protects the channel from the river. Once downstream of this, you rejoin the river at a westerly bend. If the powerhouse is generating, prepare for a sharp easterly current set in the bend.

The channel leads you to Pathfinder Island's western side. Legend says this is where Natty Bumppo fought the Iroquois in James Fenimore Cooper's book *The Pathfinder.*

Battle Island, **Mile OS-15.0 W (SM),** is at the river's westerly bend; here Captain John Bradstreet and his

British forces repulsed an attack of French and Indian forces in 1758.

Lock OS #5, **Mile OS-18.5 W (SM),** in Minetto, has its dam powerhouse alongside the lock on the western shore; its horseshoe dam extends from the lock to the eastern bank. Upper- and lower-pool damside approach walls are 0.1 mile long, so the upper-pool wall extends nearly to the upstream bridge. If you need to wait for a descending lockage, do so near the bridge. If the Minetto powerhouse is generating, current is drawn into the plant at the cement cribs alongside the powerhouse intake valves immediately south of the lock gates. The plant discharge diverts under the lock into the dam tailrace east of the lock wall. Below the powerhouse is another crib; as you exit the lock, keep to its east. If the plant is generating, prepare for a westerly set when you clear the lower-pool damside approach wall. The river makes a slight easterly bend beyond the lower-lock power cables. The western channel buoys watch shoals that extend about a mile north of the lock; when the river widens again, it's deep nearly bank to bank to the next dam.

Alongside and below you to the west, the main river rushes in its last canal mile and is dashed with rapids. There are two dams, and Oswego borders both shores.

As you approach Lock OS #6, **Mile OS-21.9 E (SM),** watch for a group of cement cribs; they are the damside approach wall. If you are milling about waiting for lockage, remember that this is an open-crested dam with a dramatic current increase at the difficult-to-see sill.

Locks OS #6, #7, and #8 are timed, but you transit them much as you do at the Flight in Waterford. Once you enter the series, it's straight through. When you exit into OS #6's lower pool, keep to the eastern bank. The main river is rocky and shoal as it flows the 0.5 mile down to the open-crested horseshoe dam south of Lock OS #7. A damside lock island begins when you reach this dam, so part of the approach is in the calm water of a canal cut.

Once you have descended Lock OS #7, you remain inside a protected canal for the short 0.3-mile run under a pair of bridges to Lock OS #8. Have the camera ready—there's an excellent westerly river rapids view.

Lock OS #8 is the canal's last and the only siphon lock in this system—locking crews open lower gates slightly to empty the lock and open upper gates slightly to fill it.

After you exit Lock OS #8 and clear the bridge and the riverside approach wall, continue to hold to the eastern shore. The channel has a 14-foot depth from Lock

OS #8 to Seneca Street, but the river's western side is shoal and rocky. When the powerhouses upstream are generating, there's a boiling increase in main river current, but it holds to midchannel and along the western shore. Once you clear **Buoy #4,** the river is deep bank to bank.

Oswego, or Choueguen, as the Iroquois called it, is "the place of the pouring-out-of-waters." In the 1700s the French, the English, and the Americans all wanted to possess it, as it was strategically positioned on the lake. It was also at the Oswego River's mouth—the shortest water route to the Atlantic Ocean and interior North America.

In 1722 the British, worried about the armed French post at Niagara, constructed Fort Oswego on the bluff overlooking what is now called Oswego. It was the first of three forts the British built and named over the years. (The last was Fort Ontario.) Once the area was part of the United States, settlement began with Fort Ontario its nucleus. Today pentagonal Fort Ontario is visible east over the terminal buildings; it overlooks land, lake, and river. It's reconstructed to its 1870 appearance and is open to the public.

Early Oswego was a center for the fur and salt trades; in 1810, 30,000 barrels of Syracuse and Onondaga salt were shipped out to ports along the lake. It was also a shipbuilding center; its yards built the world's second steamship.

After the state built the Oswego and Erie Canals, the port shipped more grain and produced more flour than any other lake port. It became known as the Flour City, usurping that title from Rochester. Granaries are still a dominant part of Oswego's waterfront—one elevator stores up to 16,000 bushels of grain in its star bins and 4,000 bushels in its side bins.

The Port of Oswego steamship terminals, located on both sides of the river, are a major American south-shore lake port. The largest lake vessels can dock without aid of tugs; the outer main harbor is their turning basin.

Three breakwaters protect the outer harbor. The western jetty is more than a mile long. It begins about 0.8 mile west of the river mouth at the lakeshore Niagara Mohawk Power Plant. The plant and its six smokestacks (two are 710 feet high and well lighted) are an excellent Oswego offshore landmark. The western breakwater ends at 57-foot West Pierhead Light, built in 1934; the port's original 1822 lighthouse still stands at Fort Ontario. At West Pierhead Lighthouse this section of your cruise ends; it intersects Lake Ontario's American shore, **Mile AONT-118.7 (NM)** (see Region

Downtown Oswego Terminal, looking south at Lock OS #8.

4, "Lake Ontario, The American Shore," beginning on page 188). American lakeshore harbors—much like this one at Oswego—dot the shoreline to the west. To the north-northeast are the New York islands and harbors of the far eastern lake. These islands are the gateway to the Thousand Islands (see Region 5, "The Thousand Islands, the St. Lawrence Seaway, and the Far Upper St. Lawrence River," beginning on page 250). To the north is the lake's Canadian shore, with more than 212 miles of coastline to explore (see Region 4, "Lake Ontario, The Canadian Shore," beginning on page 214).

WALTER ISLAND ANCHORAGE

★★

NO FACILITIES

Chart: N 14786, page O-5, *See sketch map, page 103*

Mile OS-4.7 E (SM)

This anchorage is between Walter Island and the river's

Sketch Map Depths

Sketch map depths are given at normal average summer canal pool level. When you venture outside the sketch map confines, you must adjust the NOAA chart to chart datum. For convenience in adjusting, use the following:

Mile OS-0.0 (SM) to **Mile OS-23.1 (SM)**: Plane of reference, Normal Pool Level

Mile OS-23.1 (SM) to Lake Ontario: Plane of reference, Lake Ontario Low Water Datum, 242.8 feet

eastern shore, on the island's upstream side. Depths are marginal for 6-foot-draft vessels, so approach slowly and sound carefully. If water stage is high or the Phoenix power plant is generating, current can be swift; take extra care, as it's a downcurrent approach.

The eastern entry is wide and shoals extend from both island and mainland. Wait to leave the river until midway between **Daymark #34** on the island's southeastern shore and **Buoy #32** about 500 feet farther east; then hold to the middle of the back channel. Go far

Walter Island Anchorage

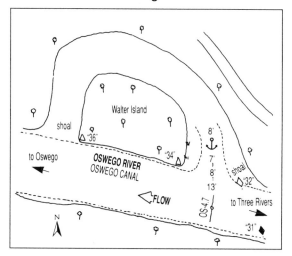

enough behind the island to be clear of wake roll, then swing into the current and sound for swinging-room depth by angling into shores. You don't have a lot of room due to shoaling. Bottom is mud.

Except for passing river traffic, this is a quiet anchorage. A local fisherman trolling along the shallows caught a nice string of bass on a Crickyhopper; they're sold in Oswego's K-Mart.

FULTON

Chart: N 14786, page O-3

Mile OS-11.5 (SM) to Mile OS-12.0 E (SM)

Fulton has two stops, one an exposed-to-traffic terminal, the other a basin marina. The city center is about 100 yards from either one. Both are between Lock OS #2 and Lock OS #3. If you plan to lay over, tell the lockmaster during your transit through either lock.

On the terminal just south of Lock OS #3 is a two-story overlook—a place to watch lockages and the dam's waterfall. Next door is Lock 3 Restaurant. Immediately east is a Midland Bank and a pharmacy. The Canalview Center, a walking mall, overlooks the river and terminal and has a fair collection of stores. On Saturdays, the farmers' market is held from 9 until noon in the mall's parking lot. Another block north on South Second Street is a Woolworth's and more shopping; the IGA supermarket is about four blocks south. The library, chamber of commerce (for information and

Fulton: Fulton Terminal, Canalview Marina

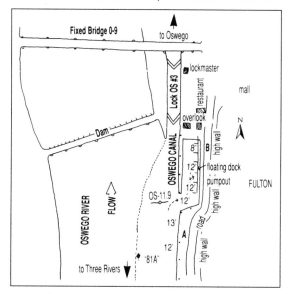

maps), and the post office are on South First Street between the two locks. The Fulton Historical Society is also there; have a look at their collection of local business and industry exhibits.

In mid-July Fulton hosts the two-day Central New York International Air Show at the Oswego County Airport, about 2.5 miles north of town. It's too far to walk, but there's a taxi and a Rent-a-Wreck car rental, (315) 598-2215.

River Fest is held in August, with many activities taking place at the terminal and lock. The Cracker Barrel Fair weekend is held in mid-September in even-numbered years at Lake Neatahwanta's Recreation Park on the lake's eastern shore. It's about a mile away; cross the Broadway Street Bridge over Lock OS #2, then bear southwest.

The large complex of Nestlé Foods Corporation is in Fulton—also too far to walk—but if you have transportation, the company usually offers tours.

Fulton Terminal

★★★   5

Chart: N 14786, page O-3, *See A on sketch map*

Mile OS-11.9 E (SM)

The eastern canal bank from Lock OS #2 through Lock OS #3 is a bulkheaded wall that serves as an approach to both locks. West is the rocky river flowing through the Falls of the Oswego. Though the wall is a popular stop for pleasure boats, be aware that it's a straight lock approach. When commercial traffic—seldom as it appears—enters and exits locks, it's going to pass very close. If you plan to stop, contact lockmasters to find out if commercial traffic is due that day or night and stay over only at their recommendation.

Downtown Fulton and a waterfront mall are just over the treetops behind the terminal—walk up the access road and you are there.

Canalview Marina

★★★

Chart: N 14786, page O-3, *See B on sketch map, page 103*

Mile OS-11.9 E (SM)

You would never know that this marina's enclosed basin existed; so far it's not charted. It is immediately south of Lock OS #3 on the eastern shore. The narrow entrance is at a break in the approach wall nearly at the upper-pool lock gates. Once you make your turn off the river, the basin bulkhead angles northeast, then north, and extends about as far as the lock on the inside of its approach wall. There are floating finger piers on the basin's eastern side with occasional parallel bulkhead parking everywhere else. Though a sign reads "Marina is by permit only," they do take transients.

The basin is backed on the east by the access road; across it is a forbidding bluff faced with a brick structure and an overhanging grey building. There's little marina landscaping—it's cement heaven. The pumpout is at the eastern corner at the entrance. The marina offers 110-volt electric hookups.

Immediately north of the basin is the lock and river overlook and the Lock 3 Restaurant.

BATTLE ISLAND ANCHORAGE

★★★

NO FACILITIES

Chart: N 14786, page O-2

Mile OS-15.9 W (SM)

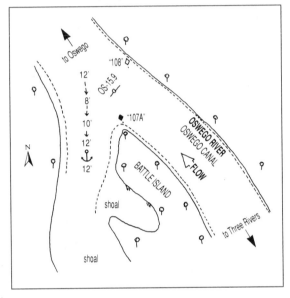

This anchorage is west of Battle Island. Enter northwest of the island; the upstream (southeastern) entrance is shoal and filled with rocks. **Buoy #107A** watches the island's northern end, and you must clear this before leaving the main channel. The entrance bar grows more shoal each year; enter cautiously and sound carefully. Once over the bar slightly favor the river's western bank to avoid the island's shoal western shore. Anchor in mud just far enough off the main channel to be clear of traffic wake roll.

The island is part of Battle Island State Park, where British Captain Bradstreet repulsed French and Indian forces. In 1916 Frederick Emerick gave the park's land to the state. Its bulk is taken over with a golf course.

You can circumnavigate the island by dinghy, but be cautious exiting into the main channel at the island's southeastern end. It's rocky and shoal, but a good place to catch some nice-size panfish. Across the river from the southeastern entrance is an old Oswego Canal section; there's a way into it at the southern end by the old ramp.

OSWEGO

Chart: N 14786, page 0-1

Mile OS-23.0 (SM) to Mile OS-23.8 (SM)

This is one of Lake Ontario's major south-shore ports and a convenient supply and crew-change port. If you are arriving from the south, Oswego is the Oswego Canal's northern terminus. If you are coming in from offshore, excellent landmarks are two very tall smokestacks and four small stacks at the Niagara-Mohawk Power Plant at the harbor's western end.

The city is divided by the river; no matter where you stay you can walk to just about everything, though some stops are more convenient for certain necessities and carry-home weight. You have a choice of two marinas and three terminals.

On the eastern shore within a few blocks of the waterfront are most city stores, banks, library, pharmacies, restaurants, Washington Square (with more than 20 early homes to admire), the Richardson-Bates House Museum, and a Price Chopper supermarket. Midtown Plaza includes a Fays Drug Store, Radio Shack, and Computer Center. Fort Ontario, on the lakeshore's northern point, is about a 0.5-mile walk from all eastern-shore dockage.

A first western-shore stop should be at the chamber of commerce, 46 West Bridge Street. You can ask directions and pick up stacks of Oswego literature; be sure to get the Washington Square walking-tour guide. On the western bank around the Bridge Street area there is a drugstore, a variety store, shoe stores, all sorts of small city shops, and a six-screen theater. The post office is on Highway 48 about a mile south. There are taxi and car rental services in town.

Star-shaped Fort Ontario is worth a visit, but don't start hiking off up the road until you check the day of the week; the fort is usually open—though not always—Wednesday and Saturday from 10 to 5 and Sunday from 1 to 5. On the way you can rest up at a park with picnic

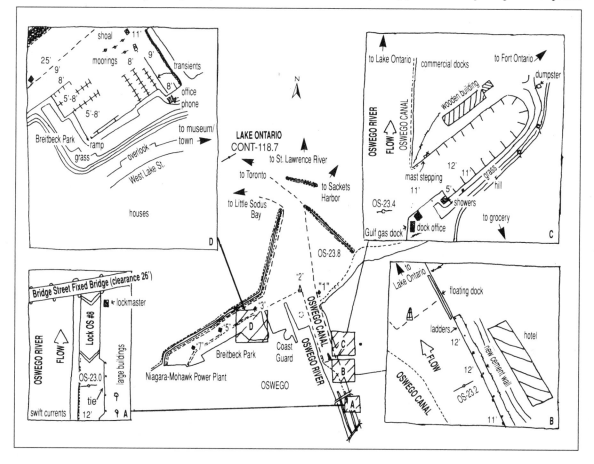

tables, ball fields, and a public swimming pool.

On the river's commercial pier by the tank farm is the Lee White Marine Museum, presided over by Rosemary Nesbitt. It presents a 300-year history of Oswego Harbor and Lake Ontario. The museum also has a collection of books written by Jewish refugees; from 1944 to 1946 Fort Ontario served as a haven for 982 German Holocaust survivors. The museum is open daily during the season.

Oswego Harborfest is held the last weekend in July. Festivities include antique and art shows, bazaars, arts and crafts, historical exhibitions, tournaments, street entertainers, parades, rock 'n roll revivals, boat parades, a Civil War encampment at Fort Ontario, water rescue demonstrations, and a fireworks display.

Though too far to walk—it's about 1.6 miles out of town to the east—the Oswego Speedway has a super-modified track and features NASCAR modifieds. Two Oswego Speedway drivers who went on to win wider fame are Indy 500 winner Gordon Johncock and Daytona 500 winner Geoff Bodine. Races are held from May into September, Saturday and Sunday starting at 7:30 P.M.

Lock OS #8 Upper

★★★   5

Chart: N 14786, page O-1, *See A on sketch map, page 105*

Mile OS-23.0 E (SM)

This eastern-bank terminal is in Lock OS #8's upper pool immediately outside its upper gates. Though barely discernible on the chart, there's an approach wall indentation, so you have protection from the rare passing commercial traffic. Old concrete fence posts, conveniently spaced, serve as bollards. If you plan to stop, be certain to tell Lock OS #5's lockmaster when downbound, or Lock OS #8's when upbound, as this group of locks is manned by roving personnel.

This stop has a view across the river at the parklike western shoreline, which is festive with flying flags. The lawn is manicured, there are flowers next door on the lock grounds, and it is backed by thick woods. Canalview Drive runs beside the terminal; follow it around the fringe of trees to downtown.

This is a preferred stop over the Downtown Terminal below Lock OS #8 during heavy northerly weather conditions. Though Oswego Harbor is protected by three offshore breakwaters, northerly quadrant strong winds sustained more than two days bring in a heavy surge down the main thoroughfare from the lake. In this scenario any vessel tied on the main river soon finds it too rough for comfortable dockage.

If you walk north on Canalview Drive about a block, you arrive at the Downtown Terminal alongside a motel. Turn right and go up the hill two blocks and you'll find the Midtown Plaza and Price Chopper supermarket. On Bridge Street you are within about two blocks of Washington Square, at the start of its historic walking tour. Off to the north is Fort Ontario. Bridge Street is your closest route to the western side of town.

Oswego Downtown Terminal

★★★   3

Chart: N 14786, page O-1, *See B on sketch map, page 105*

Mile OS-23.2 E (SM)

This terminal is along the eastern bank below Lock OS #8 about opposite midriver **Light Buoy #4.** The terminal is easy to spot; it's in front of the Best Western motel's parking lot. There are bollards and cleats on the terminal rim.

This is a very high wall; access to your boat is down a perpendicular ladder. If you have a choice of dockage, choose a space by a ladder. At the terminal's northern end is a floating dock and an access ramp intended for runabouts so they do not take up main-wall ladders.

This is a popular stop due to its convenience to eastern downtown. The Captain's Lounge Restaurant serves lunch and dinner; it's across the street from the motel. You are also near Washington Square or the bridge across to western Oswego. If you take the road at the motel's southern end and go up the hill two blocks, you are at the Midtown Plaza and the supermarket.

Oswego Marina

★★★

ALL FACILITIES

Chart: N 14786, page O-1, *See C on sketch map, page 105*

Mile OS-23.4 (SM)

This eastern-shore marina—open April 1 to October 15—is in a northeasterly basin immediately north of the Downtown Terminal. If no one answered on VHF, pull in to the main river fuel dock (gas and diesel) adjoining the terminal. At the small dock office up the ramp, you can make arrangements for a slip, yard, or mast work. Electric hookups (110-volt) and block and cube ice are available.

The office has a few basic marine supplies, local charts, guides, snacks, and soda pop. Call (315) 342-0436 for information.

Dockage is usually in the fixed-pier slips along the inner basin's southern perimeter. This is an attractive area with plots of grass, flowers, picnic tables, and grills. The repair yard and 12-ton Travelift are in the basin's northeastern end. This is the only marina in Oswego that does mast stepping; the gin pole is just inside the basin on its northern shore. There's usually a line of boats waiting to use crane facilities, so it's a good idea to call ahead for stepping schedules.

Admiral Woolsey's Restaurant overlooks the channel and basin entrance. It has a patio porch with festive umbrellas for fair-weather outside dining.

This is about the closest dockage in town to Fort Ontario. Ask at the office for directions for a shortcut after determining whether the fort is open that day. You are about three blocks from the Midtown Plaza and supermarket.

Wrights Landing Marina

★★★★

Chart: N 14786, page O-1, *See D on sketch map, page 105*

Mile OS-23.8 + 0.5 W (SM)

This municipal marina—open April 1 to November 1—is south of Oswego's western breakwater. Leave the Oswego River at the river's mouth at **Buoy #2** and bear westerly through the wide ship channel south of the breakwater that leads to the power plant. The first mole you pass contains the large granaries. The basin between this and the next mole has a southern inner basin for a U.S. Coast Guard Station. West of the main wooded mole is **Buoy #3,** which helps watch Wrights Landing. There are also a number of No Wake buoys and a few moorings.

If no one answered on VHF 16/9, pull in to the transient piers; they have parallel parking, and the rest of the marina has individual wells. The pumpout is on the longest transient dock's northern end; at its foot are the office, bath house, ice (block and cube), and phones. Electric hookups (110-volt/30-amp) are available.

Unless you arrive late at night, you'll have a lot of assistance tying up. The dock crew are recognizable by their red shirts.

The complex has three more piers with individual slips that extend northerly and a western basin section with three piers with slips that extend easterly. The northern face of the most northerly of these piers is also for transients when the eastern section fills to capacity—which it does; this is a very popular stop. The marina's land line number is (315) 342-8172.

The waterfront not taken up by parking lots is attractive, with grass and flowers. There's a sheltered picnic area by the ramp area. If you climb the southern bluff staircase, take along the camera—there's a splendid lake and harbor view. Over the hill that adjoins the western slips is Breitbeck Park, with more lawns, picnic facilities, and playgrounds.

You are farther from the eastern part of town, the supermarket, and Fort Ontario at this marina, but still within a long walk. A triangular information display in the office complex gives you directions to most town facilities.

Your exit afoot is at the parking lot's eastern end. Bear easterly; in about two blocks you face the tank farm along the harbor's western shore. The H. Lee White Museum nestles amongst the tanks. After a museum visit, take the road on south and you pass the U.S.S. *Brig Oneida* hulk, the first United States Great Lakes warship. Nearby is a favorite Oswego waterfront restaurant, Cahills Fish Market and Summer Café. Another block and you are in western Oswego's downtown section, with access east over the Bridge Street Bridge.

The Erie Canal West
Three Rivers to North Tonawanda

Mile E-159.8 (SM) to Mile E-333.2 (SM)

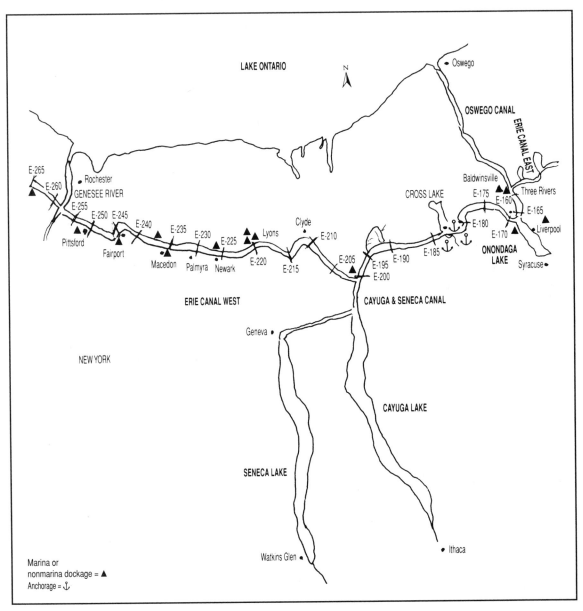

Three Rivers to East Rochester, Mile E-159.8 (SM) to Mile E-265.0 (SM)

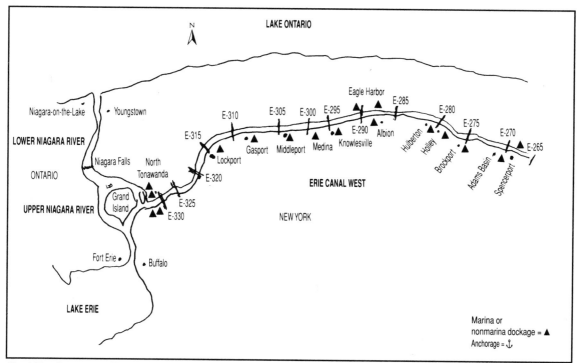

East Rochester to North Tonawanda, Mile E-265.0 (SM) to Mile E-333.2 (SM)

LOCKAGE, THREE RIVERS TO NORTH TONAWANDA

Lock	Mile	Land Line	Lift*	Tie-ups
Lock E #24	E-171.6 (SM)	(315) 635-3101	11.0 feet	Lines
Lock E #25	E-202.0 (SM)	(315) 365-3241	6.0 feet	Lines
Lock E #26	E-208.0 (SM)	(315) 923-9720	6.0 feet	Lines
Lock E #27	E-220.0 N (SM)	(315) 946-4062	12.5 feet	Lines
Lock E #28A	E-221.3 (SM)	(315) 946-4410	19.5 feet	Lines
Lock E #28B	E-225.3 (SM)	(315) 331-3296	12.0 feet	Lines
Lock E #29	E-234.8 N (SM)	(315) 597-4691	16.0 feet	Lines
Lock E #30	E-237.3 N (SM)	(315) 986-5631	16.4 feet	Lines
Lock E #32	E-252.8 (SM)	(716) 586-1837	25.1 feet	Cables
Lock E #33	E-253.9 (SM)	(716) 244-2150	25.1 feet	Cables
Lock E #34	E-315.0 S (SM)	(716) 434-3140	24.6 feet	Cables
Lock E #35	E-315.0 S (SM)	(716) 434-3140	25.5 feet	Cables

*At normal pool level

All locks monitor VHF 13. If no answer, use 3 long horn blasts. Enter on green light only. Ladders furnished (four per lock).

Daily operating hours for pleasure craft: 0700 to 2230 (may vary annually).

Call (800) 422-1825 for updated canal information, including schedules and operation hours.

Canal superintendents:

Mile E-159.8 (SM) to E-237.3 (SM): (315) 428-4589; (315) 946-6192

Mile E-237.3 (SM) to E-315.0 (SM): (716) 589-5689

SPECIAL RULES AND REQUIRED CHAMBER POSITIONS

Lock	Rule
Lock E #24	Westbound on hour; Eastbound on quarter-hour*
Lock E #34	Westbound may be required to use south chamber wall
Lock E #35	Westbound may be required to use south chamber wall

*Call ahead. Schedule often not in effect.

> *Let posterity be excited to perpetuate Our Free Institutions And to make still greater efforts than their ancestors to promote Public Prosperity By the recollection that these works of internal improvement were achieved by the Spirit and Perseverance of Republican Freemen.*
>
> 1825 Lockport Capstone

MOVABLE BRIDGES, THREE RIVERS TO NORTH TONAWANDA

Name	Mile	Land Line
Fairport	E-244.9 (SM)	(716) 223-9412
Spencerport	E-268.2 (SM)	(716) 352-5451
Adams Basin	E-270.7 (SM)	(716) 352-3548
Brockport (2)	E-275.2 + (SM)	(716) 637-4530
Holley	E-279.8 (SM)	(716) 638-6456
Hulberton	E-282.2 (SM)	(716) 638-8183
Albion (2)	E-288.4 + (SM)	(716) 589-6255
Eagle Harbor	E-291.5 (SM)	(716) 589-6700
Knowlesville	E-294.5 (SM)	(716) 798-2050
Medina	E-299.0 (SM)	(716) 798-0140
Middleport	E-303.6 (SM)	(716) 735-7250
Gasport	E-308.5 (SM)	(716) 772-7700
Lockport (2)	E-314.0 + (SM)	(716) 434-7368

All bridges monitor VHF 13. Signals: Lights and Horn (3 long blasts).

Nearly all bridges are numbered on one abutment; these can be locating points.

Clearance for movable bridges (at normal pool level) is less than 15.5 feet closed, 15.5 feet open.

Clearance for fixed bridges (at normal pool level) is 15.5 feet.

Daily operating hours for all movable bridges: 0700 to 2230 (may vary annually).

Call (800) 422-1825 for updated canal information, including schedules and operation hours.

Canal section superintendent: (716) 589-5689

Roving bridge tenders and bridges they man (* = home base):

    Spencerport*/Adams Basin

    Brockport Park Avenue/Brockport Main Street*/Holley

    Hulberton/Albion Ingersoll Street*/Albion Main Street

    Eagle Harbor/Knowlesville*/Medina

    Middleport*/Gasport

    Lockport Adams Street*/Lockport Exchange Street

The Erie Canal West's eastern terminus is Three Rivers, **Mile E-159.8 (SM),** where the Oneida and Seneca Rivers meet to form the Oswego River headwaters. This canal is the most scenic in this region. It is also the most isolated between canal ports, and has the most canal sections.

The three main destinations westbound when traveling the Erie West are Onondaga Lake, Cayuga and

Seneca lakes, and the Upper Niagara River.

In this section you transit 12 locks to ascend to the 564-foot Upper Niagara River elevation. Most lock lifts are slight; the maximum is 25.5 feet, the minimum 6 feet. The state maintains depth at 12 feet, but shoaling is more common in this less-traveled section; mind the watched channel or hold to midcanal. A slight current flows easterly. Commercial traffic is almost nonexistent.

Westbound at Three Rivers, you are on the canalized Seneca River—its source is the Finger Lakes. Around the first southeasterly bend at **Mile E-160.2 (SM),** hold to the easterly shore for over a mile to clear the shoals and rocks extending to midriver; clear of these obstructions the river is generally deep bank to bank for the next 10 miles to Baldwinsville.

If you plan to visit Liverpool or Syracuse on Onondaga Lake, make your southerly turn at Klein Island, **Mile E-166.5 (SM);** if eastbound, at **Mile E-166.9 (SM).** At the middle of the bend on the island oxbow, your lake route is via the 0.6-mile-long Onondaga Outlet. The 1862 Mud Lock site—once part of the first Oswego Canal—is on the outlet's eastern side near its northern entrance.

Onondaga Lake is 4.6 miles long, about a mile wide, and about 60 feet deep on average. Its most prominent features are the western shore's Lakeview Point, which faces Liverpool on the east, and the southern end's industrial Syracuse smokestacks.

An abundance of salt brought the Indians—the first area inhabitants—to the Onondaga area. The Jesuits arrived in 1656 near Liverpool, founded a mission, developed the Jesuit Well at the LeMoyne Salt Spring, and built Fort Saint Marie de Gannentatha. Anglos founded Syracuse in 1805. By the time the state built the first Erie and Oswego canals, Syracuse was supplying nearly all America with salt.

East of Klein Island on the Erie Canal West, the river winds through forests and farmland to Baldwinsville's Lock E #24, **Mile E-171.5 (SM).** The lock's eastern approach is alongside a 0.4-mile-long lock island. Jonas Baldwin founded the town in 1807. Its hardy first settlers survived the lowlands malaria; they were Revolutionary War veterans taking their "bonus lands."

For the next 8 miles mind the buoys and stay in the channel; shoal water often extends to the buoy line.

If you have shoal draft and need gas, ice, or a pumpout, the Midway Marina is in a small basin at **Mile E-187.6 N (SM).** A travel-trailer park near **Mile E-188.8 S (SM)** also welcomes boaters; tie-up is on both sides of the launching ramp. Approach cautiously; depth is minimal. The park serves breakfast Saturday and Sunday and pizza every evening. If you need gas, soda pop, or ice, stop at Eagle Bay Marina, **Mile E-192.7 S (SM),** just west of **Daymark #494.** This small facility is usually decked out with festive flags.

In late May and June watch for Canada geese with goslings throughout this area. Though not apparent, the land on both banks has become low and swampy—a haven for wildlife. In the area north of **Mile E-192.8 (SM)** it becomes a maze of ponds and creeks.

The unnavigable Owasco Outlet, **Mile E-193.0 (SM),** bears off south to Owasco Lake—one of the six main Finger Lakes once on the Iroquois Trail. Watch for a well-preserved portion of the early Erie's 31-arch Richmond Aqueduct at **Mile E-199.7 (SM)** near **Daymark #537.**

At **Mile E-200.5 S (SM), Daymark #543,** the Erie intersects the Cayuga and Seneca Canal, the route to Cayuga and Seneca lakes (see "The Cayuga and Seneca Canal," beginning on page 138).

The Montezuma Marsh National Wildlife Refuge begins at the Cayuga-Seneca junction. It borders the Erie westward to the Armitage Road Bridge (BR E-92), **Mile E-204.6 (SM),** and extends south to Cayuga Lake. This is only a small portion of the original marsh. In the 1800s it extended 12 miles north of the lake and was a productive North American marshlands. It was also deadly; malaria nearly brought the first Erie construction to a complete halt. Workers building a 2-mile-long, 70-foot-high canal embankment contracted the disease while toiling chest deep in the mosquito-infested swamp.

Only a few hundred acres of marsh remained after the completion of the Cayuga Lake Outlet dam and the modern canal. As a wetlands the marsh hardly functioned; wildlife, plants, and the once immense flocks of waterfowl nearly disappeared. The U.S. Fish and Wildlife Service purchased 6,432 acres of the old marsh in 1937 and built dikes to retain water. The state has restored several thousand acres, and the marsh is again a major Atlantic Flyway stopover.

Lock E #27 is in downtown Lyons, **Mile E-220.0 (SM).** If water level is up, its dams are an impressive sight. The Clyde has a movable dam and taintor gate. The open-crested dam is the Canandaigua Outlet, which connects to Canandaigua Lake, another Finger Lake inaccessible from the Erie. If a lot of water is flowing over any of the dams, watch for a current set toward the

Montezuma Marsh National Wildlife Refuge Calendar

The best sightings are nearly always in the early morning and late afternoon.

Spring

Late February through April (depending on weather and thaw): Up to 85,000 Canada geese; up to 15,000 snow geese in blue color phase; and many varieties of ducks, including common mergansers, goldeneye, and scaup.

May 1 to mid-June: Wading birds.

May 15: Warblers.

Summer

March through August: Waterfowl nesting with broods by May, including Canada geese, great blue herons, and black-crowned night herons.

Fall

Mid-September until freeze up: Canada geese peak (to 50,000) in mid-October; ducks peak (to 150,000) in November; wading birds peak mid-September.

Year-round

White-tailed deer, rabbits, and foxes.

---

lower pool's northern approach wall.

The Lyons canal park, just downstream of the lock and dams, encompasses two landscaped terminals, one on each bank. Though both are convenient to town, this is a difficult area if water level is even slightly up; current along the walls can be severe and drift heavy.

The first settlement at this river junction was the Forks. Charles Williamson renamed it Lyons; he thought it resembled the junction of France's Rhone and Saone. Most early residents were farmers, and the first Erie's opening helped move their produce—mostly apples and cherries.

Just east of Lyons is the eastern entrance of Ganargua Creek; the early Erie crossed it on a five-arched aqueduct. The upper-pool basin at Lock E #28A, **Mile E-221.4 (SM),** is the approach for a state dry-dock facility; its lock is on the northern shore.

Chart N 14786 ends at this lock, though you still need to navigate nearly 112 more miles to the canal's western terminus. This distance is primarily a canal cut with a few canalized creeks. There are also small wide waters, a great number of fixed bridges, 16 lift bridges, and many canal towns. You cannot possibly get lost. In wide waters or the wide mouths of intersecting creeks, buoys or daymarks watch the canal.

For a few miles west of Lock E #28A the canal runs between 600-foot hills and forested marshland. In this area the new Erie crisscrosses the old; spot the early canal's location by the marsh grass contours.

The eastern outskirts of Newark and Lock E #28B, **Mile E-225.4 (SM),** are just west of a railroad bridge at a sharp northerly turn. Captain Joseph Miller founded the original settlement in 1819 when he came with a contract to build part of the first Erie (old Locks #55 through #59) and eventually a five-arched 130-foot aqueduct.

The Wide Waters' eastern end, lined with south-shore cottages, begins at the Stebbins Road Bridge, **Mile E-227.3 (SM).** The mile-long, 0.2-mile-wide lake's southern shore is shoal and watched by large white nuns with green tops. Westbound at the Port Gibson Bridge, **Mile E-229.0 (SM),** you begin a sharp right-hand bend around Hog Back Hill, and once more your route becomes a canal cut. Two miles later you make a sharp left-hand bend around Galloway Hill to the south and pass the dam across Ganargua Creek's

---

western entrance off to the north. Once you make the Galloway Hill turn, you are in a fair straightaway to Palmyra on the southern shore.

On the Hill of the Camorah near Palmyra, two miles inland, Joseph Smith is said to have had his religious vision and received the golden plates from the Angel Moroni. From these he translated the *Book of Mormon*, which resulted in the founding of the Church of Jesus Christ of the Latter-day Saints. The Grandin Building on Main Street (the bridge street) was where the first *Book of Mormon* was printed in 1830.

Palmyra's unattractive terminal has no bollards. If you can arrange some way to tie up, you can visit the town; it's just up the rise. There's a taxi in town if you want to visit the Hill of Camorah or the Smith Farm. Both are open daily from 9 until 7.

It's also worth a stop and a pleasant walk to see the four churches at the Church Street and Highway 31 intersection; or pick a residential street to see Palmyra's beautiful Victorian-style homes.

Lock E #29 is on the northern bank about a mile west of Palmyra's terminal. A lock island separates it from the southern bank. Westbound you are introduced to the infamous zebra mussels that have spread eastward from Lake Erie. Make certain line handlers wear gloves; the mussels attached to lock lines have razor-sharp shells.

As you leave the lock you pass under bridge BR E-119 and begin the approach to two islands on the northern shore. The first is at an upcoming sharp right-hand bend; the second, larger island is about 0.5 mile farther west. The channel is south of both. On the southern shore across the canalside highway is the West Wayne Plaza with an auto parts store, a McDonald's, a bank, a department store, and a Price Chopper supermarket. As yet no dock is available; if it's inconvenient to dinghy ashore for a quick shopping spree, Fairport's canalside plaza is 8 miles farther west.

Lock E #30, **Mile E-237.3 (SM)**, at Macedon, is similar to Lock E #29; it's north of a lock island and the first Erie. The town is on the southern bank's hill.

Another mile-long wide waters is about 1.25 miles west of Lock E #30; its watched channel is along the northern shore. Waynesport, once a busy old Erie port, is on the southern shore beyond the trees at the bridge over the wide water's western end. In the upcoming straightaway, don't venture south of the pilings spaced along the channel's southern side; it's the old Erie Canal filled with debris and obstructions.

Fairport, **Mile E-244.7 (SM)**, a large residential community about 8.5 miles from downtown Rochester, has its city center on the canal's southern shore. When westbound, you come to the first of the canal's 16 movable bridges at Fairport. Though bridges are timed during the day, most are manned by roving bridge tenders. Delays occur when isolated boats travel within a roving tender's sector. If you plan a layover between movable bridges, always tell the bridge tender of your plans and make arrangements for your next day's departure and next bridge opening.

The Fairport Bridge has a down clearance of 6 feet with a difference in elevation on each side of 5.54 feet. Bridge height is difficult to judge due to this height variation and the fact that it's at a canal bend. If your clearance is critical, signal for an opening.

The 1825 Erie Canal routed through downtown. Canallers called it a "fair port." It was a place for canalboats to prepare for the difficult western section, which for a long time was either under construction or under repair due to embankment breaks.

One of early Fairport's exports was potatoes; for a time the local area produced more potatoes than any other in the country.

The DeLand Chemical Company, an early Fairport business, refined the process of leaching potash, saleratus, and soda from hardwood ashes for chemicals. Watch for the old chemical works building on the northern shore just east of the bridge. Henry DeLand, "the Baking Powder King," also founded Deland, Florida.

The Oxbow Canal Section is coming up at Fairport's western fixed bridge bend. The Oxbow suffered an embankment break in 1870 during the early canal widening project; it flooded the neighborhood. In early June the stands of black locust trees are in bloom, making the upcoming canal section especially fragrant. It's also the time when cottonwood tree seed capsules fly in the wind. Just before a rain you often travel in a flurry of cottonlike puffs and flower petals.

At **Mile E-246.6 E (SM)** you pass Lake Lucan, another wide waters. A mile farther west at a canal horseshoe bend is Bushnell Basin, once called Hartwell's Basin. The state found this a difficult section of canal to build and maintain. Canal embankment breaks here stopped traffic in 1825 and 1912. In 1975 a contractor drilling under the canal to install a pipeline misjudged distances and breached a hole 100 feet across. Once again Erie West's through-traffic shut down for the rest of the season. Today two guard gates watch Bushnell Basin on an 80-foot embankment. Closing

Zebra Mussels

Waterways in the northern United States are under assault by an unlikely foe: an inch-long Caspian Sea bivalve called the zebra mussel.

About the size of your thumbnail, the zebra mussel closely resembles its saltwater cousins, down to the siphoning beard used to strain plankton from the water. It also shares a prodigious reproductive capacity: over a typical life span of five years, a single female can produce more than 300,000 offspring!

Zebra mussels probably came to North America in 1985, when dumping of water ballast by a European freighter released immature microscopic mussels into Lake Saint Claire. As they multiplied, the mussels began to choke water intakes, weigh down buoys, and suffocate local bivalve species.

In 1989, the city water and power units in Monroe, Michigan, had to be shut down because of infestation. Zebra mussel densities had grown to 700,000 per square meter, infiltrating every part of both plants open to lake waters. Removal required hydroblasting and hand scraping at staggering cost.

When the mussels take over an area, little food is left for native species. Each mussel strains about a liter of water through its "beard" each day while feeding on plankton. It's estimated there are enough zebra mussels in western Lake Erie to siphon all the area's water every four days.

Zebra mussels cause problems for boaters, too. Although they avoid bottom areas covered with antifouling paint, they still attach themselves to unprotected surfaces such as bottom fittings, rudder cables, and bait tanks, and they can plug water intake valves. The chemical tributylin (TBT) mixed in bottom paint can be a boat saver, but the Environmental Protection Agency controls its use, and boaters must be EPA-certified before applying the pesticide.

How to prevent them? There are no large-scale controls. The mussel's only natural predators are a few species of freshwater fish and diving ducks, and these are not available in sufficient quantities to stem the tide. Chlorine is an effective zebra mussel killer, but it destroys many other marine species as well, including helpful ones.

gates and nearby locks prevent massive flooding.

For two years Bushnell Basin was the first Erie's turnaround while the state built the first Great Embankment, a major 1822 western-Erie engineering project. Irish immigrants hand-built a 61-foot-high hill to carry the canal over the Irondequoit Valley.

Just west of the bridge, **Mile E-248.2 (SM),** watch on the southern bank for the 150-year-old buff-colored restored Richardson Canal House—the oldest surviving canal tavern. Adjoining it to the east is Oliver Loud's Inn, a restored 1812 stagecoach stop whose gardens overlook the canal. On the northern bank west of the bridge between the inn and the restaurant is a terminal—a convenient stop to visit these very popular facilities. Across the street on the canal road is a shopping center with a Big M supermarket.

As you cross Irondequoit Creek near the terminal you will see the manhole covers that provide access to shaft ladders used by safety teams to inspect the embankment to the creek 80 feet below the canal.

Cartersville has the second guard gate for this area. It

was a bustling community during the first embankment construction. Barge cargoes moved to Bushnell Basin by horse and cart—hence the settlement's name. Like so many old Erie ports, it disappeared when transshipping ended.

Pittsford, **Mile E-251.0 (SM),** is on a bend on the canal's southern side. Captain Simon and Lieutenant Israel Stone founded the settlement in 1789; it became another thriving port on the first Erie. Today it's a residential Rochester suburb.

At the Pittsford Main Street Bridge you make a hard left-hand bend and enter the mile-long approach to Lock E #32. You didn't miss Lock E #31—it doesn't exist. Instead the state has two Lock #28s.

In this area the first Erie struck off toward Rochester, a main old-Erie port. About 4 miles northeast it passed by Cobbs Hill, the location of one of its turning basins. Today this is part of Cobbs Hill Park, and the turning basin is Lake Riley.

If there has been heavy rainfall to the south or if water level has been generally high, ask the lockmaster at Lock E #33, **Mile E-253.9 (SM),** about guard gate condition on each side of the Genesee River—this locking crew mans the gates, which are coming up in about 4 miles. The Genesee drainage is vast; flooding far in its southern reaches can cause such a significant river rise at the canal junction that crews may close guard gates to protect the canal. If increased river current makes the crossing unsafe, they close gates to protect traffic, too—they stop it.

Whether the Genesee is flooding or not, always ask the lockmaster about junction depths on both sides of the river. This is a persistent shoaling area due to junction silt collection during springtime river runoff.

The Genesee flows north from its Allegheny Mountains headwaters near the Pennsylvania border. South 35 miles it passes through the canyons and 600-foot gorge—with three waterfalls—in the Letchworth State Park, often called "the Grand Canyon of the East." In 1856 the river was the main route of the Genesee Valley Canal, which ran from Rochester to Olean near the Pennsylvania border. By 1862 the state extended the canal to the Allegheny River. Eventually it was more than 100 miles long, with 114 locks and many sidecuts. It never was a productive canal; by the time it was fully operational the railroads had moved in and taken over most of the canalboats' seasonal business.

West of Lock E #33 is a unique area of Rochester's canal bridges as you pass Monroe Community College, the University of Rochester, and the Genesee Valley Park.

As you approach the Genesee River, check to see what sort of current is running—it can be up to 5.5 knots. If there is a lot of flow, take care. Once you begin to leave the protection of the canal, there's a severe northerly set. Make an effort to reenter the canal's western entrance in midchannel—difficult to do with a strong current. You won't be bothered by current if it's a low-water year; nor is river depth a problem. The critical depth area is at the intersection—both sides. Unless the lockmaster at Lock E #33 gave you other instructions, best depth across these bars is in midchannel. Usually, if depths drop to less than 7 feet, dredging takes place.

The Genesee's mouth is 11 miles north on Lake Ontario. If bound for the lake, this is NOT the route to take; there's a 100-foot waterfall about 4 miles downstream. Rochester's marine accommodations are accessible only from the lake (see Region 4, "Lake Ontario, The American Shore," beginning on page 188).

The Genesee's two western guard gates are about 0.4 mile west of the river. West over the southern bank is Greater Rochester International Airport. Coming up next is a 5-mile canal cut with perpendicular rocky banks. It is spanned by 13 bridges. At the Pond Street Bridge, **Mile E-263.0 (SM),** you are traveling alongside extensive Kodak Park, which stretches westward nearly 10 miles from downtown Rochester. By the time you reach the Elmgrove Road Bridge, **Mile E-264.6 (SM),** and Captain Jeff's Marina, you are back into upper New York's farm country.

Spencerport, **Mile E-268.2 (SM),** was the boyhood home of John T. Trowbridge, an early writer of boy's adventure stories. His book, *Neighbor Jackwood,* sold more copies than any other American book before *Uncle Tom's Cabin.*

In 1840 Cyrus McCormick invented the first agricultural reaper in Brockport, **Mile E-275.2 (SM).** This was also the hometown of Mary Jane Holmes, a popular post–Civil War novelist whose handsome heroes and fainting heroines peopled the earliest paperbacks.

West of Brockport's fixed Smith Street Bridge you pass the campus of the State University of New York at Brockport.

The Holley Lift Bridge, **Mile E-279.8 (SM),** is about 0.3 mile north of Holley—called the "Salt Port" in early canal days, though most exports were local farm produce and quarried stone.

As you wind on west of the Hulberton Lift Bridge, **Mile E-282.2 (SM),** you are alongside sea-green pools just out of sight down and over the northern bank. These are the remains of Medina's sandstone quarries. At one time more than 50 quarries were active between Holley and Medina; they lasted until about 50 years ago, when portland cement became the major building material. The pinkish rock that lines the canal banks is sandstone.

At **Mile E-286.5 (SM),** look south—the hill and observation tower is Mt. Albion. In 1821, in anticipation of the Erie Canal, Nehemiah Ingersol and his partners bought a hundred-acre plot, including what is now Albion's Main Street Bridge area, and laid out the town as a port. Quarrying and exporting Medina sandstone began in 1860; it was Albion's major industry. George Pullman, known as the founder of first-class railroad travel, lived in Albion and learned his trade of crafting fine furniture there.

This is orchard country; cherries and more than 30 varieties of apples are grown in the state. Legend says a canaller gave a young girl named Rachel Lovewell a few seeds, with which she planted the state's first apple trees.

Just west of Knowlesville, **Mile E-296.1 (SM),** the canal becomes an aqueduct. You cross over the top of Culvert Road.

West of the eastern Medina guard gate, **Mile E-298.0 (SM),** you make a sharp left-hand bend and clear the Erin Road Bridge, and the canal widens into Medina's downtown turning basin. This was an important packet and freight boat stop for the first Erie. Its wide basin was off the canal thoroughfare and a midway point between Rochester and Buffalo. Canalboats exported local farm produce in both directions; Medina sandstone was primarily bound for New York City's "brownstone" homes and Greek Revival and Gothic churches. One of modern Medina's industries is growing roses; more than 3 million are sold annually.

The canal bend in downtown is over the Oak Orchard River, where the Niagara-Mohawk Power Plant uses its water to run three generators. The river then flows north through mile-long Glenwood Lake—visible over the northern canal wall—to 4-mile-long Lake Alice's Waterport Dam, and then into Lake Ontario at Point Breeze, a pleasure-craft harbor 12 miles overland from Medina.

About 0.5 mile west of the Medina Lift Bridge you pass the grounds of the Apple Grove Inn—a popular canal restaurant—on the southern shore in an old apple orchard. There may be a small float for boat-in diners, though lately it has been used by *Miss Apple Grove,* a mule-drawn packet boat that tours to the downtown turning basin.

At **Mile E-303.0 (SM),** just west of the Shelby Basin guard gate, you enter Niagara County and begin the approach to southern-shore Middleport. Original residents named the town for its location midway between Lockport and Albion. Franklin D. Roosevelt canalled across the state on his 1930's election campaign. Residents remember Eleanor coming ashore to shake hands while F.D.R. made his speech from his wheelchair aboard the campaign barge.

George W. Clinton and a group of scientists were somewhat responsible for naming Gasport, **Mile E-308.5 (SM).** When at the settlement—originally called Jamesport—they noted that "quantities of gas bubbled through the water." When they returned in 1826, residents had painted Gasport on the bridge; the village was renamed.

You are now in the eastern outskirts of Lockport and the Niagara Escarpment. About 0.5 mile west of the Nelson C. Goehle Marina, you come to the Market Street fixed bridge and begin a pretty canal section lined with waterfront parks. In this area you have the last of the Erie West's movable bridges, at Adams Street, **Mile E-314.2 (SM),** and Exchange Street, **Mile E-314.4 (SM).**

The handsome flagstone Church of the Living God, the Pillar, Ground, and Truth, and the nearby restored 1800s Governor Hunt home are part of Lockport's Lowertown Historic District. As you approach the train trestle, known since early times as the "Upside Down" Bridge, the Lockport gorge closes in. Just ahead are today's southern-bank locks. The small open locks on the northern shore are the 1800s Lockport Combine remains.

A waterfall once gushed over a precipice here and carved out the gorge. When the state proposed the canal in the 1800s, De Witt Clinton gave the formidable task of designing a method to surmount this barrier to canal engineer Nathan Roberts. The result was a succession of five combine locks, #67 through #71, that allowed navigation in both directions over the escarpment. Though they were expected to last indefinitely, the state replaced the locks a decade later with the enlarged Lockport Combine. Their northern tier is what you see today. When the state replaced the old Erie in the early 1900s, they demolished the southern downbound combine. While they built the modern locks, the northern combine tier continued in use for two-way commercial traffic. After 1918, pleasure boats used the locks until the 1920s, when the state converted them to a spillway.

Lockport owes its existence and prosperity to the old Erie Canal. From a small village of 2,500 in 1825, it quadrupled in 30 years. It was a transportation center and a major industrial center—the tailrace water supplied power for grist- and sawmills. Today's Locks E #34 and E #35, **Mile E-315.0 (SM),** are the only tandem locks in the Erie West. There are two sets of upper gates at Lock E #35. One set is for emergencies—these two gates and a guard lock up ahead near Pendleton are all that protects the canal from the invasion of Lake Erie. As you exit the lock westbound, you pass under Lockport's 452-foot-long Big Bridge, one of the widest automobile bridges in the world. Once out of this tunnel-like structure you pass under the Genesee Street Bridge and begin a fairly straight 5-mile-long canal section blasted through solid rock.

A short distance west is a state terminal—not too well maintained—with bollards and a smooth bulkheaded face. Tour boats from the marina below the locks have a loading dock at the terminals' western end; this is their turnabout area. The wall's eastern end can be an emergency or possible overnight tie-up.

At **Mile E-319.6 (SM)** you pass through the Sulphur Springs Guard Gate Lock, and 0.5 mile later you begin a long left-hand bend. Immediately south of the fixed bridge at **Mile E-321.8 (SM)** the canal joins canalized Tonawanda Creek, which you carry to the Niagara River. On the way there is an increase in creekside homes and pretty parks. Water color progressively becomes more emerald green—a preview of what to expect in crystalline-clear eastern Lake Erie.

At Ellicott Creek Island Park, old Three Mile Island, **Mile E-329.5 S (SM),** you begin to parallel Ellicott Creek to the south. It joins the canal at Long's Point 3 miles west in downtown North Tonawanda.

The Iroquois named this area Tonawanda, or "swift-running water," in reference to the creek rushing downstream toward the cataract at today's Lockport. French missionaries joined the Indians in the 1600s; later came the traders. After the Revolution, to protect the new country's frontier from hostile Indians and British brigands, the Americans built a log blockhouse on the creek's southern bank at the Niagara River. With this protection a few settlers filtered in to begin farming in what they called the "North Woods." When the state authorized the first Erie Canal and the western terminus construction began, workers arrived in force and founded Tonawanda.

Originally the town was part of Buffalo, but by 1836 it had become a township, and in 1854 North Tonawanda became a ward of the village. In 1897 it became a separate village. The lumber trade put the two Tonawandas on the map; they became the chief lumber-supply centers for the country, until eventually the tree supply ran out. Today North Tonawanda is the larger of the two, with a population of 36,000.

As you leave downtown on the canal, you are nearly at its western terminus. Just beyond the westernmost old railroad swing bridge, which no longer operates, you enter the Niagara River behind Tonawanda Island. Here a green freeway directional sign announces that Buffalo and Lake Erie are south (See Region 3, "North Tonawanda to Port Colborne Breakwater," beginning on page 163).

NOTE: There are no navigational charts published for

much of the Erie West; as we mentioned earlier, Chart 14786 ends at Lock E #28A, **Mile E-221.4 (SM).** Therefore, there are no charts listed for many of the following anchorages. Use the maps at the beginning of this section (see pages 108–109) as a guide.

ONONDAGA LAKE PARK MARINA

★★★★   [5]

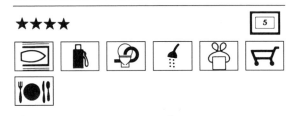

Chart: N 14786, page E-11 and E-12, *See A on sketch map, page 119*

Mile E-166.4 + 3.2 S (SM)

This marina—open May 1 through October 31—is about 3.2 miles off the Erie West on Onondaga Lake's eastern shore at Liverpool. Leave the Erie either southwest or northeast of Klein Island. Take an oxbow south around the island, into Onondaga Outlet, pass under the freeway bridge, and enter the lake.

The marina, protected from the lake's wind and waves by breakwaters, is about opposite the western shore's prominent Lakeview Point. Its northern breakwater, which overlaps the main southern breakwater, has a green lighted marker with a nearby offshore green daymark. The southern breakwater has a westerly extension and then curves south; it's low, built of rock, and has a red post at its most westerly point.

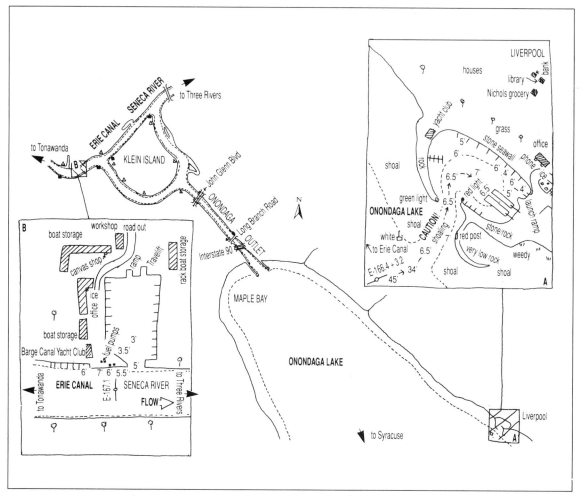

Enter the harbor between the main northern and southern breakwaters and stay in the middle. If it's a low-water year, 6-foot-draft boats may not have depth and will need to anchor offshore. Park slips line the basin's perimeter. If no one answered on VHF 16, pull in to the dock in front of the office in the basin's southeastern corner. If you need electricity, tell the dockmaster. Though most slips have 110-volt/50-amp service, some smaller slips do not.

Liverpool, a few blocks east, has fast-food establishments, banks, a library, stores, and Nichols Grocery. Taxis and car rental services are available if you plan to visit downtown Syracuse, a few miles southeast.

The marina, which can be reached at (315) 453-6721, is in the center of a landscaped park with extensive lawns, trees, flowers, park benches, and picnic facilities. It's a day-and-night promenade well used by joggers, skaters, bicyclists, strolling sightseers, and bench sitters. A tram operates from 10 A.M. to dusk; for an enjoyable outing, take the 45-minute round trip. The tram routes to the Salt Museum, the western lakeshore Long Branch Amusement Park, northern Willow Bay, Children's Landing, and Hiawatha Point—named for Chief Hiawatha, who settled there in 1570.

The waterfront Salt Museum has displays and exhibits of the early salt manufacturing trade that gave Syracuse its nickname, "Salt City." It's open daily.

The Saint Marie Among the Iroquois is a reconstructed 17th-century French settlement and Jesuit Mission. The visitor center is about 0.6 mile southeast. Costumed staff recreate the early day life. A museum complex has exhibits and a gift shop.

The bicycle path—access at the marina—takes you around the lake's northern end as far as Lakeview Point.

There are bike rentals on the lake's eastern side by the complex on the Outlet Canal, which is a tram stop.

The four-day Onondaga Lake Waterfront Extravaganza is held in late July at the Willow Bay area. It features a water circus, a juggling jamboree, mimes, a Wild West show, arts and crafts, concessions, a speakeasy, and antique cars. Each evening a musical group entertains until about 10. A fireworks display is the climax.

J & S MARINE

★★

Chart: N 14786, page E-11, *See B on sketch map, page 119*

Mile E-167.1 N (SM)

This northern-shore marina is just west of Klein Island. The fuel dock (gas and diesel) and a few permanent slips are on the canal, but the main marina is in an enclosed basin whose entrance is just east of the fuel dock. If no one answered on VHF 16, pull in to the fuel dock. If your draft is 6 feet or more, approach cautiously. Enter the inner basin with even more caution; depths are barely 6 feet.

In the basin's northern end is the ramp, Travelift well, and several large dry-storage buildings. In the westernmost building is a canvas shop. The office, at (315) 622-1095, has a ship's store with a selection of marine supplies.

The grounds have lawns, shade trees, and picnic facilities. This is a peaceful place to watch passing traffic and Klein Island's wooded shoreline.

BALDWINSVILLE UPPER TERMINALS

★

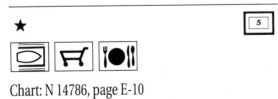

Chart: N 14786, page E-10

Mile E-171.7 N (SM)

Baldwinsville Upper Terminals

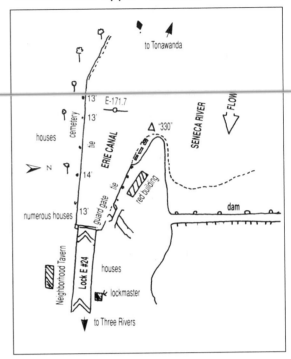

These upper-pool terminals are on the northern or southern terminal wall.

Northern Terminal

This is not an attractive stop, but it is handy to downtown. Once out of the lock and through its guard gate, pass the runoff spillway crossed by a small bridge immediately to your west. The terminal west of this angles slightly to the northwest.

The terminal wall is short and not in good shape; be careful when you tie up. There are bollards and use holes in the steel bulkhead to tie short spring lines. West of the solid bulkhead are cribs—it's not possible to tie to these. Immediately west of the cribs, the canal rejoins the river. The dam, which has an open crest with a taintor gate, is around the corner east of the water tank.

You are on the lock grounds but alongside a derelict boatyard building. To get to town, walk back to the lock, tell the lockmaster where you tied up, go out the lock access road at the bridge, turn north, and you're there. Stores include a pizza parlor, small grocery, Buille Diner, laundromat, and post office. The larger stores have moved inland to River Mall on the river's southern side about 2.5 miles west.

This long approach wall is on the canal's southern side alongside the northern boundary of Baldwinsville's cemetery. This stop is a longer walk to shops and stores because you must cross the bridge. Canal traffic passes close alongside, and the area is well used by talkative late-night bank fisherman.

COOPER'S MARINA

★★   ⬜ 4

Chart: N 14786, page E-10

Mile E-172.4 N (SM)

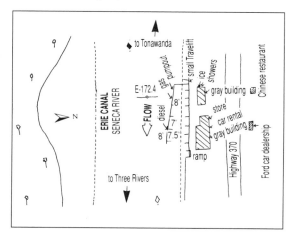

This northern-shore marina is about 0.7 mile west of Baldwinsville Lock about midway between **Buoy #336** and **Buoy #337.** It's the only large marina complex around.

If no one answered on VHF 16, pull in to the fuel dock (gas and diesel) on the outer fixed pier paralleling the river. The office is in the larger building on shore. This outer pier also serves as an inner basin's southern breakwall; the basin is primarily for resident runabouts. Transients usually tie on the canalside outer dock.

The marina has a large land complex—part of it is across the main road. It has a propane-filling facility, a

lift and a 9-ton Travelift, and 110-volt/25-amp electric hookups. If you need a diver, check at the office. The ship's store carries marine equipment, some navigation supplies, local charts, guides, nautical clothing, and snacks. The marina's land line number is (315) 635-7371.

There is a Rent-a-Wreck car rental service on the grounds. Across the street are two restaurants—one is the Hong Kong Chinese Restaurant.

The River Mall is about a four-minute drive away. Get on the main road west, cross the expressway's bridge, and go south about 0.5 mile. Among the stores are a pharmacy, a Pizza Hut, an Ames department store, a bank, a McDonald's, and a large supermarket. East about 0.7 mile is downtown Baldwinsville.

STATE DITCH CUT SOUTH ANCHORAGE

★★★   ⬜ 5

NO FACILITIES

Chart: N 14786, page E-9 (left)

Mile E-180.6 + 0.1 S (SM)

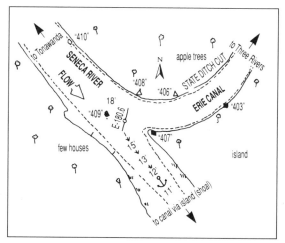

This anchorage is in an old Seneca River oxbow at its upstream (southern) end. The narrow State Ditch Cut makes a westerly bend at its southern end, so complete the turn far enough that the river is clearly open to the southeast. The oxbow entrance is wide, but hold to mid-channel. Go just far enough to be away from traffic wake roll, and anchor in midstream in mud. There are a collection of western-bank waterfront homes, though the forested cutoff island is uninhabited.

BIG ISLAND EAST ANCHORAGE

★★★

NO FACILITIES

Chart: N 14786, page E-9 and E-10, *See A on sketch map*

Mile E-181.4 N (SM)

This anchorage is between wooded Big Island's northeastern shore and the mainland. The island is near Cross Lake's southeastern end. When westbound, the channel makes a hard southwesterly turn at Big Island's eastern tip; from there it runs between the island's southern shore and the mainland before entering the lake. In a strong northwesterly wind the anchorage can be very choppy; a better stop in these conditions is a mile back southeast at the State Ditch Cut South Anchorage.

Leave the channel at the island's eastern tip between

Buoy #414A and **Buoy #416A. Buoy #414A** is usually in the center of the off-channel route leading northeast of the island. Try to ignore it as much as possible and hold to the middle of the back channel as you leave the river. Anchor in mud and weeds about 0.1 mile northeast of **Buoy #414A.**

~~This is a good place to swim; or try fishing for perch~~ along the island's western shore.

If you exit into Cross Lake by continuing on through the anchorage cut, watch for stumps off the island's northwestern shore.

CROSS LAKE SOUTH ANCHORAGES

★★★

NO FACILITIES

Chart: N 14786, page E-8, *See B and C on sketch map*

Mile E-182.6 + 0.1 E (SM)

The lake is a good stop during hot summer days; it usually has a refreshing breeze. It's possible to anchor just about

Big Island East Anchorage, Cross Lake South Anchorages

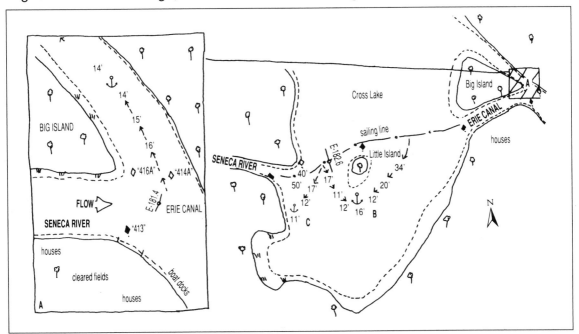

anywhere, but pick comfortable depths of 10 to 20 feet.

There is good fishing on the lake's southern end and Little Island's southern side; catch is usually panfish and a few bass. Use worms for bait.

A favorite stop is along the wooded western mainland shore just far enough from the western canal entrance to be away from wake roll. Another good fishing area is south in the marshy lake bight.

Anywhere you anchor, prepare for mosquitoes at dusk and dawn.

LOCK E #25 UPPER

Chart: N 14786, page E-4

Mile E-202.1 N (SM)

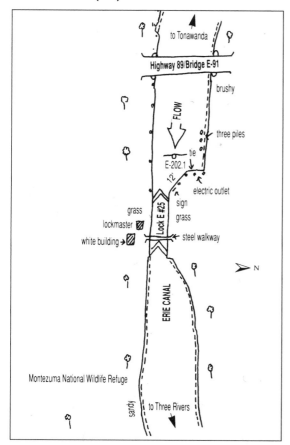

This northern-bank stop is in the lock's upper pool where the approach wall makes two fairly abrupt jogs to the north; this keeps you out of traffic. Upstream of the wall are a group of pilings. If boats fill the wall—not unusual since this is a pretty stop—you might be able to tie to the pilings. No matter where you stay, ask the lockmaster for permission to spend the night. The lock house is on the southern shore.

The lock grounds has lawns and flowers—masses of lavender irises surround the lock house in spring. It's a peaceful stop with scores of birds—cardinals, warblers, robins, phoebes, orioles, and mourning doves. It's also popular with browsing rabbits.

There is a pet shop a short way up the gravel access road. If this is a destination, prepare to be accosted on the way by a large gaggle of fleet-footed, mean-spirited farm geese.

If you cross to the lock's southern side and walk out that access road, there's a view of a group of Clyde River dams.

LOCK E #27 UPPER

Chart: N 14786, page E-1, *See A on sketch map, page 124*

Mile E-220.1 N (SM)

This northern-bank stop is in Lock E #27's (Lyons) upper pool. This is a straight but exceptionally long terminal wall, and the river is wide. The lockmaster normally gives you permission to spend the night as long as you stay well upstream of his lock.

There's a strip of well-maintained lawn backed by tall trees alongside the wall—downtown is behind the trees. Within three blocks is a post office, stores, and the Red Apple Food Mart. If visiting on a Saturday, the Lyon's farmers' market is at the village square from 8 until 5.

The Wayne County Historical Museum is a short walk away at Butternut and Church streets; it's open weekdays from 9 to 4 (but closed for lunch), and Saturday and Sunday from 2 to 4. The museum is in an

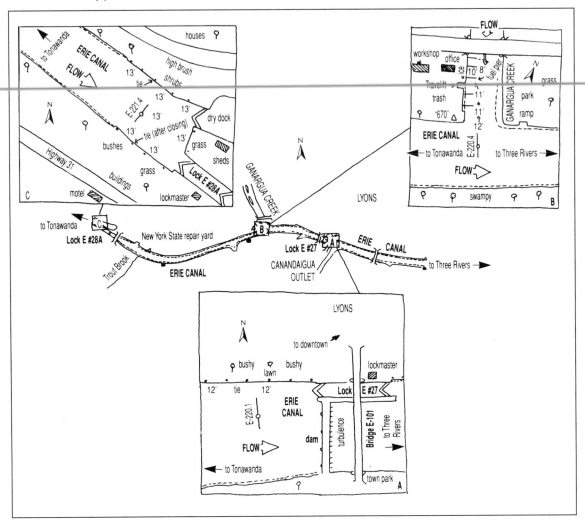

1854 two-story brick Italianate sheriff's residence with a stone jail attached—in use until 1961. It has local and old-Erie displays and exhibits, antiques, early farm implements, and transportation artifacts.

MILLERS MARINA

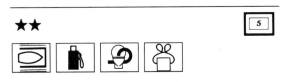

Chart: N 14786, page E-1, *See B on sketch map*

Mile E-220.4 N (SM)

This small marina—open seasonally with the canal—is in the mouth of Ganargua Creek on its western bank. If you plan a layover, tell the roving lockmaster at Lock E #27 (downtown Lyons) when westbound and Lock E #28A when eastbound.

Make your turn into the marina when the creek opens fully. The fuel dock (gas and diesel) is about halfway to the creek bridge and just north of the Travelift well. The office is in the building nearest the creek. The dry-storage area with a large service shed extends west.

Electric hookups (110-volt) are available. The marina's land line number is (315) 946-9363.

Across the creek is a park, a picnic area, a playground, and a canalside launching ramp.

Downtown Lyons is a long walk out the access road to the main highway, and then easterly another 0.6 mile.

LOCK E #28A UPPER

★★

5

Chart: N 14786, page E-1, *See C on sketch map, page 124*

Mile E-221.4 N (SM)

This stop is in Lock E #28A's upper pool alongside a northern bulkheaded wall by a state dry-dock lock. A few barges may be stored on the wall, but you usually have plenty of room. You are out of the way of all canal traffic, though if a state workboat or barge should come in to use the dry-dock lock, you are in the way. Therefore, ask the lockmaster for permission to spend the night.

Come in with long lines; bollards are spaced for barges. There is some old dredge equipment and machinery stored about on land, but it's not objectionable since it's usually covered with wild sweet peas. If you walk down the northern bank, you can stroll through a pleasant residential neighborhood. If you cross to the southern bank over the lock gates and go down that hill, there's a main road and a few businesses geared toward tractors and farm machinery.

NEWARK CANAL PARK

★★★

5

Mile E-225.8 N (SM)

This improved terminal is between two downtown fixed bridges. Once you exit Lock E #28B westbound, you pass under the Ontario-Midland Railroad Bridge; 0.3 mile farther is the East Avenue Bridge, the most easterly of the two downtown. Immediately west of this bridge

Newark Canal Park

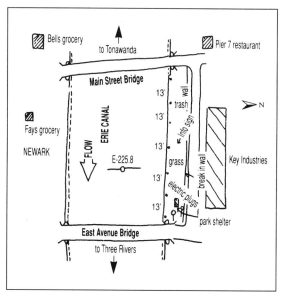

on the northern bank is the Newark Canal Park. It stretches a block as far as the next bridge (Main Street).

If you want an electric hookup (110-volt), tie by one of the standards. Have some change; the hookup is on a meter.

The terminal is also a town park and has shade trees, flower beds, manicured lawn, garbage bins, a directional map of town, and, near the East Avenue Bridge, a pagoda with picnic tables. The park closes to walk-in traffic from a half hour after sunset until a half hour before sunrise.

Your view across the canal is of downtown Newark climbing the southern-shore slope. If this is to be a crew change port, or if you have guests visiting, the Quality Inn and restaurant are just west of the Main Street Bridge on the northern shore. There's a taxi in town (331-1234), and the RTS bus line has daily service to and from Rochester.

Most shopping is on the southern shore; you'll find most kinds of stores, shops, and services. To reach the Bells and Big M supermarkets, cross the Main Street Bridge, go two blocks south of the bridge, then make a westerly turn on Miller Street for about a half block.

The Newark Public Library on the corner of High and Mason streets—about a block south of the markets—also houses the Hoffman Clock Museum, which features over a hundred clocks, most of them 19th-century antiques. The museum is open during library hours: Monday through Saturday from 9:30 to 5:30, and weekday evenings from 7 to 9.

The Central Park bandstand—about three blocks south of the Main Street Bridge—has weekly band concerts during the summer months.

This is a large, popular park with public access day and night. There are picnic tables and grills, ball fields, launching ramp and small-boat dock, playgrounds, and two sets of rest rooms. This is a junction of the Canal Park Trailway bicycle path.

Landwise you are about midway between the shopping centers of Palmyra and Macedon—both too far to walk.

LOCK E #29 UPPER

Mile E-234.8 S (SM)

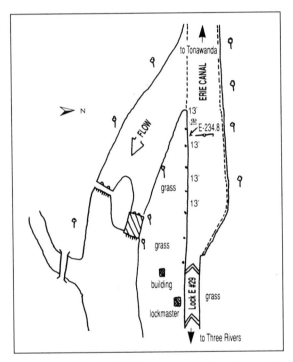

This stop is in Lock E #29's upper pool along the southern approach wall on the lock island. If you plan to stop overnight, ask the lockmaster's permission. This is a straight approach wall, and he might consider it too dangerous if he expects commercial traffic.

Lock E #29 adjoins the Palmyra-Macedon Aqueduct County Park, so you have beautiful grounds. Cross the lock island on the access road bridge for a beautiful view of its dams and waterfalls. About 50 yards beyond the island is one of the old Erie locks with its wooden gates. Beside the lock is a 94-foot-long, three-span aqueduct over the creek; most of it is still standing.

LOCK E #30 UPPER

Mile E-237.3 N/S (SM)

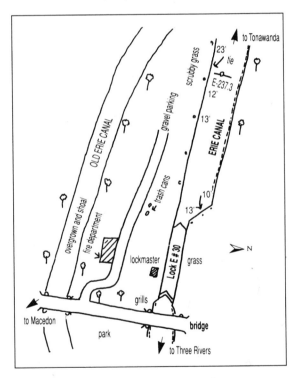

There are two places to stop at this lock, both in the upper pool. If you plan to spend the night get the lockmaster's permission. One stop is in a slight northerly jog on the northern shore; the other is at the far western end of the straight southern approach wall. Since this lock is a canal park, there may be a small-boat dock around the western end of the southern approach wall. If your vessel has very shoal draft, this would be yet another possible tie-up.

The preferred stop is on the northern shore on the northerly jog where you are slightly off the main channel. Here you have a lawn beside the terminal, which is more attractive than the southern side's dusty gravel parking lot.

If you are out for a walk, take the access road that runs in front of the fire department on the canal's southern side. Stop for a minute at the little bridge for a look at the remains of the old Erie.

Macedon is on up the hill about five blocks on Main Street. There's a post office, a beauty salon, an automotive supply, a few shops, a filling station, and a laundromat. A shopping center and supermarket are east—a bit too far to walk. If you need groceries, it's much more convenient to wait until you reach Fairport, about 7 miles west.

FAIRPORT TERMINALS

★★★★   5

Mile E-244.9 N/S (SM)

Once you have left the wide waters at Waynesport, it's 4 miles to Fairport. You have a choice of two terminals, one on each side of the canal. Each has a 48-hour time limit. Both stretch about one block between two bridges—the westernmost is the Fairport Movable Bridge. Electric hookups (110-volt/20-amp) are available.

The beautifully landscaped southern terminal is the most convenient to downtown. At the southern foot of the Parker Street Bridge, the easterly bridge, is a small picnic facility.

Directly above you on the southern terminal's terrace is Packet's Restaurant. Downtown is immediately south of the movable bridge. The Village Landing is next to the waterfront at the bridge and includes typical large-mall shops and stores, the town library, and a Tops supermarket (open 24 hours). On Saturdays from 7 until noon the Fairport farmer's market is in town.

Fairport is a residential village within commuting distance of Rochester. There's a taxi service, and the

Fairport Terminals

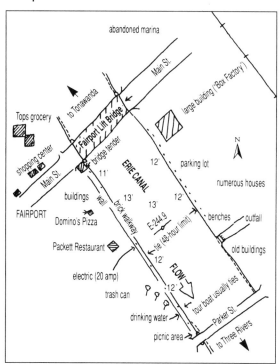

city bus runs into Rochester and to its airport.

Fairport Canal Days is usually held in early June. It's an arts and crafts fair—one of the state's largest—with hundreds of booths set up along the waterfront and on Main Street. There's also musical entertainment, mime, jugglers, dance performances, wandering street performers, and dozens of food stands. Boaters arrive from east and west and raft two to three deep along the terminal walls.

PITTSFORD TERMINAL

★★★   5

See sketch map, page 128
Mile E-251.0 S (SM)

Pittsford is on a riverbend about a mile west of the Cartersville guard gate. Westbound you first sight the Newcomb Oil tanks on the northern bank just east of the Pittsford Main Street Bridge. Next are a group of red

Pittsford Terminal

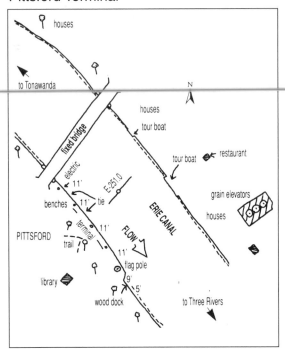

CAPTAIN JEFF'S MARINA

★★★

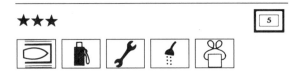

Mile E-264.6 S (SM)

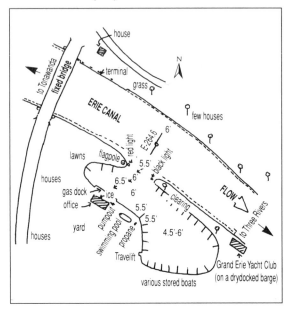

buildings that house a picturesque Schoen Place shopping area, a dock for the large tour boat *Seneca Chief,* and what appears to be a zillion resident farm geese and ducks. The Pittsford Terminal is directly opposite on the southern bank.

If you want one of the two 110-volt electric hookups, tie very close to the bridge. This is a pretty terminal maintained as the Town of Pittsford Park. It has winding, asphalted paths amidst lawns and flower beds and well-placed park benches, picnic tables, and garbage bins.

Downtown is convenient; it begins at the bridge's southern side with a collection of stores, banks, doctors and dentists, barber shops, hardware stores, and a pharmacy. Wegmans supermarket is about a mile west on Monroe Street. At Schoen Place on the northern bank you can rent a bicycle. Pittsford is an access point for the Towpath Trail, a 65-mile canalside path stretching from near Macedon to Lockport.

There's public access to the terminal, though its park restrictions note land access closes after dark. Its main drawback and distraction are all those geese and ducks; they spend their days and nights enjoying the terminal.

The annual three-day Pittsford Village Colonial Days is on an early June weekend; its festivities include musical groups, crafts, and assorted food concessions.

This southern-bank marina—open May 1 to November 1—is in an enclosed basin just east of the Elmgrove Road Bridge. The marina is not readily visible for any distance, and the entrance is narrow. In order not to pass it by, keep watch for boats' pilothouses and a few burgees and flags flying over the top of the canal's southern bank.

If your draft is more than 5 feet, depth may restrict your access. If depth is critical stay in the middle of the entry, come in cautiously, and sound carefully. If no one answered on VHF 13, pull in to the fuel dock (gas only) in front of the two-story office building about opposite the entry. The fuel dock has parallel parking; the rest of the marina has basin perimeter slips at 90 degrees to shore.

The marina has a propane-filling facility, a 10-ton lift, and 110-volt/30-amp electric hookups. The land line number is (716) 426-5400. If you need a diver, check at the office.

This is a pretty marina with flowers, a picnic area, and a swimming pool just east of the office. It's a long way to the market but the marina offers a courtesy car.

SPENCERPORT TOWPATH PARK

★★★

5

Mile E-268.1 N (SM)

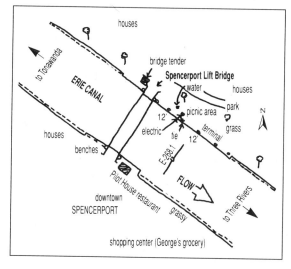

This northern-shore town terminal is immediately east of the Spencerport Lift Bridge. Directly opposite is the Pilot House Restaurant with festive flags and red, white, and blue umbrellas. There also may be a sign that says "Welcome to Spencerport's Business Area." If you want a 110-volt electric hookup, pull in close to the bridge; outlets are on the pole. It's also the area for the one water faucet and garbage bin. Bridge traffic is slightly noisy in this spot. If you are a light sleeper, you may prefer the terminal's eastern end.

This is a town park with a lawn and shrubs and a picnic table. Adjoining the park on the northern shore is a quiet residential area. If boats fill this terminal, there's an adequate southern-shore tie-up just west of the bridge.

The lift bridge is Union Street. If you cross to the southern bank you are downtown. To reach the Village Plaza walk three short blocks south of the bridge and make a left at Slayton Avenue for a half block. You'll find a Midland Bank, a post office, a variety store, a restaurant, a bookstore, a laundromat, a liquor store, and George's supermarket and pharmacy. In early June the village usually hosts a waterfront festival.

ADAMS BASIN TERMINAL

★★★

5

Mile E-270.3 S (SM)

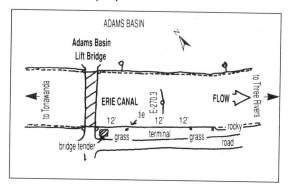

This southern-shore terminal is east of the Adams Basin Lift Bridge. This is a long terminal banked with shade trees and wildflowers. Come in with long dock lines; bollards are far apart. About a half block from the bridge on the northern shore is the Adams Basin post office. Keep going and you are in farm country with apple orchards and cabbage fields.

BROCKPORT TERMINAL

★★★★

5

Mile E-275.2 S (SM)

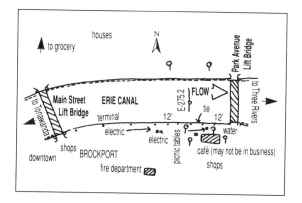

This southern-bank stop is between the Brockville Park Avenue and Main Street lift bridges. Preferred tie-up is alongside a canalside restaurant with yacht-spaced cleats in a grassy, tree-shaded area. There's one water faucet in a brick 2-foot-by-2-foot cubicle on the lawn. Electric hookups (110-volt) are available. Though the rest of the terminal is landscaped to the western bridge, it's next to a paved parking lot and has a higher noise level.

Brockport is a university town, home to SUNY Brockport. If you walk a half block to the Main Street Bridge, you are in downtown with most village stores, banks, restaurants, and a three-screen theater. The post office is at the southern foot of the bridge. The nearest supermarket and large pharmacy are a short walk north of the bridge.

Four blocks south of the bridge at the corner of South Street you can visit the headquarters of the Western Monroe Historical Society and the Morgan-Manning House, a family homestead since 1850, with eight fireplaces, gold parlor and staircase, authentic furniture, and an extensive collection of local history records. It's open Sunday afternoon between 2 and 4.

The preferred section of this southern-bank stop is west of the newly refurbished Holley Lift Bridge. Bollards are far apart; come in with long lines. There is a grassy area and a line of tall shade trees alongside. Across a small road are a few well-kept homes; across the canal is a private home with a small dock.

Town is a pleasant walk through a quiet neighborhood. Take East Avenue at the bridge and head south. In a block or two you come to the Baptist Church, dedicated in 1834. Turn west at the church, go another block, and you arrive at a church whose clock is missing its hands. You are now in the town square area, where you have a bank, a diner, a hardware store, a library, and a Super Duper Grocery.

HULBERTON TERMINAL

★★

Mile E-282.2 N (SM)

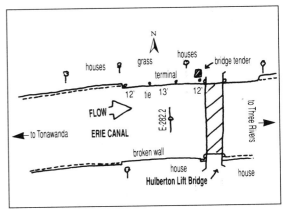

This northern-bank terminal is west of the Hulberton Lift Bridge. Come in with long dock lines and tie at the terminal's western end—the section nearest the bridge tender's house appears to be someone's improved canalside front yard.

This is a quiet stop with a small residential area on both canal banks.

HOLLEY TERMINAL

★★★

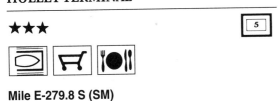

Mile E-279.8 S (SM)

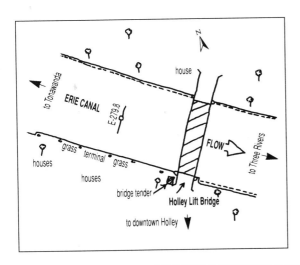

ALBION

Mile E-288.1 (SM) to E-288.5 (SM)

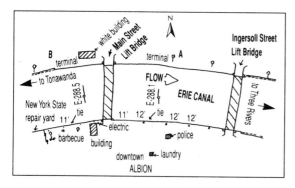

In downtown Albion there are four terminals for overnight within 0.2 mile. Those on the southern shore are more convenient since that shore has the village center on Main Street.

No matter where you stay you are within about seven blocks of most village businesses, including a NAPA Auto Parts, banks, a True-Value Hardware, a variety store, a Dollar Store, a post office, restaurants, a Radio Shack, and a Super Duper Grocery. A laundromat is about 600 feet from the southern shore's eastern terminal. About a half block north of the Main Street Bridge is a Getty gas station with a convenience store for a few basics and ice.

Stop by the chamber of commerce at 53 North Main Street and pick up a walking-tour map of Albion's Historic Courthouse District. This area is only a few short blocks from the waterfront. Also stop at the post office to see the 1939 Judson Smith mural.

At the corner of State and Main streets is the 1874 Presbyterian Church, built of Medina sandstone in the Gothic Revival Style. Its stone spire is 175 feet high. The library is across from the church.

A block farther, on the corner of East Park Street, is the impressive Pullman Memorial Universalist Church—also of Medina sandstone, with windows of Tiffany glass. George Pullman had it built in 1894 in memory of his parents. The 1857 brick county courthouse with its imposing dome with cupola and Medina sandstone sidewalks dominates the center of the square across the street. The 1896 Saint Joseph Church, across from the Universalist Church on Park Street, and the brick Baptist church are worth a trip.

Albion Terminals East

★

 [5]

See A on sketch map
Mile E-288.4 N/S (SM)

The eastern terminals are on both sides of the canal and between the two lift bridges. Distance between bollards varies, so you may need long dock lines. In this area the preferred stop is on the southern bank near a brick building—the fire department/police station. Though they appear run down, the electric standards have 110-volt service activated. There's a bit of grass fronting a back street and a parking lot, and you are within a block of downtown.

The northern-shore terminal has bollards and is a place to stop, but it's farther from town—you have to cross a bridge.

Albion Terminals West

★★★

 [5]

See B on sketch map
Mile E-288.5 N/S (SM)

The western terminal on the southern bank was at one time a marina. It's immediately west of the Main Street Lift Bridge and east of a fenced state canal complex. West of the fence, state workboats and barges are usually in residence.

This is a grassy area shaded with prolific apple trees. There are yacht-spaced cleats and bollards. It's within a few steps of downtown.

There's also a northern-bank terminal with bollards. It's similar to the eastern terminals, though there's a slight chance the state workboats and barges might overflow onto this side.

EAGLE HARBOR TERMINAL

★★

Mile E-291.6 N (SM)

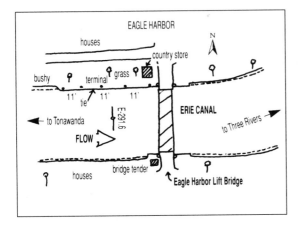

This northern-bank stop is west of the Eagle Harbor Lift Bridge. Come in with long lines; bollards are far apart. There's a table and grill at the terminal's eastern end that appears privately maintained by the Harbor Crafts Country Store at the foot of the bridge. Tie up west of the picnic area.

The terminal is a popular spot for residents to swim and picnic. The canal road runs along the northern shore. It's down the canal bank, so passing traffic is not noticeable, but you do hear bridge traffic. This is a quiet, well-kept residential area.

KNOWLESVILLE TERMINAL

★★★

Mile E-294.5 S (SM)

This southern-shore terminal/marina is immediately west of the Knowlesville Lift Bridge. This is a grassy area with shade trees and (usually) a large Open sign.

Knowlesville Terminal

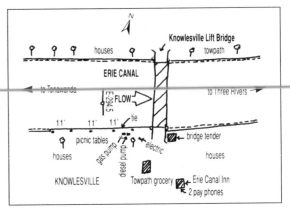

Unless you need fuel, tie west of the pumps (gas and diesel). At the bridge's southern foot is the Towpath Grocery—the owners man the fuel pumps.

Within a block and a half of the southern bridge approach is a fire hall with a bingo night, a church, the Erie Canal Inn, and more homes. The phone booths are across the street at the inn. The Towpath Grocery has a post office and a selection of food and supplies.

MEDINA PARK AND MARINA

★★

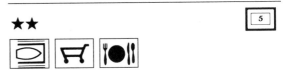

Mile E-298.6 S (SM)

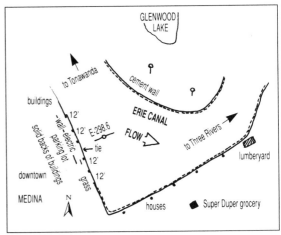

This southern-bank improved canal terminal is in the downtown canal bend. You can't miss it; "Welcome to Medina" is painted on the wall immediately behind the terminal. Behind this is the backside of Medina's business district.

The terminal has a lined, wooden wall with pilings that extend about 4 feet above the bulkhead. A black iron pipe fence separates the marina promenade from a paved parking lot. Electric service (110-volt) is available.

Your first stop should be at the chamber of commerce at 433 Main Street—practically right behind you. These friendly people will give you Medina directions and tell you about sights to see and things to do. Pick up a village guide and map and a walking-tour map of the business district; the terminal may have one posted.

Medina is a compact town; Main Street is its business center. Banks, clothing and department stores, a pharmacy, J. C. Penney, Murphys, Corky's Bakery, restaurants, office supplies, liquor stores, NAPA Auto Parts, and video stores are within a few blocks.

You dock behind the brick Medina Journal Register building, which has been there since 1920; before that, the building was the Eagle Hotel, a famous old-canal lodging house.

A block south on Main Street is the junction of East and West Center streets; Bernies Wash N' Dry is at 143 East Center Street. Go another two blocks and you have a Super Duper supermarket. On the way, note the 1833 Medina sandstone Saint John's Episcopal Church in the middle of Church Street. It's the oldest public building still in use in Medina.

An interesting stop is the Bancroft Artisans and Canal Museum at 345 North Main Street Lower, in the canal basin's fieldstone building. This artists' co-op features quilts, baskets, weaving, hand-painted china and jewelry, antiques, rag rugs, and pen and ink canal scenes. It's open Monday through Saturday from 10 to 4 and Sunday from 11 to 4.

The Medina Canal Festival is held in mid-July. Alongside will be a small midway, food concession stands, craft and art displays, and a lot of visitors.

MIDDLEPORT TERMINAL

★★★   5

Mile E-303.6 S (SM)

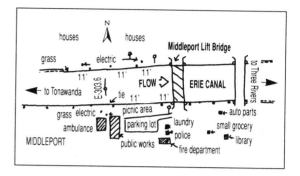

The preferred terminal is west of Middleport Lift Bridge on the southern bank behind and west of the Middleport Public Works Garage, a low blue building with a black roof. Here you do not have public parking lot noise directly alongside the boat. A favorite stop is at the terminal's western end by a small dam over the creek. Cleats are spaced for pleasure boats.

Most of the southern terminal has a well-maintained lawn and picnic tables, and it is shaded by crabapple trees. Not all the 110-volt electric outlets work, so you may need a long cord. Near the ambulance-rescue squad garage is one water faucet.

The lift bridge is Main Street; downtown is about 300 feet away. The laundromat is across the parking lot immediately west of the bridge behind the village stores; look for its sign on the covered back entrance. Within a block or two you have a Midland Bank, a barber shop, the fire department, a large auto parts store, a restaurant, a hardware store, a post office, and some other small stores. If you take State Street, the first street eastbound off Main, for a block, then turn south on Vernon, you have Mr. Bills Convenience Store, with the public library across the street.

If you are out for an afternoon constitutional, pick one of Middleport's quiet residential streets shaded by tall trees. These two-story older homes are restored with pleasant gardens and very friendly owners.

In August is the Middleport Kiddies Parade. Call the

Middleport Tourism Committee, 735-7631, for information.

On weekends this terminal may be full; in this case tie at the terminal west of the lift bridge on the northern bank. It, too, has 110-volt outlets and yacht-spaced cleats.

GASPORT MEMORIAL PARK

★★

Mile E-308.5 S (SM)

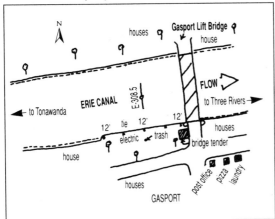

This southern-shore terminal is west of the Gasport Lift Bridge. It's a small village park with lawn, shade trees, picnic table, garbage bin, a few 110-volt electric hookups, and a water faucet.

Kitty-corner to the park is the Gasport post office. A few stores east is a pizza parlor and laundromat. In midsummer you may find street vendors selling farm-fresh fruit and vegetables.

The Gasport Pumpkin Festival is in October; call the Niagara County Tourism bureau, (800) 338-7890, for annual dates.

NELSON C. GOEHLE MUNICIPAL MARINA

★★★★

Mile E-313.3 S (SM)

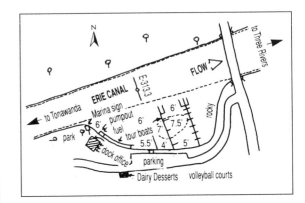

This marina—open May 19 through October 7—is on the southern bank of a wide waters just west of Cold Springs Road Fixed Bridge #226. This is about 4.8 miles west of the Gasport Lift Bridge after a pronounced left-hand bend. The small wide waters begins at the bridge. If you draw 5.5 or 6 feet, approach with extreme caution; you may not have depth except at the western end of the marina's fuel dock (gas and diesel) at the basin's western end. Continue west in the channel until you are opposite the pumps; then cross the bar.

Though some slips parallel the bank, most are on three floating docks that extend north from the basin's southern bank. The middle dock's western face has parallel-parked tour boats—they take parties through the Lockport Locks.

If the dock attendants aren't in evidence—their hours are 9 to 9—pull in by the fuel pumps for a slip assignment. The office is at the head of the ramp. The land line number is (716) 433-9795.

There is a picnic table at the marina and a wooded park west of the facility with tables, covered picnic sites, and grills.

South across Market Street is the popular Wide Waters Drive In, volleyball courts, and a playground.

The marina is an excellent base from which to tour historic Lockport, though it's a bit far to walk to town—

about 1.5 uphill miles. It's more comfortable to call Carl's Niagara Taxi. Have the cabby drop you off at the chamber of commerce at 151 West Genesee Street—about three blocks from the locks. Here you can pick up maps, brochures, and directions.

Lockport's historical area and supplies are concentrated within a few blocks of the canal locks. On the southern side you have banks, stores, pharmacies, restaurants, a surplus store, and more. The post office is on the corner of East Main and Elm streets; the library is just down the block.

The Niagara County Historical Society, 215 Niagara Street (north of the canal) has a complex of buildings with exhibits and displays of the local area. It's open Thursday through Sunday from 1 to 5.

The 1825 Colonel Bond House, the first brick home in Lockport, is at 143 Ontario Street. It's furnished in 19th-century style, and is open Thursdays and weekends from 1 to 5.

The Canal Museum on the lock grounds is in the easternmost lock building located between the old and new locks. Inside are displays and artifacts of the old canal, beautifully reproduced photos of its construction, and outdoor displays.

The Lockport Canal Fest is held in July. The three-day festival has arts and crafts, music, food, entertainment, and a boat parade. Call (716) 433-3828 for annual dates.

THE TONAWANDAS

See sketch map, page 136
Mile E-332.6 (SM) to Mile E-333.0 (SM)

As you approach downtown North Tonawanda (northern bank), Tonawanda (southern bank), and the Niagara River, there are five bridges in 0.6 mile. The most distinguishable locating landmark is the old hulking railroad bascule bridge at **Mile E-332.5 (SM).** West of this you have a choice of two terminals and a marina. In a few places a 6-foot-draft vessel may have some problem with depth if water level is down slightly, so use caution during any approach.

If it's late in the day and you have a low-powered vessel you might want to consider a layover in the Tonawandas when bound for Lake Erie. Once you leave the Erie Canal West and enter the Niagara River, you are traveling upstream to Buffalo. For 8.5 miles—as

far as the Black Rock Lock Canal—you have up to 4 mph—or more—of current against you.

Your first stop should be at the chamber of commerce at 84 Sweeney Street on the canal in North Tonawanda. They'll give you instant directions and maps to find nearly anything you might need. No matter where you stay in the Tonawandas you are within walking distance of village stores and facilities. There's a supermarket in each town, a Bells in Tonawanda, a Tops in North Tonawanda; they're about four to six blocks away, depending on your selected tie-up.

The Historical Society of the Tonawandas is worth a visit; it's in an 1870s railroad station and includes a museum with displays and exhibits.

The restored 1829 Benjamin Long Homestead at the confluence of Tonawanda and Ellicott Creeks is accessible at 24 East Niagara Street in Tonawanda. It was the first permanent home in Tonawanda and is now furnished in the 1810-to-1840 style. It's open on Sunday, May through October, from 2 to 5.

North Tonawanda has long been home to carousel and band organ factories. In 1883 Allen Herschell made the first steam-driven "riding gallery," and today at 180 Thompson Street you can visit the Herschell Carousel Factory and Museum. You can see carousel memorabilia, watch demonstrations of intricate woodworking and carving, and ride on one of the first carousels produced by the company. The museum is open from May through Labor Day. Hours vary seasonally, so call (716) 693-1885 before you start walking. If possible, plan to visit on a Sunday about 2 P.M. when they have special performances.

Canalfest, a week-long festival in July, has parades, boat races, arts and crafts, concerts, and a midway.

Pleasure boating on the Niagara River downstream of the Erie Canal junction is not recommended; there is the danger of ever-increasing current as you near Niagara Falls, 11.5 miles downstream. The tour boat *Niagara Clipper* is a fine substitute for this Upper Niagara River cruise; she docks at 650 River Road in North Tonawanda and makes a circle tour around Grand Island. You can see the mists rising over the falls; it's as close to them as you want to be in a boat.

By land, North Tonawanda is your most convenient layover to visit Niagara Falls. Gray Line Tours, at 3466 Niagara Falls Boulevard, (716) 692-4288, offers a selection of tours and a pickup point. The Niagara Frontier Transit Metro System and a choice of taxi services will also get you to the falls area and its attractions.

The Tonawandas: Twin Cities Terminals East and West, Wardells Marina, Riverview Trail Terminal

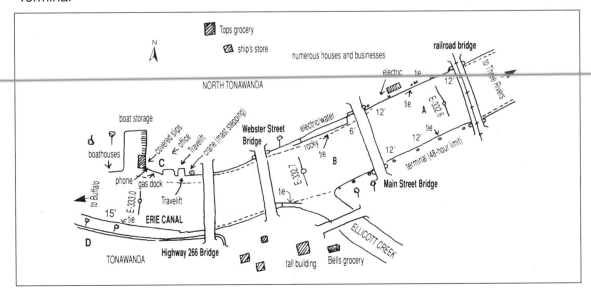

Twin Cities Terminals East

★★

See A on sketch map
Mile E-332.6 N/S (SM)

If you draw 6 feet, this is one of two layover areas with good depth in the Tonawandas. The other is Riverview Park Terminal, close to the canal entrance.

Twin Cities Terminals East are typical cement terminals with a 48-hour time limit. They are on both sides of the canal and extend for a block. They are between the old movable railroad bridge and the Main Street Bridge. With so many bridges in a short distance you might be slightly confused as to your location. The railroad bridge is heavy, hulking, and black and has a canal fixed-bridge clearance—it doesn't open for passage. Once to its west, you can identify the terminals by their red, white, and blue bulkhead rims. The preferred terminal is on the northern shore. It has a small red building on the grounds. There is a 110-volt electric hookup, a few shade trees, and a small plot of grass.

Twin Cities Terminals West

★★★

See B on sketch map
Mile E-332.7 N/S (SM)

These terminals on both banks are pretty stops, but depth might be a problem; approach carefully—bottom is rock. Both are west of the Main Street Bridge and extend a block to the Webster Street Bridge. Midway between the two bridges on the southern shore is the mouth of Ellicott Creek; it's crossed by its own bridge at Long's Point. The preferred stop is on the northern shore.

This side does not have a conventional Erie Canal concrete or steel-plated terminal wall but is a fixed dock that runs parallel to shore. Depths vary over a rocky bottom. Ashore you have grass, shade trees, picnic tables, drinking water, and garbage bins. Electric hookups (110-volt) are available. Across the street is the Packet Center and the Harbor House.

If you decide to stay on the southern bank, you have good depth at a regular cement terminal wall between the Main Street Bridge and Ellicott Creek, but it's not very attractive. West of the creek you have another fixed dock paralleling the bank.

Wardells Marina

★

ALL FACILITIES

See C on sketch map, page 136
Mile E-333.0 N (SM)

This northern-shore marina—open March to December—is immediately west of the Highway 266 Bridge, the last westerly highway bridge across the canal. Pull in to the dock by the blue lighted marina sign for fuel (gas and diesel), information on dockage, mast stepping, or yard work. This is a busy fuel dock; keep to one end or the other. If no one is manning the pumps, check the office, which is in the large building north of the dock. It can be reached at (716) 692-9428.

This is a very popular mast-stepping stop for canalling sailboats; there are usually three or four tied up or rafted off waiting for service. The mast-stepping area is at a canalside dock alongside the bridge just east of the Travelift well. If you need to haul out a sailboat, do it with your mast on deck; the Travelift is not open-ended.

The canalside part of this marina always appears filled to capacity, but the Wardells always seem to find a place to put you. Most slips, part of which are in a partially covered shed, are in a long bight extending north just south of the fuel dock; these are normally for residents. The ship's store—at the office—has a selection of marine supplies and equipment and local charts. Block and cube ice and 110-volt electric hookups are available.

To get to town, walk up the marina's access lane that leads to the main highway. Once there, cross the road to the Tops supermarket. Another few blocks east you are in downtown North Tonawanda.

Riverview Trail Terminal

★★★★

See D on sketch map, page 136
Mile E-333.0 S (SM)

This public terminal—a Tonawanda favorite—is west of the Highway 266 Bridge and almost directly opposite Wardells Marina. You tie to a corrugated steel bulkhead; there are no cleats, but the steel sheets have large holes to serve as tie-up points. Watch where you tie at the waterline; there are a few projecting bolts.

The terminal faces the paved, very popular Riverview Trail—a bicycle, roller skating, jogging, and strolling path that goes to Buffalo. Alongside the terminal is a manicured lawn and a few shade trees; across the trail path are attractive townhouses. This is an excellent trail access point if you brought along your bicycle or roller blades.

For access to Tonawanda, take the trail east and under the bridge, then up to the main road. Across the main thoroughfare is Fay's Plaza, which includes a large pharmacy, auto parts store, Family Dollar, and McDonald's. If you need the Bells supermarket, bear easterly, and cross to the multistoried apartment house; the market is just to its east.

Plan a cockpit supper. In late afternoon and early evening you can watch an endless parade of idling pleasure craft going up and down the canal.

The Cayuga and Seneca Canal and Cayuga and Seneca Lakes

Mile SEN-0.0 (SM) [Mile E-200.4 (SM)/E-200.7 (SM)]
Mile LKCAY-0.0 (SM) to Mile LKCAY-36.1 (SM)
Mile LKSEN 0.0 (SM) to Mile LKSEN-32.5 (SM)

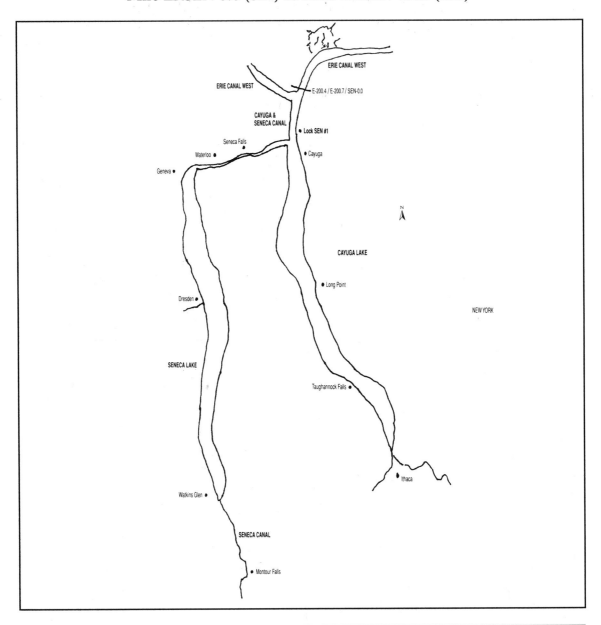

> *The Great Spirit stretched forth his hand and said, 'You should know your lands, for I have pressed my hand upon them and in my fingerprints rest the blue waters.'*
>
> Iroquois Legend: Origin of the Finger Lakes

The Cayuga and Seneca Canal first opened to navigation in 1829. The state enlarged and improved them for the modern 1900s system. The Cayuga canal portion encompasses 17 miles and connects the Erie West with Cayuga and Seneca Lakes. In this distance you have four locks, one taintor gate dam, and four guard gates. The Seneca canal portion is at Seneca Lake's southern end and connects to Montour Falls.

Cayuga and Seneca are two of the Finger Lakes, a group of long, narrow lakes in New York State. Less romantic geologically than they are in the Iroquois legend, the lakes are the result of the progressive grinding of Ice Age glaciers advancing and retreating over Canada and the northern United States. The pressure of these massive ice walls resulted in the creation of prehistoric rivers with deep gorges and long, narrow valleys. After the retreat of the last glacier more than 10,000 years ago, these became the Finger Lakes.

Originally the basin and valley rivers flowed south into the Susquehanna River system. When glaciers dropped moraine across southwestern New York State, it dammed streams already deepened and sloped by the receding ice; drainage became northerly. All the lakes lie in an almost due north and south direction, and their tributaries flow in from east and west.

Though all the lakes are navigable, only Seneca and Cayuga lakes are accessible from the Erie Canal.

Lock SEN #1 on the Cayuga and Seneca Canal.

The Erie Canal to
North End Seneca Lake

Mile SEN-0.0 (SM) / Mile E-200.5 (SM) / Mile E-200.7 (SM)
to Mile SEN-17.0 (SM)

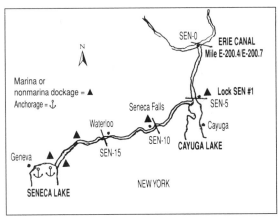

Mile SEN-0.0 (SM) to Mile SEN-17.0 (SM)

LOCKAGE, CAYUGA AND SENECA CANAL			
Lock	*Mile*	*Land Line*	*Lift**
Lock SEN #1	SEN-3.9 (SM)	(315) 253-7523	7.5 feet
Lock SEN #2	SEN-7.7 S (SM)	(315) 568-5797	26.8 feet
Lock SEN #3	SEN-7.7 S (SM)	(315) 568-5797	23.0 feet
Lock SEN #4	SEN-12.0 (SM)	(315) 539-3242	14.5 feet

*At normal pool level

All locks monitor VHF 13. Signals: Lights and Horn (3 long blasts to transit). Normally furnish lines. Ladders are furnished (four per lock).

Daily operating hours for pleasure craft: 0700 to 2230 (may vary annually).

Call (800) 422-1825 for updated canal information, including schedules and operation hours.

Canal Superintendent: (315) 946-6192

You can leave the Erie westbound at **Mile E-200.5 S (SM)** or eastbound at **Mile E-200.7 S (SM).** These entrances are on both sides of a small island on the Erie's southern shore. The Cayuga and Seneca Canal's numbering system begins at the Erie junction at **Mile SEN-0.0 (SM);** it ends upstream at the northern end of Seneca Lake, its summit level.

After you enter the canal southbound, you cross the Clyde River, which winds off west; then you pass under the New York State Thruway. This is part of the Montezuma Marsh National Wildlife Refuge. Its main pool is not far behind the fringe of thick trees along the canal banks. The flooded timber and marsh are a haven for waterfowl and wildlife. Watch for deer along the shoreline in early morning.

Near the end of this 3-mile canal cut you pass Bridge S-1, make a slight easterly bend, and approach Lock SEN #1, **Mile SEN-3.8 (SM).** The lock has an accompanying southerly guard gate. South of the lock and gate is your departure point if you plan to visit Cayuga Lake (see "Cayuga Lake," beginning on page 147).

If bound for Seneca Lake, the canals make a hard westerly bend at the junction. You leave the Montezuma Refuge at the Highway 89 Bridge (BR S-3), make a southwesterly bend, and go under the railroad bridge. The northern outskirts of Seneca Falls and its two tandem locks are coming up at **Mile SEN-7.6 S (SM).**

Seneca Falls owes its name and early industrial development to the 50-foot waterfall that provided its power. Today's northern-shore power plant has two dam spillways and an open crest. There's another guard gate as you exit the locks and enter the northern end of small Van Cleef Lake—named for George Van Cleef,

one of the first white children born in the area.

Women's Rights Park is up the street from the large building on the lake's southwestern shore; it's within walking distance of the town terminal. On the lake's southern shore is Elizabeth Cady Stanton's home; she promoted the first Women's Rights Convention.

The canal makes a bend at the first of the three downtown bridges. West of town the channel holds south of a pair of islands in a wide riverbend. In a few more miles the northern shore begins Waterloo's eastern outskirts. In 1966, by Congressional and Presidential proclamation, Waterloo was named "the Birthplace of Memorial Day"; the town held its first Memorial Day a hundred years earlier. In the center of town is Lock SEN #4, **Mile SEN-11.9 (SM).** About two blocks away is an ice cream parlor, a post office, and a few stores; a few more blocks up Main Street is the Big M supermarket.

About 2 miles west of town is Waterloo's historical Scythe Tree. Before local farm boy James Johnson left for the Civil War, he embedded his scythe blade in a fir

Seneca Falls, New York, looking south. Downtown is in the middle of the photo on the left.
(From the Archives of the Seneca Falls Historical Society)

tree with the announcement, "Let it hang there till I get back." He was killed in battle in 1864. In time the scythe handle rotted and disappeared, but the blade is still there, wrapped in the tree's trunk.

Once past southern-bank Kendig Creek and two large, wooded, cutoff islands, you begin a 2-mile approach to Seneca Lake. Near the canal's end you pass under four bridges. There has been a collection of marinas along this stretch from Waterloo, but depths are very critical for 5.5 feet, and bottom is primarily rock.

South of the bridges is Seneca Lake State Park's eastern border. Ahead is the lake entrance with a stone breakwater that extends southwesterly from the park marina. Enter the lake very cautiously because of risky depths. Though this is a deep lake—in places over 575 feet—its canal entrance shoals more each year. For best lake entry depths try to hold about halfway between the northern breakwater and the eastern-bank yacht club docks; then make for the offshore buoys and you are home free. Seneca Lake is covered beginning on page 155.

Sketch Map Depths

Sketch map depths are given at normal average summer canal pool and lake levels. When you venture outside the sketch map confines, you must adjust the NOAA chart to chart datum. For convenience in adjusting, use the following:

Mile E-200.4 (SM)/Mile E-200.7 (SM)/Mile SEN-0.0 (SM) to **Mile SEN-3.9 (SM):** Plane of reference, Normal Pool Level

Mile SEN-3.9 (SM) to **Mile SEN-7.6 (SM):** Plane of reference, Cayuga Lake Normal Lake Level, 381.5 feet

Mile SEN-7.6 (SM) to **Mile SEN-11.9 (SM):** Plane of reference, Normal Pool Level

Mile SEN-11.9 (SM) to **Mile SEN-17.0 (SM):** Plane of reference, Seneca Lake Normal Lake Level, 445.0 feet

LOCK SEN #1 LOWER AND UPPER

★★

Chart: N 14786, page CS-4 or CS-5

Mile SEN-3.9 E (SM)

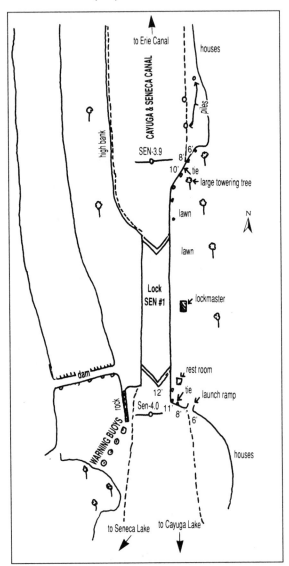

Lock SEN #1 Lower

The preferred stop for best scenery and a quiet atmosphere is north of the lock on the eastern approach wall at the northern end of the portion that angles easterly. If the space on this jog is taken, don't stay. The rest of the approach is on a lock straightaway and commercial traffic needs this space to maneuver. Come in with long lines; bollards are far apart. If you plan to stop, call the lockmaster on VHF 13, tell him your intentions, and ask permission to stay. If you don't, he may prepare the lock once you are in sight.

This is a tree-shaded stop with a lawn and flowers. To your north are a few waterfront homes. This is a place to watch lockages or cross the lock gates and have a look at the Taintor Gate Dam. There are rest rooms above the lock on the eastern shore.

Lock SEN #1 Upper

This stop is in the upper pool, through the Guard Gate, on the eastern approach bank where it jogs east. Here, too, you must be certain you do not tie on the short, straight approach wall. Commercial traffic uses this area during transit.

The area where you tie is the Mud Lock Fishing Access Site. There is a launching ramp at the jog's eastern end. This is active during daylight hours on weekdays, and very active day and night on weekends. Alongside is its parking lot, though there's a well-kept grassy plot and flower beds on the straightaway approach. Toward the lock are the rest rooms.

There's an access road that runs alongside the lock and by the residential area, but no supplies close in either direction.

SENECA FALLS TERMINAL

★★

5

Chart: N 14786, Page CS-4

Mile SEN-8.5 N (SM)

West of tandem Locks SEN #2 and #3 and through Van Cleef Lake, there are three bridges within 0.5 mile. The terminal is in downtown Seneca Falls on the northern shore between the easternmost bridge at Highway 414 (BR S-6) and the middle bridge (BR S-7). Opposite on

Seneca Falls Terminal

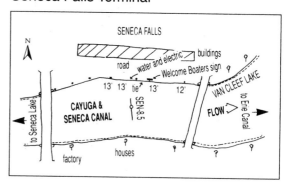

the southern shore is a smokestack and the Knitting Mills. Behind the terminal is a solid bank of buildings—the back of downtown Seneca Falls. You'll spot a sign that says "Welcome Boaters to the Village of Seneca Falls."

This improved terminal has yacht-spaced cleats, clean grounds, a few shade trees, 110-volt electric outlets, and water faucets. Downtown has shops, hardware and clothing stores, banks, a drugstore, a post office, and a Super Duper supermarket.

Seneca Falls is the birthplace of the women's rights movement. It was home to suffrage leader Elizabeth Cady Stanton and activist Amelia Bloomer. In 1848 the first Women's Rights Convention was held about a block from today's terminal.

The Women's Rights National Historical Park at 116 Falls Street has a visitor center with displays and exhibits; it's open Monday through Friday from 9 to 5. Farther on, at 32 Washington Street, is the Elizabeth Cady Stanton Home, built in 1836. The park service offers daily tours from 9 to 5, May through September.

At 76 Falls Street is the National Women's Hall of Fame, honoring outstanding American women. It has portraits, photographs, and memorabilia of its honorees. It's open May through October from 10 to 4.

INLAND HARBOR

★★★★

5

Chart: N 14786, Page CS-2, *See A on sketch map, page 144*

Mile SEN-15.6 NW (SM)

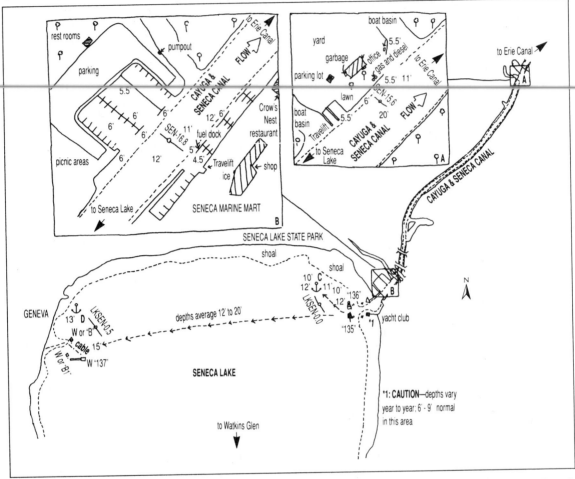

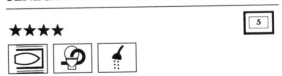

This northern-shore marina is in two basins midway between **Daymark #120** and **Daymark #122**. If your draft is more than 5 feet, use caution; it shoals abruptly as you close the channel bank, and bottom varies from mud to rock.

If no one answered on VHF 16, pull in to the main-channel fuel dock between the two basins; the pumps (gas and diesel) are in front of the blue-and-white office. The land line number is (315) 789-7255. The pumpout is just off the fuel dock on the angle leading into the northern basin. Watch your depth here; a 6-foot draft usually has to ooze through the mud to get there. If your draft is too much for the basin, the dockmaster may allow transients to stay along the canal by the fuel dock on weekdays.

The marina has a Travelift. The grounds are well maintained, and the friendly resident boatowners do not mind

answering questions on local cruising. You are about 3 miles from Waterloo or Geneva; taxis are available.

SENECA LAKE STATE PARK MARINA

★★★★

5

Chart: N 14786, Page CS-2, *See B on sketch map*

Mile SEN-16.8 W (SM)

This western-shore park marina—open April 1 to October 24—is immediately south of the canal's southerly four bridges at Seneca Lake's entrance. It's protected from the lake by a southerly mole from which extends the northern lake breakwater.

Unless water level is up, depth is critical for drafts more than 5.5 feet. Lake wind tide also alters water levels, so monitor depths carefully. Use caution during your approach; bottom is mud and rocks.

At the marina's northern extremity is a long cut filled with runabout slips that extends about 0.3 mile west to a launching ramp. The main facility is south of the cut in a basin whose northern side is a mole shared with the small-boat canal. Its southern side is the mole that protects it from the lake. Extending from the basin's western bank to the main channel are two piers with slips; both have T-piers on their eastern ends. Each mole has perimeter slips.

This is a very popular marina and dockage is limited, especially if you need a slip with deep water. For a slip assignment pull in to one of the T-piers. If a park employee is not around and you don't want to stay aboard and worry about whether a slip is available, you can hike off 0.3 mile down the access road and ask for instructions at the main park office complex. The phone number is (607) 387-7041. Electric hookups (110-volt/50-amp) are available.

Archaeological studies have determined that the 140-acre main park was once the site of the 4,500-year-old pre-Iroquois Lamoka culture. Today it's a popular area for bicycling, jogging, and pleasant walks along the lakefront. It has extensive shade trees and lawns, public phones, rest rooms, and covered picnic shelters with fireplaces and grills. There are playgrounds, a lakeside swimming beach, and baseball, volleyball, soccer, rugby, and football playing fields.

SENECA MARINE MART

★★

Chart: N 14786, Page CS-2, *See B on sketch map, page 144*

Mile SEN-16.8 E (SM)

This eastern-shore marina begins near the southernmost of the four bridges. It's opposite the Seneca Lake State

Park Marina. If your draft is more than 5.5 feet, use caution; it shoals abruptly as you close the bank. Bottom varies but is mostly rock.

The marina is a collection of three docks, each with a T-pier, extending from the eastern bank. Dockage for drafts more than 5 feet usually must be here. At the southern end is a partially enclosed basin protected by a long pier that extends northward. In this area there are some small runabout slips and a Travelift well—risky depths for more than 4.5 feet.

If no one answered on VHF 16/13, pull in to the fuel dock; it's the third T-pier south of the most southerly bridge. You can see the pump—gas only. If no one is about there, the office is in the big building. That's also the location of the ship's store, which has basic supplies. Electric hookups (110-volt) are available. The land line number is (315) 789-5520.

Toward the bridge on the marina grounds is the Crow's Nest Restaurant with its festive porch umbrellas.

GENEVA ANCHORAGES

★★★

NO FACILITIES

Chart: N 14786, page CS-2, *See C and D on sketch map, page 144*

Mile LKSEN-0.5 W (SM)

In fair weather it's possible to anchor at the lake's far northern end along the Seneca Lake State Park shoreline. You can also anchor off Geneva on the lake's western shore behind a partially submerged breakwater. Neither is a secure anchorage. Any southerly-quadrant wind shift builds an untenable sea in a very short time, requiring immediate departure. Leave someone aboard capable of moving the boat if you plan excursions ashore. A safer stop is at the Seneca Lake State Park Marina or the Seneca Marine Mart (see page 144 and this page). If you plan a leisurely day seeing the sights and shopping from one of these anchorages, you can taxi into Geneva, about 2 miles away.

Geneva touts its South Main Street as "the most beautiful street in America" due to its century-old trees and lovely homes overlooking the lake. This is a large town, so your first stop should be at the chamber of commerce at 1 Lakeside Drive. Here you can pick up a walking tour of Geneva's historical district or find directions on the quickest route to reach any supplies you might need.

Pulteney Square on South Main Street has a 19th century atmosphere. This is beside Hobart College for men, established in 1822; it's the oldest college in the state. Beside it is William Smith College for women, established in 1908.

Located at 543 South Main Street is the Prouty-Chew House. Charles Butler, a Geneva attorney, built this Federal-style home in 1829. The restored and period-refurnished house is also the Geneva Historical Society and Museum office. It's open Tuesday through Saturday from 1:30 to 4:30. The museum includes a costume collection dating from the 1700s and local area displays and exhibits.

Once in downtown Geneva, you can find nearly all city supplies near the lakefront. These include banks, restaurants, clothing and hardware stores, auto supplies, pharmacies, all sorts of shops, a post office, and grocery stores.

Cayuga Lake
Lock SEN #1 to Ithaca

Mile LKCAY-0.0 (SM) to Mile LKCAY-36.1 (SM)

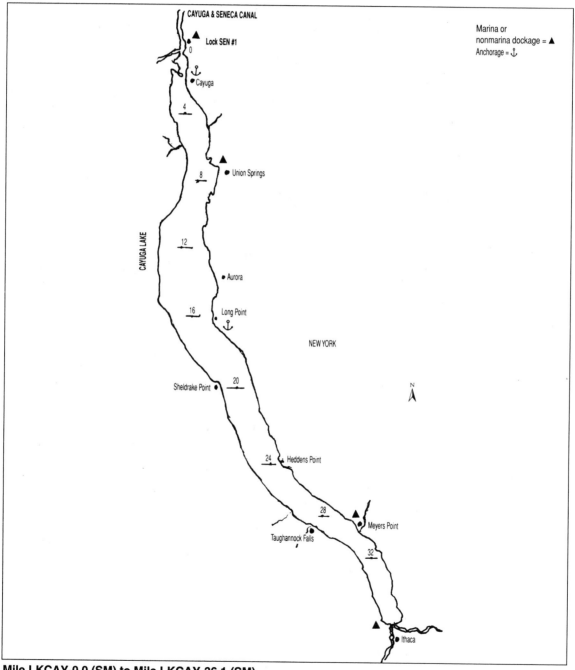

Mile LKCAY-0.0 (SM) to Mile LKCAY-36.1 (SM)

Cayuga Lake is 36.1 miles long, about 3 miles wide, and deep—at one point more than 400 feet. Lake mileage begins in the upper pool of Lock SEN #1 on the Cayuga and Seneca Canal at **Mile SEN-3.9 (SM).**

As you leave the lock, the canal widens at a junction. Your route is south—a westerly turn takes you to Seneca Lake. Ahead is a marshy island; your destination is to its east, where you enter Cayuga Lake's upper reaches. Mind the buoys in this upper lake basin; it's shoal outside the channel. At the basin's southern end is railroad bridge BR S-2, **Mile LKCAY-1.8 (SM);** to its south is open water.

The lake's lengthy, deepwater fetch produces unpleasant seas in northerly or southerly quadrant strong winds. If weather is making up and your draft is more than 5.5 feet, plan now for a secure place to stop at day's end. Once on the lake you are restricted for offlake protection until you reach Ithaca, 34 miles away. The lake's shores offer only a few prominent points with poor lees. Except for its northern and southern extremities, pleasant anchoring depths are only found very close to shore.

South of the bridge along the wooded eastern shoreline are the homes in Cayuga. The northern lakeshores are low; this is a vast agricultural area. As you make your way south, rolling forested hills appear and steadily increase in height as you approach the lake's southern reaches.

The Cayuga, Seneca, and Onondaga Indians, three Iroquois Confederacy nations, controlled the Finger Lakes region when early missionaries arrived. Most Finger Lake names—Seneca, Cayuga, Canandaigua, Keuka, Otisco, Owasco, Skaneateles, Honooye, Conesus, Hemlock, Canadice—reflect this Indian heritage.

The Iroquois—traditionally warlike tribes—had survived all French efforts to usurp their power. Throughout the colonial period their confederacy was a buffer between lands claimed by the French and the English. From 1755 to 1763 the French and the British were at war with one another; this finally resulted in British control of most of central New York.

During the American Revolution the Iroquois Confederacy tribes could never agree on whom to support; finally all but two nations sided with the British. This alliance eventually destroyed them. During the war George Washington ordered General John Sullivan and 2,500 men to take all territory in western and central New York and to destroy the Iroquois countryside. General James Clinton joined Sullivan; his detachment

came overland from Canajoharie on today's Erie Canal East. By the time this campaign was over, America had devastated all Indian villages east of Fort Niagara, including those in the Finger Lake area.

Few settlements are visible as you travel down the lake today. Union Springs, **Mile LKCAY-7.0 E (SM),** is in a slight eastern-shoreline indentation. From offshore you only notice a few homes dotting a rising wooded shoreline. Small Frontenac Island, the only natural lake island, is close to shore by the village. Hibiscus Point, the most northerly of two easterly reaching projecting points, is a mile north of the village.

Once you pass **Light Buoy #51A** at **Mile LKCAY-8.5 E (SM),** you are free of shoreline shoals until within about a mile of Ithaca. Just inland of the buoy is the site of Goi-o-gouen, the Cayuga Castle Capital of the Cayuga Indian nation, which extended nearly 4 miles eastward. In 1779 Lieutenant Colonel William Butler and a detachment of General Sullivan's army captured and then destroyed the castle and neighboring villages.

Near the eastern-shore village of Levanna, **Mile LKCAY-11.0 E (SM),** is a typical lake lighthouse. Aurora, **Mile LKCAY-13.5 E (SM),** is in a slight eastern lake curve—spot the town by the spire of a church and the half-demolished three-story stone building on the bluffy wooded shore. Originally this was a Cayuga village called Deawendote, "the Village of Constant Dawn," but like every Indian settlement in his path, Sullivan destroyed it. With the Indians gone, pioneers settled in. By 1817 they had the first steam-powered flour mill west of the Hudson River; it's still in town. In 1868 Henry Wells, creator of Wells Fargo and the American Express Companies, founded Aurora's Wells College for Women. Its 360-acre campus overlooks the lake.

In very settled weather you could anchor off near the old stone structure and make a short visit ashore. Landing is not particularly easy; don't end up trespassing in someone's front yard. Once ashore head for the church about a block up the hill; it's on the main street, along with the post office, library, and IGA supermarket.

Long Point, **Mile LKCAY-15.7 E (SM),** is a pronounced point about 2 miles south of Aurora. Wetting its feet at its easternmost projection is **Light #143,** a wire tower. In 1907 the lake steamer *Frontenac* burned and sank off the point.

By now the rolling hills on both sides of the lake are increasing in size. They are home to vast vineyards around inland winemaking centers. There are large wineries at Ovid and Interlaken high on the western hill and at King Ferry to the east. The Finger Lakes region ranks next to California in American wine production and is noted for its native New York strains of grapes—the principal source of kosher wines.

The retreating glaciers that formed the Finger Lakes increased valley slopes that terminated at the lake. Some of these consisted of layers of soft limestone and sandstone that in time eroded away. Taughannock Creek—Iroquois for "the Great Falls in the Woods"—is an example. Silt washing out the creek mouth eventually built Taughannock Point, **Mile LKCAY-28.0 W (SM).** The rushing creek created an impressive gorge, up to 400 feet deep, with 215-foot Taughannock Falls, one of the highest straight-drop American waterfalls. It's about a mile upstream of the creek's mouth.

There were large Iroquois villages on Taughannock Point by 1677. The Indians farmed beans, corn, and potatoes. They abandoned the settlements when General Sullivan came through on his razing frenzy. In 1797 Benjamin Goodwin and a group of settlers built a gristmill and distillery on the creek, and for a time the waterfall and point became Goodwins Falls and Point. Later residents built a paper mill, began a tobacco industry, which flourished, and developed an important lake port.

The Erie Canal ruined the shipping industry in 1828, but eventually the railroads helped the economy. Railroad owners built a station above the falls by the upper gorge at the rock quarries and then built a planing mill by the tracks. Large quantities of sandstone were shipped off to be used for New York City sidewalks.

Even in early days tourists discovered the spectacular Taughannock Gorge and waterfall. In 1860 entrepreneurs built spacious, luxurious hotels, Taughannock House and Cataract House, on the gorge's rim on opposite sides of the waterfall. Tourists arrived by steamboat and railroad. Today this area is the popular Taughannock Falls State Park, with maintained hiking trails through the forest and along the gorge. There's a launching ramp and an enclosed marina on the point, but depths are geared toward runabouts. In settled weather it's possible to anchor outside in the point's lee. With permission you can land the dinghy in the marina and then have a hike up the gorge trails.

Across the lake at the mouth of Salmon Creek, **Mile LKCAY-30.5 E (SM),** is Meyers Point, which extends nearly to midlake. For many years the town of Lansing was a leading producer of Finger Lakes salt. Some

mines are more than 2,000 feet deep, with tunnels running under the lake—often as much as two-thirds of the way across.

At Meyers Point the lake makes a slight southerly bend. At **Mile LKCAY-34.6 (SM)** you approach **Ithaca Front Light #146.** Ahead are two breakwaters, one with a red lighthouse, **Rear Light #148,** the other with a white light, **Light #147.** These watch the entrance to Ithaca Harbor's Cayuga Inlet. Extensive shoals lie north and west of the Rear Light and shoals extend north and east of **Light #147.** Between these shoals the depths hold between 9 and 12 feet. Once you make the slight easterly jog at **Light #147,** you are well inside the cut and depths increase slightly.

As you enter Cayuga Inlet the Allan H. Treman State Marine Park is to your west. The park was redeveloped for recreation in the 1960s from land that had been a squatters settlement, a railroad switch yard, and an old airport.

Ithaca is a city of pretty gorges and waterfalls. East over the eastern jetty is Fall Creek's mouth. From its source north of Dryden—off to the east—Fall Creek rushes downward into Beebe Lake, runs through the Cornell University campus, plunges more than 150 feet at Ithaca Falls, and finally drops down to Stewart Park on the lake.

Cascadilla Creek flows into Cayuga Inlet's western side about 0.5 mile south of the Marine Park marina's entrance. Easterly reaching Cascadilla Gorge nearly parallels Cornell's southern border.

Six Mile Creek, even farther south in the inlet, also flows in from the east. Beginning at Ithaca Commons there's an improved walk along this creek with a beautiful view of its gorges.

South of the Flood Control channel—the southern end of the Cayuga Inlet—is Buttermilk Creek. It has high cliffs, sculptured pools, meadows, and a series of 10 waterfalls through two gorges. Cayuga and Tutelo Indians inhabited the village of Coreorgonel that once was near Buttermilk Falls. They lived in log cabins while they cultivated fields and tended apple and plum orchards. A 200-man detachment of Sullivan's army burned the village.

The influx of Europeans began in 1788. They farmed land once owned by the Iroquois, built dams in the gorges, and operated gristmills. One dam built in 1872 supplied Ithaca with water until 1903. For a long time no official name was given to the settlement; inhabitants referred to it as the Pit, Forest City, Sodom, and Storm

Country. Eventually Simeon De Witt, New York's surveyor general, named it for its resemblance to a valley on Itaka Island in ancient Greece.

Ezra Cornell founded Cornell University in 1865; it was the first university in America to grant a Doctor of Veterinary Medicine degree. An important discovery made at the university, a technique for storing apples for long periods, greatly helped area apple orchard owners. Today's campus includes more than 14,000 acres; enrollment is nearly 13,000 students.

From 1912 to 1920 Ithaca's beautiful gorges brought the movie industry to town to produce films with lots of action, daring escapes, and breathless moments. For the 1916 film *Patria* a film company sent a trolley car off the Stewart Avenue Bridge into the gorge. Such noted stars as Francis X. Bushman, Pearl White, Irene Castle, and Lionel Barrymore came to Ithaca for filming.

Sketch Map Depths

Sketch map depths are given at normal average summer water level. For convenience in adjusting NOAA charts to chart datum for long anchorage approaches, use the following:

Mile LKCAY-0.0 (SM) to **Mile LKCAY-36.1 (SM):** Plane of reference, Cayuga Lake Normal Lake Level, 381.5 feet

---

CAYUGA ANCHORAGE

★★

NO FACILITIES

Chart: N 14786, page CS-4, *See A on sketch map, page 151*

Mile LKCAY-1.9 E (SM)

This anchorage is adequate if you want to wait temporarily for lake conditions south of the bridge to improve. If wind is strong northerlies, it's not recommended. The preferred tie-up in this situation is at Lock SEN #1 Upper, where you are out of a long wind sweep.

The anchorage is on the eastern lakeshore north of

railroad bridge BR S-2. As you approach the bridge southbound, watch for an eastern-shore upper range. Just south of it there may be two privately maintained buoys. At one time the buoys marked the channel into a commercial facility that lately has not been in operation. If the shoreside industry should start up, towboats and barges may become a threat and this is definitely not a recommended stop.

Anchor in mud and weeds east of the two buoys and a bit north of the shoreside facility.

HIBISCUS HARBOR

★★★★

Chart: N 14786, Page CS-1, *See B on sketch map, page 151*

Mile LKCAY-6.0 E (SM)

This well-protected marina—open April 15 to October 15—welcomes travelers. It's on the lake's eastern shore at about **Mile LKCAY-6.0 (SM).** At normal lake stage drafts more than 4.5 to 5 feet may not have depth, though water level varies seasonally and with wind tide. Bottom is rocky with some mud. The marina stands by on VHF 16 and will gladly give you an estimate on daily depths.

First find the marina on your chart. On the eastern lakeshore locate the first prominent westerly extending point about 4.5 miles south of the Cayuga Bridge; this is Hibiscus Point. Included on this point is a small basin. This is the marina.

Try to leave midlake about 0.5 mile south of light **Buoy #50** and **Buoy #51,** located about 3.4 miles south of the Cayuga Bridge; they are the southernmost navigation aids through the upper lake shallows.

There is fair depth as you leave midlake, but it shoals as you close the wooded shore. As you approach the point, you can see homes scattered along the waterfront on both sides of the marina's narrow entrance. Just west of the entrance, a red and a black stick mark the channel and help lead you through the shoreside shallows to

Cayuga Anchorage, Hibiscus Harbor, Long Point Anchorage, Lansing Town Park Marina

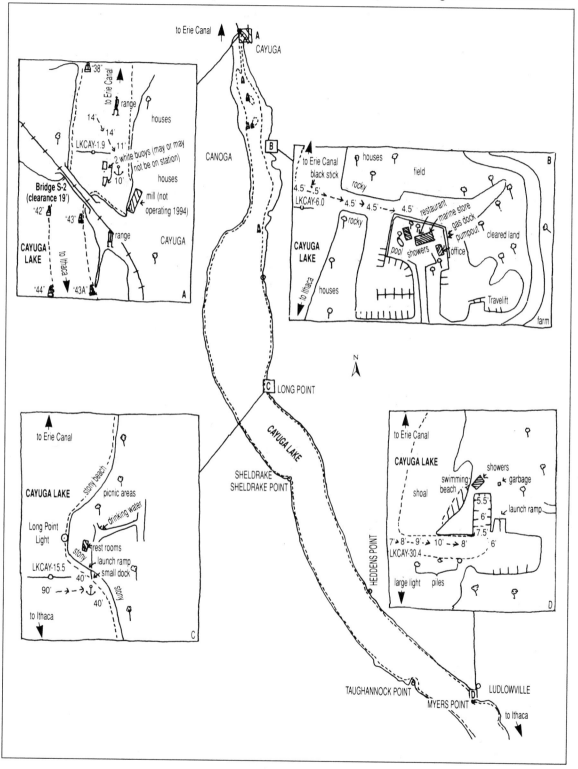

the entrance. Stay in the middle; bottom and banks are rocky. If no one answered on VHF, head for the fuel dock for assistance.

The marina has two basins, the old and new harbors. A mole with the marina facilities separates them. To reach the fuel dock (gas and diesel) come straight in the harbor. Immediately to your south you pass the channel into the new basin; there are slips on the mole side of this channel. Continue east, pass along the mole's northern end to its eastern end, then swing around the corner. The fuel dock is on the mole's eastern side. Dock personnel are usually waiting to handle lines.

The marina's 35-ton Travelift is in the old harbor. Before setting a haulout date, check to see if you have depth.

The marina, which can be reached at (318) 889-5086, is a pretty stop, with shade trees, lawns, flowers, and picnic tables. There's a swimming pool on the main mole's western side. The ship's store, at one end of the building, has a large selection of marine and navigation supplies, nautical clothing, and local charts. The marina restaurant/bar serves inside and on their deck; there's a band on weekends. Block and cube ice and electric hookups (110-volt/30-amp and 220-volt/50-amp) are available. If you need a diver, check at the office.

The marina says that Union Springs and shopping is about 0.5 mile away—it seemed five times that distance to us, so check at the office for their shortcut.

LONG POINT ANCHORAGE

★★★

Chart: N 14786, Page CS-1, *See C on sketch map, page 151*

Mile LKCAY-15.5 E (SM)

This is a fair-weather-only anchorage. Long Point does not offer protection for prolonged or strong winds out of the southerly, west, or northwest quadrants and only slight northerly protection; it's secure only in easterlies. The lake is now up to 400 feet deep and has a 12-mile fetch, so seas can run remarkably high in the

anchorage. If you do anchor and southerly weather starts to make up, you can find a little protection about 3 miles south on the western shore north of Sheldrake Point.

Anchorage at Long Point is on its southern side. To find slightly comfortable depths go in as close to shore as is safe. Anchor off a floating dock next to the launching ramp. This is a state park, and you are welcome to go ashore; land the dinghy at the dock's northern end out of the way. This is a popular fair-weather dock and picnic stop for runabouts. There are shade trees, lawns, a playground, picnic tables and grills, a water faucet, and rest rooms with showers.

LANSING TOWN PARK MARINA

★★★

Chart: N 14786, Page CS-1, *See D on sketch map, page 151*

Mile LKCAY-30.4 + E (SM)

This small eastern-shore off-lake marina is at Myers Point, which extends some distance west of the shoreline where the lake makes a pronounced southerly curve. It's watched by **Myers Point Light.**

Come south nearly as far as the light and then slow down; the marina entrance is a narrow cut a short distance north of the light, and it's difficult to spot. There's a marina on the point's southern side, but it does not take transients of any size, power or sail.

A good location mark is the park's long lakefront swimming beach whose southern limit begins at the park marina basin's northern entrance. It has no marker. The southern entrance is not watched either, nor does the land there extend westerly as far as on the northern side. However, there are three unmarked pilings that note the channel's southern side edge. The westernmost pile extends some distance west of the northern landmass. This is a very narrow channel and not exceptionally deep, so stay in the middle during your entry. Monitor your fathometer closely if you draw more than 6 feet. Silting due to high surf conditions changes entrance depths seasonally. Also be aware of your monthly lake level, as well as any wind tide that might have increased depths on that particular day. You want to get back out of the harbor when it is time to leave.

The marina is in two basins. If you continue straight east, you enter the first basin. This is open to the west, and it's a busy area due to the park launching ramp. You are better off once in the entrance to go into the northerly basin. It has slips around its perimeter. Depths of 6 feet need to take a slip at this basin's southern end; it shoals as you move north. Pick a slip, tie up, then walk off to find someone in charge.

This is not as easy as it sounds. The ramp area is usually busy but without an attendant. During the day there's nearly always a lifeguard on duty at the lakefront swimming beach; you can report in to him.

This compact little harbor is a popular stopover because of its guarded swimming beach and volleyball court. If a slip is available, you usually can make some sort of arrangements for a 110-volt electric hookup.

Supplies are up to 20 very long blocks away.

Allan H. Treman State Marine Park

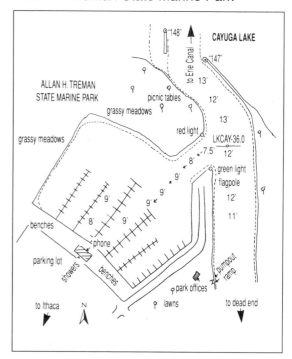

Allan H. Treman State Marine Park

ALLAN H. TREMAN STATE MARINE PARK

★★★★   5

Chart: N 14786, Page CS-1

Mile LKCAY-36.0 W (SM)

This large state marina—open May 15 to October 27—is on Cayuga Inlet's western side in an enclosed basin.

Slow down when you approach Ithaca's offshore **Front Light #146.** If seas are up out of the northerly quadrant it can be rough, and it's essential you judge any vessel drift until you are inside the inlet. About 1,700 feet ahead is the outer offshore breakwater **Rear Light #148** on the entrance's western side. The breakwater lies in a north-south direction. There are extensive shoals north and west of this light, and a direct course line between **Light #146** and **Light #148** brings you over bad water. There's a breakwater on the channel's eastern side with **Light #147** on its northwestern end. This breakwater extends from the inlet's eastern shore in a northwesterly direction, and it ends about opposite the western offshore breakwater's southern end. Shoals

extend north and east of the eastern breakwater. Between the two breakwater shoals, the channel depths hold between 9 and 12 feet. Once you make the easterly bend at **Light #147,** you are home free.

The marina's narrow entrance is just ahead on the west. If your draft is 6 feet or more be cautious, as entrance depth varies seasonally. Usually, you have about 7.5 feet. Once over the bar, basin depths increase. If your entry depth is critical, you might try to raise a local marina boat for updated entrance channel depths.

The basin's entrance is toward its southern end. There are six piers with slips extending from the southwestern bank. The transient area begins at the southerly entrance breakwall and extends all along the basin's southeastern bank. If the dockmaster is not around, find an empty spot to tie up temporarily, and walk to the office—it's in the nearby trees. The land line number is (607) 273-3440.

The coin-operated pumpout is outside the basin on the bulkhead on the inlet south of the marina entrance and just north of the launching ramp. Electric hookups (110-volt/30-amp and 220-volt/50-amp) are available.

The Marine Park has acres of manicured lawns, flowers, shade trees, picnic tables, and grills. Next door is the city swimming pool, tennis courts, ball fields, and the park paths—popular with roller skaters and bike riders.

It's a long way to grocery stores, but if you have an outboard you can dinghy up the main channel to a small canalside dock and walk about a block to small Pete's Grocery. For a supermarket or a visit downtown, you need to call a taxi, rent a car, or take the local bus. The bus stop is about 0.3 mile southeast down the road at the theater building at the park's entrance. If this is to be a crew change port, Tompkins County Airport is about 4 miles from downtown. It has major airline flights in and out.

At the entrance of adjoining Cass Park is Hangar Theatre. It has professional musicals, classics, and latest-hit productions May through September, Tuesday through Saturday. Call (607) 273-8588 for information.

Popular with visitors is Ithaca Commons, a three-block downtown pedestrian marketplace with modern shopping in a historical atmosphere. Storefronts have turn-of-the-century facades, and there are outdoor displays and sales, many trees and flowers, and an occasional entertainer. In this general area are hundreds of stores and unique little shops, restaurants, banks, hotels, a museum, a library, parks, and a post office. De Witt Park is a block up Cayuga Street; the blocks that surround it make up the De Witt Park Historical District. More than 50 buildings in this area represent Ithaca's changing architectural styles. One is the three-story 1821 restored Clinton House, a Greek Revival–style mansion, at Cayuga and Seneca streets. Nearby is the De Witt Historical Society, open Tuesday through Friday from 12:30 to 5 and Saturday 10 to 3.

Another popular attraction is the Cornell Plantations. It is spread over a large area on the university's eastern side, and you will need transportation. It includes the botanical garden and the arboretum, which specializes in shrubs and trees native to New York State. The Plantations are open from sunrise to sunset. A good way to see everything is to take its guided tour; call (607) 255-3020 for details.

On Saturdays from 9 to 2 and Sundays from 11 to 3 you can dinghy down to Steamboat Landing on Cayuga Inlet to Ithaca's farmers' market. If you are downtown on a Tuesday between 9 and 1, the market is in De Witt Park.

The three-day Ithaca Festival is held in June, with downtown festivities that include a parade, crafts, food, music, country dancing, and performances.

Seneca Lake
North End to Watkins Glen

Mile LKSEN-0.0 (SM) to Mile LKSEN-32.5 (SM)

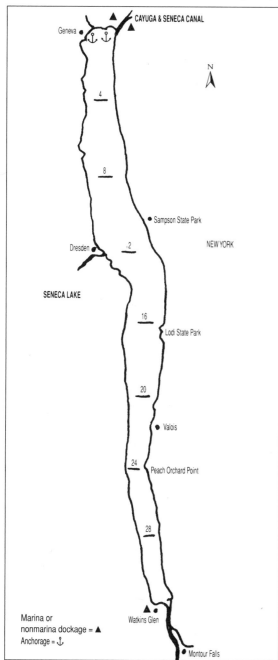

Mile LKSEN-0.0 (SM) to Mile LKSEN-32.5 (SM)

Seneca Lake is 32.5 miles long and 3 miles across at its widest. Water is clear and deep—in places more than 600 feet—and fed by natural springs. Mileage for the lake begins at the breakwater at the southwestern terminus of the Cayuga and Seneca Canal at the lake's northern end.

If wind is strong out of the northerly or southerly quadrant, the resultant long fetch can produce unpleasant seas. Choose your traveling weather with care; the lake has no deepwater off-lake harbors or inlets. Similar to Cayuga Lake, the silt deposits at stream mouths have built up small headlands, but they offer almost no protection. The western shore's Long Point, 14 miles south, is the lake's only major point; it offers little lee. To wait out bad weather, you have full protection only inside the Cayuga and Seneca Canal's southwestern end or behind the breakwater at Watkins Glen, 32.5 miles south.

Once you are clear of the canal mouth shoals and reach **Light #135** and **Light #136** offshore, have a look around. North is part of Seneca Lake State Park, which extends west from the breakwater for 1.8 miles to Geneva's outskirts.

During the early 18th century warring Indians kept white settlers clear of the lake's northern end. The original Geneva townsite included the Iroquois village of Kanadesaga. During the French and Indian Wars, Sir William Johnson built the village a log fort and 50 longhouses; he hoped for a British-Iroquois alliance. The Indians were unimpressed until 1779, when General Sullivan's army arrived and destroyed everything in sight.

With the Indians removed, Revolutionary War veterans moved in on their government land grants. West of town was the lime-rich spring that had attracted the Indians. The settlers put in Geneva's first water system, using hollow logs as the pipes.

Many early residents had arrived by water from the south by traveling up the Susquehanna River, then into its northerly running tributaries. For years the settlers floated grain and regional produce on the same water route back south.

By the early 1800s Geneva had become a wealthy community filled with palatial homes. Many of these Greek Revival and Federal-style buildings still overlook the lake. Today Geneva claims its South Main Street of century-old trees and homes is "the most beautiful street in America."

Look to the lake's eastern shore by offshore **Light #135.** That elegant 1839 Greek Revival mansion overlooking the lake is Rose Hill, built by General William Strong, a Geneva banker and New York City wool broker. Rose Hill reflects the prosperity of Geneva's general population in the 1840s. The mansion is open to the public from May 1 to October 1.

Villages are sparse along Seneca Lake's shores. As you travel down lake your vista is primarily of wooded, rolling hills that steadily increase in size. Though you can't see them, miles of vineyards cover the hilltops.

Kashong Point, **Mile LKSEN-7.0 W (SM),** is the lake's first small point. On the eastern shore is the western boundary of 1,741-acre Sampson State Park, **Mile LKSEN-10.5 E (SM).** This was the World War II site of the Sampson Naval Training Station, and later an Air Force training area.

Western shore Dresden's landmarks are four large smokestacks at the power plant on the town's southern outskirts. On the lake's shore is the U.S. Naval Underwater Systems Center. At least one large navy barge is usually moored well out in the lake. Just offshore of the center's buildings are pilings, buoys, and assorted floats. If coming past at night keep well offshore; large obstructions are lighted, but not all little floating objects wink.

The Keuka Lake Outlet's mouth is at Dresden. Between 1833 and 1877 the Crooked Lake Canal ran to Y-shaped Keuka Lake, 5 miles west. Today the abandoned canal is the 6-mile Outlet Trail, a Yates County linear park and a historic treasure, well used by hikers and bicyclists. Penn Yan boats, "the official boat of the Finger Lakes," have been built for 65 years in Penn Yan, the county seat.

As you approach western-shore Long Point, watch for another moored navy offshore barge.

Lodi Point State Park at Lodi Landing, **Mile LKSEN-17.0 E (SM),** is at another small eastern-shore projecting point. The park has a 22-slip marina, primarily for runabouts, and a large ramp. If weather is fair,

Rose Hill Mansion, 1839 Greek Revival restoration, Geneva, New York.
(Photo courtesy Rose Hill Mansion)

you can anchor off—you need to be very close to shore for decent depths—and visit the park. Tie the dinghy by the ramp. There are tables and grills, rest rooms, and drinking water.

At Valois, **Mile LKSEN-22.5 E (SM),** the lake is only about a mile wide. Shores are steep and wooded and there are a few visible homes. At Peach Orchard Point Light, **Mile LKSEN-25.0 (SM),** the town of Hector sits just back from shore. In 1818 a temperance society was founded there. Since it was unlikely that a policy of total abstinence as a cure for drinking would succeed in the local winemaking society, they omitted beer and wine from their list of prohibited intoxicants.

This is productive vineyard country with award-winning wineries. If you rent a car in Watkins Glen and enjoy winery tours, include those at Hector and Lodi and the Glenora Wine Cellars and Castel Grisch Winery just north of Watkins Glen on the western shore.

A few miles north of Watkins Glen on the eastern shore is another slight point; this is the mouth of Hector Falls Creek and its three waterfalls.

At the lake's southern end is Watkins Glen. Three stone breakwaters, all very large and high, partially protect the harbor. The offshore lighthouse is east of the

The New York Wine Region

Western New York lays claim to one of the finest wine-growing regions in the United States. In fact, New York boasts three distinctly different varieties of wine grape: the native American labruscas, fruity and hearty; the classic European viniferas, including chardonnay, gewurztraminer, and riesling; and hybrids of the two, developed to produce wines that could withstand New World climes.

Europeans initially looked down their noses at American wines, finding that labruscans tasted too much of the grape—a tendency known as "foxiness" among connoisseurs. Attempts to grow viniferas failed miserably; the plants withered and died. Vintners had to make do with various cross-bred types, some of which produce wines rivaling their European counterparts in body and flavor: cayuga, melody, seyval blanc, verdelet.

Doctor Konstantin Frank changed that in the early 1950s. His research determined that the villain in vine deterioration was phylloxera, a microscopic plant louse native to the New World. Frank's solution: grafting native American root stock to the European vines. The resistant plants thrived, and the rest was wine history.

We recommend picking up one of the many books on wine epicureanism available. Two excellent ones: Jan Aaron's *Wine Routes of America* (1989, E. P. Dutton, New York) and Tom Dial's *The Wines of New York* (1986, North Country Books).

The Finger Lakes and Cayuga Lake are home to nearly 50 wineries, many with other added attractions for nondrinking family members: picnic areas, hay rides, displays, and a variety of activities. You'll be able to visit and view wineries in operation, sample some of the best wines in the world, and learn first-hand the fascinating and complex process of winemaking. A sampling:

Fox Run Vineyards, 670 Route 14, Penn Yan. Eight miles south of Geneva. Open May through November, Monday through Saturday from 10 to 6. Tank room and tasting room.

Anthony Road Wine Company, 1225 Anthony Road, Penn Yan. Ten miles south of Geneva on Route 14. Wine tastings and tours.

Lakewood Vineyards, 4024 State Route 14, Watkins Glen. Four miles south of Watkins Glen. Open April through November, Monday through Thursday from 10 to 5:30 and Sunday from 12 to 6. Tours and tastings.

Rolling Vineyards, Route 414, Hector. Several miles north of Watkins Glen. Several varieties of grape, including viniferas, hybrids, and labruscans. Open April through October, Monday through Saturday from 10 to 5 and Sunday from 12 to 5. Tours and tastings.

Six Mile Creek Vineyard, Route 79 East, Ithaca. Open May through December, 12 to 5:30 daily.

easternmost offshore breakwater. The eastern end of this breakwater and the offshore light are your leading marks for entering the Seneca Canal, which leads to Montour Falls. If your overhead clearance is more than 18 feet, you can't get in. The fixed Highway 414 Bridge crosses the canal just inside the two land points.

Long before the white man came to this area, Indians inhabited the natural fortifications in the gorge that is now Watkins Glen State Park. It's the area of the Iroquois' death drums, subsurface earth rumblings said to be supernatural war drums. Some scientists say the groans come from the salt beds riddling the area; others say it's the popping of natural gas released from rock rifts on the lake's bottom.

European settlement began in 1791. In 1852 the town became Watkins, in honor of its early promoter, Samuel Watkins. It became Watkins Glen when outsiders discovered its lovely gorge. In 1863 this 763-acre glen became one of the first Finger Lakes State Parks, touted as one of America's prettiest natural wonders.

Early Watkins Glen was one of New York's major salt producers—for years salt-well derricks dotted the hillsides. Water was pumped into the mines, some of which were more than 1,800 feet deep, to bring brine to the surface. The salt was extracted by evaporation. In the 1940s the Watkins Glen Salt Plant had an output of 170,000 tons a year—mostly table salt.

Salt is still a leading area industry, but Watkins Glen is probably more famous today as the home of American road racing. Races are no longer held on the village streets; now they're at the Watkins Glen International Racing Circuit. The Watkins Glen Grand Prix, the international sports car race, has long been a favorite of racing fans.

The Seneca Canal, nearly 2.5 miles in length, is navigable through Bad Indian Swamp and the Queen Catherine Marsh Wildlife Management Area to Montour Falls. This village is on the site of Catherine's Town, once ruled by Queen Catherine Montour of the Iroquois Nation. Catherine is said to have been the granddaughter of Count Frontenac, the French Governor of Canada.

Seven glens and beautiful cascades still surround Montour Falls. Chequagua Falls, at the head of Main Street, is 165 feet high. Louis Phillipe—later to be Louis XVII of France—visited the site and was so impressed by the fall's grandeur he made a sketch of it that now hangs in the Louvre.

Around the falls is the Historic T, a group of 1850

buildings that includes the Governor Hill Museum and Governor's Hall of Fame, two historical museums, the Old Brick Tavern, and the Lee School Museum. The town is also home of the New York State Academy of Fire Sciences, built in 1858; it's still the training center for New York State firefighters.

After the first Erie Canal's great success, New York State ordered surveys for canals and feeder routes to expand water traffic over the state and the northeast. One of these, the Chemung Canal, was constructed in 1833 with 53 timber locks. It ran from Seneca Lake's southern end to Elmira, about 16 miles south. The state also built the navigable feeder canal that year. It ran to Corning, where there was access by railroad to the Pennsylvania coal fields at Blossburg. In time the Junction Canal crossed the Pennsylvania border to connect the Chemung with the North Branch. This in turn gave canalboat access to Pittsburgh, Philadelphia, and the Chesapeake Bay. Railroads eventually became too much competition, and by 1878 the Chemung, like many other early American canals, was closed to traffic.

Sketch Map Depths

Sketch map depths are given at normal average summer lake level. When you venture outside the sketch map confines, you must adjust the NOAA chart to chart datum. For convenience in adjusting, use the following:

Mile LKSEN-0.0 (SM) to **Mile LKSEN-32.5 (SM):** Plane of reference, Seneca Lake Normal Lake Level, 445.0 feet

---

THE VILLAGE MARINA

★★★★★

Chart: N 14786, Page CS-1, *See sketch map, page 159*

Mile LKSEN-32.5 (SM)

The harbor of Watkins Glen is at the lake's southern end. It's protected by three offshore white stone breakwaters that nearly parallel shore. The yacht harbor is

The Village Marina

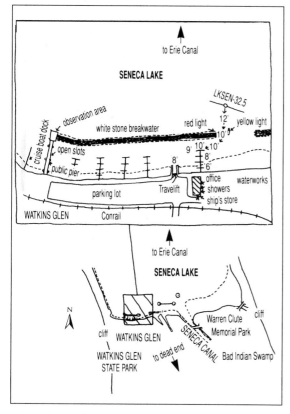

behind the westernmost of the three.

Use your fathometer during entry; lake water is exceptionally clear and the bottom looks unpleasantly close. Make your approach north of all three breakwaters; there are shoals south of the eastern and middle breakwaters. To enter the yacht harbor, keep between the red light on the eastern end of the westernmost breakwater and a post with a yellow light. This post is between the western and middle breakwaters but closer

to the westernmost. Once south of the red light, the harbor appears. Its western end is open for flushing but not navigable to the lake; it's blocked by a low-level walkway leading to an observation area on the breakwater's western end. West of the walkway are cruise-boat docks.

The marina has five finger piers extending north from shore; each has slips. For service pull in to the T-pier in front of the office building at the complex's eastern end. The marina has a Travelift and 110-volt electric hookups, and both gas and diesel fuel are available. If you need repairs, check at the office.

The ship's store has a collection of marine hardware and supplies, nautical clothing, gifts, and a few basic groceries. Call (607) 535-7910 for information.

The village is very convenient. Walk across the dirt parking lot, south of the slips and winter storage cradles, cross the railroad tracks, and make a right to North Franklin Street. Take time to look at the street signs; a Watkins Glen race car tops each one.

You are now on Watkins Glen's main street. There are banks, restaurants, a pharmacy, antiques, office supply, and all sorts of other shops, a bowling alley, a Radio Shack, and a post office. The Acme supermarket is about a mile up the street.

Watkins Glen State Park is in the center of town. Plan your visit so you can walk along the gorge and enjoy the waterfalls, but return at dusk to enjoy Timespell, a sound and laser light show within the gorge. The chamber of commerce is across the street, so stop in for directions, brochures, and maps.

From June to September, world-class motorsports events are held at the Watkins Glen International race track. The course is outside town, but taxis and rental cars are available.

Region 3
THE UPPER NIAGARA RIVER, EAST END
LAKE ERIE, AND THE WELLAND CANAL

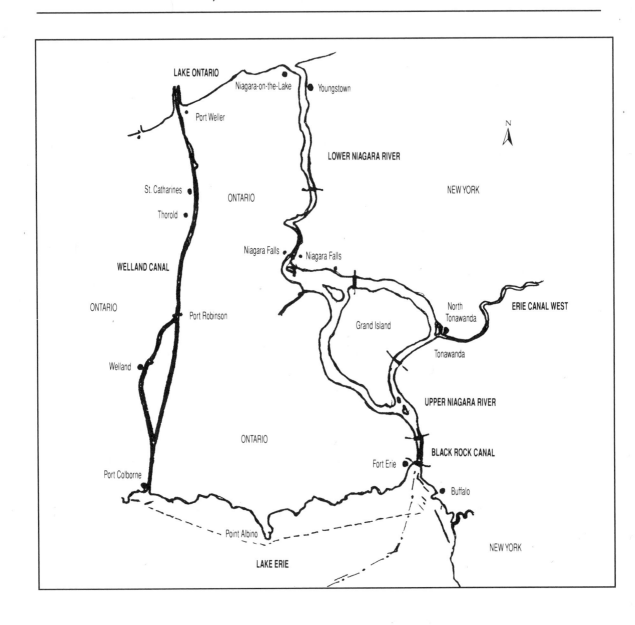

Mile UNR/LE-0.0 (NM) to Mile UNR/LE-29.3 (NM) and Mile WEL-23.4 (NM) to Mile WEL-0.0 (NM)

CURRENT DIRECTION AND SPEED		
Place	*Direction*	*Speed in mph**
Mile UNR/LE-0.0 (NM) to **UNR/LE-7.5 (NM)**	North	1.0 to 4.5
Mile UNR/LE-7.5 (NM) to **UNR/LE-11.2 (NM)**	North	About 0.15
East End Lake Erie (near Niagara River entrance)	Northeast	About 1.0
Welland Canal	North	Minimal

*In normal river, lake, and canal stage

MOVABLE BRIDGES, NORTH TONAWANDA TO BUFFALO			
Name	*Type*	*Mile*	*Clearance (Closed)**
International	Swing	**UNR/LE-7.7 (NM)**	17.0 feet
Ferry Street	Bascule	**UNR/LE-8.8 (NM)**	17.3 feet**

*At normal Black Rock Canal level

**Clearance 17.3 feet for width of 86 feet from pivot pier, from there decreasing to 12.3 feet at the western abutment.

Both bridges monitor VHF 16/12. International Bridge often has no radio and uses loudspeaker. Horn Signals: International Bridge, 1 Long; Ferry Street Bridge, 1 Long 2 Short. Northbound vessels have right-of-way.

The Upper Niagara River and East End Lake Erie
North Tonawanda to Port Colborne Breakwater

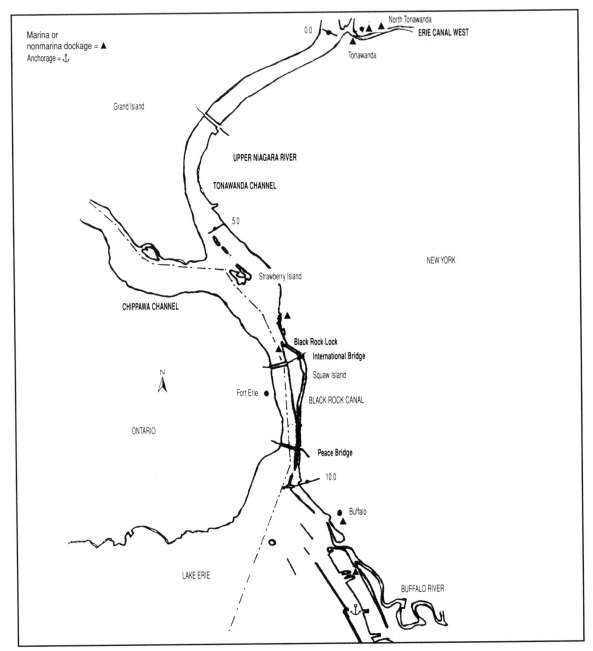

North Tonawanda to Buffalo, Mile UNR/LE-0.0 (NM) to Mile UNR/LE-10.8 (NM)

> *Rivers are roads which move, and which carry us whither we desire to go.*
>
> PASCAL, *Pensées*, 1670

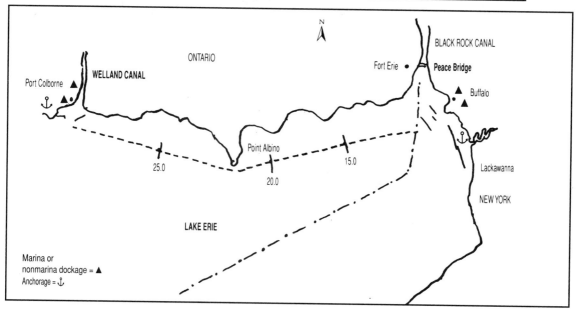

Buffalo to Port Colborne, Mile UNR/LE-10.8 (NM) to Mile UNR/LE-29.3 (NM)

This regional section and its mile numbering system begin on the Niagara River at North Tonawanda—the Erie Canal West's western terminus—and extends to Port Colborne on the north-northeastern shore of Lake Erie—the Welland Canal's southern end.

The Niagara River, outlet of Lake Erie, is a strait that flows into Lake Ontario. The American Fall and the Horseshoe Fall, which together make up Niagara Falls, divide the river into the Upper and Lower Niagara rivers. There's no navigable river route between Lakes Erie and Ontario; they are only accessible in this area by transiting the Welland Canal.

The head of the Niagara River—at Buffalo and Fort Erie—is about 20 miles upstream of Niagara Falls. Five miles north of the two cities, the upper river divides into two channels at Strawberry Island. East of Strawberry and Grand islands is the Tonawanda Channel; it's on

this channel you begin your journey south. The river is never more than a mile wide—usually far less—with a depth of about 21 feet.

The Upper Niagara River has other channels; the Niagara River Channel, a northwestern continuation of the Tonawanda Channel, extends downstream from Tonawanda Island to the city of Niagara Falls; the Chippawa Channel routes downstream west of Strawberry and Grand islands. At the northern end of Grand and Navy islands these two channels meet—off Chippawa, on the Welland River's southern shore—the 1800s upstream outlet of Canada's first Welland Canal. The International Boundary follows midriver from its head via the Chippawa Channel, and from there to Lake Ontario.

Grand and Navy islands are about the end of Upper Niagara River navigation; 3.5 miles to their north are the rapids and falls. This is an extremely dangerous area for pleasure boating; it's not recommended you navigate downstream of the Erie Canal West's junction.

The Upper River descends only about 10 feet from Lake Erie to the upper Niagara Rapids—about 2 miles upstream of Goat Island. Here the river's descent increases through the rapids, over the falls, and down the lower rapids to Lake Ontario—a fall of about 316 feet.

Glacial ice recession created the falls. The land rose behind the receding ice and formed the Niagara Escarpment. The melting ice sheet created the lake we now call Erie, which eventually overflowed near Lewiston, 7 miles downstream of today's falls. The lake water falling over the truncated edge of the escarpment's dolomite formation—into what is now Lake Ontario—eroded the soft shale and sandstone at the base of the falls and began breaking off the overhanging ledge. The falls began moving south, forming the gorge and the whirlpool, and ended about midway between the two lakes. Unless stopped by man, the falls eventually will reach Lake Erie and disappear into a collection of rapids.

The first European credited with exploring Lake Ontario and describing Niagara Falls was Samuel de Champlain, in 1604. Seventy-four years later René-Robert Cavelier de La Salle built the first Niagara Frontier forts and brought in shipbuilders to build 60-ton *Griffon*, the first vessel to sail the upper Great Lakes. This site is on Cayuga Island, about 5.5 miles downstream of **Mile UNR/LE-0.0 (NM).**

The French established the first permanent, 7-mile "carry" around the falls and built two forts to guard the upper portage. When the British occupied the area in 1759, they renamed one of them Fort Schlosser. Part of the fort still stands on the Carborundum Company grounds at Niagara Falls.

Current on the Upper Niagara River depends on water stage; Tonawanda Channel's normal current varies from 1 to 4.5 mph. Southbound you have this against you for 8.2 miles to the Black Rock Canal's northern entrance. This canal bypasses much more main river current in the remaining distance to Lake Erie. It's especially severe between the northern end of Squaw Island, **Mile UNR/LE-7.0 (NM),** and the Peace Bridge, **Mile UNR/LE-9.35 (NM).** In this area the river topography changes to a narrow, shallow gorge where current can be up to 8 mph in normal river stage. South of the Peace Bridge to Lake Erie, the shallow, rocky river widens and current averages about 3 mph.

If you have been traveling the Erie Canal West, you exit into the Niagara River south of industrialized Tonawanda Island, **Mile UNR/LE-0.0 (NM).** North and east of the island is the industrial waterfront of North Tonawanda, which is crossed by two bridges.

Once clear of **Buoy #1** south of the island, you enter Tonawanda Channel at **Buoys #37** and **#38.** Bear south upstream; a northerly turn at this point takes you downstream to Niagara Falls. Your upbound speed is now dramatically reduced, with current most severe in midchannel in midriver. Since the Grand Island shore is an outer bend, always the place on fast-flowing rivers most susceptible to increased current, hold close to the south-southeastern shore while carefully watching the fathometer.

To your southeast is Tonawanda's waterfront, with a collection of homes and parks. It was a French trading center from the 1600s until the British took control in 1759; they had to give it up to the Americans 37 years later. Tonawanda's last conflict came during the War of 1812, when the British burned it along with Buffalo and Black Rock.

The 17,381-acre Grand Island has no land more than 30 feet above the river. Its settlement began in 1823 when the Erie Canal construction laborers arrived. Later, lumber companies shipped white oak from the island's great stands by canalboat to New York City; it was prime shipbuilding material. Steam sawmills and piers lined the island and the Tonawanda shoreline. The lumber trade flourished nearly to the 20th century, until the mills ran out of trees and industry migrated off the island. Owners sold off land for farms and home sites, many of which still dot the shoreline.

In mid-island is Fantasy Island, a large amusement park.

As you close Grand Island's southern end, you no longer have most of the river for navigation; extensive shoals extend north, west, and south of Motor Island and large, U-shaped Strawberry Island. The watched channel hugs the eastern shoreline, and in midriver current steadily increases. This is the river's division point; the Chippawa Channel bears west and then northwest around Grand Island.

Grand Island's southern end is 1,081-acre Beaver Island State Park, which has a marina. If you plan a visit, take care where you depart from the main channel. The combination of rocky shoals and very swift current means you could go aground and never get off again.

At light **Buoy #1,** about a mile south of the Niagara-Mohawk Power Plant, **Mile UNR/LE-5.0 E (NM),** you begin your approach to the Black Rock Canal and Lock, the old site of Black Rock. The lock is not visible until you make the southeasterly bend, though you can see its long western lock approach. No matter the river stage, swift currents, boils, and eddies are immediately west of this wall; do not wander off into the main river here. Hold to the channel along the eastern shore. Once south of the western approach wall, you have no more current until in the lock's upper pool.

Before Buffalo had any sort of breakwater system, Black Rock had the only natural harbor at Lake Erie's eastern end. It was a shipbuilding center for the upper lakes. Black Rock shipyards built gunboats and brigs used by the American navy in the War of 1812. In 1819 its shipyard launched the first Lake Erie commercial steamboat, *Walk-on-the-Water.*

Black Rock also became Buffalo's chief rival as a trading center. This rivalry reached its peak during the search for a western terminus for the proposed first Erie Canal. Black Rock had the best natural harbor; however, Buffalo built a new breakwater that could withstand the spring freshets, and won the prize. In time, fast-growing Buffalo absorbed Black Rock.

Today's 3.5-mile-long Black Rock Canal takes you along Buffalo's waterfront. At the canal's downstream (southern) end, wooded Squaw Island separates you from the river. Here, in 1679, La Salle's ship, *Griffon,* was towed through the main river rapids and sailed off on her maiden voyage. Bird Island Pier breakwater—seasonally awash—begins at Squaw Island's southern end and extends to the canal's upper end, **Mile UNR/LE-10.6 (NM).**

Flag-adorned, high-level Peace Bridge, **Mile UNR/LE-9.35 (NM),** crosses to Fort Erie. The two nations chose its name to commemorate over a hundred years of Niagara Frontier peace.

Across the river is old Fort Erie on the city of Fort Erie's southern outskirts. The fort was built in 1764 as an outpost following the French and Indian Wars. Loyalists and a group of Butler's Rangers settled there after the American Revolution and by 1804 began to rebuild the British fort. It had been destroyed twice—first by a flood and ice and then by a storm. They hadn't finished it when war was declared in 1812.

At the start of the War of 1812 American Lt. Jesse D. Elliot set out from Buffalo at three in the morning with 100 men in two boats and rowed across the river. They boarded and captured two British ships, the *Caledonia* and the *Detroit;* no shots were fired. Returning home with their prizes, they ran the *Detroit* aground. Unable to get off, they destroyed the ship. They did manage to get the *Caledonia* to Buffalo; it became the American Lake Erie Fleet's first ship. The irritated British retaliated and nearly destroyed Black Rock and Buffalo. Both villages rebuilt, but later the British burned them again along with Fort Schlosser and Tonawanda.

The British repeatedly attacked Buffalo. After the Battle of Cook's Mills, the Americans realized they could never evict the British from the Niagara area. General George Izard ordered Fort Erie destroyed, and the Americans retreated across the river.

Your first glance at Buffalo's waterfront appears to be a mass of breakwaters. The harbor extends from the Black Rock Canal to Lackawanna, about 4.5 miles south; it also includes the winding, commercialized Buffalo River. The Outer Harbor's main breakwater primarily shelters industrial areas—eastern Lake Erie is subject to strong southwesterly storms. The tall smoke-

Black Rock Lock

Black Rock Lock, at **Mile UNR/LE-7-5 (NM),** has a lift of 5.2 feet. Operating hours (which may vary annually) are: March 23 through June 14, 0600 to 2300; June 15 through September 6, 24 hours; September 7 through November 30, 0600 to 2300. Daily lockages are: downbound (northbound) on the hour; upbound (southbound) on the half hour. The lock furnishes lines. The signal to transit is 2 long and 2 short blasts, and the land line number is (716) 876-5454.

The first thing you see in the lock's upper pool is the low-level swing section of the International Bridge to Canada. This can be a frustrating encounter. The bridge over the canal is only a small portion of the whole, and if a train is anywhere on the bridge, all-clear signals do not switch at the swing span. Since locomotive engineers generally creep their trains across the river, your wait can be a very lengthy one.

The Black Rock Lock and Canal retain the pool from the south; they keep it at the same elevation as the water surface of Lake Erie. In normal lake conditions the canal has only a slight current flowing north.

Border Crossing Do's and Don'ts

Crossing from the United States to Canada and back may be the easiest international exchange in the world. Just follow these simple rules.

Be Informed

You can get information on U.S. Customs procedures by calling your nearest customs office and asking for the pamphlet entitled "Know Before You Go"; it's a handy compendium of the most up-to-date information on U.S. Customs requirements. For Canadian Customs information, get the pamphlet "Canada: Travel Information" at any U.S. Customs office or Canadian consulate; or call (800) 387-1510 for information on Canadian Customs.

Be Prepared

Have all registration, documentation, and citizenship papers in order and accessible before you go, and be sure your decal is up to date. U.S. citizens should keep citizenship documentation, such as a birth certificate, on hand. Naturalized citizens, permanent residents, or aliens need a certificate of naturalization, alien registration card, or equal proof of status.

You'll have to pass customs inspection on your return to the United States. There's no duty or tariff placed on items you took with you to Canada, if purchased in the United States. However, it's smart to keep purchase receipts for your expensive belongings. You may have to prove that you legally purchased them prior to leaving on your voyage.

Follow Proper Landing Procedures

Make your first landing in Canada at a customs port or other official entry point. After tying up or anchoring, send *one* designated crewmember to the customs office with the vessel's documentation. All other crewmembers must remain aboard. If there isn't a local office, you can telephone toll-free, (800) 387-1510.

When checking in, you'll receive an official clearance number. Write this down in your log—you may be challenged on it later in Canada, and will need to provide it upon your return to the United States.

Reenter the United States at a designated entry port. Again, have your designated crewmember report to the customs officer on landing, while the rest of the crew stays aboard. If you can't dock at an entry port, call the office nearest you. You will need your documentation and registration information, as well as personal information on your crew. You'll be asked for your Canadian clearance number and your U.S. Customs decal number. The latter is issued by the U.S. government. Buy it on your first entry; there is a $25 annual fee.

Failure to report can result in fine, imprisonment, and possible confiscation of your boat. Each time you report to customs, you'll receive a release number. Note it in your log, along with the arrival date, time, and port of entry.

(*continued on next page*)

stacks of Bethlehem Steel at Lackawanna at the Outer Harbor's southern end make fine landmarks when you approach from the west. In bad weather offshore the 3.5-mile-long, 0.3-mile-wide Outer Harbor is a popular smooth-water pleasure boat area.

Buffalo has a well-watched North and South Entrance Channel and breakwaters with lighthouses. Your destination westbound dictates which entrance you use, but the North Entrance is the usual. This is also the ship entrance for vessels bound up the Buffalo River.

The Buffalo River entrance is watched on its southern side by **Buffalo Main Light**, which watched the first Erie Canal's western terminus. Early residents dubbed the old lighthouse "Chinaman's Light," not only for its pagodalike tower but also because the government used the tower to watch for illegal Chinese immigrants crossing from Canada. Originally built in 1818, it was one of the first on the Great Lakes. After the Erie Canal opened and water traffic increased dramatically, the tower's height and light intensity were

Observe Customs Restrictions

Canada has only minimal restrictions on articles brought in for private use. Clothes and personal items are duty-free. Smoking materials are limited to 200 cigarettes, 50 cigars, and up to 2 pounds of tobacco. Legal-age crewmembers can bring in 40 ounces of liquor or wine and four six-packs of 12-ounce cans of beer.

On return to the U.S., you won't be assessed duty on items you took with you. Declare all items you purchased while in Canada. An oral declaration usually suffices, unless you exceed your legal exemption amount, bring back more than a liter of alcoholic beverages, or purchase more than 200 cigarettes or 100 cigars. You're entitled to a $400 personal exemption when bringing goods into the U.S., subject to the limits on alcohol and cigarettes. You must remain in Canada for 48 hours for the exemption to apply, and it's good only once every 30 days.

There are also restrictions on certain food items such as citrus fruit, meat, and other perishable products. The customs service enforces the importation of agricultural products. Pets fall into the same inspection category—even if it's not your intent to eat the ship's cat.

increased twice. Its last renovation was in 1851.

Westbound to the lake you pass south of the offshore North Breakwater; its northern end is built over Horseshoe Reef's island. Next you approach the Outer Harbor breakwater. It has a break at its northern end; you pass south of the **North Side Light** on its short northern section. Your last offshore breakwater is West Breakwater, with white 71-foot **Buffalo Harbor Light** on its southern end.

Lake Erie, the last-discovered Great Lake, is the fourth largest and the shallowest—210 feet at its deepest. It's the only lake with a bed above sea level. Waters flowing from Lake Huron out the Detroit River, Lake St. Clair, and the St. Clair River feed the lake at its western end. The eastern lake level is extremely subject to wind tides and variations of barometric pressure during storms. Strong southwest and northeast winds produce a

Things to Do and See in Buffalo

Allentown. A restored historic area between Main, Edward, Cottage, Pennsylvania, and North streets. Shopping, restaurants, galleries, and antiques.

Buffalo and Erie Historical Society, 25 Nottingham Court. Features the history of the Niagara frontier, with frontier life and Pan-American Exposition exhibits. Open Tuesday through Saturday from 10 to 5 and Sunday from 12 to 5. Closed major holidays.

Buffalo Museum of Science, 1020 Humboldt Parkway. Exhibits of dinosaurs, Chinese jades, animals and birds of the northeast; observatory; discovery room for children. Open daily from 10 to 5, and until 10 on Fridays between September and May. Closed major holidays. Observatory hours: Fridays at dusk from October to May, with sun shows weekdays in July and August.

Naval and Servicemen's Park, 1 Naval Park Cove. Exhibits include the U.S.S. *The Sullivans*, the guided missile cruiser *Little Rock*, a submarine, and history of the services. Museum of naval history on shore. Open daily from 10 to 5, April through October or November; weekends 10 to 4. Closed December through March.

Roosevelt Inaugural National Historic Site, 641 Delaware Avenue; (716) 884-0095. In 1901, while in Buffalo visiting the Pan-American Exposition, President William McKinley was assassinated. His successor, Vice President Theodore Roosevelt, took the oath of office here. Restored in the late 1960s, the site now features exhibits, tours, and a Victorian garden. It's open Monday through Friday from 9 to 5 and weekends from 12 to 5. Closed major holidays, and Saturdays from January to March.

sizable sea that can be unpleasant. If poor weather is forecast, stay in port until wind and seas subside. It could be a fair wait; summer's strong prevailing wind is southwest.

When bound for Port Colborne and the Welland Canal from Buffalo, your departure point is from the red-and-white offshore Buffalo entrance bell. If it's a clear day—common in the Great Lakes—an excellent landmark on the way is the 83-foot white tower of Point Albino, **Mile UNR/LE-22.0 (NM),** on the Canadian shore 9 miles west. Keep clear of the shoals off the point; you don't want to end up like the 1,274-ton steam sidewheeler that grounded there in 1851.

Waterfront homes dot the wooded shoreline from Fort Erie to Point Albino. Albino Bay, in the point's lee, is often a Canadian and American pleasure boat weekend destination. After you change course at Point Albino you have another 8.7 miles to Port Colborne via **Light Buoy #EA2.** Port Colborne's large granaries inside the breakwaters and a single stack just east of the granaries are landmarks easily visible from well offshore. You may also see ship traffic as it plies in and out of the harbor; the Welland Canal is a very busy place for commerce.

Port Colborne, **Mile UNR/LE-29.3 (NM),** is protected by two breakwaters paralleling shore that enclose Gravelly Bay's western end. The wide, clear entrance is between **East Breakwater Light,** located at the eastern breakwater's western end, and **Inner Light** on the western breakwater's eastern end. The western breakwater also has a long southerly reaching extension that terminates at **Outer Light,** your landfall. This is the southern entrance to the Welland Canal (see "The Welland Canal," beginning on page 172).

HARBOUR PLACE MARINE

★★★

5

ALL FACILITIES

Chart: N 14832

Mile UNR/LE-7.0 E (NM)

This marina—open March 30 to November 20—is in an enclosed basin on the Niagara River's eastern shore

south of the junction of the Chippawa and Tonawanda channels. The basin parallels the river and is south of two Niagara-Mohawk Power Plant stacks and Strawberry Island, and about opposite **Light Buoy #1.** The entrance is toward the basin's northern end. Though there is strong main-river current west of the channel, there can be a slight entrance-area reverse current.

Slips line the marina's main perimeter, and there's one finger pier in the easterly extension. If no one answered on VHF 16, pull in to the fuel dock on the basin's eastern side immediately south of the easterly cut. The dock office is at the head of the ramp.

The main office is at the complex's southern end.

Harbour Place Marine

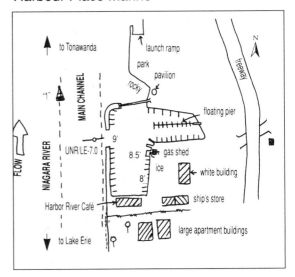

The ship's store has a fair selection of marine equipment, local charts, nautical clothing, and gifts. The Harbor River Café is also at this end of the harbor overlooking the river.

Cube ice, 110-volt/30-amp and 220-volt/50-amp electric hookups, and a 35-ton Travelift are available. If you need a diver, check at the office. The land line number is (716) 876-5944.

There's a taxi service, but town is convenient. Go under the freeway bridge and across the main street; there's a large pharmacy and a few shops. Another three blocks is the Kwik Check supermarket. Downtown Buffalo is about 4 miles south.

BLACK ROCK LOCK LOWER

★

Chart: N 14833

Mile UNR/LE-7.3 W (NM)

This stop is north of Black Rock Lock on the western approach wall on a slight east-west jog about midway

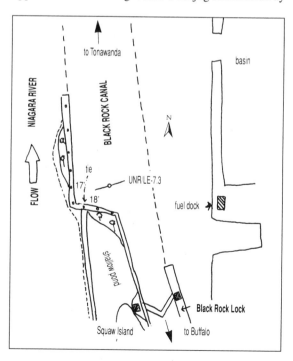

between the long wall's northern end and the lock. You cannot tie on the straight approach leading into the lock or at the approach wall's very northerly end—there's insufficient room for commercial traffic to pass.

Before considering a stop at Black Rock Lock Lower, contact the lockmaster for permission. Usually this is cheerfully granted, but you are not allowed access to lock grounds other than the approach wall's far northern end where you tie up.

If you can find an opening through the stunted trees along the western approach wall, you have an excellent view of the boisterous Niagara River.

ERIE BASIN MARINA

★★★★★

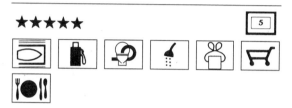

Chart: N 14833, *See sketch map, page 170*

Mile UNR/LE-10.8 E (NM)

This marina—open May 1 to October 15—is on the river's eastern shore in downtown Buffalo in enclosed Erie Basin. Southbound out of the Black Rock Canal continue straight ahead. The tall cement structure with a wide observation deck is on the basin's western entrance. This puts it just southeast of the white-based navigational red light on the point. The basin's eastern entrance is the Buffalo shoreline.

Erie Basin is about 0.5 mile long. On its eastern shore are a few harbor indentations faced with condominiums and private docks. On the mole to the west is the marina; its piers extend east. Landscaped lawns and parking lots face the slips. The road to the observation tower holds along the mole's western side. The lakeside mole face is lined with rock. During heavy southwesterly weather, seas roll in Buffalo Harbor, break along these rocks, and splash onto the street. This sea condition initiates a basin surge.

For fuel (gas and diesel) or a slip assignment pull in to the floating fuel dock immediately inside Erie Basin on the mole's eastern side. Dock attendants usually help you in. The office is at the top of the ramp in the obser-

Erie Basin Marina

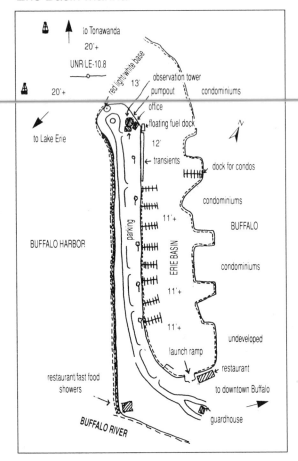

vation tower complex.

Transients are usually assigned a space paralleling the mole just south of the fuel dock. If room is available (it normally is) you can also be assigned a slip with a four-way tie on one of the main piers. The eastern-wall parallel parking is not recommended if onshore winds have been blowing for any extended time; the surge entering the basin causes an uncomfortable jerking of lines and scraping of fenders.

Block and cube ice and electric hookups (110-volt/30-amp and 110-volt/50-amp) are available. The land line number is (716) 842-4141.

The basin is a Buffalo showplace and promenade. There's a lot of daytime and early-evening automobile sightseeing traffic and many pedestrians strolling the marina bulkhead walkway. The lawns facing the slips are a favorite local picnic area.

Showers for the marina are west of the road near the basin's southern end. Using them is an involved process that is hardly worth the effort. Take a long walk to the entrance guard house, show I.D. and your slip rental agreement, and get a key; take another long walk back to the shower, another to return the key, and another back to the boat.

The office has a very limited selection of fishing supplies, snacks, film, drinks, postcards, and sun hats. If you need a few basic groceries, a Yellow Goose convenience store is in the large brick apartment building on the access road just outside the marina gate. Crawdaddy's Restaurant is at the basin's southern end, also just outside the gate.

Erie Basin is a good crew change port and a secure place to leave the boat for a tour of Buffalo. Taxis, car rentals, bus tours, an international airport, and hotels are available in the city.

Within walking distance and just outside the entrance is the Naval and Servicemen's Park extending along the Buffalo River's eastern side. It's a pretty walk with rose gardens and attractive landscaping.

RCR YACHTS

★★

NO FACILITIES

Chart: N 14833, *See sketch map, page 171*

Mile UNR/LE-11.2 + 0.8 (NM)

This large marina caters primarily to sailing vessels and has extremely limited dockage, but for canalbound sailboats it's a mast-stepping yard. It's on the Buffalo Ship Canal, a Buffalo River offshoot. You can easily spot the river's southern entrance by the 76-foot **Buffalo Main Light** with its pagodalike top. If a laker or saltie is inbound or outbound on the river, wait until she's passed. This is a narrow, shoal river for large ships; they can neither stop nor change course once committed to the channel.

At the river entrance you pass the northern-shore Naval and Servicemen's Park. Once the river makes its bend back south, you can see that the channel divides. Take the western Buffalo Ship Canal, a mile-long, deep-water, dead-end cut.

On the canal's eastern shore are the immense

RCR Yachts

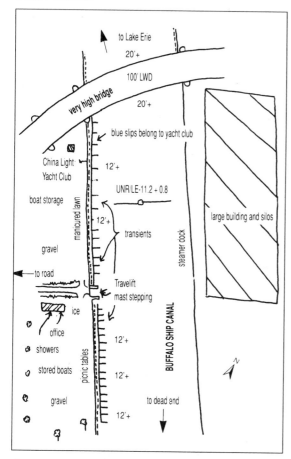

General Mills and Pillsbury grain elevators; on the western shore south of the Skyway Bridge (clear height 100 feet) is the marina and yacht club.

Slips are perpendicular to the bank. Midway down the line are the Travelift fingers at the foot of a road; at the top of the ramp is the office area. If the lift is not in use, let a crewman ashore on one of its fingers to walk to the office for information on mast stepping or a possible spot to spend the night.

The slips face a manicured lawn. West of this is a gravel lot for parking and winter boat storage. A yacht club's slips near the bridge are blue.

OUTER HARBOR ANCHORAGE

NO FACILITIES

Chart: N 14833

Mile UNR/LE-11.2 + 1.2 (NM)

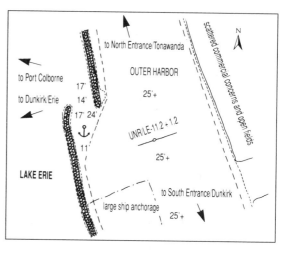

This anchorage is east of the Outer Harbor breakwater. Take your departure when midway between the Buffalo River's south entrance and the main harbor's **North Entrance South Side Light.** Bear southeast, which puts you on the breakwater's eastern side and in Outer Harbor. After about 1.4 miles, you reach the break between the Outer Harbor's two main breakwaters. Preferred anchorage is fairly near the break—north of the charted anchorage area. Ships seldom anchor in this designated spot; if they do, they won't close the break since it's too shallow and narrow for their passage.

You haven't much of a view here. East is an open area with a few industrial facilities; you can't see over the breakwater unless you have a sailboat and climb to the top of the mast. You can look through the break, however, and get some idea of the size of the seas running. If they are breaking high on the rocks, Lake Erie is going to be rough.

Perch and bluegill fishing is good along the breakwater rocks, though it's as pleasant touring the rocks with a skiff and viewing the underwater life. Since the invasion of the zebra mussels, the water in Lake Erie's northeastern end has turned crystal clear. Whether the lake is rough or not, the breakwater's eastern side is always a very popular fishing spot for the runabout fleet.

The Welland Canal
Port Colborne Breakwater to Lake Ontario

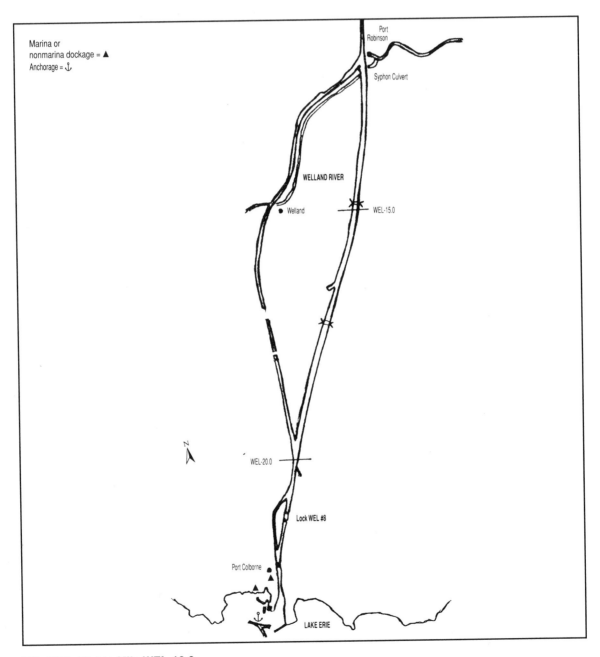

Marina or
nonmarina dockage = ▲
Anchorage = ⚓

Port Robinson

Syphon Culvert

WELLAND RIVER

● Welland

WEL-15.0

WEL-20.0

Lock WEL #8

Port Colborne

LAKE ERIE

Mile WEL-23.4 to Mile WEL-10.3

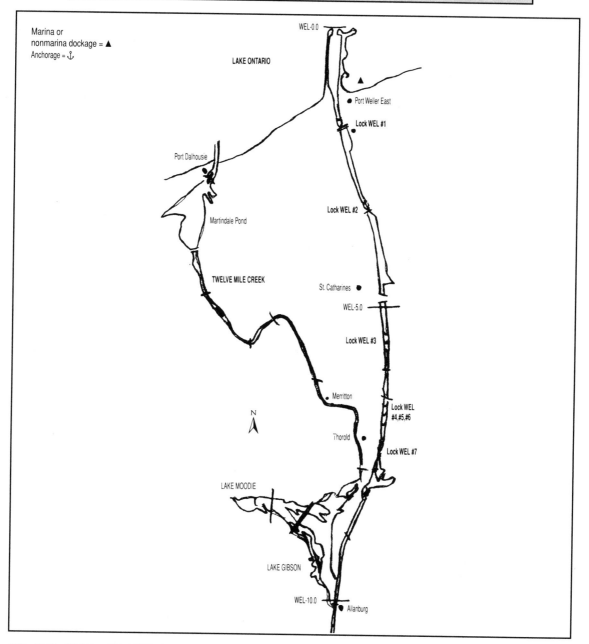

Marina or nonmarina dockage = ▲
Anchorage = ⚓

LAKE ONTARIO

WEL-0.0

Port Weller East

Lock WEL #1

Port Dalhousie

Lock WEL #2

Martindale Pond

TWELVE MILE CREEK

St. Catharines

WEL-5.0

Lock WEL #3

Merritton

Lock WEL #4, #5, #6

N

Thorold

Lock WEL #7

LAKE MOODIE

LAKE GIBSON

WEL-10.0   Allanburg

Mile WEL-10.3 to Mile WEL-0.0

LOCKAGE, WELLAND CANAL

Note: Pleasure boats using the Welland Canal should carry aboard the "St. Lawrence Seaway Pleasure Craft Guide." Lock regulations and requirements in this system are too numerous to cover in this table.

Lock	Mile	Lift	*Required Chamber Side
Lock WEL #8	WEL-21.8 (NM)	0.6+ meters	**Up-starboard/Down-port
Lock WEL #7	WEL-7.5 (NM)	14.1 meters	Up-port/Down-starboard
Lock WEL #6	WEL-6.8 (NM)	13.3 meters	Up-port/Down-port
Lock WEL #5	WEL-6.8 (NM)	14.6 meters	Up-port/Down-port
Lock WEL #4	WEL-6.8 (NM)	14.6 meters	Up-port/Down-port
Lock WEL #3	WEL-5.5 (NM)	14.1 meters	Up-port/Down-starboard
Lock WEL #2	WEL-3.2 (NM)	14.1 meters	Up-starboard/Down-port
Lock WEL #1	WEL-1.7 (NM)	14.0 meters	Up-starboard/Down-port

*At normal canal pool level

**At most water levels lockmasters have pleasure craft mill about during lockage and not secure in chamber.

All locks furnish lines for bow and stern ascending and descending.

Fees: A $10 fee is charged for each of the eight locks. A lockmaster collects the $80 (Canadian) canal transit toll at Lock WEL #3 when you are "up." American currency is accepted, but no premium is allowed for currency exchange.

Required call-in area with direct land line contact:

   Port Colborne: **Mile WEL-21.9 (NM)**. West bank south of lift bridges #21 and #22 at Sugarloaf Harbour Marina Annex. Phone on telephone pole at top of revetment.

   Port Weller East: **Mile WEL-1.3 (NM)**. East bank 0.25 mile north of Lock WEL #1. Phone on grounds.

Attempts to control the portage around Niagara Falls historically led to bad feelings and bloodshed between the inhabitants to its north and east and those to the south and west. The Falls were the one interruption on an all-water route on North America's inland lakes and rivers.

In the mid-1800s the Erie Canal gave access to the lakes from the Hudson River, but it required a long, expensive voyage to divert Lake Ontario and Lake Erie traffic into it at Oswego. Also, it was an American canal, and the United States and Canada were vying for economic supremacy. To ensure peace and prosperity for both nations, direct access between Lake Ontario and Lake Erie was needed.

William Merritt, a St. Catharines native and the owner of sawmills, potash furnaces, cooper shops, smithy, distillery, and general store, was well aware of the delays and high cost of transporting goods overland on the Niagara River portage or using New York's canal system. Even more important, he needed water to supply power to his industries. A canal seemed his best solution. With little money for building an Upper Canada canal, he went to New York and convinced an American investor to buy 600 shares in the project. With this start, Merritt convinced Canada's governor-

general to pass a bill supplying funds. Construction of the first Welland Canal began in 1824.

There were two major problems—the Niagara Escarpment and the Welland River level. To keep the need for excavation—and therefore the expense—to a minimum, contractors used natural waterways. Port Dalhousie at the mouth of Twelve Mile Creek, about 3.2 miles west of today's northern canal terminus, was chosen as the canal's northern entrance. It then routed along the creek and through St. Catharines and Marritton. Once south of the Lake Ontario–shore flatlands, it was up and over the escarpment in 35 locks to Thorold. Next came a land cut that ended at Port Robinson on the Welland River.

To enable shipping to use the river, the canal builders dammed the Grand River to the west. A new feeder canal brought water over the Welland River in a wooden aqueduct to a deep cut. Two locks at Allanburg, at its northern end, lifted the canal summit to maintain depths. Two more locks at Port Robinson, at the cut's southern end, lowered it back to the Welland River. Now shipping could transit the river as far as Chippawa, just upstream of Niagara Falls, where commerce used the Upper Niagara River.

In 1829 the first schooner transited upbound.

MOVABLE BRIDGES, PORT COLBORNE TO LAKE ONTARIO

Name	Type	Mile	Place
Bridge #21	Lift	WEL-21.95 (NM)	Port Colborne
Bridge #20	Lift	WEL-21.9 (NM)	Port Colborne
Bridge #19A	Bascule	WEL-21.36 (NM)	Port Colborne
Bridge #19	Bascule	WEL-21.03 (NM)	Port Colborne
Bridge #11	Lift	WEL-10.37 (NM)	Allanburg
Bridge #10	Lift	WEL-9.08 (NM)	South Thorold
Bridge #6*	Bascule (2)	WEL-6.58 (NM)	Thorold
Bridge #5*	Lift	WEL-6.12 (NM)	St. Catharines
Bridge #4	Bascule	WEL-4.88 (NM)	St. Catharines
Bridge #3A	Bascule	WEL-3.3 (NM)	St. Catharines
Bridge #1	Bascule	WEL-1.75 (NM)	Port Weller

Open clearance, all bridges: 116.5 feet (at normal canal pool level)

Signals:

Flashing amber: Bridge operator has seen your approach.

Flashing red: Bridge is opening. Bring vessel up to Limit Approach sign.

Steady green: Bridge open; transit.

*Opening exceptions:

Bridge #6: Pleasure craft whose height above the waterline does not exceed 39.5 feet may pass under lowered spans at their own risk.

Bridge #5: This bridge will be partially raised for pleasure craft whose height above the water is not more than 39.5 feet; they may proceed at their own risk.

Exception procedure: Pleasure craft transiting these bridges are asked if passing under fully lowered span of Bridge #6 or partially raised bridge for Bridge #5 is acceptable. If yes, pleasure craft may pass through these bridges only when blue signal light is displayed on each bridge. Permission for this procedure may be obtained upbound at Lock WEL #3 and downbound at Lock WEL #4.

Understandably, upbound canal traffic soon demanded an easier method of reaching Lake Erie; battling the extreme current of the Upper Niagara River was nearly impossible.

For this reason, four years later contractors moved the canal's southern terminus to Gravelly Bay—today's Port Colborne. By now this first Welland had developed into a canal 24 miles long and 8 feet deep, with 40 wooden locks measuring 22 by 110 feet.

After the Union of the Provinces in 1841, the government of Upper Canada voted to purchase the privately owned Welland Canal Company, which was struggling to pay for canal improvements and maintenance. At the same time, in order to join Upper and Lower Canada, the government made plans for St. Lawrence River canals and locks.

For all systems to be somewhat similar in size, the government upgraded the Welland; it became the second Welland Canal. They replaced and enlarged the wooden locks with 28 of masonry; 25 were between Port Dalhousie and Thorold. Two deep locks were built at Allanburg and Port Robinson, and a guard lock was added at Port Colborne. These increased canal depth to 9 feet. The canal route remained about the same; it still ran from Port Dalhousie to Gravelly Bay.

Meanwhile the canal opened on the St. Lawrence River to Montreal. It had been built slightly wider than its Welland counterpart; in time this width difference would again affect the Welland. By 1870 large steamers were beginning to replace the sailing ships. Grain, lumber, copper, and iron shipments were increasing beyond all expectations. The Welland was not wide enough to accommodate much of the commercial shipping that moved this cargo, so the government approved another canal upgrading.

The third Welland took a more direct route from Port Dalhousie—it completely bypassed Twelve Mile Creek. About 3 miles above the escarpment it rejoined its old route to Lake Erie. Now there were 26 larger stone locks. However, except for three very large locks with access to St. Catharines, the government had built the locks too narrow for the upcoming sidewheel steamships that were already navigating through the Cornwall Canal on the St. Lawrence. All the Welland could handle was the narrow-beamed schooners, sloops, and canalboats.

The third canal's depth started out to be 12 feet, but during construction was changed to 14 feet. By 1889 the system electrically powered and night-lighted the locks. There was still a towpath, but most traffic used tugs for towing. In 1903 the government abolished tolls on all Canadian canals; they wouldn't be reintroduced until the St. Lawrence Seaway opened in 1932.

Steam propulsion brought a new type of steamboat to the Welland. Called "canalers," they were the fore-runners of today's lakers and steered from forward. Built as bulk carriers, they had large box-shaped holds amidships capable of transporting immense cargoes. Larger versions of the canalers—able to carry 15,000 tons—began to dominate lake shipping. Inevitably the time-costly transfer between the bulk carrier ships and the small canalers meant another canal enlargement.

The plan for the fourth Welland Canal was to reduce the number of locks, increase their size, and find a more direct route between the lakes. Port Weller became the northern terminus, which required the building of a complete new harbor. Construction began in 1913 but was interrupted by World War I. Building resumed in 1919 and was completed in 1932.

After the opening of the St. Lawrence River section of the seaway, more problems developed on the Welland. Increased traffic caused long delays in its older, more complex system. In 1964 it became so great a problem that more improvements were begun: a traffic control center; signal light displays; better canal lighting; automation and centralization of controls at Locks WEL #1, #2, #3, #7, and #8; extension of approach walls; and widening of some canal areas. Eventually the government eliminated the guard gate at Lock WEL #7 and rewidened the canal at Port Robinson.

In 1973 the Welland Realignment opened. This channel—the one you use today—replaced a stretch of canal bisecting the city of Welland and crossed by many bridges.

As you begin your downbound journey from Lake Erie, you are on a system already mile-numbered; it begins at **Mile WEL-23.4 (NM)** at the Port Colborne entrance. As you enter the harbor, its most outstanding feature is the tall Maple Leaf Mills grain elevators on the western mole. From 1911 to 1960 the mills were the largest flour-milling operation in the British Empire.

To the northwest is Sugarloaf Hill—it's the high point in a fairly level area—and an early Port Colborne navigation landmark. It was also an observation outpost during the War of 1812.

Originally Port Colborne was called Gravelly Bay—so named for its stony shoreline. It was sparsely settled until workers arrived in 1832 to build the first Welland's Lock #40. The same year a cholera epidemic stopped all canal work and nearly decimated Gravelly Bay. William Merritt bought the land a few years later, laid out surveyed lots, and named it Port Colborne in honor of Upper Canada's governor-general. When the first Welland's southern canal entrance moved here from the Niagara River, the village became the prosperous trading center for lake ships and canalboats.

To be northbound at Port Colborne means only one thing: you plan to transit the canal. Pleasure craft should remember that this St. Lawrence Seaway system portion is for commercial traffic. To even begin the process of transit, you must report to the authorities. There are two places to do this: Downbound your direct-line phone is south of the Port Colborne Lift Bridges on the western bank, at the Sugarloaf Harbour Marina Annex and Harborview Park. Upbound from Lake Ontario, your call-in dock and phone are in a canal indentation at Port Weller East, **Mile WEL-1.3 E (NM)**. A call at the canal's southern end is a direct line to Lock WEL #8's lockmaster. He gives you general transiting instructions for the system. When calling in, take along your vessel documentation or certificate number. There's often a list of the other information requested posted near the phone. Once you make your call-in for transit, you are expected to conform to the laws that govern canal usage. Have aboard an up-to-date copy of the "St. Lawrence Seaway Pleasure Craft Guide." There are countless regulations, restrictions, and requirements to transit; they are far too many to list here. Usually—but not always—an attendant hands you a copy at the first lock you transit. Transit is straight through. There is no stopping except in designated areas that Welland Control carefully monitors. Expect delays of more than 12 hours. There's a fee to transit.

We are very reluctant to recommend pleasure craft transit "up" from Lake Ontario to Lake Erie on this

Port Colborne Lift Bridge with the laker Canadian Hunter, *northbound.*

canal. It's difficult and often very dangerous work for a family crew—which is why this guide's route-of-travel leads "down" the Welland. The reason for not going "up" is a system lock design that causes extreme turbulence in seven of the canal's high-lift locks. Due to the difficulty of ascending lockages, the Welland Canal requires three people aboard a pleasure craft when upbound. These include one operator and two persons capable of handling lines.

A transit "down" the Welland (from south to north) may be a time-consuming episode, but commonsense seamanship and strict adherence to the Canadian Seaway's regulations make for a very easy, safe, and enjoyable transit.

The Welland is 27 miles long and about 27 feet deep, and is spanned by 11 movable bridges. There are eight locks. Locks WEL #1 through WEL #7 have an average lift of about 46.5 feet. Lock WEL #8, a control or guard lock, has a lift that varies from 1 to 4 feet. It is used to adjust the canal to the daily level of Lake Erie. Seven locks are in the northern section between the Niagara Escarpment and Lake Ontario and include the canal's Flight Locks, Locks WEL #4, #5, and #6.

Locks WEL #1 through WEL #7 each require the

displacement of 20 million gallons of water, and it takes about 10 minutes to gravity-fill or empty a lock. What, then, is the reason for such an extended transit delay in this 27-mile-long canal? It's a combination of a 6-knot speed limit and excessive ship traffic already in the system that has priority of passage.

At one time Welland Control expected all pleasure craft to lock through with a ship. In doing so, every upbound small craft took a life-threatening risk at seven locks. Fortunately for the pleasure craft, this practice of locking upbound with ships more than 328 feet long is no longer allowed. This means small boats transiting must wait until commerce is not in a lock's vicinity.

Transiting requires extreme patience; a steady stream of commerce moves lake to lake. A semiconscious snail moves faster than a ship entering a lock and securing in the chamber—it can take up to an hour or more. Exiting takes just as long.

Canadian canal systems are much more regimented than their American neighbors. Welland Control may contact you at any time—if you are misplaced momentarily—and want to know your precise position. Bankside mileage numbers are on square yellow signs mounted on striped black and lime green poles; they are also charted every mile. Never exceed speed limits in this canal, nor advance beyond flashing signs, lights, or instructional placards when they warn you not to advance.

Once you have called in to Welland Control at Port Colborne, know your chamber companions (usually other pleasure craft or tour boats) and exact lockage position, tune your VHF to Channel 14, and have your "Seaway Pleasure Craft Guide" in hand, off you go.

Your first obstructions are Port Colborne's two movable bridges. The government built the Clarence Street Bridge in 1929; its cement block counterbalance weights each weigh 558 tons. Alongside the western bank at this bridge is the second Welland Canal's guard lock. Adjacent is one that was electrically operated and used on the third Welland.

North of the lift bridges the channel divides. Your route is east to Lock WEL #8. The channel that bears west was the first Welland's route when it moved to pass through Port Colborne in 1833. The wall north of the lift bridge is its original stonework.

Lock WEL #8 and the weir west of the island control the supply of water from Lake Erie. Waste weirs discharge surplus water to the canal's lower levels; each lock has one. The total flow of water that enters the Welland from Lake Erie can be as much as 300 cubic meters per second. Amount depends on the number of lockages, though only about 15 percent of the water is for navigation purposes. Seaway power plants and assorted local water facilities take most of the water.

The Port Colborne Tourist Lighthouse and the lock viewing platform are in Fountain View Park on Lock WEL #8's western approach wall just south of Main Street West's Jackknife Bridge.

There are bascule bridges at each end of the lock. This is common during your transit; the bridges function with lockages. Usually, when downbound at this lock, a smartly uniformed attendant steps forward and informs you, "Just mill about in the middle a bit." Lift is minimal; the usual procedure is to close the upper gate and open the lower—it takes about that much time to idle through the 766-foot-long lock.

Once in the lower pool and past the island's northern end, you'll see the large Robin Hood Mills on the west. It and the Maple Leaf Mills have a combined output of nearly 35 percent of Ontario's milling operations.

The canal ahead is wide enough for two ships to pass. It has smooth grass-covered banks, a few scattered trees, telephone and light poles, and an occasional flock of Canada geese—you left civilization behind at Port Colborne.

There's a junction at **Mile WEL-20.0 (NM);** your channel is on the Realignment Canal east of the island. To the west is the original fourth Welland, which is no longer open for through traffic. The Realignment opened in 1973, replacing a 9.1-mile portion that cut through the middle of Welland. The section always had been an irritant to city inhabitants and ship operators due to the cut's many bridges. The canal was too narrow for modern lakers; in any kind of wind it was nearly impossible to get a 700-foot, high-freeboard ship with a 75-foot beam through a 92-foot horizontal clearance bridge. One railroad bridge was hit six times in one season.

When the Realignment construction began, Welland also underwent a major overhaul. The government moved commercial industries to new locations; the railroad rerouted with new track, yards, station, freight depots and control center; and the province relocated 50 miles of highways and added two underwater tunnels.

Today's Realignment is a straight cut to Port Robinson with no overhead obstructions; the system maintains water level at 569 feet.

You cross the $40-million auto and train Townline Tunnel at **Mile WEL-17.5 (NM).** Its location is by the western shore's cement abutment. Once past the active ship slip you cross the Main Street Tunnel at **Mile WEL-15.4 (NM).**

Canal laborers settled what is now the city of Welland during construction of the aqueduct that carried the first canal over the Welland River. Today the city maintains the old canals with landscaped walks, parks, and hiking and bicycle trails. The waterfront is primarily for recreational organized boating and sporting events. Welland is famous for its giant outdoor murals. These permanent paintings—some more than three stories high and 80 feet long—depict Welland's historical past and its part in the building of the canal.

Near the Realignment's northern end, **Mile WEL-13.3 (NM),** you cross the Welland River flowing through the four-tube Syphon Culvert, 94 feet wide and 638 feet long. It can handle a water flow of 12,000 cubic feet per second.

Port Robinson once had a bridge, but in 1974 a laker hit and destroyed it. Now the divided town—part of which you can see on the canal—is connected by a tiny passenger ferry. Workers on the first and the upgraded Welland canals settled Port Robinson. During the steamboat era it was a transfer point for passengers bound upstream along the navigable feeder canal to the Grand River or downstream along the Welland River to Chippawa and from there upstream to Buffalo.

The Allanburg Lift Bridge, **Mile WEL-10.5 (NM),** is coming up in a wooded canal section. Allanburg was the first Welland's ceremonial sod-turning, speechmaking location. To the northwest are Lakes Gibson and Moodie, fed by water from the canal here at Allanburg. North of the bridge and the pipeline crossing, the canal raceway bears northwest. Here the route of the first two canals turned northwest and the old canal outlets to Lake Ontario in Port Dalhousie. At Merritton these old canals overcame the Niagara Escarpment. The second canal, just slightly south of the first system, contained six locks called by assorted names—the Mountain Locks, Neptune's Staircase, and Bradley Park.

As you make your way north of the raceway, your channel makes a slight easterly bend and you begin to see the industry of South Thorold. At the bend is another lift bridge. South Thorold had its beginnings as a canal industrial center dominated in the early 1900s by the Ontario Pulp and Paper Company. During the time of the third Welland, Thorold imported pulpwood by water from Baie-Comeau, Quebec. They exported much of the processed product to Chicago.

Before canal improvements began on the fourth Welland, there was a functioning guard gate at **Mile WEL-8.3 (NM);** it was no longer needed when they added the sector gates at Lock WEL #7.

North of the old gate you pass an easterly reaching industrial cut, then cross over the Thorold Tunnel—built over a period of three winters when engineers drained the canal.

Downtown Thorold is on the canal's western side. Construction gangs building the locks and channel of the first Welland settled the town; they named it Stump Town. Once the locks functioned, water power brought in a variety of industries and a more complimentary name. Industry ranged from lumber, flour, and knitting mills to the manufacture of soap and farm implements. The second Welland routed in nearly the same area, so population increased with the canal traffic. The Welland Mills of Thorold began in 1846 and became one of the largest producers of flour in Canada. They shipped out by canalboat up to 500 barrels of flour a day. For years downtown businesses catered to villagers but depended on the purchasing power of the canal traffic. The canal closed downtown in 1915; the government built the third canal off to the east.

This is the 1813 site of the Battle of Beaverdam. During the War of 1812 the Americans, forced to abandon Fort Erie and Fort Chippawa on the Canadian side of the Niagara River, were trying to hold Fort George on Lake Ontario. They weren't succeeding; the British had laid siege. A battalion of more than 500 Americans managed to slip out and head south for the settlement at Beaverdam. Indians began a systematic annihilation of the soldiers. Rather than lose everyone, the Americans surrendered to the British. An obelisk commemorating this event is in Battle of Beaverdam Park about four blocks west of Lock WEL #7.

Lock WEL #7, in downtown Thorold, is just above the Niagara Escarpment, 575 feet above sea level. Downbound in the lock take note of the large cable stretched at surface level across the lock near the chamber's northern end—all locks have one. They are ship arresters, installed so ships won't touch and damage the forward gate. The yellow crane at one end of the cable is responsible for getting the cable hooked into position on the chamber's opposite side.

Lock WEL #7 is typical of a downbound high-lift Welland lockage. Lock attendants wave you to your chamber position; as you approach, they hand you neatly coiled lines for bow and stern. Once you have descended and the lock gates begin to open, the attendants give a tug on the line, you let it go, and they recoil the line on the rim without it ever getting wet. You are then on your way.

Once in Lock WEL #7's lower pool you face the Twinned Flight, Locks WEL #6, #5, and #4, that takes you down the Niagara Escarpment. One twin set is for upbound traffic, the other for downbound. The Flight has their locks in tandem—lock gates of one lock are also the gates of the next. These twins replaced the 14 locks needed on the third Welland.

The large eastern-shore industry you see when in Lock WEL #4's lower pool is General Motors of Canada. The plant, which started in the 1800s in downtown St. Catharines, once produced carriage hardware and castings. After expanding several times, it entered the automobile industry and eventually moved to the fourth Welland's banks.

Set back on the western shore are the offices of the St. Lawrence Seaway Authority, Western Region. This is the traffic control center—Welland Control—that monitors vessels through the system.

You have another Lift Bridge (BR 5) midway between the Flight and Lock WEL #3, **Mile WEL-5.5**

(NM). This is the lock where you pay your toll. You'll benefit if you pay in Canadian currency; no premium is allowed for exchange rates.

Lock WEL #3 has a very popular tourist visiting center with a viewing platform on the western bank; expect a large audience when you lock. Since a locking vessel cannot let crews ashore, you miss an interesting area. If you plan a stop at the marina at the canal's northern end and have transportation, try to return to enjoy Lock WEL #3's exhibits. There's a dining room overlooking the canal, galleries, a museum, displays, and canal memorabilia. In the lock chamber you can peek over the chamber rim and see the anchor planted in cement in the center's front yard. This came from the ship *Black River,* built in 1896 and operated on the canals for 30 years to the Ontario Paper Company at Thorold.

Once in Lock WEL #3's lower pool you have the South Service Road bascule bridge (BR 4). Immediately to its north is the 123-foot high-level QEW Garden City Skyway. North of the QEW the canal is in a raised embankment 30 feet above the land on either side. Lock WEL #2 is coming up at **Mile WEL-3.2 (NM).**

St. Catharines, an early Underground Railroad depot, was a small farming center and Loyalist settlement before the first Welland came into existence. When the canal opened, its raceway was put to work for mill power. The center of town was on the old canal—then about 3 miles west. By the time the second Welland arrived, the well-established flour and lumber mills and manufacturing centers increased in size and production. Population in 1830 was 3,500, making it one of the largest towns in Ontario. Much of its success was due to its excellent port convenient to Lake Ontario, its water power, and shipping expertise. Within 30 years it ranked fifth in Ontario's urban centers, surpassed only by Ottawa, Hamilton, Toronto, and London.

As industry boomed and the town grew, the population of nearby settlements also increased. These included industrialized Merritton, Thorold, Port Dalhousie—the Lake Ontario entrance of the first three canals—and later Port Weller, when the canal's northern terminus moved east. In time these outlying towns became one large urban area that not only reaped the canal's benefits and its shipping potential but also became the center of a large agricultural area.

Once in the lower pool of Lock WEL #2, the Port Weller Dry Docks are just above Lock WEL #1 on the eastern bank. Originally, this was a canal embayment used to store spare gates. The dry dock is only one of many shipyards that were in service throughout the history of the canals. Originally this one was called the Muir Brothers Dry Dock, and it was in Port Dalhousie. When the fourth Welland opened, it moved to Lock WEL #1 and changed its name. The yard is not only a repair and hauling facility but also builds ships; many Great Lake bulk carriers and tankers have their origin in this yard.

Lock WEL #1 is your last lock northbound on the Ontario Plain. In its lower pool you enter Port Weller Harbor. On the eastern bank is the pleasure craft call-in dock for southbound transit.

Many of the early canal town names honored canal engineers, contractors, or entrepreneurs. Port Weller honors J. L. Weller, the engineer in charge of planning the fourth Welland.

The town's population increased dramatically when laborers arrived at the two breakwater and Flight lock construction sites. The new entrance was an enormous project; there was no inlet at Port Weller, so it had to be built from scratch. Due to currents along the beach, and for storm protection, the two breakwaters had to extend a mile offshore. These north-south–reaching fingers needed massive quantities of fill. It came from the Flight locks and channel between the breakwaters; contractors excavated it all to bedrock. Tall trees line today's breakwater, which is a popular area for fishing, picnicking, and ship watching.

As you approach Lake Ontario, the breakwaters' arms close; at the entrance there's only 400 feet between them. Watch for large-ship traffic coming in; it's going to be riding the channel range up from Lake Ontario.

Port Weller Outer Light, a 49-foot red skeleton tower on a white building, is on the west breakwater's end. Here this section of your journey ends; it has intersected Region 4's Lake Ontario, The Canadian Shore (see that section, beginning on page 214) at its **Mile CONT-6.5 (NM).**

Sketch Map Depths

Sketch map depths are given at normal average summer canal pool level. When you venture outside the sketch map confines, you must adjust NOAA and Canadian charts to chart datum. For convenience in adjusting, use the following:

Mile WEL-23.4 (NM) to **Mile WEL-22.0 (NM):** Plane of reference, Lake Erie Low Water Datum, 568.6 feet

Mile WEL-22.0 (NM) to **Mile WEL-1.7 (NM):** Plane of reference, Normal Pool Level

Mile WEL-1.7 (NM) to Lake Ontario: Plane of reference, Lake Ontario Low Water Datum, 242.8 feet

PORT COLBORNE

Chart: C 2042, *See sketch map, page 182*

Mile WEL-23.0 to Mile WEL-21.9

Port Colborne has an anchorage and one marina in the western section of Gravelly Bay's outer harbor. Another marina is on the canal in downtown.

An outer eastern and western breakwater protects the port's Lake Erie ship channel. The western one has a long extension jutting southeast. Four breakwaters inside the main harbor west of the canal enclose a yacht harbor.

Northbound into the port the western breakwater's southwestern extension is the first you pass. The inner main ship entrance is 0.3 mile farther north and between **East Breakwater Light** and **Inner Light.** Once clear of **East Breakwater Light,** the buoys begin. Your departure point for the outer harbor marina and anchorage is at a red main-channel buoy nearly alongside the lighthouse. To the northwest is a black spar—depending on the season there may be two—designating the entrance channel to the mill docks and the yacht harbor. Follow this channel until you see the first inner harbor breakwater that extends north and south paralleling the granaries. Now follow the directions found for individual stops.

Downtown, where you'll find a post office, pharmacy, banks, restaurants, meat market, bakery, super-market, and assorted stores, is within a long walk of Sugarloaf Marina or the anchorage area. You might enjoy the walk in, see the sights, then taxi home if you have a heavy load. To get to town, head north across Sugarloaf's facilities and go out the entrance gate alongside Lakeview Park. This is nearly as far as the remaining distance to town. Take Elm Street about five blocks north. The A & P supermarket is on Clarence Street, which you intersect.

If you walk east on Clarence Street about three blocks, you come to the canal and the town's two movable bridges. This is the location of the Sugarloaf Annex, a very convenient downtown marina. If you have yet to transit the Welland, this is a good place for a preliminary inspection. At first glance the canal does not seem especially noteworthy, but find a comfortable park bench in Harborview Park bordering the canal, sit back, and wait for a laker or saltie to appear. Notice how the size of the canal and bridges has shrunk; the ships nearly fill every inch of available space.

While in the park, walk along the canal at West Street and have a look at the remains of the first and second Welland canals. The white building is the Harbour Master's and Pilot's Office; the pilot boat is docked on the canal. Also note the location of the call-in phone; you must stop here before you can transit. You are overlooking the Annex. Part of its dockage is reserved for pleasure craft waiting a canal transit. West Street, between the old train station and Kent Street, has a collection of interesting shops. Many buildings date to the 19th and early-20th century.

A block north and one west brings you to the corner of Princess and King streets, where you can visit the Port Colborne Historical and Marine Museum. It has a steam towboat's wheelhouse planted in the yard, and six heritage buildings on the grounds. There are displays and exhibits about the area and the canal, and a collection of photographs of early Port Colborne and canal construction. A favorite stop is Arabella's Tea Room, a cottage on its original site operated by the Museum Auxiliary. It has a pleasant atmosphere—shining wooden floors, lace curtains, elegant white table covers, and silver and china place settings. The waitresses, dressed in vintage attire, serve tea and hot homemade biscuits and jam. The museum and the tea room are open from 2 until 4.

On Fridays from 6 to noon the farmers' market is at Charlotte and Catherine streets—a few blocks from the museum—with local vegetables and fruit, seafood, sausages, baked goods, and boxed and cut flowers.

If you want a preview of Welland lockages, you can walk to Lock WEL #8. Head north to Main Street, turn east, cross the weir onto the lock island, and spot the small tourist information lighthouse on the canal's western side. There's a posted daily schedule of when ships are due. Alongside is a lock viewing stand in Fountainview Park; there are picnic tables and washrooms. The tourist center is an excellent stop for brochures, maps, and general information.

Harborview Park—alongside the Clarence Street Bridge—is the Merritt Trail's southern terminus. The path crosses the Niagara Peninsula to Port Dalhousie on Lake Ontario. It has many interesting and scenic spots that include old canal channels, parts of today's canal, antique locks and mills, and routes through pretty village parks. Yellow paint blazes on signposts, trees, and telephone poles mark the trail. Try it if you brought along your bicycle and are quite fit. If you plan the whole excursion, pick up a trail brochure at the tourist center.

In mid-July is the International Week Festival, with music, dancing, and theatrical performances in the Lakeview Park bandstand by the Sugarloaf Marina. There's also a downtown parade if you are at the Annex.

Canal Days is about the first of August. There are many marine-related displays and items on sale, as well as arts and crafts, food, a model regatta, and marine demonstrations.

Port Colborne Anchorage

★★★

NO FACILITIES

Chart: C 2042, *See A on sketch map*

Mile WEL-23.0 + 0.3 W (NM)

First follow the main entry instructions. Once inside the harbor, leave the side channel at the black spar and bear southwesterly toward the breakwater. Go slowly and be very careful; there are extensive shoals all over Gravelly Bay and close to your approach route. Before anchoring make certain you are well clear of the cable area between the shore to just west of the area where the

Port Colborne: Port Colborne Anchorage, Sugarloaf Harbour Marina

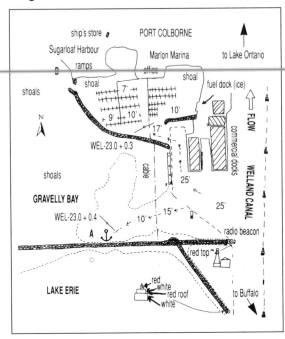

western breakwaters southeasterly extension reaches into the lake. Preferred anchorage is close to the outer breakwater rocks for convenient fishing for perch and bass. The water is very clear; you can also enjoy snorkeling along the rocks.

Though this bay was named for its stony shores, bottom seems to be mud with good holding. There's good protection from prevailing southwesterlies—they usually die down by sundown—but if wind is strong from the west or northerly quadrants, the anchorage becomes badly windswept.

Sugarloaf Harbour Marina

★★★

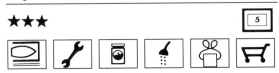

Chart: C 2042, *See B on sketch map*

Mile WEL-23.0 + 0.4 W (NM)

Follow the directions for the anchorage approach to the side channel's black spar. At this point you can see the breakwater that parallels the granaries and extends south of the mole. Keep east of this north-south breakwater and follow along the granary's western side. At the granary dock's northern end the breakwater has a small opening—intended for circulation, not entry or exit. Here, nearly at 90 degrees, is the start of another breakwater that extends in a westerly curve and nearly encloses the entire basin. Dead ahead at the break is a short breakwater that reaches west from the granary mole. If you need fuel or a pumpout, go south around this short breakwater's western end and follow it back to the eastern shoreline. You'll see the Marlon Marina's square Petro-Canada fuel sign on a pole on the breakwater.

If you do not need fuel but want to spend the night, the Sugarloaf Marina—open April 15 through October 15—is west of the short breakwater and west of Marlon Marina, which is also in the lee of the long 90-degree westerly reaching arm.

If no one answered on VHF 68, pull in to a dock—the long dock's western face is open and convenient. If no dock attendant is on duty, the main office is on a southerly reaching mole located about in the center of all the slips. Extending south from the office mole is a long floating pier with easterly reaching fingers of slips; west of the office mole is another marina section with a long center pier with fingers of slips extending east and west.

In the office complex are rest rooms and showers, ice, phone, and a laundry room. If first entering Canada, there's a posted 800 number for customs. The ship's store offers marine equipment, navigation supplies, charts and publications, basic groceries, and picnic and camera supplies.

Electric hookups (110-volt/30-amp and 220-volt/50-amp) are available. The land line number is (416) 834-6747. If you need a diver, check at the office.

Lakeview Park is near the marina's drive-in entrance, with picnic facilities, playgrounds, a bandstand, and a wading pool. This is where the annual International Festival, Canada Day festivities, and fishing derbies are held. Usually during the summertime there are concerts at the bandstand starting at 7:30 P.M. The large building well west that faces the bay is the hospital.

Sugarloaf Marina Annex (Municipal Boat Docks)

★★★★

Chart: C 2042

Mile WEL-21.9 (NM)

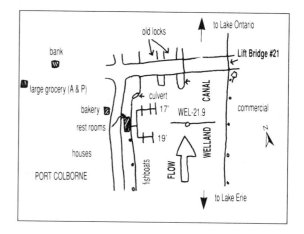

This marina is on the main canal thoroughfare's western side immediately south of the two Port Colborne lift bridges. A blue sign in front of a small white dockside building notes it's the Municipal Boat Docks, City of Port Colborne, Harborview Park. It's also the Sugarloaf Marina's Annex.

Slips extend 90 degrees from the western bank in two sections. The center section directly under the sign is reserved; it's the Welland Canal Pleasure Craft call-in dock. All docks are sturdy with large snubbing posts. Pull in to any open slip other than the call-in dock unless you plan an immediate canal transit.

There's usually no one on duty since there's no charge for use from 0800 to 1900. The dockmaster normally arrives from the Sugarloaf Marina on Gravelly Bay in late afternoon to collect the night fee. The Annex has no electric hookup, but there's a water faucet under the blue sign. Garbage bins are on the upper level. Once the dockmaster arrives, he unlocks the washrooms for your use.

You are in downtown Port Colborne on West Street. Your view north is of the old Welland Canal locks, the interesting lift bridges, and the city park. All the downtown attractions are within a short four-block radius. Be sure to stop by at the Quality Bakery just across West Street. Its delicacies are a grand addition to coffee in the cockpit while you watch the parade of ships passing through the bridges.

ST. CATHARINES MARINA

Chart: C 2042

Mile WEL-0.0 + 1.4 E (NM)

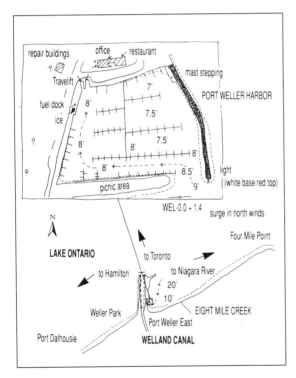

This enclosed-basin marina is convenient to the Welland Canal's northern entrance. It's on Lake Ontario on the eastern side of the canal's Port Weller Harbour Breakwater's eastern arm.

At the eastern breakwater's northern end there's a long finger of land that extends easterly about 0.4 mile. The finger's eastern end is watched by a red spar. From

this point the marina is about 0.8 mile south-southwest. If visibility is good, you can make out its stone breakwater not far from the shoreline.

The basin's eastern breakwater extends southeasterly from the Port Weller Harbour Breakwater. The basin entrance is at the southern end, watched by a lighthouse with a white base and a red top. Once at the lighthouse you can then see another mole extends northeasterly from the Port Weller Harbor Breakwater; it protects the basin from south and southeasterly winds.

If wind is strong northeasterlies, there will be a lake swell running and some water turmoil as you make your swing around the lighthouse into the entrance. This swell also brings a basin surge.

Once in the entrance you face a basin full of slips. If no one answered on VHF 68, head for the fuel dock (gas and diesel) for a slip assignment. Make a westerly turn at the entrance and follow along the southern mole to its western end, then turn back north. Here you can see the 25-ton Travelift's well and launching ramp in the northwestern corner. The fuel dock is alongside the Travelift. If no one is about, the office is in the large building to the northeast.

The basin has slips on all bulkheads except for the inside of the eastern breakwater. Stay clear of this; south of the mast-stepping dock at the breakwater's northern end, it's shoal and rocky. If assigned a slip in that vicinity, your best approach depth is alongside the docks' ends.

The bulk of the marina slips extend east and west off a main pier whose access ramp is on the northern shore about in front of the restaurant alongside the office.

Electric hookups (110-volt) are available. There's a ship's store with some supplies in the office complex. The marina restaurant, the Captains Table, also has a snack bar and a pretty view of the marina's landscaped grounds and Lake Ontario.

If you go off the grounds and plan to come home late, get instructions on getting back in after dark—gates are loaded with locks and timers. The marina's land line number is (416) 935-5522.

Downtown St. Catharines is about 5 miles away across the canal; you'll need a taxi for a day of city sightseeing. Especially interesting is a walking tour of the city's old town. Before starting, you may want to call the St. Catharines "hotline," (416) 641-8788, to find out what events are planned.

Region 4
LAKE ONTARIO

AMERICAN AND CANADIAN SHORES

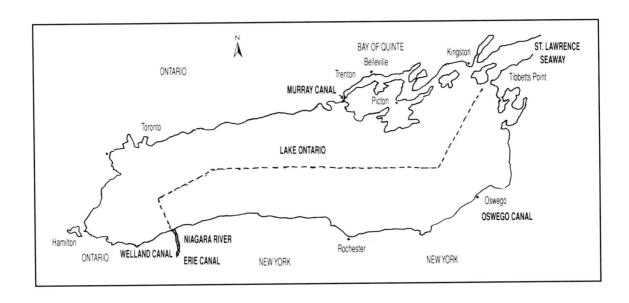

Mile AONT-0.0 (NM) to Mile AONT-156.7 (NM) and Mile CONT-0.0 (NM) to Mile CONT-212.3 (NM)

MOVABLE BRIDGES, FORT NIAGARA TO TIBBETTS POINT (AMERICAN SHORE) AT LAKE ONTARIO LOW WATER DATUM: 242.8 FEET		
Name	*Mile*	*Place*
Conrail	**AONT-67.6 + 0.9 (NM)**	Rochester
Stutson Street*	**AONT-67.6 + 1.2 (NM)**	Rochester
Schedule* for pleasure craft: April 1 to December 15, bridge opens on signal except:		
Monday through Friday except federal holidays, from 0700 to 0900 and 1600 to 1800		
Monday through Friday except federal holidays, from 0900 to 1600 and 1800 to 2300, opens on hour and half hour		
Saturdays, Sundays, and federal holidays, from 0700 to 1100, opens on hour and half hour		

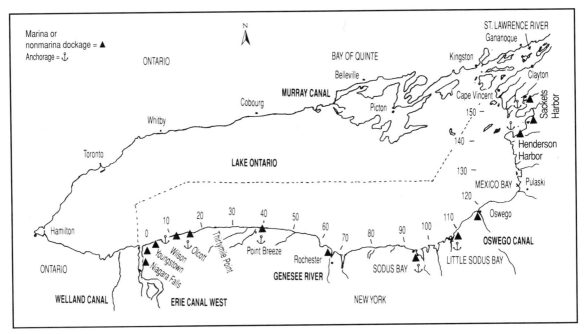

Mile AONT-0.0 (NM) to Mile AONT-156.7 (NM)

> *Geography has made us neighbors. History has made us friends.*
>
> JOHN F. KENNEDY, 1961

Lake Ontario, easternmost and smallest of the five Great Lakes, is 53 miles across at its widest, 193 miles long, and has a 700-mile coastline. Its drainage basin, including the Niagara River and the St. Lawrence River above the Iroquois Dam, is 34,850 square miles. The main lake is primarily fed by Lake Erie waters by way of the Niagara River; it drains at its northeastern end into the St. Lawrence River.

Never regard Lake Ontario as "just a lake"; treat it as an ocean. Your vessel should be sound, and you should have full comprehension of coastal navigation.

Current on Lake Ontario flows east. Speed is minimal; however, note that there is an increase of about 1.1 to 2.2 mph off the Niagara River and 1.2 mph just upstream (west) of the head of the St. Lawrence Seaway at Tibbetts Point and Kingston.

This regional section begins at the Niagara River's mouth—about 36 miles from the lake's western end. Fort Niagara is on the river's eastern point, Fort Mississauga on the west. The international boundary is in midriver. The route generally follows the lake's perimeter a few miles offshore as far as Oswego, **Mile AONT-118.7 (NM).** At this port you must bear northerly on the steamer route to cross Mexico Bay to reach the head of the St. Lawrence River. Northbound on this route there is a departure point, **Mile AONT-140.0 (NM),** from which to visit the Golden Crescent, the islands and bays at the lake's northeastern end. You can leave this area and rejoin the shipping channel at Charity Shoal, **Mile AONT-152.0 (NM),** to carry on to Tibbetts Point at the head of the river, **Mile AONT-156.7 (NM).**

The American-shore mileage system begins at the Niagara River, **Mile AONT-0.0 (NM),** and works eastward. Protected harbors dot the coastline, and the maximum distance between ports is about 45 miles if you visit the lake's eastern islands and bays.

The Lower Niagara River is navigable about 7 miles to Lewiston and Queenston; upstream of the cities, extreme current and river rapids make it a dangerous place for pleasure craft.

In its early history the Lower Niagara River was of strategic importance in the water-portage link between Lakes Erie and Ontario. It was an uneasy border that was controlled at various times by the Iroquois Confederation, France, England, and the United States.

At the river's mouth, Fort Niagara stands bluff on the point. The first fortified house on the site was Fort Conti, built in 1678 by René-Robert Cavalier de La Salle; later the French rebuilt it as Fort Denonville. In 1725 they rebuilt again and called it Fort Niagara. By this time they had an uneasy truce with the Seneca Indians, who demanded that the building be a "house of peace." The French, however, gave the renovated fort massive 1,500-pound entrance doors and 4-foot-thick walls in case relations broke down. Later the fort, also known as the Stone House or the Castle, was occupied by the British. England relinquished it to America for good in 1815, when the two nations signed the Treaty of Ghent.

Lewiston, 7 miles upstream, was a trading and transportation center as the frontier moved west; it was known as the jumping-off point on the Great Overland Route. In 1812 American General Stephen Van Rensselaer's army crossed the Niagara at Lewiston in hopes of capturing Queenston; they were defeated at the Battle of Queenston Heights.

As you cruise eastward on the lake, keep over 1.5 miles offshore to Thirtymile Point—there are a few charted offshore dangers. Your first deepwater harbor is about 12 miles east at Wilson, **Mile AONT-10.8 (NM).** Wilson-Tuscarora State Park's western boundary is on Twelvemile Creek and extends for a mile east to the Wilson Harbor entrance. Wilson, on the East Branch of Twelvemile Creek, has been a summer resort since the mid-1800s, and at one time was a noted shipbuilding center.

The next harbor eastbound is Olcott, **Mile AONT-**

15.9 (NM), at Eighteenmile Creek. Keep well offshore as you approach the harbor. Though no buoy watches it, there is a submerged rock about 3.3 miles west of the Olcott entrance. A hillside water tank about 0.4 mile up the creek serves as an Olcott Harbor–area landmark.

Olcott was an early-19th-century port of entry with a lighthouse and a customs house. It was a major lake shipping point, and the creek became the power supply for its lumberyards, gristmills, and woolen mills. The British patrolled this section of coast during the War of 1812 looking for American supply ships bound for the Niagara frontier; they discovered and captured two in the creek's mouth.

Your next port eastbound is 27 miles away at Point Breeze Harbor. A waypoint 6 miles east of Olcott is the Somerset Power Plant's single stack. Another 6 miles brings you to the 72-foot wire tower with its red-and-white diamond-shaped daymark at Thirtymile Point Light.

In the 1800s there was an extensive, dangerous shoal off Thirtymile Point at the mouth of Golden Hill Creek. After the British warship H.M.S. *Ontario* was wrecked, the government constructed a 60-foot lighthouse. Its limestone building blocks came in by sailing ship from the quarries at Chaumont Bay. The old light is still on the point at the creek's mouth, but the shoals the light watched eventually washed away on their own. Hold well offshore east of Thirtymile Point to avoid outlying rocks.

About 12 miles east of the point is the mouth of Johnson Creek, named for Sir William Johnson; he camped here with his army and Indian allies on the way to capture Fort Niagara for the British in 1759.

Farm silos are commonplace along this coastal area, but one compact group of four is about 0.2 mile up Oak Orchard Creek not far from its eastern bank. They are usually black with white tops, although fickle farmers paint them every few years; they're an offshore landmark for the Point Breeze Harbor area, **Mile AONT-39.3 (NM).**

Point Breeze Harbor has had many names. The first settlers called it Tonawanda Bay. Next it was Oak Orchard Harbor, because it is at the mouth of Oak Orchard Creek; many area residents still refer to it as

The 19th-century Thirtymile Point Lighthouse. Its limestone building blocks came in by sailing ship from quarries in Chaumont Bay.

Things to Do and See in Rochester

Charlotte-Genesee Lighthouse, 70 Lighthouse Street. A maritime museum featuring exhibits on Great Lakes ships from the 19th century to the present.

Elwanger Garden, 130 Spring Street. A Victorian garden featuring trees and perennial flowers. Open May to July on Tuesday, Thursday, and Sunday from 12 to 4.

International Museum of Photography at George Eastman House, 900 East Avenue. Eastman's 49-room mansion houses both a regional historical museum and a photographic museum that displays prints, movie stills, and 11,000 cameras. Open year-round, Tuesday through Sunday from 10 to 4:30.

Rochester Museum and Science Center, 657 East Avenue. History, science, and anthropology displays; planetarium. Open year-round, Monday through Saturday from 9 to 5 and Sunday from 1 to 5.

Seneca Park Zoo, 2222 St. Paul Boulevard, in the Frederick Olmstead–designed county park. There are some 200 species of animals from around the world here, and a children's zoo. Open weekdays from 10 to 5 year-round, and weekends and holidays from 10 to 7 from May 15 to October 9.

Strong Museum, 1 Manhattan Square. Industrial Revolution–era arts, history, clothing, and dolls; children's activity center. Open Monday through Saturday from 10 to 5 and Sunday from 1 to 5; closed Thanksgiving, Christmas, and New Year's Day.

---

such, as do older-issue NOAA charts. Today it is named for a village on the entrance's eastern side.

Eastbound at Point Breeze it's about 33 miles to Rochester. For the first 10.5 miles east, hold well north. Arrive at Devils Nose, a fairly prominent wooded knob, at least 1.5 miles offshore. The stretch of coastline from Devil's Nose to Braddock Point Light is very dangerous; a boulder bank lies almost a mile offshore. A wreck that hit the rocks is even farther offshore; it, too, is a menace, so stand clear.

Fifty-five-foot Braddock Point Light, **Mile AONT-58.3 (NM)**, is on Bogus Point—Braddock Point is 2.7 miles on east. The light is a white tower with a red-and-white diamond-shaped daymark. Nearby is the old Braddock Point Lighthouse, which had the lake's first 20,000-candlepower lens.

When bound for Rochester, Braddock Point Light means a course change. On the way you will pass Braddock Point Bay; it has a shoal entrance that allows passage only to runabouts able to run the inlet.

Smokestacks west and east of the Rochester entrance are good city landmarks. The harbor is on the Genesee River and has two entrance breakwaters, each 0.4 mile long. The westernmost breakwater is watched by 59-foot Rochester Harbor Light, **Mile AONT-67.6 (NM)**, which looks like a red box mounted on four wire legs.

Rochester, as an early harbor, was in the middle of the swamps at the Genesee River's mouth. The Seneca Indians called the river "Casconchiagon," or "river of many falls." When the first Erie Canal opened, canal-boat construction became big business just above the falls. With transportation available on the lake and inland, more flour mills began to line the river, and Rochester acquired the nickname "Flour City." Later it was called "the Flower City"; its nursery industry had become one of the world's largest.

About the time of the Civil War, Rochester's specialized industries began to develop. A local company developed a sewing machine capable of stitching shoes, and Rochester became a noted military boot- and shoe-making center. John Bausch opened an optical store and ground lenses; for $60 he sold a half-interest in the operation to Henry Lomb. The Gleasons invented and manufactured the first cutting-bevel gear teeth. George Eastman began to manufacture photographic dry plates, camera film, and Kodak cameras. In 1906 the Haloid Company—today's Xerox Corporation—started in a loft over the shoe factory.

Leaving Rochester eastbound, your next deepwater port is about 32 miles away at Sodus Bay. The 4-mile-long, 0.5-mile-wide Irondequoit Bay—about 3.5 miles east of the Rochester breakwater—was the ancient

Genesee River mouth. Today the bay has a pair of entrance breakwaters, though the shifting entrance shoals of a newly dredged channel still restrict deep-draft facilities. Marinas cater primarily to runabouts.

The multistoried square building on the way to Sodus Bay is the Genna Nuclear Power Plant on Smoky Point, **Mile AONT-80.3 (NM).**

You pass Pultneyville, **Mile AONT-86.0 (NM),** at Salmon Creek's mouth. In the 1800s the harbor was a port of entry and a terminus for the Underground Railroad. It boasted a large shipbuilding industry and was noted for its supply of capable ships' captains.

There's a harbor at Pultneyville, but depth is very marginal for 5.5-foot-draft vessels, and the channel seems to shift annually. The entrance is difficult to locate on the wooded shoreline, but it has one visible western entry breakwater about 100 feet long. The eastern breakwater is submerged and watched by a collection of buoys and private ranges.

Eastbound at Pultneyville you round prominent Fairbanks Point for the final stretch to Sodus Bay, **Mile AONT-95.2 (NM).** The bay is more than 5 miles long and 2.5 miles wide and has three large islands in its northeastern section. The village is on prominent Sodus Point and narrow Sand Point, two peninsulas that reach easterly from its northwestern shoreline. Long, wooded egg-shaped hills called drumlins surround the bay; they were formed during the Ice Age. The most interesting earth formations are at Chimney Bluffs on the bay's eastern shore; centuries of lake winds and waves have eroded the drumlins into knife-sharp peaks, ridges, and pinnacles.

Eastbound at Sodus Bay your next deepwater harbor is about 14.5 miles away at Little Sodus Bay. Deep Port Bay, **Mile AONT-101.4 (NM),** is at the mouth of Wolcott Creek, but the unimproved entrance is fit only for shoal-draft runabouts.

Southerly reaching Little Sodus Bay, **Mile AONT-107.6 (NM),** is about 2.5 miles long and about 0.5 mile at its widest. The Cayuga and Seneca Indians called it "Date-Ke-a-shote," which means "little baby cradle." The earliest European inhabitants were the French, who used the bay as a place to trade with the Indians. By the late 1800s residents had developed a harbor and named their town Fair Haven. East of the Pond was Sterling, whose early settlers dammed Little Sodus Creek to power more than 15 mills. Sterling grew into a major milling town; Fair Haven was its shipping port, first for sailing ships and eventually for the railroad.

Eastbound at Little Sodus, your next deepwater port is Oswego, 11 miles away. Look for the strobe-lighted smokestacks at Oswego's inner-harbor power plant. At least six creeks puncture the hilly shoreline along your route. None are navigable for most drafts.

When you reach West Nine Mile Point, **Mile AONT-112.0 (NM),** make certain your next easterly course takes you northwest of dangerous Ford Shoals, 3 miles ahead. The shoals are watched by a lighted buoy that is very difficult to locate when seas are up.

During the War of 1812, the government chose Oswego as an official naval base because it had long been a strategic transportation center. It was noted for its shipbuilding—it built the first warship for the Great Lakes Fleet, the 85-foot U.S.S. *Oneida*. Without a fleet at the start of the war, the government purchased merchant ships and brought them to Oswego shipyards for conversion to warships. This proved impractical; British ships would lay offshore and lob shells into town. Most of the larger shipbuilding companies moved farther east to safer Sackets Harbor, but Oswego continued to build the small transports and bateaux needed to haul military supplies, troops, stores, and armaments that came in by way of the Hudson, Mohawk, and Oswego rivers.

Today Oswego has a large harbor enclosed by man-made breakwaters (see Region 2, "The Oswego Canal," beginning on page 98).

The next nearest deepwater harbors are in the lake's northeastern end in the Golden Crescent, an area of islands, large bays, small villages, marinas, and anchorages. It extends from Stony Point, **Mile AONT-140.0 + 8.0 E (NM),** to Tibbetts Point, **Mile AONT-156.7 (NM),** the St. Lawrence Seaway's upstream end.

Your route from Oswego depends on your destination. If bound north for Canada or northeast for the Seaway and the Thousand Islands, your quickest route is the main shipping channel as far as Galloo Island, **Mile AONT-143.0 (NM).** Here you must change course if bound for the North Channel near Kingston. If heading for Tibbetts Point and the upstream Seaway entrance, at Galloo Island you have another 14 miles to go. If the Golden Crescent is your destination, lay off a course straight for Stony Point Light, about 22 miles from Oswego's offshore buoy.

As you leave Oswego you are nearing Lake Ontario's eastern end. Mexico Bay, in the lake's southeastern corner, has no notable deepwater ports. It consists of countless drainage rivers and creeks with shoal inlets and narrow barrier islands that protect marshy ponds and swamps.

A prominent shoreline feature about 6 miles east is Nine Mile Point Nuclear Power Plant. When in working order, the plant's one chubby cooling-tower stack normally belches steam. This plant and the Oswego Harbor power plant stacks make excellent waypoint landmarks when southbound from the Seaway and Canada.

Selkirk and Port Ontario are on Mexico Bay's southeastern side at the Salmon River's mouth. In the 1800s a government survey party reported that the Salmon River entrance was navigable, so a lighthouse was built. Residents had great hopes for the port, but shifting sandbars and river silt continually made the entrance dangerous and useless to large shipping. The old lighthouse is still there, but the government decommissioned it in 1850.

Another 9 miles north on the shoreline is the entrance to Sandy Creek.

As you make your way northbound, Stony Point, **Mile AONT-140.0 + 8.0 (NM),** is recognizable as a bold peninsula reaching northwesterly from the mainland. It's watched on its southwestern point by **Stony Point Light,** a 30-foot wire tower with a red lighted daymark. Alongside is the decommissioned 1869 lighthouse and keeper's residence.

Henderson Bay is the first protected Golden Crescent harbor. Eastbound your approach off the main lake is between Stony Point and offshore Stony Island—3 miles to the point's north. Here, in 1813, British Commander Sir James Yeo captured a fleet of American transports loaded with 200 soldiers bound for Sackets Harbor Naval Base.

Henderson Bay is about 6.5 miles long and 2 miles wide and lies in a southwest-northeast direction. A collection of islands and shoals somewhat protects its fairly open northern side. You enter the bay north of Six Town Point's rocks, a northeasterly reaching extension of the bay's southwestern corner, and south of Lime Barrel Shoal, watched by **Light Buoy #1.** Northeast of Lime Barrel are Gull and Bass islands and their dangerous rocky shoals. A mile northeast of Bass Island is 24-acre Horse Island and Sackets Harbor Lighthouse.

In Henderson Bay's southern corner is the hamlet of Henderson Harbor, founded because of its stands of timber and fertile farmland. Though it became an early shipbuilding center and lake port, it never gained the 1800s fame that Sackets Harbor did.

The Black River, at Black River Bay's northeastern end, has a long history as a transportation route into southern New York. Indians used it first; they needed only a few portages when bound south for the Mohawk and Hudson rivers. Dexter, at the river's mouth, was once the northern terminus of the state's Black River Canal, which ran between Black River Bay and Rome. The canal brought into being and then prosperity such river towns as Watertown, Carthage, and Lyons Falls.

Sackets Harbor—settled in 1801—is near Black River Bay's southwestern end in a southeastern shore bight. It began as a deepwater port for shipping timber. In hopes of enforcing the unpopular Embargo Act restrictions, the government sent an armed contingent to Sackets Harbor in 1807. The military dominated the harbor until World War II. During the War of 1812 one-third of the American army and one-fourth of the navy was stationed at Sackets.

When the War of 1812 began, the Americans had only one Great Lakes warship, *Oneida*. Commodore Isaac Chauncey came to Sackets with orders to build the Lake Ontario fleet. As a result, half the warships on Lake Ontario were built or outfitted in the harbor. At the same time, the British were building their own fleet of warships at Kingston, just across the lake. Expecting attack, the navy fortified Sackets with breastworks, walls, powder magazines, cantonments, blockhouses, and forts around the harbor perimeter. They built barracks to house thousands of incoming army troops, sailors, carpenters, shipwrights, teamsters, and camp followers. At war's end Sackets Harbor remained a base for the military, though the building of warships came to an abrupt halt.

The next large Golden Crescent sections are Guffin Bay and Chaumont Bay, separated by Cherry Island and Point Salubrious. In strong prevailing summer southwesterlies, these bays can seem almost as rough as the main lake.

Three of Chaumont Bay's natural harbors are along its northeastern shoreline. At the end of Sawmill Bay is Chaumont—originally part of a land purchase made after the American Revolution by James LeRay de Chaumont. Chaumont also named Point Salubrious, which is just northeast of Cherry Island; he found that the point's settlers were immune to the malaria that continually devastated the rest of the area.

Chaumont has a long history of quarrying and shipping Bird's Eye Limestone, a large portion of which went into the Oswego Canal's locks and bulkheads. For nearly 40 years in the 1800s it was also a famous fishing

Fishing in Lake Ontario

Ontario's waters harbor a prolific variety of smaller gamefish. Smallmouth and largemouth bass, walleye, and bullhead abound. There are larger species, too, like muskellunge and Chinook salmon.

You'll need an Ontario fishing license, available from the Ontario Ministry of Natural Resources or at most local sporting goods stores. In the St. Lawrence/Thousand Islands area, the Ontario Ministry can be reached at 13 Amelia Street, Box 1749, Cornwall, Ontario, Canada K6H 5V7; (613) 933-1774.

Some of the best gamefish:

Northern Pike: These fish, with their large mouths and fierce teeth, remind us of freshwater barracuda. Use a tough wire leader (preferably black) with 20-pound test or heavier. We prefer live bait, like minnows, trolled shallow over weed beds or other bottoms with good hiding places. When the pike strikes, let it run a bit before you set the hook, or it will spit it out.

Muskellunge: Muskies average 20 pounds or more. They resemble pike but have a snakier body, often with prominent spots or vertical bars. Shoal areas along the mouth of the St. Lawrence, from Cape Vincent east, are the best spots. Muskies aren't that common, but you'll know when you hook one; they often roll out of the water behind the lure before they strike. Try casting or trolling over weed beds, usually in about 20 feet of water—but seek local knowledge, because trolling is not always legal. Use at least 30-pound test if you're trolling, with a spoon or spinner lure and a wire leader. If you use live bait you have to be more careful, because muskies play with their food before gulping it down. Yank too soon and you come up with air.

Chinook Salmon: In the spring these fish—royalty among salmon—average about 10 pounds, but they will triple their weight by the end of summer, so gauge your tackle accordingly. Trolling is the best way to catch a Chinook, especially around river mouths or schooling fry. You can use a spinner or a bright-colored tail, although anchovies or other small baitfish are best. Use a weight with a long leader—10 feet or more—because you need to get down about 20 feet to colder water for a hit.

center. Local fishermen shipped thousands of barrels of ciscoes (lake herring) and whitefish all over the country. For a time ciscoes were so important they became legal tender, or "Chaumont currency."

If after visiting the lake's northeastern islands and bays you are bound northerly for Tibbetts Point, you normally are traveling along a lee shore with a full lake fetch. This area has some dangerous shoals and a slight increase in easterly current, and you are approaching an area with an unusual amount of local magnetic disturbance. Wherever you take your departure from the islands, be certain you lay off a safe course to **Charity Shoal Light, Mile AONT-152.0 + 1.5 (NM).** This is on the lake's main shipping channel; it's your safest passage to enter the St. Lawrence Seaway.

On the way to Tibbetts Point, stay clear of Grenadier Island's shoals.

The 1854 **Tibbetts Point Lighthouse** watches Tibbetts Point. It's on the ship channel's southern side and sports a 69-foot conical tower. The keeper's residence alongside is now a youth hostel. Tibbetts Point marks one entrance to the St. Lawrence River. The portion upstream of Montreal is the St. Lawrence River section of the St. Lawrence Seaway (see Region 5, "The Thousand Islands," beginning on page 252).

Sketch Map Depths

Sketch map depths are given at normal average summer lake level. When you venture outside the sketch map confines, you must adjust NOAA charts to chart datum. For convenience in adjusting, use the following:

Mile AONT-0.0 (NM) to **Mile AONT-164.5 (NM):** Plane of reference, Lake Ontario Low Water Datum, 242.8 feet

LOWER NIAGARA RIVER (YOUNGSTOWN)

Chart: N 14816

Mile AONT-0.0 (NM)

The middle of the Lower Niagara River is the international boundary; Canada is to the west, the United States to the east. When entering the river from the lake, watched shoals extend up to 3 miles off the river's mouth. Expect current to exceed 2.0 knots. As you near shore, the 91-foot Fort Niagara Light is prominent on the eastern point; there's also a range. A U.S. Coast Guard station is inside the river mouth; Niagara-on-the-Lake is on the western bank. As the river makes its first southerly bend, locate a large eastern-shore pleasure-craft mooring area; it's off downtown Youngstown. It has two public docks, yacht clubs, and a boatyard/marina. Dockage along the waterfront is subject to surge when winds are northwesterly.

This is a fairly convenient area from which to visit Niagara Falls, but you'll need transportation. Fort Niagara is in Fort Niagara State Park—you passed it as you came in the entrance. It's a long walk from the waterfront. On display is the fortified French Castle with its historical moats, entrance doors, walls, and blockhouse. Daily features include costumed soldiers on duty, reenactments of barracks life, musket and cannon firing, and drills and reviews; seasonal events include tent camps, drum and fife corps, and encampments that feature the French and Indian War, the American Revolution, and the War of 1812. It's open April 1 to Labor Day from 9 A.M. to 7:30 P.M. Call (716) 745-7611 for special event times and dates.

The Salt Battery, part of the War of 1812 Niagara River defense, is on the waterfront cliff; it overlooks Youngstown's mooring area and Canada's Fort George and Niagara-on-the-Lake.

Downtown Youngstown is up on the cliff; access is either up the stairwell near the northern dock or via the road behind the yacht club. All routes take you to Main Street and a small business district. Take Lockport Road at the town hall a few blocks to the library and a mini plaza with a grocery store.

Lower Niagara River (Youngstown): Youngstown Public Docks, Williams Marine

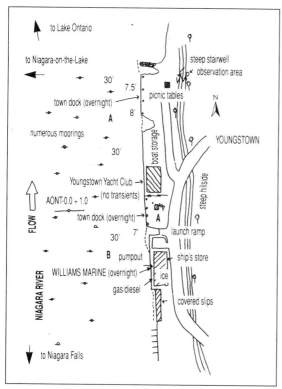

Youngstown Public Docks

★★★★

Chart: N 14816, *See A on sketch map*

Mile AONT-0.0 + 1.0 (NM)

The public docks in Youngstown parallel shore; both are a little difficult to find in the facilities squeezed together along the waterfront. Neither one has a great deal of dockage; you are normally allowed to spend one night.

Northern Public Dock: This dock is the easiest to find. Near the northern end of the moored boats, locate the zigzagging wooden stairwell that climbs the eastern cliff face to the Salt Battery's gazebo; it's above the dock. Though difficult to see if a boat ties alongside, a sign notes that it's a public dock.

There is parallel parking alongside a bulkhead with bollards; make your approach into the current, though this close to shore you are in a fairly stillwater area.

Between the dock and the stairwell is an unused concession stand, a dusty lot, and stored boat cradles.

Southern Public Dock: This is another bulkheaded dock with bollards. It's immediately south of the largest yacht club (they don't want transients); a cement fence separates the two areas. The public dock extends from the fence south to a launching ramp indentation. Make your approach heading into the current and parallel park.

This is the more attractive of the two docks; alongside is a tiny park with a lawn, most of which is taken up by an ice cream stand.

Williams Marine

★★★★

ALL FACILITIES

Chart: N 14816, *See B on sketch map, page 195*

Mile AONT-0.0 + 1.1 (NM)

This marina and yard—open April 1 to November 1—is south of the southern public dock. The marina's parking lot begins just south of the launching ramp; next is the marina's large shoreside building. South of this and extending into the river from the eastern bank are a group of the marina's covered and open slips.

If no one answered on VHF 68, pull in to the fuel dock (gas and diesel) in front of the main building; the office and the ship's store are in its northern end. The store stocks local charts and guides, marine equipment and supplies, picnic items, beer and soda, and fishing licenses. It's an official fishing weigh-in station and has a collection of rental boats.

Block and cube ice, a Travelift, and electric hookups (110-volt/30-amp and 220-volt/50-amp) are available. The land line number is (716) 745-7000.

WILSON HARBOR

Chart: N 14806, *See sketch map, page 197*

Mile AONT-10.8 (NM)

This harbor is at the East Branch of Twelvemile Creek's mouth. There are marinas, yacht clubs, and an anchorage on Tuscarora Bay, the improved inner creek that extends about 0.7 mile back east paralleling the lakeshore. Though the chart lists a public dock on the entrance's eastern side north of **Buoy #5,** it's not recommended. There is only a few feet of water, and northerly quadrant winds bring in an untenable surge.

The harbor has two 500-foot breakwaters, the western one has a red daymark and a light. From the light the entrance is straight forward—you may have a bit more depth by slightly favoring the eastern side. Once clear of the southern ends of the breakwaters, the first set of harbor buoys, **Buoy #4** and **Buoy #5,** begins. From this point on east, best water is in midchannel; it's well watched.

Wilson is about a mile inland southeast of the harbor. Young Street has a bank, a pharmacy, liquor stores, a hardware store, and a few shops. The post office is nearby. Lakeside Market is at Young and Lake streets.

Wilson is a noted fishing hotspot from early spring through December. It has a large runabout and charter fleet. The town hosts assorted fishing festivals and derbies; call (800) 338-7890 for dates.

Wilson Boatyard

★★★

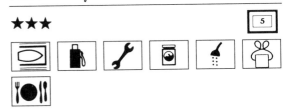

Chart: N 14806, *See A on sketch map, page 197*

Mile AONT-10.8 + 0.3 (NM)

This marina is just inside the entrance at the harbor's eastern end. It's a comfortable and protected stop during northerly quadrant weather, when much of the eastern harbor experiences heavy surge.

Leave the main channel at **Buoy #5** just south of the breakwaters. Make an easterly turn into a side channel that separates the harbor's northern point and the Tuscarora Yacht Club island. The yacht club and marina have finger piers extending from their respective banks; for best water, approach midway between them.

The marina extends along the mainland shoreline to a brick house on the bank near the yacht club island's access bridge. The office is in the northeastern corner.

Wilson Harbor: Wilson Boatyard, Beccue Boat Basin, Tuscarora Bay Anchorage

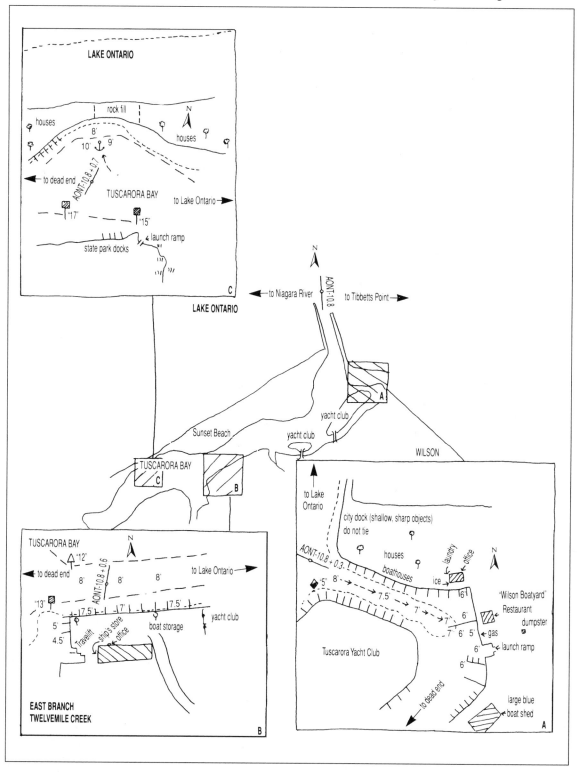

To its south on higher ground is the Wilson Boatyard Restaurant; it has a long pier extending west.

If no one answered on VHF 16, pull in to the fuel dock along the bulkhead south of the restaurant; if your draft is more than 5.5 feet you may not have depth except at its southern end. If you haven't water there, then take any open slip in front of the restaurant, walk to the office, and check in.

Block and cube ice, gasoline, a crane for haulout, and electric hookups (110-volt/20-amp) are available. The land line number is (716) 751-9202.

Beccue Boat Basin

★★★★

Chart: N 14806, *See B on sketch map, page 197*

Mile AONT-10.8 + 0.6 (NM)

Once inside the harbor at **Buoys #4** and **#5,** daymarks watch the rest of the main channel. Make a slight southwesterly turn to pass northwest of the yacht club's island. The channel makes another westerly swing and you pass more mainland yacht clubs. The large complex of buildings south at **Daymark #12** is the Beccue Boat Basin; nearly all its slips are 90 degrees to the bank.

For a slip assignment pull in to the fuel dock (gas and diesel) at the western end of the yard's large building alongside the 30-ton Travelift's well. It's in a southerly cut at the East Branch of Twelvemile Creek's mouth where it flows into Tuscarora Bay—it's visible when you approach **Daymark #13.** The office and ship's store are in the large building's western end. The store offers marine equipment and supplies.

Electric hookups (110-volt/30-amp) are available. The land line number is (716) 751-6466.

A shuttle bus—you have to call for it—runs to downtown's shopping area about every half hour.

Tuscarora Bay Anchorage

★★★★

NO FACILITIES

Chart: N 14806, *See C on sketch map, page 197*

Mile AONT-10.8 + 0.7 (NM)

The westerly end of Tuscarora Bay widens once you reach **Daymarks #12** and **#13.** At **Daymark #18** the bay swings more southwesterly, narrows, shoals, and ends. Though you can anchor in the bay's far westerly end, 6-foot drafts have slightly restricted swinging-room depth. More important—there are mosquitoes.

Best anchorage is on the bay's northern side between **Daymark #16** and **Daymark #18** and by fresh-looking northern-shore stonework. Bottom is mud. This is a popular anchorage; it's not uncommon to find 15 to 20 boats anchored here.

On the southern shore west of the creek's mouth are Tuscarora State Park's docks. These slips are available, but depth out of the main channel on that shore is very minimal. Approach cautiously if you plan to tie up or use their pumpout. You can leave the dinghy there for an excursion ashore to enjoy the park's facilities.

OLCOTT HARBOR

Chart: N 14806, *See sketch map, page 199*

Mile AONT-15.9 (NM)

This harbor at the mouth of Eighteen Mile Creek is navigable a good distance but blocked 0.2 mile upstream by an overhead cable (55 feet) and 0.4 mile upstream by a fixed bridge (50 feet). There are three marinas, a yacht club, and, if you can clear the 50-foot bridge, an anchorage.

The harbor has two breakwaters extending about 400 feet off the beach; the western one has a red lighted daymark. The entrance is straight forward, with best water usually in midchannel. At the western breakwater's southern end the channel makes a slight easterly bend and holds to that shore nearly to the bridge.

No matter where you stay in the harbor, there is a severe surge in strong northerly quadrant winds.

Olcott Harbor: Hedley Boat Company, Town of Newfane Marina, McDonough Marina, Olcott Anchorage

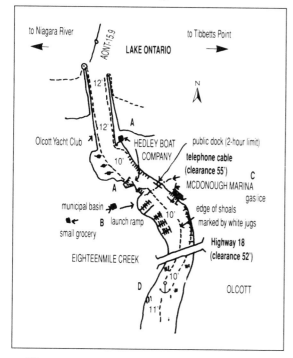

If you need basic groceries and are on the harbor's western side, get on Main Street—by the ramp—then bear westerly about a block to the Olcott Mini Mart. Nearby is a liquor store. If on the harbor's eastern side, you are near downtown Olcott; it has a few small shops, cafés, a deli, the fire department, and a filling station. The post office is at the bridge's eastern foot next to a red caboose and town park. A public dock—2-hour time limit—is about under the overhead cable on the creek's eastern side; it's a place to land the dinghy if you need access to that shore.

Olcott is a popular fishing area with charter boats, fishing piers, and bait and tackle shops. It's known for Chinook salmon fishing in September and October, rainbow/steelhead trout in the spring, and its fishing festival in June.

Hedley Boat Company

★★

ALL FACILITIES *(no diesel fuel)*

Chart: N 14806, *See A on sketch map*

Mile AONT-15.9 + 0.2 (NM)

Wherever you stay in the marina complex, you have access to its main facilities. A 30-ton Travelift, gasoline, and 110-volt electric hookups are available. Call (716) 778-7771 for more information.

Hedley East: This marina is in two main sections. Its office, a two-story barn-shaped building with an adjoining boatyard, is on the eastern shore just south of the breakwater. Almost directly opposite at the western breakwater's southern end is the Olcott Yacht Club clubhouse and a few moorings. If no one answered on VHF 16, pull in to the fuel dock in front of the marina building.

Hedley West: This is the preferred spot to spend the night in regard to protection, surge, and good depth. It's on the creek's western shore in a bulk-headed basin with a very small entrance, about opposite a group of eastern-shore covered slips located just where the creek narrows. More obvious, to the basin's south on the western bank are slips at 90 degrees to the shore—they belong to the yacht club. The basin has restricted turning room.

Town of Newfane Marina

★★

Chart: N 14806, *See B on sketch map*

Mile AONT-15.9 + 0.2 (NM)

This marina is on the creek's western side just south of the 55-foot overhead cable. This is the shoal side of the creek, and it is usually watched by at least one buoy at the cable. The marina may not have enough depth if your draft is more than 4.5 feet. The office, a small brown building, is at the marina's northern end next to the Olcott Yacht Club slips. The Harbor Patrol boat docks in front of it.

The marina is primarily for shoal-draft fishing runabouts—a multiple launching ramp is in midcomplex.

McDonough Marina

★★

Chart: N 14806, *See C on sketch map, page 199*

Mile AONT-15.9 + 0.2 (NM)

This marina on the eastern bank is across from the Town of Newfane Marina and just south of the 55-foot overhead cable. It maintains only a few floating slips, primarily for use by small fishing boats. If there's room and your boat is not immense, you usually can spend the night. Gasoline and 110-volt electric hookups are available.

Olcott Anchorage

★★

NO FACILITIES

Chart: N 14806, *See D on sketch map, page 199*

Mile AONT-15.9 + 0.4 (NM)

This anchorage is south of the 55-foot overhead cable and the 50-foot fixed bridge. Once you have cleared the overhead cable, the channel is along the eastern shore. There may not be standard navigation aids in this reach, though normally some sort of floating objects indicate the western shoal line. As you approach the bridge, the channel swings toward midstream; at the bridge you are fairly close to the western abutment.

The upper creek—upstream of the bridge—has a limited deepwater channel, so anchor in mud in midstream; sound for swinging-room depth. There's a lot of traffic when runabouts are confined to the harbor because the lake is rough, and on weekends. Have a bright anchor light.

POINT BREEZE HARBOR

Chart: N 14805, *See sketch map, page 201*

Mile AONT-39.3 (NM)

This is a crowded harbor with high wooded banks at Oak Orchard Creek's mouth. The creek is navigable for over 1.5 miles, but there are restrictions. About 0.6 mile upcreek a pair of 54-foot-clearance fixed bridges cross the creek. If you can clear these, you can continue upstream around a horseshoe bend to three low-level fixed bridges and overhead cables. Be cautious here; clearance varies, but is about 8 feet.

The entrance has two northerly-extending stone breakwaters watched by a red and a green daymark, and an offshore steel-bulkheaded breakwater paralleling the coast. The latter protects the harbor from northerly quadrant seas. On the offshore breakwater's western end is a 25-foot daymark marked "**C**"; on its eastern end is one similarly marked "**A**"; in the middle is a 30-foot-high daymark marked "**B**". Since you must round this offshore breakwater to reach the two main breakwaters, you may have buoys set south of both ends that watch beach shoals. **Buoy #2** is shoreward of the western end; **Buoy #1** is shoreward of the eastern end. Best entry depth is usually at the western end. If wind and seas are out of any northerly direction, the water discoloration south of the offshore breakwater can be disconcerting. Though color variation does not necessarily indicate that shoaling has occurred, it might. Make your approach with extreme caution.

Point Breeze is a popular trout- and salmon-fishing area; a local boat caught the King salmon that earned the Great Lakes record.

Point Breeze Harbor: Four C's Marina, Oak Orchard Anchorage

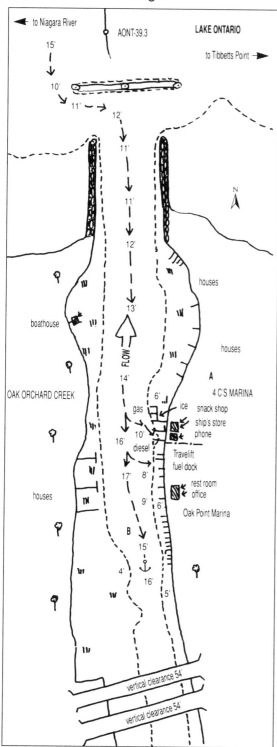

Four C's Marina

★★★

Chart: N 14805, *See A on sketch map*

Mile AONT-39.3 + 0.5 (NM)

Once you have reached the end of the two inner breakwaters the harbor widens, but continue to hold to mid-channel. Two 54-foot high-level bridges are visible ahead. As the creek begins to narrow, you can see a collection of slips along the eastern shore. Your destination is the northernmost facility—open April 1 to October 31.

If no one answered on VHF 16, pull in to the fuel dock at 90 degrees to the shore—you can see the pumps (gas and diesel). If your draft is over 6 feet, come in carefully; it shoals as you close the bank. The office and the ship's store are up the ramp; the store offers a selection of marine equipment, navigation supplies, local charts, camera supplies, and nautical clothing.

The marina has 12 boats (18-footers) and outboards for rent, and offers motel accommodations. Block and cube ice, 110-volt/30-amp electric hookups, and a 20-ton Travelift are available. If you need a diver, check at the office. The land line number is (716) 682-4224.

There is a café with a porch overlooking the creek; it's open from 5 A.M. to 9 P.M. Two large restaurants are near the eastern breakwater's southern end.

Oak Orchard Anchorage

★★★

NO FACILITIES

Chart: N 14805, *See B on sketch map*

Mile AONT-39.3 + 0.7 (NM)

Once the creek narrows, about opposite Four C's Marina, the channel holds to the eastern shore. The anchorage is north of the bridge in a muddy bottom with some weeds.

Though it's possible to anchor farther upstream if you have bridge clearance, you need to go some distance to avoid blocking access into a long line of docks.

The anchorage has little traffic except on weekends, or when the lake is too rough for small boats, or when a fishing derby is in progress. At that time runabouts putter up and down the creek day and night. Have a bright anchor light.

ROCHESTER HARBOR

Charts: N 14804; N 14815

Mile AONT-67.6 (NM)

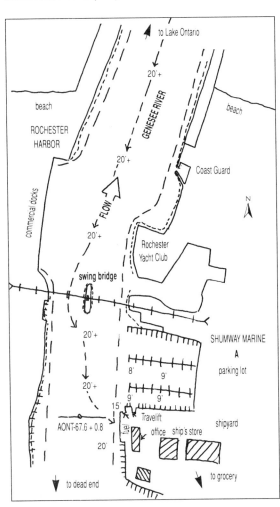

Most of Rochester's facilities, including yacht clubs and marinas for overnight, are within a mile of the harbor's entrance.

The Genesee River is deep for about 4 miles above its mouth, but a few miles more and it's blocked by a group of dams and waterfalls north of which is the Erie Canal. There's no navigable route between the two; the state never found it feasible to overcome the Genesee River Gorge's 260-foot drop. Access into the Erie Canal from Lake Ontario is east at Oswego.

In the 1800s the canal crossed the river above the falls on an aqueduct—today's Broad Street. Rochester's city center settled there and stayed. It's within visiting distance of the harbor by taxi, rental car, or city bus.

Shumway Marine

★★

ALL FACILITIES

Chart: N 14815, *See A on sketch map*

Mile AONT-67.6 + 0.8 (NM)

Once you have navigated through the ship channel entrance breakwaters and have arrived at their southern ends, the Ontario Beach Park is to your west, followed by a collection of commercial facilities at the Port of Rochester. A U.S. Coast Guard Station is on the eastern shore; to its south is a yacht club in an enclosed basin.

The untimed Conrail bridge is usually in the open position. Once through this, you will find Shumway Marine—open March 1 to November 1—in an eastern shoreside indentation filled with slips. The facility's buildings are blue with white roofs.

If no one answered on VHF 9, pull in to the fuel dock south of the slip area and along the river channel. The pumps (gas and diesel) on the bulkhead are in front of the one-story ship's store and office. Transient dockage is usually in the northern slip area. A 40-ton Travelift and electric hookups (110-volt/30-amp and 220-volt/50-amp) are available.

The very large ship's store includes equipment, charts and navigation supplies, books, hardware, nautical clothing, paint, gifts, and a large motor parts department. Their fax number is (716) 342-3142. The marina's land line number is (716) 342-3030.

The Stutson Bridge Plaza is on the highway that crosses the Stutson Street Bridge. When you exit the marina's grounds via its access road, you are across the street from the plaza. The stores include a laundromat, Fays Drugs, hardware and liquor stores, and Bells Supermarket. If you cross the Stutson Street Bridge and turn north a block from the river on Lake Avenue, there's a selection of restaurants.

SODUS BAY

Charts: N 14804; N 14814

Mile AONT-95.2 (NM)

This large protected bay with wooded shoreline hills has marinas and anchorages. Access into the bay is by way of two 1,000-foot breakwaters in its northwestern corner. The western breakwater extends northerly from Sodus Point. Charles Point, a narrow strip of land, reaches westerly from the eastern shore. From its western end is a manmade quarter-mile breakwater extension that makes a 90-degree northerly turn to become the eastern entrance breakwater.

Once you are in the entrance, the southeasterly reaching peninsula of Sand Point is dead ahead. Be careful of the shoals to its north and west; **Daymark #6** watches them. Nearly all bay dockage is on Sand Point's southern side. East and southeast are the bay's three islands.

The village of Sodus Point is partly on Sand Point and the Sodus Point peninsula; it caters to summer visitors and fishermen. On Sand Point are small marine-oriented businesses, tourist attractions, a deli, snack

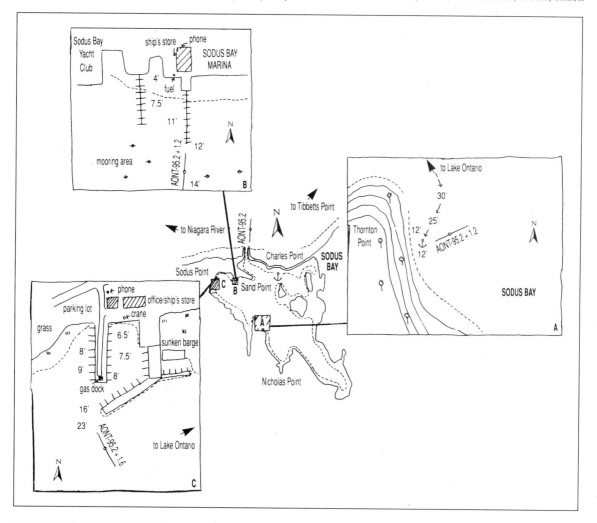

shops, and restaurants. The post office and two convenience stores, Don's and Shirtz Grocery, are up the hill on the peninsula.

The 1870 Sodus Point Lighthouse Maritime Museum is worth a visit. It's a long walk—pack a lunch. Take Greig Road on Sand Point up the hill and get on Bay Street. At the firehouse, turn north on Ontario Street; the old light is on the hill at the lake. The museum is open for tours on summer weekends; every Sunday at 4 P.M., there's a concert on the lawn. Call (716) 483-4936 for the current program.

The Fourth of July Gala Week End features the Lighthouse Run, a flea market, a farmers' market, breakfast on the bluff, and musical performances. At night there is the Wall of Fire Around Sodus Bay and fireworks.

Sodus Bay Anchorages

★★★★

NO FACILITIES

Chart: N 14814, *See A on sketch map, page 203*

Mile AONT-95.2 + 1.2 (NM)

A favorite isolated anchorage is off Thornton Point; it has a superb view, good swimming, and perch and bluegill fishing.

After you enter the harbor and round Sand Point, Thornton Point is about 0.8 mile south; it's high, narrow, wooded, and northerly reaching. Anchor in mud off its eastern shore about 0.2 mile south of its northerly end. In prevailing southwesterly winds, this is a peaceful anchorage; if wind is out of the northerly quadrant, it can be rough. In these conditions anchor south of Sand Point immediately east of the mooring area. If you visit over a weekend, expect this anchorage to be rough during daylight hours from constant traffic wakes.

Another anchorage in mild northerly winds is along the Charles Point spit. Leave Sand Point and head for Charles Point; keep north of **Buoy #2** at the northern end of Newark Island. Anchor very close to the spit about midway between Newark Island and Le Roy Island. Don't go too close to Le Roy Island; a long shoal makes out south of the spit. Bottom is mud, with a pro-

voking cover of weeds—though these make for excellent fishing. If wind is strong northerlies, the anchorage is very windswept.

Sodus Bay Marina

★★★

Chart: N 14814, *See B on sketch map, page 203*

Mile AONT-95.2 + 1.2 (NM)

This small marina is on Sand Point's southern side. After rounding the point's eastern end, stand clear of the shoal shoreline. Though waterfront homes have piers, most are for shoal-draft runabouts. The marina is the first large facility as you bear west; it's east of Sodus Bay Yacht Club, which is usually decked out with festive banners. There are offshore moorings.

If no one answered on VHF 16, pull in to the T-pier's eastern end or to the fuel dock; it's west of the main finger pier along the bulkhead in front of the office. If you draw more than 4 feet, approach cautiously. Dockage is limited, but they offer moorings; if you take the latter, ask where to tie the dinghy when you go ashore. The land line number is (716) 483-9376.

You are only a few steps from the main thoroughfare and close to a popular restaurant, Papa Joe's.

Sills Marina

★★★

ALL FACILITIES

Chart: N 14814, *See C on sketch map, page 203*

Mile AONT-95.2 + 1.6 (NM)

This marina is southwest of Sand Point in the central part of the bay's northwestern corner. Once you arrive at the easterly end of Sand Point, take a close look at the land format on the chart. Where the Sodus Point railroad track ends is the Sills Marina complex.

The marina has two moles extending from the southern side of Sodus Point; the most easterly has two extensions. The largest reaches south and then makes a southwesterly jog; it has slips on its northwesterly face. A shorter easterly reaching pier with slips on its northern face also extends off the eastern mole. This eastern mole and its extensions protect the inner western mole; you must round its western end to access the marina complex. The western mole has slips on both sides. On its southern face is the fuel dock (gas and diesel); pull in to ask about dockage. If no one is about, check the office; it's in the most westerly of the mainland's large buildings. The land line number is (716) 483-9102.

A Travelift is available for haulout.

The distance to the small grocery stores is slightly less than when at Sand Point; it's about the same to the post office and the old lighthouse. It's a long walk to Sand Point's main attractions and restaurants.

LITTLE SODUS BAY

Chart: N 14803

Mile AONT-107.6 (NM)

This 2.3-mile-long bay with high wooded banks extends in an almost due-south direction from its entrance. There is a selection of marinas and an anchorage.

Enter the bay through two breakwaters; the western one is 500 feet long and is watched by a red lighted daymark. Extending westerly from the eastern shore at Sabin Point is a long manmade barrier wall enclosing the bay's northern end. This makes an abrupt northerly jog to form the eastern entrance breakwater, which is watched by a green lighted daymark.

When you begin passage through the breakwaters, hold to midchannel. Once past the eastern barrier's jog, continue this course to clear the bay's extreme northern

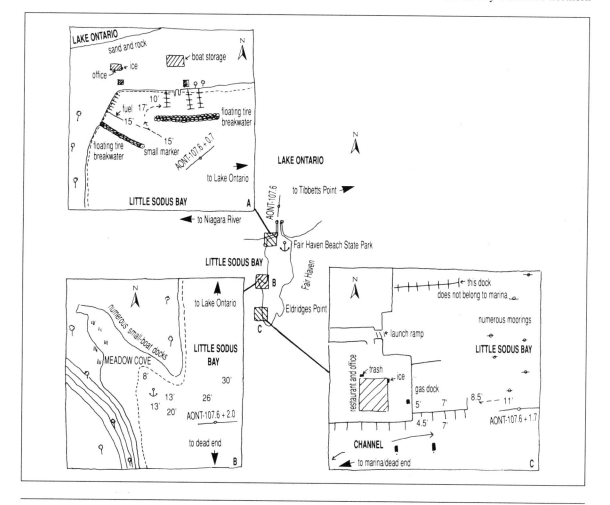

shoreline shoals. The bay has one major unwatched off-shore shoal at Grass Island—not visible in most lake levels. It's about 800 feet off the western shore and about 2,000 feet south of the entrance-barrier jog. It stretches south nearly 1,000 feet. There are other bay shoals, but these are mainly restricted to ends of coves or off extending points.

Fair Haven's supplies and groceries are not easily accessible from marinas or by hiking from anchorages; it's more convenient to visit by dinghy. At the bay's southern end is a cove to the east of Eldridges Point; it has a ramp near its southern end where you can land the dinghy. Walk a block up the access road to Richmond Avenue and you are downtown, with a post office, a hardware store, a museum, a restaurant, an ice cream stand, and a Big M supermarket.

The 865-acre Fair Haven Beach State Park is in the bay's northeastern corner. The complex surrounds Sterling Pond and faces the bay and lake. It has camping facilities, playgrounds, picnic areas, telephones, showers, and a launching ramp. Its one finger pier is open to prevailing winds. Dockside depths—especially on the northern face—are very minimal. You can anchor off, however, and tie the dinghy at the pier's easterly end to enjoy the park.

The bay's annual Fair Haven Fourth of July Field Days has midway rides, games, entertainment, races, fireworks, and a Fair Haven Wall of Fire.

Boathouse Marina

★★★

Chart: N 14803, *See A on sketch map, page 205*

Mile AONT-107.6 + 0.7 (NM)

This marina—open April 15 to October 31—is in the bay's northwestern corner. After you enter the bay and clear the barrier wall and the breakwater's shoreside shoals, bear westerly toward the visible marina buildings. Slips extend from the northern shore and are protected by two floating tire breakwaters. One is offshore; the other extends from the western bank. Make your entry between the two.

If no one answered on VHF 16/9, pull in to the long

fuel dock extending from the northwestern shore just north of the southern breakwater—as you enter the marina, it's nearly dead ahead. The office is off the parking lot and boat storage area nearer the main lake. Nearby is a travel trailer park and a small motel.

There are a few slips for shoal-draft vessels along the bank north of the fuel dock (gas and diesel), but most slips are in the three finger piers that extend from the northern shore. The bathhouse is at the head of the middle finger pier.

Block and cube ice, a 20-ton Travelift, and 110-volt electric hookups are available. Credit cards are accepted for purchases over $50. The marina's land line number is (315) 947-6111.

Fair Haven Beach State Park is across the bay; if it isn't too rough for your dinghy, it's an area worth visiting.

Meadow Cove Anchorage

★★★★

NO FACILITIES

Chart: N 14803, *See B on sketch map, page 205*

Mile AONT-107.6 + 1.7 (NM)

Meadow Cove is about halfway down the lake on the western shore. It's open to the southeast. Stand clear of Grass Island; it's near your approach route. During your cove entry don't hug its shoal northeastern point as you round up northwest. Take care; the cove's upper reaches are shoal and the heavy weed growth gives false fathometer readings. Bottom is mud with weeds.

Homes and a few private docks nestle along the cove's wooded shoreline. Fishing for perch, bluegill, and crappie is excellent. If you need groceries, it's about 0.7 mile to town by dinghy.

Chinook Harbor Marina

★★

Chart: N 14803, *See C on sketch map, page 205*

Mile AONT-107.6 + 2.0 (NM)

This marina—open April 1 to October 15—is on the western shore near the bay's southern end. There are a group of facilities here, but the marina's Shell fuel pump (gas only) is in front of the restaurant and store—a rather large building just south of a ramp. On its southern side is a buoyed channel that leads to an inner basin. There are moorings just offshore.

For dockage pull in to the fuel dock directly in front of the restaurant/office along the bulkhead. If you draw more than 5 feet, you may not have depth, in which case pull in temporarily on the main finger's eastern end.

Electric hookups (110-volt) are available. The marina's land line number is (716) 436-0338.

The family-style restaurant overlooks the bay—try the Harborburger for lunch. The store sells fishing tackle, marine supplies, charts, camera supplies, nautical clothing, a fair selection of groceries, and fishing licenses.

OSWEGO HARBOR

(See Region 2, "The Oswego Canal," beginning on page 98.)

The Bays of Lake Ontario's Golden Crescent

Mile AONT-140.0 + 18.2–24.0 (NM)

North of Mexico Bay, Lake Ontario's northeastern section has three favorite large bays: Henderson, Black River, and Chaumont. Though islands, shoals, and reefs abound, they are well watched. There are protected marinas and anchorages.

When northbound at Oswego, a safe Golden Crescent entry is between Stony Point Light and Stony Island. After a visit, when northbound again, a safe exit is south of Point Peninsula and north of Stony Island on a course for East Charity Shoal Light on the steamer channel. Remember: At this end of the lake, no matter where you come from or are heading to, current, and therefore set, is increasing as you approach the St. Lawrence Seaway. Mind the increased magnetic variation as you plot courses; it's a major factor in landfalls in restricted visibility. During normal conditions this portion of the lake is open to prevailing afternoon winds and can be rough.

Regional mileage for this end of the lake follows the steamer channel that runs nearly due north out of Oswego to off **Galloo Shoal Buoy #3.** Departure from this channel into the Golden Crescent can be at **Mile AONT-140.0 (NM),** which puts it about 8 miles west of Stony Point Light.

This area played a significant role in early history—especially the War of 1812. Residents are proud of their heritage; their museums, walking tours, and historical sites lure history buffs.

HENDERSON BAY

Charts: N 14802; N 14811, *See sketch map, page 208*

Mile AONT-140.0 + 15.0 (NM)

This 5-mile-long bay is on Stony Point peninsula's northeastern side. The bay's northwestern side is an extension of the northern end of Stony Point peninsula and a collection of islands and reefs. There is an anchorage on the northwestern shore near the middle of Henderson Bay, and there are marinas in Henderson Harbor, at the bay's southern end.

When off **Stony Point Light,** hold about midway between Stony Island and Stony Point peninsula; then bear in a northeasterly direction. Stand clear of the rocks and shoals northwest of the northeasterly extension off Stony Point. **Light Buoy #1** watches the southwestern end of Lime Barrel Shoals. This is the small-craft-channel entry point into Henderson Bay.

Once inside the bay bear back into the southerly quad-

Henderson Bay: RCR Yachts, West View Lodge and Marina, Snowshoe Bay Anchorage

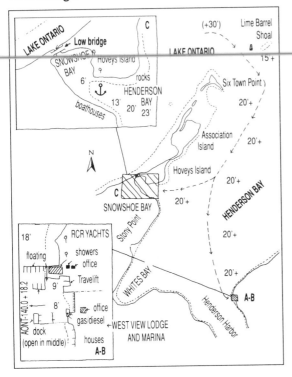

western end of one of the two finger piers or by the 25-ton Travelift's well—it's along the shore south of the large work buildings.

In very strong north and northeasterly winds, the marina is subject to some surge, though it's not uncomfortable.

The marina's land line number is (315) 938-5494. There's a ship's store, and since the complex is also a large charter company—fax (315) 938-5536—there's marine equipment, basic groceries and picnic supplies, and local charts. Block and cube ice and electric hookups (110-volt/30-amp and 220-volt/30-amp) are available. If you need a diver, check at the office.

Town is about 1.7 miles away; there's a courtesy car. The Harbor Inn restaurant is about 20 yards away, and the Gillhouse Inn is about a block north on the main road.

West View Lodge and Marina

★★★ | 3 |

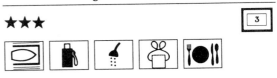

Charts: N 14802; N 14811, *See B on sketch map*

Mile AONT-140.0 + 19.0 (NM)

This marina and lodge—open April 25 to October 15—is immediately south of RCR Yachts. The marina slips extend along the eastern shore and wrap around the westerly extending shoreline. This is a popular fishing resort, and though the marina appears to cater only to powerboats, it welcomes sailing vessels.

If no one answered on VHF 10, pull in to the fuel dock (gas and diesel) on the eastern shore south of an indentation filled with slips. The office is in the main lodge. If you plan to stay ashore during the fishing season, make reservations. The land line number is (315) 938-5445.

There's a ship's store with some marine equipment, charts, nautical clothing, camera supplies, a fine supply of fishing equipment, and fishing licenses. Ice (block and cube) is available. More extensive supplies and groceries are still 1.7 miles away.

rant. The marinas are in Henderson Harbor, 3 miles off in the bay's southerly corner. This harbor—about a mile long and 0.7 mile wide—is open to northerly winds.

RCR Yachts

★★★ | 3 |

Charts: N 14802; N 14811, *See A on sketch map*

Mile AONT-140.0 + 19.0 (NM)

This marina—open April 1 to November 1—is on Henderson Harbor's eastern side near its northeastern point. It's the first large group of slips and buildings once you clear the point. Though you might see a sign noting Exclusively Sail, the marina welcomes powerboats. If no one answered on VHF 16/71, pull in on the

Snowshoe Bay Anchorage

★★★

NO FACILITIES

Charts: N 14802; N 14911, *See C on sketch map, 208*

Mile AONT-140.0 + 18.2 (NM)

This anchorage is in Snowshoe Bay, a small cove on Henderson Bay's western side. It's well protected from all winds except easterlies, though this is normally a fair-weather wind direction. Once you reach **Lime Barrel Shoal Buoy #1** and enter Henderson Bay, your route is 2 miles along its western shore. Keep *well* clear of the rocks and shoals that extend southeast of Six Town Point, Association Island, and Hoveys Island. The latter makes up Snowshoe Bay's northeastern shoreline.

Enter the harbor when the eastern portion of Snowshoe opens fully. You can see the low-level bridge crossing the narrow neck of land along the lake shoreline as you enter. The bay's northwestern half is shoal; in midsummer's extensive weed growth, a fathometer does not give an accurate reading.

Anchor in mud in midbay about opposite a northeastern shore point. This usually puts you outside the heavy weed line. Fishing for bass and perch is very good; use worms or troll with the dinghy by the inlet's bridge or on Hoveys Island's northeastern side.

There's almost no access ashore; it's all private property.

BLACK RIVER BAY

Charts: N 14802; N 14811, *See sketch map, page 210*

Mile AONT-140.0 + 18.0 (NM)

This bay, located at the mouth of the Black River and smaller Perch and Muskalonge creeks, is 5 miles long and 1 mile wide. Sackets Harbor, the bay's deepwater port, is toward its western end. It has a selection of marinas.

Your approach to Black River Bay is the same as your approach to Henderson Bay as far as Lime Barrel Shoal. Instead of bearing into Henderson Bay continue another 2.9 miles as far as Horse Island—Sackets

Harbor Light is on the island's northwestern shore.

Navy Point—it has a red lighted daymark on its eastern end—protects Sackets Harbor's northeastern side. The point was the town's main shipbuilding site in the 19th century. An approach landmark is a large gold-painted building to its west—part of the Navy Point Marina. Once you reach the daymark, there's a collection of moorings watched by a group of yellow lighted yellow buoys. Along the point's shoreline is a Travelift well. Watch your wake during harbor entry or the local jet-ski-riding marine patrol officer may ticket you.

Though you can find plenty of restaurants, snacks, and fudge shops downtown, there are only a few stores, an antique shop, a post office, and a Key Bank. The supermarket is about 0.7 mile northeast up the main road in a housing development partly built around the old Madison Barracks complex.

Much of Sackets Harbor's modern economy caters to summer visitors touring its historical sites—it's a New York State Urban Cultural Park, many of whose buildings are on the National Register of Historic Places. Most are within easy walking distance, as downtown is along the harbor's southern shore.

A good first stop in town is the four-columned Sacket Mansion, circa 1803, on Main Street near Market Square; it's open from 9 to 5. Here you can pick up a walking-tour map to help you find more than 150 nearby historical buildings.

At Main and Ray streets in the stone Union Hotel (circa 1817) is the visitor center for the 30-acre downtown Sackets Harbor Battlefield Site. Madison Barracks National Historic District is a short walk northeast of downtown. Built at the close of the War of 1812 around Fort Pike and Fort Volunteer, its fortifications protected the thousands of troops on war duty.

From mid-June through Labor Day the Sackets Harbor Historical Society hosts Sunday concerts on the waterfront. These are held either at Market Square Park or Battlefield State Park.

The annual four-day Sackets Harbor Days includes parades, craft shows, concerts and dances, rides, games, the Firemen's Chicken Barbecue, waterfront concerts, and fireworks.

Navy Point Marine

★★★★★

ALL FACILITIES

Charts: N 14802; N 14811, *See A on sketch map*

Mile AONT-140.0 + 19.6 (NM)

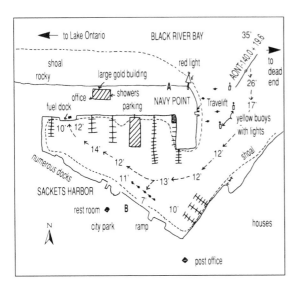

Once clear of the outer mooring area, round the southerly reaching arm of Navy Point to enter the harbor. The marina complex extends along the northern shore with piers extending from Navy Point. If no one answered on VHF 9, pull in to the fuel dock (gas and diesel) near the harbor's western end. Continue along the ends of the marina piers, pass two open piers with fingers, one covered, two more open, and then the fuel dock along the bulkhead. If no one is on duty, check in at the office; it's the gold building by the road. If a slip is unavailable, ask about a mooring.

There's a ship's store with marine equipment, charts and navigation supplies, basic groceries, and picnic supplies. Electric hookups (110-volt/30-amp), block and cube ice, and a 20-ton Travelift are available. The land line number is (315) 646-3364.

There are at least six restaurants nearby.

Market Square Dock

★★★

Charts: N 14802; N 14811, *See B on sketch map*

Mile AONT-140.0 + 19.6 (NM)

Once you round the southerly reaching arm of Navy Point and are inside the harbor, the public dock is on the southwestern shore northwest of a visible launching ramp. Other landmarks are a group of small mooring buoys off a bulkhead. Rising up a grassy knoll behind the bulkhead is Market Square, a public park.

You are expected to pick up a mooring and put your boat's most convenient boarding end up to the wall. If you have a large deep-draft vessel this could be tricky; the buoys are not that far offshore and depth is minimal close to the bulkhead. It's a first-come first-served arrangement; if the dockmaster is not visible to point out a spot, pick up whatever offshore buoy (line attached) is appealing and go through the gyrations of getting your other end up to the bulkhead cleats. Then walk to the top of the rise to the dockmaster's office and check in.

This stop has a lot of surge during strong northeasterlies and when a chop is running on Black River Bay. Any slight wave action coming around the point intensifies as it ricochets off the bulkhead.

This is a pretty park and local promenade, so expect a parade of dock walkers peering curiously into your cockpit—if that's what you put up to the wall. There are picnic tables and garbage bins, and the lawns are favorite suntanning salons, especially on weekends.

The park borders Main Street, so you are downtown. During the historical society's Sunday concerts on the waterfront, your boat is the best seat in the house. This also holds true during the village's large annual festival, held in July.

POINT PENINSULA

Charts: N 14802; N 14811

Mile AONT-140.0 + 15.0–21.0 (NM)

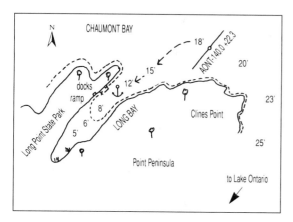

This large peninsula is almost an island; it is part of Chaumont Bay's southern shoreline. The point is connected to the mainland by a narrow causeway on its northwestern side. The prevailingly southwesterlies make the point's Lake Ontario shoreline nearly untenable. Those that face Chaumont Bay are badly exposed to the easterly quadrant, but it has one pretty cove that is open to the northeast but otherwise well protected.

Long Point State Park Anchorage

★★★   3

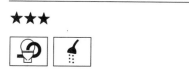

Charts: N 14802; N 14811

Mile AONT-140.0 + 22.3 (NM)

When you arrive at Stony Point Light off the southwestern side of Stony Point peninsula, lay off a course for lighted **Buoy #2** off Stony Island's northeastern end; then one to Point Peninsula's southern shoals, marked by **Light Buoy #3.** From here head for Cherry Island, about 5 miles northeast and accessible through the 0.5-mile-wide channel between Point Peninsula and the headland of Pillar Point.

Narrow Cherry Island lies in a southwest-northeast direction off Point Salubrious and is watched on its southwesterly end by a light. The channel is wide, so don't approach the light closely; there's no navigation aid on the dangerous rocks that extend to its southwest. Pass northwest of Cherry Island; your anchorage appears when you round the northeasterly end of Point Peninsula.

Wait until the cove opens fully, then enter in mid-cove. There's a northwestern shore ramp that can be very busy on weekends—don't anchor in front of it. There's also limited transient dockage. If you decide to tie up or come in to use the park pumpout, approach with care; it shoals along the shoreline. Preference is to anchor, since even light northeasterly winds make dockage uncomfortable if not dangerous. Anchor in mud near the entrance to the cove; farther inside there is heavy weed growth as the season progresses and the water warms.

The cove is part of 23-acre Long Point State Park. To go ashore, tie the dinghy at the park docks, but don't block space usable for large boats. There are picnic tables, shelters, and a camping area with showers and rest rooms.

CHAUMONT BAY

Charts: N 14802; N 14811

Mile AONT-140.0 + 21.0 (NM)

This large bay is often windswept from midmorning until dusk. Sawmill Bay is in its east-northeastern corner near Chaumont and offers a pleasant, protective tie-up.

Crescent Yacht Club

★★★   4

ALL FACILITIES

Charts: N 14802; N 14811, *See sketch map, page 212*

Mile AONT-140.0 + 24.0 (NM)

This yacht club—founded in 1901—accepts visitors affiliated with other lake clubs and those that are not. There's limited space.

The club is about 16 miles from Stony Point Light.

Crescent Yacht Club

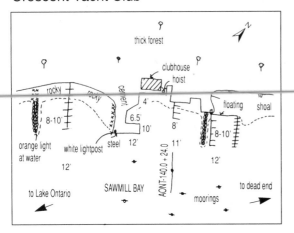

Follow the approach directions to Long Point State Park Anchorage as far as the northeastern tip of Point Peninsula. Continue to bear somewhat northeast for another 3.5 miles. Take care; Chaumont Bay's east-northeastern end has a number of dangerous shoals near your course line. You pass Point Salubrious on your east and Johnson Shoal on your west. About opposite on the Point Salubrious mainland is a shoal shoreline indentation. Point Independence divides narrow Sawmill Bay and a larger bay at Chaumont River's mouth. Off the end of Point Independence's shoals is midchannel **Buoy HBC.** Bear into 1,000-foot-wide Sawmill Bay and pass east of Chaumont Harbor Light.

The club is on the bay's western shore near its north-eastern end; you'll see a few boats on the offshore club moorings. At the complex's southwestern end there is a tire breakwater extending off the western bank with its land-side connection on a very short, partially submerged rock breakwater. Next are a main pier with finger slips, then an L-shaped mole, the clubhouse set back of the mole, the small boat ramp, a short finger of slips, another tire breakwater, and finally another pair of piers with slips.

Pull in to the fuel dock (gas only) next to the ramp, walk to the clubhouse, and find the officer of the day for fuel and dockage information. If you need repairs, check at the office. Most transients tie up on the pier nearest the southern breakwater; in strong prevailing winds its southern end can have quite a surge. If dockage is limited, ask about an available mooring. On weekends the club is very active. It has a large Lightning class fleet.

The clubhouse, which can be reached at (315) 649-2150, is very comfortable, and there's an outdoor patio with picnic tables and a fireplace. There's also a playground. Haulout by railway or 20-ton Travelift, block and cube ice, and 110-volt electric hookups are available.

If you need groceries or a few supplies, Chaumont is a long but pretty walk away. The club's long lane is narrow and wooded. Once you reach the main road, bear northeast about two blocks to Highway 12E. There's a post office, a library, a hardware store, a pizza parlor, and Dick's Mid-State Grocery Store.

The Canadian Shore
Fort Niagara to Kingston

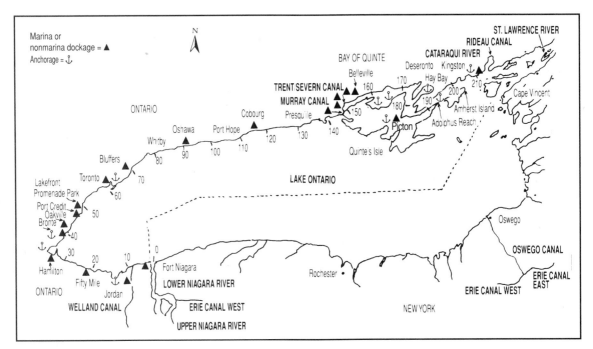

Mile CONT-0.0 (NM) to Mile CONT-212.3 (NM)

> *I love a people who have always made me welcome with the best they had. . . .*
>
> GEORGE CATLIN

MOVABLE BRIDGES, FORT NIAGARA TO KINGSTON

Name	Type	Mile	Clearance (Closed)*
Burlington Canal			
Combined Hwy./RR**	Lift	CONT-34.3 + (NM)	10 feet
*Murray Canal****			
Brighton Road Bridge	Swing	CONT-145.9 (NM)	8 feet
CN Railroad Bridge****	Swing	CONT-148.5 (NM)	10 feet
Carrying Place Bridge	Swing	CONT-148.8 (NM)	10 feet

*At normal lake level

**Operates 24 hours. Opens for pleasure craft on hour and half hour, and for commercial/government vessels any time.

***All vessels: Pass through south reach of spans. Navigation daymarks watch all bridge approaches. To open any bridge requires one toll collected at Brighton Road eastern side.

****Usually remains open unless a train is due.

This section includes more than 210 miles of Canadian shoreline. Mileage begins at the Niagara River's mouth, **Mile CONT-0.0 (NM).** The route generally follows the lake's perimeter about 1 to 2 miles offshore. It bears westerly to Hamilton, **Mile CONT-34.3 (NM),** then begins a northeasterly curve to Presqu'ile, **Mile CONT-141.0 (NM).** Mileage is then through the Bay of Quinte, a protected inland passage, to reach the northwestern head of the St. Lawrence River at Kingston, **Mile CONT-212.3 (NM).**

The main lakeshore has many harbors. The longest distance between them is about 28 miles—less if you have draft under 6 feet. Lake harbors are usually improved basins at river or creek mouths. Many are very small—only the width of a creek or river—and most are full. Transient dockage is often determined by how many residents are on holiday, leaving their wells empty. Large harbors—Hamilton, Toronto, and Cobourg—have room for anchoring. The Bay of Quinte, a popular area, takes the overload of visitors unable to find space in the Thousand Islands.

At the Niagara River's mouth, Fort Mississauga's earthworks and blockhouse sit near the western point's edge; beside it is Niagara-on-the-Lake. Loyalists came across the river after the American Revolution and settled the village.

Westbound at the Niagara River, it's about 6.5 miles to the Welland Canal's northern entrance. Its mile-long northerly reaching breakwaters, the 49-foot Port Weller Outer Light on the west, and the 33-foot eastern light are all very visible. In fog, cross the canal's entrance with caution; a stream of ship traffic plies to and from Lake Erie.

Though it's certainly possible for pleasure craft to transit the Welland upbound, it's not a recommended procedure for a family crew due to extreme ascending chamber turbulence (see Region 3, "The Welland Canal," beginning on page 172).

Port Dalhousie, **Mile CONT-9.0 S (NM),** is at the

mouth of Twelvemile Creek. It's a pleasure-craft harbor, though for more than 130 years it was one of Lake Ontario's busiest commercial ports. Between 1828 and 1889 it was the northern terminus of three different Welland Canals. Even after the Welland's northern entry moved to Port Weller, Port Dalhousie stayed a commercial harbor until 1961. Today's entrance is not the original; in early days the creek's mouth was a barely navigable sandbar. For deep-draft vessels the first Welland contractors built Lock #1 through the bar, near the western end of today's Lakeside Park.

When the railroad routed to town, immense quantities of wheat came in from Port Colborne and offloaded to sailing ships and schooners. In one four-year period Port Dalhousie shipped more than 11 million bushels of grain. In the early 1900s Lakeside Park was a large, popular day-and-night amusement park; excursion boats brought in tourists from as far away as Toronto.

Westbound at Port Dalhousie, there's a yacht harbor at Grimsby, **Mile CONT-22.0 S (NM).** It has a pair of watched breakwaters, but vessels that draw 6 feet or more will have problems with the entrance and harbor shoals. There is far better depth at Fifty Point, **Mile CONT-25.4 S (NM).**

Hamilton is at Lake Ontario's southwestern end. The 1780 pioneers called their natural harbor Lake Geneva, then Burlington Bay, and finally Hamilton Harbour. It covers nearly 5,000 acres and is protected from the lake by a narrow neck, the Beach Strip.

You enter the harbor via the 0.5-mile-long Burlington Canal, **Mile CONT-34.3 (NM);** it has two concrete breakwaters extending about 500 feet into the lake. South Pier Light is a white lighthouse; North Pier is a red-topped chubby cylindrical tower. There are two canal bridges; they are offshore landmarks.

The 5-mile-long harbor's first (1823) canal consisted of cribwork piers; storms demolished it within a few years, so the government built the more substantial one you use today. Once cargo ships began to transit the first canal, Hamilton became a major transportation center. When the steel industries became established, it gained its nickname, "Steeltown." Today it produces more than 60 percent of Canada's steel.

Burlington, to the north and northeast, began as "Brant's Block," a 3,450-acre land tract granted to Iroquois Chief Joseph Brant (also known as Thayendinagea) for his alliance during the American Revolution. James Gage bought a parcel of Brant's land on what is now the Beach Strip's northern end. His

settlement, made up of Loyalists and British immigrants, became a shipbuilding center and shipping point for exporting timber and wheat.

When you leave Hamilton Harbour you begin a northeasterly swing around the lake's western end. Inland to the west are the Niagara Escarpment bluffs. The conspicuous steep face rising out of the high land is Mount Nemo; its prominent neighbor is Rattlesnake Point. Between the escarpment and the wooded lakefront is a metropolitan suburb that extends around the lake to well east of Toronto.

Though it's only 25.7 miles to Toronto, the shoreline route has several enjoyable stops. The first is 6 miles away at Bronte on Twelvemile Creek. Waypoint landmarks about 1.4 miles southwest of Bronte's entrance include the 2,000-foot Shell Canada oil terminal and, to its west inland, the Shell and Petro Canada refineries—their chimneys periodically belch burnoff flames.

Bronte, part of the town of Oakville, has two main breakwaters and a separate basin adjoining the northern breakwater—the basin's white stone is very visible offshore. In 1846 Bronte was a commercial fishing port and shipbuilding center, noted for its fishing boats and schooners.

Oakville Harbour, your next port, is 3.4 miles northeast at the mouth of Sixteen Mile Creek. Hold about 0.8-mile offshore; about a mile to Bronte's northeast is a 3-foot obstruction marked by a hard-to-see private buoy. South of Oakville's entrance two pipelines extend about 0.4-mile offshore; they may be watched by up to three unlighted buoys—also difficult to pick up.

One Oakville landmark is a cluster of tall harborfront apartment buildings. The entrance has a pair of offshore breakwaters; a white tower with a red top and bottom watches the northern pier.

Today Oakville is a pleasure-boat harbor, but its settlers developed it as a timber shipping port. Its early industries included sawmills, gristmills, and shipbuilding. Due to its large forests, swimming beach, and peaceful isolation, it also became a summer spa for visitors from Toronto and Hamilton.

When bound northeasterly your next protected harbor is 7 miles away at Port Credit. Hold more than 0.5 mile offshore on this stretch to clear a submerged pipeline about 2 miles northeast and two wharves with causeways at an industrial complex at Clarkson Harbour, **Mile CONT-47.2 (NM).** The southwestern causeway's eastern end has a pair of visible hoppers; lakers use the dock to take on cement and discharge coal and limestone. The wharf/causeway 0.7 mile farther northeast—a Petro-Canada refinery—has no outer structure, but on the lakeshore east of the refinery are quantities of flat tanks and two 400-foot smokestacks—good landmarks. There may be two yellow buoys watching two pipelines.

Port Credit, on both Port Credit River shores, **Mile CONT-51.0 W (NM),** was named by the French, who traded with the Indians there. Later the British paid the Mississaugas 1,000 pounds for 700,000 acres at the river's mouth. By 1844 the town had riverfront wharves and warehouses and exported quantities of timber, grain, sawn lumber, flour, and sand, gravel, and stone for Toronto's roads and buildings.

Continuing northeasterly the next harbor, Lakefront Promenade Park, is immediately west-southwest of the four 485-foot-tall smokestacks and the powerhouse at the Lakeview generating station, **Mile CONT-52.5 (NM).**

As the shoreline begins a more easterly curve, there's a stop on Humber Bay's western side. It's just south of Mimico Creek in an enclosed basin in Humber Bay West Waterfront Park. Its white stone-faced moles are visible from offshore. Enter from the south at the red and the black offshore buoys and come in on the range. It carries you between an elongated northwest-southeast-oriented westerly mole and the beach. The first facility is Etobicoke Yacht Club along the basin's southern and eastern shore; the Mimico Cruising Club is along the basin's northern end—more convenient to Lakeshore Road's shopping.

You have long been able to see Toronto's 1,808-foot-high CN tower, but now on most days you can also see the silver sphere at Ontario Place low on the harborfront's western entrance. Etienne Brule claimed Toronto for France in 1615. French fur traders set up a trading post 20 years later; to be prepared in case their Indian partners turned hostile, they added a blockhouse and named it Fort Rouille. Later they built Fort Toronto. Jean Baptiste Rousseau, Toronto's first permanent settler, set up housekeeping nearby. A few years later the French left, and for years Rousseau was the only inhabitant.

In 1787 the British bought another parcel of land from the Mississaugas, and Toronto became English. Lord John Graves Simcoe and his entourage named the settlement York; it became the capital of Upper Canada in 1797. In 1812 the Americans, with 1,750 men and 13 ships, captured York, which was defended by only 700 British troops. After looting homes and burning most of town, they left with everything they could carry.

It wasn't until war's end that York was rebuilt.

Because of its protected harbor, shipping was York's major industry until population increased and the demand for goods and services grew. In 1834, when it became Toronto, the town had 9,000 residents. The railroad's arrival secured Toronto's prosperity; today it is Ontario's capital and Canada's largest city.

Toronto Harbour has two parts, the Inner and the Outer Harbour. The Inner Harbour is bounded on the east and north by the city waterfront and on the west and south by the Toronto Islands. It has two deepwater outlets: the Western Gap opens southwesterly into the lake; the Eastern Gap opens into the Outer Harbour.

Early Toronto's harbor was a large marshy bay with vessel access only at its western end; its eastern section was adjacent to Ashbridges Bay. The area where the two bays joined is now a landfill and Toronto's industrial complex. The Outer Harbour and the Eastern Gap went into use in 1970 to give shipping access to the industrial centers. It's now the main harbor entrance.

The most convenient entry when eastbound is via the Western Gap. Just west of this entrance is Ontario Place, a cultural and amusement park on three manmade islands. The short Western Gap's bulkheaded channel is between the northern end of Toronto Island's northern end—the Island Airport—and the waterfront breakwater along the mainland. Watch for a ferry dashing from mainland to island near midcanal.

At the channel's eastern end you face the 2-mile-long Inner Harbour. North and east is downtown; south are the Toronto Islands. Ferries, water taxis, and tour boats run patterns across the harbor bound to and from the islands' intricate channels and canals.

To reach the Outer Harbour, exit via the Eastern Gap at the Inner Harbour's eastern end. On the way you have a spectacular city view dominated by the CN Tower. Harbourfront, a 2.5-mile-long section west of the Ferry Terminal, is a Toronto cultural and recreational showplace. Metro Toronto's Sky Dome is at the CN Tower's base; it's home to Toronto's Blue Jays and Argonauts.

The Eastern Gap is south of the industrial piers, industries, tank farms, and steaming chimneys. Its eastern bulkhead is part of an industrial container-loading facility; its western side has a breakwater extending northwest-southeast of the northeastern end of Wards Island, the most easterly of the Toronto Islands.

As you exit the Eastern Gap southbound, you enter the Outer Harbour and begin the Main Harbour Channel. The Outer Harbour is bordered on the north by the mainland

Things to Do and See in Toronto

With over 3 million citizens speaking nearly 100 different languages, you'll find modern Toronto sophisticated and multiethnic—with a resultant diversity in restaurant fare. There's a great public transportation system, too; the Toronto Transit Commission's subway, buses, and streetcars are a real help to waterbound boaters. Fare was $1.20 one way on our last visit.

There are plenty of attractions to keep you occupied during your stay here. Our own favorites:

Black Creek Pioneer Village, at Jane Street and Steeles Avenue. Reenactments of 19th-century Canadian pioneer life, including displays of frontier skills such as blacksmithing, woodcarving, and cabinetmaking. The costumed staff really know their stuff! There are also exhibits and a theater. Open year-round except Christmas; admission is $4.50 for adults and $2.25 for children.

Fort York, Garrison Road and Fleet Street. John Simcoe's restored fort, with exhibits and military demonstrations. Open Monday through Saturday from 9:30 to 5 and Sunday from 12 to 5, except New Year's Day, Good Friday, and Christmas.

Harborfront, Queens Quay West. Restored 90-plus acres of Toronto waterfront, with shopping, art exhibits, street mimes, theaters and concerts, restaurants, and crafts. Great fun to walk.

Marine Museum of Upper Canada, in the Ontario Place complex, 955 Lakeshore Boulevard West. Displays covering the development of the Canadian waterways, ships, and exploration. The site was once the officers' quarters for Fort York. Open from 9:30 to 5 Monday through Saturday and from 12 to 5 on Sunday, except New Year's Day, Good Friday, and Christmas; admission $2.50 for adults and $1.50 for children.

Metro Toronto Zoo, Highway 401 at Meadowvale, in nearby Scarborough. Over 700 acres of animals from around the world, as well as a children's zoo. Eight ecosystem pavilions show the world's environmental systems. Open from 9:30 to 4:30 every day except Christmas, and until 7 in the summer.

The Ontario Science Center, 770 Don Mills Road. Space and technology exhibits, with many participatory experiments. Laser displays, film presentations, and a lot more. Open from 10 to 6 daily except Christmas; admission $5.50 for adults, $3.50 for youths, $1.75 for kids under 12.

The Royal Ontario Museum, 100 Queens Park. There are over six million objects in the museum's art and science exhibits, all under one roof. Highlights include displays on prehistoric Ontario, Egyptian, Greek, and Etruscan art, dinosaurs, and life sciences. There is also a replica of a Jamaican bat cave and a Ming Dynasty tomb. Open daily from 10 to 6, and until 8 Tuesday and Thursday; admission $5 for adults and $3 for children.

Toronto as seen from the West Gap.

shore; its southern and eastern sides are an immense land-fill area, the Outer Harbour East Headland—it's continually under development. If you go south on the Main Harbour Channel, you exit into Lake Ontario at the headland's southern-end lighthouse, **Mile CONT-61.6 (NM)**.

Eastbound at Toronto there are two harbors in the next 8 miles, Ashbridges Bay and Bluffers Park. If your draft is 6 feet you may have depth problems in the bay, but there's good water at the park.

If bound for Ashbridges Bay, take a course roughly paralleling the Outer Harbour East Headland's southeastern side. The bay is at the headland's most north-northeasterly end. A landmark is the 855-foot smokestack at the sewer treatment plant 0.2 mile west of the harbor.

There are two places to stay. You can access the inner harbor via Coatsworth Cut—home of the Toronto Hydroplane and Sailing Club. Monitor depths carefully. The enclosed outer harbor, a sprawling landfill whose lakeside beach begins just northeast of Coatsworth Cut, extends in a large four-fingered easterly oriented peninsula known as the Ashbridges Bay Waterfront Area. Its entrance from the lake is on its southwestern side immediately east-southeast of the Coatsworth Cut entrance; 6-foot drafts must watch depths with extreme care. Ashbridges Bay Yacht Club is in the basin's western section; the Toronto Parks Department manages the remainder—it has risky depths for drafts of 5.5 feet. You can anchor with a bit more depth on the bay's eastern side.

If you decided not to visit Ashbridges Bay, your next harbor eastbound is Bluffers Park in the city of Scarborough. Once you clear Toronto's Outer Harbour East Headland and the area of Ashbridges Bay, the coastline—the Scarborough Bluffs—gradually rises to 380 feet just east of the Bluffers Park enclosed basin, **Mile CONT-69.5 (NM)**.

Eastbound at Bluffers the cliffs diminish to a height of about 60 feet at the prominent point at **Mile CONT-73.6 (NM)**. The tall smokestack near the point is Port Union's industrial complex. Enclosed Frenchman's Bay is coming up in a coastline indentation at **Mile CONT-76.0 (NM)**. It's the pleasure-craft harbor for Pickering, another Toronto residential suburb. Pickering Village was once a Quaker settlement known as Duffins Creek, noted for exporting lumber and flour.

Frenchman's Bay's breakwaters are about midway along narrow Fairport Beach spit. This is a fairly shoal harbor; drafts of 6 feet usually are too deep for the entrance. You may find the breakwaters difficult to pick up from offshore. A fair landmark is the Pickering

Nuclear Generating Plant at Moore Point, about a mile east of the entrance. The bay facilities with best depths are in its eastern corner, or you can anchor.

Whitby, **Mile CONT-84.0 (NM)**, is the next deep-water harbor when eastbound. Early Whitby was a prosperous lake port. The local economy was based mainly on the exportation of grain to the United States via the railroad. Whitby is called "Home of the Marigold"; these colorful flowers line downtown streets and parks.

Oshawa Harbour, **Mile CONT-89.3 (NM)**, at the mouth of Oshawa Creek, is the next port eastbound; it's a commercial harbor with a separate inner-harbor basin for pleasure boats. The French had a fur-trading post at the creek's mouth in the mid-1700s, though it was another 40 years before the site had its first permanent residents. The manufacture of spinning wheels and looms were early industries. Robert McLaughlin moved to town in 1869 and built horse carriages. At the beginning of the 20th century the same family began the McLaughlin Motor Car Company; eventually its owners sold the factory to General Motors of Canada, with R. S. McLaughlin as president. Today Oshawa is one of Canada's leading automobile-industry centers.

Eastbound at Oshawa it's about 29 miles to Cobourg. If you have shoal draft, you have a chance to visit Port Darlington, Newcastle Harbour, and Port Hope along the way.

When you leave the Oshawa breakwaters keep over a mile offshore; about a mile east you have dangerous rocks extending nearly 0.7 mile off McLaughlin Bay's beach. Though **Spar Buoy #MV2** marks the shoal's southern edge, it's very difficult to pick up in any kind of sea.

The Darlington Nuclear Generating Station is a landmark for Raby Head, **Mile CONT-94.0 (NM)**. A mile on west is a 288-foot smokestack just inland of the St. Mary's Cement Company's lakeside mole, about 1.2 miles from the Port Darlington Harbor entrance.

Port Darlington, **Mile CONT-95.7 (NM)**, is on Bowmanville Creek and the harbor for Bowmanville about 2 miles inland. If you draw 6 feet be very careful attempting the harbor entrance, especially if you come in on a following sea. The entrance has two stone breakwaters about 150 feet long; the western one is watched by a green-topped cylindrical tower. The Port Darlington Marina is a place to stay overnight; it's on the creek's eastern side about 0.4 mile upstream of the outer light.

Newcastle Harbour, **Mile CONT-99.6 (NM)**, at the mouth of Graham Creek, has very risky depths in the narrow entrance at summer lake level. The port has two entrance breakwaters—the western one extends into the lake about 300 feet and is watched by a green-topped white tower. The short eastern breakwater juts from a narrow spit on the creek's eastern shore. Enter the harbor heading northwesterly; once clear of the two breakwaters, the channel makes a fairly hard northerly swing.

Port of Newcastle Marina is on the creek's western side in a lakelike basin. The center of town, with shops and supermarket, is inland about 1.4 miles. Newcastle started the first fish-breeding station in North America in 1868; it operated for 46 years.

Eastbound at Newcastle the partially wooded shoreline consists of low, sandy bluffs. Landmarks about a mile east of Crysler Point, **Mile CONT-107.5 (NM)**, are the strobe-lighted, 650-foot-high smokestack and the large buff-colored building that are part of the closed Wesleyville Generating Station.

Port Hope, **Mile CONT-112.8 (NM)**, on the Ganaraska River, is the settlement east of Crysler Point. Peter Smith settled on the river in 1778 and set up a trading post, and incoming settlers built a profitable gristmill. Much of the town's early economy depended on transporting goods to York and Kingston—its river mouth became a thriving port for exporting flour, bran, wheat, and seeds. In one year more than 400 lake steamers and 150 commercial sailing ships used the harbor. In 1932 the Eldorado Gold Mine Company established a plant for extracting and refining radium; it has been there ever since. It became the Cameco Fuel Services in 1944; today it's a Crown Corporation uranium refining and conversion operation and metallurgy facility. A nearby company manufactures fuel bundles for nuclear power stations.

The harbor has two breakwaters. The western one is a concrete pier; the one to the east is stone and is watched by a red-topped cylindrical white tower. Just inside the breakwaters a large mole with commercial warehouses divides the harbor. The Ganaraska River and the Port Hope Marina are east of the mole; to its west is part of the nuclear facility. At the harbor's end in an enlarged basin is Port Hope Yacht Club. If you draw 6 feet, it's very doubtful you will have depth. Local boats discourage visitors from anchoring; they report the harbor's bottom sediment is radioactive.

Downtown has preserved architecture, stone churches, and antique and craft shops. A branch of the Architectural Conservancy of Ontario publishes a walking-tour map; you can usually pick one up at the yacht club.

Eastbound at Port Hope keep well offshore; you need to clear a reef about halfway to Cobourg. It extends nearly 0.7 mile from the beach to terminate at Peter Rock, **Mile CONT-114.9 (NM)**. The rock supports its steel-faced, 31-foot-high, white, red-topped cylindrical tower.

Cobourg Harbour, **Mile CONT-117.6 (NM)**, has a very conspicuous lighthouse; another landmark is a large blue ship secured alongside the eastern harborfront—it's a restaurant.

Loyalists founded Cobourg in a cedar swamp in 1798. The timber attracted other settlers, and before long the village had sawmills, stores, and gristmills. The harbor developed into a major shipping port, new roads brought in local products for export, and the railroad arrived in 1854. With transportation routes established, residents felt Cobourg would be chosen as Ontario's political capital. Work started on a grand civic building to be the capital's focal point. Though the Prince of Wales opened Victoria Hall with great fanfare, Cobourg was in a state of economic disaster. Bankruptcy was imminent due to the hall's price tag, a bridge collapse that lost them the railroad, and poor forest management that doomed the lumber industry. Cobourg never again became a thriving commercial port, though now it is a noted pleasure-craft harbor.

Eastbound at Cobourg you cruise along a wooded shoreline. A waypoint is a chemical works with white silos and tank just inland of Lucas Point, **Mile CONT-120.0 (NM)**. Ogden Point, **Mile CONT-130.8 (NM)**, has a commercial pier for loading limestone from its nearby quarry.

Proctor Point, **Mile CONT-136.0 (NM)**, on High Bluff Island's southern end, is part of the Presqu'ile headland. North of the point is Popham Bay; it is open to the west and southwest and has dangerous reefs along its southeastern shore. High Bluff Island has an elevation of 60 feet and consists of shale cliffs called the Bluff. Proctor Point Light watches from a 40-foot-high, red-topped white cylindrical tower. In mid-June the tower is prominent; acres of buttercups surround it. High Bluff and Gull islands are a part of a lakeside chain that extends southwesterly off Presqu'ile Peninsula. Both are nesting grounds for more than 70,000 pairs of gulls, herons, cormorants, and terns. The ring-billed gull colony alone produces about 200,000 chicks each year.

Presqu'ile Point, **Mile CONT-141.0 (NM)**, 3 miles

east of Proctor Point, is Presqu'ile Peninsula's eastern end; it has a 76-foot-high white octagonal lighthouse that dates from 1840. This is the western access into the Bay of Quinte, where you leave the open lake for a 71-mile inland passage to Kingston.

The Bay of Quinte is a collection of bays, narrows, reaches, and channels; none are much more than 2 miles wide, some less than 0.5 mile. Length of reaches varies. Some overlap, so one stretch of water may be up to 20 miles long. Generally the bay is well protected, though this doesn't mean you can ignore upcoming weather. Strong winds blowing up or down lengthy reaches create an uncomfortable chop.

The Bay of Quinte has two other Lake Ontario access points. One is farther east at Adolphus Reach's northeastern end via the Upper Gap. Another is at North Channel's eastern end via the Lower Gap—4 miles from Kingston.

Make your approach into the watched entry channel at Presqu'ile Point from the offshore lighted **Fairway Buoy P.** Shoal water extends east of Presqu'ile Point and southwesterly from Quinte's Isle. At the Fairway Buoy pick up the Brighton Range to help carry you through the shoal narrows and clear of Middle Ground, Salt Reef, and Calf Pasture Crib. From the lake to the Murray Canal entrance, weeds are a problem. Passing traffic keeps the growth down in the channel to some extent, but fathometers are nearly useless. If your draft is 6 feet or more stay in the channel, where depths vary from 6.5 to 12 feet.

The range carries you through Presqu'ile Bay's shoal marshlands. Its entire western section, the Presqu'ile Peninsula, is the 2,000-acre Presqu'ile Provincial Park, which has campgrounds, swimming areas, sand dunes, forests, marshes, wet meadows, and walking, hiking, and bicycling trails. It's a noted bird-watching area; the park's on the Atlantic and Mississippi flyways.

You leave the Briton Range about 0.5 mile southeast of Gosport and bear easterly to the Murray Canal's western entrance; it divides the isthmus between Presqu'ile Bay and the Bay of Quinte. The isthmus's southern end became an island after the canal opened; residents call it Quinte's Isle.

Pleasure craft are the primary users of the 4.5-mile-long canal. It's about 124 feet wide, has a bottom width of 80 feet, and has a 12-km speed limit. It has good depth, averaging about 9 feet (more than Presqu'ile Bay), but don't skim the banks; they're lined with rock.

The Brighton Road Bridge, the canal's first movable

Murray Canal Seasonal Hours of Operation

May 18 to June 21: Monday through Thursday, 0900 to 1620; Friday through Sunday and holidays, 0900 to 1920

June 22 to August 19: Daily, 0830 to 2020

August 20 to September 3: 0830 to 1920

September 4 to October 10: Monday through Friday, 0900 to 1650; Saturday, Sunday, and Thanksgiving, 0900 to 1750

bridge at Lovett, **Mile CONT-145.9 (NM),** swings easterly. The tender on the bridge's southern side collects the $2 (Canadian) toll by extending a long pole with an attached cup. Price is by vessel, not length. American money is accepted, but no premium is allowed for currency exchange.

Coming up at **Mile CONT-147.4 (NM)** is an old bridge island in midcanal; daymarks hold you to its southern side. The CN Railroad Swing Bridge, **Mile CONT-148.5 (NM),** is usually kept in the open position; the Carrying Place Swing Bridge is the one farthest east. A mile farther is Twelve O'Clock Point, the canal's eastern terminus. Navigation aids begin immediately outside the outer canal piers; shoals border the channel for the next 0.5 mile.

The French named the isthmus you just crossed Presqu'ile, which means "almost an island." The narrow neck of land is a 1,000-year-old portage route. It extended from the Carrying Place—just south of the eastern canal piers—for 1.4 miles to Young Cove on Wellers Bay on the southern side of the isthmus, where there was main-lake access. Indians traveled the portage; Champlain used it in 1615, and so did La Salle. In 1787 the Gunshot Treaty was enacted at the Carrying Place; the Indians signed over an immense section of their lands stretching as far west as Toronto—all for government gunshot and blankets. Travelers called the overland trek between bay and lake "the Portage Road"—it's still there, and it has the same name. It's the oldest continuously used road in Upper Canada. At one time it was the busiest travel route in Ontario; many thought the Carrying Place would have a better future than Toronto because of its transportation and transshipment economy. It was a bustling 1800s community with supplies and accommodations for travelers. As population increased, a faster method of transporting heavy goods became urgent. The government started the canal in 1882; when it opened seven years later it took the shipping away from the Carrying Place, and the town nearly disappeared.

Your next 4.5-mile eastbound stretch is through a large bay as far as the Narrows. For the first 2 miles to Onderdonk Point, **Mile CONT-151.5 (NM)**, the channel is along the southeastern shore to clear Indian Island Bank's mile-long easterly reaching shoals.

Trenton is on this bay's northern shore at the Trent River's mouth. If it's your destination, there are two watched secondary channels to the river. One is intended for very shoal-draft runabouts; it passes west of wooded Indian Island. The 2.7-mile-long deepwater secondary channel begins at **Mile CONT-153.0 (NM)** at **Light Buoy QTB**, just northwest of the southern shore's Way Point.

Trenton's settlement began in 1790 when Europeans came for the timber. By 1870 it was a port of entry and a port of call for settlers heading west and north. An early industry was the Trenton Bridge and Engine Works; they built iron bridges, piers, boilers, tugboats, and steamboats. In the early 20th century it boasted a munitions plant—until one night it blew up.

Trenton is known to most boaters as the southeastern terminus of the 210-mile-long Trent-Severn Canal; its northwestern terminus is at Port Severn. This is a scenic trip if you plan to access Georgian Bay off Lake Huron. The system makes use of a series of rivers, lakes, and land cuts. It has 36 conventional locks, 2 hydraulic lift locks, a marine railway, and 2 flight locks. There is a toll.

The Trent-Severn's route between Lake Ontario and Lake Huron was used early on by the Indians and by Champlain. In those days it was not an easy trip; portages were commonplace. When Loyalists settled the area, they used part of the system for rafting log booms. In time their need for an improved waterway resulted in a piecemeal canal construction through critical, highly used areas. It was 1920 before the government interconnected the navigable Trent-Severn sections. By that time the logging industry had moved away, threats of an American invasion were gone, and pleasure boats took over. This canal is a cruising destination in itself; to include it here would make this guide too large for easy portability.

Continuing eastbound at main channel **Buoy QTB**,

the 2-mile-wide bay begins to close at its northeastern end. Off to the north over Baker Island—near the water tower—is the Trenton Canadian Forces Base Aerodrome; it's the Great Lakes–area Rescue Coordination Center.

The Narrows, **Mile CONT-154.0 (NM),** is the western end of the navigation channel between the southern shore's Pine Point and Narrows Shoal, a reef extending southwesterly from wooded Makatewis Island. Narrows Shoal light tower, at the reef's west-southwesterly end, is a red-topped white cylindrical tower; it replaced a lighthouse that had watched the Narrows Shoal since 1894.

Once through the Narrows eastbound you have a 4.8-mile-long, 0.8-mile-wide reach to the Norris Whitney Skyway Bridge at Belleville. An early ferry ran from Hennessey Point to town; the government replaced it in 1891 by a movable bridge, Canada's longest highway bridge at that time. Keep clear of the old bridge's standing portions west of the Skyway.

Belleville, **Mile CONT-159.9 (NM),** is on the northern shore just west of the bridge at the Moira River's mouth. Loyalists and Mohawk Indians settled at the site of Belleville in 1789 and developed the town into a major Canadian cheese marketing center. In 1866 gold was discovered in Eldorado, 30 miles north. Gold Rush miners arrived by ship and railroad and gave Belleville its nickname, "the Golden Gate of Hastings County."

Eastbound at Belleville you cross a 3-mile-long bay to another narrows and pass north of low, wooded Cow Island and south of Snake Island. A northern-shore landmark about halfway across the bay is the Bakelite plant's buildings, water tower, and smokestack. The Narrows, **Mile CONT-162.5 (NM),** is between wooded Ox Point peninsula on the north and Massasauga Point on the south. **Light Buoy Q53** keeps you north of dangerous Rush Bar. Massasauga Point was a noted 1800s recreation spa with an extravagant tourist hotel, picnic areas, boating, fishing, and lawn tennis courts.

Clear of the Narrows you enter 4.5-mile-long Big Bay; it ends at Trident Point, **Mile CONT-167.0 (NM),** though the easterly reach continues to Telegraph Narrows. Well-watched North Port Shoal, **Mile CONT-167.8 (NM),** is about in midbay.

The southern shore's Big Island and North Port were active lake ports between 1860 and 1890 and exported millions of bushels of barley—most destined for America. During the steamboat era, North Port was a scheduled stop with a hotel, stores, a cannery, a tannery, and a tin smith.

Telegraph Narrows, a mile-long bay section, has its western terminus just west of Telegraph Island, **Mile CONT-171.0 (NM);** it's watched by a green-topped white tower. This short section has a shoal-water reputation; hold to the watched channel for at least 15 feet at summer lake level.

As you approach the eastern end of Telegraph Narrows, the large Tyendinaga Indian Reserve is to the north. The reserve, and the village, a mile north of Sucker Creek's mouth, honor Mohawk Chief Joseph Brant.

Coming up at **Mile CONT-172.7 (NM)** is another high-level Skyway bridge. A mile later you pass north of wooded Foresters Island. Deseronto, **Mile CONT-174.5 (NM),** is on Mohawk Bay's northern shore—its name is on the town's white standpipe. Here Captain John Deserontyou and his party of Mohawk Loyalists landed on 2,000 acres granted to the Indians for their support during the American Revolution. They brought with them a revered silver communion service presented to them in 1841 by Queen Anne. It was kept in Her Majesty's Mohawk Chapel—one of only two chapel royals outside Great Britain. Now it resides in the local museum.

H. B. Rathburn built a lumber mill in town and started small diversified manufacturing factories. By the late 1800s Deseronto had grown to support a railroad, a railway car factory, flour mills, an iron company, and a boiler and gas works. It was a major port for tugs and barges, freighters, and passenger ships.

Today it has a marina and a watched entry channel.

The Napanee River mouth is in Mohawk Bay; it's navigable for 5 miles upstream to the falls at Napanee. It's pleasant for dinghy exploring and has excellent pickerel and bass fishing.

Long Reach begins at Mohawk Bay's northern end. It's a 6-mile-long, 0.5-mile-wide stretch that extends south-southwesterly as far as Picton Bay. It's a pretty area with high wooded shores, deep water, and a few waterfront homes. Boats often anchor in the cove on Long Reach's western shore between Grassy Point and Green Point, **Mile CONT-175.3 (NM)** and **176.0 (NM),** but the bottom is very risky; this was the old log storage area during Deseronto's early lumbering years.

Nine-mile-long Hay Bay extends east-northeast off Long Reach. Ram Island, 3.5 miles northeast of Shermans Point, **Mile CONT-179.5 (NM),** is one of Bay of Quinte's more famous anchorages.

The route to Kingston makes a hard bend easterly at **Fairway Buoy Q, Mile CONT-182.0 (NM),** off Mallory Bay. Near the prominent Lake Ontario Cement Company—west-southwest of the Fairway Buoy—at Long Reach's southwesterly end is Picton Bay's western entrance. Picton Harbour, at the bay's southwesterly end, is protected behind Chimney Point, the harbor's western entrance.

Eastbound at Picton Bay you leave Long Reach and bear for Adolphus Reach's western entrance between Glenora and Young's Point, **Mile CONT-184.0 (NM).** If it's foggy, watch for the *Quinte Loyalist* and *Glenora,* two cross-reach ferries.

Loyalists founded southern-bank Glenora. By the 1800s it was one of the busiest and most profitable Bay of Quinte industrial centers. There were grist-, plaster, flour, and carding mills; one of the large limestone buildings you see at the water's edge was Loyalist Peter Van Alstyne's flour mill. The other building was the Little Giant Water Wheel Foundry; it built turbines for water-powered industrial machinery. The foundry became a munitions plant during World War I. Later the government converted it into a fish hatchery—today's Ontario Fisheries Research Station.

On top of the 180-foot escarpment is 3-mile-in-circumference, 125-foot-deep, turquoise-colored Lake-on-the-Mountain. It has no known inlet, though it retains a constant level despite its large outflow. It's been in use as a Glenora water-power source since the time of the waterwheel works. Today the fisheries station uses the water for their fish tanks. One local legend says the lake is bottomless and somehow connected to Lake Ontario by subterranean passages. Another tells of rum-runners' treasures hidden in its depths.

Adolphus Reach, oriented northeast-southwest, is about 10 miles long and 1.5 miles wide. It ends at the northeastern end of Quinte's Isle's Cressy Point at Indian Point, the westerly entrance of the Upper Gap. The inland route to Kingston is north of Amherst Island via North Channel, another 10-mile-long northeast-southwest-oriented reach. Except for shoreline shoals, this 20-mile stretch is deep.

As you leave Glenora bound for Kingston, pass north of Keith Shoal, **Mile CONT-186.7 (NM),** watched by **Light Buoy Q1.** On the northern shore is a bay formed between Pull Point and Cole Point, with Lyons Island (once Bass Island) sitting near the eastern end. From a distance, the partly wooded island looks to be in two parts.

Just inland on the bay's northern shore is Adolphustown. Loyalists founded the settlement in 1784 and named their grant to honor Prince Adolphus Frederick, 10th son of King George III. Though not a secure anchorage in prevailing winds, in a northerly blow it's a pleasant stop. Enter west of Lyons Island and anchor as close to the northern shore as depth allows—it's not so far to row ashore. Bottom is mud, stones, and weeds. On the northern shore is Adolphustown Provincial Park. Land the dinghy at its launching ramp—it's almost in front of the United Empire Loyalist Museum. If you are seeking information or genealogical records of Loyalist ancestors, this is the place to visit.

On Cressy Point's northern side is Prinyer Point, **Mile CONT-192.5 (NM),** Prinyer Cove's western entrance. Lieutenant Archibald MacDonnell and his refugee Loyalists landed in the cove in 1784. A hundred years later docks and wharves for sailing schooners lined the banks; it had become the center of Bay of Quinte's fishing industry.

At **Mile CONT-194.0 (NM)** you reach Quinte's Isle's northeastern end; if you plan to continue the inside passage to Kingston, cross the Upper Gap. On Adolphus Reach's northern shore at **Mile CONT-195.5 (NM)** are the powerhouse and two 678-foot-high smokestacks of the Lennox Generating plant, the largest of Canada's oil-fueled plants. The plant is a landmark when making a landfall from Lake Ontario through the Upper Gap.

Your next course is along the northern shore of 9-mile-long Amherst Island. It was part of an extensive land grant made in 1675 to explorer René-Robert Cavelier de La Salle by Louis XIV. The island—with Simcoe, Wolfe, and Howe islands—was one of Ontario's original 19 counties.

The Canada Lafarge Cement plant, **Mile CONT-199.0 (NM),** is a landmark on North Channel's northern shore. Another 1.6 miles northeast is Bath, settled by Loyalists in 1784. It was a bustling 1800s port and rivaled Kingston as an industrial and commercial center. Finkle's Shipyard built one of Lake Ontario's first steamboats. When the Grand Trunk Railroad bypassed Bath it began to decline, while Kingston grew.

There are a few popular anchorages on Amherst Island's northern shore in indentations at Kerr Bay, Wright Bay, Stella Bay, and Preston Cove. Though badly exposed to the northeast, they do have prevailing wind protection. If you plan a visit from an eastbound course, be careful of dangerous Kerr Shoal, which lies about 0.3 mile off Amherst Island's northern shore just west of Kerr Point. If visibility is restricted, watch for the ferry that crosses between Millhaven and Wright Bay. This is a year-round ferry; it can run an ice-free winter course due to a cross-channel bubbler system.

At the eastern end of Amherst Island you enter an area of erratic magnetic disturbances that may range from 3 degrees east to 27 degrees west. Take care if traveling in fog; you are approaching a dangerous area off Amherst Island's north-northeastern end. It includes the Brother Islands (three of them), which are part of the Amherst Bar. The bar extends north-northeasterly from Amherst Island's eastern end. Some of Amherst Bar is low, bushy, and above water; much is awash. West Brother is watched by a green-topped white cylindrical tower; wooded Center Brother is the largest, somewhat higher in elevation, and watched on its northern side by a tower with a triangular white daymark. Keep to their north.

Across the channel from the Brother Islands is 2-mile-long Collins Bay. It curves northeast and then east; its entrance is more than 0.5 mile wide. Early Collins Bay Loyalists based their economy on rafting timber to the United States and Quebec. If you plan a bay visit, you must go nearly 2 miles—stay in the middle—around the slight easterly bend to find protection from the prevailing lake winds. A charted government dock on the upper bay's western side is usually too rough, due to wind chop and wakes, for an overnight stay, but it's a place to leave the dinghy if you want to visit the supermarket. Near the bay's easterly end on the southern shore is Collins Bay Marina, protected by a breakwater.

Eastbound at the Brother Islands and Collins Bay you are in Kingston's outskirts. The control tower over Lemoine Point to the north is the city airport. Pass north of Salmon Island, **Mile CONT-207.3 (NM);** it's nothing more than a gravel lump. The island marks North Channel's western terminus as well as the Lower Gap's western entrance—Kingston's main lake entrance. On Simcoe Island's southwestern end—3.5 miles southeast—is Nine Mile Point Light with its red-topped white cylindrical tower. This is the major landmark when approaching from the American shore, the Ducks Islands, or East Charity Shoal. At Salmon Island you enter the geographical northwestern entrance to the St. Lawrence River.

Your course to Kingston is easterly at Lower Gap. If weather makes up in this last 3 miles, a protected anchorage is in northern-shore Cataraqui Bay, **Mile CONT-210.0 (NM);** it's just east of the conspicuous Dupont of Canada plant. The bay has a 0.5-mile-long breakwater extending easterly from Carruthers Point; enter around its eastern end. At one time this was a busy commercial port; it's now a residential area.

Portsmouth Olympic Harbour, **Mile CONT-210.6 (NM),** is another all-weather harbor chock-a-block with resident pleasure boats; there's seldom space for transient dockage and no room to anchor. You can't miss the harbor; it shares its eastern shoreline with the penitentiary's bluff buildings and high, well-guarded walls.

You have been in Kingston Harbour since Carruthers Point at Cataraqui Bay, but the main part of the city lies along the Cataraqui River shores, **Mile CONT-212.3 (NM).** Kingston, one of Lake Ontario's loveliest cities, has much to offer a visitor, and most of it is within walking distance of a downtown marina and anchorage. Kingston also lies at the western end of the Thousand Islands on the Canadian Middle Channel (see Region 5, "The Thousand Islands," beginning on page 252).

Sketch Map Depths

Sketch map depths are given at normal average summer lake level. When you venture outside the sketch map confines, you must adjust NOAA and Canadian charts to chart datum. For convenience in adjusting, use the following:

Mile CONT-0.0 (NM) to **Mile CONT-212.3 (NM):** Plane of reference, Lake Ontario Low Water Datum, 242.8 feet

NIAGARA-ON-THE-LAKE SAILING CLUB

★★★★★   5

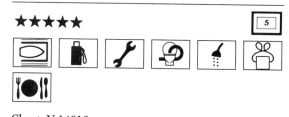

Chart: N 14816

Mile CONT-0.0 + 1.0 (NM)

This club—open May 1 to October 31—is on the west bank close to the Lower Niagara River's mouth; it welcomes all vessels.

When entering the Niagara River remember that current can be up to 2 knots flowing into the lake. In strong

Niagara-on-the-Lake Sailing Club

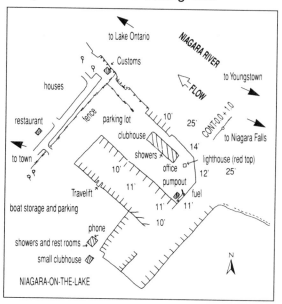

northerlies, it's going to be rough with wind and current in opposition. Use the ship range coming in; your destination is at the northern range structure. It's a red-topped white square tower on the southerly end of the club's south-reaching mole. The Customs dock is just north of the club's property.

North of the range is the two-story clubhouse. Though some club dockage is on the riverfront, most wells are on the mole's western side. If no one answered on VHF 68, pull in to the bulkhead in front of the club or at the fuel dock. The latter is on the mole's southeastern end; you can see the pumps (gas and diesel) when you get to the mole's end. If you choose the riverfront, come in heading upstream; if you choose the fuel dock, watch the northerly current set as you make the turn. Once at the pumps you are nearly current-free. If no one is on duty at the pumps, check in at the main office at the clubhouse's southeastern end. The club's land line number is (905) 468-3966.

Block and cube ice, a 14-ton lift, and 110-volt/30-amp electric hookups are available. If you need repairs, check at the office.

There are three restaurants just outside the club grounds and more uptown. If this is a crew-change port, a motel's nearby.

Downtown Niagara-on-the-Lake is about 0.5 mile away. Go out the gate to Melville Street and up the hill to Byron. Make a right, then go one block to Wellington (there's a newspaper stand on the corner); make a left and take it to Picton. The large building across the street is the Shaw Festival Theatre. Make your final right on Picton; in a few blocks, at the Historical Marker, it becomes Queen Street and the business district's southern end. Shade trees and flowers, banks, a pharmacy, department stores, quaint shops, cafés, and tea rooms await you. The Value Mart grocery is at Gate and Queen streets.

Stop at the chamber of commerce, 153 King Street, and pick up a guide to the old town's restored buildings. The Niagara Apothecary, at the corner of King and Queen Streets, was built in 1820 and is the oldest continuously operating pharmacy in Upper Canada.

Across the street is the 1848 Court House; its old assembly room is one of three Shaw theatres. The other two are the Royal George, across the street in the next block, and the main 861-seat Festival Theatre you passed on the way to town. Today the theater, which began performing George Bernard Shaw's plays in 1962, has one of the world's largest casts of actors who work on an ongoing basis. Pick up the three-theater schedule at the chamber of commerce.

At 106 Queen Street is the 1835 McClelland's West End Store—the "T" sign notes it once was a ship supplier.

The Niagara Historical Society Museum, at Castlereagh and Davy streets in the old Niagara High School, is one of the oldest in Ontario. It has a large collection on the history of Niagara-on-the-Lake and the Niagara Peninsula. It's open daily from 10 to 6.

The Cobble-Stone Galleries has art shows from May through October; it's at 223 King Street, across from the 1864 Prince of Wales Hotel. The Doug Forsythe Gallery is across the street from the club, by the gate.

If you brought along your bicycle, you have access to the bike path along the river to Fort Erie on Lake Erie.

PORT DALHOUSIE PUBLIC DOCK

★★★ [3]

Charts: C 2077; C 2070

Mile CONT-9.0 + 0.4 (NM)

Port Dalhousie offshore landmarks include two parallel breakwaters and two green-topped white lighthouses

that serve as a range. One light is on the eastern breakwater's northern end; the other is at the beach end. An outer harbor addition extends easterly off the eastern breakwater near its midpoint. If you plan to visit the eastern harbor, bear around the eastern end of the breakwater that's watched by a red light on a white tower.

The public dock is in the main harbor. If the upstream power plant is operating and its sluice gates are open, current flowing out of the harbor can be 2 knots or more. In strong northerlies this much current means a rough entrance until inside the breakwaters. Be careful of the shorter western breakwater watched by a small red daymark; during high lake level it's awash.

The public dock is at the western breakwall's southern end at the point where it makes a slight southwesterly jog. It's alongside Lakeside Park and north of a fenced area enclosing Port Dalhousie Yacht Club slips. It has parallel parking. If wind is out of the northerly quadrant, tie around this southwesterly jog to have some surge protection. For easier fendering pick a spot with a wooden bulkhead extending above the top of the cement walkway.

Port Dalhousie Public Dock

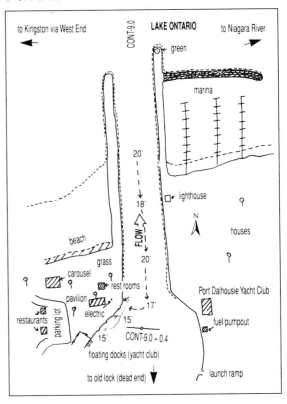

If you need electricity (110-volt service), keep close to the southwesterly jog; the only outlets are in a box on that light pole. The park's rest rooms are north of the large picnic pavilion. A dock attendant arrives around dusk to collect a fee.

Walk south across the park's parking lot and you are about in the center of downtown—it's mainly cafés, bars, and gift shops. Bear southwest about five blocks on Main Street to find the Main Street Laundromat and an Avondale convenience store.

South along the waterfront are Front and Lock streets, which were developed during the old Welland Canal era. There are taverns, a hotel, banks, shops, and a customs house. The Second Welland Canal Lock #1 is about opposite Murphy's Restaurant. Here you have a view of the harbor, dam, and locks from the bridge crossing Martindale Pond's northern end. The pond is an international rowing course and permanent home of the Canadian Association of Amateur Oarsmen. Their annual Royal Canadian Henley Regatta is held on the pond—usually the first week in August.

Be sure to ride the 1800s carousel at Lakeside Park's western side—it costs a nickel. It was part of Port Dalhousie's famous 19th-century amusement park.

JORDAN HARBOUR ANCHORAGE

NO FACILITIES

Chart: C 2077

Mile CONT-14.0 (NM)

This well-protected, relatively new pleasure-craft harbor has good depths. Though not yet noted on the chart, it's at about latitude 43-11-01 N, longitude 79-22-04 W. If weather makes up unexpectedly and you need refuge, this can be a stop; however, even though the government built the breakwaters and there are no marina facilities, the hotel complex along the harbor's shoreline prefers that no one anchor in the basin. Therefore, in severe and dangerous conditions with the safety of crew and vessel at stake, make your own decision about using this harbor.

Offshore landmarks include the harbor's high white

Jordan Harbour Anchorage

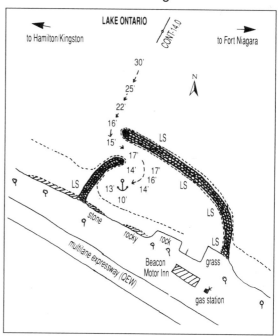

stone northern breakwater, the entrance's green-topped white cylindrical tower, a large hotel bordering the harbor, and, about 0.5 mile west, a Wet and Wild Water Slide on a high, grassy knoll.

The harbor has two breakwaters. The longest begins just east of the visible hotel and curves north and west to end at the light. The shorter breakwater extends northerly from the beach at about the point of the main breakwater's light. The short breakwater curves slightly northeast and terminates at a red daymark. Entry is between the two breakwaters. Since you would only be entering the harbor seeking safe haven during bad conditions, you may have a heavy sea during entry. The entry has fair depth but it's narrow and very close to the beach. Keep alert and stay in the middle as you round up easterly to roll your way inside.

This is a large basin, but to keep clear of the hotel, anchor close to the harbor's southwestern end. Don't go ashore, and once storm conditions abate, exit the harbor. In time the government and the hotel will reach an agreement on harbor use; watch for new reports.

FIFTY POINT MARINA

★★★★

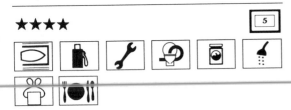

Chart: C 2077

Mile CONT-25.4 (NM)

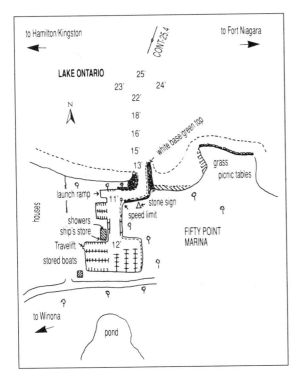

This enclosed harbor at Fifty Point is immediately west of the Canadian Land Forces, Grimsby Small Arms Range. When approaching from the east, hold north of the firing range prior to entry—it's defined by yellow spars and light buoys. The eight red-and-white radio towers on the lowlands to the entrance's east provide a fair shoreside range landmark. Also obvious is the wide white-stone northerly face of a manmade 500-foot peninsula jutting into the lake immediately east of the breakwaters.

Approach west of the most westerly firing range buoys and the peninsula to clear the range and avoid a 6-foot shoal just east of the approach and north of the peninsula.

The harbor has two short white-stone breakwaters.

The most easterly is the longest; it's watched by a green-topped white cylindrical tower. The westerly breakwater watched by a red daymark is practically on the beach. In strong northerlies you may encounter a large swell as you close the beach.

Be prepared for a sharp westerly turn—it's lined with white stone—once you reach the western breakwater's southern end. After the turn, be prepared for a southerly swing. Entry depths are most shoal at this last turn—about opposite the western shore's ramp.

Here the full basin opens. There's a northerly harbor indentation with slips along with the ramp; to its south is the two-story office complex with the fuel dock along its easterly face. The harbor's southerly end has two piers of slips in the westerly section, three piers in the easterly section, and perimeter wall docking. If no one answered on VHF 68, pull in to the fuel dock (gas and diesel).

In the office complex there is a restaurant called the Landing and a chandlery with a collection of marine equipment, supplies, nautical clothing, and basic necessities.

Electric hookups (110-volt/30-amp) are available. If you need repairs, check at the office. The land line number is (905) 643-2103.

The marina is part of the 187-acre Fifty Point Conservation Authority lands. It's an attractive park with trees, lawns, playing fields, playgrounds, picnic areas, and a fishing area. It has a swimming beach, rest rooms, a changing room, and a snack bar on the outer manmade peninsula's eastern side.

Winona, a small village, is about 1.5 miles southwest across the QEW and the railroad tracks. It doesn't have a taxi.

HAMILTON HARBOUR

Charts: C 2077; C 2086; C 2067

Mile CONT-34.3 (NM)

This triangular enclosed harbor is about 5 miles long and 3 miles wide. Clustered about the harbor's southern shore is Hamilton; along its northern shore is Burlington. Though Hamilton is recognized as one of Canada's leading industrial cities, its industry is concentrated in the harbor's southeastern end. The city also has much to offer travelers.

Hamilton's yacht facilities are near the harbor's

western end; residential Burlington's facilities are about midway on the northern shore.

Enter Hamilton Harbour at its eastern end via the Burlington Canal, which cuts through the Beach Strip. You can identify the canal from offshore by its bridges. Time your entry so you needn't idle about waiting for the timed movable bridge. In prolonged east and north-easterly winds there's no calm-water waiting area.

At the canal's western end on the northern shore is the Canada Centre for Inland Waters, a complex of two-to seven-story buildings. It has a harborfront north-south-oriented breakwater for its fleet of research and hydrographic ships.

At this point you have a choice of destinations.

Harbour West Marine Basin

★★★★   5

ALL FACILITIES

Charts: C 2077; C 2086; C 2067

Mile CONT-34.3 + 3.7 (NM)

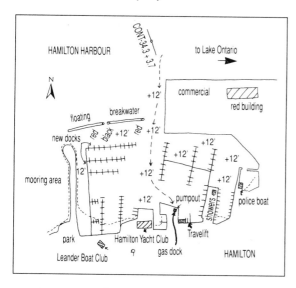

This marina—operated by the Hamilton Harbour Commissioners—is near the harbor's western end on the southern shore about 3 miles west-southwest of the Burlington Canal's Skyway Bridge. It's protected by a collection of in-harbor breakwaters.

Except for its northeastern and northwestern corners, Hamilton Harbour is generally deep. There are navigation aids scattered about and a number of confusing yellow buoys—lighted and unlighted—watching ship anchorages.

Your destination is near the western end of Pier 8, the most westerly of the southern shore's commercial piers; it has a prominent, low, red-roofed building. At the pier's western end is one end of a submerged gas-line crossing watched by an obvious "Danger Do Not Anchor" sign. This pier end has a square corner; round it closely to reach the marina basin. At this point, you can more easily see the floating metal breakwaters that protect the marina from north and northwesterly harbor chop. Enter east of the most easterly floating breakwater section; there is a red light on its easterly end.

There are two breakwaters; where they meet is another entry/exit. The easterly breakwater's western end is watched by a black daymark; the westerly breakwater's easterly end is watched by a red daymark.

Once you are in the basin you will see the facilities. The older section is on the harbor's eastern side. In mid-basin on the southern shore is the Hamilton Yacht Club; to its west is a collection of piers with slips that extend north. At the harbor's far western end is a small boat and rowing club and a large, fairly new collection of floating marina slips. Three piers of fingers extend easterly from a floating main pier that parallels a fixed north-south-oriented breakwater.

If no one answered on VHF 12, pull in to the fuel dock (gas and diesel) in the basin's southeastern section just west of the visible 50-ton Travelift's wells. The small dock office is by the pumps on the bulkhead's northerly face. Your slip assignment may be almost anywhere in the harbor; it depends on available space. If you have a choice, the western docks offer a pretty view of the hills across the bay.

Block and cube ice and 110-volt/50-amp electric hookups are available. The land line number is (905) 525-4330.

No matter where you stay, a small shopping center is about a block away. Go up the slight hill behind the yacht club to James Street; it's near condominiums with blue porches. There's a grocery store, a laundromat, a gas station, and a donut shop. Dowsar Marine Supplies at 522 James Street North has equipment, books, gifts, charts, and guides. Another block or so is the library and a meat market.

There are taxis and rental cars. The local bus runs

about every 20 minutes to Jackson Square and a large downtown shopping area—a 15-minute ride.

The 2,700-acre Royal Botanical Gardens is about 3.5 miles away at Plains Road at Highways 2 and 6. If you check the chart, it's almost due north of the marina across the bay not far north of Willow Cove. It has lovely flower gardens, acres of roses, arboretums, and greenhouses. It's also a nature park and wildlife sanctuary—Cootes Paradise—with trails winding through forest and marshland.

Dundurn Park is near the intersection of Dundurn Road and York Boulevard—the highway that curves across the bay's western end. It has a historical museum and restored 35-room Dundurn Castle. Sir Allan Napier MacNab built the Tuscan-style villa in 1835; it's open from 11 to 4. The Hamilton Military Museum, also on the Dundurn Park grounds, is in the old Battery Lodge. It features military displays, equipment, uniforms, and memorabilia dating from the 1790s. It's open from 12 to 5.

If you're a football buff, visit the CFL Hall of Fame and Museum at 58 Jackson Street; it has an impressive football sculpture in its front yard. It's open Monday through Saturday from 9:30 to 4:30 and Sunday from 12 to 4.

Whitehern, a Georgian mansion at the corner of Jackson and McNab streets, has most of its original furnishings, some dating from 1852; it's open daily from 1 to 4.

LaSalle Park Anchorage

 ★★★   3

NO FACILITIES
Charts: C 2077; C 2086; C 2067

Mile CONT-34.3 + 2.4 (NM)

This anchorage is about midway along Hamilton Harbour's northern shore about 1.9 miles west-northwest of the Burlington Canal's Skyway Bridge. You can't miss it; it's by a tall condominium and an obvious group of boats moored and docked at LaSalle Park Marina.

The moorings are outside a collection of low floating tire breakwaters protecting marina slips. Anchor east of the most easterly moorings as close to shore as depth

LaSalle Park Anchorage

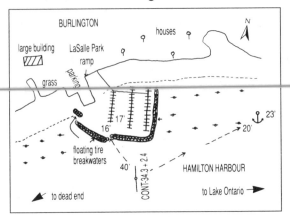

allows. Bottom is mud with weeds.

During periods of strong southerly quadrant winds, this is a bouncy stop. Don't anchor inside any of the floating breakwaters to gain a lee; it's not allowed.

The marina is operated by the Hamilton Harbour Commissioners. If you prefer to tie up, transient slips are available. If you anchor and go ashore, leave the dinghy by the ramp on the mole's eastern side.

LaSalle Park has playing fields, a playground, trails to roam, and picnic areas. Band concerts are held Sunday and Wednesday at 7:30 in the park's pavilion. If you need supplies, the shopping mall is on Highway 2. It's a long way away, but it has a supermarket, a bank, a drug store, and a Canadian Tire (a department/automotive/hardware store).

The park is within taxi distance of the Royal Botanical Garden—it's west of LaSalle Park and back toward the bay's western end.

BRONTE HARBOUR

★★★★   5

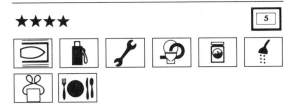

Charts: C 2086; C 2070, *See sketch map, page 231*

Mile CONT-40.3 (NM)

The main Bronte Harbour is on Bronte Creek; its Outer Harbour is on the lake. Places to stay include Bronte

Bronte Harbour

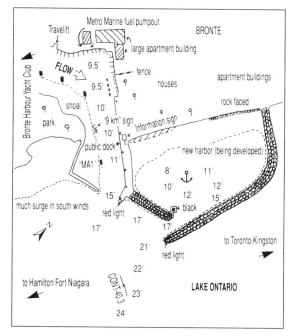

Map labels:
Metro Marine fuel pumpout
Travelift
BRONTE
large apartment building
FLOW
fence
apartment buildings
houses
9.5'
9.5'
rock faced
Bronte Harbour Yacht Club
shoal 10'
park
"9 km" sign
Information sign
10'
public dock
new harbor (being developed)
"MA1" 11'
8' 11'
10' 12'
15' 12' 15'
much surge in south winds
red light
17' 17' 17'
21'
red light
to Toronto/Kingston
22'
to Hamilton/Fort Niagara
CONTOUR 3
23'
LAKE ONTARIO
24'

Harbour Yacht Club, Metro Marine, a public dock, and an anchorage. Finding dockage in the main harbor is difficult—it's packed with resident boats—but you can usually find most facilities (such as gas and diesel fuel and 110-volt electric hookups) at Metro Marine or the yacht club. You can anchor in the enclosed outer harbor until it's filled with developing marina facilities.

Offshore approach landmarks include the following: oil refineries with tall black-topped gray chimneys that may puff smoke and steam, visible inland about 1.5 miles south-southwest of the entrance area; with them a collection of other stacks that intermittently spurt fire; buildings along the creek's western shore with very bright green roofs; and visible white stones of the high outer-harbor breakwater. Closing the entrance there's a collection of navigation aids.

The Outer Harbour has two breakwaters. The longest begins on the beach north of the creek's entrance and curves southeast to terminate in a red-topped cylindrical white tower. The harbor's southern side makes partial use of the main harbor's northeastern entrance breakwater. From near its easterly end, a short stone extension reaches northeasterly to terminate just north of the outer breakwater; it's watched by a black daymark. If your intention is to anchor, the outer harbor's entrance is between the black daymark and the outer breakwater. Bottom is mud and holding poor. Land the dinghy on the beach in the basin's southeastern corner.

The main harbor's entrance has two breakwaters. The northeasterly one terminates at the end of a slight outer southerly hook—it has the stone appendage for the outer harbor. It's also watched by a red-topped white tower. The southern main harbor breakwater extends southeasterly from the grassy beachfront, then makes a sharp northeasterly bend to terminate nearly opposite the main harbor's northeastern breakwater light; it's not watched. Once you enter the old harbor your channel is along the creek's northern side; it's watched by black spars. The large covelike area at the southern breakwater's bend is very shoal. You have good depth as far as Metro Marine's Travelift well. Upstream of this point, shoal water usually restricts drafts of 6 feet.

The public dock is along the main harbor's northern side and extends from the entrance to the bulkhead's western end as far as a group of moorings; it has a dangerous surge in strong southeast winds. The dock has parallel parking; pick a spot that has a decent fendering bulkhead.

Metro Marine is at the point where the creek makes a southerly bend. Its ship's store has a collection of marine supplies and charts. The yacht club is south of the bend.

You can contact the harbormaster by calling the Town of Oakville offices, (905) 845-6601, extension 3601, between 8:30 and 4:30 weekdays, excluding holidays. The town's general information line is (905) 338-4200.

No matter where you stay on the creek's northern side, you are close to downtown. There is a park and promenade alongside the public dock and up the rise to the street; it's especially busy on weekends, as Bronte is a designated tourist area—shops are open Sundays.

Most stores are on the creek's northern side on the main highway, Lakeshore Road, about two blocks from the yacht harbor. Around and in the Bronte Village Mall are banks, a pharmacy, a hardware store, restaurants, shops and boutiques, and a Food City supermarket. The Oakville Transit bus runs in an intricate pattern around the town of Oakville, of which Bronte is a part.

The Bronte Summerfest is held over the July Canada Day holiday and includes street dancing, buskers, arts and crafts, and fireworks.

OAKVILLE HARBOUR

★★★★

ALL FACILITIES

Charts: C 2077; C 2086; C 2070

Mile CONT-43.4 (NM)

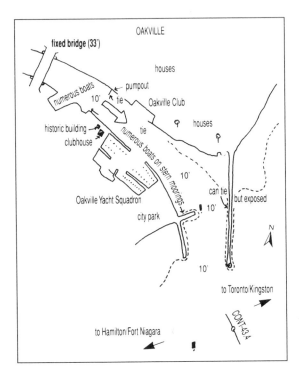

You can find most facilities, including 110-volt electric hookups, at any club in this packed harbor, but there's no room to anchor. Slips are operated by the town of Oakville, Oakville Yacht Squadron, and other clubs, and there's a breakwater tie-up. Trying to find someone to direct you to a vacant well is often difficult.

An offshore landmark is a group of tall apartment buildings near the entrance; closing shore, pick up its two breakwaters. The longest is the one to the northeast; it's watched by a white tower with a red top and bottom. The southwestern breakwater is not watched, but there's one offshore black spar. Prominent at this breakwater's northern end is waterfront Tannery Park's low grassy bluff with flags flying. At the land end of this breakwater is a short inner jetty that juts northeast; it helps protect the inner harbor from southeasterly swells and surge. Its channelside end is watched by a black spar.

The northeastern breakwater's western end is a popular tie-up. If you draw 6 feet or more approach its far northern end cautiously; there are shoals. This is not a recommended stop in strong southeasterly winds due to surge.

West of the short breakwater on the creek's southern side are moorings—bow to bulkhead and stern to mooring. This securing method is generally standard for the rest of the harbor. About midway along this line of moored/docked boats is a creek indentation—a partial basin filled with boats. Some of this area is managed by the town of Oakville and some by the Oakville Yacht Squadron. Trying to locate a dockmaster may require going upcreek to the town pumpout on the creek's northeastern side near the bridge. A town dock attendant assists in pumpouts and collects its fee; he may or may not know of a place to spend the night. Or call the town office for help; see "Bronte Harbour," page 230, for phone numbers.

The Oakville Yacht Squadron's officer of the day may know of a space. The clubhouse is on the main creek slightly west of the basin, but it has no dock to tie to while searching for the dockmaster. This club bustles with activity, so as a last resort standoff, hail a member, and ask him to point out "authority."

Securing in an assigned space nearly anywhere in the harbor is an adventure. Boats are bumper to bumper and there are no finger piers. Procedure is to belly in, gently shoving neighboring boats slightly aside. Pick up the offshore tire mooring line on the way in. You need an agile crewmember to leap ashore with bow line in hand. If the boat is equipped with bowsprit or awkward forward protuberances, all shoreside activity ceases to more closely observe a landing.

On upstream on the harbor's northeastern shore are assorted clubs that tend toward squash playing, elegant dining, and extreme physical fitness. East of the bridge on the northern shore are more town docks—the pumpout is at the property line between the town and the Oakville Club. More town docks, another yacht club, and a launching ramp are on the creek's southern side—most in another creek indentation. Except for the reserved ramp dock, all are stuffed with small boats.

The only marina fuel (gas) we could find in the harbor is on the creek's northeastern side at the Oakville Power Boat Squadron immediately west of the upstream fixed bridge—clearance 32 feet. The downstream fixed bridge has a clearance of 33 feet.

It's uphill from the yacht harbor to downtown; convenience depends on where you dock. Most of the stores, boutiques, banks, and quaint restaurants are on the creek's northeastern side on Lakeshore Road—the downstream bridge. About a block north of the bridge is Hennesseys of Oakville, a small convenience/grocery store. About nine blocks north at Allen Street is Jubilee Fresh Fruits and Vegetables. If you need a supermarket, a taxi is recommended; it's west about a mile.

Sightseeing convenient to the harbor includes waterfront Shipyard Park on the downstream bridge's western side. There's a display of oaken timbers and rails that were part of one of Oakville's famous 1800s shipyards. By the ramp in this same general area is a restored log cabin, once the home of George and Mary Lyon and their fours sons and five daughters, who immigrated here from England in 1868.

Oakville Museum has three units in the Lakeside Park vicinity on the creek's northeastern side. On Navy Street is the Erchless Estate, home of William Chisholm—Oakville's founder—and the old Custom House, the estate's business center. This section has a collection of Oakville memorabilia. The Old Post Office is in the park; it opened in 1835 and has a selection of historical displays. The nearby Thomas House has costumed guides demonstrating early lifestyles. The museum's units are open Tuesday through Friday from 1 to 4:30 and weekends from 12 to 5.

Many of the town's historic homes are on Front Street, which borders Lakeside Park. Plaques note when a house was built, the original owner's name, and his occupation.

Golf buffs will enjoy Oakville's Glen Abbey Golf course, designed by Jack Nicklaus; it's one of Canada's top courses and home of the Canadian Open. The Canadian Golf Hall of Fame, Golf Museum, and Library are at the club, on Dorval Drive about 4.5 miles to the harbor's northwest.

Downtown Centennial Plaza includes the Oakville Centre for the Performing Arts, a 500-seat theatre that hosts a variety of local and out-of-town artists. Call (905) 842-2555 for the current program.

PORT CREDIT HARBOUR

★★★

Charts: C 2077; C 2086; C 2048

Mile CONT-51.0 (NM)

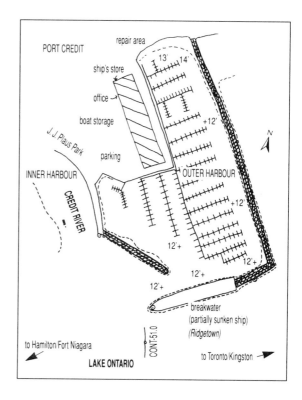

Port Credit Harbour has two places to stop. One is on the Credit River at the J. J. Plaus Memorial Park public dock; it's badly exposed and not recommended in strong southeast winds. The other is a full-service marina (including gas and diesel fuel and 110-volt electric hookups) in an enclosed Outer Harbour.

Offshore harbor landmarks include two 400-foot smokestacks at the Petro-Canada refinery 3.3 miles to the southwest, and Lakeview Generating Plant's four 485-foot stacks in a northeast/southwest line about 1.5 miles to the northeast. As you close the harbor, it looks as if a laker is on its way out; it's not. The grounded *Ridgetown* is in use as a breakwater.

Port Credit Harbour consists of three breakwaters. The original harbor, the Inner Harbour on the river, has a breakwater and a training wall. The latter is an extension of the river's northern shoreline; it curves slightly south and is watched at its end by a red-topped white tower. Added to this original training wall is a 1,000-foot-long easterly extending arm that terminates at a green-topped white tower. This wall and its extension serve as the Outer Harbour's southwestern side. To add to this harbor's protection, a 2,300-foot second breakwater extends southeasterly from the beach. It terminates at a red-topped white tower near the *Ridgetown*'s stern. The laker lies on a southwesterly line and overlaps the southern breakwater; at its bow is another red light. The Outer Harbour entrance is between the laker's bow and the southern breakwater's western end.

When bound for the Inner Harbour and J. J. Plaus Park, favor the wall during your entry. An extensive shoal extends northeast of the river's southern bank; it's watched by a collection of green spars.

Dockage at the J. J. Plaus Park is at the training wall's western end; it's an improved old commercial terminal. Check the weather very carefully before planning a long layover; it has an appalling 30-mile deep-water open-lake fetch. If weather is fair this is a pretty stop, as you have a lake view. The park has a lawn, picnic tables, park benches, and some wildlife—Canada geese, ducks, and black squirrels.

The Port Credit Harbour Marina—land line (905) 274-1595—is in the Outer Harbour—an immense basin packed with boats. Enter at the *Ridgeway*'s bow and the southern breakwater. The marina office is in the mole's large building on the harbor's southern side near its two Travelifts. To get there follow along the laker's starboard side, then follow the northern breakwater back to the beach. Any open dock can serve as a temporary stop while a crewmember checks in at the office. Dockage is seldom available despite a large supply of empty wells. If there's space, find out your charge in advance. On one visit, the numerous staff couldn't agree if our overnight fee was to be $8, $10.50, $21, $53.25, or nothing.

Either place you stay, you are convenient to a portion of Port Credit's rambling business center, most of which is on Lakeshore Road—the bridge road. Port Road East is about the first street accessed from either stop; if you take it to Elizabeth Street—about 1.5 blocks north from the river and south from the marina—you end up about in the parking lot of a large supermarket. This is not a compact town, though there's also a convenient bank, hardware store, post office, drugstore, and laundry. There are two chandlers: Mason's, in the northwestern end of Port Credit Harbour Marina's large building; and the C & C Yachts Ship's Store, at 55 Port Street.

You have easy access to the Mississauga transit system; it connects to the Islington Station in Etobicoke for the Toronto subway.

The Credit River's mouth is a noted fishing area. Most productive in spring until the end of June are the migratory rainbows (steelhead). In mid-June the town holds its River Hooking Festival; festivities include an arts and crafts show, a Midnight Madness sale, live bands, and strolling musicians. A jazz and rock festival is usually held at the harbor.

LAKEFRONT PROMENADE PARK MARINA

★★★★★

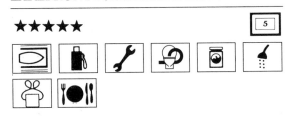

Charts: C 2077; C 2086

Mile CONT-52.5 (NM)

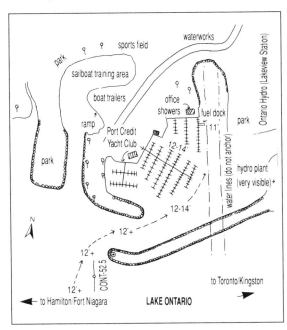

This marina—open May 1 to November 1—is in the Mississauga environs and in Lakefront Promenade Park. It's immediately southwest of the Lakeview Generating Plant's four 485-foot-tall smokestacks. The harbor has two white stone breakwaters. The northeasterly is the longest and extends southwesterly from the power plant to terminate in a slight westerly hook. It's watched by a red-topped white tower; it overlaps a short inner breakwater—a stone-faced mole—that extends south from shore, then hooks sharply east. Enter the main harbor heading northeast. Southwest of the inner-breakwater mole is another harbor, home to the Mississauga Sailing Club.

As you enter the main harbor you are confronted by a packed boat basin. In immediate view in the southwestern section is the Port Credit Yacht Club; its clubhouse is prominent between its two main piers. To reach the marina keep northeast of the piers and make a swing north. It's at that basin's end; as you round the club docks you can see the two-story building that houses the office.

If no one answered on VHF 68, pull in to the fuel dock (gas and diesel) on an easterly extending pier off the facility's most easterly pier—you can see the gas and diesel pumps.

Electric hookups (110-volt/30-amp) are available. If you need repairs, check at the office. The land line number is (905) 274-7061.

If you plan to walk off and then return to the marina grounds late, ask about getting back in the gate that separates the marina from the public park grounds. It may be locked after hours.

Supplies are not convenient. The access road winds westerly to Lakeshore Road, the main highway—it's nearly a mile. When you get there make a left toward Cawtha Road. There is a convenience store, a few shops, and a fast-food restaurant. This is also your access to the Mississauga Transit System to Pearson International Airport or Islington Station in Etobicoke for the Toronto subway.

HANLAN'S POINT MARINA

★★★★★

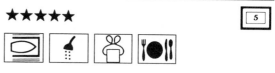

Charts: C 2077; C 2086; C 2085

Mile CONT-59.0 + 2.3 (NM)

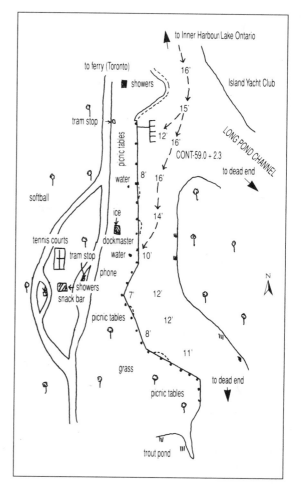

This marina is in Hanlan's Memorial Park in the Toronto Islands, about a dozen islands trailing easterly from large Toronto Island. Access is from Toronto's Inner Harbour, which is most conveniently reached from offshore when you enter the Inner Harbour via the Western Gap. If you enter at the Eastern Gap, cross the Inner Harbor to near the Western Gap for entry.

Your destination is Blockhouse Bay. Once through the Western Gap continue easterly about 0.3 mile before making your southerly turn to keep clear of the airport's easterly runway landing pattern's danger buoys. Once south of this area head into the channel west of Muggs Island and east of the prominent Hanlan's Point Ferry slips. You are then in Blockhouse Bay. Island Yacht Club is on the bay's eastern side on Muggs Island's western shore; Hanlan's Memorial Park is on the bay's western side.

Hanlan's Point dockage is an auxiliary mooring area of the Toronto Island Marina, a municipal facility for permanent-based pleasure craft. The main marina is in enclosed basins on the island just east of Muggs Island off Long Pond. Though the main marina stands by on VHF, transients are directed to Hanlan's Point for dockage.

There are slips about opposite Island Yacht Club and just south of a rather prominent park point. Choose one that is appealing and pull in. If your draft is over 7 feet, this may be your only deepwater stop. The rest of the marina—the most popular part—is all parallel parking alongside a bulkhead. It begins south of the slips at about where the Long Pond channel bears off southeast at Muggs Island's southern end. It extends for nearly a half mile on the bay's western side. Choose a likely spot beside the extensive lawns and shade trees—preferably by a picnic table—and pull in. If you draw over 6 feet, approach cautiously. Most wall depths can handle 7 feet, but not all. If you arrive on a summer weekend, the entire area may be jam-packed—any empty space may very well be shoal. If you want 110-volt power, pick a spot near an electric standard.

The dockmaster's small office is near the water just south of the Long Pond channel turn. He has a large area to manage, so he's not always there, but he will appear to collect about sundown. A rest room/shower/snack bar complex for the parallel parking docks are across the one-way northbound road in a traffic island. On the traffic island's eastern side is a phone. Drinking water must be carried from widely spaced water standards in the lawn. Another rest room/shower/snack bar complex for the slip area is north of its docks. The ice machine is at the office. Check-out time is 2 P.M., and there's usually a 48-hour maximum mooring period.

If you need repairs, haulout, gas, diesel, pumpout, laundromat, a ship's store, and a small convenience store, they are usually available at the main marina. Provisions can be delivered; call (416) 360-1430.

Nearly all the Toronto Islands are part of a public park. Some islands are used by yacht clubs, government centers, a waterworks, and a school; at Wards Island there's a small residential area.

Weekend and evening sporting team competitions are held on assorted fields, many of them near the marina. Babe Ruth hit his first home run at the old Hanlan's Point Stadium. The park is named for world champion sculler Ned Hanlan, and rowing races are a normal weekend activity on Long Pond. There are night-lighted tennis courts, and west across the south-bound one-way road there's a beach with bathing stations. There are also playgrounds and a trout pond.

Except for official and supply vehicles, there are no cars on the island. A free tram system routes from the Hanlan's Point Ferry Dock to access park highlights. Board at any of the snack bar complexes scattered around the islands. If you want to see the other island areas, you either walk or bicycle. There are bicycle rentals at the ferry docks.

Though Centre Island Amusement Center—a tram stop—is apparently intended for children, adult visitors outnumber youths. There are concessions, gentle mid-way rides, a large miniature golf course, swan-shaped paddle boats, cafés and snack bars, souvenir and gift shops, and formal flower gardens. Far Enough Farm, which adjoins the Centre, is stocked with pleasant-tempered barnyard animals.

A good way to enjoy Hanlan's Point is to have a grilled supper at your bulkhead picnic table and watch Toronto come alight.

The city ferries take about 10 minutes and run about every 20 minutes from 6:30 A.M. until 11:30 P.M. If you expect to get home very late, check at the terminal for the exact close-down time.

AQUATIC POND ANCHORAGE

★★★★

NO FACILITIES

Charts: C 2077; C 2085

**Mile CONT-61.6 + 1.3 (NM)
(via Main Harbour Channel)**

**Mile CONT-59.0 + 2.7 (NM)
(via Western Gap, east end)**

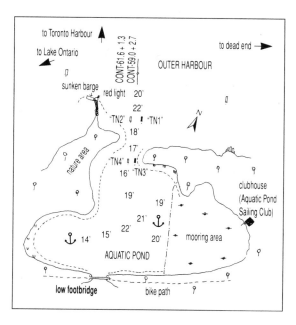

Toronto's Outer Harbour includes a collection of northern-side yacht clubs, large Outer Harbour Marina complex in its northeastern section, and another yacht club and the anchorage in an enclosed basin on the Outer Harbour East Headland's northwestern side. You have a choice of two ways to approach Aquatic Pond's outer breakwater light.

Via Main Harbour Channel: Toronto- or lake-bound ship traffic in the Outer Harbour is confined to the Main Harbour Channel. This is the area from the southerly tip of the Outer Harbour East Headland to the Eastern Gap's southern entrance. The rest of the harbor—its 1.5-mile-long northeastern end—is your destination. The landfill project is ongoing, so what

you see may not agree with the latest chart.

Leave the lake and begin the Main Harbour Channel entry. It has a very visible ship range to the Eastern Gap that begins at the lighthouse on the Outer Harbour East Headland's barren southern end. The range markers are on the mainland just east of the Eastern Gap's southern end. The channel is also watched by light buoys. Carry the range to the point where you can see the Outer Harbour's far northeastern end. Make your turn northeast and hold well off the headland. Continue along this shoreline for about 0.5 mile, depending on where you made your turn.

Along the headland's northwestern side, the landfill project includes long southeasterly reaching indentations or bays. Your destination is the third of these. The first large indentation or bay when northeast-bound is about 0.2 mile long and has a narrow entrance; the next bay is about the same length but is wide and has a wide entrance. This bay's eastern entrance point is the Outer Harbour East Headland's most northerly projecting point. This point is also part of Aquatic Pond's western entrance. The point has a northerly reaching breakwater with a sunken barge on the end; the barge juts off northwest. There's a navigational light on the breakwater's northern end, but none on the barge.

Via Western Gap East End: The chances are very good your pond approach comes after a visit to Toronto's Inner Harbour. From the Western Gap's eastern end, follow the watched channel to the Eastern Gap's southern end. At this point you must lay off a generally east-southeasterly course to pick up the pond's entrance breakwater. It's not easy to see against the Outer Harbour East Headland's wooded shoreline. Depending on where you start your course line, you may come across a collection of secondary channel buoys watching the route to the Outer Harbour Marina at the Outer Harbour's far northeastern end. Once you begin to close the headland shoreline, you are more able to see the pond's breakwater and its sunken barge extension.

From whichever route you arrived at the breakwater, you must now enter the pond. The entrance channel has two pairs of secondary channel buoys to lead you in; they carry the prefix "TN". Do not make your turn south until the channel between these pairs of buoys opens clearly. Once you arrive at **Buoys TN1** and **TN2**, slow down. Coming up is a small point. It projects easterly from the western land form, and a shoal makes out from the point. As long as you keep clear of this yet do not venture too far east, you have good depth.

South of **Buoys TN4** and **TN3,** large Aquatic Pond opens clearly. Almost dead ahead on the pond's southern shore is a low-level bridge that separates another landfill project taking place on the Outer Harbour East Headland's southeastern side. To your east in the pond is a mooring area for the Aquatic Park Sailing Club. When you reach midpond you can see a cove in the western end.

Anchor either in the western cove or west of the mooring area. In midsummer, the former locale is well filled with weeds and mosquitoes. During the week this is a quiet anchorage. On weekends the club is active and the western cove fills with boaters seeking a haven from Inner Harbour bustle.

The pond's western entrance headland is a nature preserve—a great area for birdwatching. If you brought along your bicycle, you can access the path at the footbridge. The path, also used by hikers and joggers, runs along the Outer Harbour East Headland. Grocery stores, shopping centers, and downtown Toronto are definitely *not* within walking distance.

BLUFFERS PARK

★★★★★ | 5

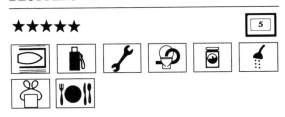

Chart: C 2077

Mile CONT-69.5 (NM)

This enclosed harbor has a collection of stopovers but no room to anchor. Four main yacht clubs and a large public marina offer standard marina facilities.

A landmark from a mile or more offshore is the white stone harbor breakwaters; they are about at the point of the highest Scarborough Bluffs. Inland on the bluff's top almost directly behind the harbor is a patina-colored dome—part of the former St. Augustine Seminary.

The harbor is on the lake and is protected by breakwater moles. The longest extends from the beach at the basin's northeastern end and curves south-southwest. It terminates in a curved southerly T at the basin entrance. On the T's southerly tip is a red-topped cylindrical

Bluffers Park

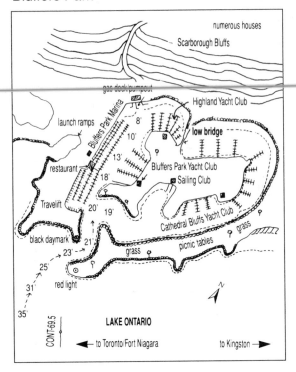

white tower. The basin's southwesterly mole extends southeast from the beach and makes a right-angle hook northeast to terminate near the T. It's watched by a green daymark. Don't confuse the harbor with another harbor project west of the basin. So far the one to the west is not lined with white stone. Enter at the light tower from the south and proceed in a slow curve around the stone-faced "T". The Scarborough Bluffs Sailing Club (launchable-class boats) is to the north-northeast, then northerly around the first mole. Cathedral Bluffs Yacht Club, which can be reached at (416) 261-0537, is also off to the north-northeast on the complex's most northeastern corner.

Along the mole on the basin's southwestern section is Bluffers Park Marina—(416) 266-4556. It has repair facilities, a Travelift, and a restaurant and ship's store. Across the channel to the northeast is Bluffers Park Yacht Club—(416) 261-6993. If you continue north and make a swing northeast around the end of the center island, you'll arrive at Highland Yacht Club—(416) 267-0224.

The park's fuel dock (gas and diesel) and pumpout are in the harbor's northwestern corner.

Supplies are about a mile away—an uphill walk

★★★★

5

through the cleft in the cliffs. Once at the top, take Brimley Road to the main northeast-southwest thoroughfare, Highway 2, where you enter busy Toronto suburbia with all variety of stores and a market.

PORT OSHAWA MARINA

★★★

5

Charts: C 2077 or C 2058; C 2050

Mile CONT-89.3 (NM)

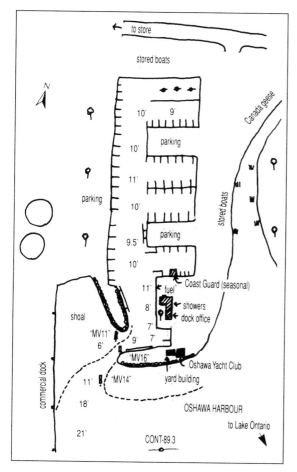

This marina is inside commercial Oshawa Harbour in a separate enclosed basin.

If you approach Oshawa from the west close to shore, the harbor entrance will be obscured until you clear a fairly prominent bluff about 0.5 mile west of the entrance. Arriving from the southeast, landmarks are a collection of gray domelike structures (covered piles of materials), blue cranes, and usually two offshore buoys. The harbor has two 500-foot-long breakwaters extending southeast from the beach. The northeastern breakwater's outer end has a very short hook southwest. Once you are lined up with the buoys and breakwaters, ride in on the ship's range. The triangular front range is on the southwestern breakwater's southeastern end; it's a green-topped cylindrical white tower. The rear range is on the entrance mole's northwestern side. Once you clear the front range and are between the breakwaters, there's usually a collection of spars watching shoals extending southwest of the northeastern breakwater.

Oceangoing ships and lakers visit the harbor often and normally require a pair of towboats to help pivot them into their piers. If you see a ship preparing to enter or exit the harbor, give it right-of-way.

Inside the harbor, both shores have commercial facilities. Bear west and then northwest along the industrial site's ship-pier bulkhead to reach the yacht basin. The yacht harbor approach begins nearly at this commercial bulkhead's northwestern end. Usually there are one or two very large commercial vessels stored close to this end. By going hard aground alongside them, we discovered they sit in depths of 0.5 to 3.5 feet.

The yacht basin has two entrance moles. The easterly mole extends westerly from the harborfront; it's just west of an auxiliary creek mouth. **Spar Buoy MV14** watches a long shoal making out south and southwest from this mole. The northwestern entrance mole extends from the northwest on the eastern side of a bridge over Oshawa Creek. The area between this northwestern mole and the commercial pier is shoal and unwatched.

The yacht basin entrance is very narrow. It is watched at the two mole ends by **Spar Buoys MV11** and **MV16.** You usually have best depths if you favor **Buoy MV16**—but not always.

Once you are inside the basin, Port Oshawa Marina is almost dead ahead. The Oshawa Yacht Club's land facilities are on the mole's southern end just east of the marina. For dockage pull in to the fuel dock (gas and diesel); usually transients are assigned the fixed dock along the northwestern side of the southeastern mole near the basin entrance. Electric hookups (110-volt) are available. The marina's land line number is (905) 723-3112.

Downtown Oshawa is nearly 3 miles away. If you need a supermarket, convenience store, or Dollar department store, you have about a 0.5-mile walk through a residential area once off the marina grounds. Go out the marina's access road, turn west on Harbour Road, and take it to Simcoe Street South. To get to the IGA and the Dollar store, turn northwest on Simcoe and walk a few blocks.

Simcoe Street is also the place to catch the local bus to the city center. There are also taxis and rental cars in town.

The Canadian Automotive Museum is at 99 Simcoe Street South. Its displays trace the development of the Canadian automobile industry, of which Oshawa has been a major part, from 1898 to the present. The museum is open weekdays from 9 to 5 and weekends and holidays from 10 to 6.

Closer to the marina is landscaped Lakeview Park at Simcoe Street South and Henry Street; it's west of the harbor's western commercial facilities. In the park is the Oshawa Sydenham Museum complex, open from 1 to 5. It includes three 1800s homes that serve as repositories of local history, period furnishings, and memorabilia.

COBOURG HERITAGE HARBOUR

★★★★

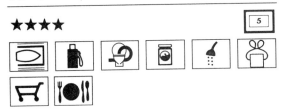

5

Charts: C 2058 or C 2061; C 2054

Mile CONT-117.6 (NM)

This marina is in Cobourg Harbour's northern end. The main harbor's two breakwaters extend about 0.3 mile into the lake, and bowling-pin-shaped East Pierhead Light is easy to pick up when offshore. The eastern breakwater reaches south from the beach and terminates at East Pierhead Light—it's white with a red top. About half of the western breakwater extends south from the beach; then it makes a 1,000-foot southeasterly jog before angling easterly to terminate south of the end of the eastern breakwall at West Pierhead Light, a green-topped white cylindrical tower. These two breakwaters are made up of a collection of different materials and

Cobourg Heritage Harbour

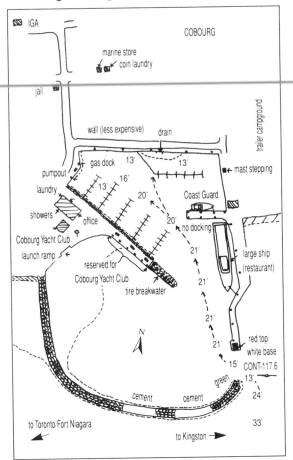

have assorted jogs and crooks—each added at a different stage of the harbor's life.

You enter heading northwesterly. Be prepared for your fathometer to drop violently at the entrance. Stay in midchannel—it's very narrow, and there are shoals just outside and at the entrance.

Once inside the outer harbor bear northerly along the eastern breakwater—it's dominated by a large ship. Your destination is in the harbor's northern end in another enclosed basin. Extending from the northwestern bank is a southeasterly reaching permanent breakwater that has a floating tire breakwater extending off its southeastern end. You enter the inner basin by holding east of the tires and its green light. Once north of this you confront marina slips extending northeast off the inner basin's permanent western breakwater. To the north is another permanent breakwall extending west from the harbor's main eastern breakwater; it's watched by a red light. Moored on the northern side of this short breakwall are the Cobourg-based Coast Guard cutters.

If no one answered on VHF 68, continue northwesterly around the ends of all the marina finger piers. There are more finger piers at the basin's northern end. At the western end of this section by the access ramp is a place for transients to tie up to check in. If you need fuel (gas or diesel) or don't want to walk around the harbor to access the office, pull in to the fuel dock. It's along the bulkhead just northwest of the last pier of slips extending off the southwestern shore and the conspicuous office complex.

Block and cube ice and 110-volt electric hookups are available. The land line number is (905) 372-2397.

Normally—at a much lower cost than if you take a slip—there is parallel-parking bulkhead dockage around the part of the harbor perimeter that is not taken up with docks; however, it's without electric hookup or convenient drinking water access. Nearly all this area has good depth; it was Cobourg's coaling pier for lakers.

Downtown is convenient. Walk up Third Street—it accesses the office complex—for two blocks to King Street. There are banks, a pharmacy, restaurants, fast foods establishments, hardware stores, and shops. If you need a supermarket, bear westerly about three blocks; the IGA is tucked behind its parking lot on the street's northern side. If you need a laundromat—the one at the marina usually has a long waiting line—there's one on Albert Street, about a block away; next door is Dean Marine, a ship's store with equipment, gear, and charts.

Victoria Hall—Cobourg's legal, political, and cultural center, and the most impressive building in town—is at 55 King Street. It has four Corinthian columns, a Greco-Roman roofed porch, a crown-topped cupola clock with four faces, and an ornate weathervane. It's home of the Art Gallery of Northumberland and the Town Hall Theater and Concert Hall. The building has been restored to look much as it did when the future King Edward VII arrived for its dedication. (It's named for his mother.) Guided tours are given on Friday, Saturday, and Sunday at 2 P.M. The art gallery—in the West Wing on the third floor—is open Tuesday through Friday from 9 to 5 and weekends from 11 to 5. The concert hall has musicals and live theater throughout the year; call (905) 372-2210 for curtain times.

The chamber of commerce is in the Marie Dressler House, the renovated home of the Oscar-winning actress, a few blocks west at 212 King Street West.

Victoria Park, on the basin's northeastern side, has manicured lawns, picnic areas, wading pools, shade trees, a playground, a ball field, a miniature golf course, a bowling green, and flower beds, one of which is planted in the shape of a 30-foot-diameter clock. The Cobourg Concert Band usually performs in the park's band shell Tuesday evenings at 8.

If you are a weathervane buff, take time to visit the 1852 United Church. It's a few blocks from the marina at Division and Chapel streets, near the library. The church vane's finger points from all directions upward, to its business center.

Canada Day Holiday is a Cobourg event attracting pleasure boats from all over the lake. It encompasses the northern end of the basin parking lot, Victoria Park, an uptown park, and downtown. There are concerts, crafts, food concessions, street dances, art shows, a parade, races, games, a carnival, and fireworks.

MURRAY CANAL WEST END

★★★

Chart: C 2031 or C 2069, *See sketch map, page 242*

Mile CONT-145.1 (NM)

This stop is at the Murray Canal's western end alongside some approach cribs. In strong westerly winds, it can have an uncomfortable chop, in which case a better choice is inside the canal at Brighton Bridge or at its eastern end.

The canal's western entrance approach walls are interconnected cement cribs with cleats. Tie on the channel side of the cribs. A single crib is of insufficient size for most boats to tie entirely alongside, so you'll need to utilize one crib to fender against and a few more—depending on your length—for a decent scope on bow and stern line.

Preferred tie is on the southern side of the northern approach, only because there's more access to deepwater fishing. It's an excellent place to catch bass and perch; use worms.

Put up mosquito screens at dusk.

Murray Canal West End

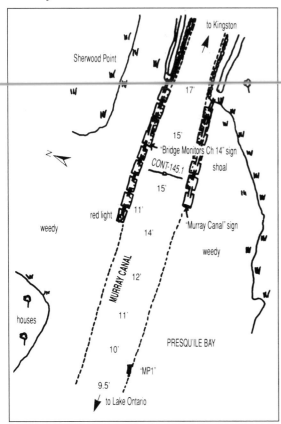

Brighton Road Bridge

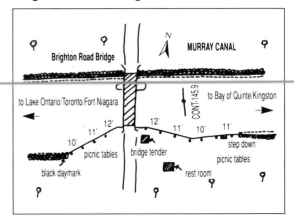

BRIGHTON ROAD BRIDGE

★★★

Chart: C 2031 or C 2069

Mile CONT-145.9 (NM)

This stop is on the canal's southern side on either side of the Brighton Road Bridge. Dockage is parallel parking on a bulkhead fitted with cleats. The grounds have rest rooms, manicured lawns, park benches, and picnic tables. If you need a grill, tie east of the bridge.

The bridge is on a daily time schedule, so opening and closing noise is eliminated after hours; however, road traffic continues all night, and there may be some talkative late-evening bank fishermen.

Button up for mosquitoes.

MURRAY CANAL EAST END

★★★★

Chart: C 2031 or C 2069

Mile CONT-149.5 (NM)

This stop is similar to the one at the canal's western end; tie alongside large cement interconnected cribs. In strong east or northeasterly winds, it's not recommended due to an uncomfortable chop. A better choice is either at Brighton Bridge or at the canal's western end.

Preferred tie is on the northern approach's southern side. Though there's a lot of daylight-hours fishermen

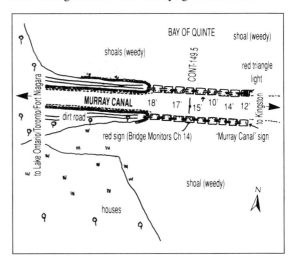

on the southern approach's northern side, there's good perch fishing on the northern crib's northern side.

This stop is at Twelve O'Clock Point. An 1800s stagecoach line left Picton every morning at eight and arrived here at noon. If you walk west out the canal's northern-bank access road to the Carrying Place Bridge, then bear northerly, there's a phone and a small store with a selection of camping supplies aimed at drive-in visitors.

Mosquitoes arrive at dusk and dawn.

FRASER PARK MARINA (Trenton)

★★★

ALL FACILITIES

Charts: C 2069; part of C 2031

Mile CONT-153.0 + 2.7 (NM)

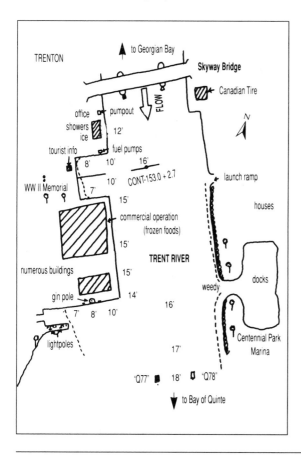

This Trenton marina is at the Trent River's mouth on the southern side of the Dundas Street Fixed Bridge—the first bridge spanning the Trent upbound. Strong southeasterly winds tend to cause a surge and make the marina rolly; there's also continual runabout wake roll during daylight hours.

A watched secondary channel intended for deep-draft pleasure craft is the safest route to reach Trenton from the Bay of Quinte's main channel. This channel begins at **Light Buoy QTB, Mile CONT-153.0 (NM),** off Way Point. Bear westerly; navigation aids bear the prefix "Q". As you close the river's mouth, you intersect a shoal-draft watched route coming in from the southwest. By that time you can clearly spot a bulky two-story building on the river mouth's western point—it's the Cold Storage Plant. Your destination is just to its northwest in a riverbank indentation. The dock office is on the river just south of the bridge. The fuel dock is partly on the southern side of the indentation's northern end and on the main river—you can see the pumps (gas and diesel). There's normally a long line waiting to fuel up and pump out at the start or end of a Trent-Severn Canal trip.

There's usually no charge for daytime dockage; many boats come in for supplies, then go off again. Some of the overnight slips do not have an electric hookup, so if you need 110-volt service, tell the dockmaster. If you need repairs, check at the office; it also has a few guidebooks on the Trent-Severn Canal. The land line number is (613) 394-2561.

There is a mast-stepping gin pole at the public dock just south of the Cold Storage Plant. It's alongside a bulkhead beside a small building. There's a fee for its use; contact the dockmaster at Fraser Park Marina. This is not an ideal spot for stepping masts due to bay chop and passing boat wakes. Best time is usually at daylight calms.

Fraser Park's manicured lawns, shade trees, park benches, and flower gardens are at the marina indentation. Beside the eastern park gate is a Tourist Bureau kiosk offering directions, maps, brochures, and a walking-tour guide of Trenton's business center. Across from the park's western entrance is the Memorial Library; it often has displays of local historical interest.

Dundas Street West—the southeasterly bridge street—is downtown; it has banks, drugstores, office supply shops, dime stores, Jeffry's Value Mart Grocery, restaurants, and fast food establishments. The A & P supermarket and Speed Queen laundry are in a shopping complex off Dundas Street at Division and Quinte, about four to five blocks from the marina. There's a farmers' market every Saturday, Tuesday, and Thursday morning along the riverfront.

The Dundas Street Bridge is the longest automobile/pedestrian bridge in North America to be slid into place. In 1990 it was moved 33 feet from the point on the river where it was originally built.

A hike to Mt. Pelion Park makes a breathless outing. It's west up 445 feet and is charted as The Mountain—you probably saw it on your way in the secondary channel. It has 26 acres of trails and a fantastic lookout tower view.

The Quinte International Air Show is held the last weekend in June at the CFB Trenton aerodrome. Vintage planes, flying acts, and the Snowbirds (the Canadian Forces air demonstration team) are featured.

In July, during the annual four-day Trenton Summerfest, there are arts and crafts sales, fiddlers, sidewalk sales, concessions, square dancers, and cloggers. At the waterfront is a farmers' market, canoe races, a boat parade, a bathtub race, and fireworks.

VICTORIA PARK MARINA (Belleville)

★★★★

Charts: C 2069; C 2007; C 2011

Mile CONT-159.9 + 0.5 (NM)

Victoria Park Marina

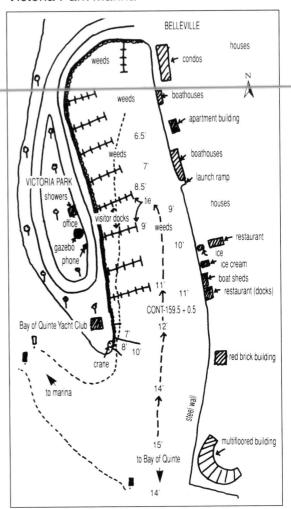

This marina is in Belleville—the largest city between Oshawa and Kingston—on the eastern side of the Moira River and Victoria Park Peninsula. There's a collection of places to stay, but Victoria Park is convenient to downtown.

Eastbound on the Bay of Quinte, clear the Norris Whitney Skyway Bridge and follow the main channel another 0.5 mile to miss the extensive shoals at the Moira River's mouth.

The Belleville secondary entrance channel begins off the river's eastern mouth at **Buoys QMB and Q54.** Once you make this northerly turn, the secondary channel's aids have a "QM" prefix. The most prominent landmark on this channel is a multistoried condominium on the river's eastern point—you are going to pass alongside

it. The channel also takes you just west of an old concrete wharf extending about 500 feet off the same point. The wharf forms the western side of Meyers Marina's offshore basin. If you need gas or diesel this is a good stop with an easy approach. To reach Victoria Park's southern end continue down the secondary channel.

The park—once an island—is a peninsula extending off the harbor's eastern side; it's open at its southern end. Leave the secondary channel when the bay formed by the peninsula opens clearly. Your departure point is normally at **Buoy QM9**—if it's on station. At the buoy the secondary channel bears off northwesterly to access western-shore marinas farther upriver.

At the southerly end of Victoria Park peninsula are the Bay of Quinte Yacht Club's piers; they extend easterly from the peninsula's eastern side. The marina piers are north of the club; they also extend easterly. The farther you go inside the bay, the more severe is the weed growth. The eastern end of the third and fourth marina piers are the check-in docks—they usually have signs. Before securing for the day see the dockmaster; you may need to move to another slip. He's at the head of the dock at the snack bar—he also runs the concession.

Electric hookups (110-volt) are available. The marina's land line number is (613) 962-9593.

The peninsula is a park with lawns, shade trees, benches, pretty views, picnic tables, and grills; it's a local drive-around promenade.

Belleville encompasses a wide area. Large, busy Valdi Discount Foods is a convenient grocery. It's on Dundas Street East, which crosses the southernmost bridge. Walk out the park's access road to Front Street South and bear northerly; it's on the corner just north of the railroad tracks. Valdi doesn't carry refrigerated products, but if you need quantities of major stores, it's an economical stop. There's a butcher shop downtown on Front Street North—about eight blocks away. It's a long walk or taxi ride to a regular supermarket. Belleville's farmers' market is held Tuesday, Thursday, and Saturday mornings in Market Square on Pinnacle Street—that's close; it's behind City Hall.

All conveniences are available downtown, north of Dundas Street and centered on Front Street North. Before you start out, ask the dockmaster for a downtown walking-tour map. Many of Belleville's historical buildings are on the way. About the first you come to is the 1872 City Hall at 169 Front Street; you can't miss its Gothic Revival–style clock tower and pointed arches.

Keep going north on tree-lined Front Street and you are in the city center. There are banks, pharmacies, dime stores, a post office, restaurants, department stores, chip wagons, and countless small shops selling everything imaginable. Find one that sells local cheese and try the Canadian fresh curd.

Walk out on the Foot Bridge and have a look at the crystal-clear, rapid-filled Moira River. It's about a block and a half north of the Bridge Street Bridge.

The Belleville Waterfront Festival and Folklorama is held annually at the beginning of July. This is a three-day multicultural festival with dance, costumes, and food. Over 100 uptown stores have sidewalk sales. There are 50 opening-day parade bands, a midway, waterfront sports, musical events, a boat parade, water-ski shows, and fireworks.

SANDY COVE ANCHORAGE

★★★

NO FACILITIES

Chart: C 2069 or C 2007

Mile CONT-163.0 + 0.5 (NM)

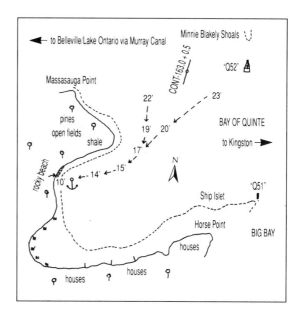

This anchorage just east of the Narrows at Massasauga and Ox points is on Big Bay's southwestern side. It's a good anchorage during northwest, west, southwest, and southeast winds, but it is badly exposed to wind and seas from north through east.

The 0.5-mile-wide cove mouth is difficult to pick up from offshore as it blends with the rest of the wooded shoreline. Best approach is to lay off a course for mid-cove from fixed departure point **Light Buoy Q52** off Minnie Blakely Shoals. Landmarks include a few cottages on the cove's southern shoreline, pines and open fields on the cove's northern point, and usually one or two local boats on moorings in its southwesterly section. Dangers include Ship Islet, a collection of rocks extending off Horse Point. Many reach east-northeasterly about 0.3 mile; they are watched by **Buoy Q51.** Those that extend northerly are not watched.

Anchor off the wooded shoreline by a rocky beach on the cove's northwestern side. Though the shoreline is shale and rocks, bottom is mud and holding is generally good. If you prefer the southwesterly side, take care—the bight is shallow. If you anchor in this area, expect heavy weed growth.

NORTH PORT ANCHORAGE

★★★

NO FACILITIES

Chart: C 2069 or C 2007

Mile CONT-168.0 + 0.5 (NM)

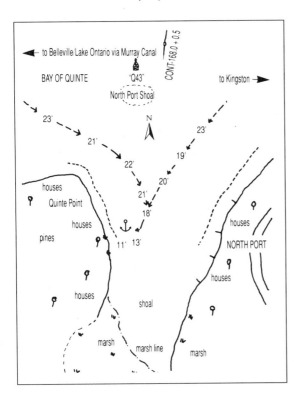

This anchorage is on the Bay of Quinte's southern shore between Quinte Point and North Port and nearly due south of dangerous North Port Shoal. It's in a funnel-shaped bay just east of Big Island's northeastern end. The anchorage is wide open to the northerly quadrant. If strong winds are forecast from this direction, don't stop; if they arrive when you're anchored, day or night, be prepared to seek safe haven elsewhere.

North Port Shoal is watched by **Light Buoy Q43;** it takes Bay of Quinte's navigation north of the shoal. You cannot take a southerly course for the anchorage at the buoy since its placement over its shoal varies. Leave the main channel at least 0.75 or 1.0 mile from **Buoy Q43** whether bound east or west on the Bay of Quinte. Favor the southern coastline to the bay's mouth.

The 1.5-mile-long bay is about 0.6 mile wide. Only its northerly 0.4 mile has good depths; the southerly area is marsh. Though you have a choice of places to anchor in the deepwater section, if you plan to fish the weedy marsh, anchor as far south as depth allows. If you choose this area, come in cautiously; your fathometer will be erratic due to weed growth. Bottom is mud and weeds. You may be more comfortable anchored in midbay with clear swimming water and more breeze; the latter helps confine marsh mosquitoes to their habitat.

RAM ISLAND ANCHORAGE

★★★★

NO FACILITIES

Charts: C 2064; C 2006, *See sketch map, page 247*

Mile CONT-179.8 + 3.3 (NM)

Ram Island is in Hay Bay, an offshoot of Long Reach. The bay's mouth is 1.2 miles wide; Shermans Point is its northern entry point. It has a 0.3-mile-long southerly extending shoal watched at its southern end by **Spar Q8.** Once you clear this spar and head up Hay Bay, you have clear water to Ram Island. On the way you pass Witlow Point on the bay's southern shore. In the slight cove formed southeast of this point there's a popular local anchorage, though it is weedy and badly exposed to the northeast.

Wooded Ram Island isn't visible until you round the bay's slight northerly bend near Gosport. Even as you make the bend, the island is difficult to make out—it sits in midbay at a bend and blends with the wooded shoreline. The prettiest anchorage is on the island's eastern side just north of its protruding southeastern point. There is one navigation aid, **Spar QH1,** just south of the island. For depths from 15 to 27 feet during your final approach, hold east of the buoy and slightly favor Hay

Ram Island Anchorage

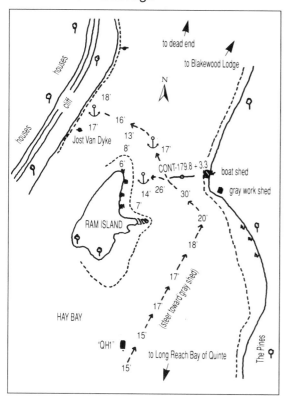

PICTON HARBOUR

★★★★★

ALL FACILITIES

Charts: C 2064 or C 2069; C 2006

Mile CONT-182.0 + 3.8 (NM)

Well-protected Picton Harbour is at the southwesterly end of Picton Bay; the bay is Long Reach's southwest-

Picton Harbour

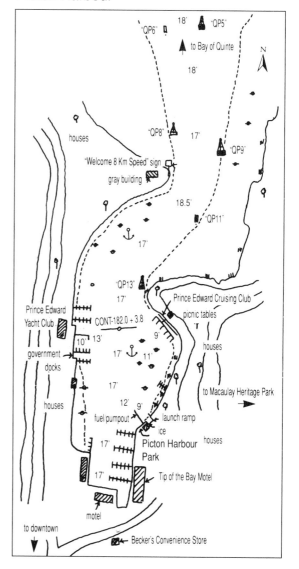

Bay's eastern shore. There's a gray shed about on the eastern mainland's prominent point, nearly opposite the island. It's a good leading mark from **Spar QH1.**

Once north of the island's southeasterly point, you can see that it forms the southerly side of a slight island cove. For some protection from the prevailing afternoon breeze, anchor as close to shore as depth—or room—allows. As you close the shoreline, sound carefully; weed growth interferes with fathometer readings. Bottom is mud and weeds.

The anchorage is usually overflowing with boats, so you may have to anchor farther off the island. If you do, depths range up to 30 feet; use sufficient scope.

Severe winds in summer often come from the northwest. Good protection in these conditions is in mud in the lee of the bay's steep northwestern shoreline just north of the island.

Blakewood Lodge is 1.2 miles on up Hay Bay's southeastern shore. It has a popular restaurant specializing in farm-style meals. You can either take the big boat and anchor off, or outboard up. Breakfast is served from 8 to 10 A.M.; dinner is at 6 P.M.

erly end. In the harbor you have a choice of marinas and clubs with the usual facilities, or you can anchor.

When eastbound take a main-channel departure at **Fairway Buoy Q, Mile CONT-182.0 (NM)**, and bear into large Picton Bay. If westbound you have good water close to shore west of Glenora, so follow the coastline as it makes a slow bend into Picton Bay. A prominent landmark to let you know when you are in Picton Bay is the western shore's Lake Ontario Cement complex. There are good depths throughout Picton Bay until you begin the approach to Picton Harbour—the last 0.5 mile of Picton Bay. As shoreside depths decrease the channel becomes watched—buoy prefix is "QP"—so you have no problem rounding Chimney Point, the harbor's western entrance point. Your destination is south of Chimney Point.

As you round this point, there is a collection of moorings in its lee. You can anchor close to them, but don't swing into the watched channel. Land the dinghy at the Picton Harbor Park ramp dock, or if that's too far, make paying arrangements with the Prince Edward Yacht Club.

Ahead on the eastern shore is prominent Brick Kiln Point at **Buoy QP13.** In this point's lee on the eastern shore is the Prince Edward Cruising Club, with slips and offshore moorings. It has most conveniences, including a laundry room, a swimming pool, lovely grounds, and friendly management. If the docks are filled, ask about a mooring. You can also anchor close to their moorings, but don't swing so you clutter the fairway or the approach to the club's slips. If you anchor, tie the dinghy at the town dock at Picton Harbour Park.

Across from the cruising club on the western bank is what appears to be one marina; it's not. The northernmost piers are those of the Prince Edward Yacht Club; the southernmost are government docks. Both are managed by the yacht club. Price of dockage varies dramatically and depends on whose slips you occupy.

Back on the bay's eastern side south of the cruising club's moorings is the Picton Harbour Park, operated by the town of Picton. This is the place to go for fuel (gas and diesel), ice, and a pumpout; they have a few spaces for overnight. Just south of the park on the eastern shore is the Tip of the Bay, another marina with a large collection of slips; their facilities include a restaurant and laundry room.

No matter where you stay in the harbor, you are convenient to downtown. The city center is primarily west of the harbor on Main Street. If you're on the eastern side, cross the Bridge Street Bridge. There's a small convenience store close by, west of the bridge on the street's southern side. Continue up the hill and you come to Main Street; bear southerly and you are downtown, with a drugstore, banks, a restaurant, a laundromat, a bakery, shops, and boutiques. The supermarkets and laundromat are the farthest away—still southeast on Main Street. The IGA is on Main Street's western side at Washburn; the A & P is a tad farther west at Main Street's "Y" intersection at Talbot and East Lake Road. If you have a heavy load, Dan's Cab, (613) 476-4622, might help on the carry home.

Nearby sights include Macaulay Heritage Park— open Monday through Friday from 10 to 4:30 and weekends from 1 to 4:30. It includes the restored 1850s home of William Macaulay. The 1823 St. Mary Magdalene Church is beside the Macaulay House. The church is the Prince Edward County Museum and has area memorabilia and historical artifacts.

The Royal Canadian Legion Museum is in the 1863 Ross-McMullen House at 347 Main Street East. It includes a collection of weapons, photographs, flags, models, and world war history. It's open Wednesday, Friday, and Saturday from 1:30 to 4:30.

If you enjoy walking tours, pick up a guide at the Quinte's Isle Tourist Office at 116 Main Street.

The annual Quinte Summer Music Festival is centered around Picton. It's held in July over a two- to three-week period and presents a collection of Canadian musicians with children's shows, classical and popular performers, dance bands, folk music, choirs, country music, and gospel. Call (613) 476-7042 for times. Performances are held in various churches and the Community Center. The latter is at the fairgrounds, which is very close the harbor's western side.

PRINYER COVE ANCHORAGE

★★★★

NO FACILITIES

Charts: C 2064; C 2006

Mile CONT-192.6 (NM)

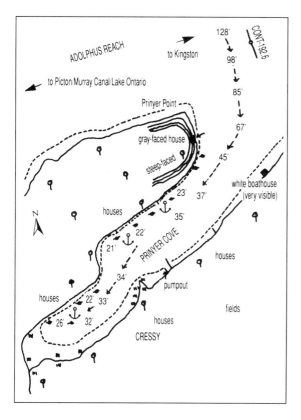

tors seeking a lee. Remember, if you have a view up North Channel after anchoring, you are at risk in northeasterly weather. Bottom is weeds with rocks, mud, and clay. In fair weather many boats anchor in midcove, but if you do, use sufficient scope—depths range from 30 to 45 feet.

There's a lower or westerly end of the bay around a slight point projecting southeasterly off the northern shore. This point offers some northeasterly weather protection; however, the bay is packed with moored boats.

Waterfront cottages and private docks make access ashore only by invitation. The open area on the southeastern shore about midcove was once a marina. Though not open as such, there may be an operating pumpout on a remaining pier/bulkhead.

This 0.8-mile-long cove is on the northern side of Cressy Point, the northeasterly end of Quinte's Isle. The cove's western entrance point is Prinyer Point. When eastbound on Adolphus Reach, the point and mouth of the cove—known as the Gap—is difficult to spot; it's about 1,000 feet wide. Wooded Prinyer Point blends in with Cressy Point's shoreline. The cove is badly exposed to northeasterly weather; it has a 10-mile-plus North Channel deepwater fetch.

You have good depth if you hold to mid-entry. For northeast wind protection, anchor close to the cove's northern bank. This isn't easy; the bank is filled with private docks, boats on moorings, and anchored visi-

Region 5
THE THOUSAND ISLANDS, THE ST. LAWRENCE
SEAWAY, AND THE FAR UPPER ST. LAWRENCE RIVE.

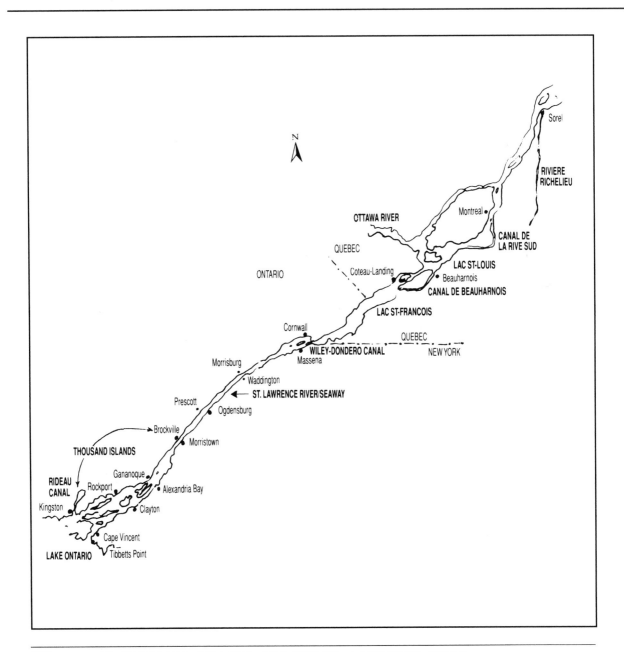

Mile SW-164.5 (NM) to Mile SW-0.0 (NM); Mile MDCH-29.5 (NM) to Mile MDCH-0.0 (NM); and Mile SLR-136.3 (NM) to Mile SLR-99.7 (NM)

CURRENT DIRECTION AND SPEED*

The St. Lawrence River flows northeasterly

Place	Mile	Speed in knots**
The Thousand Islands		
Tibbets Point	SW-164.5 (NM)	0.5 to 1.3
Kingston	MDCH-29.5 (NM)	0.5 to 1.2
Clayton	SW-147.0 (NM)	0.5 to 1.3
Gananoque	ADM-4.2 (NM)	0.5
Thousand Islands Bridge	SW-141.3 (NM)	2.8
Alexandria Bay	SW-138.0 (NM)	1.2 to 1.5
Ash Island	MDCH-7.0 (NM)	1.3 to 2.0
Rockport	MDCH-3.8 (NM)	1.4 to 1.8
Brockville Narrows	SW-122.0 (NM)	1.3 to 2.4
The St. Lawrence Seaway and the Upper St. Lawrence River		
Ogdensburg	SW-109.3 (NM)	2
Galop Island	SW-104.9 (NM)	2
Ogden Island	SW-94.2 (NM)	2.4 to 2.7
Long Sault Islands	SW-80.0 (NM)	2.0
International Bridge (Cornwall)	SW-70.4 (NM)	1.0 to 3.4
Lac Saint-Francois	SW-72.5 (NM) to SW-41.0 (NM)	1.0
Lac Saint-Louis	SW-27.0 (NM) to SW-17.0 (NM)	1.1
Montreal	SW-0.0 (NM)	1.5 to 2.0
Sorel	SLR-99.7 (NM)	1.5 to 2.0

*In normal river stage

**An average speed only. Water-level fluctuations, placement of islands, power plant generation, and regulated outflows of Lake Ontario may increase or decrease current flow. When extreme natural changes occur, they are so noted in the text.

The Thousand Islands
via the Seaway Channel and/or the Canadian Middle Channel

Mile SW-164.5 (NM) to Mile SW-118.7 (NM) and
Mile MDCH-29.5 to Mile MDCH-0.0

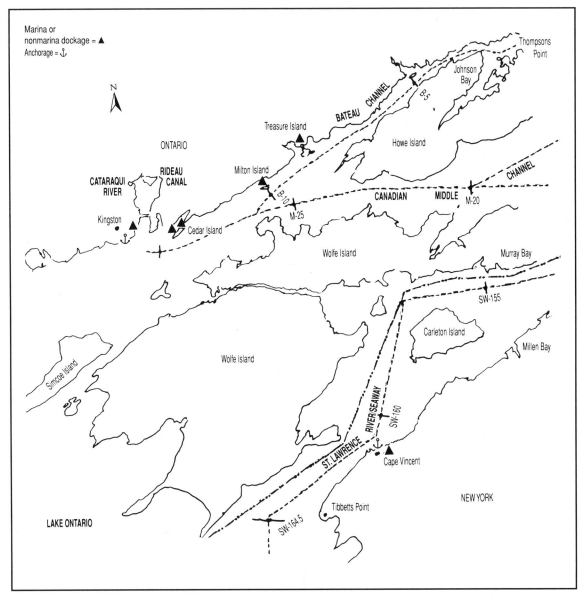

Tibbetts Point to East Wolfe Island, Mile SW-164.5 (NM) to Mile SW-154.0 (NM), and Kingston to Thompsons Point, Mile MDCH-29.5 (NM) to Mile MDCH-18.0 (NM)

Maritonna, Garden of the Great Spirit

IROQUOIS, The Thousand Islands

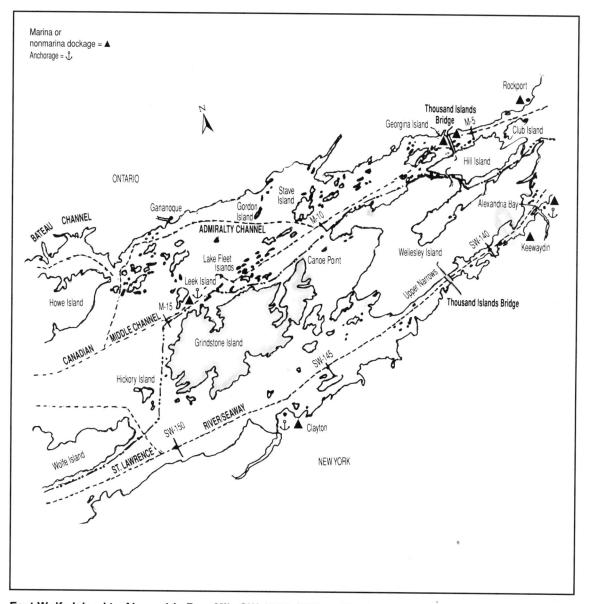

Marina or
nonmarina dockage = ▲
Anchorage = ⚓

Rockport

Thousand Islands
Bridge
Georgina Island
M-5
Club Island

Hill Island

ONTARIO

Stave
Island

Alexandria Bay

Gananoque

Gordon
Island

M-10

Keewaydin

ADMIRALTY CHANNEL

SW-140

BATEAU CHANNEL

Lake Fleet
Islands

Canoe Point

Wellesley Island

Leek Island

Howe Island

M-15

Upper Narrows

Thousand Islands Bridge

CANADIAN MIDDLE CHANNEL

Grindstone Island

SW-145

Hickory Island

SW-150

RIVER/SEAWAY

Clayton

Wolfe Island

ST. LAWRENCE

NEW YORK

East Wolfe Island to Alexandria Bay, Mile SW-154.0 (NM) to Mile SW-138.0 (NM), and Thompsons Point to Rockport, Mile MDCH-18.0 (NM) to Mile MDCH-3.0 (NM)

Alexandria Bay to Morristown, Mile SW-138.0 (NM) to Mile SW-118.7 (NM), and Rockport to Ironsides, Mile MDCH-3.0 (NM) to Mile MDCH-0.0 (NM)

The 2,342-mile-long St. Lawrence River system extends from the river's mouth at the Gulf of St. Lawrence, through the five Great Lakes, to Lake Superior's major ports, Duluth and Thunder Bay. Region 5 makes use of part of this immense system.

This region begins at Lake Ontario's northeastern end on both sides of Wolfe Island where the St. Lawrence River's 744-mile-long easterly section starts its final run to the sea. At the same time it becomes the St. Lawrence Seaway south of the island. In the 1950s a Canadian and American St. Lawrence Seaway navigation project improved a 164.5-mile-long section between Lake Ontario and Montreal to bypass the river's narrow channels and shallow river rapids. It's a composite of canals, natural rivers, and expanses of open lakes with a maintained depth of 27 feet.

For the most part the region uses official Seaway mileage, beginning in downtown Montreal with **Mile SW-0.0 (NM)** and ending at Tibbetts Point with **Mile SW-164.5 (NM)**. River mileage from Montreal to Sorel has its own numbering system. All mileages count upstream.

The St. Lawrence River Valley, an 18-mile-wide lowland north of the Adirondack Mountains, reaches northeast from Lake Ontario. It has a mean altitude of about 300 feet. The river's upper 46 miles between Lake Ontario and Morristown resembles a lake. This river section is studded with about 1,700 islands, known collectively as the Thousand Islands. A few of them have an area of 20 square miles and are settled with farms and homes. Most are small, with room for one or two cottages, a camp, a few old homes, or a mansion. Some are only inches high; many are awash.

River current varies here; it depends on channel depth, narrowness of reach, and seasonal lake and river levels. From Lake Ontario to Morristown the river's natural fall is about a foot, so in many areas normal current is about 0.6 knot. In very constricted channels it can be up to 2.5 knots or more. Most marinas, park docks, and anchorages are in areas of slight current.

The Thousand Islands have two popular cruising areas accessed by separate channels. They are the Seaway Channel, Tibbetts Point to Morristown, **Mile SW-164.5 (NM)** to **Mile SW-118.7 (NM)**, and the Canadian Middle Channel, Kingston to Ironsides Island, **Mile MDCH-29.5 (NM)** to **Mile MDCH-0.0 (NM)**. The channels intersect at Ironsides Island, **Mile SW-133.4 (NM)/Mile MDCH-0.0 (NM)**. The 29.5-mile-long Canadian Middle Channel is north of Hill,

Wellesley, Grindstone, and Wolfe islands and has secondary channels to access island groups. The mileage system for this channel begins at **Mile MDCH-0.0 (NM)**, downstream on the Seaway at Ironsides Island, **Mile SW-133.4 (NM)**. At that point it branches west from the Seaway and favors the river's northern shore. It routes through the Thousand Islands on the Canadian side of the international boundary. Its mileage system ends upstream at Kingston, **Mile MDCH-29.5 (NM)**. Until the Seaway was completed the Canadian Middle Channel was heavily used by commerce; it's still well watched and has depths ranging from 20 to 200 feet. Today it's primarily a pleasure-boat cruising area.

Wooded islands have a microclimate with cool, damp, shady northwestern slopes and dry, sunny southwestern shores. The islands and nearby mainland are composed of pinkish Precambrian granite and limestone and offer some fantastic scenery. It's a rocky area with an unforgiving bottom. Most rocks are circled by deep water, so a fathometer may give no warning of impending danger. Nor are all rocks charted—a fact we discovered when we came to a grinding halt on a pinnacle in charted depths of 42 feet.

While cruising the Thousand Islands, you will come across lime-green buoys referred to by local boaters as "gum-drops." These are seasonal buoys placed by the Thousand Islands Association and mainly intended for shoal-draft runabouts; they mark obstructions. The buoys are helpful aids, but never entirely depend on them to mark a charted obstruction.

Careful navigation is absolutely imperative once you leave a maintained channel. *Always travel the Thousand Islands with up-to-date charts;* every newly issued chart notes dangerous shoals in what once was charted as good water. The shoals are often discovered the hard way by the increasing number of deep-draft vessels visiting the area—they hit them. Once a shoal is reported, verified, and noted in the Coast Guard's "Notice to Mariners," it eventually will be charted.

Always know your location. Be familiar with Canadian spar buoy configuration, which differs somewhat from that of United States buoys. Spar coloration and the shape of the small top—cone or flat—is often difficult to distinguish at a distance. Closely approaching buoys when in rocks is a dangerous practice unless you absolutely know the buoy and its placement over its obstruction.

Throughout this region you can easily spot the tall, cylinder-shaped, white light towers with red or green tops. Use them as leading marks, but watch carefully for intermediate buoys.

Picking out a destination island in the midst of a look-alike group can be confusing. To be safe, use clear-cut departure points from fixed navigational aids and steer a compass course. Leave a watched channel slowly and with utmost caution, and sound carefully. Allow for river current and its set; memorize how you came in to a destination so that you can safely exit exactly the same way. Remember that the descriptions in this guide are general and are intended only to give you a sense of direction.

Downbound you can enter the Thousand Islands from the west either at Tibbetts Point on the Seaway Channel, **Mile SW-164.5 (NM),** or at Kingston on the Canadian Middle Channel, **Mile MDCH-29.5 (NM).** In the river's upper 30 miles you can skip back and forth between the two channels through one recommended well-marked deepwater cut. Many other routes between the two channels exist; some are watched, some are not.

The islands are a pleasant but extremely crowded summer cruising area. There are convenient supply points at Cape Vincent, Clayton, Alexandria Bay, and Morristown on the southern shore, and at Kingston, Gananoque, Rockport, and Brockville on the north side. There are many marinas and anchorages. Island parks are the favorite destinations. Though often very crowded, they are well worth a wait to visit.

Since there are two major routes through the Thousand Islands for 30 miles downbound, they are described separately as far east as Ironsides Island, **Mile SW-133.4 (NM)/Mile MDCH-0.0 (NM),** where they rejoin. Both offer lovely scenery, pleasant stops, and short runs.

The Seaway Channel
Tibbetts Point to Ironsides Island

Mile SW-164.5 (NM) to Mile SW-133.4 (NM)

The St. Lawrence Seaway's western terminus is 1.75 miles off Tibbetts Point at **Light Buoy A.** The buoy is also the eastern terminus of the 157-mile-long American shore of Lake Ontario (see Region 4, "The American Shore," beginning on page 188).

As you begin your downbound Seaway journey, Tibbetts Point is to the east and Wolfe Island to the north. The 6-mile-wide island, the largest in the Thousand Islands group, stretches downstream 16 miles. In 800 A.D. its inhabitants were Point Peninsula Indians; 700 years later it was an Iroquois summer fishing ground for eel, drum, and sturgeon. The Iroquois called the island Ganounkouesnot, or "a long island standing up"; later, French residents named it Grande Island. After the American Revolutionary War it became a British shipbuilding and farming community. Its present name honors General James Wolfe.

In 1850 the Wolfe Island Barge Canal was established as a quick route to American markets. It ran from the western shore's Barrett Bay to the eastern shore's Bayfield Bay. It is no longer in use.

If you approach the narrows at Cape Vincent, **Mile SW-161.0 (NM),** in fog, watch for cross-river Horne's Ferry, which plies to Wolfe Island's Alexandria Point. A ferry service has worked between the Cape and Wolfe Island since 1801. This is the only American community left with an automobile-passenger ferry crossing the Seaway.

An offshore breakwater protects Cape Vincent. The Cape Vincent Seaway Pilot Station is in the harbor; all salties must take on a river pilot.

The village was once part of James LeRay de Chaumont's vast northern New York lands—he named the settlement for his son, Vincent. Chaumont encouraged a group of Napoleon Bonaparte's contemporaries to immigrate to the village; the Emperor was to arrive after his expected escape from Saint Helena. Though Napoleon never saw the settlement, his sister Caroline and his brother Joseph lived in town for a time. Cape Vincent never became a major early river port, but it was noted for its lumber, shipbuilding, wood pulp, and coal.

Downbound at Cape Vincent the Seaway Channel routes west of 2-mile-long Carleton Island, an early supplier of stone for Cape Vincent's homes. It was also site of a Revolutionary War British outpost, Fort Haldiman, a staging area for British, Tory, and Indian raids south into the Mohawk Valley. The Treaty of Paris required the British to give up the fort, but they refused to leave until the Americans paid reparation to Loyalists fleeing the new United States. The British were still on the island in 1812 when American Captain Abner Hubbard and a military force came from southern-shore Millens Bay and captured the fort without much problem—its complement was a sergeant, three wounded soldiers, and two women.

Wolfe Island Cut at Wolfe Island's eastern end is a deepwater watched access into the Canadian Middle Channel. From Quebec Head, the Wolfe Island Cut's northern end, it's 4 miles to the Admiralty Islands parks and 7 miles to the Lake Fleet Islands. Both areas are north of Grindstone Island.

Ahead the Seaway Channel holds south of the Eagle Wing group's small islands and those surrounding prominent Calumet Island, **Mile SW-147.1 (NM).**

During the War of 1812, American General Jacob Brown's brigade established a battery on Bartlett Point, **Mile SW-148.0 S (NM).** Brown was the forward vanguard of General James Wilkinson's 8,000-man army, which had been ordered to capture Montreal. The main British fleet—eight gunboats, two schooners, and two brigs, all filled with infantry—discovered the American battery. While Brown repelled the British in two engagements, Wilkinson's main troops slipped by downstream toward their eventual defeat.

Clayton, **Mile SW-147.0 S (NM),** founded in 1822, is on a southern-shore peninsula at French Creek's mouth. It became a noted river port, the center of a large shipbuilding industry, and a lumber port. Later its economy catered to summer visitors, with eight hotels and other tourist amenities.

Xavier Colon, owner of the 1868 St. Lawrence Skiff,

Canoe, and Steam Launch Company, developed the St. Lawrence Skiff, the dominant boat for the Thousand Islands resort trade. The double-ended lapstrake cedar skiff was light, fast, and easy to row and sail.

Downbound at Clayton the Seaway Channel takes you north of North Colborne, Little Round, and Round Islands. Outside the channel there are unwatched isolated rocks awash. Be careful if you plan to route to the Canadian Middle Channel through the passage south of Grindstone's northeasterly end and northwest of Picton Island.

Coming up is the American Narrows (Upper Narrows), a 6-mile reach. Its western entrance routes through small islands and shoals south of Wellesley Island. Currents increase in the reach and peak at the bridge.

The 1882 Rock Island Lighthouse, **Mile SW-143.2 S (NM),** is prominent on the channel's southern side. Until 1941 it was a manned light. Today the Thousand Islands Parks Commission maintains it; it's open from 8 to 4:30.

On the southern shore is Fishers Landing. Its border proximity made it a busy but surreptitious port during Prohibition. Downstream at **Mile SW-142.6 (NM),** south of Niagara Shoal, is Grass Point State Park on Mullet Creek Bay's northeastern side. The shoal, weedy bay sprinkled with rocks is a popular spring and early summer fishing area for bass, bluegills, pumpkinseeds, and crappie.

The 152-foot-clearance Thousand Islands Bridge crosses at **Mile SW-141.3 (NM).** This span is only part of its link between nations. On Wellesley Island, the highway rounds north of the Lake of the Isles, then crosses a concrete viaduct at the International Rift to Hill Island. Another span jumps over islands to cross the Canadian Middle Channel's Raft Narrows to Ivy Lea Park.

At the eastern end of the American Narrows there's another large collection of southern-shore islands. Keewaydin State Park, **Mile SW-139.0 S (NM),** is one of New York's island parks. Keewaydin once had an elegant castle; its remaining gazebos and boathouses are along the waterfront.

Cherry Island, **Mile SW-138.3 S (NM),** is the site of Casa Blanca, a 27-room 1895 Victorian mansion nestling among the island trees. It's typical of the early Thousand Islands summer homes, with elaborate landscaped grounds and gardens.

In 1974 the 640-foot ship *Roy A. Jodrey* hit Pullman Shoal on the channel's northern side carrying a cargo of iron pellets. She stayed afloat nearly four hours, then capsized and sank. She's still on the bottom.

Another son of James LeRay de Chaumont settled Alexandria Bay, **Mile SW-138.0 S (NM),** in 1818. Residents based their early economy on the area's pine and oak forests and sent log rafts downriver. For a time exports also included potash and oaken barrel staves. During the steamboat era the port was a woodlot. Stevedores loaded fuel for ships' boilers.

By 1870 vacationers had turned Alexandria Bay into a spa. Entrepreneurs built elegant hotels and associated tourist attractions; the wealthy made it their summer base and built grand "cottages" on nearby islands. Tourism remains Alexandria Bay's leading industry.

Six-story Boldt Castle, built by hotel owner George C. Boldt as a gift to his wife, is on Heart Island at **Mile SW-137.6 N (NM).** Boldt started the castle in 1900 and intended it to have more than 120 rooms, but he abandoned the $2.5 million project when his wife died. The Thousand Island Bridge Authority assumed ownership in 1977; it's now open to the public. Across on Wellesley Island is the yacht house built for the family's three yachts and their enormous houseboat. Daily tour boats access the island from Alexandria Bay and Gananoque. There is a U.S. Customs dock on the island's northern side.

Sunken Rock Light, **Mile SW-137.4 (NM),** watches the eastern end of the American Narrows. The 1847 brick lighthouse, now faced with wood, and its associated wooden house, are still in service.

North of **Whiskey Island Shoal Light #182, Mile SW-134.6 (NM),** is Grenadier Island. On its southern shore, north of the Slim Island group, is Centre Grenadier island park. Part of the island is private, but West, Centre, and East Grenadier are open to the public. There are also park areas on Grenadier's two main satellite islands, Squaw Island (off the Small Craft Route near Centre Grenadier's northern shore) and Adelaide Island (off East Grenadier).

Northeast of Whiskey Island Shoal at the Canadian Middle Channel's eastern terminus is Ironsides Island, **Mile SW-133.4 S (NM).**

The Canadian Middle Channel
Kingston to the Thousand Islands Bridge

Mile MDCH-29.5 (NM) to Mile MDCH-5.8 (NM)

The Canadian Middle Channel's western terminus, **Mile MDCH-29.5 (NM),** is at Kingston. This is also the eastern terminus of the 212-mile-long Canadian shore of Lake Ontario (see Region 4, "The Canadian Shore," beginning on page 214). The mouth of the Cataraqui River, in downtown Kingston, is the western terminus of the Rideau Canal.

The Canadian Middle Channel is the favorite pleasure-boat route through the Thousand Islands. From it, you have easy access to the most popular section between Kingston and Brockville, the Canadian St. Lawrence Islands National Park islands, which are about the only uninhabited areas in the Thousand Islands.

Nearly all park islands have one or more docks available for overnight. A few have moorings. It's a first-come first-served arrangement, and there is a layover time limit of three consecutive nights. The docks are heavy-duty fixed cribs, floating finger piers, or a combination of both; depths at docks vary with river stage. There's a fee for day or overnight use of docks, firewood, and camping. All have onsite self-registration and a fee box. You can pay by cash or check; there's a posted current rate of exchange for foreign boats. All islands have picnic tables, grills, shelters, garbage bins, wood, rustic pit toilets, and camping areas. None have electricity. There's well water on nearly all islands; it's tested periodically by the park service. Nevertheless, signs warn you to boil water before drinking or cooking.

Check at registration desks or bulletin boards for trail locations. Most follow an island's perimeter; some go inland. The trails are there to prevent hikers from destroying sensitive habitats.

All the islands have naturalist programs on certain days; wardens come in on a floating interpretation center. Maintenance crews arrive daily by workboat to tend to facilities, take off garbage, and tidy up nature trails. There's one dockage site per area—marked with a yellow line—reserved for warden boats.

Mileage for the Canadian Middle Channel begins at Ironsides Island, **Mile MDCH-0.0 (NM),** downriver on the Seaway Channel at **Mile SW-133.4 (NM).** Roughly, the mileage works upstream from Ironsides Island to the north of Hill Island, through Raft Narrows, then north of Wellesley, Grindstone, and Wolfe islands and finally to Kingston. Most Canadian Middle Channel navigation aids carry the prefix "H".

Branching off the Canadian Middle Channel are four major charted secondary channels. Mileage on these deepwater offshoot channels also reads heading upstream. The secondary channels off the Canadian Middle Channel include the Small Craft Route, the Admiralty Channel, the Wolfe Island Cut, and the Bateau Channel. These are generally the safest way to travel through dicey areas. From these watched secondary channels you can make your approach into off-channel anchorages with a minimum distance to travel through rocky shoals. Most secondary-channel navigation aids carry a "J" prefix.

Kingston, Canada's second oldest city, was settled because of its strategic position at the junction of the Great Lakes, the head of the St. Lawrence River, and the mouth of the Cataraqui River. The site was Iroquois territory until 1678, when the French built Fort Frontenac as a defense against British fur traders encroaching from the east. The British named it Kingstown when they captured the fort in 1758.

The Rideau Canal links Lake Ontario and the Ottawa River between Kingston and Ottawa. Construction on the original canal began in the 1820s. Today's canal climbs 160 feet over the Canadian Shield in 14 locks to its highest point in Upper Rideau Lake; 31 locks lower boats more than 250 feet to the Ottawa River. The locks accommodate vessels up to about 134 feet in length and about 33 feet in width. Though the canal maintains an available navigation season depth of 5 feet at chart datum, vessels drawing more than 4 feet must contact canal staff before attempting transit.

If bound for the Rideau's entrance, travel upstream on the Cataraqui River through the La Salle Causeway bascule bridge; it's open to pleasure craft from 0600 to

2200 and raised every half hour except at 0800, 1230, 1630, and 1700. The Rideau Canal is a cruising destination in itself; it is so extensive that including it here would have made this guide too large for convenience.

As you leave Kingston downbound on the Canadian Middle Channel at **Point Frederick Light Buoy KH2,** be very careful, especially when visibility is limited. You are cruising in rocky islands in an area of unusual magnetic disturbance, there is a slight easterly current, and navigation aids are often 2 or more miles apart. Watch for the cross-river ferry *Wolfe Islander III;* it barrels briskly between Kingston and Marysville in Barrett Bay.

Point Frederick forms the eastern side of the Cataraqui River mouth and Navy Bay's western bank. Old Fort Frederick, with its cylindrical gray stone martello tower, is on the point. The Royal Military College's impressive stone buildings and clock tower are nearby. East across Navy Bay is Point Henry; you'll see Fort Henry with its red roof.

Point Frederick is also part of Deadman Bay's northwestern side. Near the entrance is another redoubt. This bay's southeastern shore is partly made up of Cedar Island, the most westerly of the St. Lawrence Islands National Park islands. The Cathcart Tower is on Cedar's western end. Deadman Bay was named during the tower's construction when a rowboat transporting workers from the mainland capsized and 17 of the 23 men aboard drowned.

Downbound you pass north of rocky **Bayfield Shoal Buoy H43** a mile west of Wolfe Island's Knapp Point, **Mile MDCH-26.0 (NM).** At Knapp Point you have a route decision coming up; you can take the Bateau Channel, which is a secondary channel from the Admiralty Island group to within 4 miles of Kingston, or you can continue on the Canadian Middle Channel. If bound for the Admiralty Islands and Gananoque, the distance on either is about the same. The Canadian Middle Channel has more exposed water, so if wind and seas are up, the Bateau Channel offers more comfort. The Bateau Channel's eastern terminus is at Gillespies Point on the Admiralty Islands group's northwestern side.

The Canadian Middle Channel route is closer if you want to access safe passage into the Seaway Channel via the Wolfe Island Cut; or if you are bound for the southeastern Admiralty Islands park at Leek Island; or if you are heading farther east to the Lake Fleet and Navy island groups.

The Bateau Channel

Mile BAT-10.3 (NM)/MDCH-26.0 (NM) to Mile BAT 0.0 (NM)/ADM-6.0 (NM)

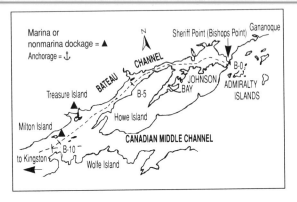

The Bateau Channel's western terminus is between Milton Island and the Spectacles. The former is an island park; the latter is a collection of rocks, shoals, and two low, bushy islands.

The 10.3-mile-long channel averages about 0.5 mile in width. It has been a major transportation route since the days of the fur traders; unlike the Canadian Middle Channel, it had calm waters and offered less risk of losing cargoes carried by bateaux, canoes, and skiffs as they plied between Kingston and Gananoque. The wooded shores are sprinkled with waterfront cottages and homes. Depths range from 30 to 50 feet as long as you mind the well-watched channel. Shoals extend far from shores and tend to be rocky and weedy—excellent fishing areas if you lay over enroute. There are a few islands and a few small bays. Current is usually about 0.2 knot but increases to near 0.6 knot when the channel narrows to 300 feet at the Narrows, **Mile BAT-4.0 (NM).**

Trident Yacht Club, **Mile BAT-3.0 (NM),** is on the northern shore. Across from the club is Howe Island's 3-mile-long Johnson Bay—an ideal place to fish for northern pike and bass. For the most part the marshy bay is shoal and rocky, especially at its entrance; for safe access, use your dinghy.

At Thompson's Point, **Mile BAT-2.1 (NM),** the downbound channel opens to nearly a mile across. Watch for the ferry that crosses from Gillespies Point to the eastern mainland; it's at the Bateau Channel's eastern terminus, **Mile BAT-0.0 (NM).** The rocky, wooded Admiralty Islands litter the river ahead. Gananoque is about 2 miles east via the Admiralty Channel, which routes through these islands.

You may decide not to travel the Bateau Channel back at the Spectacles. If that's the case, at **Mile MDCH-26.0 (NM)** continue downbound on the Canadian Middle Channel (with about a knot of current) and approach the narrows between the western end of Howe Island to the north and Wolfe Island's Oak Point to the south. The Canadian Middle Channel leads you north of a rocky patch at **Cold Bath Shoal Light Buoy H39, Mile MDCH-23.4 (NM),** which lies south of Hickey's Point.

Now the Canadian Middle Channel begins a gradual 3-mile widening process. Off Holliday Point on Wolfe Island, **Mile MDCH-20.4 (NM),** you have another choice of routes. If bound for the Seaway Channel south of Wolfe Island, choose the recommended route that leads east along the northern shore of Wolfe Island past large Irvine Bay, Rattray Point, and Brakey Bay to Wolfe Island Light on Quebec Head. This is the northern end of the mile-long Wolfe Island Cut back into the Seaway Channel.

If eastbound for the southern access to the Admiralty Islands, or if bound even farther east, at Holliday Point continue on the Canadian Middle Channel. **At Light Buoy H34, Mile MDCH-17.0 (NM),** you have another route decision. If bound for the northern Admiralty Islands and Gananoque, you will change course to travel the watched Admiralty Channel, a secondary channel north of the Canadian Middle Channel that generally follows the Admiralty Island's perimeter.

The Admiralty Channel

Mile ADM-7.8 (NM) to Mile ADM-0.0 (NM)

See sketch maps, page 262, 263

The Admiralty Channel routes for 7.8 miles off the Canadian Middle Channel in a wide northerly arc and back again. It accesses the Admiralty Islands group and many other islands. Downbound mileage is **Mile ADM-7.8 (NM)/Mile MDCH-17.0 (NM)** to **Mile ADM-0.0 (NM)/Mile MDCH-10.1 (NM).**

The channel is well watched, but use extreme caution when leaving it to get to an anchorage area; there are many unwatched rocks and shoals.

The Admiralty Islands are in a 2.0-mile-by-3.5-mile area toward the Admiralty Channel's western portion. There are 9 large islands and more than 100 small islands and islets. The larger islands were named in honor of British Admiralty members who held posts during the War of 1812. Some have been renamed, and local reference to islands is often a confusing mixture of old and new. For instance, Bostwick Island was Yorke; Sagistawika was Campbell; Hay was Melville; and Leek was Thwartway.

This is a popular area offering five St. Lawrence National Island Park islands, many anchorages, and a supply point. There is another island park on the Admiralty Channel in its far eastern portion. These stops are easily accessible; most are on the perimeter of the Admiralty Islands fairly close to the Admiralty Channel.

Downbound your departure point from the Canadian Middle Channel is at its western terminus at **Mile MDCH-17.0 (NM)** at **Light Buoy H34.** This buoy lies about 0.7 mile off Howe Island's southern shoreline, east of Rush Bay. **Buoy H34** gives you a fixed departure point from which to lay off a compass course to Aubrey Island Light, about 1.6 miles off in a northwesterly direction. The light is a 49-foot-high white wire skeleton tower with a square fluorescent orange daymark; it's on Aubrey's eastern side at **Mile ADM-6.4 (NM).** Laying off a course is very important because from a distance the overlapping Admiralty Islands all look alike against the wooded background of other islands and the mainland.

As you close Aubrey Island Light, you first pass west of Mermaid Island, **Mile ADM-6.5 (NM).** Aubrey and Mermaid are St. Lawrence National Island Park islands.

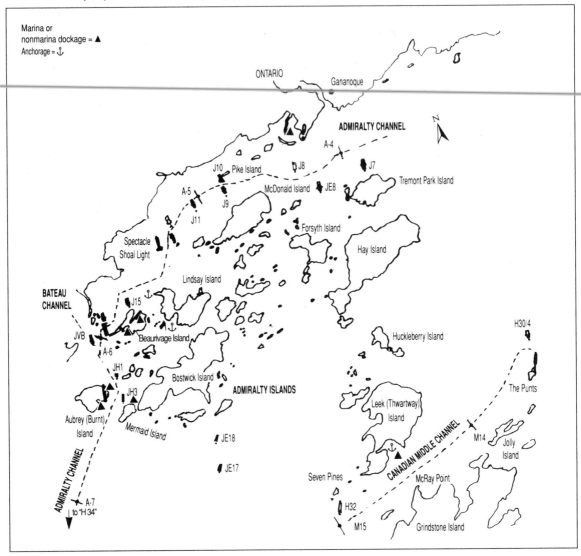

Marina or
nonmarina dockage = ▲
Anchorage = ⚓

At Aubrey Island Light the channel bears northerly to red and green **Light Buoy JVB** off Anchor Shoal, **Mile ADM-6.1 (NM).** This is about midway between Beaurivage Island, another island park, and Gillespies Point, the Bateau Channel's eastern terminus.

At Anchor Shoal the Admiralty Channel zigzags its way northeast, vaguely paralleling the mainland shoreline. It passes south of Spectacles Shoal Light's red-topped white cylindrical tower, and north of Spectacles Rocks. You continue to bear northeasterly and northwest of McDonald Island, part of which is another island park, and south of Pike, Cherry, and Ormiston islands and Ormiston's neighbor island, to Gananoque,

Mile ADM-4.0 (NM), at the Gananoque River's mouth.

After Kingston, Gananoque is the largest town in the Canadian Middle Channel area. It's a fairly convenient supply point and a very busy yachting center. It's also base for a booming summer tourist trade and home port for a large Canadian tour boat fleet.

Gananoque, Indian for "rocks rising out of the water," was originally a western wilderness fur-trading outpost. After settlers built a river dam for power, the town became a noted lumbering and milling port. By 1826 a quarter of all flour consumed in Montreal came from Gananoque mills.

If you feel in an exploratory mood after visiting

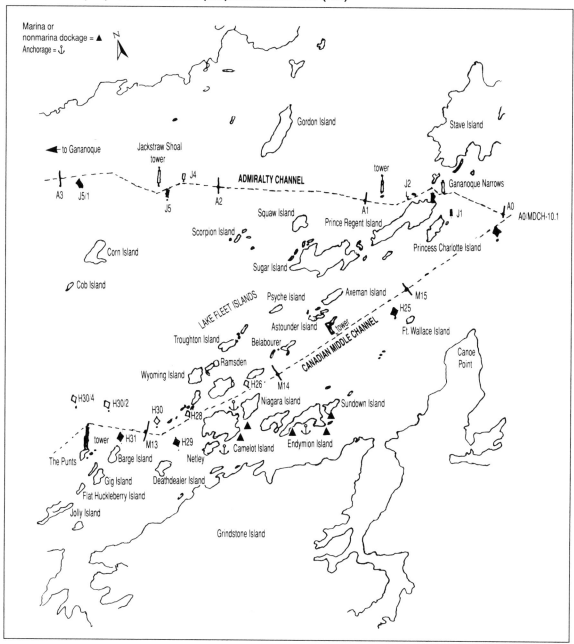

Gananoque, there's a watched route off the Admiralty Channel south from Gananoque. It accesses more of the Admiralty Islands, most of which are private. Roughly, this channel begins off Gananoque and routes between the White Calf Islands and Tremont Park Island and their satellite islets. It then winds between Forsyth Island and its islets and Hay Island; and then between Polaris Island's shoals and Hay Island's western shore. Here the channel bears around the southwestern tip of Hay Island; then in a southwesterly direction to clear Juniper Island's extending shoals and those south of Hemlock Island. Finally, it bears back southeast and eventually regains the Canadian Middle Channel at its spar buoy at **Mile MDCH-15.2 (NM).**

This places the channel's southeastern end about a mile southwest of the anchorage at Leek Island, another island park. If you plan to take this route, go slowly and be extremely careful. Shoals extend well off islands, and though some are watched, many are not. Ignore other vessels that pass you at 30 knots; most are long-term island residents with uncanny local knowledge.

Downbound at Gananoque the Admiralty Channel continues easterly and you leave the Admiralty Islands group. Islands begin to thin out, the river widens, and navigation aids are far apart. There are offshore reefs and rocks near your course line, so mind the channel that takes you southwest of red-topped white cylindrical Jackstraw Shoal Light tower, then wind through its collection of watched rocks and reefs. You pass to the southwest of Gordon Island, another island park. Continue north of Scorpion Island, its satellite rocky islets, and Squaw Island, and finally bear for Gananoque Narrows, a 100-foot-wide passage between Stave Island and Prince Regent Island. The passage is your access back into the Canadian Middle Channel at its **Mile MDCH-10.1 (NM)** at **Light Buoy H23.**

If you decided against traveling the Admiralty Channel back at your departure point south of Howe Island at **Light Buoy H34, Mile MDCH-17.0 (NM),** continue easterly on the Canadian Middle Channel. At **Mile MDCH-15.2 (NM)** you intersect that exploratory route to and from Gananoque.

Now the Canadian Middle Channel bears more northeasterly and passes south of tiny, bare Bass Rock Island and large Leek Island. It routes north of shrub-covered Potter Island and McRay Point on Grindstone Island. You enter the Lake Fleet Islands when you pass north of the Punts, a broken island with a green-topped white cylindrical light tower, **Mile MDCH-13.3 (NM).** Here the channel shifts slightly so you pass northeast of Barge Island's **Spar Buoy H31** at **Mile MDCH-13.1 (NM).**

The Lake Fleet Islands

Mile MDCH-13.0 (NM) to Mile MDCH-10.1 (NM)

(See the Admiralty Channel map for Mile ADM-3.2 (NM) to Mile ADM-0.0 (NM)/Mile MDCH-10.1 (NM), page 263.)

The Lake Fleet Islands include 10 large and more than 60 small islands and islets. Their names honor British gunboats and surveying vessels that operated on the river from 1812 to 1817.

Two very popular park islands, Camelot and Endymion, are in this group; the remaining islands are private.

As you enter the main Lake Fleet group downbound, the channel bears south of Dumfounder, Bloodletter, and Belabourer islands and north of Camelot, Niagara, and the Endymion Island group. At the northeastern tip of Grindstone Island is New York's Canoe Point State Park.

The northeastern boundary of the Lake Fleet Islands is Gananoque Narrows, **Mile MDCH-10.1 (NM),** at **Light Buoy H23.** Here you also intersect the Admiralty Channel's eastern terminus; it bears off west.

If you are bound for Clayton on the Seaway Channel, **Mile SW-147.0 (NM),** and you feel like exploring again, this is a Seaway access point. The route is south along Grindstone Island's eastern end and north of Picton Island. Many unwatched shoals exist; lay off clear-cut compass courses and steer small.

At Gananoque Narrows, **Mile MDCH-10.1 (NM),** you are also at the eastern end of the Navy Islands.

The Navy Islands

Mile MDCH-10.1 (NM) to Mile MDCH-8.2 (NM)

All the Navy Islands are north of the Canadian Middle Channel. There are five large islands, a peninsula that resembles an island, and nearly 90 small islands and islets. Some island names honor the commanders of the gunboats and survey vessels that worked the river in the 1800s.

The group is roughly bounded on the west by Gananoque Narrows and on the east by **Steeple Shoal Buoy H20.** Nearly all these islands are private. Mulcaster is the Navy Islands' only Canadian island park.

Also nearby is New York's Wellesley Island State Park. It covers much of the island's northwestern peninsula-like tip. Its main marina dockage—best suited for shoal-draft vessels—is in a large southwesterly reaching cove that lies south-southwesterly from **Steeple Shoal Light Buoy H20.** If you plan on a Wellesley Island visit with Steeple Shoal as a departure point, be very careful of Island 70's shoals. A rock lies about 0.1 mile west of Island 70; a reef also extends off the islands' eastern end. Park dockage gives you access to its golf course, hiking trails, playgrounds, and nature center. You can anchor in the cove if you haven't depth at the docks.

At the Canadian Middle Channel's Steeple Shoal your view east is slightly disconcerting—islands are everywhere. Don't start following one of the gaily-bedecked tour boats expecting it to be bubbling down the channel. This is tour boat heaven; they pop in and out of narrow cuts and chutes and abruptly charge around ends of seemingly shoal rocky islands only to disappear behind others.

The Canadian Middle Channel course takes you south of **Sir William Shoal Buoy H18, Mile MDCH-7.8 (NM).** Next it bears north of Myers Island. Myers Island Light is on the channel's northern side on a red-topped cylindrical white tower. From there you make for **Spar Buoy H17,** which lies west of Lyndoch Island Light tower, **Mile MDCH-7.0 (NM).** This places you at the northeastern end of Fiddlers Elbow Reach; the reach is to Ash Island's southeast and to Wallace Island's northwest. This is a pretty area; island cottages and palatial homes cling to cliffs.

Current steadily increases; it can reach 1.3 knots. Dead ahead in midreach are Wood Island's bluffs.

Downbound bear south of the island and northwest of Hines, Bratt, and Georgina islands. At the western end of Georgina, **Mile MDCH-6.0 (NM),** your route bears more easterly and you come to the 120-foot high-level Thousand Islands Bridge northern suspension span, **Mile MDCH-5.8 (NM).**

The Canadian Middle Channel
The Thousand Islands Bridge to Ironsides Island

Mile MDCH-5.8 (NM) to Mile MDCH-0.0 (NM)/Mile SW-133.4 (NM)

The bridge straddles Georgina and Constance islands. The latter is to Georgina's south across Lost Channel. These are island parks; the remaining 28 islands are private. The conspicuous tower to the south is the 400-foot-high Thousand Island Skydeck on Hill Island.

Downbound at Georgina you enter Raft Narrows. Here the channel favors the mainland Palisades before swinging to the opposite shore to pass close to large Club Island, **Mile MDCH-3.8 (NM).** Northeast of Club Island Light is Rockport, a small Canadian Middle Channel village. St. Brendan's Church is on the town's western side. Beside it on the Cliff is the statue where the annual Blessing of the Fleet takes place in June.

At **Mile MDCH-3.1 (NM)**—at 2-mile-long Tar Island's southwestern end—you have another route decision. This is the upstream terminus of the Small Craft Route secondary channel, which bears northeasterly and eventually regains the Seaway Channel at **Light Buoy #152, Mile SW-125.1 (NM).** This is a good route if bound for Mallorytown Landing or if downbound toward Brockville and Morristown; you will very slightly lessen the mileage for your return to the Seaway Channel.

The Small Craft Route

Mile SCR-10.9 (NM)/MDCH-3.1 (NM) to Mile SCR-0.0 (NM)/Mile SW-125.1 (NM)

Most of this secondary channel between the Seaway Channel and the Canadian Middle Channel is in a wide river area. Navigational aids—they have a "U" prefix—are often over a mile apart. Channel width averages about 0.1 to 0.2 mile. Depths range from 20 to 50 feet except in the mile-long shoal area east of Haffie Shoal, **Mile SCR-4.9 (NM);** there depths drop to 7 to 8 feet.

When you leave the Canadian Middle Channel downbound and enter the Small Craft Route, you are traveling along Tar Island's southeastern shore. Within the first mile, you leave Doctor and Buck Islands to the south and begin (roughly) to parallel 4.5-mile-long Grenadier Island's northwestern coast. The channel takes you north of Duck Island Shoal, **Mile SCR-9.4 (NM).** Be careful downbound by the two buoys watching this area; the shoal extends west-northwest of **Spar Buoy U19.** Duck Rock Light is a green-topped white cylindrical tower at **Mile SCR-9.0 (NM);** it's on an islet just to Duck Island's northwest. At Duck Island the river slowly opens to over a mile with a sprinkling of islands.

You can easily pick up Goose Island's red-topped white tower; it's to the island's northeast. In the shoal cove of Senecal Bay on Grenadier Island's northern shore is a portion of Centre Grenadier island park. Shoal water allows access only to runabouts. The parklands continue to the island's southern shore. Though depths there are risky and it's open to prevailing winds, the docks do have slightly more depths than those on the northern shore. Access to the park's southern docks is off the Canadian Middle Channel.

Squaw Island, a park island, is just ahead; access is for shoal-draft vessels. Adelaide Island, another island park, is off Grenadier's easterly tip, but it's out of your safe reach from the Small Craft Route. Access is from the Seaway Channel.

Nathaniel Mallory founded Mallorytown Landing, **Mile SCR-5.6 (NM),** in 1840; it was the first glassmaking site in Upper Canada. Today it's headquarters for the St. Lawrence Islands National Park and home base for the park's naturalists. There's overnight dockage if you want to lay over. Leave the Small Craft Route about 0.2 mile southwest of **Buoy U9** and bear northwesterly. The park's visitor center and dock are at a slight peninsula's southeastern end; it extends from the northern mainland. This southeastern end is oriented southwest-northeast; the dock is at its southwestern end.

If you draw more than 5.5 feet, come in cautiously and mind river stage. The most protected area is the pier's northwestern side. The outer face is badly exposed to a long southerly fetch; if severe, it's untenable. If dockage is limited, you can anchor off. Holding is difficult in weeds. Ashore there are picnic facilities, shelters, hiking trails, a swimming area, a playground, rest rooms, and access to drinking water. The visitor center introduces you to the area's natural and cultural history. In a special display building is the 15-meter-long, 1815 British gunboat salvaged from Brown's Bay. The center is open from 10 to 5; evening programs begin at 8 and may include films, plays, skits, and slide shows.

The camping area is across the highway. You are welcome to attend their dusk campfires, sing-alongs, and story hours. Over the July First holidays the park hosts its annual Heritage Day Picnic with displays, crafts, programs, games, and plays; hours are 1 to 5.

Slow down at upcoming red-topped Haffie Shoal Light tower, **Mile SCR-4.9 (NM).** This is the start of the mile-long shoal area midway between Haffie Shoal Light and Chimney Island Light, **Mile SCR-4.2 (NM).** Chimney Island Light is not on Chimney Island, which is conspicuous because it has a stone chimney in its center; it's on Bridge Island. Weeds are a major problem in this section; they prevent a fathometer from finding a bottom contour and they quickly clog an engine's water intake.

At **Mile SCR-3.9 (NM)** you are back in depths more than 20 feet. Don't go wandering off south looking for access to Adelaide Island or the Seaway Channel; ugly shoals exist. Better now to stay with the Small Craft Route roughly paralleling the northern coast. Pass north of the Griswold Shoals, the Amateur Island group, unwatched Perry Shoal, the far outlying rocks at Crossover Island, and Bay State Shoal. Ahead is Seaway Channel **Light Buoy #152;** you have returned to the Seaway Channel at the northwestern end of the charted Ship Anchorage Area southeast of Butternut Bay, **Mile SW-125.1 (NM).**

If you decided not to route easterly on the Small Craft Route when you were at **Mile MDCH-2.9 (NM)** on the Canadian Middle Channel, continue easterly downstream and pass to Yeo Island's north. There's another island park at Grenadier Island's southwestern tip, **Mile MDCH-2.3 (NM).** Now make a reach for **Ironsides Shoal Light #180,** a skeleton tower with a metal base and a red daymark. It's just northwest of Ironsides Island and its impressive channel-side cliffs. Ironsides Island Shoal Light is **Mile MDCH-0.0 (NM);** you have intersected the Seaway Channel at its **Mile SW-133.4 (NM).** Downbound at this intersection you hold to the Seaway Channel.

The Eastern Seaway Channel
Ironsides Island to Morristown

Downbound at Ironsides Island the channel bears to Long Brother Island's southeast, northwest of the unused skeleton tower on Third Brother Island Shoal, which is now watched by **Light Buoy #177.** There's a laker on the bottom here; it hit the upper Brother Island shoals and sank with its cargo of coal.

Northwest of Third Brother Island Shoal is **Sister Island Light #178,** a white pole with a white triangle with a red border. Sister Island is really three islets joined by a causeway. Beside the modern light tower is the 1870 lighthouse; the two-story slate-roofed limestone structure is now a summer cottage.

Jorstadt Island, **Mile SW-129.6 (NM),** was long known as Dark Island. It was once a Chippewa campsite—they used the sunken depressions on the rocks for their cooking fires. Frederick Bourne of the Singer Sewing Machine Company built red-roofed Jorstadt Castle as a summer home in the early 20th century. The mansion has more than 47 rooms, vaulted stone chambers, secret passages, and a dungeon. A nondenominational evangelistic association now owns the island and uses it as a religious retreat. All are welcome to Sunday morning services. The boat-in visitor's dock is on the island's southeastern side.

Southeast of Jorstadt Island is the Cedar Island group in Chippewa Bay near the mouth of Chippewa Creek. Part of the Cedar Islands is a New York State Island Park.

The Seaway passes northwest of the rocks off the southwestern end of **Superior Shoal Light #165;** it's a steel tower with a green daymark just off Chippewa Point.

The Indian Chief Islands, **Mile SW-128.5 N (NM),** are a dangerous group if you have the bad habit of cutting channel corners. Many of these islands are bare and unimpressive; the dangerous obstructions are the submerged and just-awash rocks extending up to 0.6 mile northeast of the larger low islands.

Near the entrance of Blind Bay the channel makes a jog north-northeast. Follow the Chippewa Point Range

if you can't quickly pick up **Light Tower #160;** it's east of wooded Crossover Island. At one time Crossover was the point at which shipping crossed from the river's American Channel to the Canadian Channel. To mark the junction the government built the Crossover Island lighthouse in 1848. It was manned for more than 80 years. Today it's a bright red summer cottage.

Continuing north-northeast from Crossover, you pass southeast of Bay State Shoals; don't confuse the shoals' old tower for the new **Tower #156.** At **Mile SW-125.6 (NM),** north of **Light Buoy 153,** the channel swings more northeasterly. At **Light Buoy 152, Mile SW-125.1 (NM),** you intersect the Small Craft Route's eastern terminus; it bears southwesterly to access the Canadian Middle Channel above Grenadier Island.

Notice that the navigation towers are now a slightly different shape; this aids them in diverting ice floes.

Downbound at Oak Point you begin a 2-mile reach to the western end of Brockville Narrows; you can follow the De Watteville ship channel range on northern shore De Watteville Island. Current increases in the Narrows to 2.3 to 3.5 knots.

The islands in the Narrows are the last in the Thousand Islands area. The easternmost St. Lawrence Islands National Park, Stovin Island, is in this group at **Mile SW-121.8 (NM).** In 1933 the government deeded 27 Narrows islands, the Brock group, to Brockville for $3,600; they're east and west of Stovin. They are public islands, and most of the ones that border the channel have small city docks available for a fee. Most are in shoal water. If you plan to visit, take care; remember the strong current and approach docks heading upstream. Most back channels are watched by small secondary buoys and a collection of gum-drops.

Loyalists founded Brockville, **Mile SW-119.8 (NM),** when they came to Canada after the American Revolution. In time the settlement became known as Elizabethtown. In February 1813 American Major Benjamin Forsyth and 200 soldiers crossed the frozen river from Morristown, attacked the village, and overpowered Elizabethtown's Leeds Militia. Two weeks later the British retaliated and attacked downstream Ogdensburg.

It was during the war that Brockville changed its name to honor Major-General Isaac Brock, the victor at the Battle of Queenston Heights and an Upper Canada national hero.

In 1854 Brockville villagers laid the cornerstone of the 1/3-mile-long Brockville Railway Tunnel, intended to give the Brockville and Ottawa Railway quick river access. It was 6 years before the first train transited. The tunnel was in use for 100 years and only became obsolete because new locomotives did not fit inside.

Brockville Municipal Harbor is in the lee of Blockhouse Island. The island is now connected to the mainland. During the War of 1812 the island was a signaling station, and in 1832 it was a hospital island during a cholera epidemic. By 1840 the government had built a small blockhouse on the island to defend town.

Downbound at Brockville mind the dangerous unwatched reefs and rocks surrounding Brockville Rock; it's about 0.5 mile south-southeast of Brockville Harbor Light and north-northwest of Old Man Island. The Seaway Channel holds near the Canadian shore northwest of McNair Island, the northernmost of the Three Sisters Islands. If you plan to visit Morristown, Brockville's neighbor across the river, your safest departure point is northeast of the Three Sisters.

In 1792 Gouverneur Morris purchased Morristown, **Mile SW-118.7,** at the mouth of Louce Creek, from the Macomb Purchase. Most residents left during the War of 1812, fearing attack from across the river. After war's end the settlers returned and Morristown became a river port for naval stores heading downriver. Today's Morristown is much as it was in the 1800s. One of its famous structures is the Stone Windmill, built by Scotsman Hugh McConnel to process grain.

Morristown is the eastern end of the Thousand Islands regional section; it's also the western end of the regional section on the St. Lawrence Seaway to Montreal and a portion of the Upper St. Lawrence River downstream to Sorel (see "The St. Lawrence Seaway and the Upper St. Lawrence River," beginning on page 300).

Sketch Map Depths

Sketch map depths are given at normal average summer water level. When you venture outside the sketch map confines, you must adjust your NOAA and Canadian charts to chart datum. For convenience in adjusting, use the following:

Mile SW-164.5 (NM) to **Mile SW-118.7 (NM):** Plane of reference, Lake Ontario and Upper St. Lawrence River Low Water Datum, 242.8 feet to 242.2 feet

CAPE VINCENT

Chart: N 14767

Mile SW-161.0 (NM)

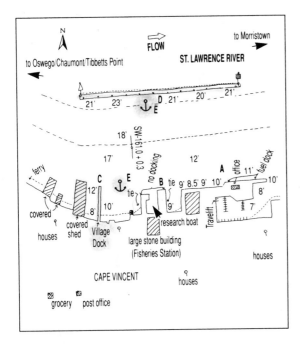

American-shore Cape Vincent offers a choice of a marina, a village dock, tie-ups, and an anchorage. An offshore breakwater paralleling shore protects the harbor. Enter at either end; daymarks watch both. There's harbor surge when winds are westerly; it increases in strong northeasterlies.

Broadway, about a block from the waterfront, is downtown; it has a few shops, a bank, a laundromat, a post office, a library, restaurants, and Aubrey's Supermarket. The chamber of commerce is across the street from the ferry ticket office at the foot of James Street.

Cape Vincent Fisheries Station—originally an 1856 gristmill—has an information center and an aquarium.

The latter, in the building's basement, displays lake and river fish.

The Community House Historical Museum is about four blocks from the water on Market Street. It has early French memorabilia and sunken-ship artifacts; it's open Wednesdays from 10 to 4 and evenings from 7 to 9.

Cape Vincent holds "La Fete Francaise" the second Saturday in July. There are arts and crafts, historical exhibits, concerts, and a parade. Downtown there are decorated carts offering French pastries, ice cream, bread, cheese, candy, and wines.

Anchor Marina

★★★★

3

ALL FACILITIES

Chart: N 14767, *See A on sketch map*

Mile SW-161.0 + 0.3 (NM)

This marina—open April 15 to November 15—is about opposite the breakwater's eastern end; a landmark is its long transient dock paralleling shore. If no one answered on VHF 16, pull in to the fuel dock (gas and diesel) in front of the office—it resembles a railroad station.

The marina also has an enclosed basin primarily for shoal-draft resident vessels; entry is at the outside dock's eastern end. The 12-ton lift is in the basin's northwestern corner.

The office stocks a few supplies, some marine equipment, and local charts. Block and cube ice and 110-volt/30-amp electric hookups are available. The land line number is (315) 654-2300.

Downtown is a few blocks away.

Cape Vincent Fisheries Station

★★★★

Chart: N 14767, *See B on sketch map, page 270*

Mile SW-161.0 + 0.3 (NM)

The Fisheries Station, a four-story stone building, is behind its piers—wide solid bulkheads. The easterly pier's northern end has a slight westerly hook that helps protect a small slip area. Don't tie here or on the dock's northern face; they're for the Fisheries Research boat. Tie on the outer eastern or western bulkhead; choose the one with the best lee. Since the harbor is prone to surge, use stout springs and many fenders.

Once secured, check in at the office in front of the building up the steps. There's a picnic area on the building's east side, with a lawn, grills, table, shade trees, and a soda machine. The building's western garbage area is set up for recycling.

You are practically downtown.

Cape Vincent Village Dock

★★★★

Chart: N 14767, *See C on sketch map, page 270*

Mile SW-161.0 + 0.3 (NM)

This dock—time limit 48 hours—is about opposite the breakwater's western end. It's very wide and extends northerly. A western landmark is a large, faded red covered boat shed. Dock area weed growth may tangle keels and rudders, but depths are fairly good on both sides, except at the extreme southern end. It's usually taken by runabouts. Parallel park and have good fenders; some of the dock face is rough, and surge can be severe. The covered shed helps protect the southern end and the middle of the dock from westerlies. If there's no surge, vessels often ask to raft. At the dock's southern end is a grassy plot, picnic tables, and a water tap.

Downtown is about a block away.

Cape Vincent Breakwater

★★★★

Chart: N 14767, *See D on sketch map, page 270*

Mile SW-161.0 + 0.3 (NM)

The breakwater, about 500 to 700 feet off downtown's waterfront, is a protective barrier that can be a tie-up bulkhead if you are seeking safe haven. Its southern face has bollards and a smooth fendering surface. This is a good stop if dockage is unavailable and severe weather is forecast; anchoring could mean standing an all-night anchor watch. In northerly weather, it has almost no surge.

You may share the breakwater with sea birds, and if northeast seas are up, you may also get some spray when waves crash into the riverside wall. However, you have an exceptionally pretty view of the town's lamplighting.

If going ashore, tie the skiff in the village dock's shallows or ask permission to use the picnic bulkhead at the Fisheries Station.

Cape Vincent Anchorages

★★★★

Chart: N 14767, *See E on sketch map, page 270*

Mile SW-161.0 + 0.3 (NM)

Though this area is more than 20 feet deep, preferred anchorage is near the breakwater. Bottom is mud and gravel and less weedy than close to shore. This is the harbor thoroughfare, but a No Wake zone limits wake roll. During weather conditions that cast a waterfront surge, it's one of the harbor's calmest areas.

If you have a shoal-draft small boat there is space to anchor close to shore between the village dock and the Fisheries Station. Often there are one or two small boats on moorings here; be careful not to foul them. Holding is poor due to heavy weed growth.

CLAYTON

Chart: N 14774

Mile SW-147.0 (NM)

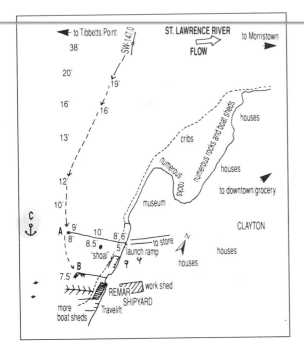

Clayton is on a peninsula at French Creek's mouth. You can anchor or tie at a marina or a municipal dock. You are fairly protected from prevailing conditions, but any strong northwest or north winds bring an uncomfortable chop and surge into all areas.

No matter where you stay, you're downtown. Most of Clayton takes up the northern half of the six-block-wide peninsula. Facilities include a post office, a library, shops, banks, a pharmacy, supermarkets, hardware and marine stores, night clubs, and restaurants—don't forget to ask for the Thousand Island Dressing, which was created in Clayton by Sophia LaLonde. The chamber of commerce, Great American supermarket, and a laundromat are on the peninsula's northern end. For shopping by dinghy, there is a convenient village dock—2-hour time limit—in the middle of the peninsula's northern end. A Big M supermarket is farther away but offers free dockside pickup and return; call (315) 686-3601.

The Antique Boat Museum, at Mary Street's western end beside the municipal dock, has a collection of historic freshwater boats and engines. Most were built within 35 miles of Clayton. The museum also offers boatbuilding courses. The annual three-day Antique Boat Show, held in early August, includes an antique boat parade.

The Craft School and Textile Museum, 314 John Street, has a carving loft, a gift shop, gallery exhibit rooms, a pottery shop, and a collection of hand-woven textiles and spinning tools. The school offers classes in weaving, basketry, duck and bird carving, pottery, sculpture, painting, and miniature furniture building. They host Spring Festival in mid-May and an antique and art auction in July.

The Town Hall Museum, 403 Riverside Drive, has a turn-of-the-century Clayton village under its roof. It's open from 10 to 5. In mid-July they host the Decoy and Wildlife Art Show.

Clayton Municipal Dock

★★★   3

Chart: N 14774, *See A on sketch map*

Mile SW-147.0 + 0.6 (NM)

The municipal dock is on the peninsula's western side. Note that it has a three-day time limit. From the main channel, you have clear water as far as the peninsula's northern end; it then begins to shoal gradually. Keep clear of the northwestern side bight; it's full of rocks and old cribs. Head for the municipal dock, the longest pier with parallel parking, about 0.2 mile from the peninsula's northern tip. It's charted extending west-southwesterly from Mary Street. There are pilings north of the dock toward the pier's western end, and there may or may not be two privately maintained buoys nearby. Once you begin to close the pier's end, weed growth begins.

If you have a choice of dockage, choose the southern side. In severe weather the northern face may become untenable if seas make up. The dock's southern side has a shoal buoy near the ramp; stay close to the municipal dock if in that vicinity. A dock attendant is usually on duty; if not, he arrives to collect about sundown. The Harbor Inn Café is at the ramp.

Electric hookups (110-volt) are available.

You are practically downtown. The Antique Boat Museum is about 100 feet from the pier.

Remar Shipyard

★★★

ALL FACILITIES

Chart: N 14774, *See B on sketch map, page 272*

Mile SW-147.0 + 0.7 (NM)

The marina—open April 1 to November 1—is just south of the municipal dock, so use its approach (see page 272). A launching ramp separates the two facilities.

There's good water as far as the end of the municipal dock, but if you draw more than 6 feet be cautious after that point. The shipyard has one large building at the head of its two longest piers. For service, parallel park on the northernmost long dock's hooked end; you can see its sign, gas and diesel pumps, and dockhouse. If no one is on duty, the office is in the big building.

Block and cube ice, a 10-ton lift, and electric hookups (110-volt/30-amp) are available. If you need a diver, check at the office. The land line number is (315) 686-3579.

The ship's store has a selection of marine equipment, a parts department, charts, and guides. The facility is base for their large charter fleet of 38- to 55-foot houseboats and 18- and 19-foot runabouts.

Downtown is a short walk away.

Clayton Anchorage

★★★★

Chart: N 14774, *See C on sketch map, page 272*

Mile SW-147.0 + 0.5 (NM)

Anchor northwest of the municipal dock and the privately maintained buoys that may or may not be in place. Bottom is mud, weeds, a few rocks, and submerged logs; the latter are remains of Clayton's lumbering days. Holding is fair.

You'll find the best harbor view here. Governors and Calumet islands are north, and the village lamplighting

is a pretty backdrop for a cockpit supper.

You can usually tie the dinghy at the public dock shallows, but first check with the dock attendant. If you tie by the ramp, don't block its access. If you tie anywhere else, make certain you know the charge. It can be as much as overnight dockage for a big boat.

In your dinghy, you can explore up French Creek beyond its low-level bridge. This area is base for an immense runabout fishing fleet. Bait is available at the marina just south of the bridge.

KEEWAYDIN STATE PARK MARINA

★★★★★

Chart: N 14772, *See sketch map, page 274*

Mile SW-139.0 + 0.2 (NM)

This park is inside a small bay in the American (Upper) Narrows. The clearest approach is a downstream entry; keep this in mind, as the Narrows has up to 2 knots of current.

Leave the Seaway just southwest of **Comfort Island Shoal Light #199;** it's a black skeleton tower with a small white house just southwest of Comfort Island. Make your turn and bear southeasterly about 0.1 mile to the mainland's small bay, which lies south of Comfort Island's bulk. Make certain you clear the unwatched rock northeast of the small islet off Bella Vista.

As you close the little bay, you can see a floating tire breakwater extending southwest from the bay's northeasterly point. At the breakwater's land end there's a stone cupola; at the entrance is a square daymark.

It's possible to make your approach heading upstream. Do this by leaving the Seaway west of **Stony Crest Island Light #197,** which lies to Comfort Island's northeast. The light is a white pole with a white square daymark edged with black. If you choose to come in this way, be certain you clear the dangerous rocks extending off the end of the narrow northeast-southwest-oriented, sparsely wooded, unnamed island to Stony Crest Island's east. Current will set you in the rocks' direction. Once you pass this slim island, hold

Keewaydin State Park Marina

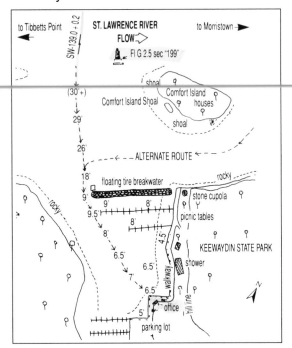

ALEXANDRIA BAY

Chart: N 14772

Mile SW-137.6 (NM) to SW-138.0 (NM)

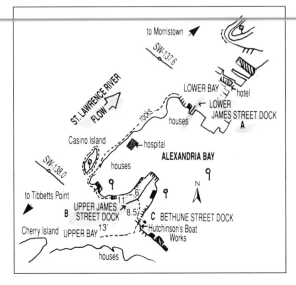

midway between Comfort Island and the mainland until you reach the breakwater's end.

Once you enter the basin, draft dictates your destination. The office and fuel dock (gas only) are in the bay's southeastern corner; be careful if you draw 5 feet. For deeper drafts best water is on the two piers extending westerly off the bay's western shore just inside the breakwater. You may need to pull in to a slip if you can't see the dockmaster. South of these slips is a bulkhead that extends to the fuel dock and to two more piers of slips at the bay's southern end. If you draw 4 feet, this can be a place for you.

The marina is usually full, but it has a large transient turnover. If you arrive between 9 and 10:30 in the morning you have a fair chance at a space.

The office—land line number (315) 482-3331—has some supplies. By the piers there's a collection of picnic tables and grills. Electric hookups (110-volt) are available.

The park is a good place for hiking, jogging, or ambling; it also has camping and trailer sites. Take your wallet if you leave the complex; there's a park access fee to get back in. If out sightseeing watch for hidden gazebos and boathouse buildings that were once part of the Keewaydin castle grounds. There's a castle painting in the administration building.

Alexandria Bay is on a semipeninsula east of Cherry Island. Facilities are upstream and downstream of the peninsula in Upper Bay and Lower Bay. Dockage depths anywhere in Alexandria Bay rarely exceed 9 feet.

You have a choice of town docks close to downtown. If these are filled, check for dockage at area marinas. Protection is generally good unless prolonged wind is severe; then a chop and surge enters the bays. West-northwest winds affect boats in Upper Bay; north winds affect those in Lower Bay.

If bound for the peninsula's western side, do not cut the mouth of Upper Bay's western point; there are a few unwatched outlying rocks. Favor the peninsula. You can carry depths of 50 feet nearly as far as the peninsula's western-side indentation. Once shoaling begins, it's fast. The indentation on Upper Bay has two town docks.

If bound for Lower Bay, watch out for a 6-foot shoal just off the peninsula's northeastern tip. Once clear of that, Lower Bay's southerly section has best depths along the eastern waterfront. This is the pier area for the tour boat fleet, so watch for their fast approaches and departures. Depths in the eastern half of Lower Bay's southern part are often less than 6 feet.

Though the village is spread over a wide area, most of downtown is on the peninsula. Facilities include a post office, a library, banks, a marine store, a pharmacy, a liquor store, restaurants, and a Great American super-market.

The 1800s Greek Revival T. A. Graham Thompson Memorial Museum is open Tuesday through Sunday from 10 to 4. Originally home to an early settler, it has an impressive collection of family heirlooms, china, silver, photographs, and a research library.

The restored Cornwall Brothers Store on the Market Street waterfront is open from 10 to 7. The Cornwall family built the store in 1829 and operated it for over a hundred years.

For a beautiful view of Boldt Castle and area islands, walk out to Cranberry Lookout; it's up the hill at the corner pharmacy.

Village events begin near the end of May, when boats parade along the waterfront and receive the Blessing of the Fleet for another season. On the Fourth of July there are fireworks—often set off at Boldt Castle—and an Antique and Classic In-the-Water Boat Show. The Bill Johnston's Pirates Weekend in August celebrates the pirate's Thousand Islands escapades. The Labor Day weekend International Hot Air Balloon Festival includes the annual Parade of Yachts, which ends the season.

James Street runs east and west through downtown across the peninsula; it's about two blocks from the northern point. At each street end are village docks; each is accessible by different routes.

Lower James Street Dock

 ★★★

Chart: N 14772, *See A on sketch map, page 274*

Mile SW-137.6 + 0.3 (NM)

Leave the Seaway west of **Sunken Rock Shoal Light #199**—it's a black skeleton tower with a small white house. Bear southerly to the peninsula's eastern end. After clearing the small shoal off this point, enter Lower Bay with its two southerly arms. These are filled with boats and docks.

There is frenetic activity around the Thousand Island Tour Boat docks in the bay's southwestern prong, which is your destination. The other side of this prong

has somewhat risky depths for a 6-foot-draft vessel, so favor the bay's southwestern side. Your dock is just south of a small ferry dock. It's a long pier extending northeast, with parallel parking. Pull in wherever there's space; either side has depth. You may find a water tap at the dock.

The dockmaster works all three village docks; he arrives in the afternoon to collect. Call (315) 482-2648 for further information.

Alexandria Bay bustles with activity, and this dock has its share. Passengers waiting to board tour boats mill about and walk the dock, boats idle in from the main river sightseeing, tour boats rumble in and out on a tight schedule, and the ferry next door is active. However, if you plan to sightsee and shop, it's only a few blocks to uptown.

Upper James Street Dock

 ★★★

Chart: N 14772, *See B on sketch map, page 274*

Mile SW-138.0 + 0.25 (NM)

For this village dock leave the Seaway about **Mile SW-138.0 (NM)** at the peninsula's upstream side. Favor the village shore as you bear southeasterly into Upper Bay as far as the large northeasterly reaching indentation. Your destination is a very long pier extending south-west. The pier, which has parallel parking, has a slight westerly hook near its bayside end. Where the hook begins is a small gazebo. This is the dockmaster's main base; he may be about by the gazebo and suggest a place to tie up. If you draw 5 feet or more, depth usually restricts you to the pier's westerly section. Call (315) 482-2648 for further information.

Both sides of this harbor indentation are stuffed with boating facilities, slips, restaurants, and waterfront homes. You are near the center of downtown. At the dock's end is Wings and Things, a combination restaurant and convenience store. The Great American super-market is about 4.5 blocks away.

Bethune Street Dock

★★★

Chart: N 14772, *See C on sketch map, page 274*

Mile SW-138.0 + 0.25 (NM)

This is another village dock in Upper Bay, but you need
shoal draft to stay. It's southeast of the Upper James
Street Dock at Bethune Street, just northwest of the
Hutchinson Boat Works Marina and yard facilities. Use
the Upper James Street Dock's approach (see page 275).
Depth southeast of the Upper James Street facility is
possible for 6 feet, but the dock itself has only about
4.5 to 5 feet of water at its southwesterly end. It's also
visited by the village dockmaster. If you stay here, you
are still very close to downtown.

Canadian Middle Channel Anchorages
Kingston to the Thousand Islands Bridge

Mile MDCH-29.5 (NM) to Mile MDCH-5.8 (NM)

KINGSTON

Charts: N 14768; C 2017, *See sketch map, page 278*

Mile MDCH-29.5 (NM)

Kingston is at Lake Ontario's northeastern end at the Cataraqui River's mouth. The Canadian Middle Channel's western terminus is just off the harbor mouth at Point Frederick. Kingston Harbour extends along the city's southern side as far west as Cataraqui Bay; it's also along the Cataraqui River north of the LaSalle Causeway

---

Things to Do and See in Kingston

The Confederation Tour Train makes hour-long tours around historic sites and attractions including Queen's University, the Olympic Harbor, the home of Sir John Macdonald (Canada's first prime minister), and the Royal Military College. The train leaves every hour between 10 and 7; board at the park.

Downtown Kingston's seasonal festivities begin in June with Confederation Basin's Kingston-In-The-Water Boat Show. The Buskers Festival in early July includes magicians, jugglers, mimes, and musicians competing for prizes in downtown streets and Confederation Park. Fanfayre, a three-day arts and crafts show, is held in the park over the Canada Day holidays.

More attractions:

City Hall, 216 Ontario Street, across the street from Confederation Park. The building, with its massive columns and domed tower, was built in 1843, when Kingston was capitol of the United Provinces of Canada. Tours are held Tuesday through Saturday.

Fort Henry, Junction of Highway 2 and Highway 15. This museum of Canadian and British military history overlooks the river and lake. Many of its 126 rooms are equipped and furnished as they were when they were British garrisons. Try to arrive when the Fort Henry Guard performs. Ceremonial Retreat, held on Monday, Wednesday, and Saturday at 7:30 P.M., includes infantry drill, tactics, and salutes fired by the fort's 1700s muzzle-loading cannon.

Marine Museum of the Great Lakes, 55 Ontario Street. Exhibits covering the history of Great Lakes shipping from 1678. On display is the 3,000-metric-ton icebreaker *Alexander Henry.* The museum is open Tuesday through Sunday from 10 to 4.

Murney Tower Museum, Barrie Street and King Street West. This tower, built in 1846, was part of Kingston's defense during the Oregon Crisis. It overlooks the river and the lake. You'll notice quite a few of these cylindrical stone redoubts scattered about the Kingston area; this is an opportunity to go inside one and see its collection of artifacts. It's open from 10 to 5. *MacDonald Park,* landscaped with flower gardens and shade trees, is across the street. Have a look at the monument that honors Sir John MacDonald.

Pump House Steam Museum, 23 Ontario Street. Now completely restored, this was Kingston's pumping station in 1849. On display are its immense main steam pumps and one of the world's largest working steam engine exhibits. It's open Tuesday through Sunday from 10 to 5.

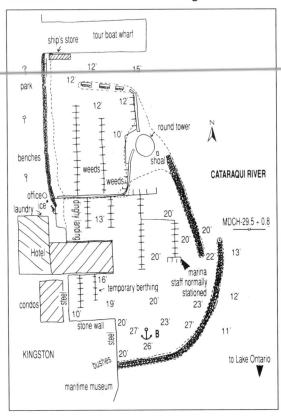

Confederation Basin

★★★★★ 5

Charts: C 2017; N 14768, *See A on sketch map*

Mile MDCH-29.5 + 0.8 (NM)

and the approach to the Rideau Canal's western terminus.

You have a choice of a marina or an anchorage on the Cataraqui River. Downtown is a few blocks away.

At the yacht basin take Ontario Street for a block or two, then turn west and you'll find just about every city attraction. If you need the A & P supermarket, continue north on Ontario to Barrack Street, then bear northwest for about a block and a half; the bus station is across the street. If you have a heavy load, call a taxi or rent a car. You can see the city and the townships of Kingston, Pittsburgh, and Ernestown via the Kingston Area Transit System.

A farmers' market with fresh local produce, flowers, baked goods, and crafts is held every Tuesday, Thursday, and Saturday at Market Square behind City Hall. Confederation Park, at the marina, is beautifully landscaped with flowers and shade trees. Some event seems to be in progress every day—usually band concerts or craft fairs. Stop by the tourist bureau at the park's western end to pick up brochures, schedules, and maps.

This enclosed basin marina is on the Cataraqui River's western side. There are about 400 floating slips, but by sundown—especially on weekends—they may all be taken. Best arrival time is about 11 A.M., when transients usually depart.

Since the Cataraqui River is not all that deep, leave the Canadian Middle Channel, bear to the western river shore, and arrive about at the Kingston Yacht Club mole. Best water is along the river's western shoreline. As you make your turn upriver, your destination is the prominent pinkish rock breakwater.

A green-topped white cylindrical light tower watches the narrow entrance. Though its pedestal is in place, there may or may not be a northern-point red daymark. Once inside the basin, the multistory Ramada Inn juts from the western shoreline. Bear northerly to the slips off the hotel. Dock attendants watching your arrival will hail you by loudspeaker with directions to a slip. Usually this is in the "new" basin. If not, it's in an older section that requires you to exit the harbor and go about 1,000 feet north to the old basin's entrance. On the way there you pass the stone Shoal Tower, another historical redoubt.

As you make for your assigned slip, a number of dock attendants split from the main body and trot off to meet you at your assigned spot. These attendants watch your progress, and if you appear hesitant, they shout you into position and then take your lines.

Once secured, register at the office; it's at the water's edge across the street from the hotel's northern side in a little lighthouse. It can be quite a hike over docks and piers.

There's a floating ship's store at the old basin's northeastern end; it offers nautical gifts, clothing, marine supplies, and charts. Electric hookups (110-volt) are available. If you need repairs, check at the office. The land line number is (613) 544-9842.

Temporary dockage is usually available at no charge on the western shore immediately south of the hotel. If you plan to stay in Kingston for only a few hours, swing by and so inform the pack of attendants with their bull horns; otherwise, they become badly confused. Dockage assistance is not supplied at the temporary slips, and they have very short fingers. Fender accordingly and land with a spring line in hand.

Confederation Basin Anchorage

★★★★★   5

Charts: C 2017; N 14768, *See B on sketch map, page 278*

Mile SW-29.5 + 0.8 (NM)

Follow the entry instructions to enter Confederation Basin (see page 278). Once inside you can see that most of the basin's southern end is without slips. Those on the Ramada Inn's southern side are for a temporary visit. There are plans for slips in the remainder of this basin; if this occurs, the anchorage will no longer be available.

Before you anchor, swing by the bevy of dock attendants to inform them of your intent. They will ask you to check in at the office. There's an anchoring fee; it allows use of marina showers, rest rooms, garbage bins, and laundry, and a place to tie the dinghy.

Do not anchor near the harbor entrance. In some wind conditions the shoal Cataraqui River is subject to a bad swell. Since the harbor entry is narrow, first-time visitors entering in heavy weather often have a difficult time as they violently roll themselves between the breakwaters. They usually erupt into the calm basin at high speed; a boat anchored close to the entrance is a target.

Bottom is mud and holding good, but this is a deep harbor; it requires a commonsense judgment on scope. During Kingston's festive summer weekends the anchorage is usually packed.

Leave the dinghy by the access ramp at the temporary docks. If off to the showers, laundry, ice machine, garbage bin, downtown, or the grocery store, you are closer if you tie it by the office lighthouse. Before you leave it in this area, check with a dock attendant about where it won't be in the way.

Plan a cockpit cookout at dusk for a splendid city lamplighting view.

CEDAR ISLAND

Charts: C 2017; N 14768

Mile MDCH-28.7 (NM)

This St. Lawrence National Islands Park is about 0.3 mile southeast of Point Henry and about 1.5 miles east

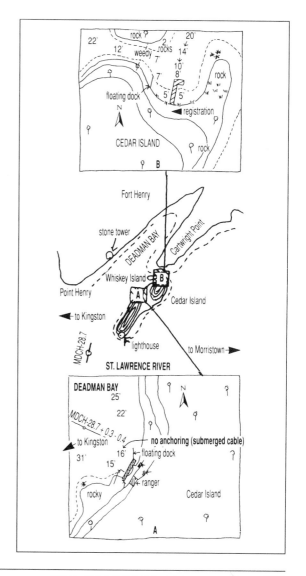

of downtown Kingston. The island partially forms mile-long Deadman Bay's southeastern shore.

There are two dockage areas on the island's northwestern side. If you arrive late and docks are filled, you can anchor off either area. Holding is not good; bottom is uneven rocks and weeds.

~~Both stops access the round-the-island trail, which~~ takes you past the Cathcart Redoubt.

A clear approach is at the island's southwestern end. Landmarks here are red-topped white cylindrical Cedar Island Light and, 500 feet away, the 100-foot-high red-roofed cylindrical redoubt.

Leave the Canadian Middle Channel about **Mile MDCH-28.7 (NM),** round the island's end, and continue northeasterly up Deadman Bay. At this point follow individual approaches.

Cedar Island Mid-Island

★★★★

Charts: C 2017; N 14768, *See A on sketch map, page 279*

Mile MDCH-28.7 + 0.3 (NM)

Your destination is about the middle of Cedar Island in a slight island indentation. Once clear of the indentation's southwesterly point, you can see the crib and two floating docks. Head in to shore and choose your dockage.

The cove is fairly protected from the southwest by the point, but if wind is strong, there's a surge. Fender well; wakes are a problem, especially on weekends.

The registration desk and fee box, warden's cabin, picnic tables and grill, garbage cans, and rest rooms are up the ramp. More rest rooms and a shelter are by the inland campsites.

Keep small pets below. One day a large owl made off with a visiting boat's energetic adult cat.

Cedar Island Northeast

★★★★★

Charts: C 2017; N 14768, *See B on sketch map, page 279*

Mile MDCH-28.7 + 0.4 (NM)

This cove is on Cedar's northeastern end. There's a narrow finger of land that arcs from the island's eastern end toward Whiskey Island; it forms a slight cove. The park docks are in this bight.

Follow the approach directions from the Canadian Middle Channel as far as Mid-Island dock (above). At that point continue northeast. Keep offshore slightly to more easily make out Cedar Island's small satellite, Whiskey Island, off Cedar's northeastern end. Off north on Deadman Bay's northwestern shore are a few boats on private moorings.

There's a narrow passage between Whiskey Island and Cedar Island that barely takes a 6-foot draft at summer level. Bottom is rock covered by weeds. Safest entry is to continue around Whiskey Island's northwestern end and pass between it and the unnamed island off Cartwright Point's southwestern tip. Keep clear of Cartwright's little island; it has outlying reefs. Your entry into the park docks is midway between Whiskey Island's eastern shore and the western end of Cedar's northerly peninsula. Depths are good to the docks, but beware of rocks covered by weeds; read the clear water as you go.

There is a crib with an eastern hook at its northern end and one floating dock. These docks are more protected than the ones at Mid-Island, but there still is weekend wake roll.

The registration desk, fee box, and picnic shelter are on shore; garbage cans and rest rooms are in the trees.

Bateau Channel Anchorages
(A Secondary Channel)

Mile BAT-10.3 (NM)/MDCH-26.0 (NM) to Mile
BAT-0.0 (NM)/ADM-6.0 (NM)

MILTON ISLAND

★★★★

Chart: N 14768

Mile BAT-9.9 + 0.2 W (NM)/MDCH-26.0 + 0.5 (NM)

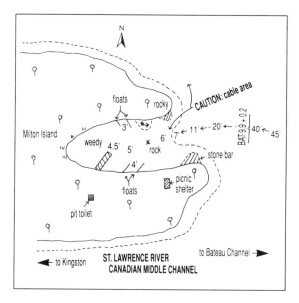

This park island is near the Bateau Channel's western end, so it's close to the Canadian Middle Channel's departure point into this secondary channel.

The island is about 0.5 mile northwest of the Spectacles, a collection of rocks, reefs, and two bushy islands off Howe Island's extreme western end.

Dockage is at Milton's easterly end in a natural cove. It's badly exposed to the east and northeast; if wind from these directions is forecast, choose another stop.

When downbound, leave the Canadian Middle Channel at **Mile MDCH-26.0 (NM),** the Bateau Channel's western terminus at its **Mile BAT-10.3 (NM).** This junction is just north of Wolfe Island's Knapp Point Light. Bear north-northeasterly to a point off Milton Island's eastern end. When the cove opens fully start straight in toward the cove; you'll see the four docks and the crib. Do not become so absorbed in looking for an empty space that you don't pay attention. You have a clear approach *only* as far as the cove's mouth; that's where shoaling begins. The cove's two entrance points have gravel and rock bars that extend toward the middle of the entrance. Best entry water is in the middle—if you draw more than 5 feet you probably won't even get this far. Now come in very cautiously and bear slightly to the southern side; there's a rock in midcove near the entrance. Don't depend on the fathometer to register accurately; weeds blanket rocks extremely well. Best dockage water is at the crib's northeasterly end toward the cove's end on its southern side.

The registration desk and fee box, picnic tables, grills, and a shelter are at the crib's end. More tables and garbage bins are close to the other dock areas. Rest rooms are down the path in the trees. There are park trails and camping facilities.

If you plan to anchor off, check the chart. Underwater cables litter the most protected areas.

TREASURE ISLAND MARINA

★★★★

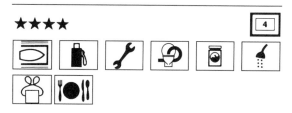

Chart: N 14768, *See sketch map, page 282*

Mile BAT-9.0 + 0.5 N (NM)

This marina is off the Bateau Channel's northern shore in an enclosed basin. Treasure Island is not really an island, but the southern end of a peninsula extending from the northern mainland at Abbey Dawn Creek's mouth.

Leave the Bateau Channel about a mile east-northeast of Milton Island. Head for the cove to Treasure

Treasure Island Marina

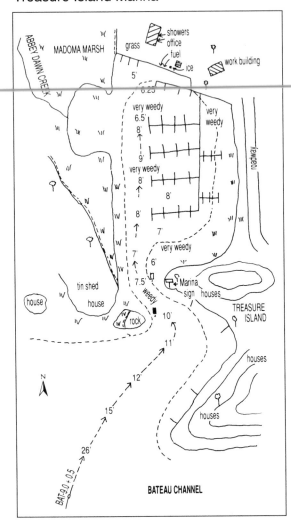

BATEAU CHANNEL

this channel; favor the docks. If you draw more than 6 feet you may have some summer-level depth problems once you reach the pier just south of the bulkhead, and from there to the pumps.

Block and cube ice, a 20-ton Travelift, and electric hookups (110-volt/30-amp and 220-volt/50-amp) are available. The land line number is (613) 548-8444.

This is a quiet stop with friendly staff and boat-owners who are ready to give you information on cruising and fishing the islands.

Admiralty Channel Anchorages
(A Secondary Channel)

Mile ADM-7.8 (NM)/MDCH-17.0 (NM) to Mile ADM-0.0 (NM)/Mile MDCH-10.1 (NM)

THE ADMIRALTY ISLANDS

Mile ADM-6.5 to Mile ADM-4.2; Mile MDCH-14.5

There are hundreds of Admiralty Islands in an area of approximately 2.0 miles by 3.5 miles. Roughly, they are between Grindstone Island's northwestern point, Howe Island's eastern extremity, and Gananoque on the group's northern perimeter.

Approach directions for the Admiralty Islands anchorages are given downbound off the Admiralty Channel, except for Leek Island, which is alongside the Canadian Middle Channel. The Admiralty Channel, **Mile ADM-7.8 (NM)/Mile MDCH-17.0 (NM) to Mile ADM-0.0 (NM)/Mile MDCH-10.1 (NM),** a secondary channel north of the Canadian Middle Channel, is discussed in the main text, beginning on page 261.

A few times a week during the season an entrepreneur in a runabout visits most of the Admiralty Islands with a fair selection of groceries, drinks, and ice. You may even order special items for delivery on his next visit.

The island parks' naturalists and their floating interpretation center come to each island about twice a month. You can visit the boat museum and nature dis-

Island's west; waterfront cottages surround it. Once you arrive at this point, it's slightly easier to tell that the cove has two prongs at its northern end. You want the eastern prong; bear in that direction and watch for the basin's entrance buoys—one red and one green. The green buoy is usually alongside a large boulder that helps enclose the basin. At the buoys the weed growth is excessive; a fathometer is nearly useless.

Inside the basin there are five main piers that extend westerly. If no one answered on VHF 16, make for the fuel dock (gas and diesel) on the most northerly bulkhead by the prominent two-story brown building. This is the office. The narrow channel to get there is along the pier's westerly ends. Depth increases as you approach the first pier. There's an extensive marshland alongside

play and attend an afternoon lecture. Check your island bulletin board for time schedules.

On Bostwick (Yorke) Island's southern side near its northeastern end is Half Moon Bay. Since 1887, summer residents and visitors have met here on Sundays for vesper services held in an outdoor chapel. You are welcome to attend these hour-long nondenominational services, which usually begin at 4 P.M. They include music, prayers, familiar hymns, and a sermon. Tie your dinghy—it's your pew—to a rocky bank's eye ring.

MERMAID ISLAND

★★★★★

Chart: N 14774

Mile-ADM 6.5 + 0.1 (NM)

Mermaid Island, a park island, is on the Admiralty Channel's western perimeter. It has good protection—the island is surrounded by more islands—but in strong northerlies you may have a slight surge.

When you leave the Canadian Middle Channel at its **Mile MDCH-17.0 (NM)** and begin the Admiralty Channel downbound, your first landfall is between Aubrey and Mermaid islands at Aubrey Island Light, **Mile ADM-6.4 (NM).**

When you reach a position on this course where you can see along Mermaid's northern shore, immediately locate **Tin Cap Shoal Buoy JH3,** which lies north of Mermaid. It watches a very dangerous rock you must avoid. Make your turn northwest and hold between Tin Cap Shoal and Mermaid. Follow along Mermaid's northern shore to its northeasterly section.

Most docks are floating and extend north from a crib's arm that reaches northeasterly. There's good water in all slips. If you plan to lay along the crib's northeastern end, feel your way in. Rocks are very close and you may be disconcerted by bathers sitting on these barely submerged boulders. Nevertheless, there's room and good water along that end. There's more dockage on the crib's southern side, but parts of this area are shoal. To reach this spot bear alongside any boat lying on the crib's northeasterly face to get around the southerly corner. You may not have a lot of maneuvering room, and may need to walk the boat in. Normally a beamy boat on the crib's end has to move out while the other vessel goes in behind. We moved four times in one morning for this reason.

The registration desk and fee box are at the dock's end. There are picnic tables on the crib and a few nearby; rest rooms are in the westerly trees.

If you are off for a hike, take along the camera; it's high land and you have a splendid view.

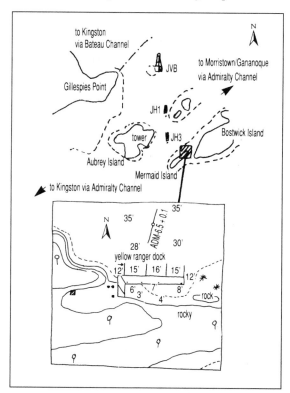

LINDSAY ISLAND
SOUTHWEST ANCHORAGE

★★★★★

NO FACILITIES

Chart: N 14774, *See sketch map and the Admiralty Channel map for Mile ADM-7.8 (NM)/Mile MDCH-17.0 (NM) to Mile ADM-3.2 (NM), page 262.*

Mile ADM-6.4 + 0.7 NE (NM)

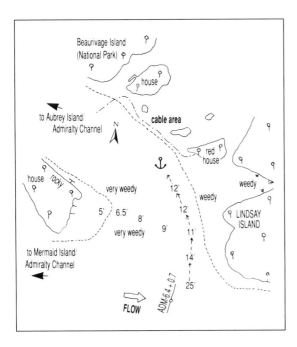

If you can't find island park dockage, this anchorage is near most Admiralty Channel Islands and is a place to wait for dockage to open. It's about 0.7 mile off the channel's western perimeter.

When you leave the Canadian Middle Channel and begin the Admiralty Channel downbound, your landfall is between Aubrey and Mermaid islands at Aubrey Island Light, **Mile ADM-6.4 (NM).** Locate **Tin Cap Shoal Buoy JH3** to the east-southeast—it watches a dangerous rock. Now pick up **Spar Buoy JH1** off to Tin Cap's north. Both buoys are on the Admiralty Channel's eastern side. Position yourself about midway between the two buoys. Before you start wandering off northeast, sort out individual islands.

South of Tin Cap Shoal is Mermaid Island. The large island to Mermaid's northeast is Bostwick Island. From this point Bostwick has only one visible satellite island; it's about 200 feet off Bostwick's northwestern shore. On this satellite island is a large house. Slowly head for this inhabited satellite island; we usually pass to its northwest. During this approach, you pass south of the southernmost islands watched by main-channel **Spar Buoy JH1, Mile ADM-6.3 (NM).** As you round Bostwick's satellite island, a group of three islands are visible to your north. Keep south of these, favor the deepwater channel off Bostwick's northwestern shore, and go to near Bostwick's northeastern end. Lindsay Island is now to your north. Your destination is off Lindsay Island's southwestern side, south of the satellite islands that lie southwest of Lindsay's northern half.

If you find bottom through the dense weeds, it's mud. Holding is poor.

The surrounding islands are all private except for Beaurivage, the large park island to the anchorage's northwest. If you want to go ashore, that's your closest place. If it's Sunday and you want to attend church, Half Moon Bay's worship area is close enough to reach by dinghy.

AUBREY ISLAND

Chart: N 14774, *See sketch map, page 285*

Mile ADM-6.4 + 0.1 (NM)

Wooded, rocky Aubrey Island is often called Burnt Island, depending on what issue chart or publication you happen to be reading. Aubrey suffered a devastating fire years ago and became known as "the burnt island." Now green and lush, it's charted as Aubrey again.

Aubrey is a park island on the Admiralty Islands' western perimeter. A small corner at the island's northwestern tip is private land. There are two main dockage areas, one on the island's southeastern side and one on the northeastern side. The northeastern dock has best depths. Each area has its own registration desk and fee box, picnic facilities, garbage bins, rest rooms, and access to park trails that lead past the camping area and to high island viewpoints. One trail passes near the 1800s Aubrey Lighthouse site. Before the Seaway was widened, deepened, and straightened, the Canadian

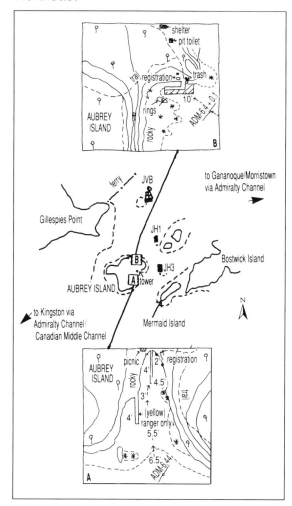

Middle Channel and its secondary channels were major watched routes for ships.

If docks are filled at the two usual Aubrey stops and you have very shoal draft, one other dock is on the island's northwestern end. Be very cautious during your approach to this stop; dangerous unwatched rocks extend nearly 0.5 mile southwest from Gillespies Point. Best water is favoring Aubrey's shoreline.

Aubrey Island Southeast

★★★★

Chart: N 14774, *See A on sketch map*

Mile ADM-6.4 + 0.1 (NM)

When you leave the Canadian Middle Channel downbound, your first landfall is Aubrey Island Light, **Mile ADM-6.4 (NM)**. These docks are in a natural cove on the island's southeastern side immediately southwest of the light. It's a fairly shoal docking area, and if you draw 5.5 to 6 feet, you may not have summer depth. If southerly quadrant wind is strong and prolonged, there can be a surge as waves ricochet against the cove's northern bank.

Enter the cove only when it opens fully. Come in cautiously. There's an islet off the western entry mouth with rocks extending toward the middle of the entrance; the eastern bank also has rocks extending westerly off the cliffs. Best dockage depths are at the end of the cove on the main dock's southern end.

Aubrey Island Northeast

★★★★

Chart: N 14774, *See B on sketch map*

Mile ADM-6.4 + 0.1 (NM)

There's good depth at this dock. In strong and prolonged northerly or northeasterly winds, it can be choppy. More of a problem is wake roll caused by passing pleasure craft; fender well.

Aubrey Island Light, **Mile ADM-6.4 (NM),** is in a very slight island indentation. The dock is just around the light's northerly point in its own island indentation. When you approach from the light and round its point and see the crib, do not start straightaway for the dock. Dangerous rocks litter the dockage indentation's western side.

The crib extends west from its land connection near

the indentation's eastern point. There are more dangerous rocks extending southeast from this point. Stay in good water until you can approach the crib's eastern corner by heading in a northwesterly direction. This approach brings you in about midway between the two outlying reefs.

There's room for 6-foot-draft vessels on the crib's far eastern end and all along its southern face. When you tie on the southern face, approach all dockage from its eastern end. The rocks extending from the cove's western shore are extremely close. If you tie along the crib's southern face's western end, walk the boat in; keep the bow facing east in case you need to leave abruptly. An immense boulder is almost within fendering distance.

A small boat may want to tie along the crib's extreme western end. If a boat of any size is on the southern face's western end, it has to move for the other to have access. This is an involved process due to the nearby boulder and adjacent rocks and normally involves assistance of all visiting boats' crews.

If you plan to anchor off to wait for space, be advised that holding is poor; it's rocky and very deep. If you anchor off and want your stern to the island, the crib's western-end boulder has tie-up rings; they are only accessible by dinghying in a stern line.

BEAURIVAGE ISLAND

Chart: N 14774

Mile ADM-6.0 (NM) to ADM-5.6 (NM)

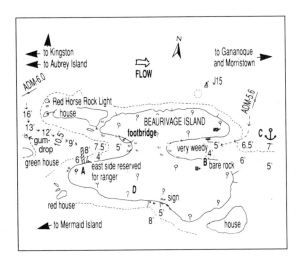

This island park is on the northwestern perimeter of the Admiralty Islands. It has two main dockage areas, one on the island's southwestern side and one on the northeastern side. Before preparing to leave the Admiralty Channel for either area, study the chart and locate your destination.

Beaurivage has the bulk of its island to the southeast. A narrow neck separates the southwest-northeast-oriented narrower northern section. Possibly this was awash at one time; it's low, marshy, and full of biting flies and mosquitoes.

The southwestern dockage is on the northwestern shore of the island's main bulk. It's at the southwestern end of a small cove whose northeastern end reaches as far as the island's narrow neck.

The northeastern docks are on the island's northeastern side in a cove separating the island's northern section from the larger southern section. This cove extends southwest to the narrow neck; just across the bulrushes on this neck is the cove for the southwestern docks.

The southwestern cove has the best approach and crib depths; the northeastern cove has the most dockage. Both areas are well protected, though each has a wind direction that's slightly unfavorable. Each has its own registration desk and fee box, rest rooms, garbage cans, shelters, grills, and picnic tables. Both are subject to an annoying invasion of flies; also, expect mosquitoes at dusk and dawn.

There are a few other small Beaurivage docks. All are in shoal water, usually less than 4 feet for approach and dockage; they may be of use if you have shoal draft. Two are just east of the northeastern cove on the main bulk of the island's northern shore. Two more are on the island's southeastern side, and two are on the northwestern shore. All have picnic tables, garbage bins, and access to trails that lead to rest rooms, registration desks, and fee boxes. Be extremely cautious during your approach to any of these areas, as extensive rocks and reefs exist in nearly all approaches.

There is a perimeter trail, as well as trails through the middle of the island that enable you to see island wildlife—chipmunks, squirrels, at least one bad-tempered hissing raccoon, kingfishers, owls, herons, gulls, songbirds, and mosquitoes.

Beaurivage Island Southwest

★★★★★

Chart: N 14774, *See A on sketch map, page 286*

Mile ADM-6.0 + 0.3 (NM)

Dockage is on the island's southwestern side. Watch out for rocks and shoals during your approach. The main dock is a wide crib on the small cove's southwestern end on the northwestern shore of Beaurivage Island's southern bulk. The crib extends northwest. The cove's northern shore is made up of rocks, awash reefs, and a collection of bushy and wooded islets. These terminate at Beaurivage Island's extreme western end at Red Horse Rock Light, a green-topped white cylindrical tower.

Begin your approach off Red Horse Rock Light to have a fixed departure point. Another entry landmark is a two-story brown house that fills an islet almost completely; it's just to the light's south in the collection of satellite islands and rocks forming the southwestern cove's northern shore. Bear south and west of Red Horse Rock Light; then continue far enough south so you are south of the most northern satellite islands and the brown house. In doing this, keep north of the small, high offshore islet with a prominent green cottage. In fact, don't come near that cottage islet at all; a very dangerous rock is about 200 to 300 feet to its northwest. It's occasionally watched by a seasonal gum-drop, but don't depend on it being there or assume that it marks the rock's top. Now head for the crib's northerly end; it's very visible.

The most protected stop is on the crib's northeastern face; the southwestern face has an unpleasant chop during strong southerly quadrant winds. If you tie at the cribs' southerly end on either side, read the water for rocks near the beach. On the crib's northeastern side you overlook the small northwesterly cove; outside you have a view of islands everywhere.

Inside the cove alongside the crib is a short floating dock suitable for shoal drafts; one side is for the warden. Inner-cove depths range from 4 to 7 feet. If you have depth, this is a good anchorage. Due to restricted space, anchor in midcove and take a stern line ashore; there are eye rings on the cove's southern cliff.

Beaurivage Island Northeast

★★★★★

Chart: N 14774, *See B on sketch map, page 286*

Mile ADM-5.6 + 0.2 (NM)

These docks are on the island's northeastern side; if you draw more than 5 feet, you may not have depth. Hold to the Admiralty Channel until well northeast of **Light Buoy J15,** which watches an isolated shoal off Beaurivage's northern section. About opposite the island's northeastern end, bear southeasterly toward Beaurivage's most northeastern point, but give it a fair berth—depths close in are risky for drafts of 4.5 feet. Continue southeasterly until a long, southwesterly reaching cove opens fully. Docks are on both cove banks. If you draw 4 feet or more, come in cautiously; you may have depths only on the dock's most northeasterly ends.

These docks are mainly used by shoal-draft powerboats, and can be noisy—portable generators sitting on docks run from dawn till late night.

Beaurivage Anchorage

★★★★

NO FACILITIES

Chart: N 14774, *See C on sketch map, page 286*

Mile ADM-5.6 + 0.1 (NM)

This anchorage is in the area bounded on the southwest by Beaurivage's Northeast Cove and on the northeast by the northern section of Lindsay Island's southwestern shore. The anchorage may be windswept and choppy during strong northerlies, but it's still tenable.

Leave the channel when about 0.1 mile northeast of **Light Buoy J15**—it watches the shoal off northern Beaurivage. Hold slightly closer to Lindsay Island for best depths. Try to anchor far enough southeast to clear upper Lindsay Island's northern tip for a little protection in case of northeasterly weather. If you draw 6 feet, you may not be able to get that far; go as far as you can with good swinging-room depth. On the other hand, if you have shoal draft, don't go as far southeast as Beaurivage's large eastern satellite island. If you do, you may come to a crashing halt on an isolated ~~unwatched, uncharted dangerous rock. It's off the satel~~lite's northeastern side about midway between Beaurivage and Lindsay islands.

Bottom is mud and weeds; holding is poor.

Land the dinghy at Beaurivage Northeast or one of the smaller docks. Tie in the shallows; don't block a space for incoming, hard-to-maneuver, shoal-draft large boats.

GANANOQUE MUNICIPAL MARINA

★★★★

Chart: N 14774

Mile ADM-4.2 + 0.2 (NM)

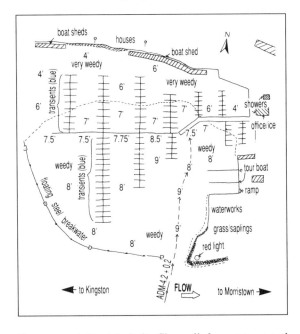

Gananoque is the Admiralty Channel's largest town and a supply point. The marina—open mid-May to mid-October—is in a partially enclosed basin. Finding a slip

may require waiting for one to be vacated; best chance is in midmorning, the usual transient departure time.

The basin is just southwest of Gananoque River's mouth. This area resembles a peninsula. On its southwestern end is a southerly reaching mole that forms the basin's eastern entrance. A long floating metal breakwater curves northwest, giving prevailing wind protection.

Leave the main channel at **Mile ADM-4.2 (NM)** east of **Light Buoy J8**—it watches a shoal north of the channel. Bear north-northeasterly to the basin entrance. The eastern entrance point is watched by a red light above a rocky revetment topped with grass and a few saplings. Enter between the light and the breakwater.

Once inside, bear around the slips' northeasterly perimeter; go past the waterworks, a ramp, and some tour boat service slips, to the main crib dock extending southwest from the peninsula. This is the pumpout area; attendants are usually on duty, but if not, tie up and check in at the office on shore.

Block and cube ice and 110-volt/30-amp electric hookups are available. If you need repairs, check at the office. The land line number is (613) 382-4088.

Downtown and most stores are on the river's other side. It's a long way, but you can walk to town, finish the day with a visit to the market, then taxi home. To get to town take Clarence Street, then make a left on Main Street and cross the river bridge. Northwest is Gananoque City Park; a laundromat is across the street. Large stores, banks, a hardware store, pharmacies, small shops, restaurants, the chamber of commerce, and the A & P supermarket are around King Street.

The Gananoque Museum, near the park at 5 King Street, used to be the Victoria Hotel. It dates from the mid-1800s and is furnished in that period's style. The collection includes military memorabilia, costumes, old photographs, and Indian artifacts. It's open Monday through Saturday.

A favorite attraction is the Thousand Islands Playhouse, a 300-seat summer theater on the riverbank at 690 South Charles Street. Many patrons come in by launch and tie on the bulkhead in front of the theater. Performances are at 8:30 P.M. Occasionally there is a matinee. Call (613) 382-7020 to find out what's currently playing.

The Gananoque Craft Fair is held in the town park over the Canada Day holiday. Local weavers, painters, woodworkers, and knitters display their work, and there is music and other entertainment. In August King Street has a large sidewalk sale, a farmers' market, and performances by musicians and dancers.

LEEK ISLAND

★★★★

□ (moorings)

Chart: N 14774

Mile MDCH-14.5 + 0.1 (NM)

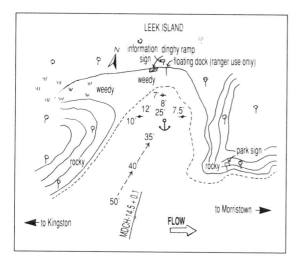

Though it is charted as Leek, this park island is often called Thwartway. It is one of the Admiralty Islands, but it's conveniently accessible from the Canadian Middle Channel. It's north of Grindstone Island's northwestern end. The Canadian Middle Channel passes between Leek's southern shore and Grindstone's McRay Point.

Leek's most popular anchorage is a large southeastern-shore cove. It has good protection, though in strong southwesterlies its northeasterly end tends to be rolly.

Downbound leave the Canadian Middle Channel at **Mile MDCH-14.5 (NM).** This is about opposite Grindstone Island's McRay Point and about 0.3 mile northeast of bare Bass Rock Island. This satellite islet lies off Leek's southerly shore near its southwestern end. The only nearby navigation aid is Canadian Middle Channel **Light Buoy H32,** about 0.25 mile to Leek's southwest. A small National Islands Park sign is on the

cove's northeastern point. Though a mooring buoy is charted off the cove's western entrance, it's not there; the moorings are farther inside the cove.

There's good depth in midcove during entry. If you decide on a mooring, all are close to the cove's northern shore—much too close if you draw 6 feet; sound for swinging-room depth or you may come to a crunching stop on a rock when the wind shifts.

Anchoring is the normal procedure since the moorings are usually taken. Holding is poor; bottom includes some mud, rolling rocks, and extensive weeds. The farther south you anchor in the cove, the deeper the water.

If wind picks up and you're anchored, keep vigilant. It seems every time we are here, at the merest whisper of wind, the anchorage turns itself into a muddle of dragging boats with an immense tangle of interwoven anchor lines that wrap around someone else's keel and rudder. Then, as a collective immovable group, we all end up bouncing on the beach boulders.

There's a quiet trail walk. The island is uninhabited, though the trails pass the ruins of a camp, a house, a barn, and silo foundations. There's a dinghy ramp at the cove's end, a small dock for the warden, an information sign, and rest rooms.

The Lake Fleet Islands on the Canadian Middle Channel

Mile MDCH-13.0 (NM) to MDCH-10.1 (NM)

The Canadian Middle Channel passes through this island group; anchorage directions are given downbound off the channel.

There are two popular island parks here, Camelot and Endymion. Both are toward the group's western section south of the main channel. The grocery boat and park showboat visit these islands.

Approach directions nearly all begin at the same point. It's the clearest approach near a fixed Canadian Middle Channel departure point. The reason we do not enter the islands from other Canadian Middle Channel areas is the difficulty in sorting out islands during a landfall and judging locations of uncharted dangerous rocks. We exit these islands by the same route for the same reason. For years we exited easterly at Endymion and Sundown Islands, but as new charts were issued, rocks and shoals appeared in areas we had transited. Other boaters apparently had found obstructions we had managed to miss.

Leave the Canadian Middle Channel about 0.1 mile east of **Light Buoy H26, Mile MDCH-12.1 (NM).** It's just south of Bloodletter Island and north of Niagara Island's northeastern tip—Camelot's easterly neighbor. Bear southwesterly between Niagara Island's southern side and a large unnamed island just west of Endymion.

Near the middle of Niagara Island, about opposite its pink house, start to slightly favor the eastern unnamed island. There's an unwatched rock in depths charted as more than 40 feet off Niagara Island's southwestern end. The rock normally doesn't show by discolored water; it's occasionally marked by a seasonal gum-drop.

At this point follow individual anchorage approach directions.

CAMELOT ISLAND

Chart: N 14773

Mile MDCH-12.1 (NM) to Mile MDCH-12.3 (NM)

There are four main areas in which to stay at Camelot. Most have docks; a few have only a dinghy ramp. Most are well protected except in very severe weather.

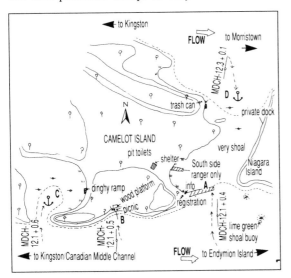

Though vessels with greater than 6-foot draft may be restricted to certain areas, they usually can find good water somewhere at each stop. Two places offer a few moorings.

Camelot East with its large crib is the usual base for information, park show boat, and main shelters, but most mooring and dock areas have their own registration desk and fee box. Rest rooms, grills, picnic tables, and camping facilities are nearby at all docks. The rocky, wooded island has well-used perimeter trails with inland offshoots.

Camelot Island East

★★★★

Chart: N 14773, *See A on sketch map*

Mile MDCH-12.1 + 0.4 (NM)

When you have passed the pink house on Niagara Island's southern shore and cleared the outlying rock off Niagara Island, continue to slightly favor the unnamed island until opposite Camelot's southeastern shore. Not until then should you turn northwest to the dock.

If you draw more than 5.5 feet, approach with caution; you may only have depth on the eastern half of the crib's southerly face and across the crib's eastern end. If you draw about 1.5 feet and are frustrated about waiting for a space to open, continue around the main crib's end and bear northwesterly. Another crib is in a small shoreline indentation with space for very shoal drafts. The passage between Camelot and Niagara Islands accessing Camelot's northern shore is only for cautious dinghies.

Camelot Island South

★★★★★

Chart: N 14773, *See B on sketch map, page 290*

Mile MDCH-12.1 + 0.5 (NM)

This dock is on Camelot's southern shore a few hundred feet west of Camelot East's docks, so use its approach (see page 290). The island is rocky and steep in this area. Your destination is a small dock extending southeast from the bluff. There's a camping area directly inland on the hill; you may or may not see it. It's a very short dock—about 15 to 20 feet—so if you're of fair length, have a stout spring ready in case you misjudge forward speed; boulders line the bank. There's good depth on both sides of the dock.

Weekend wake roll is a problem, primarily due to the short dock and spring line dependence. Take an anchor or grapple to the side and drape it around a nearby rock to hold you off.

Since there's room for only two boats, it's quieter than most Camelot docks. Swimming and snorkeling at the rocky cliff edge is excellent. Steps up the cliff access the camping area; halfway up is a porch with a picnic table.

Camelot Island Southwest

★★★★★

 (moorings)

Chart: N 14773, *See C on sketch map, page 290*

Mile MDCH-12.1 + 0.6 (NM)

This cove is on the island's southwestern side. Use the same approach as for Camelot East and Camelot South docks (see above). Once at South dock, continue westerly another few hundred feet to the end of the island's southwesterly hook. Here there is an opening north between Camelot and Netley islands. Your destination is in this cove.

Enter midway between Netley's eastern end and Camelot's southwestern arm. It's narrow. There are usually up to three moorings available, but if your draft is more than 5 feet and you plan to pick one up, sound for swinging-room depth; there's not a lot of good water. There's a cove dinghy ramp.

Deep-draft boats usually put a stern anchor in mid-cove and take a bow line to the cliffs' rocks.

Camelot Island North

★★★★★

 (moorings)

Chart: N 14773, *See D on sketch map, page 290*

Mile MDCH-12.3 + 0.1 (NM)

This anchorage and mooring area on Camelot's northeastern shore is convenient to approach from the Canadian Middle Channel. Though assorted northern islands surround the anchorage, they do not sufficiently stop a severe chop and swell produced by a prolonged, strong, northerly quadrant wind. Choose proper weather for a visit—it's a nervous business here moving in the dark of a bad night.

Leave the Canadian Middle Channel about 0.2 mile west of **Light Buoy H26** about midway along Dumfounder Island's high southern shore. Bear southerly. Your destination is just west of a tiny islet off Camelot's northeastern side and east of a slightly projecting point on Camelot. East of the islet is the cut between Niagara and Camelot islands. The islet, not charted on all issue charts, helps form a tiny cove. You probably can see two or three moorings near the islet; they indicate your course direction. There's a dinghy dock off the point.

If the moorings are taken, anchor. If you plan to tie a line ashore, put a bow anchor to the northerly quadrant and your stern to the rocks. If weather worsens, the bow facing your exit makes departure easier. There is one large eye ring in the cliff for securing. Holding is poor in weeds, rock, gravel, and a smattering of mud.

This is a pretty stop with an extraordinarily attractive view; sunsets can be spectacular. You have access to island trails, rest rooms, and shelters. If you plan to attend any sort of evening function at the east dock's main shelter, take along a dependable flashlight.

ENDYMION ISLAND

Chart: N 14773

Mile MDCH-12.1 (NM)

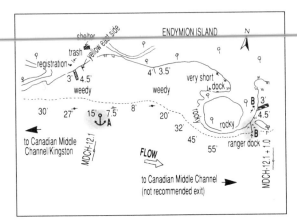

```
ENDYMION ISLAND          N
shelter
trash
registration
          3'  4.5'        4'  3.5'
          weedy           weedy        very short
                                        dock
   30'   27'   15'  7.5'    8'      20'        rocky      B  3'
                    A                    rocky          4.5'
                              32'                        B
   to Canadian Middle        45'        ranger dock
   Channel/Kingston               55'
                    FLOW
                    to Canadian Middle Channel
                    (not recommended exit)
```

This island has park docks, moorings, and an anchorage on its southern shore. Dock depths are usually less than 4.5 feet.

The stops have the usual registration desk and fee boxes, picnic tables and grills, bulletin boards, shelters, rest rooms, and access to trails. If you plan a visit ashore at sundown, leave your small pet below; an owl made off with another boat's cat on this island.

If moored or anchored, tie the dinghy in any dock shallows. Leave room for large shoal-draft boats that tend to scrape in over rocks to tie up. All docks access trails that in turn access camping areas with friendly campers that have great sing-alongs.

Your clearest approach to the Endymion docks, anchorage, and mooring areas is the same as that for visiting Camelot's southern docks (see page 291). After you clear the uncharted rock off Niagara Island's southwestern end, continue to Camelot. There's a dangerous uncharted reef off the southwestern end of the large unnamed island to Endymion's west. It lies about 200 to 400 feet off the island; a seasonal gum-drop might mark the reef's general area. Swing wide around the unnamed island before bearing east-southeasterly toward Endymion. Now follow the individual area approach directions.

Another popular island anchorage is on the northern side of a cut that leads between Endymion and its southwestern unnamed neighbor. This anchorage is badly open to a 10-mile-plus fetch to the north and east. If this exposure doesn't make you nervous, you can

anchor. Holding is poor in rock, weeds, and some mud. The only approach is from the Canadian Middle Channel to Endymion's northern shore.

Endymion Island South

★★★★

Chart: N 14773, *See A on sketch map*

Mile MDCH-12.1 + 0.65 (NM)

Once you round the unwatched reef off the unnamed island west of Endymion and are bearing east-southeasterly, pass the cut between the two islands. You may see boats anchored on the cut's northern side in the anchorage exposed to the north and east. Do not make an approach to that anchorage through the cut; there are dangerous rocks there.

When you pass Endymion's long southwesterly reaching finger of land, your destination is in sight. This finger and Endymion's southeastern end form a wide indentation that contains the anchorage and mooring area. It's usually filled with boats. You can now bear more northeasterly.

The western crib extends south-southwest and has the best depths at its southern end—though if you draw 4 feet, come in very carefully. Dense weeds cause erratic fathometer readings. There's a floating dock just west of the crib with space on its western side; the other face is for the warden. Farther east another short floating dock *may* have water for 4-foot-draft vessels. The third floating dock is in the cove's eastern-end bight; depths are about 2 feet.

Since dockage depth restricts most boats, pick up a mooring or anchor. If you choose the latter, try to stay in the moorings' vicinity—but not so close you foul one. However, if you go south much, water depth plummets. Bottom is mud, rock, and weeds; holding is poor. The prevailing wind usually pipes up fair by afternoon; an anchorage pastime is to count the boats that drag anchor and disappear downriver.

Endymion Island East

★★★★★

Chart: N 14773, *See B on sketch map, page 292*

Mile MDCH-12.1 + 1.0 (NM)

There are two stops at Endymion's broad eastern end, and both are best approached by the same route as to Endymion South (see page 292). Once you reach its large anchorage/mooring area, continue east to the island's end. The first dock is in the lee of a small, wooded islet and Endymion's shore. Half this short dock is for the warden; tie on the other side. Read the water as you come in; rocks are abundant.

You'll see a concentration of boats on the wooded islet's other side. This crib extends from Endymion's eastern end and toward Sundown Island, which is off to the east. On Sundown's western end there are rocks, a few islets with adjacent shoals, and rocks extending east from the wooded islet off Endymion's southeastern end. Approach very cautiously from the east and start your entry about mid–Sundown Island. Approach depth is about 5 feet; it shoals to about 4 feet at the crib. This is a pretty stop, but usually unbelievably noisy. Since the dock has fairly shoal depths, it's normally occupied by large shoal-draft powerboats that raft up to four deep. These vessels need quantities of electricity; their portable generators run day and night.

THE NAVY ISLANDS/MULCASTER

N O   F A C I L I T I E S

Chart: N 14773

Mile MDCH-10.1 (NM) to MDCH-8.2 (NM)

The Canadian Middle Channel routes south of this island group. It has one park island, Mulcaster. The rest are private and occupied.

For many years we visited Mulcaster; we now are reluctant to do so. Every new chart issue shows unexpected rocks on off-channel deepwater routes we previously traveled to the island. We hesitate to recommend it to first-time visitors; other dangers may lurk undiscovered.

If you are fearless and plan to visit Mulcaster, use caution. There's a moderate current and therefore set through this group, rocks are often outlying off visible landmarks and not always marked by seasonal gumdrops, and distances are difficult to judge, as in profile the islands overlap.

Mulcaster has dockage on its southwestern side and on its eastern end. The eastern end is the prettiest and the most popular, but it requires the most care in its approach; it nestles northwest of a group of satellite islands, rocks, and reefs.

Canadian Middle Channel Anchorages
The Thousand Islands Bridge to Ironsides Island

GEORGINA ISLAND

Chart: N 14772

Mile MDCH-5.9 (NM) to MDCH-5.7 (NM)

This island park is one of a compact group of more than 20 islands scattered near the Thousand Islands Bridge along the southern shore north of Hill Island. It is easy to find; the northern bridge section crosses above

Georgina Island West

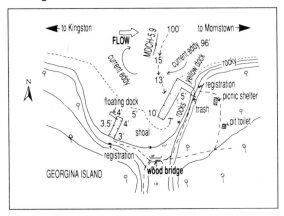

Georgina Island East

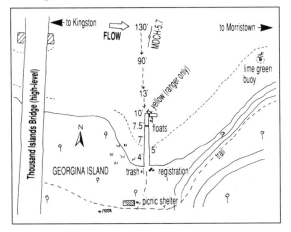

Georgina's easterly third. The island's northern shore is the Canadian Middle Channel's southern side.

This is an area of strong river current. Approaches must be made from flow up to 1.5 to 2.5 knots, though docks are in a generally slackwater area. There are two main dockage areas, both on the island's northern shore. Both have good weather protection, but weekend wake roll can be severe; fender well.

Two other docks are on the island's southern side. Their approach requires finding the entrance and your way on a side trip up Lost Channel. The preferred stop on this side is a floating dock just east of Georgina's bridge abutment. Another cove is about mid-island west of the bridge. Noisy generators with tangles of cords usually line this dock, and power-hungry anchored boats float portable generators astern on inner tubes—power cords may be supported by wine bottle corks. Except for the noise, the risk of electrocution when swimming, and the appalling overhead bridge hulk, this is an attractive stop; islands are everywhere.

All dock areas have picnic tables, grills, and access to park trails that lead to shelters, registration desks and fee boxes, rest rooms, and some of the most spectacular of Thousand Islands viewpoints.

Georgina Island West

★★★★

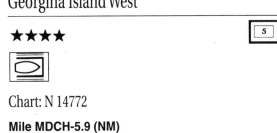

Chart: N 14772

Mile MDCH-5.9 (NM)

Dockage is in an indentation on Georgina's northern shore about 0.1 mile upstream of the bridge; you can see the docks from the channel. Make your turn slightly favoring the eastern point. There is a lot of channel current, but south of the point it's minimal. There may even be a reverse current as you approach the outer docks; it tends to swirl the boat back west, leaving line handlers out of dock-leaping range.

There are two docks in this cove; if your draft is more than 6 feet, best depths are at the crib nearest the channel. For better wake roll protection, walk your boat around inside this crib; it normally has fair depth.

The crib farther inside the indentation has one floating finger pier extending west off its northern end; part of this is for the warden. This entire inner-crib area is shoal; drafts over 3.5 feet may not have depth. This dock is usually very noisy, as it's littered with portable generators.

Georgina Island East

★★★★

Chart: N 14772, *See lower sketch map, page 294*

Mile MDCH-5.7 (NM)

This dock is on Georgina's northern shore about 0.1 mile east of the bridge in a slight shoreline indentation. The crib extends from the island's northern shore and has a floating extension. Off the end of this is another floating section that branches easterly. There's good depth on the dock's northern half; the remaining section gradually shoals as you close shore.

Channel current is strong; you are very close to the bridge abutment, always an area of increased flow on a river.

Approach the dock heading for its northern end. To do this, you must angle in upstream due to the current's set. Don't let this set put you too far east of the dock area; there's a dangerous offshore rock down there. It may be marked with a seasonal gum-drop, but don't depend on it. As you close the dock, current decreases.

The dock's shoreside end is normally base for shoal-draft powerboats that tend to fill the walkway with their portable generators and power cords. Deep-draft sailboats usually occupy the dock's outer end. Conflict has occurred between these groups due to generators running long after midnight.

ED HUCK MARINE (ROCKPORT)

★★★

ALL FACILITIES

Chart: N 14772

Mile MDCH-3.8 + 0.5 (NM)

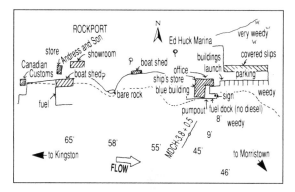

Downbound take a departure at Club Island Light, **Mile MDCH-3.8 (NM),** and bear northeast across the channel. Rockport is home port to the double-decker Rockport Tour Boat Lines; you can see their docks along the bulkhead in front of town. Your destination is slightly farther to their northeast. Continue past the Customs pier toward the eastern end of Rockport's slight point. The marina is the last large facility east in that area; its outer dock parallels shore just east of a large blue office building.

If no one answered on VHF 16, pull in to the fuel dock; you can see the gas pumps. Most marina dockage, with open and covered slips, is around the north point; transients usually stay on the exposed outer dock. The ship's store has some supplies and sells fishing licenses. The owners operate a water taxi service for island campers. Block and cube ice, 110-volt electric hookups, and a 30-ton Travelift are available. Call (613) 659-3408 for information.

The village is back southwest on the waterfront road. There are a few snack shops, a nearby marina with ice cream and a few staples, and a small village store that includes the post office.

Late in June Rockport holds it Blessing of the Fleet at St. Brendan's Church, on the waterfront road north of town overlooking the river. St. Brendan the Navigator is the town's patron saint.

GRENADIER ISLAND WEST

★★★★

4

Chart: N 14772

Mile MDCH-2.5 + 0.2 (NM)

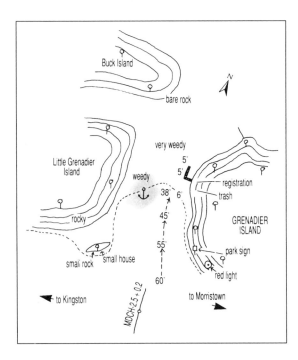

Most of large Grenadier Island is private, but it has three island park areas. This stop is at the island's southwestern end.

Leave the Canadian Middle Channel off red-topped white cylindrical Grenadier Island Light and make for the channel between Grenadier's southwestern end and Little Grenadier's eastern end. Just south-southeast of Little Grenadier is an islet that is fully occupied by a cottage; keep that islet to your north as you enter. There's excellent depth nearly to the most southerly of West Grenadier's two dock areas. Once weed growth begins depth drops to 6 feet.

If you draw less than 5 feet, the southerly crib is a place to stop. It extends westerly from the steep bank, then jogs northerly. The second dock is around the slight northeast point; it has less depth than the southern dock.

If you haven't depth to tie up, anchor off. Search about for a small area with about 8 feet slightly west of midway between Little Grenadier and Grenadier at about the drop-off line. There's a lot of weed growth; under the weeds it's mud. Tie the dinghy in either park dock's shallows.

You'll find the usual registration desk and fee box, picnic tables and grills, garbage tins, shelter, and rest rooms. There's a trail between the two docks. About 0.5 mile down the main island road is a golf course.

Eastern Seaway Channel Anchorages
Ironsides Island to Morristown

Mile SW-133.4 (NM) to Mile SW-118.7 (NM)

ADELAIDE ISLAND

★★★★★

 3

 (moorings)

Chart: N 14771, *See sketch map*

Mile SW-130.7 + 0.5 (NM)

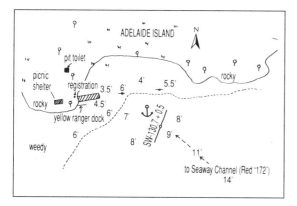

This park island is off Grenadier Island's northeastern end; it's one of more than 20 islands in this area. There's a dock, though it's in such shoal water that usually only runabouts have depth. You can anchor off or pick up a park mooring. If you anchor, you must struggle with extensive weed growth; if you take a mooring and draw 6 feet, sound for swinging-room depth; the three moorings are in fairly shallow water.

The dock and anchorage/mooring area is fairly well protected from prevailing southwesterlies, but if east and southeast wind is severe, there's a bad surge on the dock's southeasterly face and the anchorage is rough and windswept.

Since there are so many islands off Grenadier's northeastern end, and in order not to confuse one island for another during your approach, use a fixed departure point. At **Light Buoy 172, Mile SW-130.7 (NM)**, lay off a 0.5-mile west-northwesterly course to the dock—it's charted. This course takes you south of wooded Peel and Robert islands, and occupied Rough and Bagot islands; it's about midway between Adelaide Island and St. Helena Island and its northerly satellite islet. When you are in a general line midway between St. Helena and Rough islands, slow down. Once you cross the 12-foot curve, depths drop quickly.

If anchored or moored, tie the dinghy in the dock's shallows. If you plan a hike ashore, use insect repellent; most of the island is a mosquito marsh.

Runabouts use the cut between Rough and Adelaide islands to reach a noted pike and bass fishing area—try trolling with a Mepps #2 gray minnow.

BROCKVILLE MUNICIPAL HARBOUR

★★★★★

 5

Chart: N 14770, *See sketch map, page 298*

Mile SW-119.8 + 0.2 (NM)

Northern-shore Brockville marina—open May 15 to October 15—is behind a protective breakwater mole extending southwesterly from Blockhouse Island. The latter is not an island but is connected to the mainland by a causeway that secures the harbor. The mole is a landscaped park.

Leave the Seaway south of the city and bear for the breakwater mole's red-topped white cylindrical Brockville Breakwater Light. Beside the light is a Canadian Air Force jet airplane mounted on a pedestal. The entrance opening faces southwest. Round the breakwater, then follow its inner face to the northeast. This is called Tunnel Bay; it's a Brockville tourist showpiece. Marina

Brockville Municipal Harbour

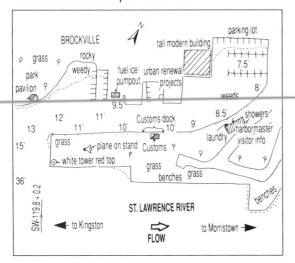

dockage is all along the mole's inner face, save one space reserved for Customs. You'll be closer to showers and town if you tie as far northeast as possible.

The office—land line number (613) 342-8772—is in the large building east of the Customs cottage. Block and cube ice and 110-volt/30-amp electric hookups are available. There is fuel and a pumpout at the private marina on the other side of Tunnel Bay.

You are in the Armagh S. Price Park. The James Auld Harbor Services Building is the hub of activities. There are picnic areas, landscaped flower gardens, park benches, a playground, a beautiful river view, and, on the building's eastern end, a canteen.

Before walking off to town, stop by the services building; the chamber of commerce has a lobby corner packed with brochures and tour maps. Downtown is a five-minute walk and has most city facilities—post office, library, small shops and large retail stores, banks, hardware stores, and restaurants. West on Key Street are two supermarkets. Key Street, Brooksville's main street, is two blocks up the marina access road. If you don't want to walk to the store, there are taxis, rental cars, and a bus.

"The Oldest Railway Tunnel in Canada" is in Brockville; it was in use for 100 years. Nineteenth-century Italianate Brockville City Hall is just up from the tunnel on Market Street. Historical Court House Square and the 1809 village green are a few blocks from the marina.

The 1800s Brockville Museum—open from 10 to 4—is about seven blocks from the marina; go west on

Water Street to Henry and turn toward the river. It has early documents, vintage photographs, and artifacts of Brockville and the nearby area.

The Brockville Arts Center, at 225 King Street West, is the city's cultural activities center. Performances include touring ballet companies, concerts, and community presentations. Call (613) 342-7122 for information.

From 7 to 1 on Tuesday, Thursday, and Saturday there's a farmers' market next to City Hall; the market has been held since 1833.

Riverfest, an annual Brockville event, takes place for 10 days in late June and over the July 1st holiday. The harbor and park area are in the midst of the activities. There are land and water parades, canoe races, fish fries, barbecues, pageants, craft shows, a historical military encampment, musical entertainment, a fishing derby, and outdoor concerts. It's climaxed on Canada Day with flag raising, speeches, birthday cake, and evening fireworks.

MORRISTOWN

Chart: N 14770, *See sketch map, page 299*

Mile SW-118.7 + 0.7 (NM)

Southern-bank Morristown is on Louce Creek. You have a choice of an anchorage, a marina, or a village dock off the main river current. The harbor is open to the northwest. If northwest wind is severe, you'll have better protection across the river in Brockville. When wind subsides, return to Morristown for a visit.

Best approach is from the northeastern side of the Three Sisters Islands. Leave the Seaway near the river's northern shore when northeast of McNair Island, the northernmost of the Three Sisters. Lay off a course to Louce Creek's eastern mouth, making certain you keep clear of the shoals off the northeastern ends of all the Three Sisters islands. The marina and the village dock are inside the creek on its eastern side about halfway to the low-level bridge. If these are filled, anchor off the town dock; it's where you tie the dinghy.

All stops are within two blocks of Main Street up on the hill. There's a post office, a hardware store, a liquor store, a café, and Morristown Market. Just south of the village dock is the Harbor Inn, a waterfront restaurant.

A historical landmark is the restored Stone Wind-

Morristown: Wright's Marina, Morristown Village Dock

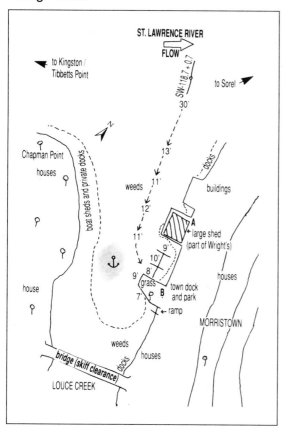

Wright's Marina

★★★ ☐ 4

Chart: N 14770, *See A on sketch map*

Mile 118.7 + 0.7 (NM)

Locate this marina by its large service shed, flying flags, and small floating breakwater. The latter is just off the covered shed and helps protect the marina from the northwest. For dockage pull in to the fuel dock—you can see the gas pump. If no one's on duty, there's a speaker alongside the building that connects you with the management up on the hill. Depth is best for drafts of 4 and 5 feet.

The small ship's store has some marine equipment and supplies, clothing, and local charts. The marina's land line number is (315) 375-8841. Block and cube ice, 110-volt electric hookups, and a 9-ton lift are available.

Walk up the hill to town.

Morristown Village Dock

★★★ ☐ 3

Chart: N 14770, *See B on sketch map*

Mile SW-118.7 + 0.7 (NM)

This village dock—time limit 24 hours—is immediately south of Wright's Marina. It's a good stop if you need more depth. Dockage is along the creek on a bulkhead. It's exposed to northwesterly wind chop; in severe conditions it may become untenable.

Dockage is in a grassy, tree-shaded, well-maintained village park with a picnic table and garbage cans. Check the park bulletin board for a walking-tour map, or pick one up on Main Street at the village offices.

mill, east on Morris Street. A Scottish miller built the fieldstone mill in 1825.

The town and village clerk's office on Main Street houses a display of Morristown's history. The building, which was formerly the 1906 Frontier National Bank, has interesting pressed-metal siding.

The 1820 Paschal Miller House is at the intersection of Main and Morris streets. Miller, a mid-1800s town supervisor, built the house in the "cup and saucer" style. This type of architecture has a rounded roof crowned with a cupola and resembles an inverted cup in a saucer.

The St. Lawrence Seaway & the Upper St. Lawrence River
Morristown to Sorel

Mile SW-118.5 (NM) to Mile SW-0.0 (NM)

and Mile SLR-136.3 (NM) to Mile SLR-99.7 (NM)

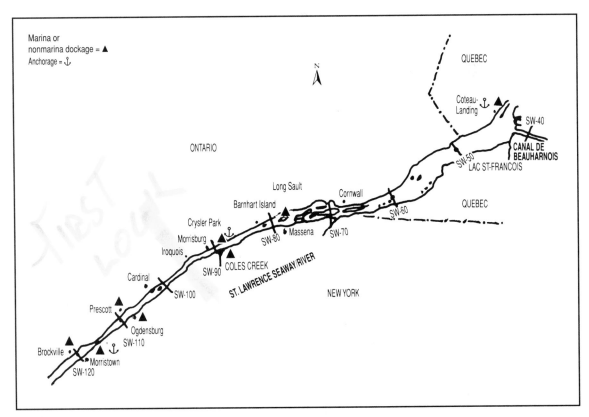

Morristown to Coteau-Landing, Mile SW-120.0 (NM) to Mile SW-40.0 (NM)

> *Row, brothers row, the stream runs fast,*
> *The Rapids are near and the daylight's past.*
>
> TOM MOORE,
> "A Canadian Boat Song," 1806

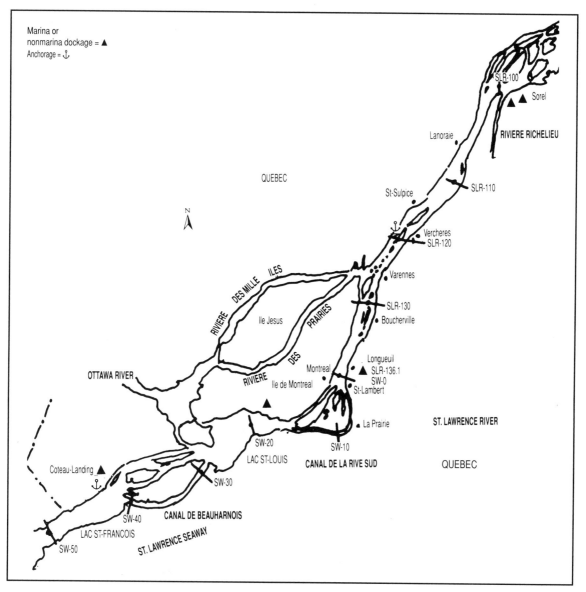

Coteau-Landing to Sorel, Mile SW-40.0 (NM) to Mile SLR-99.7 (NM)

The St. Lawrence Seaway
Morristown to Montreal

Mile SW-118.7 (NM) to Mile SW-0.0 (NM)

LOCKAGE, MORRISTOWN TO MONTREAL

Note: Pleasure boats using the St. Lawrence Seaway should carry aboard the "St. Lawrence Seaway Pleasure Craft Guide." Lock regulations and requirements in this system are too numerous to note in this table.

Name	Mile	Lift*	Required Chamber Side
Iroquois	SW-98.0 (NM)	0.5 to 6.0 feet	Down-starboard/up-port
Eisenhower	SW-76.55 (NM)	38 to 42 feet	Down-starboard/up-port
Snell	SW-72.5 (NM)	45 to 49 feet	Down-starboard/up-port
Beauharnois Upper	SW-28.3 (NM)	36 to 40 feet	Down-port/up-starboard
Beauharnois Lower	SW-27.5 (NM)	38 to 42 feet	Down-port/up-starboard
Cote-Ste-Catherine	SW-10.0 (NM)	33 to 35 feet	Down-starboard/up-port
St-Lambert	SW-2.8 (NM)	13 to 20 feet	Down-starboard/up-port

*At normal Seaway pool level.

All locks furnish lines and collect fee.

Required call-in area with direct land line contact:

Iroquois—Upper and Lower, Southeast side

Eisenhower—Upper, Northeast side (also contact VHF 12)

Snell—Lower, Northeast side

Beauharnois Upper—Upper, Northeast side

Beauharnois Lower—Lower, Northeast side

Cote-Ste-Catherine—Upper and Lower, South side

St-Lambert—Upper and Lower, South side

Pleasure craft transit fees: A $10 fee is charged for each of the five Canadian and two American locks. Canadian lockmasters collect ascending and descending tolls at each lock. For both American locks, Snell and Eisenhower, fees for upbound traffic are collected at Snell Lock; fees for downbound traffic are collected at Eisenhower Lock. All locks accept American or Canadian currency. No premium is allowed for currency exchange.

MOVABLE BRIDGES, MORRISTOWN TO MONTREAL

At Normal Seaway Pool Level.

Name	Type	Mile	Place
Iroquois Bridge*	Bascule	SW-97.8 (NM)	Wiley-Dondero Canal
Pont Valleyfield (#10)	Lift	SW-38.8 (NM)	Canal de Beauharnois
Pont St-Louis (#9)	Lift	SW-33.8 (NM)	Canal de Beauharnois
Bridge #8*	Swing	SW-28.4 (NM)	Canal de Beauharnois
CPR** (#7A/#7B)	Lift	SW-14.3 (NM)	Canal de Rive Sud
Bridge #5*	Bascule	SW-10.1 (NM)	Canal de Rive Sud
Victoria Bridge (#3)*	Lift	SW-2.9 (NM)	Canal de Rive Sud
Victoria Bridge (#2)*	Lift	SW-2.7 (NM)	Canal de Rive Sud

* Works in conjunction with adjacent lock.

** CPR = Canadian Pacific Railroad

Signals for all bridges:

   Flashing amber—Bridge operator has seen your approach.

   Flashing red—Bridge is opening; bring vessel up to Limit Approach sign.

   Steady green—Bridge is open; transit.

The St. Lawrence River served well as an early major transportation route, except in a 118-mile section between Morristown and Montreal. Most of this area was shoal, filled with dangerous rapids, and prone to excessive current.

In 1700, to safely bypass the rapids, settlers built a short, 1.5-foot-deep canal. Subsequently, to increase the commercial potential of the area, private companies and the government-in-residence built more short canals with 3-foot depths.

It was 1848 before the first real canals and locks with a 9-foot depth went into operation. The Galop, Rapide Plat, Farran Point, and Cornwall canals bypassed the dangerous International Rapids; the Canal de Beauharnois linked Lac St-Francois to Lac St-Louis; and the Lachine Canal allowed access from Lac St-Louis to Montreal.

The canals were for upbound traffic; downbound vessels shot the rapids. In 1901 the government built new locks with a depth of 14 feet, but this was insufficient for the ships that were now able to ply the western lakes and the Welland Canal. Boats with deep-sea draft could access downstream only as far as Prescott and Ogdensburg; upbound from the sea they could reach only as far as Montreal. Transshipping became a major industry.

When the government rebuilt the Welland Canal for 25-foot-draft vessels, access to Montreal and the sea became economically imperative. The Seaway finally eliminated the 14-foot bottleneck in 1959.

Strong river currents in this section remain a dominant factor for pleasure craft travel. At Brockville/Morristown current steadily increases; it is most pronounced in narrow reaches. Amount depends on the season, Iroquois Control Dam's water release, and hydroelectric generation. Current is usually minimal in Canal de la Rive Sud, Canal de Beauharnois, and the Wiley-Dondero Canal. Lake St. Lawrence, Lac St-Francois, and Lac St-Louis have current; intensity depends on how close you are to rapids and dam tailwaters.

Downbound to Montreal, **Mile SW-0.0 (NM),** you transit seven locks; lift depends on river stage. Except for the Iroquois Control Lock, whose lift varies from 0.5 to 6 feet, locks have lifts from 13 to 50 feet. Downbound locks are very easy to negotiate. Upbound in large lift locks with only a family crew, transit can be very difficult due to excessive lock turbulence. Commerce has first priority of lockage, so transit time varies. This is a busy system, and hours of delay are not unusual.

As you start downstream at Three Sisters Islands, **Mile SW-118.7 (NM),** the mile-wide wooded river shores have waterfront homes and an occasional commercial facility. At Maitland, **Mile SW-115.5 (NM),** watch for a historic waterfront windmill tower. These fieldstone grain mills with square upper windows and large lower-level doors are frequent sights. Few have their vanes.

Major Edward Jessup, a Loyalist, founded northern-shore Prescott, **Mile SW-109.7 (NM)**. The British gave him the land in appreciation for his support during the American Revolution.

Before the canals were built, people and goods came by sailing ship as far as Montreal. From there they had to travel by bateaux, the only vessels usable for the next 118 miles upbound. Prescott, one of the first smooth-water ports after Montreal, became known for its forwarding companies, which contracted to send passengers and cargo to their destinations.

Downbound transport was easier. Though cargo often came from far upriver or on the lake, Prescott was the place to rest up, take on supplies, and "tighten chains" before starting down the rapids. Prescott's forwarding trade ended when uninterrupted canal navigation opened from Lake Ontario to Montreal.

At the start of the War of 1812 the government built Prescott's Fort Wellington. In 1837, when Canadian rebels attempting to free the colony from British rule went to the United States and began raiding across the river, the government decided to rebuild and strengthen the fort. You can see it on Prescott's southeastern hill.

American-shore Ogdensburg is on both sides of the Oswegatchie River's mouth. Around 1749 its first settler, Abbé Francois Picquet, built fortified La Presentation, an Indian mission, school, trading post, and bastion on what is now Lighthouse Point. During the French and Indian War, with British invasion imminent, the French destroyed the fort before it could be captured. The British rebuilt it and called it Fort Oswegatchie. After the American Revolution, the Jay Treaty granted the fort to American Judge Nathan Ford, a land agent.

Farther downriver is Windmill Point, **Mile SW-108.2 N (NM),** with an old red-topped white stone mill.

Downbound you pass the Lower Lakes Terminal, a major Canadian grain transshipment point. It's just west of 129-foot Ogdensburg-Prescott International Bridge, **Mile SW-106.6 (NM)**, which crosses from Johnstown to Chimney Point's western side. Johnstown is on an old Indian camping ground and 1600s French outpost, La Galette. When the British took over they changed the name to honor Sir William Johnston, a prominent figure in the early Mohawk Valley and father of Loyalist leader Sir John Johnston.

Downstream of the bridge the river widens into a collection of low, sparsely wooded islands. For a quick channel reference pick up the florescent orange-and-black range marks on Galop Island's southern end.

Isle Royale, now Chimney Island, **Mile SW-105.8 (NM)**, on the channel's southern side, is the site of old French Fort Levi. Legend says a French commander buried a chest of gold on the island before his surrender during the French and Indian Wars. A hundred years later Monsieur Pauchet, the commander's proclaimed grandson, and a riverboat pilot dug up more than 500 pounds of the treasure. When they started for the mainland, the overloaded boat foundered in a storm. Given the choice of sinking or lightening the load, Pauchet chose to tie himself to the gold and go down with the boat. The pilot swam ashore.

Chimney Island marks the upstream end of the historical Galop Rapids.

Current increases in the next 4 miles; it can be up to 3 knots. On the channel's northern side is Spencer Island Pier Light, a red-topped white tower. It's at a jog in an old pier breakwall partly covered with brush just southwest of Drummond and Spencer islands. This pier is the western end of the early-era North Channel or Cleveland Cut, a 1.5-mile-long, 400-foot-wide channel cut through rocky Drummond Island. It bypassed the upper Galop Rapids and served as an upstream Galop Canal extension; it ran along the river's northern side.

Galop Island, low, covered with grass, bushes, and saplings, was cut in two pieces during Seaway construction. The large section on the channel's southern side extends eastward to Cardinal.

Northern-shore Cardinal, **Mile SW-102.0 (NM)**, has a cornstarch plant prominent on its point. In the late 1700s the settlement based its economy on hauling boats around an uncontrolled Galop Rapids section. This ended in 1846 when the government completed the Williamsburg Canals, a three-canal system that ran between Cornwall to above the Galop Rapids. This first Galop Canal ran around Cardinal Point's southern end, by the cornstarch plant. Between 1897 and 1901 a new, deeper canal ran inland of the point; Cardinal became an island accessible by a swing bridge. After the Seaway was constructed this canal was filled in and the bridge was removed.

Parts of the old Galop Canal are accessible at different points and used by local pleasure craft. Be cautious if you decide to take this side trip; weeds and low-level overhead power lines make the area hazardous. The most used area with best water is one with an entrance at the Spencer Island Pier Light. Use the North Channel. Now pass north of Adams (Prison) Island into old Galop Canal's western end to the next embankment gap 1.5 miles to Cardinal's west.

At Cardinal you begin the 4.5-mile-long Iroquois Lock and Control Dam approach. The lock is on the river's northwestern side between Harkness and Iroquois Islands; the 2,700-foot dam extends easterly to Rockway Point. Such a long dam is necessary to provide more gates for river control. Between Montreal and Lake Ontario the Seaway regulates water levels and flows by a series of structures. One is Iroquois; it also controls the level of Lake St. Lawrence. Farther downstream are the Moses-Saunders Power Dam at Massena and Cornwall, a group of dams near Coteau-Landing, and the Beauharnois power dam.

Iroquois Dam has 32 vertical-lift opening gates. They are often operated in a fully open position. If you have a small boat with a minimum overhead clearance of 8.5 feet, you can pass downbound (at your own risk) through sluice gate #28. The upstream side of the dam piers is painted with red navigation aids and green navigation aids. Upbound traffic uses sluice gate #30, similarly marked on the dam's downstream side. Remember: *Sluice gates close or partially close without notice.*

If you plan to transit Iroquois Lock, stop at the lock's small-craft dock and call in. Since Iroquois is the first downbound lock, a bilingual Seaway official usually comes to the dock to ask questions about vessel size, draft, and destination and to distribute pamphlets containing upcoming system information. Iroquois lift varies with water level, but during the season it's generally small; attendants close one set of gates, open the others, and collect the transit fee.

The lower pool, 25-mile-long manmade Lake St. Lawrence, is contained downstream by Eisenhower Lock, Moses-Saunders Power Dam, and Long Sault Spillway Dam. During dam construction, Lake St. Lawrence inundated seven villages. Old Iroquois was the largest one affected; more than 150 buildings were moved by machine into orderly Canadian-shore blocks. The old site is now about midriver.

Rapide Plat, a series of small rapids in Iroquois, had swift 15-mph current and sufficient depth for large freight steamers on their way down from the Great Lakes to Montreal. They ran the rapids at an average of 20 to 25 mph. Upbound was another matter. In 1847 the government finished the Point Iroquois Canal, bypassing the rapids. In 1897 the government added an

800-foot lock, the longest in Canada.

Downbound, current in island-littered Lake St. Lawrence depends on the number of open Iroquois Control Dam sluice gates. The channel is on large Ogden Island's northern side; Le Petit Sault (now called Little River on the chart) flows between Ogden's eastern side and the American mainland.

Le Petit Sault was a difficult early section of the Rapide Plat; it dropped 8 feet in a narrow 800-foot stretch. Waddington, settled by the French in 1673, had a canal and lock to bypass this area. In 1800 Waddington's residents built a dam and power canal across to Ogden Island to power sawmills and gristmills. At its industrial height Waddington was a major pulpwood receiving port and had an iron ore smelter and impressive factories, one of which produced the first machine-made scythe and ax in America.

A landmark at Morrisburg, **Mile SW-91.0 N (NM)**, is its stone waterfront church just north-northeast of low, grassy Canada Island. The town, one of Canada's earliest settled areas, was once traded for a gallon of rum. The Seaway Authority transported all of Morrisburg's waterfront business district and homes farther north before the onset of the lake's rising water.

At **Weaver Shoal Light Tower 68, Mile SW-85.2 N (NM)**, look north to see needle-shaped Crysler Farm Battlefield Memorial Monument. In 1813, American forces were defeated here by British and Canadian troops. Just over Ault Island's southern tip downstream of the monument is Upper Canada Village, an attraction recreating life in Ontario during the 1860s. It includes working sawmills, a woolen factory, a steam-powered flour mill, and farms.

American-shore Wilson Hill Wildlife Refuge, a vast marshland enclosed by six dikes, is a midsummer haven for waterfowl. It's south of Bradford and Wilson Hill islands.

Old Aultsville is on the river bottom south of Cat Island Shoals. North of the Croil Islands and the Long Sault Island chain are Farran Point, Dickinsons Landing, Wales, Mille Roches, and Moulinette, whose residents also moved for Lake St. Lawrence's flooding. The islands are in the area of the famous 9-mile-long International—or Long Sault—Rapids. Collectively the rapids had a 45-foot drop filled with whirlpools, white water, and dangerous reefs. Current was so swift a downbound lumber raft transited in 40 minutes. By 1848 the government had bypassed the rapids with a series of 9-foot-deep canals and locks. In this area the

Cornwall Canal ran along the northern shore; dike remnants are charted.

Early passage downstream—only upbound traffic used the canal—was treacherous; an unprecedented number of lives and boats were lost. Travel was restricted to small boats, scows, and log rafts. It was the mid-1800s before large vessels came downbound on a regular schedule; the 200-foot steamers left Lake Ontario one morning and arrived in Montreal the next. At the rapids it took four men at the wheel to handle steering as the bow pointed down as if over a waterfall. Boilers were shut down to an idle, yet speeds up to 25 mph were the norm.

You pass only a portion of Massena at **Mile SW-78.3 (NM)**; most of the city is south on the northeasterly flowing Grass and Raquette rivers. French woodcutters founded Massena. They were after long-length pine, which they rafted downstream to be used as ships'

masts. By the 1830s woolen and grain mills replaced the lumber industry; the timber supply had been depleted, and ice jams had destroyed waterfront sawmills. Indians had long used the medicinal mineral springs on the Raquette River's northern bank. Massena profited from them; from the 1800s to the early 20th century it was a renowned health spa with luxurious hotels.

In 1900 Henry Warren's company built a 3-mile-long canal connecting the Grass River to the St. Lawrence—you pass the old canal just west of Massena's waterfront. The canal dropped 45 feet and operated a 200,000-hp generating plant. The Aluminum Company of America moved in and cast its first aluminum ingot "pig." When the Seaway built its 1950s power project, ALCOA expanded and the Reynolds Metals Aluminum reduction facility arrived. Though still classified as a village, Massena has grown into the largest municipality in St. Lawrence County.

A downbound laker prepares to leave Eisenhower Lock in Massena, New York.
(Photo courtesy St. Lawrence Seaway Development Corporation)

Looking west: the International Seaway Bridge, foreground; Pollys Gut; Snell Lock; Moses-Saunders Power Dam, upper right; Eisenhower Lock, left background; and the Long Sault Dam, middle background.
(Photo courtesy St. Lawrence Seaway Development Corporation)

Barnhart Island, north of the Seaway, has two major dams. The Moses-Saunders Power Dam, 3 miles northeast of Eisenhower Lock, extends from Barnhart Island's eastern end across the border to the Canadian mainland. Long Sault Spillway Dam connects the mainland north of Eisenhower Lock to Barnhart's western end. Because of fast river flow above the dams, pleasure boats are not allowed within 1,000 feet of sills.

Flags and banners fly in the middle of the power dam. Robert H. Saunders is the Canadian portion; Robert Moses is the American half. They are a joint undertaking of the Power Commission of Ontario and the Power Authority of New York. The 3,200-foot dam has 32 generators divided evenly between the two countries. Water flow through the system is about 2 million gallons a second, with a generating capacity of 1,824,000 kilowatts. Long Sault Spillway Dam has 30 vertical gates, each 50 feet wide, and serves as an emergency spillway. It's used occasionally when required discharge exceeds the powerhouse's capacity.

Massena is the upstream end of the 8.5-mile-long American Wiley-Dondero Canal; speed limit is 6 knots over the bottom. It connects Lake St. Lawrence to Lac St-Francois, bypassing the Power Dam and Long Sault Spillway. The canal has two locks that overcome an elevation difference of 87 feet. Eisenhower is upstream; Snell is downstream. You may call Eisenhower Lock on VHF 12 for transiting information; if there's a wait, tie at its small-craft dock.

Eisenhower Lock warns Snell of your downbound approach. If there's a wait at Snell, proceed to the standby area immediately upstream of Snell; it's

Eisenhower Lock, looking east from upper sill during concreting operations, June 17, 1957.
(Photo courtesy St. Lawrence Seaway Development Corporation)

marked by a small white buoy but has no dock.

After exiting Snell downbound you enter the western end of 37-mile-long Lac St-Francois. Immediately south is the Grass River's mouth; its current flow is minimal unless river stage is high. However, once you clear the lock's northern approach wall, you are in Pollys Gut's approaches. This narrow cut between the large lock island and Cornwall Island has the most Seaway current; amount depends on the Moses-Saunders Power Dam's outflow. If it is generating, current can be up to 6 knots; if not, and if river stage is normal, current is about 3 to 3.5 knots. There's a curving breakwall north of the channel at Pollys Gut's southern end, and if flow is severe, current deflects southeast so it runs slightly fair to the channel.

Just ahead, the high-level Seaway International Bridge crosses three areas: Cornwall Island, the island's northern channel, and the old Cornwall Canal. Cornwall is on the river's northern bank.

Loyalist John Johnson and a group of settlers founded Cornwall in 1784 as a farming area; they came from Johnstown in the Mohawk Valley. When the Cornwall Canal went into use, the village specialized in the manufacture and shipping of cotton products. Thomas Edison installed his first electric lighting system in one of Cornwall's cotton mills. When the government improved and deepened the canal, its entrance ended up downtown. It became one of the most prosperous ports below the International Rapids.

As you clear the International Bridge downbound, the channel is on Cornwall Island's southern side. If you need fuel (at an excellent price), southern-bank Ahnawate

Marina is at **Light Buoy 15.** Its long floating dock parallels the bank. Approach heading into the current—it's about 2 to 3 knots without upstream power generation.

Cornwall Island, an Indian Reserve, is a living museum whose recreated village demonstrates early 1700s Iroquois, Cree, and Ojibway life.

Just east of the Raquette River's mouth, **Mile SW-68.5 S (NM)**, you cross the Ontario border. Downbound at this point you travel in Quebec, Canada's largest province.

Settlement and land cultivation in this area began after the American Revolution. The government offered prime river land to army regiments that came to Canada for the war. Most stayed on since field officers could receive 5,000 acres, captains 3,000, and subalterns 2,000. Noncommissioned officers and privates could have 200 acres, with an added 50 for a wife and each child. In addition more than 10,000 American Loyalists arrived in western Quebec; they also had free land grants.

Because these English-speaking settlers clashed with the area's French Canadians, the British Parliament passed the Constitutional Act in 1791 and divided Quebec at this border. The eastern portion was renamed Lower Canada. The western region became Upper Canada, a separate province with an English legal system and its own government.

East at the border at the St. Regis River's mouth is St. Regis, part of the large St. Regis Indian Reserve.

Above the trees is the spire of 1700s St. James Church.

If you plan a visit to Cornwall, your course is about 3 miles westerly upstream on watched Cornwall Channel, **Mile SW-66.4 N (NM)**; the entrance is southwest of the wooded Colquhoun Islands. Marina 200 is an off-current transient marina, though if your draft is more than 5 feet, call ahead for depths. Current on Cornwall Channel can be severe and depends on the power dam's generating status and river stage.

Downstream of St. Regis Island, 5-mile-wide Lac St-Francois begins to open. This is a natural lake, but Seaway construction and resultant water-level rise made its western end a dangerous area for exploration. Just-awash islands and extensive marshlands dot the lake. Though unwatched deepwater channels exist, large uneven areas of very shoal water predominate. Current decreases slightly once the lake widens but picks up to about 2 knots at the lake's far eastern end—the approach to the next group of old river rapids.

About 2 miles northeast of **Buoy D8, Mile SW-44.0 (NM),** is the old 14.5-mile-long Soulanges Canal's eastern terminus at Coteau-Landing. Though it's no longer open to navigation, commerce used the canal from the early 1900s until the Seaway went into operation. Ships were designed and built to completely fill the Soulanges locks.

Before the canal era, downbound river navigators hated Coteau-Landing. It was the head of a collection of

The western entrance of the old Soulanges Canal, Coteau-Landing, Quebec.

very dangerous rapids between Lac St-Francois and Lac St-Louis; in 15 miles they overcame a drop of 85 feet. Each major group had a name; they included the Coteau, Cedar, Split Rock, Cascades, and Soulanges rapids.

The downbound trip began by winding through the islands between Coteau-Landing and Ile de Salaberry. Coteau du Lac, just downstream of this point on the Riviere Rouge, was for years Upper Canada's main port of entry. It was protected by octagonal Fort Coteau du Lac. Here was the small but fast Coteau Rapids, whose submerged rocks and boulders made navigation difficult.

Next came Cedar Rapids, near Cedar; this group had the fastest water and the sharpest drop in elevation. In 1759 General Jeffery Amherst lost 84 men and 40 boats attempting to transport his army downriver here.

The Split Rock Rapids were next. These were the most difficult to navigate due to a rock formation running across the river bottom. Boat operators had to cut diagonally across the river—a fault in the rock was the only way through—then turn back across again.

Next were the Cascade Rapids, named for their frothing white water. Finally the Soulanges series boiled down into the calms of Lac St-Louis. Today's Canal de Beauharnois bypasses these obstructions.

Mile SW-42.4 (NM) is a departure point if you plan to visit Valleyfield, often called the Venice of Quebec. It's on the eastern side of the Coteau Rapids, south of Ile de Salaberry on Baie St-Francois. In the late 1800s Valleyfield had one of the world's largest cotton mills. It was also at the head of the old Canal de Beauharnois, the first canal to link Lac St-Francois and Lac St-Louis with a 9-foot depth. It roughly parallels the river's southern side. In 1901 the government abandoned the old Canal de Beauharnois; they had built the northern shore's Soulanges Canal. You can trace these old canal routes on chart C 1411.

During Seaway construction the new Canal de Beauharnois—situated well south of its ancient sister—replaced everything. It is today's access between the two lakes and swings in a grand curve from **Mile SW-41.0 (NM)** in Lac St-Francois to Melocheville on Lac St-Louis. About 14 miles long and more than 0.5 mile wide, it is crossed by three movable bridges and has two locks. The locks at the canal's eastern end overcome a 78-foot elevation difference between the two lakes.

When you exit Beauharnois Lower lock downbound and enter Lac Saint-Louis, Ile Perrot is northeast. Along the island's southwestern side is an Ottawa River mouth; it's *not* the route to take if bound for Ottawa.

The navigable Ottawa River entrance is on east between Ile de Montreal and Ile Perrot's northern side.

Lac St-Louis extends easterly 15 miles to the Lachine Rapids. The downbound route bears easterly and south of Ile Perrot's eastern end and north of low-lying Iles de la Paix. Look north at Pointe du Moulin, **Mile SW-23.5 (NM), to see another 1700s stone wind-mill. This one has its vanes and miller's house.

If bound for Ottawa, Ste-Anne-de-Bellevue, or the locks at the Ottawa River's eastern terminus, a shortcut is coming up. If you have shoal draft—6 feet usually can't make it at summer level—your departure point is at Pointe a Fourneau north of Pointe du Moulin. This watched channel carries aids with the prefix "AE". It takes you through the shoals from Pointe a Fourneau to near the middle of La Grande Anse, the large bay on Ile Perrot's eastern side.

Next you transit La Passe Channel between Ile Perrot and the Iles Ste-Genevieve. This is the area where deep-draft vessels have shoal-water problems. La Passe Channel intersects the Lynch Channel at **Buoy AD42.** Lynch Channel carries aids with the prefix "AD". The Ste-Anne locks—your access from Lac St-Louis to Lake of Two Mountains and from there to Ottawa—are another 2.5 miles west via a choice of two other routes.

If you are not bound for the Ottawa River, or if you need more depth for the way to Ste-Anne, then at Pointe du Moulin your Seaway course bears northeasterly. Though here the lake widens to 6 miles across, outside the channel is very shoal water. If you plan to leave the main channel, do so only on watched secondary channels.

The northern shore of Lac St-Louis is on Ile de Montreal; the prominent island peak with its collection of radio towers is Mont Royal. Dotted along the northern shore of Lac St-Louis are yachting facilities.

At **Light Buoy A18, Mile SW-19.5 (NM),** the ship channel makes a hard easterly bend. Here secondary channels access the northern lakeshore.

Secondary Channels to Lachine, Dorval, Pointe Claire, Beaconsfield, and Ste-Anne

This collection of intersecting channels (chart C 1410) has varying amounts of current. The amount depends on how close your channel choice takes you to the Lachine Rapids. Close to the rapids it can be up to 3 knots; most channels average about 2 to 2.5 knots.

You must first access the main secondary channel. Leave the Seaway at **Light Buoy Lachine A,** just east of **Seaway Light Buoy A13.** This channel leads to Lachine; other channels to other points divert from it. The Lachine channel has a range—Dixie Island Range—and is watched by aids carrying the prefix "AC". Allow for current set and carry this channel east-northeasterly about 1.7 miles to **Lachine Channel Buoy B.** This is a junction buoy accessing other secondary channels.

TO LACHINE

If you plan to visit Lachine, bear easterly at the buoy, continuing to follow the Lachine channel "AC" aids for nearly a mile to **Light Buoy AC38,** just west of the Banc de Chateauguay. At this point bear very slightly north and carry another range for 1.8 miles. Current increases dramatically as you approach the rapids; steer small and avoid drifting out of the narrow channel. **At Light Buoy AC20** bear slightly southeasterly toward the old Lachine Canal's upstream end. Once in the old canal dike's lee, current is no longer a threat.

TO DORVAL, POINTE CLAIRE, BEACONSFIELD, AND STE-ANNE

If bound for any of these areas, at **Lachine Channel Buoy B** bear northwesterly and follow the aids prefixed by "AD" for 1.4 miles to **Light Buoy AD12** and another junction.

If you plan to visit Dorval, bear easterly about 1.1 miles to Dorval Island's north—aids carry the prefix "AS".

If bound for facilities west, at **Light Buoy AD12** bear westerly where your navigation aids continue to bear the prefix "AD". This channel bears westerly for about 6 miles to Ile Dowker, the northernmost of the

Iles St-Genevieve. Pointe Claire and Beaconsfield are about 0.8 mile off this channel.

At Ile Dowker you begin the Lynch Channel at **Buoy AD42.** Lynch Channel intersects the shoal short-cut route from Point du Moulin and Pointe a Fourneau. At **Buoy AD42** are two watched channels to Ste-Anne—the locks are still west about 2.5 miles. The deeper channel is along Ile Perrot's northern shore and still carries the prefix "AD". The most shoal channel is along Ile de Montreal's southern shore and carries the prefix "AE".

If your itinerary did not include northern-shore Lac St-Louis, then downbound at **Seaway Light Buoy A13** and **Buoy Lachine A** pass north of Ile des Soeurs Grises (old Ile St-Bernard). This island divides the Chateauguay River's mouth. Except for Le Tertre, a 120-foot-high hill at its southwestern corner, the island is low. At one time it belonged to the Grey Nunnery and was beautifully cultivated. Many Montreal-vicinity islands were governed by different orders of nuns who obtained large revenues from island farms.

Downbound at **Mile SW-17.0 (NM),** at the northern dike, you begin the 18-mile-long, 225-foot-wide Canal de la Rive Sud, which bypasses the Lachine Rapids and takes you to downtown Montreal. For about 10 miles the canal follows the river's southern shore; then it makes a slow 2-mile northerly bend to **Mile SW-0.0 (NM).** Crossing the canal are six bridges, four of them movable, and two locks that overcome a 48-foot elevation difference between Lac St-Louis and **Mile SW-0.0 (NM).**

Across the river at the head of the rapids is Lachine, once a Montreal military outpost granted to the explorer René-Robert Cavelier de La Salle.

The government built the Lachine Canal in stages with various depths. Construction started in the 17th century; the final updating, which put the town at the canal's upstream Lock #5, took place in the 1800s. Downtown Montreal was the canal's eastern terminus. Its old first lock—access into the St. Lawrence—is now filled in to make room for industry. The Lachine Canal closed to navigation in 1959; it's now a landscaped recreational park.

As you start downbound on the Canal de la Rive Sud, you pass Tekakwitha Island. After you round the first bend you are at Kahnawake (Caughnawaga), part of the Kahnawake Indian Reservation. The town was originally an early-1700s French mission intended to win the Indians over to "The Faith"; Caughnawaga means "praying Indian."

Today more than 6,000 Indians live on this Iroquois site. Their native language is Mohawk; their second is English. Now called Kahnawake, meaning "at the rapids," it's still served by the Jesuits at the St-Francois-Xavier Mission, founded here in 1719. On the southern bank are numerous No Trespassing signs; they note that this is Mohawk territory, and that very large fines will be imposed on anyone stopping by.

East of Kahnawake are the Honore-Mercier Bridge and two Canadian Pacific Railroad (C.P.R.) lift bridges. Cote-Ste-Catherine Lock is also coming up at **Mile SW-10.0 (NM).** The Boulanger Yacht Company is in two cuts west of the lock and east of the canalside industrial facility. The marina/yard has floating docks and a Travelift for deep-draft vessels.

When you make your required land line call-in at Cote-Ste-Catherine Lock's floating pleasure-craft dock, you receive a recorded message—first in French, then English. You are asked to leave your name and time of arrival and to await instructions by loudspeaker. These are normally given in French only. If you didn't understand, get underway and wait for a green light. If the command was not for you, the green light won't come on and lock personnel will make agitated hand signals.

La Prairie, **Mile SW-7.5 (NM),** was a New France pioneer town given to the Jesuits in 1667. It had a trading post but was primarily a farming community. By 1836 it was a prosperous town with railroad service connecting Montreal with southern Quebec and Saint-Jean on Riviere Richelieu.

Just upstream of the Champlain Bridge, **Mile SW-4.5 (NM),** an ice control structure reaches from Ile des Soeurs to the Seaway embankment. St-Lambert Lock, **Mile SW-2.8 (NM),** is the last lock downbound on the Seaway. Though you are unaware of its presence in relation to navigation, the lock's lower pool is head of tidewater. Tidal flow is insignificant and only begins to affect distance-run when you approach Trois-Rivieres, about 35 miles downstream of Sorel. That area is not covered in this guide.

As you exit St-Lambert lock downbound, St-Lambert is east and Ile Notre Dame is west. The latter, a 2-mile-long island, is manmade; most of its landfill came from the riverbed. The island constricted the river so badly it caused massive ice jams, which in turn caused flooding. The government had to build the Ice Control Structure in the upstream La Prairie Basin to control ice flow.

Montreal's Expo 67 was held on Ile Notre Dame and its 1.8-mile-long midriver neighbor, Ile Ste-Helene. The city removed many attractions when the World's Fair was over, but many remained or were added. Today Ile Notre Dame is home to the Palais de la Civilisation and the Gilles-Villeneuve track for Molson Grand Prix Formula One racing. An island favorite is Ile Notre Dame Floral Park. It is delimited by water—if your feet won't take long walks, rent a canoe or pedalo to cruise the gardens. Also in this water system is Regatta Lake, with a nautical center and sailing school. Olympic Basin's island canal system is a summer swimming and rental-boat area; in winter it's an ice skating rink.

Ile Ste-Helene is more clearly visible once you are through the Jacques-Cartier Bridge—your last Seaway bridge—and clear of Ile Notre Dame's long northerly extending seawall on the channel's western side. At Ile Ste-Helene's northern end is Nautique de la Ronde—old Port Ste-Helene. Once this was the gala yacht harbor at Expo; shoaling now restricts all but runabouts.

Today Ile Ste-Helene is a multifunctional park and La Ronde is an immense amusement park with rides, shops, musical shows, a children's enchanted village, a water slide, and the Aquarium de Montreal. There are also boutiques, restaurants, heated baths, pool, and terraces for sunbathing.

The Duke of Wellington ordered Fort Ile Ste-Helene built on the island in 1822; it served as an arsenal for 100 years. Today it's a place to witness reenactments and maneuvers of troops once stationed in Montreal.

Montreal, **Mile SW-0.0 (NM),** is squeezed between the river and Mont-Royal, an extinct volcano 1.7 miles inland. Monsieur Paul de Chomedy, Sieur de Maisonneuve, carried a wooden cross to the mountaintop in 1643 to thank God for sparing Ville-Marie from a Christmas Day river flood. The original cross was replaced in 1924 by the one you see today. It is 100 feet high, illuminated by 240 lights, and visible for nearly 50 miles.

The Iroquois continually threatened Ville-Marie; they disliked French interference in their fur trade and their alliance with the Algonquins and Hurons. For protection the French built fortifications and a citadel defended by cannons. By 1701 the Iroquois had signed a peace treaty, so for over 100 years the fur trade went on without interruption. Ville-Marie was renamed Montreal and became the most wealthy commercial center in New France.

Things to Do and See in Montreal

The city celebrated its 300th birthday in 1992 and retains its reputation as the best combination of old and new in Canada. Wander through Old Montreal, enjoy fine dining downtown, explore the neon intrigue of the Underground, picnic on Montreal Island—everywhere you go, you'll enjoy the confluence of English and French traditions.

Old Montreal

Chateau Ramezay, 280 Notre Dame Street. This mansion, which belonged to one of the early governors of Montreal, has displays of 18th-century furniture, costumes, and painting. It's open year-round Tuesday through Sunday from 10 to 4:30, and on Monday from June to Labor Day. Admission is $3 for adults and $2 for children.

Notre Dame Basilica, 116 Notre Dame Street West. Features neo-gothic architecture, three rose ceiling windows, the 12-ton bell "Gros Bourdon," and the bronze-paneled Chapel of the Sacred Heart. It's open year-round from 7 to 6, and June to September from 7 to 8. The adjoining museum of church history is open weekends from 9:30 to 4.

Place d'Armes, Notre Dame Street (just north of the Basilica). Here Monsieur de Maisonneuve fought the Iroquois; a statue marks the event. The Seminary du St-Sulpice, the oldest building in Montreal, is also here. The wooden clock inside is the oldest in North America.

Ile Sainte-Helene

La Ronde. This amusement park, open daily from May 29 until September 2, has rides (including the highest dual-track roller coaster in the world), musical reviews, international shows and circus, and restaurants. An adult day pass is $17.25; children under 12, $8. A family pass is $38.50. The Aqua Parc de la Ronde, with 21 water slides, is open June through August from 10 A.M. until early evening. Admission is $15 for adults and $8 for children.

McCord Museum of Canadian History, 690 Sherbrooke Street West. The history of Canada from the 1700s to the present, including prints, paintings, photographs, and costumes. Open daily 10 to 6 from May 15 to September 15; off-season hours are 11 to 4:30, Tuesday to Sunday. Admission is $2 for adults and $.50 for children under 12.

Montreal Botanical Gardens, 4101 Sherbrooke Street East. More than 25,000 varieties of plant species, including orchids, bonsai, and heath gardens. The gardens are open from 8 A.M. to sundown, and the greenhouses are open from 9 to 6. From May 15 to October 15 there is a $6 admission fee for adults.

The Old Fort. The oldest fortification in Montreal. The David M. Stewart Museum contains a collection of firearms, navigational instruments, exhibits on frontier life, and maps of the colonial period; it's open daily from 10 to 5, except Tuesday. From late June to Labor Day mock regiments perform military maneuvers Wednesday to Sunday at 11, 2:30, and 5.

In 1760 Montreal's population was all French; by 1830 the number of French and English residents was nearly equal. The old town outgrew its walled compound; population spread to St-Laurent, Les Recollets, and St-Louis. From 1844 until the decade's end Montreal was the capital of Canada. Today it is Quebec's largest city and has more French-speaking inhabitants than any city except Paris. In 1977 the official provincial language became French, and its use in the workplace and in schools was made compulsory for all residents regardless of their background.

The Upper St. Lawrence River
Montreal to Sorel

The Upper St. Lawrence River below the Seaway has another official mile-numbering system—one of many. This one begins downstream at Quebec, **Mile SLR-0.0 (NM).** Mileage works upstream to the Seaway; downbound your Upper River starting point is **Mile SLR-136.3 (NM)/Mile SW-0.0 (NM).** Ship channel navigation aids carry the prefix "M" as far as Sorel.

Though you may meet an occasional ship or see one alongside a shoreside terminal, nearly all river traffic to Sorel is an unusually large number of 26- to 32-foot pleasure powerboats. They travel day and night at top rpm, closely pass or overtake, and run through anchorages and directly alongside marinas. Most cast severe wakes and badly affect places to stop anywhere on this Upper River section. On summer weekends the wake problem becomes so severe it's dangerous.

The river to Sorel ranges from 1 to 2 miles in width; most of it is a maze of low islands riddled with small-craft secondary channels. Depth in some of these channels is less than 6 feet; some range from 9 to 30 feet. The ship channel has the most current, as it follows the natural river's deep water; secondary channels have only slightly less flow. In the past small craft drawing less than 9 feet were required to use one of these secondary channels; today more pleasure craft use the ship channel.

You cannot wander about the river in this area. If you decide to travel a secondary route, stick with it until it eventually rejoins the ship channel. Shoals, flats, marshlands, and rocky patches are everywhere. Deepwater exits on and off the secondary and ship channels exist, but they are often unwatched. The wide ship channel has much the same scenery as the secondary channels, is well watched, and offers more relaxed cruising.

Taking a watched major secondary channel to Sorel may be appealing. They include the Lanoraie-Ste-Therese and the Varennes-Ile Charron secondary channels. Current seldom flows fair with their narrow channels, and navigation aids are often up to a mile apart. If you choose one of these routes, be alert; a helmsman's lack of attention to set can lead to grounding—an unpleasant situation in strong current.

Begin your downbound journey to Sorel at the Seaway intersection in downtown Montreal. The Courant Ste-Marie—St. Mary's Current—flowing through the passage between Ile Ste-Helene and Montreal carries the bulk of the St. Lawrence River. Normal river stage current in this short passage averages 4 to 6 knots; it starts you off with gusto. Montreal's commercial waterfront along the western bank extends nearly to Pointe-aux-Trembles in East Montreal, **Mile SLR-130.0 (NM).** Longueuil, **Mile SLR-136.3 (NM),** and the river flats—a weedy area with spotty shoals—are on the river's eastern side.

About midway between **Light Buoy #177** and **Light Buoy #175** at **Mile SLR-134.25 (NM),** you have access to a small-craft secondary channel.

Varennes-Ile Charron Secondary Channel

This 8.5-mile-long secondary channel (chart C 1339) extends from Ile Charron's southern end to just north of Varennes. Navigation aids carry the prefix "MT". Mileage reads heading upstream and begins at **Light Buoy Varennes, Mile VARCHA-0.0 (NM).** The channel has a 32-foot overhead clearance restriction at the Highway #20 Bridge at its southern end and a few 5.5-foot shoals in its northern section. The major shoal is in the passage between the northern end of Ile Grosbois and the Iles de Varennes, **Mile VARCHA-2.5 (NM)** to **Mile VARCHA-3.2 (NM).** If bridge clearance and depth are no deterrent, this channel is another way to travel the river. It has a good terminus exit back into the ship channel.

Downbound on this secondary channel you pass Iles

de Boucherville's eastern side. These islands are a park with nature trails, hiking and bicycling paths, a picnic area, and a nature interpretation center. Cable ferries bring visitors from the mainland, and from island to island where there are no connecting bridges.

Boucherville, **Mile VARCHA-4.8 (NM),** is on the channel's eastern bank. Founded in 1668, it is one of Quebec's oldest towns. It has interesting architecture and historical sites, including the residence of Louis-Hippolyte LaFontaine, a former Canadian prime minister.

Near the channel's northern end is Varennes, **Mile VARCHA-0.5 (NM);** its twin church steeples are prominent on the eastern bank. It has a number of very old churches, chapels, and sanctuaries. There's a mooring area off shore; if you plan a visit, be very cautious of the few isolated shoals. There's a government wharf off downtown, though a 6-foot-draft vessel normally hasn't depth alongside; in any case, violent wake roll restricts all tie-ups to very brief intervals.

The Varennes-Ile Charron Secondary Channel intersects the ship channel about 0.7 mile upstream of Varennes at **Light Buoy Varennes, Mile SLR-126.4 (NM).**

There's a good chance that, when downbound at Montreal, you decided not to follow the Varennes-Ile Charron Secondary Channel and preferred the western bank's ship channel. At Longue Pointe, **Mile SLR-133.5 (NM),** you cross over the Louis-Hippolyte LaFontaine Tunnel. At Pointe-aux-Trembles, **Mile SLR-130.0 (NM),** Montreal's industry dwindles and you face a collection of islands.

West of Ile Ste-Therese is the Ile Lebel-Pointe aux Trembles Secondary Channel; it eventually intersects the Lanoraie-Ste-Therese Secondary Channel. The Lebel Island route is watched but not highly recommended due to its current—especially at the mouth of Riviere des Prairies and Riviere L'Assomption. Depths of 6 feet in that area are very difficult to find. If you want to visit Repentigny, which is farther north on the western bank, it's more relaxing to take the deeper, straightforward Lanoraie-Ste-Therese Secondary Channel. It's another 3 miles downstream on the ship channel.

If momentarily confused on the ship channel course at Pointe aux Trembles, follow the Ile aux Vaches Traverse. The Upper River's ship ranges are large fluorescent-orange daymarks—they're easy to see. The range is a crossover to the eastern shore between the Iles

de Varennes and Ile aux Vaches; the reach has about 2.2 knots current.

At **Light Buoy Varennes, Mile SLR-126.4 (NM),** you are at the Varennes-Ile Charron Secondary Channel's northern end; you also intersect the Lanoraie-Ste-Therese Secondary Channel.

Lanoraie-Ste-Therese Secondary Channel

This 19-mile-long secondary channel (charts C 1339 and C 1338) is on the river's western side. Its lower terminus is **Light Buoy Ile St-Ours, Mile SLR-107.5 (NM),** about 0.6 mile south of Lanoraie; its upper terminus is **Light Buoy M130, Mile SLR-126.3 (NM).** Navigation aids carry the prefix "MS".

Downbound this channel makes a 2-mile-long crossover to the western shore and comes in close to Repentigny at **Light Buoy Lebel.** This reach has buoys more than 0.5 mile apart, and there's a lot of current. Stay alert; it's easy to be set northeasterly out of the channel.

Light Buoy Lebel also marks the lower terminus of the Ile Lebel–Pointe aux Trembles Secondary Channel, whose upper terminus is upstream west of Ile Ste-Therese near downtown Montreal. When downbound to Lanoraie, **Light Buoy Lebel** is your point to bear northeasterly.

In the next 11 miles there are six ranges to help you hold the channel. They carry you west of the Iles de Vercheres. About midway in these islands you make a swing around Ile Ronde and bear easterly; across on the western bank is St-Sulpice. There's an uncomfortable and windswept anchorage here off the village church.

Another 6 miles upstream you pass east of Ile de Lavaltrie; Lavaltrie is on the western mainland bank. If you plan a visit, leave the secondary channel about midway between **Light Buoy MS25** and **Light Buoy MS21** and use a watched side channel that begins about 0.5 mile to Ile de Lavaltrie's south. Anchor off the government wharf in strong currents. If wind opposes the current, it's a very uncomfortable stop. Return to the Lanoraie-Ste-Therese Channel the same way you left it.

The channel's last 5 miles is well west of St-Ours Island; you return to the ship channel at **Light Buoy Ile St-Ours, Mile SLR-107.5 (NM).**

If you decided not to travel the Lanoraie-Ste-Therese Secondary Channel back south on the ship channel at **Light Buoy M130, Mile SLR-126.3 (NM), or Light Buoy Varennes, Mile SLR-126.4 (NM),** your route northbound on the ship channel is between Cap Ste-Michel and Ile Deslauriers. For the next 10 miles you favor the eastern bank.

Vercheres, **Mile SLR-119.7 (NM),** is where Madeleine de Vercheres fought off the Iroquois in 1692; her statue is in the waterfront park. There's a marina in Vercheres in a small enclosed basin—though drafts of 6 feet usually haven't depth in summer level. The basin's entrance is at its northeastern end, but before starting inside, look up and down the river to see if a ship is going to pass in the next few minutes. If one is close, wait until it's well past the entrance. There's a lot of current all the time—it can be a problem in itself as you try to clear the harbor's narrow opening. If a ship passes at the same time, it will be directly alongside the entrance, adding to the entry problem. Though the ship won't throw a wake, it will displace an immense amount of water inside the basin. When attempting to tie up during these surge conditions, you tend to end up on top of the dock, not alongside it. Due to this occasional surge problem, you may want to keep your stay brief—perhaps just long enough to buy fuel (gas and diesel), use the pumpout, take a stroll to see the church and Madeleine's statue, and visit the ice cream parlor and butcher shop. You can then leave and find a more comfortable anchorage on the western side of Ile aux Prunes.

At **Mile SLR-115.0 (NM)** the ship channel leaves the eastern shore and moves to midriver to clear the Iles de Contrecoeur's flats. After about 3.5 miles you swing back and pass to the east of Ile St-Ours. By the time you reach **Buoy Ile St-Ours, Mile SLR-107.5 (NM),** you are again in the middle of the 0.5-mile-wide river and nearly opposite Lanoraie.

Once past the four eastern red-and-white-striped stacks of Tracy's Hydro-Quebec power plant, **Mile SW-104.4 (NM)**, you approach Lac St-Pierre's upper end. The main lake is still another 13 miles downstream, but the lake's upstream island archipelago has more than 75 low islands of various sizes with a maze of interconnected channels. The ship channel makes a hard easterly bend at **Mile SLR-101.0 (NM)** to pass south of the islands.

Riviere Richelieu's mouth, **Mile SLR-99.7 (NM),** is on the southern shore; it's a major St. Lawrence River tributary whose source is Lake Champlain. St. Joseph de Sorel is west of Richelieu's Pointe aux Pins; Sorel is on the eastern side.

Sorel is Canada's fourth oldest city. Today it's one of the larger St. Lawrence River commercial ports. Chances are very good a few ships will be anchored off waiting their turn to load or unload at Sorel terminals. Granaries, foundries, and shipyards line the Richelieu's northern end for more than 0.5 mile.

Sorel, **Mile SLR-99.7 (NM),** is the terminus of our coverage of this regional section. If you plan to continue down the St. Lawrence River to Quebec, the province's capital, you have 100 miles to go. If you plan to exit the St. Lawrence River into the Atlantic Ocean via the Gulf of St. Lawrence, you must travel about 440 miles to Cap Gaspe.

Sorel is also the northern terminus of our next region (Region 6), which takes you south to the Atlantic Ocean in three steps via Riviere Richelieu and the Chambly Canal (see that section, beginning on page 330), Lake Champlain (beginning on page 350), and the Champlain Canal (beginning on page 398). Region 6 intersects Region 1, "The Hudson River," a way to the Atlantic Ocean at New York City.

Sketch Map Depths

Sketch map depths are given at normal average summer river level. When you venture outside the sketch map confines, you must adjust NOAA and Canadian charts to chart datum. For convenience in adjusting, use the following:

Mile SW-118.7 (NM) to **Mile SW-0.0 (NM)/Mile SLR-136.3** to **Mile SLR-99.7 (NM):** Plane of reference, St. Lawrence River Low Water Datum, 242.8 feet to 242.2 feet

St. Lawrence Seaway Anchorages
Morristown to Montreal

Mile SW-118.7 (NM) to Mile SW-0.0 (NM)

OGDENSBURG MUNICIPAL MARINA

★★★★

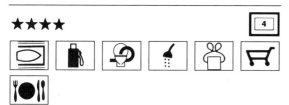

Chart: N 14764

Mile SW-109.3 + 0.7 S (NM)

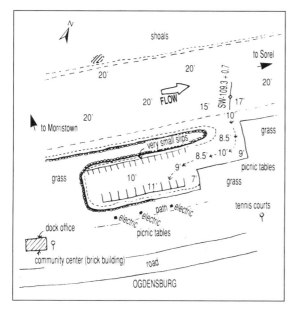

This southern-shore marina in Ogdensburg—opposite Prescott—is in an enclosed basin. A mile-wide shoal separates Ogdensburg's waterfront and the Oswegatchie River's mouth from the main channel. The shoal's southeastern side has a wide, dredged, open-ended secondary channel for waterfront access for commercial shipping. The marina basin is off this channel.

Secondary channel approach is from the southwest or the northeast; downbound the closest entry is at the channel's southwestern end. Leave the ship channel just west of **Light Buoy #133** and bear southerly into the watched channel's southwestern entry. On the west is a breakwater on a mainland protrusion, Lighthouse Point, with the old Ogdensburg Lighthouse. Once you are about opposite the old light, bear northeasterly to the St. Lawrence waterfront. The marina is about 0.25 mile northeast of **Secondary Channel Buoy #5.** There is a marina sign, and over the low riverside mole you will see masts and flying flags. The entrance is at the mole's eastern end. This "old basin" is more convenient to town; there's a new addition downstream.

During entry favor the eastern bulkhead; inside, the basin opens clearly. Slips at 90 degrees to shore line the northern and southern basin sides. The short northern slips are for runabouts; the larger slips are south. There's also parallel parking along the bulkheaded portion at the northeastern end. Pull in to any space available—the bulkhead is usually open—then check in at the dock office. It's in the brick building set back on the grass at the basin's southeastern end. The land line number is (315) 393-1980. Ice is available at the dock office, but for pumpout facilities and fuel (gas and diesel) you must go to the new harbor addition farther northeast on the river. Electric hookups (110- and 220-volt) are available.

The marina is in the center of Greenbelt Park, which has wide lawns, picnic facilities, playgrounds, and lighted tennis courts. Before you start sightseeing, stop at the chamber of commerce in the park's community center and pick up walking-tour maps and brochures.

Downtown—only a few blocks away—has banks, a library, a post office, and many shops and stores. Two shopping malls, the Seaway and the Park Plaza, are about 1.2 miles south on Highway 37 and include two supermarkets. Taxis and rental cars are available.

The Historical Downtown Battlefield Walking Tour starts at City Hall at Ford and Caroline streets, but you can join it at Greenbelt Park. Historical plaques dot an

8- to 10-block area and tell you about Ogdensburg's early relationship with Canada.

The Frederic Remington Art Museum, about a block from the marina at Washington and State streets, is a memorial to the work and life of the famous artist whose subject matter was the American West. It has the finest single collection of his paintings, bronzes, and sketches. Hours are Monday through Saturday from 10 to 5 and Sunday from 1 to 5.

The last week in July is Ogdensburg's International Festival. It's Seaway-oriented, and much of it is held in Greenbelt Park. There are fishing derbies, canoe races, concerts, amusement rides, square dancing, arts and crafts, flea markets, live entertainment, barbecues, and fireworks.

PRESCOTT HARBOUR

★★★★★

Chart: N 14764

Mile SW-109.3 + 0.3 (NM)

Enclosed Prescott Harbour is opposite Ogdensburg; a downbound landmark just upstream of the harbor is the Coast Guard's beached buoys, docked cutters, and helicopters. The harbor has two high stone breakwaters;

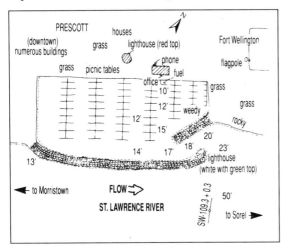

the longest roughly parallels shore and extends from the harbor's western end. A short inner breakwater extends from the harbor's eastern end, slightly overlaps the outer breakwater, and gives protection from east-north-east wind and waves. The entrance is watched by a green-topped white octagonal light tower on the river-side breakwater's eastern end.

You enter upcurrent; once inside you are current free. The entrance is very narrow. If your boat is of fair size, come in slowly. If a large boat is exiting, you may not have room to pass. Harbor weed growth is severe.

The marina has six piers of slips at 90 degrees to the bank. If no one answered on VHF 68, head for the office. It's white with a black roof and is east of a robust red-topped lighthouse up on the beach. The land line number is (613) 925-1255. The fuel dock in front of the office parallels shore. Gas and diesel are available.

Slips are rented with or without electric hookup (110-volt), so let the dockmaster know which you prefer. The marina grounds are a beautifully landscaped town promenade.

Downtown Prescott centers on tree-lined King Street, a few blocks from the harbor; it has preserved and restored heritage buildings that house modern shops. It has received Heritage Canada's Main Street Canada award. There are banks, a hardware store, pharmacies, a post office, a library, a variety of shops, and two factory outlet stores—Hathaway Shirts and Portolano Outlet Centre. The supermarket is about 0.5 mile away, but there's a convenience store within a block. The marina won't let you go hungry. If you need to stock up, they can normally find you transportation, or you can always call a cab.

Just east of Fort Wellington is 18-hole Prescott Golf Club. It has a pro shop, rental clubs, and carts. Green fees are slightly lower during the week.

Town tennis courts, at the bottom of Sophia Street, are open until midnight. Get the gate key from Becker's, at George and Kings streets. There's a modest fee.

If out sightseeing, you might enjoy Prescott's Heritage Walking Tour. Pick up a guide at the office.

A block from the harbor, at Water and Centre streets, is the Forwarders' Museum. It's open from 10 to 4:30 and recounts Prescott's role as a trade and transportation site from 1700 to 1850.

The Stockade Barracks and Hospital Museum is at 356 East Street—two blocks from the marina. The two-story cut-stone building is the oldest surviving military building in Ontario. Built in 1810, it served as a military barracks during the War of 1812 and later as a hospital for Fort Wellington. It's open from 10 to 5.

Fort Wellington National Historic Park is just east of the harbor up the hill. The park has fully restored the fort to the 1840s period, when it was garrisoned by the Royal Canadian Rifle Unit. There are interpretive programs with demonstrations by costumed staff. It's open from 10 to 6.

Prescott's Loyalist Days are from the second to the third weekend in July. Festivities include sidewalk sales, garden parties, antique car shows, canoe and rubber-duckie races, midways, talent nights, live entertainment, barbecues, and much more. The festival is climaxed by the Fort Wellington Military Pageant—an immense production. Historical reenactors dressed in authentically reproduced uniforms of the Revolutionary War years battle to control Fort Wellington.

COLES CREEK STATE PARK MARINA

★★★★   5

Chart: N 14762

Mile SW-87.3 + 2.1 (NM)

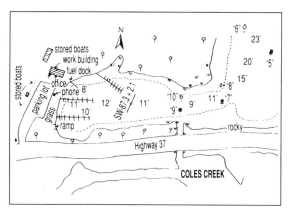

This southern-shore marina—open May 1 to November 1—is part of 1,800-acre Coles Creek State Park, developed during Seaway construction. It's in a long bight on Coles Creek's western side.

The river near Coles Creek is about 1.5 miles wide. Though there are ways to approach the marina with a shorter distance when downbound, the safest route—

and the one on which shoals are easiest to spot—is to leave the ship channel east of Goose Neck Island Shoals. In this approach you do not approach the creek coming downcurrent, though you will be broadside to river flow.

Leave the ship channel at **Light Buoy #74** and bear south-southwesterly. Your immediate destination is **Buoy #2,** about 1.3 miles away; the buoy is east of the most westerly Bradford Islands. It's to your advantage to pick up the buoy for a landmark before you leave the ship channel; current sets you downstream quickly. Since mile-long Goose Neck Island Shoals are only watched on the ship channel, this group's outlying southeastern shoals could be dangerous if you don't see the buoy and have allowed too much for current set. Don't end up aground on Goose Neck's shoals. The densely wooded Bradford Islands are obvious; you can judge their charted northwesterly shoals accurately. Use your fathometer; if depth drops below 20 feet you may be approaching bad water.

Buoy #2 is the first of the marina's entrance channel buoys, though the marina is still about a mile away. Depth remains good up to entrance **Buoy #5** and **Buoy #6.** At this point dense weed growth badly affects fathometer readings, so be cautious. Shoaling is gradual as you begin the westerly bend at the creek causeway into the marina bight. The unusually clear water is slightly disconcerting, as you can see bottom, but least depths are usually at the narrowest section once you make your westerly turn.

Once clear of the narrow section at **Buoys #9** and **#10** the marina opens fully. There are three major piers with slips at the cove's western end. Pull in to the fuel dock (gas only); it's a short single pier with parallel parking by the large work buildings at the end of the ramp.

A ship's store in the main building has a selection of marine supplies, charts, nautical gifts, fishing supplies, snacks, basic groceries, and picnic supplies. The marina also rents 14-foot boats with 9.9-hp outboards. Electric hookups (110- and 220-volt) and a Travelift are available. If you need a diver, check at the office. Call (800) 244-3486 for marina information.

CRYSLER PARK MARINA

★★★★★

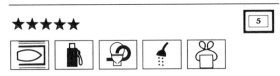

Chart: N 14762

Mile SW-86.4 + 0.5 N (NM)

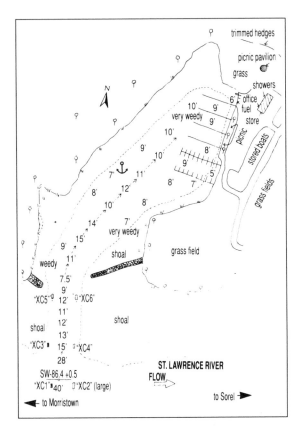

This northern-shore marina is in a long bight protected by two breakwaters. It has a watched entrance channel.

Leave the ship channel at **Light Buoy #72.** Three sets of tall spar buoys lead you to the rock breakwaters. The longest jetty extends westerly from the eastern entrance point; the shorter extends easterly from the western point. Once you clear these breakwaters, the marina is at the bight's northeastern end. This section has a watched channel, but its buoys are smaller.

The marina has six piers extending from the mainland. The southerly two have fingers; the next four have parallel parking. If no one answered on VHF 68, pull in to the fuel dock (gas and diesel). It's at the complex's

northeastern end along the bulkhead about in front of the office, which is easy to see. You must round the northernmost pier's end, then bear easterly to the bulkhead south of the ramp. Favor the pier as you come in; it's weedy next to the northern shore.

If all slips are taken or if you prefer, anchor off the western shoreline southwest of the piers. Bottom is mud and weeds. Make arrangements with the marina to tie the skiff.

Block and cube ice and 110-volt electric hookups are available. A fee is charged for shower use. At the office is a very small store that sells snacks, gifts, basic foods, and local charts. The land line number is (613) 543-3254.

The marina complex is in a large area of trees and grassy fields where Canada geese come to graze. Also on the grounds is a locomotive, a popular attraction for youngsters.

The 18-hole Upper Canada Golf Course is open to the public. It has a dining lounge, pro shop, driving range, and club and cart rentals.

This is a convenient stop for a visit to Upper Canada Village, about 0.5 mile west on the main highway. The village is a reconstructed pioneer settlement that includes a village store with Victorian games and handcrafted gifts, a working blacksmith's shop, quilting demonstrations, a flour mill, a sawmill, a wool factory, a cheese factory, two churches, working farms, a tavern, restaurants, a bakery, a doctor's office, and a one-room schoolhouse. Special activities include a horse-drawn bateau for a riverfront canal cruise, the arrival of a stagecoach, town meetings, Temperance Society demonstrations, and special Victoria Day celebrations. The village is open from 9:30 to 6. The marina can furnish transportation.

BARNHART ISLAND MARINA

★★★

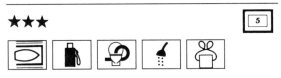

Chart: N 14761, *See sketch map, page 321*

Mile SW-78.0 + 3.7 (NM)

This very pretty but isolated upper-pool enclosed-basin marina is on Barnhart Island's northwestern side. Here you are out of the main river flow; this is important, as

---

Barnhart Island Marina

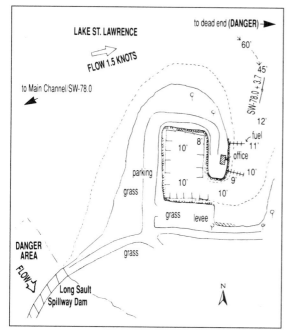

on the island's western end is Long Sault Spillway and on its eastern end is the Moses-Saunders Power Dam. As you might expect, this is an area of strong currents dependent on power generation and river stage.

Barnhart Island is east of the Croil Islands and the Long Sault Islands chain. Departure from the ship channel is possible at a number of places; preferred exit is at **Mile SW-78.0 (NM)** about midway between **Light Tower #46** and **Light Tower #44**. There's a wide deep-water channel alongside the eastern side of the chain of Long Sault Islands. This channel leads for 1.4 mile to the southern side of Long Sault Island; not all charts name this island. During this approach best water is along the Long Sault Islands. East of the channel are very dangerous unwatched rocks and shoals. Keep alert; strong current will set you in the direction of these shoals.

After 1.4 miles you face Long Sault Island at about a quarter of its distance from its western end. Bear west-northwesterly and round the western end of Long Sault Island. At this point you are midway between Macdonell Island and Long Sault Island, and you must begin a slow easterly bend around Long Sault Island back to Barnhart Island's northern shore. This may seem a roundabout route to reach Barnhart Island, but by using it you keep well away from the Long Sault Spillway Dam. If this dam is running, current is very severe.

As you approach Long Sault Island's eastern end,

there's a red spar off to your northeast; it watches a long shoal that extends well west of Sheek Island. Keep south of the spar and head toward the point extending north off Barnhart Island's western end. This point forms the marina basin's western side; it's about 0.2 mile northeast of Long Sault Spillway Dam's northeastern end. There's some shoaling off the northern end of this point, so don't come too close. Once the southerly channel opens east of the point, you can see two easterly extending piers. The northernmost pier's eastern end is the fuel dock (gas only). Pull in and check in at the office, about midway between the two outer docks. The main basin is on the south around the office mole's end.

Electric hookups (110-volt and 220-volt) are available. The marina's land line number is (800) 244-3486.

The Seaway Minimart is in the office building. It has a very small selection of drinks, snacks, and picnic supplies. They also sell fishing licenses and rent 14-foot boats and 9.9-hp outboards. Massena is the nearest supply point; taxi fare runs about $20 one way.

You are in the middle of 2,322-acre Robert Moses State Park. It has campsites and rental cabins. About 2.5 miles west of the marina is the Moses-Saunders Power Dam's visitor center. Across the Robinson Beach Bridge on the main lock island to your south—about 1.2 miles away—is the park's nature center.

COTEAU-LANDING

★★★★   [4]

Chart: C 1412, *See sketch map, page 322*

Mile SW-44.0 + 2.3 N (NM)

This Lac St-Francois stop is at the old Soulanges Canal's western end. It is at the lake's northeastern end on the northern shore. The canal is closed to through navigation; your destination is in its entrance.

Leave the ship channel at **Mile SW-44.0 (NM)**— about midway between **Light Buoy D9** and **Light Buoy D8.** This puts you in a charted ship anchorage area outlined by lighted yellow buoys. Bear 2 miles northeasterly to the Soulanges Canal's Upper Entrance Lighthouse, a green-topped white tower. It sits on a detached 500-foot-

Coteau-Landing

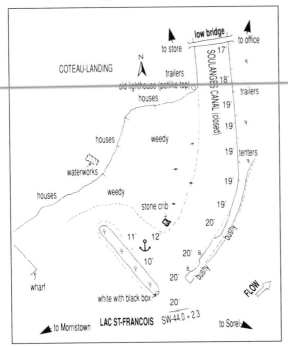

long breakwater's southeastern end. The breakwater is overgrown with trees; at a distance it looks like an island. There's one enroute buoy, **Spar DA1,** about 1.2 miles from the Seaway exit. Very visible during your approach are three bridges across the river. Their spans jump from Ile aux Chats to Ile Longueuil to Ile Giroux to the western river mainland. Avoid that area; current increases dramatically down there, as this is the head of old river rapids.

As you close the offshore breakwater's light tower, keep it to your west and make a northeasterly swing around the long manmade Soulanges Canal approach dike's southwestern end. There's a crib off northwest as you make this swing; it's in shoal water, so favor the breakwater. There may be one or two rusting spar buoys along the breakwater left over when buoyage reversed. Continue to follow the eastern breakwater northeast. West of the channel is a mooring area, and just ahead is another large old Soulanges Canal lighthouse—it's white with a blue potlike top. The light is on the southern end of the old canal's western approach wall.

At the point where the eastern wall makes a slight northerly jog, the canal opens fully. A low-level footbridge and then a highway bridge over the canal's old upper lock are just ahead. Once you make the jog northerly, the easterly wall becomes solid stone; paral-

lel park anywhere. Best protection is on the canal's western side, though this is usually filled with runabouts.

This is a government dock. A fee is charged if you stay the night; the manager of the camping and trailer park alongside the canal appears in his pickup truck late in the afternoon to collect. If you want 110-volt hookup and access to drinking water, choose a wall space—either canal side—close to the bridge. Facilities are in the trailer park.

This is a popular overnight stop; if all space is taken, anchor on the offshore breakwater's northeastern side. Choose a place near the middle of the breakwater to be out of the traffic flow. Bottom is mud and weeds. Less desireable anchorage in heavy weed growth is just east of the mooring area. There is less room to keep clear of the channel fairway here, and it's very busy, though the canal dead-ends at the bridge.

You can have a look at the Soulanges Canal lock chamber from the highway bridge that crosses its upstream end.

On the main highway you'll find a miniature golf course, a café, and a grocery store. If docked on the canal's eastern side, cross the footbridge and then trek through the campground to the main entrance. At the intersection is the miniature golf course and the café. For the market bear southwesterly about four blocks; it's on the street's western side. Try their fresh raisin and French breads. If you don't speak French, take your pocket dictionary—English is a foreign language here.

ROYAL ST. LAWRENCE YACHT CLUB

★★★★

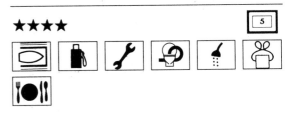

Chart: C 1410, *See sketch map, page 323*

Mile SW-19.0 + 3.7 (NM)

This primarily English-speaking yacht club in Dorval welcomes visitors. It's on the northern shore of Lac St-Louis. If you are in a sailing vessel and are bound to and

Royal St. Lawrence Yacht Club

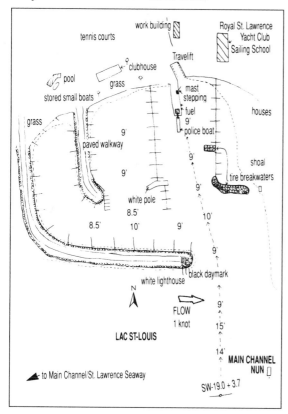

Once inside the entrance, there's a protective floating tire breakwater off the most easterly harbor pier. The rest of the harbor has piers and slips of assorted lengths and shapes running at various angles. Your destination is the fuel dock (gas and diesel) on a long southerly extending fixed/floating pier at the Travelift well and mast-stepping crane along the northern bank. The dockmaster is on duty in the office on the pier's fixed portion.

The main clubhouse is west of the Travelift well. Farther west is the swimming pool complex; behind both are tennis courts. The two-story building east of the Travelift is for the junior members. Ask the steward about the club's restaurant hours; the bar is usually open during the day. Call (514) 631-2720 for more marina information.

Electric hookups (110-volt/30-amp) are available.

Downtown Dorval, a very long but pleasant walk away, has all city conveniences, as well as a large supermarket. Taxi service is available. If the club has space for a few days, this is a chance to take public transportation into downtown Montreal—though access to the city is much more convenient from Longueuil, **Mile SW-0.0 (NM).** If you have guests arriving by plane or need a rental car, they are available at the Montreal International Airport, Dorval. This is extremely handy; the airport is in Dorval's immediate outskirts.

from low-bridge country, the club has a recommended mast-stepping facility.

The northern shore of Lac St-Louis is approached by a collection of watched secondary channels. Its main access point on the ship channel is at **Mile SW-19.0 (NM)** at **Light Buoy Lachine A.** These channels are discussed in the main text; follow the directions on page 311 to **Light Buoy AD12.** Here make a hard easterly turn into another watched secondary channel whose navigation aids bear the prefix "AS". Carry the "AS" channel for a mile to **Spar AS8.** Along the way you will pass **Cardinal Buoy Dorval** (yellow-black-yellow).

At **Spar AS8** round up north-northeast and bear for the white tower and black daymark on the Royal St. Lawrence Yacht Club's high stone breakwater's eastern end. Over the top you'll see a large collection of masts. There's very shoal water off the shoreline north of Point Marion, so mind current drift in that direction. The shoal is watched by club buoys.

Approach the breakwater slowly; this is the point where you usually confront a large flock of sailing dinghies, the club's junior-member fleet.

Upper St. Lawrence River Anchorages
Montreal to Sorel

PORT DE PLAISANCE

★★★★★

ALL FACILITIES

Chart: C 1340

Mile SLR-136.1 + 0.3 E (NM)

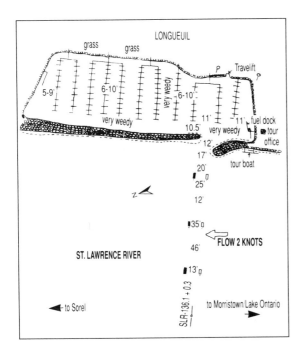

This marina is in Longueuil, across the river from downtown Montreal, in an enclosed basin free of the river's severe current. It's a safe place to leave the boat while you tour nearby attractions. There's a Metro station in Longueuil, so you have fast access to Montreal via the tunnel.

Strong river current is something with which you must cope anywhere immediately downstream of the Seaway's St-Lambert Lock and Ile Ste-Helene. It begins to subside farther downstream, but in this particular area you must constantly be aware of its velocity.

Port de Plaisance's stone breakwater is very visible on the eastern shore once you reach **Mile SLR-136.1 (NM)**. The marina has its own watched channel; it's impossible to miss, though its buoys are on a smaller scale than those of the ship channel. It's a very narrow but straightforward channel that leads directly to the basin entrance. You make this 0.3-mile entry stretch broadside to a minimum 2-knot current—it's usually much more.

Wait until the channel opens clearly before you leave the ship channel. Once you start, it's extremely important not to let the strong current set you out of the channel into shoal water. Compensate for your drift. Your fathometer may become erratic when you closely approach shore; this is an area of heavy weed growth.

As you approach the breakwater you can see a riverfront dock just west of the short western breakwater—it's for the local tour boat. Enter the basin; it has a narrow opening, so if you have deep draft stay in the middle. Once inside, you are out of the current.

The marina stands by on VHF 68, though if you don't speak French you might have a problem with this. If confused, pull in to the fuel dock in the basin's southwestern corner; you can see the dock office and fuel pumps (gas and diesel). Weed growth inside the basin is very heavy, so fathometers are almost useless; at the fuel dock depth is 9 to 11 feet. If you need a diver, check at the office.

Electric hookups (110-volt) are available. For more marina information, call (514) 442-9575.

The marina area is a prominent part of a large park complex that parallels the Boulevard Marie-Victorin. The Promenade René-Levesque is a mile-long landscaped walkway and bicycle path along the riverfront. At the marina's northern end is a large cabaret.

Longueuil is across the freeway. To get there you must cross Autoroute #20; use the pedestrian and bicycle bridges. If bound for a tour of Vieux Longueuil (Old Longueuil), use the bridge about midbasin.

Once across the highway you can bear about two blocks toward the very prominent St-Antoine-de-Padoue Cathedral steeple. It's on the corner of St-Charles Street and Chemin de Chambly and is the largest diocese church. At 205 Chemin de Chambly is the Maison Rollin-Brais, once a blacksmith shop and then a country inn; it's now the tourist bureau. If you do not speak French, there is usually someone there who speaks English and will help with directions. They can also supply you with the Metro schedule and instructions for a visit to Montreal.

Longueuil's St-Charles Street has preserved its past with picturesque cobbled sidewalks and quaint lampposts. It has interesting shops, boutiques, and restaurants. At 300 St-Charles Street West is City Hall, once a public marketplace. Next to it is St-Marc Church, an interesting example of the Quebec Neo-Roman style of architecture.

The Longueuil Metro station is about a mile from the marina, so you may want to taxi that far and save your feet for city touring. The Metro system is a treat in itself. It has more than 65 stations on four color-coded interconnecting lines that cover about 40 miles. It's integrated with Montreal's Underground City complex. The Underground has hotels, department stores, nearly 1,500 shops and stores, 150 restaurants, banks, theaters, and exhibition centers.

ILE AUX PRUNES ANCHORAGE

★★★★

NO FACILITIES

Chart: C 1339

Mile SLR-119.4 + 0.6 W (NM)

This anchorage is off the ship channel on the northwestern shore of 0.65-mile-long Ile aux Prunes. This wooded low-lying island is on the ship channel's northwestern side about midway along the southeastern shore of the Iles de Verchères.

Though it's always preferable to make an upstream anchorage approach in current, the downstream—north-

Ile aux Prunes Anchorage

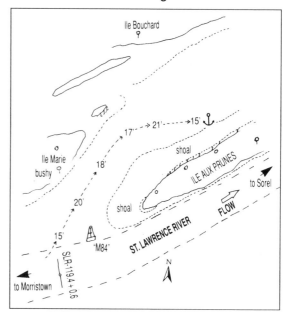

western—end of Ile aux Prunes has some unwatched off-lying shoals that are very difficult to locate. There are much better landmarks and depths when you approach at the island's upstream end, but keep in mind that you are entering with over a knot of current.

Leave the ship channel just west-southwest of **Light Buoy M84,** about 0.5 mile upstream of Ile aux Prunes. During your approach favor Ile Marie's southeastern shore to clear the shoals off Ile aux Prunes west-southwestern end. Once you are about opposite the St-Pierre Channel—it separates Ile Marie from Ile Bouchard—hold about midway between Ile Bouchard and Ile aux Prunes. Though you can anchor just about anywhere in this back channel, you are slightly out of the pleasure craft traffic's wake area if you huddle close to Ile Aux Prunes at about mid-island. This puts you just upstream of the range marker on Ile Bouchard. You won't be able to get too close to Ile aux Prunes; its western shoreline is an old spoil bank. Bottom is mud and weeds, and you swing with the current.

Except for wake roll this is a quiet stop. Most pleasure craft traffic is bound full-throttle for the bathing beach on Ile Bouchard, just downstream in the lee of Ile aux Boeufs. Much—though by no means all—of the traffic subsides at sundown.

We saw no signs indicating that Ile aux Prunes is a private island. Some boaters anchored alongside us did dinghy ashore for a walk in the trees with the family dog.

SOREL

Chart: C 1338

Mile SLR-99.7 (NM)

There are two main marinas in Sorel. Both are on the St. Lawrence River in enclosed basins. Parc Nautique de Sorel has the best depth, the most slips, and the most ambience, but it is a very long walk from downtown. Parc Nautique Federal has less depth and fewer slips, but it has a gin pole for mast stepping and is within easy walking distance of town. Bear in mind that depths are not affected by tidal exchange but by river stage, which can vary up to 10 feet.

Riviere Richelieu's mouth on the St. Lawrence River's southern shore marks the end of this guide section's mileage system at **Mile SLR-99.7 (NM).** To reach either marina you must continue on the St. Lawrence River east of the Richelieu's mouth for about 0.6 mile in order to access the upstream end of the marinas' 0.5-mile-long secondary channel. You must do this to find your way through the extensive and shifting shoals offshore of both marinas. Do not mistake the commercial basin just east of the granaries for the pleasure-craft harbors.

Since the secondary channel has only about a knot of current, you can make it a downstream passage. If you are bound for the Parc Nautique Federal basin, half of the secondary channel distance is going to be upstream. If you prefer to make your entry heading upstream to both marinas on the secondary channel, then you must continue downstream on the St. Lawrence ship channel at least a mile east of the Richelieu's mouth to access the secondary channel's eastern end.

For a downstream approach do not leave the St. Lawrence ship channel until you have the two secondary channel's upstream entrance buoys, **Buoy SN28** and **Buoy SN27,** in sight. From these two buoys proceed southeasterly to green-red-green **Junction Buoy PNF** and **Light Buoy SN26.** If bound for the Parc Nautique Federal Basin, this is your departure point to head back west to this basin entrance. If bound for Parc Nautique de Sorel, you must continue on easterly to **Light Buoy SN24.** For the remaining entry instructions see the individual anchorage directions.

Downtown Sorel is about a block from Riviere Richelieu, more than a mile from Parc Nautique de Sorel, and about 0.5 mile from Parc Nautique Federal. The city center is about three blocks south of the gra-

naries at the Richelieu's mouth. Another landmark when walking to town are the twin spires of one of the two downtown churches. They face the Carre Royal, a landscaped park that dates to the 18th century. Its floral display announces "Bienvenue a Sorel."

All city conveniences are available downtown. At Elizabeth and Augustus streets—about a block from the ferry dock to St-Ignace-de-Loyola—is a large supermarket.

At 90 Chemin des Patriotes is the Maison des Gouverneurs, where the first illuminated Christmas tree in North America was erected.

Parc Nautique Federal

★★★★

ALL FACILITIES

Chart: C 1338 or C 1350 Sheet 1

Mile SLR-99.3 + 0.5 (NM)

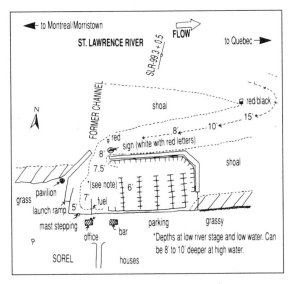

This marina is nearest town, and if yours is a sailing vessel stepping a mast, this is the facility you need. Depth is slightly less here than at Parc Nautique de Sorel, which is farther downstream.

Once you have entered the secondary channel and reached **Light Buoy SN26,** make a wide swing around **Junction Buoy PNF**—green-red-green—and pass to its southeast. After you make your swing back west around **Junction Buoy PNF,** head for a pair of spar buoys—**Buoy SF6** and **Buoy SF5**—at the basin's entrance. Water normally is good this far, but be cautious—the offshore shoals seem to shift continually. There's a white sign with red lettering on the basin's eastern bulkhead at its western end. The western bulkhead is fairly short and extends at an angle northeast. Depth inside the basin varies with river stage.

This marina may respond on VHF 68 to give you an update on depths, though usually it is the Parc Nautique de Sorel that replies. French is spoken; measurements are in metres. If in doubt, or if no one answers your call, come straight in the basin to the southern bulkhead and tie up at the fuel dock in front of the white one-story office building; you can see the pumps (gas and diesel). If no one is on dock duty, check in at the office.

Most slips are off individual piers extending from the bank; the rest are along the main bulkhead breakwater. If you have a draft more than 6 feet and it's low water stage, specify one with sufficient depth in meters. If you need to use the mast-stepping crane, it's west of the fuel dock. To use the crane you need to lie against the bulkhead; at most summer-level river stages depth here is usually very risky for any draft more than 4.5 feet.

Electric hookups (110-volt) are available. If you need repairs, check at the office. The land line number is (514) 743-2454.

Just east of the office is a bar and café. To walk to town, go out the marina access road and bear southwesterly.

Parc Nautique de Sorel

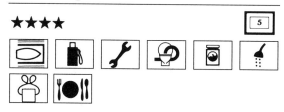

★★★★

Chart: C 1338 or C 1350 Sheet 1

Mile SLR-99.3 + 0.5 (NM)

Access into this enclosed marina is also via the secondary channel. When you reach **Light Buoy #SN26** simply continue easterly. When about midway between **Spar #SN23** and **Light Buoy #SN24** you can see the marina's

Parc Nautique de Sorel

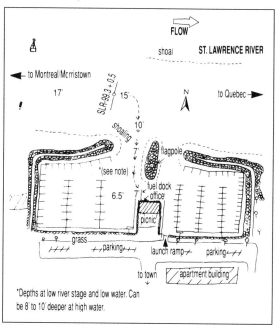

*Depths at low river stage and low water. Can be 8' to 10' deeper at high water.

rock breakwaters and its two-story brown marina buildings. The entrance is about midway in the northern breakwater. In the middle of the entrance opening there's a rock-faced island that separates entering and exiting traffic. If you draw 6 feet, you may have to use the western side for both due to eastern-side shoal water. Once south of the entrance island you are out of the current flow.

The marina stands by on VHF 68, though if you do not speak French you may have some trouble understanding their very lengthy directions. If in doubt, come in to the fuel dock, where you can more easily explain your needs. The fuel dock (gas and diesel) is south of the entrance island and extends north of the building bulkhead's western side. It has parallel parking and is very busy. The office is in the building overlooking the river. If you draw 6 feet and water stage is down, make certain the dockmaster and office attendant clearly know your depth before you start wandering about looking for your slip. Most of the marina has only about 6 feet at summer level.

Electric hookups (110-volt) are available. If you need repairs, check at the office. The land line number is (514) 742-9056.

The main building's lower level has a patio with tables, bar, phones, snacks, and a soda machine.

The marina is on the main road; take it west into town. If a mile seems too far to walk, you can always call a taxi.

Region 6
RIVIERE RICHELIEU, THE CHAMBLY CANAL,
LAKE CHAMPLAIN, AND THE CHAMPLAIN CANAL

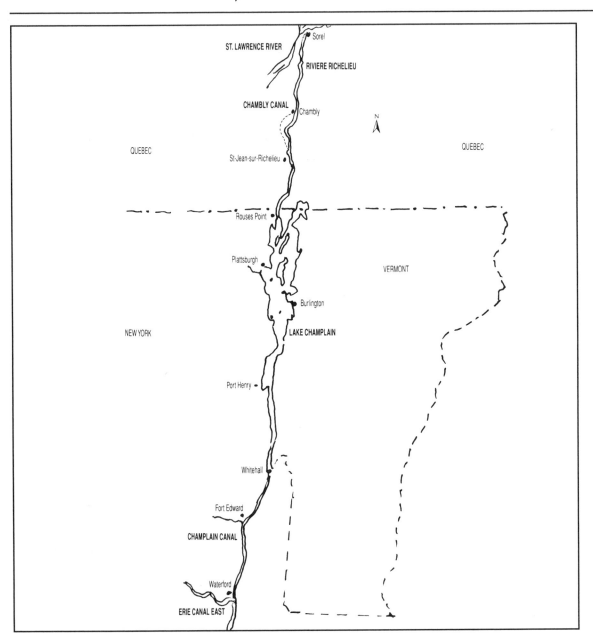

Mile RC-0.0 (NM) to Mile RC-69.3 (NM), Mile CH-0.0 (SM) to Mile CH-106.0 (SM), and Mile CC-0.0 (SM) to Mile CC-59.4 (SM)

CURRENT DIRECTION AND SPEED

Place	Flow Direction	Speed in mph*
Riviere Richelieu	North	About 0.25
Chambly Canal	North	Minimal
Lake Champlain	North/Wind tide	Minimal
Champlain Canal	North**	About 0.25
Champlain Canal	South***	About 0.25

*In normal river, lake, and canal stage

**Mile CC-0.0 (SM) to Mile CC-23.7 (SM)

***Mile CC-23.7 (SM) to Mile CC-69.3 (SM)

LOCKAGE, SOREL TO OLD ROUSES POINT (Riviere Richelieu and Chambly Canal)

Lock	Mile	Land Line	Lift*
Lock St-Ours	RC-12.12 (NM)	(514) 785-2212	4.9 feet
Lock CHM #1	RC-39.48 (NM)	(514) 658-6525	15.49 feet
Lock CHM #2	RC-39.50 (NM)	(514) 658-6525	9.75 feet
Lock CHM #3	RC-39.53 (NM)	(514) 658-6525	9.8 feet
Lock CHM #4	RC-40.0 (NM)	(514) 658-7221	7.25 feet
Lock CHM #5	RC-40.11 (NM)	(514) 658-1351	8.0 feet
Lock CHM #6	RC-40.18 (NM)	(514) 658-1451	8.25 feet
Lock CHM #7	RC-40.47 (NM)	(514) 658-1651	7.5 feet
Lock CHM #8	RC-40.76 (NM)	(514) 658-1801	9.0 feet
Lock CHM #9	RC-49.06 (NM)	(514) 348-3392	5.8 feet

*At normal river stage and canal pool level

For all locks:

During lockage you may not smoke or use external combustion devices. You must shut off your engine.

Bow and stern lines are furnished by each lock—usually they are handed to line handlers.

The lockmaster assigns rafting positions before a vessel enters the chamber; largest boats take the wall and handle lock lines.

At St-Ours, French or English may be spoken; at the Chambly Canal, usually French.

Transit fees are collected before lockage by the lockmaster.

Riviere Richelieu and the Chambly Canal
Sorel to Old Rouses Point

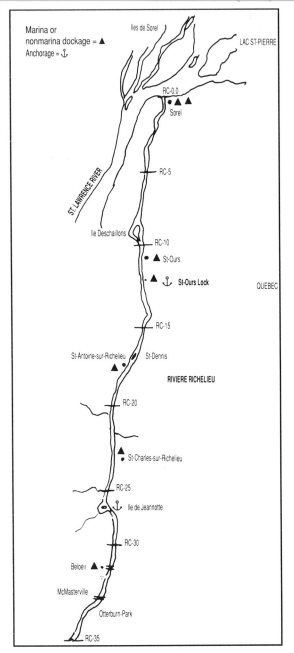

Mile RC-0.0 (NM) to Mile RC-35.0 (NM)

Mile RC-35.0 (NM) to Mile RC-69.3 (NM)

Today Riviere Richelieu and the Chambly Canal are almost entirely pleasure-boat systems, and they are easily transited. This was not always the case. Though the Richelieu has always been the first link in an age-old trading waterway between the St. Lawrence and Hudson rivers, early travelers and traders never found it an easy journey. It required at least four portages, and until 1814 Indians or Europeans battled for its control and made passage risky.

When the Americans completed the Champlain Canal in 1823, commercial traffic plied from the Hudson River to Lake Champlain and down the Richelieu as far as St-Jean. The Chambly Rapids stopped through-river traffic; for another 10 years cargoes and passengers continued to portage either to

Montreal or north to regain the Lower Richelieu.

Today you travel 70 miles upstream from Sorel to reach the Richelieu's source, Lake Champlain. The lake discharges an average of 2,992 gallons per second in normal river stage; river current is about 0.25 mph. The Chambly Canal is current free.

Navigation channel depth depends on the time of year. Charted depths are at Low Water Datum (LWD), which is normally below all water stages—though in very dry years channel depths have fallen below LWD. Highest water level, which is usually in May, averages about 4.5 feet above LWD. In June it's about 4 feet, in July about 2.3 feet, and in August and September about 1.5 feet—the lowest level.

There's an overhead clearance restriction; at normal

MOVABLE BRIDGES, RIVIERE RICHELIEU AND THE CHAMBLY CANAL

At normal river stage

Name	Type	Mile
Pont Turcotte	Bascule	RC-00.45 (NM)
Pont CN/CN RR	Swing	RC-00.64 (NM)
Beloeil/Mont-Ste-Hilarie	Swing	RC-31.48 (NM)
Pont de Beloeil	Swing	RC-32.50 (NM)
Pont #1*	Swing	RC-39.54 (NM)
Pont #2 CN/CN RR	Swing	RC-40.78 (NM)
Pont #3	Rolling	RC-40.78 (NM)
Pont #4	Swing	RC-41.23 (NM)
Pont #5	Swing**	RC-41.78 (NM)
Pont #7	Swing	RC-42.64 (NM)
Pont #9	Swing	RC-44.21 (NM)
Pont #10*	Swing	RC-46.62 (NM)
Pont CP/CP RR	Swing	RC-49.15 (NM)
Pont #12*	Draw	RC-49.39 (NM)
Pont CN/CN RR	Swing	RC-65.47 (NM)

*Closed Monday to Friday between 1145 and 1315
**Normally kept in open position.

Pleasure Craft Transit Fees

Fees for this Quebec system are per one day, six days, or the season. The fee is good for all locks—nine on the Chambly and one at St-Ours on the Richelieu. Cost depends on the size of the vessel; a goods-and-services tax is included. Permits are not transferable or refundable. There is also a mooring fee if you spend the night at the lock wall or alongside the canal.

The lockmaster collects lock fees before lockage. Government employees collect mooring fees in late afternoon.

VESSEL LENGTH	GENERAL FEE	SENIOR CITIZEN FEE
Fees may vary annually. If you speak French fluently, call lock CHM #1, (514) 658-6525, for up-to-date information.		
Lock Fee (C), Single Lockage		
5.5 meters or less	$5.25	$5.00
Over 5.5 meters to 8.0 meters	$10.75	$10.00
Over 8.0 meters to 12 meters	$16.00	$14.50
Over 12 meters	$21.50	$20.00
Lock Fee (C), One Day**		
5.5 meters or less	$7.00	$6.25
Over 5.5 meters to 8.0 meters	$13.00	$12.00
Over 8.0 meters to 12 meters	$19.00	$17.00
Over 12 meters	$26.00	$23.00
Lock Fee (C), Six Days**		
5.5 meters or less	$26.00	$23.00
Over 5.5 meters to 8.0 meters	$51.00	$46.00
Over 8.0 meters to 12 meters	$77.00	$69.00
Over 12 meters	$103.00	$93.00
Lock Season Permit**		
All vessels	$25.75 per meter	$23.00 per meter
Mooring Fee (C), Per Night		
No discount for senior citizens		
5.5 meters or less	$6.00	
Over 5.5 meters to 8.0 meters	$10.00	
Over 8.0 meters to 12 meters	$14.00	
Over 12 meters	$18.00	
Mooring Season Permit		
No discount for senior citizens		
All vessels	$17.00 per meter	

*Fees may vary annually.

**You may transit as many locks as you wish during this time period.

pool it's 29 feet. If your overhead clearance is close, monitor river stage fluctuations. There are 15 movable bridges with minimal closed clearance; they must open for all traffic.

Many river areas have posted speed limits, but they are rarely obeyed. Most river tributaries are shoal, and few river islands have depth in their lee. If good water exists at anchorage or dock, wake roll is destructive for visitors and residents and ruins an otherwise good stop. Your only respite from wake roll is in the Chambly Canal.

The river and the canal are clearly watched with numbered, lighted, and unlighted aids; upbound, red aids are to the west, green or black to the east. Follow the charted red sailing line; it has best depths. It's seldom in midriver. The one secondary channel in this regional section has a dashed red sailing line.

Official mileage begins at Pointe aux Pins, **Mile RC-0.0 (NM),** the Richelieu's western mouth at its junction with the St. Lawrence River. Each mile is charted with its number circled in red.

As you start upstream at Sorel, there's heavy industry on both banks. Ships and lakers go upriver as far as the CN/CN Railroad Bridge, **Mile RC-0.6 (NM);** most dock at eastern-shore terminals. If a ship is on the move, keep clear; it takes up the whole river.

South of the industrial outskirts of Sorel and Tracy, an area that includes three bridges, the river straightens and becomes about 0.1 mile wide. Behind a fringe of trees and waterfront homes along the shoreline's banks and low bluffs are miles of farmland—the Quebec lowlands. When you sight an impressive silver-roofed church with tall spires, it usually means a village is coming up.

The St-Onge Traverse, **Mile RC-8.3 W (NM),** is one of many Riviere Richelieu ranges. This one is intended to carry you safely east of large, low-lying Ile Deschaillons' northern shoals. It's a good idea to follow ranges; they show best depths. Unfortunately, the St-Onge Traverse markers are similar to most on the Richelieu; they are nearly impossible to find in overgrown vegetation.

Buoys take you through the island's southern shoals, then west of a marsh island at **Mile RC-10.0 (NM),** and finally to eastern-bank St-Ours and St-Roch-de-Richelieu on the west. Watch for the towns' active cross-river cable ferry.

St-Ours Lock, **Mile RC-12.1 (NM),** is on long, narrow Ile Darvard's eastern side. If the river is high and a number of dam sluice gates open, watch for a slight easterly set at the lock island's northern (downstream) end.

Looking north at St-Ours Lock on the Richelieu River.

St-Ours Canal Seasonal Hours of Operation

May 15 to May 31: open Tuesday and Wednesday, 0830 to 1600; closed Thursday to Monday

June 1 to June 18: closed June 2 and June 3 and Friday to Sunday. Other days: 0830 to 1600

June 19 to August 16: open daily 0830 to 2000

August 17 to September 13: Monday to Thursday, 0830 to 1600; Friday to Sunday, 0830 to 1800

September 14 to October 12: Thursday through Monday, open 0830 to 1600; closed Tuesday and Wednesday

---

Today's lock bypasses St-Ours shoals, the historical Lower Richelieu obstruction. Though river rock removal took place in 1758, it was 1849 before the government built the first St-Ours Dam, made of wooden cages filled with stone, and its 6.5-foot-deep cut-stone lock. The main upbound cargo at that time was St. Lawrence–region timber bound for America; downbound canalboats brought back coal, iron, and copper. In 1933 the government replaced the old lock and dam with the one you use today.

In St-Ours' upper pool, St-Ours Upper Traverse's downstream markers are on the lock's eastern side to help you pass the shoals about 0.5 mile upstream. The Laperle Range is next; it intersects the Laplante Range, which carries you as far as Laplante Creek. Its eastern-shore markers are amidst the waterfront homes at Quatre-Chemis.

At eastern-shore St-Denis, **Mile RC-17.0 (NM),** watch for the cross-river ferry to Domaine Lecours. The eastern ferry slip is down from twin-spired St-Denis church.

The channel is west of wooded Ile Larue and beside St-Antoine-sur-Richelieu, **Mile RC-17.7 W (NM),** and another twin-spired church. You can use the Marcotte Traverse to take you along the river's western shore to miss the charted shallow northern marsh flats; in reality it's an island with tall trees. The Marcotte Range intersects the Upper St-Antoine Travers; it takes you through the southern flats.

At **Mile RC-20.7 (NM)** watch for runabouts speeding full-throttle into the river from under the low-level cement bridge on the western bank's Ruisseau Coderre.

The channel bears east of midriver shoals off St-Charles, **Mile RC-23.2 E (NM);** watch for the village's active cross-river ferry.

Upcoming St-Marc-sur-Richelieu, **Mile RC-24.0 W**

(NM), is recognizable by its downtown church spire. Upstream of the village is Handfield Marina and restaurant; south of the marina in a blue-and-white converted ferry is the Theatre L'Escole.

At Ducharme Creek, **Mile RC-25.0 W (NM),** pick up the Ile aux Cerfs Range. This will carry you to the river bend and west of large, wooded Ile de Jeannotte and Ile aux Cerfs. Borchert Marina, **Mile RC-25.2 E (NM),** has fuel and overnight dockage; watch depths if your draft is more than 4 feet. A public wharf at **Mile RC-25.8 W (NM)** has better water, but wake roll makes it an unpleasant overnight stop. There's a slight current increase in the channel's narrow section as you round the two large islands.

As you pass under the fixed Highway 20 Bridge, **Mile RC-29.5 (NM),** isolated 1,300-foot Mont-St-Hilaire dominates the low-lying countryside. The Beloeil/Mont-St-Hilaire Swing Bridge, **Mile RC-31.4 (NM),** separates the two towns. South of the bridge in Beloeil a large marina parallel's shore.

Passage through the Pont Beloeil Bridge, **Mile RC-32.5 (NM),** is on the river's western bank at McMasterville at a hard westerly bend. Extremely narrow horizontal bridge clearance means one-way access for large vessels, and there is a significant current increase in normal river stage. Upbound, prepare for a nearby protective breakwall immediately south of the bridge on the span's eastern side. South of the wall are three stone cribs. Upstream of the bend, Otterburn-Park is on the eastern shore.

At **Mile RC-33.4 (NM),** between the bridge and the explosives plant's smokestacks, the white numbered floats indicate speedboat racing lanes.

The next 4 miles is a fairly wide, straight reach to Bassin de Chambly's northern end. Eastern-shore

Marina St-Mathias, **Mile RC-34.0 (NM),** has dockage—4-foot draft is about maximum—and gas; across the road is the Excalibur Restaurant, bar, brokerage, and service area.

Upbound your channel bears to large Ile Goyer's eastern side; after you pass the St-Mathias waterfront, 1.5-mile-long Bassin de Chambly opens fully. The channel holds near midbasin and is surrounded by weedy flats. As you close the southern shore, the Rapides de Chambly are in the basin's southeastern corner.

At the mouth of the rapids on the basin's southern shore is Fort Chambly. The Chambly Canal's entrance is just to its west.

Though the French had improved the Lower Richelieu at St-Ours, they found the 10-mile-long rapids between Chambly and St-Jean insurmountable. When the British claimed Canada in 1763, a lumber trade developed north from Vermont to Lower Canada. After the American Revolution, the Americans and the British agreed that their economic prosperity depended on building a Chambly Canal. When the War of 1812 was declared, however, the British decided that a canal would make it easier for the Americans to invade via the Upper Richelieu, and canal planning came to an abrupt halt.

Canal excavation finally began in 1831 and was completed as far as Chambly. Construction resumed 10 years later, and the canal was opened in 1843. Though it was improved in 1860, it was never a complete success. Its nine locks were too small for the northbound Champlain Canal coal barges; transshipment into the Lower Richelieu continued.

Today's 9.7-mile-long Chambly Canal still overcomes an elevation difference of 79 feet between Chambly and St-Jean and holds along the river's western shore. Southbound, eight of the nine ascending locks are within 1.5 miles of Chambly. On average the locks are about 111 feet long, 23 feet wide, and have a lift of about 8 feet. Lock CHM #1 has a lift of 15.5 feet. The locks are still hand-operated, and its smartly uniformed attendants are gracious, helpful, and usually speak both French and English. Lock grounds are all extremely well maintained; buildings sparkle with fresh paint, and flower gardens abound.

Though there's a restricted canal depth of 6.5 feet over lock sills, the canal itself usually is maintained at about 7 to 8 feet. If your draft is 6 feet, contact the lockmaster at your first lock—Lock CHM #1 or Lock CHM #9—and explain your depth problem. Normally, lock crews cheerfully raise the water level to make certain you clear sills and any known canal shoals.

The Chambly has a minimum surface width of 60 feet and a bottom width of 36 feet, but shoal areas reduce the latter dramatically. Usually temporary spars watch shoal areas; if not, lockmasters inform you of shoal locations. If you draw 6 feet or more, always hold to midchannel; it's a cautious procedure when two deep-draft vessels pass. The canal also has narrow horizontal bridge clearances; transit is one boat at a time.

Though restricted overhead clearance is 29 feet, do not plan to clear obstructions by bending antennas. Overhead power cables often go unnoticed, and electrical line–antenna arcing is deadly.

Canal speed limit is 5.4 knots, but examine posted signs closely. There's a crossbar under the circular speed restriction symbol. If wake wave reaches the bar, you are exceeding the speed limit.

Southbound at Chambly your first three locks are in tandem. Once in the flight, transit is straight through.

Chambly Canal Seasonal Hours of Operation

May 15 to June 5, including Memorial Day: 0830 to 1800

June 6 to June 18: Monday through Thursday, 0830 to 1600; Friday through Sunday, 0830 to 1800

June 19 to August 16: open daily, 0830 to 2000

August 17 to August 30: open daily, 0830 to 1800

August 31 to September 13: open daily, 0830 to 1600

September 14 to October 12: open Thursday through Monday, 0830 to 1600; closed Tuesday and Wednesday

The flight's upper pool is about 0.4 mile long. Locks CHM #4 and CHM #5 have very short pools—about 330 feet; the pools at Lock CHM #6 and Lock CHM #7 are only slightly larger. There's a railroad swing bridge in Lock CHM #8's approach that's usually in the open position; if not, you may have a long wait until the train clears all switches down the line.

Lock CHM #8 has a unique rolling bridge, the only one on the canal; it's immediately upstream of the upper gate and works with the lock. East at **Mile RC-44.2 (NM)** is the northern end of 2-mile-long Ste-Therese. In the 1600s the French built a palisaded island fort here to protect the portage road from warring Iroquois.

Southbound at the sharp easterly bend at **Mile RC-44.5 (NM)** the canal opens to a wide waters. Stay in the channel; there's a persistent shoal area near the Iroquois River. It flows in through the western marsh at **Mile RC-45.8 (NM)**. The most shoal portion usually has slightly less than 6 feet; it's between spar **Buoy #38** and **Buoys #40** and **#41**. If you need 6 feet tell the nearest lockmaster; he can arrange to top off the pool for more water.

At Pont #10 at Ile Ste-Therese's southern end you start another narrow section with another 6-foot shoal. It's at the western-bank culvert just north of high-level Felix-Gabriel Marchand Bridge, **Mile RC-47.9 (NM)**.

The French built Fort St-Jean in 1668 to protect the river and portage road's southern end. With safety from Iroquois attack fairly well guaranteed, a settlement developed around the fort. By 1775 the British were in residence. They built two warships in St-Jean in hopes of controlling Lake Champlain.

By 1836 St-Jean had a railroad to La Prairie on the St. Lawrence; at last Richelieu-area farms had fast access to Montreal markets. Canal commerce declined; in 1851 the last commercial steamship, the *Whitehall*, made her final stop in town.

Once clear of guard Lock CHM #9 in St-Jean, your next upstream 4.5 miles is one of the Richelieu's deeper sections. The isolated, cone-shaped knob to the northeast is 700-foot Mount Johnson.

At Pointe a la Meule, **Mile RC-54.2 W (NM)**, the river begins to widen gradually in its approach to Lake Champlain. For the next 3 miles it also begins another gradual shoaling process; weedy shallows extend off both shores and channel depths can range about 7 feet. If you are traveling during low water stage and you draw 6 feet, use the range that begins at **Mile RC-55.0 (NM)**; buoys are often over 0.5 mile apart. After an episode of strong winds and a large chop in this area,

Pont #9, a typical narrow horizontal-clearance Chambly Canal bridge.

weeds dislodge from the bottom and gather in great islands, often in midchannel; at a distance they look suspiciously like terra firma.

By the time you reach Pointe de Bleury, **Mile RC-58.5 W (NM),** channel depth increases. Here you must decide on your immediate destination; this is the northern departure point for the Richelieu's 3-mile-long secondary channel. It leads to Ile aux Noix's western side and eventually rejoins the main route south of Anse a l'Esturgeon. On the secondary channel you have a choice of marinas and an anchorage off Fort Lennox. This is a fairly deepwater secondary route for nearly 2.8 miles. If you are traveling at low water stage and you draw 6 feet, you may have a depth problem from **Buoy EA19** to just south of **Buoy EA22** and in the secondary channel's southernmost, final 0.2 mile.

You can also visit Fort Lennox from a wake-prone anchorage by continuing on the main navigation channel that routes to Ile-aux-Noix's east. If this is your plan, then at Pointe de Bleury pick up the Ile Aux Noix Range; the markers are about 2 miles ahead on Pointe du Gouvernement peninsula. At the range's upstream end the river begins its slight westerly bend around the island.

White stone Fort Lennox, surrounded by a moat, is on Ile aux Noix's southern end. The French built the original fort in 1759. Later the British replaced the wooden buildings with the stone ones you see today.

Southbound at Pointe Naylor, **Mile RC-63.3 E (NM),** a channel crossing takes you west of Ile de l'Hopital and Ile Ash (Ile aux Tetes) and to the latter's two bridges.

There's a marina south of the western-shore railroad bridge. It has two river piers, moorings, and a more shoal section in a mainland cut.

To the west the Adirondack Mountains are coming into view, and soon you'll see the Green Mountains of Vermont; both chains surround Lake Champlain.

At **Mile RC-66.3 E (NM)** you pass west of the visibly weedy Ile du Sang's marshlands. The channel has good water, but it's bordered by shoals. South of the marsh island you can pick up the Ile aux Tetes Range. The Canadian Customs dock, **Mile RC-67.7 W (NM),** is on the end of a narrow mole extending beyond the worst shoreside shoals. If you stop during low river stage, be cautious; 6-foot-draft vessels may not have depth to lay alongside.

At the international border, **Mile RC-68.6 (NM),** you leave Quebec and enter New York and Vermont—west and east, respectively. Once you cross the border,

prepare for boarding by marine police from one of these states. Their primary purpose is to inspect your holding tank installation.

Fort Montgomery, about 0.5 mile north of Old Rouses Point, is on the island's western shore; it's now connected by a causeway. Anxious to control the Richelieu's entrance, the U.S. Army began fort construction in 1816. Three years later, with the fort unfinished, surveyors determined that it was 0.7 mile north of the 45th Parallel—in Canada. It became known as Fort Blunder. Twenty-one years later the government resurveyed the site and discovered that it was south of the border after all. More construction took place over the years, but the fort was never manned. Today most of the old structure is still standing. The gaping portion in its southeastern walls went into a Rouses Point bridge.

The high-level Old Rouses Point bridge, **Mile RC-69.3 (NM),** marks this regional section's southern terminus. South is Lake Champlain (see that section, beginning on page 350).

Sketch Map Depths

Sketch map depths are given at normal average summer canal pool and river levels. When you venture outside the sketch map confines, you must adjust Canadian charts to chart datum. For convenience in adjusting, use the following:

Mile RC-0.0 (NM) to **RC-39.4 (NM):** Sorel, 3.8 m; below St-Ours Lock, 4.4 m; above St-Ours Lock, 6.5 m; below Lock CHM #1, 6.7 m

Mile RC-39.5 (NM) to **RC-69.3 (NM):** Between Lock CHM #3 and Lock CHM #4, 16.2 m; between Lock CHM #4 and Lock CHM #5, 18.7 m; between Lock CHM #5 and Lock CHM #6, 21.1 m; between Lock CHM #6 and Lock CHM #7, 23.5 m; between Lock CHM #7 and Lock CHM #8, 26.1 m; between Lock CHM #8 and Lock CHM #9, 28.3 m; between Lock CHM #9 and Old Rouses Point, 28.3 m.

ST-OURS PUBLIC DOCK

★★★

Chart: C 1350 Sheet 2

Mile RC-10.7 E (NM)

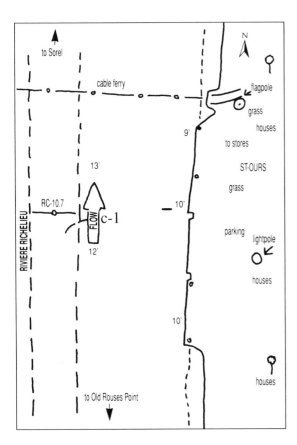

This eastern-shore dock is at St-Ours. The village is easy to locate; it's dominated by its church. The dock is a high cement bulkhead, an old commercial terminal, paralleling the river. It's immediately north of the ferry terminal to St-Roche.

There's good depth in from the channel, but tie up heading into the slight northerly current. You'll need long dock lines. The wall has two sections for low-freeboard boats. Choose space with a decent access ladder, and fender well; the pleasure-boat traffic casts immense wakes. A commercial boat may be on the bulkhead's northern end; if it's not there and you choose this spot,

watch for broken-off pilings alongside the wall about 1 to 2 feet below the surface.

Downtown is just up the access road; there's a bank, an attractive stone post office, a café, and a small supermarket.

ST-OURS LOCK

★★★★

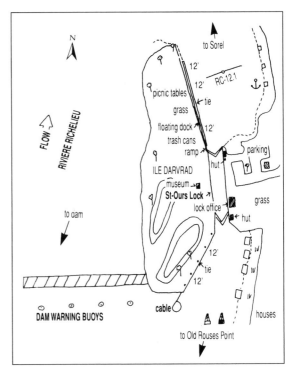

Chart: C 1350 Sheet 2

Mile RC-12.1 E (NM)

St-Ours Lock is on the eastern bank separated from the river by a lock island, Ile Darvard. There are two dockage areas on the island's eastern side; where you tie depends on your next day's direction of travel and departure time. The lower pool's dock is floating; the upper pool's dock is along a bulkhead.

Ile Darvard has lawns, shade trees, picnic tables, and garbage bins. You can watch lockages or walk across the island to see the dam. The old lockhouse is a small museum, open Wednesday through Sunday from 10 to 6. Walk across the lock gate to the eastern shore for rest rooms and a phone.

If you take the access road to the hilltop, there's an ice cream shop. A half-block south is the Terrace des Ecluses restaurant; it has all-you-can-eat fondue on Fridays. This means the docks are usually full on Friday nights. If this is the case, anchor out of the current in the lower pool near the southeastern bank in the cove formed by the approach island. Favor the isolated eastern-shore cement abutments to keep out of locking traffic. By midnight the dock is usually empty again.

This dock, another old commercial terminal, is about 0.1 mile north of **Light Buoy #135** and **Light Buoy #136**; it parallels St-Antoine's western shore. A landmark just south of the dock is the village's twin-spired church. When you see the dock bulkhead, come straight in. Mind the northerly current set; there's shoaling immediately north of the dock and launching ramp off Quarante Creek. Fender well; wake roll cast by pleasure craft is severe.

Downtown, about 100 yards away, has a small grocery; about six blocks away is a hardware store. About a block past the church is Cantine Marie L'eau, which has an outdoor patio with a river view.

ST-ANTOINE PUBLIC DOCK

★★★

Chart: C 1350 Sheet 3

Mile RC-17.6 W (NM)

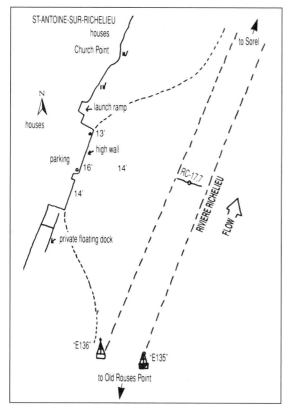

ST-CHARLES DOCKS

★★★

Chart: C 1350 Sheet 3

Mile RC-23.2 E (NM)

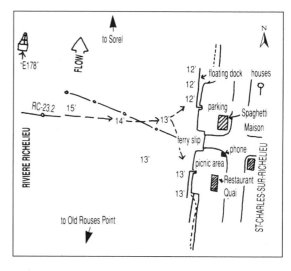

These eastern-shore docks in St-Charles are about opposite **Light Buoy #178.** One tie-up is immediately north of the cross-river ferry dock; the other two are to its south. Leave the river at the buoy and come straight in. Mind northerly current set and tie up at your dockage choice heading into the current. Fender well; passing pleasure boats cast severe wakes.

North of the ferry slip and paralleling the river is a bulkhead with a floating dock alongside it. This stop puts you in front of the popular Spaghetti Maison restaurant.

South of the ferry slip is a cement terminal. You can stop at a floating dock that's alongside the terminal's southern section or tie directly on the northern wall. Another floating dock with minimal depths extends off the end of the bulkhead's inside corner. The floating docks put you beside the Restaurant Quai, overlooking the river.

There is a convenience store on Main Street, about a half-block away. The phone is at the ferry slip.

ILE DE JEANNOTTE ANCHORAGE

★★★★ 3

NO FACILITIES

Chart: C 1350 Sheet 3

Mile RC-25.3 + 0.3 E (NM)

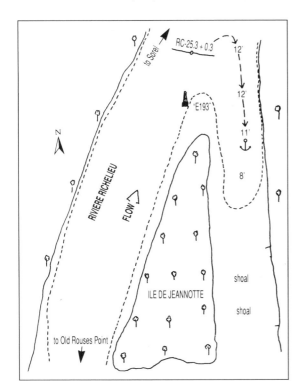

This anchorage is at large, wooded Ile de Jeannotte's northern end on its eastern side. Access is from the north. You may want to choose your weather—the anchorage is exposed to northerly winds with a fair fetch.

There are two islands in the area where the river makes a fairly sharp easterly bend. The northerly is Ile de Jeannotte; the southerly is Ile aux Cerfs. Southbound from St-Marc you normally begin the Ile aux Cerfs Range about 0.3 mile north of **Buoy E188.** The range carries the main channel west of the two islands. Though your destination is the very visible channel to Ile de Jeannotte's east, ride the range until you are about 0.1 mile north of **Buoy E193.** Do not approach the buoy closely; a long shoal extends to Ile de Jeannotte's north. Hold to the middle of the back channel during entry since more shoals extend west from the mainland. Anchor near the island's northern end in mud and weeds; you swing with the current unless wind is strong.

Shoal-draft traffic uses this channel nearly as much as the navigation channel, so wake roll is severe. They even travel full-throttle after dark, so have a very bright anchor light.

Do not take the back channel south to regain the main channel. It's shoal—often less than 3 feet—and there's an overhead power cable running between Ile aux Cerfs and the mainland.

We caught a few small bass trolling between the islands and at Le Grand Ruisseau's mouth; the latter creek is across the navigation channel about opposite the northern end of Ile aux Cerfs.

MARINA DE PHARE DE BELOEIL

★★★★ 3

Chart: C 1350 Sheet 4, *See sketch map, page 341*

Mile RC-31.5 W (NM)

This western-shore marina, named for its prominent blue-and-white lighthouse on the bluff, is just south of the Beloeil/Mont-St-Hilaire swing bridge. It's backed by a fieldstone revetment.

Marina de Phare de Beloeil

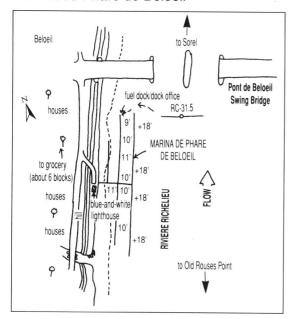

A main pier extends east from the shoreline. Off this are five long piers that parallel shore. Three extend north; two extend south. You parallel park.

The marina stands by on VHF 68 (in French) or you can approach the fuel dock (gas only) and hail the dockmaster (in French). This dock is at the northern end of the middle pier that extends north. There's a small covered dockhouse, though the dockmaster usually stays on his own boat tied alongside.

Transients usually tie on the T pier that faces the channel. It has a splendid easterly view of Mont-St-Hilaire but a lot of wake roll. Electric hookups (110-volt) are available. The marina's land line number is (514) 464-5257.

To reach town, go up the steep access road to the bluff's top and turn north. Within about eight short blocks you have a bank, a post office, a village church, shops, a restaurant, and a good-size market.

CHAMBLY

Chart: C 1351 Sheet 1, *See sketch map, page 342*

Mile RC-39.35 (NM) to Mile RC-40.8 (NM)

Chambly lies on the rapids' western bank, along Bassin de Chambly's southern and western shores and the Chambly Canal. The town is dominated by the canal; the three-lock flight is downtown. The procession of pleasure-boat lockages stops land traffic and gathers onlookers by the hundreds. No matter where you stay you are convenient to facilities; stops include a marina and a lock dock.

Downtown, generally west of Lock CH #3's bridge, has various stores, a large supermarket, and Place Chambly mall. There are a number of restaurants with outdoor dining near the locks.

About 0.3 mile east of the locks, overlooking the rapids and the basin, is 1-hectare Parc Historique National du Fort Chambly. It's open daily, but hours vary; call (514) 658-1585 to check schedules. Captain Jacques Chambly built the original fort in 1665; three more eventually came and went with military conquests. Today's stone fort was in use by the British until the mid-1800s. It's been almost completely restored; you can see the early chapel, hospital, and fireplaces, as well as exhibits on its history and restoration.

Marina de Chambly

★★★★

ALL FACILITIES

Chart: C 1351 Sheet 1, *See sketch map, page 342*

Mile RC-39.35 E (NM)

This marina—open May 15 to October 15—is at Bassin de Chambly's southern end in a small basin east of the channel; it's western-shore enclosure is Lock CHM #1's eastern lower approach wall. The entrance is between the lock wall's northern end and an east-west-oriented rock breakwater; the breakwater eventually makes a jog south. **Buoy E259** watches the entrance breakwater rocks.

Leave the channel at the approach wall's northern end and favor that side. A shoal extends west from the breakwater's western end. The marina has one main pier paralleling the eastern breakwater; from this are four finger piers extending westerly. Each pier has slips.

The marina stands by on VHF 68. If you don't speak French, pull in to the fuel dock (gas only) at the basin's southern end; approach along the western ends of the finger piers. The dock parallels shore in front of the office that's part way up the hill. There's a ramp at the dock's eastern end.

Electric hookups (110-volt/15-amp and 220-volt/30-amp) are available. If you need a diver or repairs, check at the office. The land line number is (514) 658-7308.

There are hillside picnic tables and grills with a beautiful view of Chambly Basin, and there's a restaurant within 500 feet.

Marina de Chambly

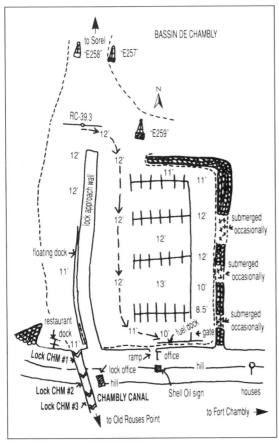

Lock CHM #3 Upper

★★★★

Chart: C 1351 Sheet 1

Mile RC-39.58 W (NM)

Lock CHM #3 Upper

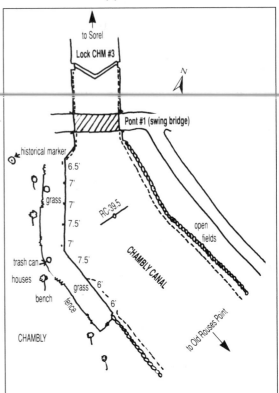

This western-bank bulkhead dockage is in Lock CHM #3's upper pool—the Chambly flight's southern end—immediately south of Pont #1. A blue line designates dockage space.

During lock hours—especially on weekends—this can be a busy place. Boats waiting hourly to transit mill about alongside the dock area and rev their engines. When the upbound group exits the lock, the milling and rumbling doubles. Adding to the commotion is the operation of the bridge, which works with the lock. Bells ring, lights flash, land traffic halts and backs up at least a mile in both directions, and sightseers arrive in droves to admire yachts.

A fence separates the tie-up from a shady park with lawns, flowers, park benches, garbage bins, and a stone pedestal commemorating the canal's 1843 completion. Across the park is a convenient yogurt and ice cream shop on Main Street.

LOCK CHM #8 UPPER

★★★★

Chart: C 1351 Sheet 1

Mile RC-40.8 E (NM)

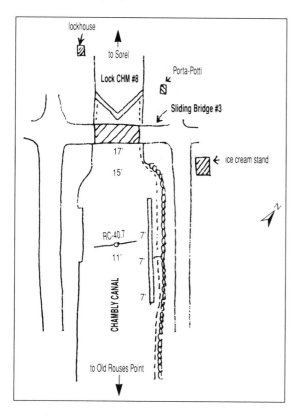

PONT #7 SWING BRIDGE NORTH AND SOUTH

★★★★

Chart: C 1351 Sheet 1

Mile RC-42.6 W (NM) to Mile RC-42.67 W (NM)

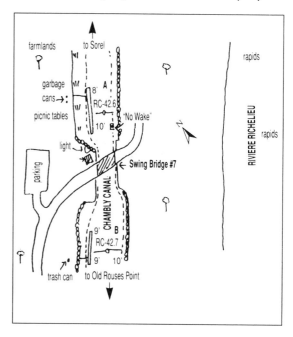

Swing Bridge North

See A on sketch map

This 100-foot-long floating dock parallels the canal's eastern bank south of Lock CHM #8.

The lock has beautiful grounds with masses of flowers and manicured lawns; it's a good place to watch lockages. The lockmaster doesn't mind answering questions about his lock and it's unique rolling bridge—the only one in this system. It rolls west on rails instead of lifting or swinging.

There's a small eastern-bank store and snack bar at the road intersection.

This western-shore floating dock is immediately north of Pont #7. Canal swing bridges look a lot alike; this one is about 0.4 mile south of the more noticeable fixed Highway 10 Bridge.

Ashore there is a large lawn, four picnic tables, garbage bins, and a Porta-Potti. During warm summer days the grounds are a sunning and picnic spot favored by area residents. The residential area across the road is a pleasant place for a stroll; most homes have beautiful flower gardens. If you cross the bridge to the eastern bank and walk up the road, you have a view of the main river Rapides Fryers.

Swing Bridge South

See B on sketch map, page 343
This western-bank dock is south of Pont #7. It has a manicured lawn and a garbage bin.

PONT #9 SWING BRIDGE NORTH

★★★★

Chart: C 1351 Sheet 1

Mile RC-44.19 W (NM)

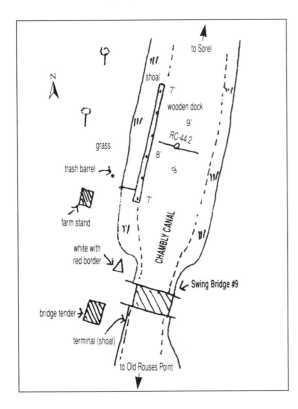

Pont #9 serves a secondary road to Ile-Ste-Marie. The western-bank dock is north of the bridge. There's a lawn, a picnic table, and a garbage bin. On the road beside the grounds a fruit and vegetable stand sells freshly picked local produce; the raspberries are excellent.

Cross the bridge to the eastern shore and you're on the 20-kilometer towpath and bicycle trail along the canal and river. It has superb canal and rapids viewpoints. Though you can access the path at all canal docks, this one is particularly handy.

PONT #10 SWING BRIDGE NORTH

★★★★

Chart: C 1351 Sheet 2

Mile RC-46.6 W (NM)

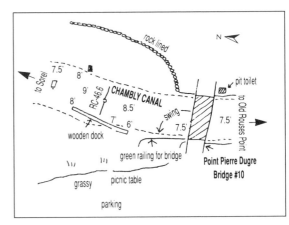

This western-bank dock is north of Pont #10. If you draw 6 feet, best depth is at the northern end. Do not tie immediately north of the bridge on the western bulkhead; this is where the bridge rests when open.

Ashore there is a plot of grass, a picnic table, and a garbage bin. The grounds adjoin a dirt parking lot, so it can be slightly dusty here. There's a snack shop nearby on the main road. If you need gas you can fill a portable container at the Shell station, about a block north. A few more blocks away is a butcher's shop.

ST-JEAN-SUR-RICHELIEU

Chart: C 1351 Sheet 2, *See sketch map, page 345*

Mile RC-49.0 W (NM) to RC-50.0 W (NM)

Western-shore St-Jean, the canal's largest city, is at the canal's southern terminus. Iberville is east across

St-Jean-sur-Richelieu: St-Jean Public Dock, Le Nautique St-Jean

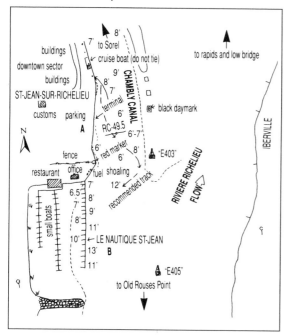

the Pont Gouin Bascule Bridge. St-Jean has a public dock and a marina.

Downtown is a short walk from your choice of dockage. There are stores, banks, a pharmacy, bars, a theater, a library, restaurants, and sidewalk cafés. The post office is at Champlain and St-Charles streets. The Metro Supermarket is slightly farther away on Jacques Cartier North; if you plan to stock up, there's taxi service.

On Rue Champlain you can see the polished boulder marking the site of Fort St-Jean.

St-Jean Public Dock

★

3

Chart: C-1351 Sheet 2, *See A on sketch map*

Mile RC-49.5 W (NM)

This 1,000-foot-long western-shore town terminal begins immediately south of Pont #12, the Gouin Bascule Bridge. Though the bulkhead has fair depth, be

careful in your approach if you draw 6 feet. You may bumble over a few isolated shoals just west of the wall as you look for a way in. The dock can be rough in strong, prolonged southerly winds.

The red space about midterminal is for a large tour boat. It's usually out between 1:30 and 5:30; don't block its space. If in doubt about where it ties, ask the attendant at the ticket kiosk.

The terminal is not especially attractive. There's a large parking lot alongside the dock and you look west at the backs of the main street's stores. There is a pleasant river view east over the canal's eastern approach dike. The dock is usually free of wake roll; traffic waits until south of the wall before speeding up.

Downtown is about a half-block away.

Le Nautique St-Jean

★★★

3

Chart: C 1351 Sheet 2, *See B on sketch map*

Mile RC-49.64 W (NM)

This western-shore marina—open April 1 to October 31—is at the downtown terminal's southern end.

About opposite **Buoy E403,** just south of a red daymark on the terminal, the western shoreline makes an abrupt westerly turn. The marina is in its lee. There are three main piers extending from the northern shore. The easterly pier's eastern face—normally the transient dock—has parallel parking; the rest of the piers have slips. Except the transient dock, the marina is protected from southerly chop by a breakwater that extends east from the western riverbank.

If no one answered on VHF 68, pull in to the fuel dock; it's at the marina's northern end along the land-mass bulkhead. If you draw 6 feet, you may have a depth problem at the pumps (gas and diesel); in this case pull in to the transient dock and check in at the office next to the northern-shore restaurant.

Block and cube ice, 110-volt/30-amp electric hookups, and a 5.5-ton Travelift are available. If you need a diver, check at the office. The land line number is (514) 347-4888.

The ship's store has marine equipment, navigation supplies, charts, nautical clothing, and 24-foot boats and outboards for rent. Within a half block is a Customs reporting station.

At Le Nautique Restaurant, at the head of the middle ramp, you can dine inside or on a pretty patio under festive umbrellas overlooking the marina and river.

ILE-AUX-NOIX VIA SECONDARY CHANNEL

Chart: C 1351 Sheet 3

Mile RC-58.47 + 1.8–2.2 (NM)

Ile-aux-Noix, a large midriver island, is noted for Fort Lennox. Nearby is a large marina, a public dock, and anchorages.

To reach the marina and one of the anchorages, you must travel a watched secondary channel. It routes along the river's western shore, passes Ile aux Noix's western side, goes through Anse a l'Esturgeon, then intersects the main channel again south of Ile Ronde at **Mile RC-61.3 (NM)**. Most of the secondary channel has good depth, but follow its charted sailing line (red dashes). If you draw 6 feet, two dicey areas in the route's southern end may give you trouble. Be cautious near **Secondary Buoy EA28** and at the channel's extreme southern end.

To enter the secondary channel southbound, leave the main navigational channel at **Mile RC-58.47 (NM)** at **Buoys E458 and E457**; they are just south of Pointe de Bleury. Secondary channel buoys carry a prefix "EA". At this point follow directions for individual stops on this route.

You can reach the island's public dock and another anchorage via the main channel.

On the secondary route there are restaurants, a grocery and a hardware store, and an Esso filling station at St-Paul-Ile-aux-Noix. It's about 0.5 mile north of the western end of the western shore's large canal cuts.

The 81-hectare Fort Lennox National Historic Park is on the island's southern end. It's open Monday from 1 to 5:30 and Tuesday through Sunday from 9:30 to 5:30. The fort has a moat and most of its original stone buildings, with well-preserved officers' quarters, a bar-

rack, a commissary, a guardhouse, and a magazine. The fort museum has a collection of artifacts and military equipment. Try to plan your visit for a summer weekend when there are battle reenactments.

Marina Gagnon et Fils

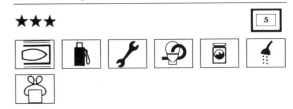

Chart: C 1351 Sheet 3

Mile RC-58.47 + 1.8 W (NM)

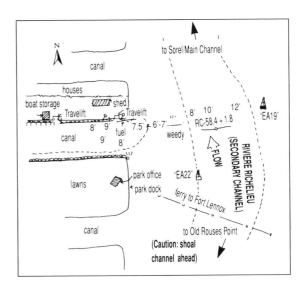

This marina is accessible via the secondary channel. Southbound from its Pointe de Bleury access, take the secondary channel south to about **Mile RC/SEC-1.8 (NM)** near **Buoy EA19**. The marina extends along the southern side of a western-bank mole; its service buildings are tan with red roofs. A landmark on the next mole south is the Fort Lennox ferry dock; it's in a park-like setting.

If you draw 6 feet be cautious of depths once you leave the secondary channel and bear into the marina's cut. Heavy weed growth interferes with fathometer readings.

For service pull in to the fuel dock (gas and diesel).

It's at the pier's eastern end and parallels the canal bank at the point where the marina's south-reaching slips begin. It's in front of the office in the large building on the canal's southern waterfront.

The marina—land line number (514) 291-3336—has a large boatyard with two Travelifts (with separate wells) and mast-stepping facilities. Electric hookups (110-volt) are available.

The excellent ship's store sells marine equipment, charts, nautical clothing, and gifts.

The grocery is about a mile hike; walk west down the mole to the main road—that's about half the distance—then bear northerly on the highway.

If you intend to visit Fort Lennox, you can take the park ferry; its another mile hike to get there. Go down the mole, turn south to the road up the next mole, and take it back to its eastern end.

This general area has surrounding marshlands; prepare for mosquitoes at dusk and dawn.

Fort Lennox Anchorage

★★★★   3

NO FACILITIES

Chart: C 1351 Sheet 3

Mile RC-58.47 + 2.2 W/E (NM)

When southbound, approach this anchorage via the secondary channel that leaves the main channel near Pointe de Bleury. Carry the secondary channel for 2.0 miles. This places you just about opposite Fort Lennox's island ferry landing and about 0.3 mile north of **Buoy EA23**. Continue south just far enough to clear the island's underwater cable; it extends to a western shoreline mole. Anchor as close to the island as depth allows to keep out of the well-used fairway. Bottom is mud and weeds. If wind is strong from the west, north, or northwest, it's very windswept.

Though it's possible to land the dinghy anywhere on the beach, unless you plan to leap the moat the only access inside the walls is at the entrance bridge in the center of the fort's northern end. Occasionally you are allowed to tie to the pier inside the ferry dock in the shallows and well out of the way; obtain permission

Fort Lennox Anchorage

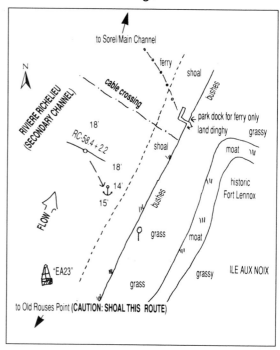

before you leave it. You can also pull it up on the beach in the same area.

Button up for mosquitoes at dusk and dawn.

FORT LENNOX PUBLIC DOCK AND ANCHORAGE

★★★★   2

Chart: C 1351 Sheet 3, *See sketch map, page 348*

Mile RC-60.7 W (NM)

This stop is on Ile aux Noix's eastern side about mid-island. It is accessed from the main navigation channel. A government dock extends southeasterly from the island, then jogs east; it has a three-hour time limit and no overnight docking. This temporary dockage is restricted to all but the pier ends; tour boats use the deep southeastern face. Rafting is common but not recommended. Though the main channel is well southeast,

Fort Lennox Public Dock and Anchorage

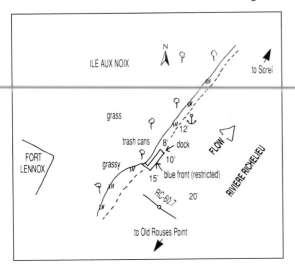

passing pleasure boaters cast high wakes that result in raft chaos. Though exposed to prevailing winds, wind usually subsides at sundown.

For overnight, anchor off the dock in weeds and mud. In severe northeasterlies you can move to the island's western side. Beach the dinghy in the eastern-dock bight by the lawn.

Lake Champlain
Old Rouses Point to Whitehall

Mile CH-0.0 (SM) to Mile CH-106.0 (SM)

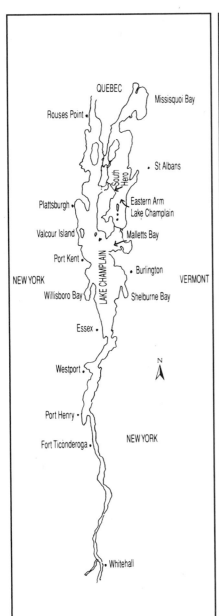

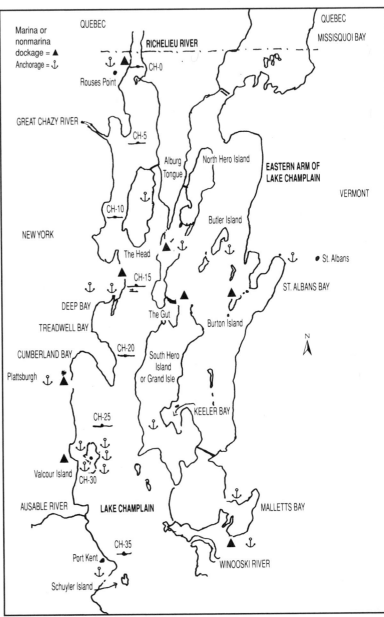

Mile CH-0.0 (SM) to Mile CH-106.0 (SM)

Old Rouses Point to Port Kent
Mile CH-0.0 (SM) to Mile CH-35.0 (SM)

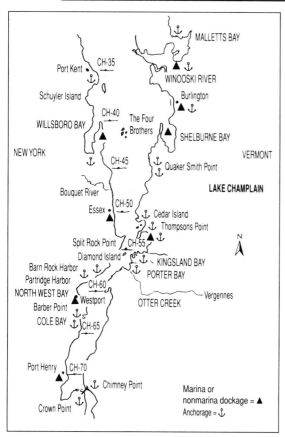

Port Kent to Chimney Point
Mile CH-35.0 (SM) to Mile CH-70.0 (SM)

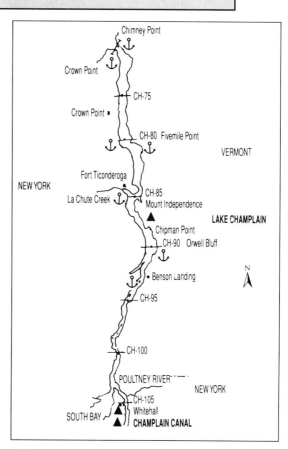

Chimney Point to Whitehall
Mile CH-70.0 (SM) to Mile CH-106.0 (SM)

Lake Champlain nestles between New York's Adirondack Mountains and Vermont's Green Mountains and extends from close to the Canadian border near Old Rouses Point to Whitehall. It is about 110 miles long, varies from 0.1 mile to 12 miles wide, and lies in a north-south direction.

This is primarily a recreational area, with densely wooded shores, lakefront hills and palisades, a sprinkling of waterside homes, and splendid mountain views. Water is clear; fishing and swimming are superb; anchorages abound. Though waterfront settlements are sparse, most have some pleasure-craft facilities.

The lake is part of an international waterway. Quebec's Upper Richelieu River—the lake's northerly

MOVABLE BRIDGES, OLD ROUSES POINT TO WHITEHALL			
Name	*Type*	*Location*	*Clearance (closed)* *
South Hero/North Hero (Highway 2)	Bascule	Eastern Arm: East side of the Gut	18 feet
Missisquoi Bay (Railroad)	Swing	Eastern Arm: South side Missisquoi Bay, East Alburg	11 feet
Missisquoi Bay (Highway 78)	Bascule	Eastern Arm: South side Missisquoi Bay, East Alburg Bay at East Alburg	18 feet

*At normal lake level

Schedules:

South Hero/North Hero (Highway 2)—May 15 to October 15, opens on signal from 0700 to 2100; from 2100 to 0700 four hours notice needed. October 16 to May 14, 24 hours notice needed.

Missisquoi Bay (Railroad) 802-527-7123—June 15 to September 15, opens on signal Monday through Friday from 0900 to 1700; Saturday, Sunday, July 4, and Labor Day, 0700 to 2300; all other times 2 hours notice needed. September 16 to June 14, 24 hours notice needed.

Missisquoi Bay (Highway 78)—opens on signal; 24 hours notice needed.

outlet—accesses the Chambly Canal, the Lower Richelieu, and the St. Lawrence River. The lake's southern end accesses the Champlain Canal, the Hudson River, and the sea. Midlake generally serves as the border between New York and Vermont, except in its northern section where the border is west of the two Heros.

A large part of the northern lake is divided into two sections, the Eastern Arm and the Western Arm. The Western Arm's northern end is the Richelieu River. It's separated from the Eastern Arm by Isle La Motte and the Isle of the Two Heros, North and South Hero. South Hero is often called Grand Isle. Alburg Tongue also separates the two arms; it's a long peninsula extending south from Quebec. Area residents often call the lake's Eastern Arm the "Inland Sea."

This is a seasonal lake for boating—accessible from May through October. Lake ice more than 2 feet thick can form in winter and has been known to pile up 30 feet high on a windward shore. July and early August are generally the warmest months; temperatures then are usually in the high 70s. Water temperature in this period averages in the high 60s and low 70s, which stimulates shallow-water weed growth.

Prevailing winds are light from the southerly quadrant and tend to follow the lake contour. Frontal pas-

sages can occur at any time, though they are most severe early and late in the season—the time of continental North America's seasonal changeover. Travel during fronts is unpleasant due to rough seas. Monitor weather so you will know when a front is expected to occur, and give yourself enough time to seek safe haven.

When a front approaches, southerly and southwesterly winds increase; after it passes, wind shifts to the northerly quadrant (usually northwest), veers northeasterly, and finally turns back south. The strongest, longest-duration winds are from May through mid-June and from mid-September through October.

Summer thunderstorms are most common in July and August, when towering cumulus clouds build over nearby mountains. If they move to the lake, be wary; most bring violent lightning and severe winds that abruptly swing 180 degrees. You may suddenly find yourself on a very dangerous lee shore, as few anchorages in this lake have total protection.

The lake has strict holding-tank regulations; expect state marine police inspection boardings day or night.

Most of the lake's shoreline is private, with limited access ashore for hiking, picnics, and beachcombing. Become accustomed to No Trespassing signs even when no habitation is in sight.

Keep watch for Champ, Lake Champlain's version

Fishing in Lake Champlain

With over 15 species of gamefish at hand, fishermen can find excellent opportunities most anywhere on Lake Champlain.

For Vermont waters, you'll need that state's fishing license if you're over 15—unless you're a resident landowner. Buy one at sporting goods or tackle shops, or by mail from the Vermont Fish and Wildlife Department, Information and Education Division, Waterbury, VT 05676. Their phone number is (802) 244-7331.

Champlain's water is free of most pollutants, so you'll find fewer constraints on catch consumption here than in New York's waterways or the Great Lakes. However, large fish may be toxic. Read New York's license guide for good rules of thumb.

There are many familiar species throughout Lake Champlain: largemouth and smallmouth bass, walleye, northern pike, and yellow perch. Some other favorites:

Chain Pickerel. These look like small pike and can be identified by the blue-green chain-link pattern on their flanks. Pickerel usually weigh only about 2 pounds, but they fight much harder than you'd expect. You'll find them in shallow, grassy areas with good protection. We use about 5-pound test with a fine wire leader—like pike, they'll often bite through line with their needlelike teeth. Cast or troll along the edge of weeds. Best lure is a spinner or a spoon, although live minnows work well too. Try jerking your lure to emulate realistic motion.

Lake Trout. Lakers differ from other trout varieties in their small scales, white-edged fins, and deeply forked tails. They average about 5 pounds, but can get much larger. Troll for these deep and slow, because in warm weather they seek colder water—20 feet or deeper, depending on the temperature. Let your lure sink periodically by varying your speed. Best lures are bright fluttering ones, such as spinners or spoons. A close second choice: dead smelt.

Landlocked Salmon. Try for these on streams or on the lake surface during salmon-run time in May. Later in the summer salmon, like trout, head for deeper, cooler waters. These fish average about 3 to 4 pounds, so an 8-pound-test line will do nicely. If you're fly fishing, streamer flies are reputed to be good, although we haven't had much luck with them. Wobbler or smelt-imitating lures, trolled moderately deep, work for us. And be prepared—salmon hit hard.

---

of the Loch Ness Monster. Explorer Samuel de Champlain was the first to report seeing the 20-foot-long serpentine creature with a horse-shaped head. Sightings continue.

Lake Champlain mileage generally follows the shortest north-south commercial route, as noted in "Coast Pilots." Southbound mileage begins at Old Rouses Point, **Mile CH-0.0 (SM),** about 0.8 mile south of Quebec's border, and follows the watched navigation channel through the reefs and shoals of the lake's upper Western Arm. At Isle La Motte's northern end, **Mile CH-6.5 (SM),** the route bears to the island's western side. At the island's southern end, the Head, **Mile CH-12.4 (SM),** the lake widens, depths increase, and mileage begins to slightly favor the lake's western side to Cumberland Head, **Mile CH-22.2 (SM).** Continuing

south, mileage bears east of Crab Island, **Mile CH-25.0 (SM),** and west of Valcour Island. It then rounds Trembleau Point, **Mile CH-35.5 (SM),** holds east of Schuyler Island, **Mile CH-37.0 (SM),** to Willsboro Point, **Mile CH-40.5 (SM).** Still favoring the western shore, the route passes west of the Four Brothers Islands to Split Rock Point, **Mile CH-53.0 (SM).** Here mileage holds to midlake and bears past Diamond Island, **Mile CH-55.6 (SM),** to the Crown Point headland, **Mile CH-71.1 (SM),** the start of the lower lake. The lower lake increasingly narrows; mileage follows the watched channel to Whitehall, **Mile CH-106.0 (SM).**

From this north-south mileage route, you have suggested **Departure Points** to reach off-route areas. A **Departure Point** normally is the start of the shortest, safest course to follow from the main mileage system when southbound. If not following the main mileage route, find your own safe course to reach a destination.

Samuel de Champlain reached and named the lake in July 1609 during his St. Lawrence River exploration. Once on the lake his French soldiers and Algonquian war party paddled their canoe fleets to near Crown Point before turning back. At this same time, explorer Henry Hudson was sailing *Half Moon* up the Hudson River.

Attempts to control the Lake Champlain area have led to many battles. Iroquois and Algonquians fought over fishing and hunting grounds. Champlain fought resident Indians to claim it for the French. The French battled the British for its control but lost it at the end of the French and Indian Wars. By 1760 the British controlled the lake—and nearly all of North America. Eventually, they clashed with the colonies, lost the lake region to the Americans during the Revolutionary War, then repeated the struggle during the War of 1812. Lake Champlain warfare came to a close after a Confederate raid during the Civil War.

You start your lake journey southbound at Old Rouses Point's high-level bridge, **Mile CH-0.0 (SM),** then pass through an old railroad trestle. Rouses Point is on the western shore in a mile-wide northern bight. Once clear of Vermont's south-reaching Windmill Point and New York's Stony Point breakwater, **Mile CH-1.8 W (SM),** the lake begins its gradual widening process.

Hold to the watched channel to clear shoals and reefs extending some distance from banks—especially at Point Au Fer Reef, **Mile CH-5.0 W (SM).** The passenger ship *Ticonderoga*, rounding Isle La Motte's northern end, hit the reef in 1919 and was holed.

Goose Island, **Mile CH-5.5 E (SM),** begins another mile-long southerly reaching shoal extending to Reynolds Point at Isle La Motte's northern end.

There's a small-boat channel between Isle La Motte's northeastern end and Alburg Tongue, but there's an 8-foot bridge clearance. For clear access to anchorages on Isle La Motte's eastern shore, round the island's southern tip at the Head, then return north into La Motte Passage.

West of Point Au Fer and across King Bay is the Great Chazy River's mouth and extensive marsh flats. The river has marinas along its lower shores, but if you draw 6 feet, be cautious; you may not have entrance channel depth.

The **Departure Point** from the main lake to enter King Bay is about 0.4 mile southwest of **Buoy #10.** This route keeps clear of rocky mile-long Point Au Fer Reef.

Bear northwesterly across King Bay; it gradually shoals. The watched river entrance channel has minimal depth. Stay in the middle to avoid rocks on the channel edges. Inside the entrance, depths increase to 8 to 10 feet.

In a pine grove near Isle La Motte's northwestern end is the site of Fort Ste. Anne, Vermont's earliest European settlement. French Captain Pierre de la Motte and 60 soldiers built the fort for protection against Indians in 1666. Forty soldiers died of scurvy, but a settlement started and the Jesuits built a chapel. Look closely in the trees along the beach in this same area to see a granite statue of Champlain; it commemorates his discovery of the lake.

In 1807 Matthew Sacks built the first lake steamboat landing at Chazy Landing, **Mile CH-8.0 W (SM);** for years it was the only steamer stop between Whitehall and St-Jean.

At Monty Bay, **Mile CH-11.0 W (SM),** you travel the area where Benedict Arnold spent 12 days in September 1776. Here he readied his Lake Champlain fleet and planned his strategy against Sir Guy Carleton, who was sailing south toward him.

The Head, **Mile CH-12.5 (SM),** is your **Departure Point** if you plan to visit waters east of Isle La Motte or enter La Motte Passage. It's from the Passage that you make your way to the cut between Alburg Tongue and mid–North Hero Island into Alburg Passage, Pelots Bay, and Carry Bay. There are shoals in this area; consult the anchorage text for approach directions.

Southbound on the main lake watch for **Buoy LR;** it's difficult to see in rough weather. It watches La Roche Reef shoals, which lie about 0.4 mile offshore west of Point Au Roche Light, **Mile CH-14.3 W (SM).** South of the light you are nearing Long Point, which is part of Point Au Roche State Park. The point forms Treadwell Bay's northeastern end. If you plan to visit Treadwell Bay's northern anchorages, your **Departure Point** is south of the long shoal that makes out nearly 0.8 mile from Long Point's southwestern end. It's watched by **Buoy #2, Mile CH-18.0 (SM).** More shoals exist in Treadwell Bay; consult the anchorage text for approach directions.

Buoy #2, off Long Point Shoal, is also a **Departure Point** from which to reach the lake's Eastern Arm without a restrictive bridge clearance. Shoals exist; consult the anchorage text for approach directions.

The entire Eastern Arm of Lake Champlain extends about 40 miles in a north-south direction. At the far northern end—north of Hog Island's two bridges—is

Missisquoi Bay, 5 miles of which are in Quebec. The Missisquoi River lowlands are at the bay's southern end, bordered by the shallows and marshlands of northern Vermont.

The most popular Eastern Arm cruising area is the 24-mile-long section extending south from the Hog Island bridges to the Sand Bar Causeway's extensive shoals. This causeway has a 16-foot overhead clearance and blocks most traffic into Malletts Bay, the remaining 5 miles of the Eastern Arm. If you plan to visit Malletts Bay, a good **Departure Point** is from the main lake near Valcour Island.

Generally the Eastern Arm has excellent depths. Its shoals are mainly along the shoreline, at extensions of points and headlands, and fringing its nearly two dozen islands. One 1.5-mile-long dangerous midlake shoal is in Gull Island Reef—it surrounds tiny Gull Island.

Though there are anchorages and marinas throughout the Eastern Arm, the most popular is Burton Island, about 4 miles east of the Gut's bascule bridge, off St. Albans Point. St. Albans endured the Civil War's northernmost Confederate raid. Lieutenant Bennett Young and 22 soldiers came in by railroad, held up three banks, terrorized the populace, tried to burn the town, stole horses, and escaped into Canada with more than $200,000. Though they refused to extradite the raiders, the Canadians did return some of the money.

Back on the main lake's mileage route near Treadwell Bay, **Mile CH-18.0 W (SM),** the lake is not nearly as wide as the Eastern Arm. It narrows even more as you close Cumberland Head. If it's foggy, watch for the fast-moving cross-lake ferry between Cumberland Head's eastern shore and Vermont's Gordon Landing.

Just south of Cumberland Head, **Mile CH-23.0 (SM),** is your **Departure Point** to reach Plattsburgh; it's on Cumberland Bay's western shore at the Saranac River's mouth.

Southbound from Cumberland Head you angle across Cumberland Bay and pass east of 0.5-mile-long Crab Island, **Mile CH-25.0 (SM).** It was a hospital island during the 1814 Battle of Plattsburgh, which left the Americans in control of Lake Champlain. To more easily see the obelisk honoring the wounded and dead, you can pass on the island's western side. Northern offshore rocks are watched by **Buoy #10.**

You route through Valcour Bay, a designated National Historical Landmark, west of 2-mile-long Valcour Island. Bluff Point Lighthouse, on mid–Valcour Island's western shore, divides the bay. South of the bluff, in October of 1776, Benedict Arnold and his 15-vessel Revolutionary War fleet met the impressive ships of Britain's Sir Guy Carleton. Though Carleton managed to sink ship after ship, the Americans eluded capture. The American gundelo *Philadelphia,* sunk by a 24-pound cannon ball in the first hour of battle, was recovered from the lake in 1935. With her four cannons still mounted, she's in Washington's Smithsonian Institution.

If you want to visit Vermont's Malletts Bay, your **Departure Point** on the main lake is at **Mile CH-30.0 (SM),** just south of Garden Island—Petite Isle in Colonial times—off Valcour's southern end. To reach Malletts Bay you must first enter the Eastern Arm's far southern end, then bear another 4.3 miles to its eastern shore. Shoals exist; consult the anchorage text for approach directions.

An old railroad causeway encloses the large outer bay of the southern Eastern Arm. It was built across the shallows from Colchester Point on the south to Allen Point at South Hero's southern tip. This railroad served the lake inhabitants in the late 19th century and lessened the need for the vast cargo fleet to transport harvests.

Near the old causeway's southern end in the main lake are a group of isolated islands, shoals, and reefs. In 1869 a lighthouse was built on Colchester Reef, which had one of the most dangerous shoals for early shipping. Although engineers anchored the 25-foot structure with iron rods sunk into 3 feet of stone and bolted it to eight-by-eight sills, it was wrenched from its foundations one April by flowing, breaking ice. The lighthouse, its keeper, and his family survived only because a last-minute wind shift turned the ice away.

Southbound from Valcour Island on the main lake, don't miss **Buoy #4, Buoy #16,** and **Buoy #18**—they are difficult to see in rough seas. They watch two extensive shoals near Ausable Point, **Mile CH-31.3 W (SM).** This is the area of the Ausable River's main mouths. The river's headwaters are about 50 winding miles southwest at Mount Marcy, the highest point in the Adirondacks. Upstream about 4 miles is Ausable Chasm. The 1.5-mile-long gorge was opened as a tourist attraction in 1870. Today boat tours and hiking trails access its narrow, rock-walled waterways, rapids, and waterfalls. Ausable River delta shoals restrict pleasure craft approach from the lake.

If it's foggy when you approach Port Kent, **Mile CH-35.0 W (SM),** watch for the cross-lake ferries that ply between the village and Burlington. Also keep watch for dangerous Ferris Rock, **Mile CH-35.4 (SM)**, about 1.5 miles east of Trembleau Point; give it a wide berth. It's watched by a lighted daymark/sign that says **"Danger Rock"** and is very difficult to see. Though charted east of the rock, the daymark appears to sit right on top of it—or one nearby. In very low lake levels, you can stand hip-deep on a rock at the marker.

Large, wooded Schuyler Island, **Mile CH-37.0 (SM)**, is just south of Trembleau Point. There is a **Departure Point** for Vermont's Burlington and Shelburne Bay at Schuyler Island Light on the island's eastern shore. There are shoals on the way to Burlington, **Mile CH-37.0 + 10.8 E (SM)**, so consult the anchorage text for approach directions.

Burlington lies in the Green Mountains foothills in a slight curve of the Vermont coastline. It's the largest lake port and Vermont's largest city.

Edward Burling, for whom the town was named, settled in the area after the French and Indian Wars. Ira, Ethan, and Heman Allen owned more than 300,000 acres along the nearby Winooski River. Ethan later became famous as the commander of the Green Mountain Boys.

Burlington's first large industries were shipbuilding, lumber, textile mills, and iron forges. Commerce came to a near halt during the War of 1812, but when safe lake travel resumed, the town prospered. Wealthy businessmen built handsome mansions along the waterfront hills; many are still there. The Lake Ferry Company, founded in 1816, continues to operate.

When the Champlain Canal and later the Chambly Canal opened, local yards designed and built boats to fit the new locks. Burlington became the major lake port. It based its economy entirely on lumber, most of which was imported from the Ottawa River, Three Rivers, and other Canadian streams. It came in by barge convoys—Canadian and American—each loaded with about 80,000 board feet. At Burlington the lumber was transshipped by railroad to New England. By 1873 Burlington was America's third largest lumber port. This trade nearly depleted the timber supply on the eastern slope of the Adirondacks, and in 1893 Congress put a duty of $2 on every 1,000 feet of lumber imported from Canada.

Ira Allen secured the original charter of the University of Vermont, which is in Burlington. Its first class of four graduated in 1804; today's enrollment is more than 10,000.

When you leave Burlington you are near south-reaching Shelburne Bay, about 2 miles south of Burlington Harbor breakwater's southern end.

After a bay visit, you may want to cross back to the lake's western shore from Shelburne Point. If this is your route, watch out for barren Rock Dunder; a long ledge extends to its southeast. Legend says the Indian Creator was so enchanted by his beautiful Lake Champlain he turned himself into Rock Dunder for an everlasting lake view. You can pass south of Juniper Island with its prominent 115-foot light tower.

Back on the main mileage route on the western shore at Schuyler Island, the tank farm in Corlaer Bay is in Port Douglas. Towboats and fuel barges ply between the port and New York City.

A few miles south of Port Douglas is deep, fjord-like Willsboro Bay, **Mile CH-40.53 W (SM)**. The bay is open at its northern end; Willsboro Point is its eastern entry. If you approach from the south, keep clear of Pumpkin Reef, watched by **Buoy #20** off the point's eastern tip.

William Gilliland, a wealthy New York City merchant, founded Willsboro in 1765; it's about 2 miles south of the bay on the Bouquet River. Gilliland tried to establish the town as a feudal manor, though his endeavor ended when British General John Burgoyne captured Willsboro during the Revolutionary War. Burgoyne finalized another alliance with the Indians in the area and greatly increased his already immense army.

Southbound at Willsboro Point the Four Brothers Islands are nearly in midlake. One is wooded; the others are nearly bare. Prominent Ligonier Point, **Mile CH-43.0 W (SM)**, on the Willsboro Point peninsula, is a **Departure Point** if you plan to visit more eastern lakeshore anchorages. To be certain of your location on the wooded shoreline, a good Vermont landfall is at Saxton Reef, **Buoy #17**. It's just northeast of Saxton Point, the location of Shelburne Farms; an offshore landmark is the mansion on the bluff.

In the late 1800s, 3,800-acre Shelburne Farm belonged to the William Seward and Lila Vanderbilt Webb family. Frederick Law Olmstead designed the farm with specially planted woods, flower gardens, rolling fields, and a 110-room summer "cottage"—the mansion. The farm was unprofitable and eventually became an independent, nonprofit educational trust. Today it offers Champlain cuisine, farm tours, swimming, fishing, hiking, wagon rides, and croquet. Mozart Festival Concerts are held on the lawn during the summer; if weather is fair, you can anchor in the small cove just below the house to enjoy the music from your cockpit.

If you plan to visit the popular Vermont-shore anchorages at Quaker Smith Point, be wary of Quaker Smith Reef, watched by **Buoy #19A**, 0.7 mile west of Quaker Smith Point. Also be careful of Quaker Smith Point's west-reaching shoal, watched by **Buoy #19.**

Back on the lake's western side and southbound at Ligonier Point, **Mile CH-43.0 W (SM),** is an isolated shoal watched by **Buoy #24.** If the lake is rough, it's difficult to pick up. At **Buoy #26** there's another long shoal reaching 0.5 mile east off the Bouquet River's mouth.

By now the lake is only a few miles wide, so skipping from shore to shore is not a long process. There are pretty anchorages and marinas on both shores.

Essex, **Mile CH-50.2 W (SM),** is in a slight indentation on the western shore. If it's foggy as you approach the village, or if you are off to visit Vermont anchorages, watch for the fast-moving lake ferries crossing between Essex and McNeil Cove.

Essex, the hub of the early lake sloop trade, was also a shipbuilding center. Yards built a number of the 200-ton lake sloops and warships for Thomas Macdonough's War of 1812 American fleet. When the early canal systems opened, new commercial boats and canal barges shipped great quantities of lumber and iron ore; many were built in Essex. Essex was also on the receiving end of thousands of tons of coal that came up the Champlain Canal; the coal fueled furnaces that manufactured iron.

The eastern lakeshore's McNeil Cove and Converse Bay have few outlying dangers. There are perimeter shoreline shoals off wooded offshore islands and the mainland shores of cove and bay.

Split Rock Point, **Mile CH-53.0 W (SM),** is a prominent slab of rock with an adjacent island. Indian legend says a great chief's spirit inhabited Split Rock. Whenever anyone passed in his canoe, he was to throw gifts to the spirit to guarantee a safe journey. If a gift wasn't forthcoming, the spirit called up the fierce mountain winds and capsized the canoe.

The Indians called Split Rock "Roche Regio"; it's a historical landmark. At first it was the traditional boundary between Mohawk and Algonquian territory. In 1713, at the end of Queen Anne's War, the Treaty of Utrecht ruled it the northern limit of British possessions. In 1760 it became the boundary between New York and Canada; this shifted in 1777 to the 45th Parallel.

This is a scenic area with steep hills rising abruptly from the western shore. Midway between Split Rock and Thompsons Point, lake depths are more than 390

feet. Partially wooded Diamond Island, **Mile CH-55.6 (SM),** sits in midlake; its 35-foot white light tower is easy to see.

The Vermont shoreline south of Thompsons Point has a collection of stops and a few hazards. If you visit Town Farm Bay south of Thompsons Point, be cautious of two watched isolated shoals in the approach; buoys are hard to find. Kingsland Bay is just south of Macdonough Point; this point is on a shoal bay's southern side at Little Otter Creek's mouth. Porter Bay's southern side ends at Fort Cassin Point at Otter Creek's mouth. Keep clear of Fields Bay shoals on the southern side of the creek's mouth. They extend well west of Fort Cassin Point and are watched only by **Buoy #23.**

If you can find the deepwater channel at Otter Creek's entrance, and if your vessel has no more than 5-foot draft, you usually have depth for 8 miles to the Vergennes dam and waterfall. This tailrace supplied power for the Vergennes shipyard to build part of Thomas Macdonough's navy. For a time the British trapped Macdonough and his ships up Otter Creek; he escaped by digging a tiny canal through the lower swamps into the main lake.

As you make your way south, the lake narrows to 0.7 mile; depths alongside the northwestern face can be up to 160 feet. These Palisades have a few indentations, but as anchorages, most are very deep and exposed to easterly winds. If calms are forecast or northwesterlies are blowing, a few offer peaceful stops with extraordinarily beautiful views.

On the Vermont shore, next to the Basin Harbor resort, **Mile CH-58.8 E (SM),** is the Lake Champlain Maritime Museum. It's open from 10 to 5 and has marine displays, artifacts, historical maps, paintings, prints, and a replica of Benedict Arnold's gundelo *Philadelphia*. The Basin Harbor Club, a century-old family resort, offers dockage while you visit the museum; if you draw 6 feet and lake level is down, be cautious of depths.

As the lake widens again, North West Bay is on the western shore. In midbay, at **Mile CH-60.0 W (SM),** is Bessboro, later called Westport. In the early 1700s it was a sawmill and gristmill settlement; in the 19th century it was a noted ferry port. In the lake's heyday, from 1901 to 1950, Westport was an overnight stop for the 220-foot, 300-passenger sidewheel steamship *Ticonderoga,* which was wrecked on Point Au Fer Reef and then repaired.

If you plan to visit Vermont's Button Bay, **Mile CH-**

60.8 E (SM), and its state park, be cautious of shoals extending south from the bay's southerly reaching western peninsula to 0.3 mile south of Button Island.

Benedict Arnold stopped in Arnold Bay, **Mile CH-62.0 E (SM),** opposite Barber Point. His tattered American fleet had just battled the British for the last time at Split Rock. Arnold knew the pursuing enemy, commanded by Sir Guy Carleton, would inevitably destroy what was left of his navy, so he beached and burned his remaining four vessels. He and his men then started south on foot, bound for the safety of Fort Crown Point.

Port Henry, **Mile CH-70.0 W (SM),** is up on the hill, overlooking its harbor. The iron ore in Port Henry's countryside and mountain foothills was early rated among the world's highest-grade ore, but little was mined until the Champlain Canal opened. With low-priced access to southern markets, the canal brought about a "golden age of iron" practically overnight. Throughout the 19th century Port Henry was the center of the western shore's iron industry.

Today the iron industry is no longer profitable, and Port Henry is geared toward recreational activities. If you plan a visit, beware of shoals; consult the anchorage text for approach directions.

South of Port Henry is 2-mile-long Bulwagga Bay. Its easterly shore is bounded by the Crown Point peninsula. At one time Bulwagga Bay was partially protected from northerly weather by a causeway, but most of this has deteriorated and is now a menace. Submerged piles and cribs dot the entrance and are marked with confusing Danger buoys.

The channel bears southeasterly at Port Henry. You enter the lower lake at the high-level Chimney Point Bridge, **Mile CH-71.0 (SM).** The lower lake is an isolated, scenic section that winds along the mountain foothills and grows increasingly narrow as you continue south.

Since earliest times the Crown Point peninsula was a stopover on the only direct water route from the St. Lawrence to the Hudson. The waterway's northern section was broken by two portages—at St-Ours and Chambly. South of Crown Point peninsula voyagers had a choice of routes. They could continue to Skenesborough—now Whitehall—and from there into swampy Wood Creek, then make one portage to the upper Hudson River. This lower route was the most difficult during low water. The preferred route was to continue downlake another 14 miles to La Chute Creek,

then portage up to the northern end of north-south-oriented 32-mile-long Lac St-Sacrement—now Lake George. Another portage was necessary at the lake's southern end into the Hudson at Fort Edward.

Disputes over the ownership of Crown Point—it was used by the Indians and claimed by the French, the Dutch, and the British—eventually developed into open warfare during the French and Indian Wars.

After the Treaty of Utrecht was signed, the French built Fort St. Frederic, whose remains sit near the water's edge immediately north of the western bridge approach. The British built Fort Crown Point after capturing Fort St. Frederic and nearby Fort Carillon from the French in 1759. Fort Crown Point was located at the tip of Crown Point, set back slightly from the lake, at what is now the Crown Point Reservation. When their fort fell into disrepair the British built the Grenadier Redoubt; at its site is a 55-foot limestone lighthouse built in 1858.

Southbound the lake narrows dramatically at Crown Point village, **Mile CH-77.0 W (SM).** Locally mined and smelted iron ore was used in the construction of the Civil War ironclad U.S.S. *Monitor*.

The lake—now more like a river—varies from 0.3 mile to 1 mile in width. Though daymarks and buoys watch the channel, they are often 2 miles apart. Take care not to miss a mark; shoal water often reaches from both shores to the channel's edge. A landmark for Fivemile Point, **Mile CH-80.0 W (SM),** is its large paper mill.

At **Mile CH-84.0 (SM),** just before you begin a righthand wheel around Ticonderoga's point, watch for the cross-lake ferry to Vermont's Larabees Point—once called Shaw's Landing. The ferry dock is alongside Teachouts Store and Wharf, homeport for the tourboat *Carillon*. This is not the first ferry at Larabees Point. In 1768 a large freight ferry operated across to Fort Ticonderoga; small sailing ferries carried passengers. By 1776 the Americans had a military bridge across to Mount Independence.

As you complete the turn, Mount Independence is to the south. Southwest is towering Mount Defiance—once called Rattlesnake Mountain. Menacing Fort Ticonderoga, flags flying, sits on the northern rise near La Chute Creek's mouth—the old Lake George portage's lower end.

By now you will have noticed that the lake water has turned a muddy green. In strong, long-lasting northerly winds, downbound current may increase to 0.25 knot. At Benson Landing, **Mile CH-93.0 (SM),** prepare for critical steering as the narrow channel winds around extensive marshlands, past wooded islands, and along mountain foothills. On this section you pass a collection of "weed-eaters," odd-looking, tractor-like floating mowers. They keep the fast-growing weeds out of the channel.

Maple Bend, **Mile CH-99.1 (SM),** once had a decent offlake anchorage to its island's east; lately both entrances have shoaled and weeds clog the back channel.

At **Mile CH-103.7 W (SM)** the mountains close in and you pass large South Bay; it bears off southwest. Only runabouts can clear its entrance's low-level railroad trestle. A half mile farther south you enter the Narrows of Lake Champlain; at it's southeastern end the Poultney River, **Mile CH-105.4 E (SM),** defines the New York–Vermont border. From this point south to near Nyack on the lower Hudson River, you cruise entirely in New York. The point that forms the southern side of the Poultney's mouth is the Elbow; here by the long island, Thomas Macdonough's warships and his prizes were stored after the War of 1812.

At the island's southern end you can see Lock CC #12 in downtown Whitehall. Southbound, prepare to lock on the eastern chamber wall; there are lines and poles for securing inside the chamber.

If you plan to stay south of the lock but need fuel—gas or diesel—you may want to stop at Lock 12 Marina

before locking through. Its floating docks are on the lake's eastern shore within a few hundred feet of the dam.

The lock and dam mark Lake Champlain's southern end and the Champlain Canal's northern terminus (see "The Champlain Canal," beginning on page 398).

Lake Champlain anchorages and marinas are listed in the order they appear downbound off the main lake mileage route. Stops may be convenient to main lake east and west shores and have limited approach instructions. Others require that you leave the main route at a **Departure Point East** and divert many miles—often up to 18—to a destination somewhere on the lake's eastern shore or in the Eastern Arm. These usually require detailed approach directions. At **Mile CH-70.0 (SM)** you begin the lower lake. It's never more than about a mile wide; its navigable width is about 100 feet. Approaches are short and are given either east or west of the channel.

Keep watch for a number of very small isolated offshore shoals; many are surrounded by depths up to 80 feet. Other than an unlighted danger buoy—red-green nun or green-red can—there's often no indication that you are approaching them.

Most dockage is on floating piers. Since they must be removed seasonally, only minimal numbers are installed. The result is very crowded marinas; transient space is often unavailable late in the day, on weekends, and on

This section of the Lower Lake near Dresden is the same route taken by Benedict Arnold's northbound fleet of gundelos and row galleys during the Revolutionary War. During the War of 1812 it was also traveled by Macdonough's fleet.

American and Canadian holidays. The best time to find weekday dockage is midmorning; on weekends and holidays make reservations or anchor out. Many marinas have moorings; most are for residents, but if a boat is on holiday, the marina might rent the space. Moorings generally are outside breakwaters and are rough.

When anchoring prepare for prolific weed growth during warm-water months.

for about 0.3 mile. There's good water as far as the shoreside shoals extending about 0.1 mile off the beach. At this point consult your destination's directions.

Rouses Point's main street is north-south-oriented Highway 223, Lake Street. Within four blocks of all stops are a post office, a library and museum, snack shops, a motel, a Key Bank, a restaurant, a pharmacy, a hardware store, and a Grand Union supermarket.

Main Lake West Shore
Rouses Point, Stony Point, and Monty Bay

Mile CH-0.0 (SM) to Mile CH-12.5 (SM)

Sketch Map Depths

Sketch map depths are given at normal average summer lake level. When you venture outside the sketch map confines, you must adjust NOAA charts to chart datum. For convenience in adjusting, use the following:

Mile CH-0.0 (SM) to Mile CH-106.0 (SM): Plane of reference, Lake Champlain Low Lake Level, 93.0 feet above mean sea level

ROUSES POINT

Rouses Point is in the lake's far northern westerly bight. You have a choice of a marina (open from May 15 to November 1), a public dock, and an anchorage. All require the same general approach.

Rouses Point is south and west of an old nonoperating cross-lake trestle whose opening is nearly in midlake. It's south of the very visible high-level bridge at Old Rouses Point. Leave the main channel south of the trestle and well south of **Buoy #2.** The buoy watches a 0.4-mile-long shoal extending to the trestle's north and south not far west of its opening.

Once you clear the shoal at **Buoy #2,** bear westerly

Gaines Garage and Marina

★★★

ALL FACILITIES

Chart: N 14781, *See A on sketch map*

Mile CH-0.5 + 0.4 W (SM)

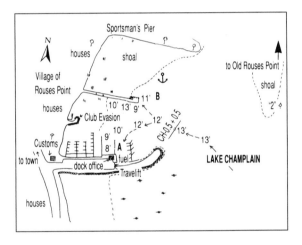

When you close the mainland, you can see three moles extending east from the shoreline; they protect the waterfront from southerly quadrant wind and seas. Your destination is the most southerly rock mole's northern side. It has a slight northerly hook; on its southern side is a mooring area.

North of the mole's end the marina opens fully; most slips extend northerly. The far, easterly pier has individual wells. The next pier extending northerly is the one you want; it has parallel parking. Pull in to any open easterly face space; if you need fuel, go to its southern end—the pumps (gas and diesel) are by the 25-ton Travelift's well. The office is in the bulkhead building.

Their land line phone is (518) 297-7000. If clearing Customs, get forms at the office and fill them out while you wait for the inspector to arrive.

Block and cube ice and electric hookups (110-volt/30-amp and 220-volt/50-amp) are available.

There's a ship's store with most marine supplies. The prettiest picnic area is at the mole's western end; there are tables, lawn, and a gazebo.

Town is nearby. The marina is on Lake Street, a few steps from the library and museum. Turn north for the rest of downtown.

Rouses Point Public Dock and Anchorage

★

Chart: N 14781, *See B on sketch map, page 360*

Mile CH-0.5 + 0.4 W (SM)

There are several marinas in Rouses Point, but dockage is often limited. The public dock, an old state barge canal terminal, is an alternative tie-up.

Once off the Gaines Marina mole, your destination is the next southeasterly extending mole. It, too, has a slight hook on its eastern tip.

The tie-up has a few problems. There is good depth only on the easterly half of the mole's southern side; the western half is shoal. Nearly all the northern side is shoal except the very eastern tip. The southern side has slight prevailing wind exposure, but except in severe winds it's tenable. Be aware that much of the southern wall's face has an underwater ledge protruding south below the surface. A well-fendered round-bilged vessel probably won't have a problem. So far there's no northerly protrusion from the deepwater northerly face's tip. There's also little to which to tie, so improvise your own cleats.

It's not an attractive stop; the mole is full of potholes, broken bottles, and trash. Its attractions: the dock is sturdy in storms and the supermarket's about a block away.

If you prefer to anchor, there's a place off the mole's northern side between it and the next wooded mole. Shoals extend off the mainland nearly to the ends of the

two moles; sound carefully. There's almost no prevailing wind protection, but it's seldom untenable. Bottom is mud and weeds.

STONY POINT ANCHORAGE NORTH

★★

NO FACILITIES

Chart: N 14781, *See A on sketch map*

Mile CH-1.8 W (SM)

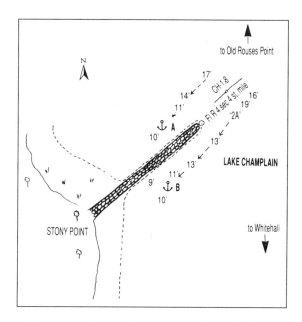

This western-shore anchorage is north of a breakwater extending east-northeasterly from Stony Point. The breakwater helps protect the lake's northwesterly bight from prevailing winds. Therefore, in southerly quadrant winds and seas you have protection; it's not protected from east, north, or northeast winds.

The breakwater is alongside the channel and is watched at its northeasterly end by **Lighted Daymark 2A.** This is your **Departure Point**; bear to the breakwater's northern side. Shoals extend well off the beach, so the best place to anchor depends on your depth. Bottom is mud; near the beach it's weedy.

You can snorkel the clear water at the breakwater; it's a browsing area for assorted lake fish and fingerlings.

STONY POINT ANCHORAGE SOUTH

★★

NO FACILITIES

Chart: N 14781, *See B on sketch map, page 361*

Mile CH-1.8 W (SM)

Your approach is the same as for Stony Point North, except when you turn west, bear south of the breakwater. The anchorage has protection from frontal winds from the west, northwest, and north. It's not protected from the northeast or southerly quadrant prevailing winds.

The western beach shoaling does not extend quite as far into the lake on this side of the breakwater, so you can anchor slightly closer to the beach. Bottom is mud and weeds.

You can snorkel by the rocks here, too.

SNUG HARBOR MARINA AT MONTY BAY

★★★

Chart: N 14781

Mile CH-12.1 + 1.5 W (SM)

This western-shore marina—open May 1 to October 1—is in Monty Bay's southern section; it's the largest facility with moorings in that area.

Though difficult to see from offshore, a very large tire breakwater protects the slips from northerly weather. The moorings are to its south. Once the breakwater is in sight, you can see two piers of slips extending easterly. The 20-ton Travelift's well is north of the northernmost pier on a short mole's easterly end. If no one answered on VHF 16, pull in to the barge fuel dock (gas and diesel) on the mole's southern side; depths at the dock are usually only about 4.5 to 5 feet. If you draw

Snug Harbor Marina at Monty Bay

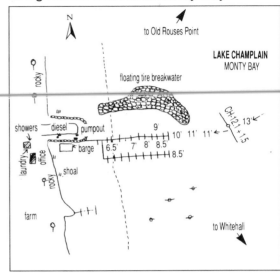

more than this and want to spend the night, pull in on the end of one of the two main piers—they're usually open—and check in at the office just south of the mole.

There's a ship's store with charts, navigation and marine equipment, camera supplies, nautical clothing, and a few groceries. A restaurant is within walking distance.

Block and cube ice and electric hookups (110-volt and 220-volt) are available. The marina's land line number is (518) 846-7900.

If dockage or a mooring is unavailable, anchor on the mooring area's edge or make the short run to Monty Bay Anchorage.

MONTY BAY ANCHORAGE

★★★

NO FACILITIES

Chart: N 14781, *See sketch map, page 363*

Mile CH-12.1 + 1.5 W (SM)

This anchorage is at Monty Bay's southern end west of Point Au Roche's North Point. It is completely exposed to northerly quadrant winds; it's protected in prevailing winds. It has a beautiful lake and mountain view.

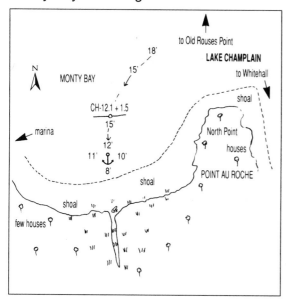

Your approach from the main lake is from the north. If northbound, give the shoals off North Point's northeastern side a fair berth. Once past these, the bay is clear as long as you don't approach the beach too closely.

La Motte Passage, Alburg Passage, and Pelots Bay

Mile CH-12.5 + (SM)

Your **Departure Point** from the main lake to reach these eastern cruising areas is **Mile CH-12.5 (SM).** This is between North Point—on Point Au Roche—and the Head, Isle La Motte's southern tip. There is an anchorage in La Motte Passage, an anchorage and a marina in Alburg Passage, and an anchorage in Pelots Bay. Take care; each has nearby shoals. Follow the individual approach directions.

LA MOTTE PASSAGE

This northeast-southwest-oriented passage separates Isle La Motte and Alburg Tongue. A low-level bridge (clearance 8 feet) crosses its shoal northerly end, so generally approach via the southern end at the Head. There are shoreline shoals at the passage's northern end and isolated shoals at the southern end.

Jordan Point Cove Anchorage

★★★   3

NO FACILITIES

Chart: N 14781

Mile CH-12.5 + 4.5 E/N (SM)

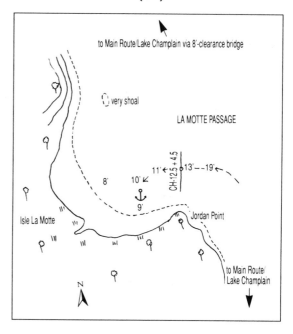

This anchorage is on Isle La Motte's eastern side. When you leave the main lake and round the Head, pay close attention to dangerous shoals. Some are watched; some are not.

Navigational aids are the dependable method of finding problem areas; anchorage approach uses them as pivotal points. Off the Head, lay off a course to the isolated rock west of Townes Reef; it's watched by red-green **Buoy H.** At this buoy lay off a course for red-green **Buoy HS,** which watches mile-long main Horseshoe Shoal's southern end. In this run you pass well east of the unwatched rock off wooded Cloak Island's east-northeastern side. At **Buoy HS** lay off a course for the 2-mile reach to Jordan Point, avoiding the shoals that are part of Horseshoe Shoal and those to Holcomb Point's south.

Jordan Point forms the anchorage's southern side. Enter the cove toward its southern limits; an unwatched isolated rock exists near the cove's northern terminus. Anchor as close to the western beach as you have depth. The cove is sufficiently indented into Isle La Motte to give protection from southwest, west, northwest, and prevailing winds. It's not protected from north, northeast, or east winds.

Bottom is mud, movable rocks, and weeds.

Try fishing for bass around Jordan Point. If you plan to barbecue your catch, do it early; mosquitoes arrive at sundown.

ALBURG PASSAGE

This passage lies on Alburg Tongue's eastern side and the western side of North Hero Island's northern portion. If you expect to enter the lake's Eastern Arm off this route, be aware that though there are two accesses for a departure into the Eastern Arm, both have restricted bridge and culvert clearances. The Gut is your main Eastern Arm access point with full clearance; it's farther south on the main lake and is reached from the **Departure Point, Mile CH-18.0 (SM).**

Alburg Passage is only accessible from the main lake through an opening in an old railroad dike. This dike extends north from Pelots Point peninsula and south from Point of Tongue, Alburg Tongue's southern tip. The opening is 0.3 mile north of the tip of Pelots Point peninsula.

To reach the Alburg Passage leave the main lake at **Departure Point, Mile CH-12.5 (SM).** At the Head, La Motte Passage is to your north; the dike opening is toward the east. As you bear easterly watch for dangerous shoals. Lay off a course to the isolated shoal west of Townes Reef; it's watched by red-green **Buoy H.** Then lay off a course for red-green **Buoy HS,** which watches the main part of mile-long Horseshoe Shoal's southern end; this route keeps you clear of Townes Reef rocks. At **Horseshoe Shoal Buoy** lay off a course for the dike

opening, which is still a mile away. A pole and a light watch each side of the opening, but they are difficult to see until fairly close.

Once through the dike opening you are in Alburg Passage's southern end. North up the passage is access into the Eastern Arm with its fixed 26-foot-clearance bridge. Dead ahead is large Carry Bay; in its south-south-eastern end there is an exit into the Eastern Arm at the Carrying Place—an early-era portage—through a culvert under Highway 2; it's accessible only to runabouts.

Marina Internationale

★★★

Chart: N 14781, *See A on sketch map*

Mile CH-12.5 + 3.7 E/S (SM)

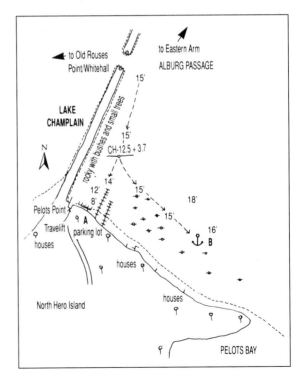

This marina is at Pelots Point in the corner beside the dike's southern end. A landmark is its mooring area east of the slips. The marina is open to the north and northeast; in strong winds from those directions, there is a lot of surge.

Start your approach after you give the dike a slight berth and follow it south-southwesterly. The marina has two long piers of slips extending north from Pelots Point and one shorter pier paralleling the shore with slips extending off its northern face. This pier is just east of the Travelift well in the harbor's western corner.

If no one answered on VHF, pull in on any T-pier or by the Travelift and then check in at the office. The staff can help you find repair facilities.

Electric hookups (110-volt) are available, and there's a small ship's store. The marina's land line number is (802) 372-5953.

If a slip or a mooring is unavailable, you can anchor off the mooring area (see B on the sketch map, page 364), though in north and northeast winds it's choppy. In these conditions better anchorage is in Pelots Bay.

Pelots Bay Anchorage

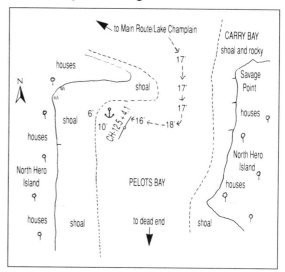

PELOTS BAY

Pelots Bay is Alburg Passage's southerly end. It's open to the north and northeast except in one deepwater area.

Pelots Bay Anchorage

  ★★★ | 3 |

NO FACILITIES

Chart: N 14781

Mile CH-12.5 + 4.1 E/S (SM)

Use the same approach from the main lake as far as Marina Internationale. At this point bear easterly along the moored boats' northern perimeter and prepare to round Pelots Point peninsula's easterly end. Be very wary of a long unwatched shoal extending south and southeast of Pelot Point's southeastern tip. However, don't give the shoals such wide berth that you bumble into North Hero Island's Savage Point shoals. Once you clear the point, round up into the bay's north-northwestern end. Go in as far as you have depth, so the point's wooded hook and its shoals gives you north and northeasterly protection.

Main Lake West Shore
Mooney Bay and Treadwell Bay

Mile CH-12.5 (SM) to Mile CH-18.0 (SM)

MOONEY BAY MARINA

★★★★ | 3 |

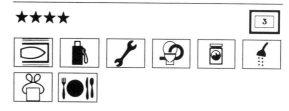

Chart: N 14781, *See sketch map, page 366*

Mile CH-15.3 + 0.2 W (SM)

This marina—open May 15 to October 15—is in a small half cove about a mile south of Point Au Roche Light tower. There is good water to come in from the lake at nearly any angle.

The marina has a collection of protective weather

Mooney Bay Marina

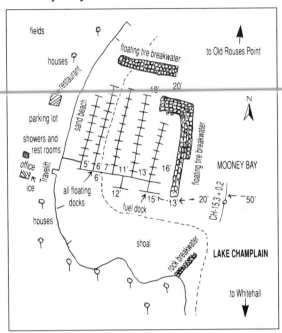

fields

houses

restaurant

floating tire breakwater

to Old Rouses Point

parking lot

sand beach

19' 20'

N

showers and rest rooms

office

Travelift

ice

all floating docks

MOONEY BAY

5' 6' 7' 11' 13' 16'
6'
12' 15' 13' 20' 50'
fuel dock

floating tire breakwater

CH-15.3 - 0.2

houses

shoal

rock breakwater

LAKE CHAMPLAIN

to Whitehall

barriers. A floating offshore tire breakwater extends east from near the beach; it gives northerly protection. A second tire breakwater extends northeast-southwest and protects from easterly weather. At this breakwater's northeastern end, it makes a right-angle bend back to the west, extending as far as the east-west breakwater. Between this right-angle jog and the east-west breakwater's easterly end is a marina entrance for use by boats tied in the northern slips. There's one more stone breakwater off the bay's southern mainland point; it extends northeast. If no one answered on VHF 16, head for the fuel dock (gas and diesel); your entrance is between the stone breakwater and the southern end of the one that runs northeast-southwest. Deep water favors the tire breakwater.

West of the tire breakwater the marina opens clearly. Most slips extend north from a long pier reaching east. Off this east-reaching main pier are two T-piers. Pull in to the fuel dock on the most easterly T's southern face. If you draw 6 feet or more, you have good depth on the two T-piers, but be cautious as you approach the main pier's westerly face; it shoals as you close the beach. The office is behind the 20-ton Travelift's well and the crane.

Block and cube ice and electric hookups (110-volt/ 30-amp and 220-volt) are available.

This is an attractive marina with fieldstone buildings, many flowers, and a brick-floored, terraced picnic and

lounging area. The land line phone is (518) 563-2960. There's a ship's store with marine equipment, navigational supplies, local charts, camera supplies, and basic groceries. Café Mooney Bay overlooks the lake.

TREADWELL BAY

Mile CH-18.0 W (SM)

This 2.5-mile-long, mile-wide bay has two anchorages in its northeastern corner, Deep Bay and Middle Bay. Both are in hilly, forested Point Au Roche State Park. There is access ashore to the park's nature trails on both peninsulas to as far north as Mooney Bay.

Both anchorages are open to the south and southwest. Strong prefrontal southwest winds result in rough anchorages due to Treadwell Bay's long deepwater fetch. Long-lasting southerly winds also cause swells to enter anchorages and make them rolly. They are protected from the southeast, the east, and the northerly quadrant.

Mile-long wooded Long Point extends southwest from the mainland and ends at Rocky Point. Extending southwest from this point is a dangerous 0.7-mile-long shoal broken by one deepwater opening that is hard to find. The entire shoal's southern end is watched by **Buoy #2.** Your safe **Departure Point** into Treadwell Bay is southwest of this buoy where you round up and head back to the bay's northeastern end.

Avoid the one dangerous shoal area watched by **Buoy #1** in the middle of Treadwell Bay.

Deep Bay Anchorage

★★★★

Chart: N 14781, *See A on sketch map, page 367*

Mile CH-18.0 + 1.5 W/N (SM)

Long Point's western side forms Deep Bay's eastern shore; Middle Point is the bay's western entry point. It's rocky off Middle Point's southern end; hold to the middle of Deep Bay as you enter. Deep Bay is nearly 0.7

Deep Bay Anchorage, Middle Bay Anchorage

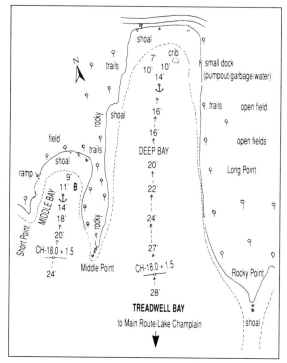

mile long and you can anchor just about anywhere, but there's easy access ashore from near its north-north-easterly end. Bottom is gravelly mud with weeds.

There's a floating dock with a coin-operated pumpout at the bay's northeastern end on its southeastern shore. Just off the dock is a buoy to mark an obstruction. If you draw more than 5 feet, approach the dock with caution; depth depends on lake level. You cannot spend the night at this dock—though some do. Up the ramp is a drinking water tap and garbage bins. If you plan a hike ashore, park the skiff behind the dock; don't block the outer face.

Expect to be boarded at anchor by the New York marine police; they check holding tank installation and border clearance.

Middle Bay Anchorage

★★★

NO FACILITIES

Chart: N 14781, *See B on sketch map*

Mile CH-18.0 + 1.5 W/N (SM)

Middle Bay is immediately west of Deep Bay. It is much shorter in length than Deep Bay and usually has fewer boats at anchor on weekends.

From the main lake use the same approach as for Deep Bay as far as Middle Point. A landmark to help spot Middle Bay is a large launching ramp on its north-north-western side. Middle Point is Middle Bay's easterly entrance point; Short Point is its western entrance point. The main danger during entry is Middle Point's outlying rocks. You can usually identify them by discoloration of clear water, but give them a good berth. Anchor wherever you please, but don't block the busy ramp.

The Eastern Arm of Lake Champlain
Sandy Point, Butler Island, Burton Island, St. Albans Bay, and Keeler Bay

Mile CH-18.0 +

The only high-clearance, deepwater access into the Eastern Arm is via the Gut, a 1.5-mile-long bay between North and South Hero islands. There are three other routes to reach the Eastern Arm, but they all have clearance or depth restrictions.

To reach the Eastern Arm, leave the main lake route at **Departure Point, Mile CH-18.0 W (SM),** at **Buoy #2** off Long Point's southerly shoals at Treadwell Bay. Choose a course that takes you across the lake to pass south of **Buoy #1;** it watches Middle Reef's southerly rocks. Now pass north of the unwatched rocks off wooded Bixby Island's eastern end. Here you must choose a clear course that takes you to the Gut's western entrance. This course leads you north of narrow Nichols Point with its bulbous northern tip, and from there 0.5 mile farther east toward an opening through an old railroad dike. If the lake level is high, be cautious approaching Nichols Point. The narrowest part of the point's peninsula is low and may be submerged. This leaves its northern tip an island. Do not confuse the submerged peninsula portion with the Gut's entrance.

The Gut is enclosed on the west by long, narrow Bow Arrow Point to the north and Tromp Point to the south. Your only entry from the west is through the opening between them. It's watched on the west by **Buoy #9,** which sits practically in front of the opening, and by **Daymark #2.** Once through the opening, your channel bears in a northerly swing and is watched by **Buoy #4** and **Buoy #6.** Next you bear east-northeasterly across the Gut. The approach to its eastern side is watched by **Buoy #5** and **Daymark #8.** This side of the Gut is enclosed by Knight Point to the north and Sandy Point to the south. They are separated by the Grand Isle bascule bridge, which you must transit to enter the Eastern Arm.

Eastern Arm approach directions are referenced from this bridge.

TUDHOPE SAILING CENTER (SANDY POINT)

★★★ [3]

Chart: N 14781

Mile CH-18.0 + 4.9 E (SM)

This marina—open May 15 to October 15—is along Sandy Point's northern end on Grand Isle Bridge's eastern side. East of the bridge you can see the marina; it's the largest group of slips on the southern shoreline. Continue east a short distance before turning southeast; this way you clear the weeds on the dike's eastern side.

The marina's two piers have slips extending northwest from Sandy Point nearly paralleling the dike; another east-west-oriented pier is set at an angle to the

Tudhope Sailing Center (Sandy Point)

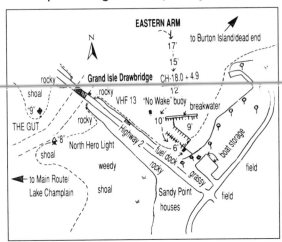

main slips. It serves as a breakwater, since the marina is wide open to the northeast. In a northeast blow the marina has some surge.

If no one answered on VHF 16, pull in to the fuel dock (gas and diesel); it's on the western side of the pier nearest the highway dike's southern end. If you draw more than 6 feet, be cautious as you close the beach slips.

The office is up the ramp. The staff can assist you in finding repair facilities. There is a ship's store with marine equipment, local charts, nautical clothing, camera supplies, and basic groceries.

Block and cube ice, electric hookups (110-volt/50-amp), and a 6-ton lift are available. The land line number is (802) 372-5320.

The 15-acre marina complex is a pretty area for walking or jogging. Town is 4 miles away; the Shore Acres Restaurant is 3 miles away. The marina has a courtesy car.

BUTLER ISLAND ANCHORAGE

★★★★ [2]

NO FACILITIES

Chart: N 14781, *See sketch map, page 369*

Mile CH-18.0 + 10.8 E/N (SM)

Wooded Butler Island is about 6 miles northeast of the Grand Isle bascule bridge. The anchorage is on the

Butler Island Anchorage

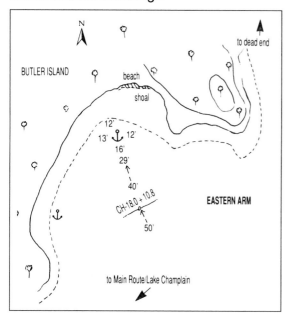

BURTON ISLAND STATE PARK

★★★★★

Chart: N 14781

Mile CH-18.0 + 10.0 E (SM)

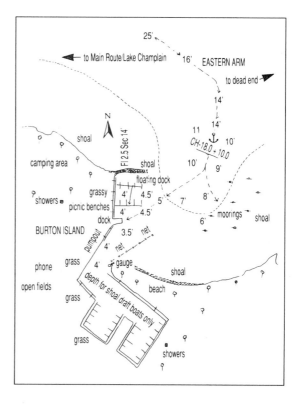

island's eastern side near its northeastern end. It's well protected from the north, northeast, northwest, and west. It's badly exposed to strong southerlies or southeasterlies. In the hot, calm days of summer this stop has excellent swimming and a cooling breeze.

Leave the Grand Isle Bridge and lay off a 5-mile-long northeasterly course to take you about 0.3 mile southeast of the wooded islet on Butler's eastern side near its southern end. On the way you pass about 0.5 mile off wooded Knight Island. When you reach Butler's satellite islet, do not use the channel between Butler and the islet; dangerous rocks exist. When east of the islet begin to bear into the 0.5-mile-wide cove near its northeastern end.

You can anchor nearly anywhere in a mud bottom with weeds, but there are pleasant depths at its northern end. The cove shoals slowly as you close the beach, and if you anchor close to shore you risk a weedy swim.

Burton Island lies easterly off St. Albans Point, a long peninsula that forms St. Albans Bay's northwestern side. The island is in a 253-acre Vermont State Park— open May 31 to Labor Day. Its marina and mooring area are on the island's northern side at its eastern end.

Once through the Grand Isle Bridge make your way 0.7 mile to Ladd Point, South Hero's northern end. Here lay off a 3.5-mile-long easterly course for Burton Island's northern side. Once you approach the island, stand off its northern shore; shoals extend north of the shoreline near its easterly end. When near the eastern end, locate a stone breakwater reaching easterly. This breakwater protects the outer marina. Do not approach the breakwater closely; shoals extend well to the breakwater's northeast.

East of the breakwater you can see a collection of park moorings that are usually filled with visiting boats. Make your turn into the marina area east of the breakwater and just west of the moorings; most moorings are in shoal water.

If you draw 6 feet you are unlikely to have sufficient depth to make the dock approach. You will have depth at a few moorings. If unable to get into the outer harbor, try to contact the dockmaster on VHF 16 to see if you can rent one of these. If you can't locate him, pick up a mooring, row in, check in, tell him where you are, and explain your depth problem. The state tries to reserve a few moorings for deep-draft vessels. You are not allowed to anchor beside the moorings.

If depth is no problem, pull in to the outer harbor's most southerly dock. This is the pumpout and fuel dock; the office is on the mainland. The park also has a large, nearly landlocked inner harbor, but it's normally only usable by very shoal draft boats and runabouts. Its entrance channel opens just south of the fuel dock.

Electric hookups (110-volt/30-amp) and cube ice are available. The office land line number is (802) 524-6353.

The park has camping facilities, a snack bar, picnic areas, trails, playgrounds, swimming areas, rowboat and canoe rentals, a visitor center, and ranger talks and walks. There are beautiful views across the Eastern Arm islands to the highest Adirondacks peaks; the one with the distinctive scar is Whiteface Mountain.

Since this is an island camping area, a daytime launch service runs every hour and a half to Kill Kare Park on St. Albans Point's southeastern tip. If you badly need supplies and are willing to pay expensive taxi fares, the boat can also shuttle crews to Kill Kare Park. There you must call a taxi from downtown St. Albans. Then return by taxi to catch the launch back to Burton Island. If you have mainland visitors coming by launch, get them on the last boat back or they're your overnight guests.

The cut at Burton Island's eastern end is *not* recommended as a north-south route to reach or leave this marina. It's not well watched, and it's filled with rocks and reefs. If you must go from one side of Burton Island to the other, be safe; take the long way around **Buoy #1,** well southwest of Ball Island, which lies southwest of Burton Island.

ST. ALBANS BAY ANCHORAGE

★★★

NO FACILITIES

Chart: N 14781

Mile CH-18.0 + 14.5 E (SM)

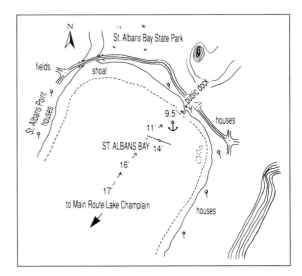

St. Albans Bay and the village of the same name are on the Eastern Arm's eastern side. The bay is 2.5 miles long, about a mile wide, and bounded on the west by St. Albans Point. It's open to prevailing lake winds and is usually windswept.

Once through the Grand Isle Bridge your **Departure Point** is off Ladd Point, South Hero's northern end. Lay off a southeasterly course for **Buoy #1** off Ball Island's southwestern shoals; this island is southwest of Burton Island. At **Buoy #1** round up east-northeasterly. Lay off a course for **Buoy #3,** which watches a rocky patch off Hathaway Point at St. Albans Bay's entrance. This course takes you well off Burton Island's southern side.

Once northeast of **Buoy #3** you are finally in St. Albans Bay. Keep clear of the unwatched rock sitting midway between Rock Island and Lazy Lady Island—old Ram Island—on the east. Most of the bay's eastern shore between Lazy Lady and Mill River is shoal, so stay in midbay to its northeastern end. The anchorage is off the public dock.

There are a few shoal areas at the bay's far eastern section; stand off until you find your destination. The large, cement dock is L shaped; the L's limb reaches northwest.

Dockage is not recommended; it can be rough due to prevailing wind chop. If you anchor in mud and weeds close to the pier, you have a short row if planning an excursion ashore; tie the dinghy in the dock's lee.

St. Albans Bay is a residential area; for supplies and supermarket, you must get to large St. Albans, about 3 miles east on Highway 36. It's too far to walk; call a St. Albans taxi.

KEELER BAY ANCHORAGE

★★★   3

NO FACILITIES

Charts: N 14781; N 14782

Mile CH-18.0 + 15.6 E/S (SM)

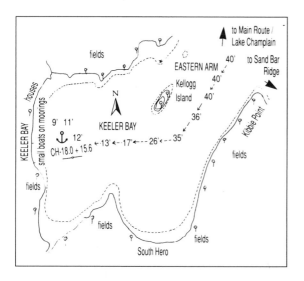

Keeler Bay is in this Eastern Arm section's southern end on South Hero Island's eastern shore.

Once through the Grand Isle Bridge, head for Ladd Point (South Hero's northern end), then bear southerly for Keeler Bay. Most of this section has good depth; you can cruise about 0.25 mile off the shoreline. You could go south along South Hero to more easily find Keeler Bay, and return along the Arm's eastern shore. This way you have new views of each shore and the wooded islands.

Shoals include those off the eastern entrance of South Hero's Pearl Bay; the perimeter shoals of large Savage Island; an isolated unwatched shoal midway between Savage Island's southern end and South Hero's Cooper Bay; and Keeler Bay's entry shoals. If you make an Eastern Arm perimeter cruise, watch out for extensive shoals north of the fixed Sand Bar Bridge.

As you start south from Ladd Point and round the prominent point south of Ladd Bay, large, wooded north-south-oriented Savage Island sits in midlake.

A few coves on South Hero make pleasant lunch stops if wind is calm and is not from the southerly quadrant. These include Pearl Bay, its unnamed neighbors to the northeast and southwest, and Cooper Bay. If you draw 6 feet and lake level is very low, don't forget the unwatched shoal 0.7 mile east of Cooper Point.

At Cooper Point you have a good view of wooded Fish Bladder and Cedar islands trailing south from Savage Island. Fish Bladder's southern end is almost due east of Kibbie Point, Keeler Bay's eastern entrance point. Stand clear of shoals to Kibbie Point's north and east.

Keeler Bay opens to the northeast. Wooded Kellogg Island sits just inside the bay nearly in mid-entrance. Enter midway between Kibbie Point and Kellogg Island's eastern side; shoals extend north-northeast from Kellogg Island nearly to South Hero's mainland.

After you enter Keeler Bay give Kellogg Island's southern end a wide berth, then bear westerly and anchor where you have the best lee. Preferred anchorage is midway on the western shore fairly close to the South Hero beach in mud and weeds. Most of the bay's western side is a residential area; it's private property.

Main Lake West Shore
Treadwell Bay to Garden Island

Mile CH-18.0 (SM) to Mile CH-30.0 (SM)

PLATTSBURGH

Plattsburgh's harbor is off the main lake on Cumberland Bay's western side just south of the Saranac River's mouth. Though an offshore breakwater protects the harbor, it's not particularly secure from north through northeasterly winds. If these winds increase, the harbor has a surge. You have a choice of a marina or an anchorage; both are within a long walk of town.

Your **Departure Point** from the main lake is near ~~Cumberland Head Light, Mile CH-22.7 (SM)~~, at Cumberland Head's southern end. Shoals extend southwesterly off the point, so give it a fair berth. Lay off a 2.5-mile northwesterly course to the 29-foot-high light tower on Plattsburgh's offshore stone breakwater's northeastern end. Town landmarks are its slender tower, blue tank, church steeples, and large buildings.

Once you clear the breakwater light, the harbor opens clearly. The large collection of docks is the marina; northwest of the breakwater is the anchorage.

Downtown Plattsburgh is a long walk away. Follow the main road west and continually bear toward the tall, prominent winged monument. Cross the stone bridge over the Saranac River, then bear northerly. You can stop for a rest in the landscaped park and have a close look at the monument. Built in 1926, it commemorates Commodore Thomas Macdonough's 1814 naval victory at the Battle of Plattsburgh. Each side of the monument represents one of Macdonough's main warships, *Saranac, Eagle, Ticonderoga,* and *Preble*.

Walk along the park and approach Cornelia Street; City Hall is across the road. The Clinton County Historical Museum—open Friday through Monday from 1 to 4—is on the top floor. It has displays, dioramas, artifacts, and memorabilia of the War of 1812 Battle of Plattsburgh and the Revolutionary War Battle of Valcour.

If you continue through the park, as the river makes its bend to the east, just across the street is the Federal-style Kent DeLord House, built in 1797. It was the home of three generations of DeLords. The house is open for tours Tuesday through Saturday at 10, 1, and 3.

In the park at the river's mouth is another monument; this one honors Champlain.

The business district encompasses a two- to three-block area east of the stone bridge. It has the usual city stores, though the supermarket is over a mile away. Sunbright Grocery on Margaret Street near the intersection of Cornelia Street is a laundromat—groceries consist of soda pop. The post office is on Miller Street, a half block north of City Hall.

Large Plattsburgh malls are not within walking distance, but there are taxis and car rentals; phone num-

bers are at the marina phone booth. If you have transportation, you might enjoy the State University of New York College at Plattsburgh campus. It was founded in 1889. The Myers Fine Arts Gallery is on campus, and the Rockwell Kent Gallery is in the university library building.

~~Plattsburgh is home of the Plattsburgh SAC Air~~ Force Base's museum, which offers military history tours; it's open Monday through Friday from 2 to 4.

Plattsburgh Harbor Marina

★★★

ALL FACILITIES

Chart: N 14782

Mile CH-22.7 + 3.0 W (SM)

This marina—open May 15 to October 15—has slips in a partially enclosed basin; others extend east from the lake's shoreline. A small floating offshore tire breakwater somewhat protects its southernmost slips.

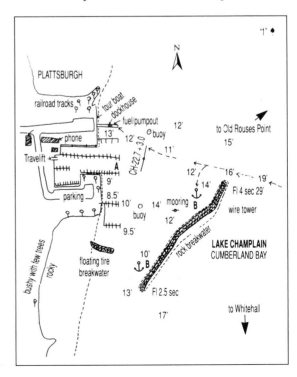

If no one answered on VHF 68, parallel park on the fuel dock (gas and diesel). It's at the slip farthest north that extends east off the mainland. If you can't find the dockmaster, check in at the quonset hut office at the enclosed basin's northwestern corner.

Block and cube ice, electric hookups (110-volt/50-amp), and a 35-ton Travelift are available. The marina's land line number is (518) 561-2800.

There's a ship's store with marine equipment and supplies, charts, guides, nautical clothing, and basic groceries.

Downtown is 0.25 mile away; getting out of the marina complex is about the longest part of the walk. At the top of the first hill is the D and H Restaurant. As you bear right toward the monument, there's another café and a large auto parts store.

Plattsburgh Anchorage

★★★

Chart: N 14782, *See B on sketch map, page 372*

Mile CH-22.7 + 3.0 W (SM)

This anchorage is northwest of the main breakwater. It is exposed to northerly winds with a 1.5-mile Cumberland Bay fetch—the same exposure as the outer marina slips. Though the anchorage is tenable in northerly weather, it's badly windswept and choppy.

There are usually one or two orange-black buoys west of the breakwater. Do not anchor to their east; it's the marina slip approach.

If you plan to go ashore, check in at the fuel dock and ask where to leave the dinghy. Offer payment if you leave trash or take on water.

SNUG HARBOR MARINA AT VALCOUR

★★★★

ALL FACILITIES

Chart: N 14782

Mile CH-27.8 + 0.5 W (SM)

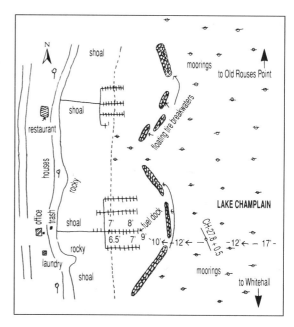

This large marina complex is on the mainland, west of Valcour Island's Bluff Point.

Southbound at Valcour Island's northern end, pick up **Buoy #2** at Valcour Shoal. Continue south in Valcour Bay another 0.6 mile. For a **Departure Point** pick up **Buoy #1**; it's north of Bluff Point's old red-roofed light-house. Your destination isn't hard to spot. At one time it was two marinas; now combined, it has a very large collection of slips and offshore moorings.

Head for the complex's southern end. If lake level is down and you draw 6 feet or more, be cautious; depths shoal as you near shore. Boats on moorings partially obscure a collection of isolated tire breakwaters protecting the slips from southeast through northeast. Nearly all usable entrances through these groups of tires are watched. If no one answered on VHF 16, your most convenient break to reach the fuel dock and check in is at the most southerly breakwater's northern end.

West of the breakwaters the southern marina complex

opens. This section has four piers with slips extending easterly. The fuel dock (gas and diesel) is the easterly end of the second pier to the north; the office is at the head of the main ramp. If a slip is unavailable, ask about a rental mooring; it won't be protected from wind or chop.

Block and cube ice, electric hookups (110-volt/30-amp and 220-volt/50-amp), and a 15-ton Travelift are available. If you need a diver, check at the office. The marina's land line number is (518) 563-5140.

The marina's two sections are some distance apart, but each has its own shoreside facilities. Ship's stores have marine equipment and supplies, charts, nautical clothing, basic groceries, and picnic and camera supplies. Nearby is a golf course, a camping area, a travel trailer park, and a motel. Within a short walk is a popular restaurant.

You are not within walking distance of a town, but there's a courtesy car for rent.

VALCOUR ISLAND

Chart: N 14782

Mile CH-27.0 (SM) to Mile CH-29.2 (SM)

Valcour Island, a Historical National Monument, has five anchorages. None offers total protection; choose which is the most desirable based on wind conditions. The western shore has anchorages north and south of Bluff Point; the eastern shore has Spoon Bay, Sloop Cove, and Smuggler Harbor. Except for a part of Bluff Point that's private, you can go ashore and hike island trails. All these anchorages tend to be very crowded.

Bluff Point North (Valcour Island West)

★★★★

NO FACILITIES

Chart: N 14782

Mile CH-27.9 + 0.2 E (SM)

Bluff Point is about mid-island on the western shore; landmarks are Bluff Point Light, an unattractive wire

Valcour Island: Bluff Point North, Bluff Point South

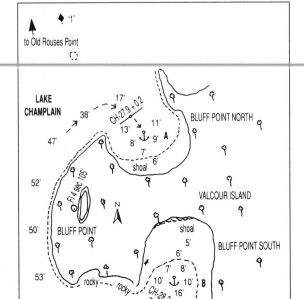

tower, and the old stone lighthouse. During prevailing southerly winds this is a protected anchorage; during north and northwesterlies it's badly exposed. If such a wind change threatens, move around to Bluff Point's southern side.

Leave mid–Valcour Channel when about due west of the lighthouse; then bear toward it. There's a dangerous shoal north of Bluff Point; it's watched by **Buoy #1.** This obstruction extends south of the buoy, which makes the shoal's location difficult to judge accurately. Therefore, when you close Bluff Point, favor its shore and bear northerly and then easterly into the cove. Bottom is mud and weeds.

Bluff Point South (Valcour Island West)

 ★★★   2

NO FACILITIES

Chart: N 14782, *See B on sketch map, page 374*

Mile CH-28.2 + 0.4 E (SM)

During north, northeast, and east winds this anchorage is well protected; it's open to prevailing southerly winds. During strong prefrontal southwesterlies, it's unsafe. During those conditions you can find temporary haven on Bluff Point's northern side. However, the frontal passage's strong wind shift is usually northwest; you would then find that anchorage untenable. Best protection in prefrontal winds and their northerly shift is at Smuggler Harbor and Sloop Cove on the island's eastern shore, at least until the front's accompanying strong northeasterlies arrive.

Continue about 0.2 mile south of Bluff Point Light before making your easterly swing around the point's southern end. Bottom is mud and weeds. The beach in this area is private property.

Smuggler Harbor (Valcour Island East)

★★★★★ 3

NO FACILITIES

Chart: N 14782

Mile CH-29.3 + 2.0 E/N (SM)

This anchorage is on Valcour's eastern side; it's well protected from all winds except from the easterly quadrant. However, this exposure depends on your draft. Shoal-draft vessels usually can tuck well inside an inner cove's southeastern or northwestern corner with good protection.

Leave the main mileage route at the southern end of Valcour Island and bear easterly. There's clear passage between Valcour and small, wooded Garden Island. If you have deep draft and are coming in from the south-

Valcour Island: Smuggler Harbor

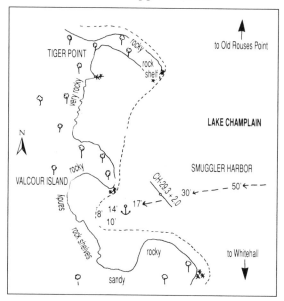

east, be careful of shoal Garden Island Ledge, which is watched by **Buoy #14.** When the eastern side of Valcour opens clearly, bear northerly along the shore for about 0.5 mile.

Smuggler Harbor is the most southerly west-reaching shore indentation. Stand off and sort out your location. At first glance it appears to be one large cove with a large mouth bounded on the north by Tiger Point. This is not the case. Shoal water reaches south from Tiger Point. Smuggler is in the southern section and south of a small inner point. At this inner point Smuggler opens and then branches north and south. If your draft is 6 feet or more, chances are very good you cannot get inside either branch and must anchor at the entrance.

Come in midway between the inner point and the southern point. A shoal extends south from the inner point. If you anchor outside the entrance, sound for swinging-room depth so you clear the shoal and rocks off to the north. Bottom is mud; inside the cove there are also rocks.

There's fair perch and bass fishing along the shoreline by Tiger Point.

Sloop Cove (Valcour Island East)

★★★★

NO FACILITIES

Chart: N 14782

Mile CH-26.5 + 2.3 E/S (SM) or Mile CH-29.3 + 2.3 E/N (SM)

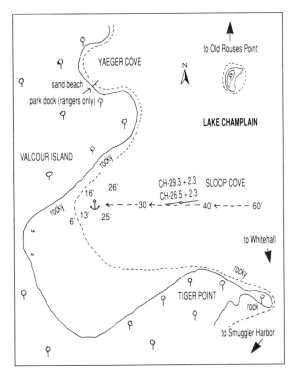

This anchorage is on Valcour's eastern side about mid-island. It's fairly protected from nearly all winds except those from the easterly quadrant. In these conditions better protection is on Valcour's western shore at Bluff Point. In strong southeasterlies the cove has a surge.

To reach this anchorage from the main mileage route you can take a departure from either end of Valcour.

From the north: Take a departure about 0.5 mile north of **Valcour Shoal Buoy #2.** Keep well clear of the island's rocky northern-perimeter shoals and then bear easterly around the end. Keep clear of the isolated rock watched by **Buoy #12;** it's not far from the island's northeastern tip and lies about 0.3 mile east of the island. The first large indentation in the shoreline south of **Buoy #12** is Spoon Bay; it has a long, wooded island

paralleling its shore at its southern entrance. Keep off-shore, then pick up the tiny, partially wooded islet that lies off Sloop Cove's northern side. Pass east or west of the islet — give it a decent berth — and once to its south bear into Sloop Cove.

From the south: Leave Valcour Bay south of the island, round its southern end and bear northerly. Keep offshore and continue past Smuggler Cove. Tiger Point forms Sloop Cove's southern entrance. You can enter about midway between this point and Sloop Cove's off-shore islet.

The cove is fairly large. The farther inside you go, the better the protection from wind and chop. Preferred anchorage is near the trees close to shore about mid-way in the cove on its northwestern side. Bottom is muddy gravel and weeds. The park employees' boat dock is in Yaegers Cove, around Sloop Cove's northern Point.

Spoon Bay (Valcour Island East)

★★★★

NO FACILITIES

Chart: N 14782

Mile CH-26.5 + 2.1 E/S (SM)

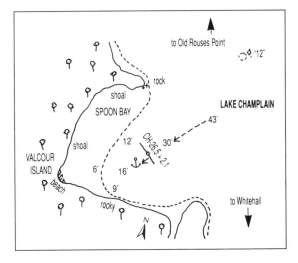

This anchorage is on Valcour's eastern side near its northeastern end. It has good protection except from the

---

northeast and the east; in winds from those directions it can be untenable. In these conditions best anchorages are on Valcour's western side at Bluff Point.

From the main mileage route that's west of Valcour, take a departure about 0.5 mile north of **Valcour Shoal Buoy #2.** Keep clear of the island's northern perimeter shoals, then bear around the end. Look for the shoal watched by **Buoy #12,** about 0.3 mile offshore near the island's northeastern tip. The first large shore indentation south of **Buoy #12** is Spoon Bay. The entrance is wide. Part of the southern entrance point is an elongated island paralleling shore.

Where you anchor depends on your draft; you might even have depth on the bay's shoal northwestern side. You'll have the most protection from prevailing afternoon breeze and chop if you hold more to the deep southeastern side near the beach. Bottom is mud with weeds.

There's fair bass fishing on the entrance's south side in the elongated island cut.

The Southern Eastern Arm of Lake Champlain
Malletts Bay

Mile CH-30.0 + (SM)

This large bay is in the Eastern Arm's far southern end on its eastern shore. It has anchorages and marinas—all busy and well filled.

To visit Malletts Bay from the main lake, your **Departure Point, Mile CH-30.0 (SM),** is south of Garden Island off Valcour Island's southern end. Plan an easterly course to the Vermont shore and leave Providence Island and the rock islet, Carleton Prize, to your north. Leave Stave Island to your south. Now you must find the entrance into the Eastern Arm's far southern end.

This Eastern Arm portion is really a very large bay. It's bounded on the north by the Sand Bar Causeway and on the west by an old 3-mile-long railroad dike that arcs from Allen Point at South Hero Island's southern tip to the Vermont mainland at Colchester Point. The

only fairly deepwater, full-clearance opening into the southern Eastern Arm is in the dike. From offshore the dike looks like a white strand.

The dike opening is about 0.5 mile south of Allen Point. Shoals parallel the dike and extend up to 0.5 mile to its east and west and more than 0.5 mile northwest. Approach to the opening is north of this latter shoal, which is extensive. The route is neither buoyed nor especially deep at low water stage. During normal lake level, once you find the channel, 6-foot-draft vessels usually have no severe problem. Note that heavy weed growth causes inaccurate fathometer readings.

East of the cut, **Buoy #1** is just ahead; it watches a northerly shoal. Malletts Bay is still 4.3 miles southeast; its mouth is between Malletts Head and Red Rock Point, so at **Buoy #1** lay off a proper course.

MALLETTS BAY ANCHORAGE

★★★★

NO FACILITIES

Chart: N 14782

Mile CH-30.0 + 11.0 E (SM)

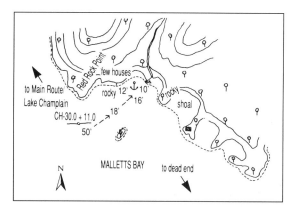

This anchorage is on Malletts Bay's northern shore not far from the bay's entrance. It's open to more than 2 miles of southerly quadrant bay winds; if they are strong, the anchorage is badly windswept and choppy. In these conditions it's more comfortable on the bay's southern side.

Mallett Bay's northern entrance point is Red Rock

Point; Malletts Head is south. Enter midway between the two, then locate an approach landmark, a small, wooded unnamed island about 0.3 mile southeast of Red Rock Point. A few shoals reach southeasterly off Red Rock Point toward this island; a few reach southwesterly off the island. Neither are a menace at normal lake level. When you are about in a line between Marble Island—close to Malletts Head's eastern end—and the unnamed island, bear north-northeast. Hold about midway between Red Rock Point and the small island.

There are a number of northern-shore coves. Most are for shoal drafts. Your destination is the second indentation east of Red Rock Point. Though that area appears unsettled, there are homes among the shoreline trees and at least one private dock along the cove's western side. Anchor as far inside the cove as depth allows; bottom is gravelly mud with weeds.

MALLETTS BAY MARINA

★★★ 3

ALL FACILITIES
Chart: N 14782

Mile CH-30.0 + 12.5 E (SM)

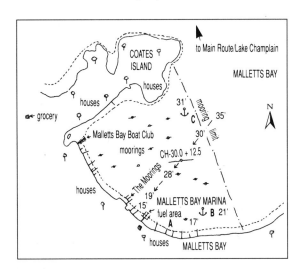

This marina—open May 15 to October 15—is in the bay's southwestern section on Coates Island's southern side about 2 miles from the bay's entrance.

After you make your entry into Malletts Bay between Red Rock Point and Malletts Head, hold northeast of the eastern shore's collection of islands. These include Marble Island, Cave Island and its western satellite, and two small unnamed islets. By now you can see marinas, yacht clubs, and mooring areas appearing along the Malletts Head shoreline between the islands; this is *not* your destination.

Once clear of the islands' northeasterly shoals, bear toward the eastern end of prominent Coates Island, a 0.7-mile-long peninsula jutting off the bay's southwestern shoreline. South of Coates Island is a huge mooring area in the peninsula's bight. Your destination is the most southeasterly of two marinas with a large number of slips; both are well southeast of the peninsula. Work that way through the moored boats.

Malletts Bay Marina has one main dock that runs parallel to shore; extending to this dock's northeast are four long piers of slips. If no one answered on VHF 16, pull in to the fuel dock—the end of the second dock from the south. You can see the gas pumps and a dock office; the main office is up the ramp.

Block and cube ice, electric hookups (110-volt/30-amp), and a 15-ton Travelift are available. The marina's land line number is (802) 862-4072.

If dockage is unavailable, you can anchor outside the mooring areas.

Across the road is Malletts Bay Campground; next door is the Beach and Boat Motel. Within a short walk you can find marine equipment, charts, navigation supplies, restaurants, roller skating, miniature golf, hardware stores, and a market.

Main Lake West Shore
Garden Island to Schuyler Island

Mile CH-30.0 (SM) to Mile CH-37.0 (SM)

PORT KENT ANCHORAGE

★★★

NO FACILITIES

Chart: N 14782

Mile CH-35.0 + 0.6 W

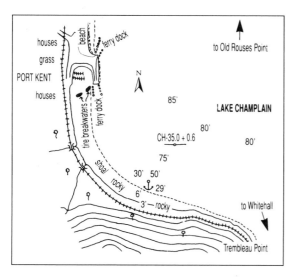

This anchorage is just south of Port Kent in Trembleau Point's lee. It's badly exposed to all winds from the northerly quadrant and from the east.

Southbound on the lake make sure you clear the Ausable River's southern shoals; they're watched by **Buoy #18.** Once south of the buoy, bear midway between Port Kent and Trembleau Point. Port Kent is the western terminus of the Burlington ferry; its piers are north-south oriented from a short shoreline mole.

Go in close to the beach to find decent depths; the headland can give you prevailing wind protection. Bottom is mud with weeds.

There's a small marina in the southern bight of the

ferry dock mole. It's protected from the south and southeast by two tire breakwaters. Slips are generally for area resident's runabouts, but it's a secure place to leave the skiff for a tour ashore; land on the beach. If you have shoal draft, occasionally a transient slip is available; check at the ferry dock office.

There's a small store, snack bar, and phone at the ferry landing.

Main Lake East Shore
Burlington and Shelburne Bay

Mile CH-37.0 + (SM)

BURLINGTON

Burlington is in the center of the curve of Burlington Bay on the lake's eastern shore. Transient dockage is limited; be prepared to anchor off.

A fixed main-lake departure point to Burlington is at **Departure Point, Mile CH-37.0 (SM)**, on Schuyler Island's eastern-side mid-island light tower. Lay off a 7-mile-long, east-southeasterly course to the northern end of Burlington Harbor Breakwater. This route brings you well north of Schuyler Reef, **Mile CH-38.0 (SM)**; its buoy is not a good departure point, as in rough weather or fog it's very difficult to find.

As you close the lake's eastern shore, hold south of Appletree Shoal, which is watched by a red-green nun—also difficult to spot.

The 0.7-mile-long Burlington breakwater is about 0.3 mile offshore. It parallels shore and offers partial harborfront protection from westerly quadrant wind and seas. Strong southerly and northerly winds bring in a chop of varying intensity and can make the harbor rolly.

Enter at either breakwater end. North Light, a 35-foot-high red skeleton tower with a small white house, is at the northern end; another light watches the southern end. Cross-lake ferries use both entrances.

Ferry Dock Marina

★★★

Chart: N 14782

Mile CH-37.0 + 7.5 E (SM)

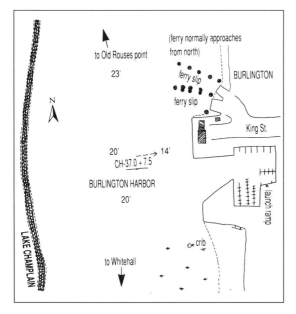

This marina—open April 14 to October 18—is the only one in downtown Burlington that welcomes transients. It has limited space, and vessels with drafts more than 4 feet may not have depth in its basin. Outside dockage can be rough.

The marina is easy to find. A mole extends from the shoreline about 0.5 mile south of North Light. On the mole's north side are the cross-lake ferry docks; the marina is on the south side. Pull in to the fuel dock (gas only) on the mole and inquire about space and depths. Depth is good to the pump and pumpout, but the basin is shoal. Large tour boats, one power and one sail, take up most of the adjacent deepwater outer dock area; they come and go, so don't tie in their spaces.

Block and cube ice and electric hookups (110-volt/30-amp) are available. The marina's land line number is (802) 864-9804.

A few blocks north of the ferry dock are two marine hardware stores. Within a four- or five-block radius are most city facilities. There is a restaurant on the mole.

The outer mall and supermarket are more than a mile away; there are taxis and a local bus.

Burlington International Airport, 3 miles east, has flights to most major cities. Rental cars are available there.

Church Street Marketplace, about six blocks east of the waterfront, is a brick-paved, tree-lined, traffic-free mall that covers about four blocks. It's decorated with hanging baskets, flower beds, and fluttering flags and has stores, a theater, banks, and cafés.

If you brought along your bicycle, pedal along the scenic 8-mile shoreline bicycle path.

You might enjoy a visit to the University of Vermont campus off Highway 2, though you'll need transportation. The Robert Hull Fleming Museum has an art collection dating from the 18th century; it's open Monday through Friday from 10 to 5.

The Shelburne Museum, founded by Electra Havemeyer Webb in 1947, is in the inland village of Shelburne. Though you are close to the museum if you visit Shelburne Bay (see page 381), it's more convenient to visit by rental car from Burlington. Displays include immense barns, a house, an 1890 railroad station, and the 220-foot sidewheel steamship *Ticonderoga*, which docks in a museum "basin" near a landbound reconstructed Colchester Reef Lighthouse. There are also collections of carriages, sleighs, guns, art, decoys, quilts, and Victorian valentines.

While in the museum vicinity, drive about 2 miles to Saxon Point to the main house of Shelburne Farm. Today the Vanderbilt mansion is a hotel and restaurant.

Burlington Harbor Anchorage

★★★★

Chart: N 14782, *See sketch map, page 381*

Mile CH-37.0 + 8.0 E (SM)

This anchorage is in Burlington Harbor's southern end along the breakwater's eastern side. It's the only harbor area in which you can anchor legally. It's not well protected except from the west and northwest. Winds from the southwest and southeast make the anchorage

Burlington Harbor Anchorage

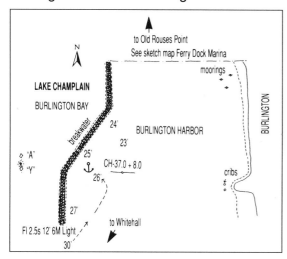

Shelburne Shipyard

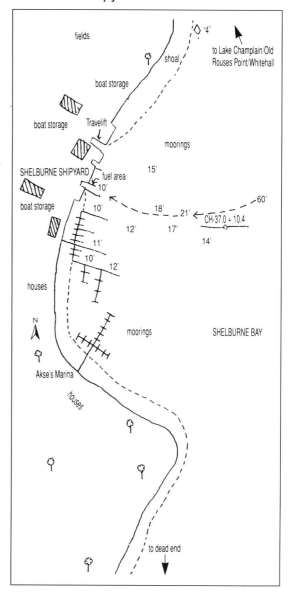

rolly; winds from the northeast make it choppy; in all these wind directions it's badly windswept.

Whichever breakwater entry you use, make for its southern end. The breakwater is a series of slight jogs; there's fair anchorage in a mud bottom just north of the southern jog. The city lamplighting is a pleasant backdrop for a cockpit supper.

Leave the dinghy at the Ferry Dock Marina, but don't tie up until you have the dockmaster's permission.

SHELBURNE SHIPYARD, INC. (SHELBURNE BAY)

★★★★   4

Charts: N 14782; N 14783

Mile CH-37.0 + 10.4 E/S (SM)

Three-mile-long, eastern-shore Shelburne Bay is one of Burlington's main yachting centers—the other is Malletts Bay. Shelburne Bay is about 2 miles southwest of Burlington breakwater's South Light; it's open at its northern end.

Your approach depends on where you came from on the lake.

From the northeast: If you visited Burlington Harbor, you come in from the northeast. Follow the

approach directions to Burlington, make your way to Burlington Harbor breakwater South Light, and from there lay off a course for the middle of Shelburne Bay's mouth. On the way watch for Proctor Shoal and its red-green buoy; there are usually two yellow fish-haven buoys, **Buoy C** and **Buoy D,** just to its north. Shelburne Point is prominent; 0.2 mile to its northeast is a rocky shoal watched by **Buoy #2.** The bay's western entrance point is reddish sandstone Redrock Point.

From the northwest: If you have fair weather and good visibility, you can come straight from Schuyler

Island on the main lake and pass south of Schuyler Reef's red-green buoy. At this buoy you can lay off a 5.8-mile course straightaway for **Shelburne Point Buoy #2.** A good eastern landmark is Juniper Island's 115-foot light tower. Wooded Juniper has outlying shoals, and as you close the island your course takes you north of Juniper's **Buoy #2.** Next you pass north of barren Rock Dunder, then to your destination, Shelburne Point's **Buoy #2.** You are now about opposite Shelburne Bay's easterly entrance at Redrock Point and ready to enter.

Your destination is in the first large indentation on the Shelburne Point peninsula, just southwest of **Buoy #4.** You can identify the marina by its mooring area. There are two facilities in this bight. Shelburne Shipyard is the farthest north, with slips extending southeast. Pull in to the fuel dock (gas and diesel) at the complex's northern end, then check in at the office.

Electric hookups (110-volt/50-amp) and a 50-ton Travelift are available, and there is a ship's store with marine supplies and charts. The land line number is (802) 985-3326.

Though you are a very long way from supermarkets, malls, or restaurants, you can call a taxi. If you didn't get to the Shelburne Museum while in Burlington, this is another chance if you can arrange transportation.

Main Lake West Shore
Willsboro Bay
(Schuyler Island to Jones Point)

Mile CH-37.0 (SM) to Mile CH-45.0 (SM)

Willsboro Bay is 4 miles long, about a mile wide, and open at its northeastern end. Willsboro Point is its eastern entry point. Your **Departure Point, Mile CH-40.0 (SM),** is northeast of the point; the main mileage route holds well offshore. If southbound, there's good water approaching the bay's entrance; if northbound along Willsboro peninsula, stand clear of Pumpkin Reef. It lies east and slightly south of Willsboro Point and is watched by **Buoy #20.**

The impressive foothill mountains rise abruptly

from the bay's western shore. Depths alongside the bank can range more than 100 feet. There's an anchorage and a marina on the bay's southeastern side near its southern end.

WILLSBORO BAY SOUTH ANCHORAGE

★★★★ | 3 |

NO FACILITIES
Chart: N 14783

Mile CH-40.0 + 5.6 W/S (SM)

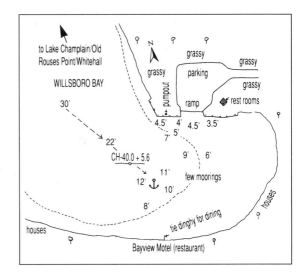

This anchorage is in the bay's very southeastern end. Monitor weather; strong northwest winds can make the anchorage untenable, in which case you might seek haven at Willsboro Bay Marina, or try to find shoal enough water to anchor hard along the bay's western bank in the hill's lee.

Once in the bay's entrance, your destination is still nearly 4 miles south. Eastern-shore Frisbies Point is prominent, so bear south-southeasterly for it. When you round the point, Willsboro Marina and its moored boats appear, but continue to the bay's southeastern corner.

The anchorage is beside a large state launching ramp in a slight northeasterly tuck in the main bay's southeastern end. You can see its bulkhead during your approach. Don't come in too far; shoals extend from the eastern and northeastern banks and include the bulk-head approach. Anchor wherever you have good depth; bottom is mud and weeds.

The launching ramp faces southwest. If you draw less than 4 feet you may have depth to tie at the bulkhead. There's a state pumpout on the section west of the ramp. The bulkhead is also a place to tie the dinghy. Ashore there's a parking lot, a lawn, and rest rooms.

Willsboro is about 2 miles south on the Bouquet River, a rushing trout stream. It's too far to walk, but if you brought your bicycle there are shops, a hardware store, and a Grand Union supermarket.

WILLSBORO BAY MARINA

★★★★★   3

ALL FACILITIES

Chart: N 14783

Mile CH-40.0 + 5.0 W/S (SM)

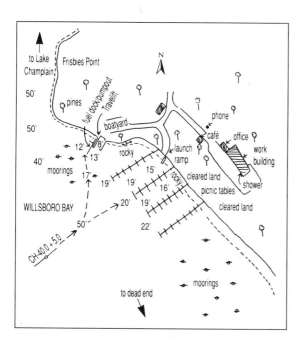

This eastern-bayshore marina—open May 15 to October 15—is about 3.5 miles south of Willsboro Point in Frisbies Point's lee; it's recognizable by its red-

and-white buildings and offshore moored boats.

The marina has four piers of slips extending from the eastern bank; each has its own access ramp. If no one answered on VHF, pull in to the fuel dock (gas and diesel) on the northern side of the Travelift well; it's at the facility's northern end. The office is in the hillside trees.

Electric hookups (110-volt) are available.

The marina has a large ship's store with marine equipment and hardware, navigation supplies, nautical clothing, charts, a dive shop, and basic groceries. The land line number is (518) 963-4472. The complex has landscaped lawns, flowers, paths through the trees, and scenic picnic areas with mountain views. There's a restaurant on the grounds.

Main Lake East Shore
Quaker Smith Point

Mile CH-45.0 + (SM)

This low, wooded, T-shaped Vermont-shore point has two anchorages. To reach the point from the main lake mileage route, take the **Departure Point, Mile CH-45.0 (SM).** This is slightly north of western-shore Jones Point and well north of the Bouquet River. Lay off about a 2.7-mile easterly course for **Buoy #19A,** which watches Quaker Smith Reef. Pass to its south, then continue another 0.5 mile and pick up **Buoy #19;** it watches a long shoal extending west of Quaker Smith's northern end. Now decide which anchorage is most appropriate for upcoming wind conditions.

The anchorage on the point's northern side is open to the northwest and may be untenable in strong west, northwest, north, and some northeast winds. The anchorage on the point's southern side is open to the southwest. If you choose an anchorage and the weather changes, it's a 1.6-mile trip to move anchorages and clear shoals watched by unlighted **Buoy #19.**

Both cove shores are private land; don't go ashore.

QUAKER SMITH POINT NORTH ANCHORAGE

★★★★ 3

NO FACILITIES

Chart: N 14783, *See A on sketch map*

Mile CH-45.0 + 3.7 E (SM)

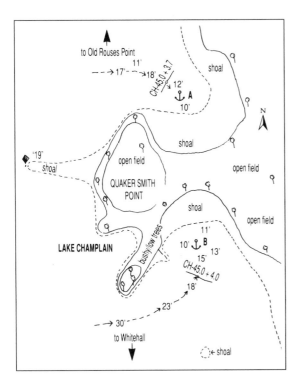

At **Buoy #19** off Quaker Smith Point, bear easterly until the northern cove opens fully, then head into midcove. You won't be able to get close to the beach; the cove's perimeter is shoal. Monitor the weather.

Try for lake trout just northeast of **Buoy #19** in depths of about 40 feet; troll a Mepps #3 Grey Squirrel Tail.

QUAKER SMITH POINT SOUTH ANCHORAGE

★★★★ 3

NO FACILITIES

Chart: N 14783, *See B on sketch map*

Mile CH-45.0 + 4.0 E (SM)

At **Buoy #19** at Quaker Smith Point, bear southeasterly to the point's southerly extension. At its southern tip round up slightly, clear the point, then bear northeasterly when the cove opens fully. If you are coming in from downlake, there's an unwatched shoal about 0.4 mile south.

As you enter the anchorage, avoid a dike extending southeasterly into the bay from the point's eastern side. Head toward midcove; you can't get close to the northern beach due to its shoreline shoals. Monitor weather.

Main Lake West Shore
Jones Point to Essex

Mile CH-45.0 (SM) to Mile CH-50.0 (SM)

ESSEX SHIPYARD

★★★★ 3

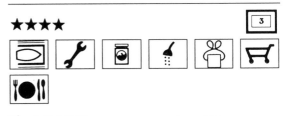

Chart: N 14783, *See sketch map, page 385*

Mile CH-50.0 + 1.0 W (SM)

Midlake landmarks for Essex are the village buildings and offshore moored boats. The waterfront is in two

Essex Shipyard

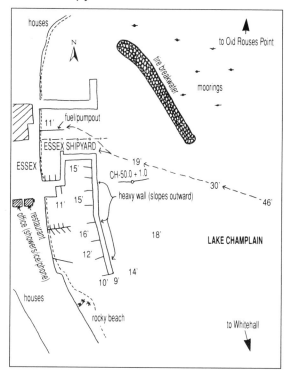

slight coastal indentations separated by an easterly reaching middle point. North of this point is the Essex–McNeil Cove cross-lake ferry dock. The marina—open May 15 to October 15—is south of the middle point.

The Essex waterfront has little natural protection. To remedy this exposure south of the point, there's a large floating tire breakwater northeast of the marina facilities. Moored or anchored boats don't have this protection.

The marina entrance is at the breakwater's southwestern end. There are two facilities. Your destination—the one farthest south—has a long dock paralleling shore. The dock's westerly face slopes slightly outward and serves as a breakwater. Access into the marina slips is at this dock's southern open end. If no one answered on VHF 16, come around the floating breakwater and head for the northern end of the marina's main offshore dock. Tie up temporarily on the section extending east and check in at the office near the head of the ramp just west of the restaurant. The office staff can help you find repair facilities if you need them; their land line number is (518) 963-7900.

Block and cube ice and electric hookups (110-volt/30-amp) are available.

Fuel and a pumpout are available at the second facility, Essex Marine Base.

Go up the steep marina access road and you are on Essex's main street. There's a small store with snacks and basic groceries at the intersection. In the village are a few shops, a post office, and a fire station. There's a village park on the point that separates the Essex waterfront indentations. The Old Dockhouse Restaurant shares the northern cove with the ferry slip.

Main Lake East Shore
Converse Bay, Town Farm Bay, Kingsland Bay, and Porter Bay

Mile CH-52.0 (SM) to Mile CH-58.0 (SM)

CONVERSE BAY

Chart: N 14783

Mile CH-52.0 + 1.2 E (SM)

This large eastern-shore bay is open to the west-southwest. Its northern boundary is Cedar Beach peninsula; its southern side is Thompsons Point's northeastern end. It has three islands. Small Picket Island is near the Cedar Beach peninsula; Garden Island, the largest, is north of Thompson's Point; north-south-oriented Cedar Island is northeast of Garden Island. There are two anchorages.

The **Departure Point** from the main lake route is at **Mile CH-52.0 (SM),** about a mile north of Split Rock Point—though you can enter from the main lake just about anywhere. All the wooded islands are visible and have only perimeter shoals. Entrance depths range from 200 to 50 feet and gradually shoal as you bear easterly to your anchorage choice.

The islands and shoreline are private property.

Cedar Island Anchorage

★★★★★

NO FACILITIES

Chart: N 14783, *See A on sketch map*

Mile CH-52.0 + 1.7 E (SM)

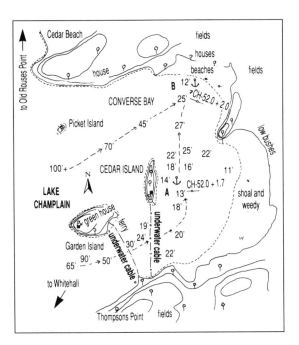

This anchorage is east of Cedar Island; it offers fair protection in nearly all wind directions, though this depends on where you anchor. Since the anchorage is usually crowded, the only space left might give you a bad northwest or southwest exposure. Strong winds from these directions cause large seas from a deepwater fetch through all but the recommended anchorage area. In strong northerly quadrant winds there's more protection in the bay's northeastern anchorage.

A scenic approach from the main bay is south of Garden Island; just give its perimeter shoals a fair berth. As you approach its southeastern end there are a few private docks and the island ferry-boat pier. Farther northeast is Cedar Island's southern end; bear to Cedar's eastern side, also clearing its perimeter shoals. Bear north to about mid-island and anchor as close to the island as depth allows. If you can see the main lake's open 10-mile fetch to your southwest or the 3-mile fetch

to your northwest, you are not in a protected area. Holding is very poor in weeds, rock, and a little mud.

Converse Bay Northeast Anchorage

★★★

NO FACILITIES

Chart: N 14783, *See B on sketch map*

Mile CH-52.0 + 2.0 E (SM)

This anchorage is in Converse Bay's northeastern corner. It offers good protection in nearly all winds except strong southwesterlies.

Downbound in the main lake a convenient approach is north of Garden and Cedar islands and south of Picket Island. As you close the northeastern shore's low land, you can see boats at anchor and on private moorings. Pick your spot to anchor; depths shoal as you close the beach. Bottom is mud and weeds.

POINT BAY MARINA (TOWN FARM BAY)

★★★★★

Chart: N 14783, *See sketch map, page 387*

Mile CH-53.0 + 2.0 E (SM)

Town Farm Bay is on Thompsons Point's southern side in a wide northeastern bight. The bay is open to the south and southwest. You have a choice of a protected marina and a pair of anchorages.

A good **Departure Point** from the main-lake mileage route is midway between Split Rock Point and Thompsons Point. You must round to Thompsons Point's far southern side. The fair-sized bay on Thompsons Point's southeasterly end is badly exposed.

Point Bay Marina (Town Farm Bay)

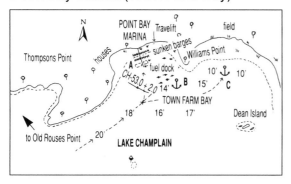

Continue around Thompsons Point and then bear north-easterly.

There are two watched isolated shoals as you make this turn; buoys are hard to see. One is about 0.5 mile south-southeast of Thompsons Point's southern point; it's watched by a red-green nun. The other shoal, which is more dangerous, is another 0.5 mile east of the southern point. It's about 0.3 mile offshore and is watched by another red-green nun. If you approach alongside Thompsons Point's southern side, the shoals are not much of a problem; if you approach from downlake, watch out for them.

By the time you reach the most easterly shoal buoy you are in Town Farm Bay. It encompasses a northerly bight west of Williams Point and an easterly cove in the lowlands south of Williams Point.

The marina—open May 1 to October 31—is in the northerly bight west of Williams Point; it's very visible in the western corner. The remaining bight is a mooring area.

The marina has one long pier extending from shore; from this are two sets of piers extending east and west. Each is filled with slips. The main pier continues into the bay between sunken barges; they serve as the marina breakwater and give protection from wind and seas from the southwest and south. If wind is very severe, there's some surge.

If no one answered on VHF 16, pull in to the fuel dock (gas and diesel) on the main pier's southerly end. The office is on shore in the trees.

Block and cube ice and a 25-ton Travelift are available. If you need a diver, check at the office.

There's a ship's store with navigation supplies, marine equipment and hardware, nautical clothing, local charts, and picnic supplies. The land line number is (802) 425-2431.

If a slip or mooring is unavailable you can anchor along the mooring area's southerly fringe or east of Williams Point. Shoreline shoals extend offshore at the point, so sound carefully. Bottom is mud and weeds. You have an attractive view west but the eastern area is flatland. Expect mosquitoes at dusk and dawn during light offshore winds.

KINGSLAND BAY ANCHORAGE (KINGSLAND BAY)

 ★★★★ 3

NO FACILITIES

Chart: N 14783

Mile CH-54.5 + 1.0 E (SM)

Kingsland Bay is 0.7 mile long and open at its northerly end. Its eastern entry point is Macdonough Point; it also

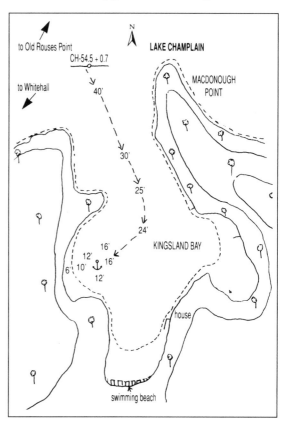

serves as the southern terminus of a large bay formed at the mouth of Little Otter and Lewis creeks. Kingsland Bay is not readily identifiable on the wooded shoreline, so steer a course to find it. Downbound your clearest **Departure Point** is at Split Rock Point. Lay off a course for the middle of Kingsland Bay's entrance, 2 miles south-southeast.

Though the bay does not offer good protection in northerly winds, this can be somewhat overcome depending on where you anchor.

There's good water throughout the Kingsland Bay entry. Once inside, you can see a slight point extending from the bay's western shore; it's about 200 feet south of the western entry. South of this slight point is a small westerly reaching bight; this is the preferred anchorage. It's usually stuffed with boats. If northerlies are predicted and you cannot tuck well inside the bight, you are subject to a very rough, possibly untenable anchorage. If the protected bight is open, go in as close to shore as depth allows. Bottom is mud with weeds.

This is an attractive anchorage with a high, wooded shoreline and good swimming.

PORTER BAY ANCHORAGE (PORTER BAY)

 ★★ 3

NO FACILITIES

Chart: N 14783

Mile CH-55.6 + 0.8 E (SM)

Small, circular Porter Bay is about 0.5 mile in diameter. A good **Departure Point** is on midlake Diamond Island's eastern side at its light, **Mile CH-55.6**. Lay off a course 0.8 mile southeasterly to the middle of Porter

Porter Bay Anchorage (Porter Bay)

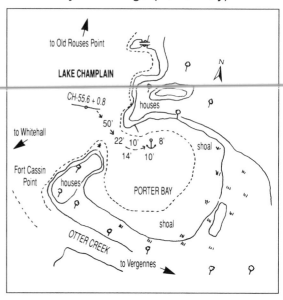

Bay's entrance to keep clear of large, shoal Fields Bay at Otter Creek's mouth. Porter Bay is a good anchorage in all winds save those from the northwest.

As you near the bay, make your entry slightly favoring its northern entrance point; rocks extend north from its southerly point. Anchor in the cove's northeastern corner off the dock; come in close to shore for best protection. Bottom is mud and weeds.

This is not a very popular anchorage, possibly because the eastern shore is rather unattractive flatland. However, there is a superb western-shore mountain view. Prepare for mosquitoes at dusk and dawn.

This is a good place to wait for calms if you plan to search about for the channel into Otter Creek. The southern entry headland for Porter Bay, Fort Cassin Point, also serves as the northern entry of Otter Creek. The creek is navigable for 8 miles to Vergennes, but it has risky depths for drafts over 5 feet.

Main Lake West Shore
Barn Rock Harbor, Partridge Harbor, Westport, Cole Bay, and Port Henry

Mile CH-58.4 (SM) to Mile CH-70.0 (SM)

BARN ROCK HARBOR ANCHORAGE

★★★★

NO FACILITIES

Chart: N 14783

Mile CH-58.4 + 0.5 W (SM)

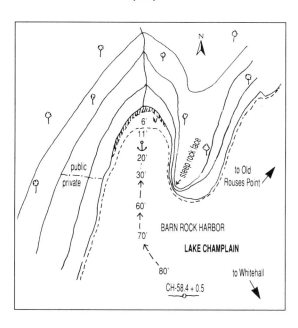

This anchorage is in a narrow finger reaching almost due north at the foot of the lake's western-shore palisades. It's open to the southerly quadrant; plan your visit for calms or northerly quadrant winds.

You must go to the cove's northerly end to find depths shoal enough in which to anchor; bottom is mud,

weeds, and rock. In strong northerly winds, prepare for williwaws whooping down the canyon.

Cliffs surround you; the view is impressive. There's fine swimming and excellent snorkeling.

PARTRIDGE HARBOR ANCHORAGE

★★★★

NO FACILITIES

Chart: N 14783

Mile CH-59.4 + 0.7 W (SM)

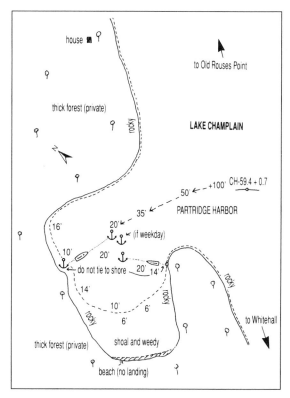

This stop is one of the smaller palisades coves. It has good protection except from the east—not a common direction for strong winds—and is nearly always crowded.

The harbor is between wide Rock Harbor to the north and wide Hunter Bay to the south. Stay in the middle of the entrance as you come in. If boats fill the place, you may not have room to swing to one anchor without a local boating revolt. Preferred anchorage with nearly complete protection is in the lee of the harbor's southerly point. If a spot is available approach with caution—the harbor's southern end is shoal. Since it's unlikely the anchorage will remain isolated, and in order not to receive threats from late arrivals, drop and set a bow anchor in gravelly mud with weeds. Now unload the dinghy, row in a stern anchor, and set it in the shallows at the edge of the beach. Do not land and do not tie to a convenient tree; this is private land that is dearly cherished.

Another option is to drop a bow anchor near mid-cove and put a stern anchor to the western or northwestern shore. Don't land or tie to trees here, either. You can now sit back and enjoy the pretty view and watch the anchoring, grumbling, and fist-shaking of other arrivals. Barbecue scents and musical entertainment normally continue throughout the evening.

WESTPORT MARINA

★★★★★

ALL FACILITIES

Chart: N 14783

Mile CH-60.0 + 1.7 W (SM)

Westport is in midbend of North West Bay. It's open to easterly quadrant weather, but an offshore, floating tire breakwater somewhat protects the harbor waterfront.

You can identify town by its homes and offshore moored boats. You have a clear approach from midlake. When you close shore, pick up the breakwater west of the moorings; harbor entry is at its northern end. If no one answered on VHF 16, pull in to the fuel dock (gas and diesel) on the bulkhead in front of the Citgo sign and the office.

Block and cube ice, electric hookups (110-volt/30-amp and 220-volt/50-amp), and a 25-ton Travelift are available. If you need a diver, check at the office. The marina's land line number is (518) 962-4356.

This is a very popular marina, due mostly to the friendliness of the Carroll family and their staff. There's a ship's store with marine equipment and hardware,

Westport Marina

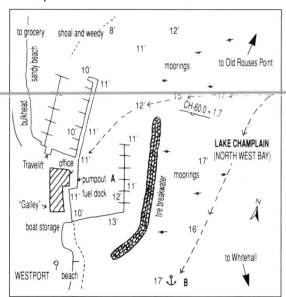

navigation supplies, guides, charts, a book exchange, camera supplies, nautical clothing, basic groceries, picnic supplies, and fishing licenses. The Galley restaurant, near the office, is open for three meals a day. Its Saturday night barbecues are one of the reasons weekend dockage is often limited; they begin at 6:30, with entertainment at 8.

The annual marina Lobsterfest is held over a summer weekend; it includes meals, live music, dancing, barbecues, a costume parade, and decorated boats. Make reservations.

If a slip or a mooring is unavailable, there is a fair anchorage outside the breakwater south of the mooring area. Bottom is mud and weeds. If you anchor north of the moorings, it's very weedy. When you go ashore, immediately check in at the office, ask where to tie the dinghy, and pay for marina facility use.

Downtown is just up the hill to the main road; most stores are north. There's a bank, a post office, a library, a pharmacy, hotels, small stores, and Everybody's Supermarket.

Pick up a walking-tour map at the marina office and have a look at some of Westport's historical homes.

COLE BAY

Chart: N 14783 or N 14784

Mile CH-63.0 W (SM)

Cole Bay, about 1 mile southeast of **Barber Point Light**, **Mile CH-62.0 (SM)**, has a pair of anchorages. Both are open to wind and seas from the south, southeast, and east but are good in nearly all winds from north through west.

Leave the main mileage route in midlake at **Departure Point, Mile CH-63.0 (SM)**, and bear westerly. Cole Island sits in the middle of Cole Bay, but at a distance it is difficult to pick out on the wooded shoreline. The bay is bounded on the south by Stacy Brook's mouth and on the north by a YMCA boy's camp. As you near shore and pick out Cole Island, it's time to choose your destination.

All the mainland is private, so don't plan to go ashore. The island appears to have no "restricted landing" signs; it may be a place to visit.

A long shoal extends off the island's northwestern end. If you have deep draft and plan to move from one side of the island to the other, safest passage is around the island's southeastern end.

Cole Bay Southwest Anchorage

★★★★

NO FACILITIES

Chart: N 14783 or N 14784, *See A on sketch map*

Mile CH-63.0 + 1.2 W (SM)

This anchorage is along Cole Island's southwestern side. As you come in from offshore, give the island's southeastern end a fair berth; shoals extend off the rocky point. For perch and bass fishing, anchor close alongside the island. There's depth if you want to be near the mainland. Bottom is gravelly mud and some weeds.

Cole Bay Southwest Anchorage, Cole Bay Northeast Anchorage

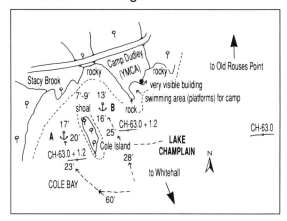

Cole Bay Northeast Anchorage

★★★★

NO FACILITIES

Chart: N 14783 or N 14784, *See B on sketch map*

Mile CH-63.0 + 1.2 W (SM)

During your entry from offshore keep in mid-entrance between the northern-point boy's camp and the island. There's a long shoal visible at low lake level off the northern point, and there are rocks extending off Cole Island's eastern end.

To get a little protection from afternoon prevailing winds, anchor toward the bay's northeastern end close to the island. Bottom is mud, but there are more weeds than on the island's other side.

PORT HENRY PUBLIC DOCK
(PORT HENRY)

★★★★

Chart: N 14784

Mile CH-70.0 + 1.2 W/N (SM)

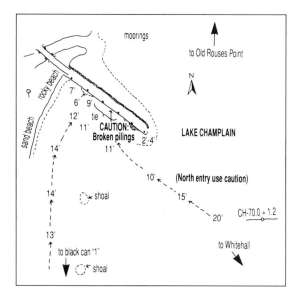

Port Henry is protected from northerly and most westerly quadrant weather, but it has a 2-mile south and southeast open-water fetch.

The village is very easy to see from midlake; it's on the hill overlooking its waterfront. You must approach the harbor from the south.

To help orient yourself on the approach from midlake, find **Buoy #27;** it watches a long shoal off Vermont's Crane Point. On the western shore about opposite **Buoy #27** is a fixed 500-foot breakwater that extends southeastward but is difficult to see. Its purpose is to protect

Port Henry's harbor from northerly weather. Your eventual destination is this breakwater's southern side; it's an old canal terminal. Just to the breakwater's northwest are boats on moorings off a small marina.

A shoal reaches 0.6 mile south and east of the breakwater and is watched at its southern end by **Buoy #1.** Round this buoy to reach the deepwater harbor that lies between the shoreline and the shoal. At **Buoy #1** bear northerly back 0.6 mile to the breakwater.

If southbound, going all the way south to **Buoy #1** and then returning north again is time consuming. If you feel like experimenting, there is an unwatched channel to and from the main lake; it's near the breakwater. The long shoal's most dangerous areas are in its midsection, so keep well to their north. However, you also must clear a perimeter shoal that extends off the breakwater's southeastern end and continues around southwest of its tip. By using this upper channel you'll normally find only gradual shoaling from the main lake. However, if you suddenly find yourself in risky depths, stop, go back, and enter the harbor the long way, around **Buoy #1.**

Whichever route you choose to reach the breakwater's southern side, at the tie-up keep in mind the shoal that has worked its way back west from the breakwater's southeastern tip. Its far northwestern end also shoals near the beach. You also need to cope with pilings—some of them broken off—set south of the terminal wall. You can usually fender against the pilings.

The breakwater is actually a mole with a northerly rock face. The land surface is dirt; it's a parking lot for local day fisherman.

If you need supplies, look west-southwest on the hill; the Presbyterian church steeple clock tower is downtown. There's a Grand Union supermarket, a hardware and other stores, a pharmacy, a bank, a hotel, a post office, and a library. There's also a café where you can sit for a few minutes to catch your breath after the hike up the mountain.

In late July Port Henry celebrates Champ Day in honor of the lake's sea serpent.

The Lower Lake
Port Henry to Whitehall

Mile Ch-70.0 (SM) to Mile Ch-106.0 (SM)

FORT ST. FREDERIC ANCHORAGE

★★★★

NO FACILITIES

Chart: N 14784, *See A on sketch map*

Mile CH-71.1 W (SM)

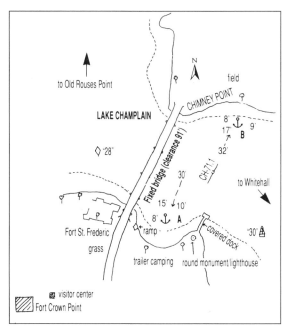

This western-shore anchorage is in a small bight just south of the high-level Champlain Bridge. It's well protected except from northerly quadrant winds. If these are forecast, move across the lake to Chimney Point Anchorage. Wakes—especially on weekends—can make this a rolly anchorage.

Once south of the bridge bear toward its southwestern end. As you near shore, the bight's southeastern point is topped by the old 55-foot lighthouse monument;

extending northeast from the point is a covered pier. Anchor as close to the pier and beach as depth permits. Bottom is mud and weeds. You can land the dinghy at the pier, or if wakes are severe, pull it up on the beach by the dock.

Fort St. Frederic and Fort Crown Point have a visitor center; it's out the monument's access road and across the highway in the one modern building. Displays, paintings, and dioramas help orient you to the two historical sites. Pick up a walking-tour map and the informative pamphlet entitled "Crown Point," and start sightseeing.

CHIMNEY POINT ANCHORAGE

★★★★

NO FACILITIES

Chart: N 14784, *See B on sketch map*

Mile CH-71.1 E (SM)

This northeastern-lakeshore anchorage is just southeast of the Champlain Bridge and about 0.3 mile from the Fort St. Frederic Anchorage. It's well protected during winds from the northerly quadrant.

If the crew becomes restless or you need a few supplies during northerly weather, you can land the dinghy—with some difficulty—at the Chimney Point bridge access. Walk about 0.5 mile northerly, past a cornfield, to the Champlain Bridge Marina on Hospital Creek. They have a small ship's store.

FIVEMILE POINT WEST ANCHORAGE

★★★   2

NO FACILITIES

Chart: N 14784, *See A on sketch map, page 394*

Mile CH-79.5 W (SM)

This western-shore anchorage is 0.5 mile north of Fivemile Point Light. It's well protected from westerly

Fivemile Point West Anchorage, Fivemile Point East Anchorage

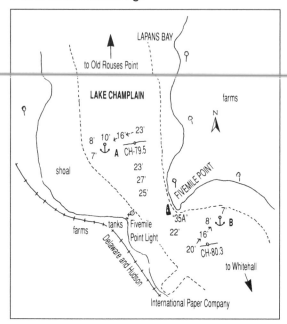

and southerly quadrant winds, though in strong southeasterlies it's often windswept. In winds from nearly any other direction there's better protection at Fivemile Point East Anchorage.

Southbound you can easily pick up the 25-foot light tower opposite Fivemile Point; when about 0.5 mile to its north, begin to bear toward the western shore. Shoreline shoals extend a long way from the bank, so come in cautiously. Go far enough to get well off the channel; towboats with fuel barge tows ply this route regularly. Bottom is mud with weeds.

There's usually a cooling breeze until sundown — that's when mosquitoes arrive. There's a large paper mill just south of the point, and it lets off periodic hair-raising roars similar to a rocket's blast-off.

FIVEMILE POINT EAST ANCHORAGE

★★★★

NO FACILITIES

Chart: N 14784, *See B on sketch map*

Mile CH-80.3 E (SM)

This eastern-shore anchorage is south of Fivemile Point. It's well protected from northerly and easterly quadrant winds. A view of the western mountains makes it slightly more attractive than the anchorage north of the point. However, there are occasional snorts, roars, and belches of steam coming from the western-shore mill.

Once you clear the narrows at Fivemile Point, continue south until about opposite the mill. Now bear northeasterly into the wide bight sheltered by the northern point. Come in as far as depth allows so errant towboats won't run you down. Bottom is mud with weeds.

FORT TICONDEROGA ANCHORAGE

★★★★★

NO FACILITIES

Chart: N 14784, *See sketch map, page 395*

Mile CH-85.0 W (SM)

This western-shore anchorage is just north of La Chute Creek's mouth and in the lee of Fort Ticonderoga's point. It's well protected from all northerly and westerly quadrant winds. It's open to the south, but because the lake is not overly wide and there's a bend a mile farther south, southerly quadrant winds tend only to make the anchorage windswept. Though there's a Special Anchorage Area just north of Ticonderoga Light, it's not recommended. It's difficult to find sufficient depth off the channel to be safely clear of passing commercial traffic.

Southbound, pass **Buoy #38;** it's just north of the narrows between Mt. Independence to the south and the point where Fort Ticonderoga sits on the hill. Once you clear these narrows and the rock off the northern

Fort Ticonderoga Anchorage

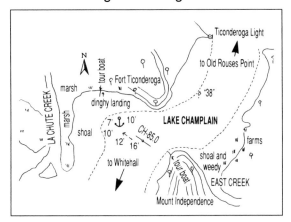

point, begin to bear into the northwest bight. It's important to find the area where depth permits you to go well west to keep clear of towboats and wake roll. Bottom is mud and weeds.

Be sure to visit Fort Ticonderoga. Unlike Fort St. Frederic and Fort Crown Point, it is on its original foundations. It was completely restored from its French architectural plans.

Though the fort overlooks the anchorage, it's about 0.3 mile back from the lake. You can land the dinghy just about anywhere, but to get up the hill without imitating a mountain goat, land on the beach beside the tour boat dock on the cove's northern bank. You can use the stairway and path intended for tour boat passengers.

The fort—open daily from 9 to 5 (until 6 in July and August)—has a museum with displays and artifacts, paintings, papers, uniforms, and military weapons covering the fort's history. The visitor center store offers historical prints and photographs, books, camera supplies, and tourist knickknacks. During July and August there are reenactments of historical cannon and mortar drills, and fife and drum parades.

Mount Defiance towers above the fort. It is part of the fort complex and is open during the same hours. Climbing the mountain is almost impossible, though early soldiers managed it toting their belongings and equipment on their backs. If you can arrange transportation, it's a worthwhile trip—the view is superb. Southwest is Lake George and the old portage route between it and Lake Champlain. Looking down on Fort Ticonderoga you can understand why General Arthur St. Clair hastily surrendered in 1777 when British General John Burgoyne aimed his artillery nearly straight down at the Patriot troops.

CHIPMAN POINT MARINA

★★★★

Chart: N 14784

Mile CH-87.8 E (SM)

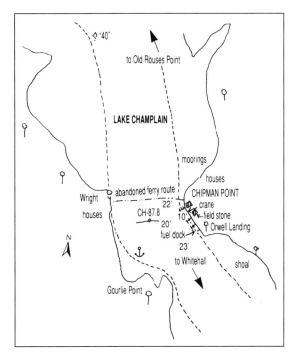

This marina—open May 31 to October 11—is immediately south of Chipman Point alongside the eastern channel; watch for its two stone buildings on the water's edge.

This is an easy approach; when opposite the docks come straight in. There are three piers with fingers extending from the bank; the most northerly is practically on the point's end. The large building ashore is the office. If no one answered on VHF, pull in to one of the T-piers, which are usually for transients, or to the fuel dock (gas and diesel); it's the one in the center.

Block and cube ice, electric hookups (110-volt/20-amp and 30-amp), and a 12-ton lift are available. The marina's land line number is (802) 948-2288.

There's a small ship's store that sells local charts and

a few supplies. It also has a book exchange. If you badly need food, the owner can usually find you transportation to the grocery store.

Up in the trees are picnic tables and grills with a western mountain view.

The marina's two stone buildings are old Champlain Canal warehouses built in the early 1800s. They once stored incoming rum, coal, and molasses destined for nearby inland settlements at Brandon and Middlebury.

If you haven't been to Fort Ticonderoga, you can visit from here. Call the tour boat office and make arrangements for the boat to pick you up, take you to the fort, and bring you home again.

If the marina is full, there's an anchorage—deep drafts use caution—with a pretty view up the lake just across the channel in the bight north of Gourlie Point.

ORWELL BLUFF ANCHORAGE

★★★

NO FACILITIES

Chart: N 14784

Mile CH-89.9 E (SM)

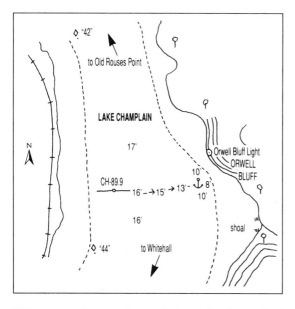

This eastern-shore anchorage is immediately south of Orwell Bluff Light in a mile-wide lake area. It's not rec-

ommended in northwest, west, or southwest winds because it can be very windswept. Anchor in mud as close to the eastern shore as depth allows.

This is a pleasant anchorage during hot weather; there's usually a breeze blowing up or down the lake. Fishing tends toward small perch.

BENSON LANDING ANCHORAGE

★★

NO FACILITIES

Chart: N 14784

Mile CH-93.2 W (SM)

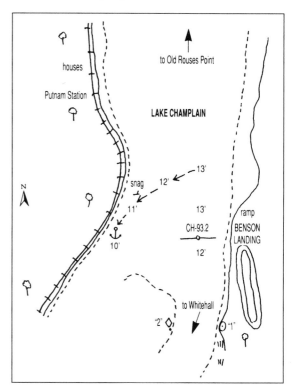

This western-shore anchorage is near the point where the lake and channel begin to narrow dramatically in the final run to Whitehall. It's also where navigation aid numbering changes. Nearby on the eastern bank is Benson Landing.

Leave the channel when just south of Benson

Landing, about 0.3 mile north of **Lighted Daymark #1.**
Bear southwesterly. Though we have never found it, a
snag is charted at about this point, so don't come in at
full throttle.

Anchor as close to the western bank as your depth
allows, since pleasure craft wake roll can be severe.
You have good protection from almost all wind directions, though in strong northeasterlies a fair chop runs
downlake.

This anchorage has some unpleasant features: trains
roar alongside, and during very strong prevailing winds
periodic williwaws shriek down the mountain gullies
and blow all loose objects into the lake.

The Champlain Canal
Whitehall to Waterford

Mile CC-0.0 (SM) to Mile CC-59.4 (SM)

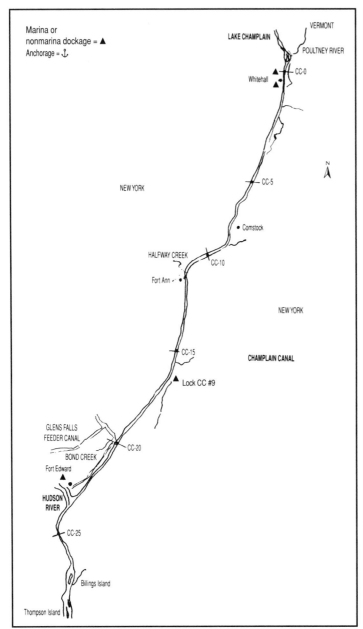

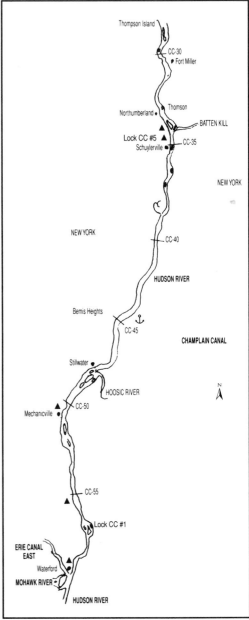

Mile CC-0.0 (SM) to Mile CC-25.0 (SM)

Mile CC-25.0 (SM) to Mile CC-59.4 (SM)

> *. . . precisely the route that an army ought to take.*
>
> British General JOHN BURGOYNE on the
> Hudson-Champlain Valley, 1777

LOCKAGE, WHITEHALL TO WATERFORD

Name	Mile	Land Line	Lift*	Poles
Lock CC #12**	CC-0.0 W (SM)	(518) 499-1700	15.5 feet	Poles
Lock CC #11	CC-6.5 W (SM)	(518) 639-8964	12.0 feet	Poles
Lock CC #9	CC-15.8 (SM)	(518) 747-6021	16.0 feet	Poles
Lock CC #8	CC-21.6 (SM)	(518) 747-5520	11.0 feet	Lines
Lock CC #7	CC-23.7 E (SM)	(518) 747-4614	10.0 feet	Poles
Lock CC #6	CC-30.6 E (SM)	(518) 695-3751	16.5 feet	Poles
Lock CC #5	CC-34.2 E (SM)	(518) 695-3919	19.0 feet	Lines
Lock CC #4	CC-48.3 E (SM)	(518) 664-5261	16.0 feet	Lines
Lock CC #3	CC-50.0 E (SM)	(518) 664-5171	19.5 feet	Lines
Lock CC #2	CC-52.5 W (SM)	(518) 664-4961	18.5 feet	Lines
Lock CC #1	CC-56.3 W (SM)	(518) 237-8566	14.0 feet	Poles

*At normal pool level

**Required chamber position: Upbound vessels usually must use eastern chamber wall in this lock.

All locks monitor VHF 13. Signals: Lights and Horn (3 long blasts to transit). Normally furnish lines; have ladders each chamber corner.

Daily operating hours for pleasure craft: 0700 to 2230 (may vary annually).

Canal Superintendent: (518) 747-4613.

LOCK TRANSIT FEES

Boat Length	Daily Pass	Unlimited Seasonal Pass
Under 16 feet	$5	$25
16 feet to under 26 feet	$10	$50
26 feet to under 39 feet	$15	$75
More than 39 feet	$20	$100

Fees may vary annually. Canal passes are available at locks and marinas along the system and at New York State Thruway offices across the state. For more information on where to purchase a seasonal pass, call (518) 436-3175. For commercial rates call (518) 471-5016.

The 60-mile-long Champlain Canal, part of the New York State Barge Canal System, extends from Whitehall to Waterford and connects Lake Champlain and the Hudson River. Canal mileage begins at Whitehall's Lock CC #12, **Mile CC-0.0 (SM),** and ends at Waterford, **Mile CC-59.4 (SM).**

The Northern Inland Lock Navigation Company made an attempt to link the Hudson River and Lake Champlain in 1792. They also had sketchy plans to join the Mohawk and Seneca rivers to Lake Ontario. From the company's limited river improvements came the conception of an Erie Canal system.

The first successful Champlain Canal was part of New York's 1817 Erie Canal project. When the Champlain opened in 1823, it was 66 miles long and 5 feet deep. Cargoes were limited to 80 tons. Its 20 locks were larger than those on the Erie, with which it connected via the Waterford Sidecut. These locks are still at Waterford's Lock E #2.

The first boat to transit the Champlain was the *Gleaner,* known as the Barque of Mountains. She came from Lake Champlain's St. Albans Bay fully loaded with wheat and potash.

Previously, cargoes brought in by lake sailing ships were transshipped south on wagon trains to the navigable Hudson River. Profitable as this was, heavy southbound iron ore and lumber and northbound coal could not be moved by wagon. The canal changed this almost

overnight. Though far shorter than the early Erie Canal, the Champlain became the state's second most prosperous system.

The immense success of the two canals brought about the "Canal Era." In 1843 Canada opened the Chambly Canal; finally there was water access from the New York harbor to the St. Lawrence River. Until railroads arrived, water travel was the preferred choice between New York, Quebec, and Montreal. In 1916 the state updated the original system; it's the one you use today.

Whitehall, **Mile CC-0.0 (SM),** is surrounded by high hills and dominated by eastern-shore Skene Mountain. British Major Philip Skene founded the town in 1759 and named it Skenesborough. That's old Skene Manor on the mountain.

In 1775 Benedict Arnold, realizing the town's strategic value, captured it for the Patriots and seized Philip Skene's schooner. It became the first U.S. Navy ship. Arnold sailed the schooner north to Crown Point, captured the British ship *Enterprize,* and added it to his fleet.

Retreating British troops burned the town in 1777, but by the 1800s Skenesborough had rebuilt. Its shipyards furnished War of 1812 ships for Thomas Macdonough. After the Battle of Plattsburgh the navy stored Macdonough's ships and British prize ships in the harbor, north of where Lock CC #12 is today. When the Champlain Canal opened in 1823, local yards became major builders of canal- and packet-boats.

Whitehall is surrounded by high hills. Skene Mountain is near the eastern shore.

Southbound at Whitehall you are in Lock CC #12's upper pool. You must ascend two more locks to reach the canal's 140-foot summit level near Fort Edward. From that point south you travel the canalized Hudson to the Federal Lock's upper pool at Troy; this section has eight locks to descend.

The canal's narrow northern portion is manmade. It has few waterside villages or homes; it's mainly woods. South of Fort Edward the river widens and settlement increases in the approach to Albany.

There are few navigational aids in the canal sections, but the canalized river is well watched with lighted and unlighted buoys and daymarks. Southbound green aids are to starboard, red aids to port.

Though it's not apparent as you leave Whitehall, you are crisscrossing Wood Creek. Before the canal existed, traffic used the creek for transport, though it was not the fastest route between Lake Champlain and the Hudson. The usual corridor was west about 10 miles via Lake George and its two portages.

The canal's western-bank indentation across from the Mettawee River's mouth, **Mile CC-1.6 E (SM)**, was once a canalboat lumber loading basin.

Lock CC #11, **Mile CC-6.5 W (SM)**, is similar to most Champlain locks. There's extremely limited space for overnight dockage. Approach walls are often very short, and active commercial traffic needs all the room for maneuvering.

South of Lock CC #11 and before Bridge C-25, a collection of white-orange Danger Buoys holds you off eastern shoals.

The state built Comstock's original Great Meadows Prison in 1810; it's about 0.5 mile inland.

Fort Ann, Mile **CC-11.4 W (SM),** is on the divide between the Hudson River watershed and Lake Champlain. Halfway Creek, just north of the Fort Ann Bridge, was an early east-west transportation route. Five forts were in use here, beginning in the French and Indian Wars. The Battle of Fort Ann in 1776 was a brief encounter with an advance party under the command of British General John Burgoyne; look east to see Battle Hill just after the canal's sharp southerly bend. Fort Ann was on the first canal and was another lumber shipping point. About 0.5 mile west of Bridge C-21, **Mile CC-15.3 W (SM),** is Smith Basin, another old canalboat stop.

Lock CC #9, **Mile CC-15.8 (SM),** is coming up. You didn't miss Lock CC #10; it was never built. Lock CC #9 takes you into the canal's summit level.

Southbound your locks are now all descending.

At **Mile CC-20.0 W (SM)** you pass the Glens Falls Feeder Canal, just south of a farm's line of tall trees that march west-northwest. The original Champlain Canal was west by Bond Creek. Northbound at Fort Edward the first canal left the Hudson River—as it does today—since the Hudson no longer headed toward Lake Champlain. Since the canal needed a water supply to get it over the summit level, part of the first canal's construction included a Hudson River dam and a 0.5-mile-long feeder canal. Within two years a flood destroyed the dam, and canal depth could no longer be maintained. Instead of replacing the old dam, the state built a new one farther up the Hudson at Glens Falls. They also built a new 7-mile-long Glens Falls Feeder for the northern water supply.

By 1832 feeder canal towns—Glens Falls, Hudson Falls, Queensbury, and Kingsbury—wanted commercial access into the profitable north-south Champlain system. The state rebuilt the feeder for navigation; it was widened and deepened, and an aqueduct and 13 masonry locks—5 of them combines—were built to overcome the 130-foot vertical drop east of Hudson Falls. This navigable feeder was in use more than 100 years; it brought prosperity to its waterside mills, factories, lime kilns, lumber-loading cranes, boat basins, and repair yards. The feeder is on the National Register of Historic Places. It's no longer navigable for commerce, but it's a popular paddle for canoeists.

Southbound you transit through Lock CC #8, **Mile CC-37.9 (SM)**; 2 miles farther south, in Fort Edward, is Lock CC #7. The lock's lower pool is the canal's midway point; here you enter the Hudson River.

Fort Edward's site was at the southern end of the Indian portage trails; Europeans fortified it at the start of the French and Indian Wars. It went by assorted names: Fort Nicolson in 1709, Fort Lydius in 1731, Fort Lyman in 1755, and finally Fort Edward.

The murder and scalping of Jane McCrea brought to an abrupt end any lingering sympathy Fort Edward's population might have had for the British. Jane planned to marry a Tory with Burgoyne's army. One day, when she was on her way to the British lines to meet her Lieutenant, one of Burgoyne's Wyandot Indian allies killed her; he wanted to collect the bounty paid for American scalps. Faced with a massive walk-out of his Indian allies if he arrested the guilty man, Burgoyne let the matter pass. Infuriated local residents became fanatic Patriots. Fort Edward's yacht basin is about a block from the site of Jane's home.

Downbound at Fort Edward you begin the wide winding canalized upper Hudson. It's well watched, and for good reason—shoals extend well out from both banks. It's not a pleasant river during high water conditions; then flow can be excessive at all dam tailwaters. Since many are situated alongside a lock approach, it makes maneuvering difficult when exiting and entering the lock. Current amount depends on seasonal runoff and power plant generation.

At **Mile CC-28.3 (SM)** the channel bears easterly into a narrow, wooded, 2-mile-long land cut. There's a long wall on the cut's western entrance with **Daymark #187** on its end. The main river on the wall's western side is watched by Danger Buoys. Don't miss the turn; just downstream are two open-crested dams.

Thompson Island Guard Gate, **Mile CC-28.7 (SM)**, protects this canal cut; during severe high water expect the gate to be closed and navigation stopped until conditions return to normal. At the land cut's southern end is Fort Miller. It's named for its early outpost, which was built for settlers' protection during the French and Indian Wars.

Once in Lock CC #6's lower pool, **Mile CC-30.6 (SM)**, the river is nearly 0.3 mile wide; stay in the channel in the tailwater area, as there are bankside rocks and shoals.

At the Highway 4 Bridge (BR C-10) you approach the Northumberland Dam. It crosses half the Hudson, and part of it forms the canal's eastern bank. The channel holds to the western shore to avoid a collection of old dam cribs. Don't miss the turn. The dam has a long open crest and is unpleasantly close to the channel and very difficult to see.

Thomson is just above the dam on the eastern shore.

The next mile-long land cut leads to Lock CC #5, **Mile CC-34.3 (SM)**. As you exit downbound you are at the Northumberland Dam's tailwaters and rapids and also at Batten Kill's mouth. There's no riverside protective grid or approach wall. If the river or kill is running high, watch for a hard westerly set. If northbound in severe current, this can be a difficult mill-about area in which to wait for lockage.

Just ahead is a midriver island. There was once a river ford at its northern end. In the 1700s, when water was up, the DeRidder family supplied transportation via the Horse Boat ferry at the island's other end.

Schuylerville, long known as Saratoga, is along the river's western shore. South of the midriver island,

winding, unnavigable Fish Creek flows in from Lake Saratoga near Saratoga Springs. Just up the creek is a remaining portion of the old canal.

The Iroquois called this area Sarach-toque, "hillside of a great river." It was a unique place. Here the Hudson Valley gave early access to Canada and the Mohawk and lower Hudson rivers. Fish Creek gave access west, and Batten Kill, about a mile back upstream, gave eastern access to the Connecticut Valley.

Saratoga's first European settlers arrived in the late-17th century. Peter Schuyler was an original landowner whose family members played major roles in the history of what would become America. By 1702 Saratoga had a few farms, mills, and two forts. All were destroyed during the French and Indian Wars. The rebuilt settlement included a supply depot and troop barrack called Fort Hardy.

During the Revolution General Burgoyne surrendered his army in Saratoga.

When the first canal opened, Saratoga became a major shipping port. By 1831 the town had incorporated and changed its name to honor General Philip Schuyler.

Downstream on the river's western shore near **Buoy #141** is a reminder of the area's dangerous early days. Fort Vrooman was built here in 1689. It was destroyed and then rebuilt as Fort Saratoga in 1702, only to be destroyed again and rebuilt in 1721. French and Indian troops destroyed it again in 1745. This time they killed a Schuyler family member and burned mills, stores, and 30 houses. The fort was rebuilt for the last time in 1746 as Fort Clinton, but the bloodshed didn't stop; a year later 45 men were killed and scalped.

As you continue downstream, the western shore often serves as boundary for 2,800-acre Saratoga National Historic Park. At the break in the western hills near **Buoy #103** is the park's entrance road, which follows the winding valley creek. The visitor center is about two miles west on Fraser Hill, the highest point in the park. Up on the first range of river hills you can see cannons placed as they were when they protected the river.

Just inland at **Mile CC-44.0 (SM)** is Bemis Heights, the site of another Revolutionary War battle. The 200-foot bluffs squeeze the Hudson Valley into a narrow corridor.

At Stillwater, **Mile CC-48.3 W (SM)**, Lock CC #4's upper-pool lock approach is along the Hudson's eastern bank to a lock island; the orange-white barrels on the west warn you off the dam's crest just downstream.

Stillwater is the site of an old Indian river crossing. Its first settlers were protected by Fort Ingoldsby, built in 1709 by Colonel Peter Schuyler. Later Stillwater's Dirck Swart House became Revolutionary War headquarters for General Philip Schuyler; it's a residence today. During the Revolution, Stillwater's ferry was a major link for moving army supplies and troops. Before the Battle of Saratoga the army put up earthworks north of the village about a block inland on a wooded river hill.

Once in Lock CC #4's lower pool, you are in the Mechanicville reach. For 0.3 mile downbound, a large island protects you from river rapids and major Hudson current. When you exit this protected area, the Hoosic River's mouth is on the eastern bank. If the Hoosic is running high, watch for a sharp westerly set. Across the canal is a cut between the lock island and its southern neighbor. If the Hudson is running high, watch for a pronounced easterly set.

Once under the railroad bridge you are in the approach to Lock CC #3, **Mile CC-50.0 E (SM).** This is the canal's highest lift lock. Hold to the channel on the eastern bank; on the west is a very large dam. Watch for a current increase near the upper lock gates.

In the lock's lower pool south of the western approach wall's protection, look for unexpected currents that vary in intensity with river stage. Here the dam's outflow enters the narrower improved channel. Since the lock's western approach wall extends well south, the outflow area is narrow. If the river is high, the restricted entrance results in a strong easterly set. When this flow strikes the eastern shore just ahead, the current ricochets westerly.

Mechanicville's waterfront, **Mile CC-50.7. W (SM),** is on Anthony Kill. The settlement was on the major route of Revolutionary War armies destined to and from the Battles of Saratoga.

Mechanicville has long been an industrial center. Early economy was based on sawmills, logging, brickyards, and woolen and cotton mills. In 1882, the Hudson River Water and Power Company founded the town's large papermaking industry. When the first canal opened, Mechanicville became a major shipping port for log rafts and canalboats plying the last 15 miles to Albany—the destination for most local products. When the railroads arrived in the 1800s the town became a freight and passenger station and a major railroad service yard.

The next 1.2-mile stretch downbound is in Lock CC #2's wide upper pool. Shoals extend off both shores. Here you begin a crossover to pass east of a large island. Be cautious of rocks at the western channel edge as you approach **Buoy #61A** just north of the island. You can see the rocks at low water. At the island's southern end the channel recrosses to the western bank. You pass the Tagson Paper Company, then pass west of the next island.

Lock CC #2, **Mile CC-52.5 W (SM),** has another large dam, and the Mechanicville Hydro powerhouse extends from the lock to the western bank. After you descend the lock, watch for current fluctuations. If generating, power plant outflow comes through a bypass channel west of the lock; it enters the main river along that bank. When it generates, there's a definite current increase and often a sharp easterly set as you leave the shelter of the lock's western approach wall. If you are unprepared and are hugging the channel's eastern side, it could force you into main-river rocks.

The lock also has a main-river dam that is nearly 0.2 mile long and stretches from the lock to the eastern bank. The lower pool lock approach does not have a riverside eastern approach island or approach wall to protect you from the main dam's tailrace. If the river is running high, there's a sharp westerly set as you exit the lock.

South of the lock the watched channel swings from one riverbank to the other to miss rocky shoals. Keep in the channel as you approach Lock CC #1, **Mile CC-56.3 (SM).** Don't go over for a look at the dams; although the large eastern section is gated, the portion by the lock has an open crest that is difficult to see.

In Lock CC #1's lower pool you are on the canal's last reach; once clear of bridge BR C-2, you'll see Waterford's outskirts on the western bank. The Price Chopper supermarket in Troy is convenient; it's south of the Waterford Bridge on the eastern bank. There is a long floating dock behind the store.

Waterford is on the Erie Canal's northern shore. At Waterford Point, **Mile CC-59.4 W (SM),** a directional sign notes that you should bear west if planning to transit the Erie to Lake Ontario, Lake Erie, or Cayuga and Seneca lakes (see Region 2, beginning on page 60). If off to the sea, your route is south (see Region 1, beginning on page 22).

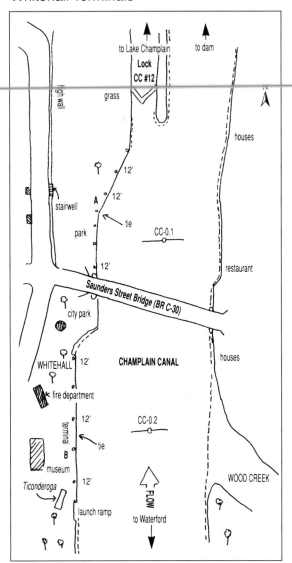

Whitehall Terminals

Sketch Map Depths

Sketch map depths are given at normal average summer canal pool level. When you venture outside the sketch map confines, you must adjust the NOAA chart to chart datum. For convenience in adjusting, use the following:

Mile CC-0.0 (SM) to **Mile CC-59.4 (SM):** Plane of reference, Normal Pool Level

WHITEHALL TERMINALS

★★★★   5

Chart: N 14786 page C-10

Mile CC-0.1 W (SM) and Mile CC-0.2 W (SM)

North Terminal (see A on sketch map): This west-bank downtown terminal is on the lock's southern approach wall just north of buff-colored Saunders Street Bridge (BR C-30). It's alongside a grassy park that rises abruptly to a high wall; access to downtown is up the stairwell.

South Terminal, Skenesborough Riverside Park (see B on sketch map): This west-bank terminal is south of the Saunders Street Bridge. It's on the Skenesborough Museum grounds. The museum is set back from the water's edge. There is a lawn and picnic tables. At one time 110-volt electric was available, but lately standards no longer function. Service may resume, so if you need a hookup give it a try.

About a block south is the village canal park. There are more picnic tables and grills as well as rest rooms, garbage bins, and a water faucet. The farmers' market is held in the park on Tuesdays from 10 to 1.

Both terminals are convenient to small shops and a hardware store. A laundromat is across the street from the north terminal; a few doors away is small Chase's market with a good selection of groceries, fresh meat, and ice. The post office and the Diner, a popular local café, are a few blocks away on the main highway.

A nearby mall on Highway 22 has a pharmacy, restaurants, another hardware store, and a Grand Union supermarket. To get there, walk south along the towpath road to Bridge C-29, then bear west over the railroad overpass to the first main street. Turn south again and the mall is nearly across the street.

Skenesborough Museum, on the south terminal waterfront, has exhibits concerning Whitehall's early history, including ship models, dolls, and military items. On the grounds is the hulk of the U.S.S. *Ticonderoga*, raised from Lake Champlain in 1958. The 1812 warship fought in the Battle of Plattsburgh. The museum is open

Monday through Saturday from 10 to 4 and Sunday from 12 to 4.

Whitehall is a designated State Urban Cultural Park. Its visitor information center is in the museum, so stop by for directions, brochures, and a local walking-tour map. Many downtown buildings are on the National Register of Historic Places.

This is a village of parks. Riverside Park, with an impressive veteran's monument overlooking the south terminal, is just south of the bridge. Concerts are usually held at the bandstand on summer weekends. On the canal's eastern bank is a ball diamond and basketball and tennis courts. Local baseball teams play most summer afternoons at about five o'clock.

Walk to the bridge over the lock and dam to see lockages, the dam, old lock buildings, Skene Mountain, and Lock CC #12's lower pool.

LOCK CC #9 UPPER

★★★★

Chart: N 14786 page C-7

Mile CC-15.8 E (SM)

This is a pretty stop out in the country, south of Lock CC #9. Contact the lockmaster; you need his permission to stay.

Since commercial traffic travels the canal at night, you must be safely out of the way. When you exit into the lock's upper pool, continue around the curving eastern approach wall. At the wall's end is a small dam runoff. It's well guarded by its own wall, so there's no danger of tumbling down into Wood Creek. Tie just north of the dam.

This is a showplace lock with immaculate grounds, lawns, and shade trees. It's an excellent place to watch passing canal traffic, lockages, and grazing rabbits.

Lock CC #9 Upper

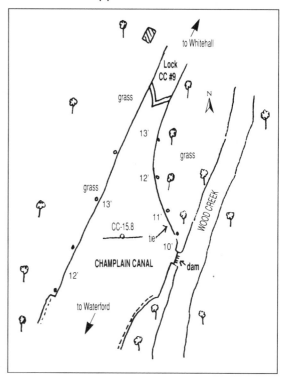

FORT EDWARD YACHT BASIN

★★★

Chart: N 14786 page C-6, *See sketch map, page 406*

Mile CC-23.7 + 0.8 W (SM)

This town terminal—72-hour time limit—is south of Lock CC #7 on a westerly secondary channel about 0.9 mile from the canal.

When you exit downbound at Lock CC #7, slow down, make an about-face in midcanal and orient yourself. The large landmass immediately north of the lock approach wall is Roger Island. About 100 feet southwest of the lock and west of the island, the unimproved Hudson River flows into the navigation channel. Your destination is on Roger Island's eastern side in a secondary channel whose entrance is not at first apparent;

Fort Edward Yacht Basin

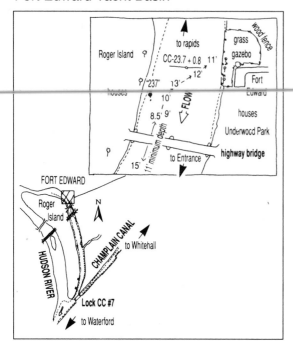

it's very narrow. To make the entry seem even more constricted, there may be barges stored by the island and lock wall. The secondary channel has very minimal current unless the river is running high.

The lock approach wall's northwestern side is the secondary channel's southeastern entry point. Don't wander over to the canal's far northwestern side for a better view of this entrance. If you get even slightly beyond the navigation channel limits you may bumble aground; shoaling extends well east of the island and river.

The secondary channel entrance has good depth, usually more than 15 feet, but you must hold close to the approach wall when you begin your entry. Once you start in and are alongside the wall, there are three buoys watching the secondary channel's first northerly turn. If barges are stored at the entrance, the buoys are often obscured. Past the three aids the channel widens, and more buoys show the way.

The terminal is 0.8 mile farther on, north of two bridges. The most shoal area is just north of the highway bridge. Give **Buoy #237** a fair berth, then begin to bear into the eastern-bank terminal; a sign notes that it's the yacht basin. Choose a spot—the best is by the tree—and parallel park.

Return to the canal the same way you came in. Do not attempt to round Roger Island's northern end and

return to the canal via the shoal, rock-strewn Hudson.

The town has provided a landscaped setting, water, electricity (110-volt), and picnic tables, but no garbage bins. Adjoining the terminal to the south is Underwood Park. If you need fuel, it's available back on the canal immediately south of the canal-river junction.

Downtown is convenient. Walk out the access road, or cut through Underwood Park, to Broadway, the first main street. A block south is the post office, shops, a restaurant, and a bank. The supermarket is about 1.5 miles away, but two convenience stores are very close by. One is about a quarter block west on Broadway; Stewarts, which is larger, is about two blocks away and has ice and a phone.

Moon Street—about a block east of the railroad bridge—puts you near the 1755 Fort Edward outworks northeastern bastion. The Old Fort House Museum at 29 Lower Broadway is open afternoons from 1 to 5. This was once the 1772 Smyth House; much of its wood came from Roger Island's old military hospital. The house was the American Revolutionary headquarters for American Generals Philip Schuyler, Benedict Arnold, and John Stark, as well as British General John Burgoyne. There are historical displays and exhibits, French and Indian artifacts, an old fort model, and a gallery.

About two blocks away, near the Stewarts convenience store, is Jane McCrea's house.

LOCK CC #5 UPPER

★★★ $\boxed{5}$

Chart: N 14786 page C-5, *See sketch map, page 407*

Mile CC-34.2 W (SM)

This stop is in Lock CC #5's upper pool on the western approach wall's western side in a small, partially enclosed basin. If you are southbound and did not tell Lock CC #6 you planned to stop, call Lock CC #5's lockmaster right away. Otherwise he may start lock preparations once you are in sight.

The basin, once part of the old canal, seems to shoal

Lock CC #5 Upper

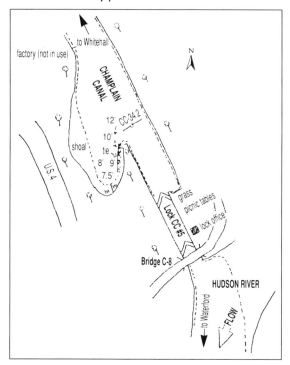

more each year, so sound carefully if you go to the wall's southern end.

The lock has pretty grounds and lawns. In early mornings and late afternoons it's a place for numerous browsing rabbits. On the lock island's eastern side are picnic tables and grills—walk across the lock gates. For a good view of the rapids and more hungry rabbits, walk north along the main road.

Schuylerville is about a mile south, a bit far to walk.

SCHUYLER YACHT BASIN

★★★★   5

ALL FACILITIES

Chart 14786 page C-4

Mile CC-35.5 + 0.1 W (SM)

This marina is in a back channel of the Hudson River portion that flows west of Bridge Island.

Make your approach south of the Schuylerville

Schuyler Yacht Basin

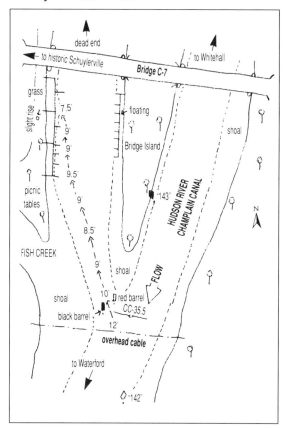

Bridge (BR C-7) but north of the overhead power cable just south of the island's southern end. This is also at the mouth of Fish Creek. The marina channel is south of a long shoal extending south of the island. Privately maintained red barrels and black barrels usually watch the entrance channel. Try to hold midway between them, because another shoal extends east off Fish Creek's mouth. If you draw 6 feet, you might want to call ahead before leaving the main river to ask about current depths.

The marina has two sections with slips at 90 degrees to the banks. The section along Bridge Island's western side is primarily for resident vessels. The rest of the marina is on the mainland's eastern shore. If no one answered on VHF 16, pull in to the fuel dock (gas only) about midway on the mainland section. If you draw more than 5.5 feet, approach cautiously; depth along the bulkhead may be risky. The office is at the head of the ramp. It has a few navigation supplies, charts, nautical clothing, picnic supplies, a book exchange, and a spot for making coffee and tea.

Block and cube ice and electric hookups (110-

volt/30- and 60-amp, and 220-volt/60- and 100-amp) are available. If you need a diver or repairs, check at the office. The marina's land line phone is (518) 695-3193.

The marina has pretty grounds with a lawn, shade trees, flowers, and a picnic area.

Downtown is convenient. Go out the marina access road and bear west. The post office is just after you cross the old Champlain Canal at the intersection of Highway 4. If you need groceries and supplies, make a turn south for a block and you'll find Sulli's Supermarket, a bank, and a few stores. If the walk to town or to the Saratoga Monument seems excessive, with advance notice the office may be able to rent you a courtesy car. There's also a taxi and car rental in town.

Schuylerville is proud of its historical past; note the life-size cutouts of Continental and British soldiers along the main street. On the way to the market you walk the Field of Grounded Arms. Here General Burgoyne consummated the articles of capitulation, and his army stacked their arms in surrender to General Horatio Gates.

At the corner by Sulli's make a westerly turn up McCoyne Avenue. Three blocks up the hill is 155-foot granite Saratoga Monument; its cornerstone was laid in 1877, 100 years after the surrender. There are four outside niches in the monument, with bronze statues commemorating the major American commanders of the Battles of Saratoga. Facing east toward his home is General Philip Schuyler; facing north is General Horatio Gates; and facing west is Colonel Daniel Morgan, Commander of the Rifle Corps. The empty fourth niche faces south. It's meant for Benedict Arnold, who fought so valiantly for the American cause at Saratoga. He became a traitor three years later, so his place on the monument was left vacant.

If you visit Saratoga Historical Park, you can also see another ironic tribute to Benedict Arnold. At the battle on Breymann's Hill, where he was shot in the left leg for the second time, is his monument: a granite boot, epaulets, and an inscription that notes his heroism, but neglects to mention his name.

South across Fish Creek on Highway 4 is the General Philip Schuyler House. The two-story white house with green shutters is beautifully restored to its 1787 appearance. The house originally was the country home of wealthy landowner Philip Schuyler. Its notable visitors included George Washington, Alexander Hamilton, and General Lafayette. General Burgoyne's invading army camped at the house not long before the battles at Saratoga. Catherine Schuyler, the General's wife, thwarted him by burning the ripening wheat fields behind the house. A few days before his surrender, Burgoyne burned the house so the Americans could not use it as a defense. Within a few weeks Schuyler began to build the house you see today.

Since you can rent a car in Schuylerville, this is a convenient place to visit the Saratoga National Historical Park. Though the park is open daily from 9 to 5, you may want to call (518) 664-9821 to verify schedules before driving the 8 miles. The visitor center has self-guided tours and theater programs.

Schuylerville is also your closest point from which to visit Saratoga Springs, about 10 miles west. This city was originally colonized after the Revolution, and its mineral springs soon made it a fashionable high-society spa. Today the town hosts Thoroughbred Racing in August and Harness Racing from April to November.

BEMIS HEIGHTS BEND ANCHORAGE

★★★

NO FACILITIES

Chart: N 14786 page C-3

Mile CC-44.5 E (SM)

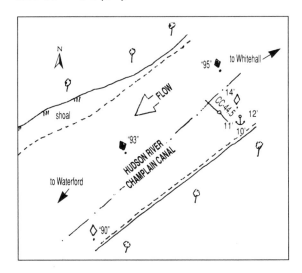

This anchorage is on the river's eastern side at **Buoy #92.** Stop here if you are delayed at a lock and prefer not to travel the river at night. Since the canal is used by commercial traffic, you must anchor so that there's no chance you might swing into the channel. The anchorage is on a long straightaway with a wooded shoreline, so you are at least visible to traffic approaching from both directions. Have a very bright anchor light.

Anchor as close to shore as depth permits east of **Buoy #92.** Let the buoy serve as your protective barrier; there's little chance a commercial vessel will pass on the wrong side of a navigational aid, or even come close to one. You will have a problem with severe pleasure craft wakes during daylight hours.

Bottom is mud, but sound for swinging-room depth. Generally you swing with river current.

Across the river's fringe of trees are the low bluffs of Bemis Heights, where Morgan's Rifle Corps were entrenched in 1777 awaiting General Burgoyne's oncoming army. Just north of the bend was one of the army's pontoon bridges, built for crossing the river with supplies.

MECHANICVILLE TERMINAL

Chart 14786 page C-2

Mile CC-50.7 W (SM)

This western-shore terminal is just south of Mechanicville Bridge (BR C-4A) and opposite **Buoy #64.** Anthony Kill, a small rivulet, enters the Hudson at the terminal wall's southern end. Some silt has built up east of its mouth, so make your approach from the main river about midterminal, heading into the current. The terminal wall is a bit rough, so get your fenders in place. If you want an electric hookup (110-volt) or drinking water, best tie-up is by one of the standards. If your preference is to tie at the wall's southern end, then once alongside move the boat back by hand as far as depth permits. In this spot watch for large carp basking in the clear, shoal water off Anthony Kill's small beach.

Downtown is convenient. Walk up the access road—Terminal Street—to the first main road. If you need groceries, bear north about two blocks, then west on Frances Street another block or two to reach a large

Mechanicville Terminal

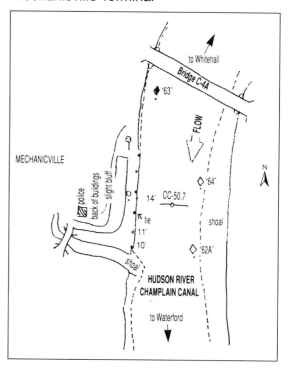

Price Chopper supermarket. Or you can turn north for about two blocks, then turn west on Park Avenue to a small midtown mall that has a Grand Union supermarket, a McDonald's, and a collection of stores.

LOCK 1 MARINA

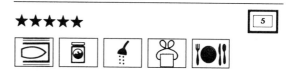

Chart: N 14786 page C-1, *See sketch map, page 410*

Mile CC-56.0 W (SM)

This western-bank marina—open May 1 to October 30—is in an enclosed basin about 0.5 mile above Lock CC #1. The entrance is about opposite **Buoy #28.** You can probably spot an old cannon and a gazebo on the basin's southern mole. If you draw more than 4.5 feet, you probably have too much draft for a visit inside the basin during normal pool; call the office on VHF 13 to ask about current depths. There may be a seasonal riverside float

Lock 1 Marina

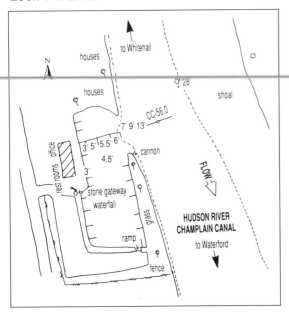

just south of the entrance; it usually has fair depth.

The basin's narrow entrance is at its northern end. Stay in midchannel during your entry and allow for southerly current set; there's no flow inside. If no one answered on VHF, there's usually an empty slip in front of the office; it's directly west of the entrance. Pull in, walk up, and check in.

Block and cube ice and electric hookups (110-volt/30-amp) are available. The ship's store has marine equipment, charts, and picnic supplies. The marina's land line number is (518) 427-6000.

This is an exceptionally clean, well-maintained marina. On the grounds are picturesque cannon, several bubbling fountains, flowers, stone archways dripping with cool water, picnic tables, masses of misty ferns, and tall shade trees. It's idyllic during the river's hot summer days.

Approximate Seasonal Opening and Closing Schedules

	OPEN	CLOSED
All opening/closing schedules are dependent on the severity of ice accumulation and breakup and the opening and closing of ice booms. Schedules may vary annually.		
The Hudson River	April 15	January 1
The New York State Barge Canal System	For updated information on canal operation and navigation, call (800) 422-1825.	
The Erie Canal East of Three Rivers, the Oswego Canal, and the Champlain Canal	May 6 to May 30 EDST (0700 to 2230)	November 27
The Erie Canal West of Three Rivers and the Cayuga and Seneca Canal	May 15 to May 30 EDST (0700 to 2230)	November 6
The Upper Niagara River and the Black Rock Canal	May 1	Mid-December to January 1
(The Upper Niagara River ice boom at Buffalo is removed between March 25 and March 30)		
East End Lake Erie	Mid-April to May 1	Mid-December to January 1
The Welland Canal	April 1	December 15
Lake Ontario	All year except near shore	Near shore from January 1
The Murray Canal	May 18	Mid-November to mid-December
The St. Lawrence Seaway and the St. Lawrence River (West of Sorel)	April 1	December 15
St-Ours Canal (Riviere Richelieu)	May 1 to mid-May	Mid-October
The Chambly Canal (Riviere Richelieu)	May 1 to mid-May	Mid-October
Lake Champlain	May 1 to May 15	January 1

APPENDIX 2
Metric Conversions

Canadian distances and speed limits are posted in kilometers. A kilometer is about 0.6 mile, and a mile is 1.6 km. To quickly find the approximate mile equivalent, drop the unit or right-hand digit of the kilometer number and multiply by 6. Example:

100 km/hr. = 10 x 6 = 60 mph
90 km/hr. = 9 x 6 = 54 mph

Note: The equivalents below have been rounded off; for example, we rounded off 1 pound to 450 grams. The exact equivalent is 453.6 grams.

Length
1 in. = 2.5 cm; 1 cm = 0.4 in.
1 ft. = 30 cm or 0.3 m; 1 m = 3.3 ft.
1 yd. = 90 cm or 0.9 m
1 statute mile = 1.6 km or 1600 m;
   1 km = 0.6 statute mile

Weight
1 oz. = 28 g; 1 g = 0.035 oz.
1 lb. = 450 g or 0.45 kg; 1 kg = 2.2 lb.

Volume
1 U.S. qt. = 0.95 liter; 1 liter = 1.06 U.S. qt.
1 U.S. gal. = 3.78 liter; 1 liter = 0.26 U.S. gal.

Temperature
Celsius to Fahrenheit:

C degrees x $\frac{9}{5}$ + 32 = F degrees

Fahrenheit to Celsius:

F degrees − 32 x $\frac{5}{9}$ = C degrees

Continuous Weather Reports

USA NOAA CONTINUOUS WEATHER

Place	Channel
New York	
New York	WX-1
Kingston	WX-3
Albany	WX-1
Syracuse	WX-1
Rochester	WX-2
Buffalo	WX-1
Vermont	
Burlington	WX-2

CANADIAN CONTINUOUS WEATHER

Place	Station	Reports on
Cardinal	CH 21B (VDQ)	Lake Ontario/St. Lawrence Seaway
Kingston	CH 83B (VDQ)	Lake Ontario/St. Lawrence Seaway
Cornwall	CH 83B (VDQ)	Lake Ontario/St. Lawrence Seaway
Toronto	CH 21B (VBG)	Lake Ontario
Cobourg	CH 21B (VBG)	Lake Ontario
Font Hill	CH 83B (VBG)	Lake Ontario
Montreal*	CH 21B/25B/83B (VFN)	St. Lawrence River
Quebec*	CH 21B (VCC)	St. Lawrence River

*Given in French followed by a short break—either music or static—then given in English.

A.M. WEATHER, a national weather service program of Maryland Public Television produced in cooperation with NOAA, is fed to the Westar IV satellite seven times each weekday morning. Coverage includes Canada. The program concentrates on satellite imagery sequences, national radar, chances of severe weather advisories, a national radar summary, current national weather maps, and 12-, 24-, 48-, and 72-hour forecast maps. There are also long-range temperature and moisture reports and severe weather watches, warnings, and advisories.

A.M. WEATHER

Station	Channel	Time*
New York		
Buffalo	WNED/17	6:45
Norwood	WNPI/18	6:45
Plattsburg	WCFE/57	6:45
Rochester	WXXI/21	6:45
Schenectady	WMHT/17	6:45
Syracuse	WCNY/24	6:45
Watertown	WNPE/16	6:45
Vermont		
Burlington	WETK/33	7:15
Rutland	WVER/28	7:15

*Morning only

Metric Conversions

Canadian distances and speed limits are posted in kilometers. A kilometer is about 0.6 mile, and a mile is 1.6 km. To quickly find the approximate mile equivalent, drop the unit or right-hand digit of the kilometer number and multiply by 6. Example:

$$100 \text{ km/hr.} = 10 \times 6 = 60 \text{ mph}$$
$$90 \text{ km/hr.} = 9 \times 6 = 54 \text{ mph}$$

Note: The equivalents below have been rounded off; for example, we rounded off 1 pound to 450 grams. The exact equivalent is 453.6 grams.

Length

1 in. = 2.5 cm; 1 cm = 0.4 in.
1 ft. = 30 cm or 0.3 m; 1 m = 3.3 ft.
1 yd. = 90 cm or 0.9 m
1 statute mile = 1.6 km or 1600 m;
    1 km = 0.6 statute mile

Weight

1 oz. = 28 g; 1 g = 0.035 oz.
1 lb. = 450 g or 0.45 kg; 1 kg = 2.2 lb.

Volume

1 U.S. qt. = 0.95 liter; 1 liter = 1.06 U.S. qt.
1 U.S. gal. = 3.78 liter; 1 liter = 0.26 U.S. gal.

Temperature

Celsius to Fahrenheit:

$$\text{C degrees} \times \tfrac{9}{5} + 32 = \text{F degrees}$$

Fahrenheit to Celsius:

$$\text{F degrees} - 32 \times \tfrac{5}{9} = \text{C degrees}$$

APPENDIX 3
Continuous Weather Reports

USA NOAA CONTINUOUS WEATHER

Place	Channel
New York	
New York	WX-1
Kingston	WX-3
Albany	WX-1
Syracuse	WX-1
Rochester	WX-2
Buffalo	WX-1
Vermont	
Burlington	WX-2

CANADIAN CONTINUOUS WEATHER

Place	Station	Reports on
Cardinal	CH 21B (VDQ)	Lake Ontario/St. Lawrence Seaway
Kingston	CH 83B (VDQ)	Lake Ontario/St. Lawrence Seaway
Cornwall	CH 83B (VDQ)	Lake Ontario/St. Lawrence Seaway
Toronto	CH 21B (VBG)	Lake Ontario
Cobourg	CH 21B (VBG)	Lake Ontario
Font Hill	CH 83B (VBG)	Lake Ontario
Montreal*	CH 21B/25B/83B (VFN)	St. Lawrence River
Quebec*	CH 21B (VCC)	St. Lawrence River

*Given in French followed by a short break—either music or static—then given in English.

A.M. WEATHER, a national weather service program of Maryland Public Television produced in cooperation with NOAA, is fed to the Westar IV satellite seven times each weekday morning. Coverage includes Canada. The program concentrates on satellite imagery sequences, national radar, chances of severe weather advisories, a national radar summary, current national weather maps, and 12-, 24-, 48-, and 72-hour forecast maps. There are also long-range temperature and moisture reports and severe weather watches, warnings, and advisories.

A.M. WEATHER

Station	Channel	Time*
New York		
Buffalo	WNED/17	6:45
Norwood	WNPI/18	6:45
Plattsburg	WCFE/57	6:45
Rochester	WXXI/21	6:45
Schenectady	WMHT/17	6:45
Syracuse	WCNY/24	6:45
Watertown	WNPE/16	6:45
Vermont		
Burlington	WETK/33	7:15
Rutland	WVER/28	7:15

*Morning only

A P P E N D I X 4
Marine Operators

VHF-FM frequencies are available through the United States Public Local Service Coast Stations and through Canadian Coast Guard radio stations with facilities for connecting ships to shore commercial telephone systems.

CALL	SERVICE AREA	CHANNEL	MARINE OPERATOR ID
New York and Vermont			
KEA	New York	25/26	New York Marine Operator
WHU 638	New York	86	Call sign
KIL 929	Ripley	84/86	Call sign
WHU 738	Staten Island	28	Call sign
WBL	Buffalo	28	Buffalo Marine Operator
KLU 788	Rochester	25	Rochester Channel 25
KGW 417	W. Beekmantown	28	Plattsburgh Marine Operator
KFL 993	Schenectady	26	Call sign
KLG 325	Fishkill	27	Call sign
KMP 846	Dryden	26	Call sign
KGW 418	Newark	28	Newark Marine Operator
KGW 416	Syracuse	25	Syracuse Marine Operator
KGW 415	Utica	28	Utica Marine Operator
N/A	Burlington	28	Burlington Marine Operator
Ontario and Quebec			
VBG	Fonthill	26/27/88	VBG Fonthill
VBG	Toronto	26/27/88	VBG Toronto
VBG	Cobourg	26/27/88	VBG Cobourg
VBG	Trafalgar	24	VBG Trafalgar
VDQ	Kingston	24/26/85	VDQ Kingston
VDQ	Cardinal	26/27/85	VDQ Cardinal
VDQ	Cornwall	26/27/85	VDQ Cornwall
VFN	Montreal	24/26/88	VFN Montreal
VCC	Quebec	24/26/21B	VCC Quebec

A P P E N D I X 5
Maintained Depth and Overhead Clearance Limitations

PLACE	LEAST DEPTH	REGIONAL CLEARANCE
Hudson River South of Albany	32.0 feet	132.0 feet
Hudson River North of Albany to Waterford	14.0 feet	20.0 feet*
Erie Canal East	13.0 feet	20.0 feet
Oswego Canal	13.0 feet	20.0 feet
Erie Canal West	12.0 feet	15.5 feet
Cayuga and Seneca Canal	12.0 feet	15.5 feet
Black Rock Canal	13.0 feet	149.0 feet
Welland Canal	27.0 feet	120.0 feet
Murray Canal	9.0 feet	N/A
St. Lawrence Seaway	26.0 feet	120.0 feet
Richelieu River	12.0 feet	29.0 feet*
Chambly Canal (lock sills)	6.5 feet	28.0 feet
Lake Champlain (the Elbow, Benson Landing)	10.6 feet	91.0 feet*
Champlain Canal	12.0 feet	15.5 feet

*Movable bridges in this system may require advance notice to open.

APPENDIX 6
Anchorages, Marinas, and Nonmarina Dockage by Mile

Place names in **boldface** type indicate marinas or dockage. Place names in standard type indicate anchorages. For each entry, the page number in standard type is the location of the text description for the marina, dockage, or anchorage. The page number in **boldface** type is the location of the associated sketch map.

A plus (+) symbol indicates dockage may be 1 to 18 miles away from route mileage.

Nonmarina dockage may require a fee.

Region 1
The Hudson River South

H-1.2 W (NM)
Newport Yacht Club and Marina	30	**30**

H-5.8 + 0.2 E (NM)
79th Street Anchorages	30	**31**

H-23.5 + 0.6 E (NM)
Tarrytown Marina	31	**32**

H-25.0 + 1.4 NW (NM)
Nyack Anchorage	33	**32**

H-27.0 + 1.0 W (NM)
Hook Mountain Anchorage	33	**32**

H-31.2 + 1.7 E (NM)
Croton Point Anchorage	33	**33**

H-33.5 + 0.5 W (NM)
Haverstraw Marina	34	**34**

H-35.2 + 0.3 E (NM)
Verplanck Anchorage	35	**34**

H-44.5 + 0.2 E (NM)
Garrison Landing Anchorage	35	**35**

H-46.8 + 0.2 E (NM)
Cold Spring Anchorage	35	**35**

H-56.0 + 0.3 E (NM)
Chelsea Low Point Anchorage	36	**36**

H-59.6 + 0.3 W (NM)
West Shore Marine	36	**37**

H-65.4 + 0.2 W (NM)
Mariner's Harbor	37	**37**

H-72.4 E (NM)
Poughkeepsie Yacht Club	37	**38**

H-79.0 + 1.2 W (NM)
Kingston City Dock	38	**39**

H-79.0 + 1.6 W (NM)
Rondout Yacht Basin	39	**39**

H-79.0 + 3.0 W (NM)
Eddyville Pond	40	**39**

The Hudson River North

H-88.0 + 0.3 W (NM)
Saugerties Marine	48	**48**

H-88.0 + 0.4 W (NM)
Saugerties Anchorage	48	**48**

H-88.0 + 0.7 W (NM)
Lynch's Marina	49	**48**

H-97.1 + 0.3 W (NM)
Riverview Marine Services	50	**49**

H-97.1 + 0.6 W (NM)
Catskill Marina	50	**49**

H-100.6 + 0.5 W (NM)
Athens Anchorage	50	**51**

H-101.4 E (NM)
Hudson Power Boat Club	52	**51**

H-104.8 + 0.4 E (NM)
Stockport Middle Ground Anchorage	52	**51**

H-108.6 + 0.3 SW (NM)
Coxsackie Anchorage	54	**53**

H-108.6 + 0.5 SW (NM)
Coxsackie Yacht Club	54	**53**

H-111.6 + 0.4 E (NM)
Houghtaling Island South Anchorage	54	**53**

H-113.3 W (NM)
Shady Harbor Marina	55	**55**

H-114.3 + 0.4 W (NM) or H-115.0 + 0.2 W (NM)
Coeyman's Landing	56	**55**

H-124.9 E (NM)
Albany Yacht Club	56	**56**

H-132.4 + 0.3 W (NM) or H-133.0 + 0.3 W (NM)
Van Schaick Island Marina (Cohoes)	57	**57**

Region 2
The Erie Canal East

E-0.2 N (SM)
Button Park	71	**71**

Region 5

The Thousand Islands

*The Seaway Channel
(Tibbetts Point to Ironsides Island)*

*The Canadian Middle Channel (Kingston
to Thousand Islands Bridge)*

The Bateau Channel (Secondary Channel)

The Admiralty Channel (Secondary Channel)

ADM-6.4 + 0.1 (NM)
Aubrey Island Northeast   285 **285**
ADM-6.0 + 0.3 (NM)
Beaurivage Island Southwest   287 **286**
ADM-5.6 + 0.2 (NM)
Beaurivage Island Northeast   287 **286**
ADM-5.6 + 0.1 (NM)
Beaurivage Anchorage   287 **286**
ADM-4.2 + 0.2 (NM)
Gananoque Municipal Marina   288 **288**
MDCH-14.5 + 0.1 (NM)
Leek Island   289 **289**

The Lake Fleet Islands (Secondary Channel)

MDCH-12.1 + 0.4 (NM)
Camelot Island East   290 **290**
MDCH-12.1 + 0.5 (NM)
Camelot Island South   291 **290**
MDCH-12.1 + 0.6 (NM)
Camelot Island Southwest   291 **290**
MDCH-12.3 + 0.1 (NM)
Camelot Island North   291 **290**
MDCH-12.1 + 0.65 (NM)
Endymion Island South   292 **292**
MDCH-12.1 + 1.0 (NM)
Endymion Island East   293 **292**

The Canadian Middle Channel
(Thousand Islands Bridge to Ironsides Island)

MDCH-5.9 (NM)
Georgina Island West   294 **294**
MDCH-5.7 (NM)
Georgina Island East   295 **294**
MDCH-3.8 + 0.5 (NM)
Ed Huck Marine (Rockport)   295 **295**
MDCH-2.5 + 0.2 (NM)
Grenadier Island West   296 **296**

The Eastern Seaway Channel
(Ironsides Island to Morristown)

SW-130.7 + 0.5 (NM)
Adelaide Island   297 **297**
SW-119.8 + 0.2 (NM)
Brockville Municipal Harbour   297 **298**
SW-118.7 + 0.7 (NM)
Wright's Marina   299 **299**
SW-118.7 + 0.7 (NM)
Morristown Village Dock   299 **299**

The St. Lawrence Seaway
(Morristown to Montreal) and the Upper
St. Lawrence River (Montreal to Sorel)

SW-109.3 + 0.7 S (NM)
Ogdensburg Municipal Marina   317 **317**
SW-109.3 + 0.3 (NM)
Prescott Harbour   318 **318**
SW-87.3 + 2.1 (NM)
Coles Creek State Park Marina   319 **319**
SW-86.4 + 0.5 N (NM)
Crysler Park Marina   320 **320**
SW-78.0 + 3.7 (NM)
Barnhart Island Marina   320 **321**
SW-44.0 + 2.3 N (NM)
Coteau-Landing   321 **322**
SW-19.0 + 3.7 (NM)
Royal St. Lawrence Yacht Club   322 **323**
SLR-136.1 + 0.3 E (NM)
Port de Plaisance   324 **324**
SLR-119.4 + 0.6 W (NM)
Ile aux Prunes Anchorage   325 **325**
SLR-99.3 + 0.5 (NM)
Parc Nautique Federal   326 **326**
SLR-99.3 + 0.5 (NM)
Parc Nautique de Sorel   327 **327**

Region 6
Riviere Richelieu and the Chambly Canal

RC-10.7 E (NM)
St-Ours Public Dock   338 **338**
RC-12.1 E (NM)
St-Ours Lock   338 **338**
RC-17.6 W (NM)
St-Antoine Public Dock   339 **339**
RC-23.2 E (NM)
St-Charles Docks   339 **339**
RC-25.3 + 0.3 E (NM)
Ile de Jeannotte Anchorage   340 **340**
RC-31.5 W (NM)
Marina de Phare de Beloeil   340 **341**
RC-39.35 E (NM)
Marina de Chambly   341 **342**
RC-39.58 W (NM)
Lock CHM #3 Upper   342 **342**
RC-40.8 E (NM)
Lock CHM #8 Upper   343 **343**
RC-42.6 W (NM)
Pont #7 Swing Bridge North   343 **343**

APPENDIX 7
Alphabetical Listing of Anchorages, Marinas, and Nonmarina Dockage

Place names in **boldface** type indicate marinas or dockage. Places names in standard type indicate anchorages. For each entry, the page number in standard type is the location of the text description for the marina, dockage, or anchorage. The page number in **boldface** type is the location of the associated sketch map.

A plus (+) symbol indicates dockage may be 1 to 18 miles away from route mileage.

Nonmarina dockage may require a fee.

Brockville Municipal Harbour	SW-119.8 + 0.2 (Region 5)	297	**298**
Bronte Harbour	CONT-40.3 (Region 4)	230	**231**
Burlington Harbor Anchorage	CH-37.0 + 8.0 E (Region 6)	380	**381**
Burton Island State Park	CH-18.0 + 10.0 E (Region 6)	369	**369**
Butler Island Anchorage	CH-18.0 + 10.8 E/N (Region 6)	368	**369**
Button Park	E-0.2 N (Region 2)	71	**71**
Camelot Island East	MDCH-12.1 + 0.4 (Region 5)	290	**290**
Camelot Island North	MDCH-12.3 + 0.1 (Region 5)	291	**290**
Camelot Island South	MDCH-12.1 + 0.5 (Region 5)	291	**290**
Camelot Island Southwest	MDCH-12.1 + 0.6 (Region 5)	291	**290**
Canajoharie Terminal	E-59.9 S (Region 2)	82	**82**
Canalview Marina	OS-11.9 E (Region 2)	104	**103**
Cape Vincent Achorages	SW-161.0 + 0.3 (Region 5)	271	**270**
Cape Vincent Breakwater	SW-161.0 + 0.3 (Region 5)	271	**270**
Cape Vincent Fisheries Station	SW-161.0 + 0.3 (Region 5)	271	**270**
Cape Vincent Village Dock	SW-161.0 + 0.3 (Region 5)	271	**270**
Captain Jeff's Marina	E-264.6 S (Region 2)	128	**128**
Catskill Marina	H-97.1 + 0.6 W (Region 1)	50	**49**
Cayuga Anchorage	LKCAY-1.9 E (Region 2)	150	**151**
Cedar Island Anchorage	CH-52.0 + 1.7 E (Region 6)	386	**386**
Cedar Island Mid-Island	MDCH-28.7 + 0.3 (Region 5)	280	**279**
Cedar Island Northeast	MDCH-28.7 + 0.4 (Region 5)	280	**279**
Chelsea Low Point Anchorage	H-56.0 + 0.3 E (Region 1)	36	**36**
Chimney Point Anchorage	CH-71.1 E (Region 6)	393	**393**
Chinook Harbor Marina	AONT-107.6 + 2.0 (Region 4)	207	**205**
Chipman Point Marina	CH-87.8 E (Region 6)	395	**395**
Clayton Anchorage	SW-147.0 + 0.5 (Region 5)	273	**272**
Clayton Municipal Dock	SW-147.0 + 0.6 (Region 5)	272	**272**
Cobourg Heritage Harbour	CONT-117.6 (Region 4)	240	**240**
Coeyman's Landing	H-114.3 + 0.4 W or H-115.0 + 0.2 W (Region 1)	56	**55**
Cold Spring Anchorage	H-46.8 + 0.2 E (Region 1)	35	**35**
Cole Bay Northeast Anchorage	CH-63.0 + 1.2 W (Region 6)	391	**391**
Cole Bay Southwest Anchorage	CH-63.0 + 1.2 W (Region 6)	391	**391**
Coles Creek State Park Marina	SW-87.3 + 2.1 (Region 5)	319	**319**
Confederation Basin	MDCH-29.5 + 0.8 (Region 5)	278	**278**
Confederation Basin Anchorage	MDCH-29.5 + 0.8 (Region 5)	279	**278**
Converse Bay Northeast Anchorage	CH-52.0 + 2.0 E (Region 6)	386	**386**
Cooper's Marina	E-172.4 N (Region 2)	121	**121**
Coteau-Landing	SW-44.0 + 2.3 N (Region 5)	321	**322**
Coxsackie Anchorage	H-108.6 + 0.3 SW (Region 1)	54	**53**
Coxsackie Yacht Club	H-108.6 + 0.5 SW (Region 1)	54	**53**
Crescent Boat Club	E-5.4 + 0.2 W (Region 2)	74	**73**
Crescent Terminal	E-4.2 + 0.1 N (Region 2)	73	**73**
Crescent Yacht Club	AONT-140.0 + 24.0 (Region 4)	211	**212**
Cross Lake South Anchorages	E-182.6 + 0.1 E (Region 2)	122	**122**
Croton Point Anchorage	H-31.2 + 1.7 E (Region 1)	33	**33**
Crysler Park Marina	SW-86.4 + 0.5 (Region 5)	320	**320**
Deep Bay Anchorage	CH-18.0 + 1.5 W/N (Region 6)	366	**367**
Diamond Reef Anchorage	E-5.7 + 0.2 E (Region 2)	74	**73**
Eagle Harbor Terminal	E-291.6 N (Region 2)	132	**132**
Ed Huck Marine (Rockport)	MDCH-3.8 + 0.5 (Region 5)	295	**295**
Eddyville Pond	H-79.0 + 3.0 W (Region 1)	40	**39**

Kingston City Dock	H-79.0 + 1.2 W (Region 1)	38	**39**
Knowlesville Terminal	E-294.5 S (Region 2)	132	**132**
Lakefront Promenade Park Marina	CONT-52.5 (Region 4)	234	**234**
Lansing Town Park Marina	LKCAY-30.4 E (Region 2)	152	**151**
LaSalle Park Anchorage	CONT-34.3 + 2.4 (Region 4)	230	**230**
Le Nautique St-Jean	RC-49.64 W (Region 6)	345	**345**
Leek Island	MDCH-14.5 + 0.1 (Region 5)	289	**289**
Lindsay Island Southwest Anchorage	ADM-6.4 + 0.7 NE (Region 5)	284	**284**
Little Falls Upper	E-79.7 S (Region 2)	84	**84**
Lock 1 Marina	CC-56.0 W (Region 6)	409	**410**
Lock CC #5 Upper	CC-34.2 W (Region 6)	406	**407**
Lock CC #9 Upper	CC-15.8 E (Region 6)	405	**405**
Lock CHM #3 Upper	RC-39.58 W (Region 6)	342	**342**
Lock CHM #8 Upper	RC-40.8 E (Region 6)	343	**343**
Lock E #10 Lower	E-34.5 S (Region 2)	76	**76**
Lock E #11 Upper	E-38.8 N (Region 2)	78	**77**
Lock E #12 Upper	E-43.1 N (Region 2)	79	**79**
Lock E #14 Upper	E-60.5 N (Region 2)	83	**82**
Lock E #20 Upper	E-105.0 N/S (Region 2)	88	**89**
Lock E #23 Lower	E-153.2 S (Region 2)	94	**94**
Lock E #25 Upper	E-202.1 N (Region 2)	123	**123**
Lock E #27 Upper	E-220.1 N (Region 2)	123	**124**
Lock E #28A Upper	E-221.4 N (Region 2)	125	**124**
Lock E #29 Upper	E-234.8 S (Region 2)	126	**126**
Lock E #3 Upper Terminal	E-1.0 W (Region 2)	72	**71**
Lock E #30 Upper	E-237.3 N/S (Region 2)	126	**126**
Lock E #7 Upper	E-12.8 S (Region 2)	74	**74**
Lock E #8 Upper Island Anchorage	E-24.0 + 0.2 N (Region 2)	75	**75**
Lock E #9 Upper	E-28.7 N (Region 2)	75	**76**
Lock OS #8 Upper	OS-23.0 E (Region 2)	106	**105**
Lock SEN #1 Lower	SEN-3.9 E (Region 2)	142	**142**
Lock SEN #1 Upper	SEN-4.0 E (Region 2)	143	**142**
Long Point Anchorage	LKCAY-15.5 E (Region 2)	152	**151**
Long Point State Park Anchorage	AONT-140.0 + 22.3 (Region 4)	211	**211**
Lower James Street Dock	SW-137.6 + 0.3 (Region 5)	275	**274**
Lynch's Marina	H-88.0 W + 0.7 W (Region 1)	49	**48**
Malletts Bay Anchorage	CH-30.0 + 11.0 E (Region 6)	377	**377**
Malletts Bay Marina	CH-30.0 + 12.5 E (Region 6)	378	**378**
Marcy Marina	E-103.7 N (Region 2)	88	**88**
Marina de Chambly	RC-39.35 E (Region 6)	341	**342**
Marina de Phare de Beloeil	RC-31.5 W (Region 6)	340	**341**
Marina Gagnon et Fils	RC-58.47 + 1.8 W (Region 6)	346	**346**
Marina Internationale	CH-12.5 + 3.7 E/S (Region 6)	364	**364**
Mariner's Harbor	H-65.4 + 0.2 W (Region 1)	37	**37**
Market Square Dock	AONT-140.0 + 19.6 (Region 4)	210	**210**
McDonough Marina	AONT-15.9 + 0.2 (Region 4)	200	**199**
Meadow Cove Anchorage	AONT-107.6 + 1.7 (Region 4)	206	**205**
Mechanicville Terminal	CC-50.7 W (Region 6)	409	**409**
Medina Park and Marina	E-298.6 S (Region 2)	132	**132**
Mermaid Island	ADM-6.5 + 0.1 (Region 5)	283	**283**
Middle Bay Anchorage	CH-18.0 + 1.5 W/N (Region 6)	367	**367**
Middleport Terminal	E-303.6 S (Region 2)	133	**133**
Millers Marina	E-220.4 N (Region 2)	124	**124**

Ram Island Anchorage	CONT-179.8 + 3.3 (Region 4)	246	**247**
RCR Yachts	UNR/LE-11.2 + 0.8 (Region 3)	170	**171**
RCR Yachts	AONT-140.0 + 19.0 (Region 4)	208	**208**
Remar Shipyard	SW-147.0 + 0.7 (Region 5)	273	**272**
Riverview Marine Services	H-97.1 + 0.3 W (Region 1)	50	**49**
Riverview Trail Terminal	E-333.0 S (Region 2)	137	**136**
Robb Island Anchorage	E-39.5 + 0.2 N (Region 2)	78	**77**
Rome Terminal	E-114.5 N (Region 2)	89	**89**
Rondout Yacht Basin	H-79.0 + 1.6 W (Region 1)	39	**39**
Rouses Point Public Dock and Anchorage	CH-0.5 + 0.4 W (Region 6)	361	**360**
Royal St. Lawrence Yacht Club	SW-19.0 + 3.7 (Region 5)	322	**323**
Sandy Cove Anchorage	CONT-163.0 + 0.5 (Region 4)	245	**245**
Saugerties Anchorage	H-88.0 W + 0.4 W (Region 1)	48	**48**
Saugerties Marine	H-88.0 W + 0.3 W (Region 1)	48	**48**
Schoharie Crossing Anchorage	E-43.4 S + 0.1 S (Region 2)	80	**79**
Schuyler Yacht Basin	CC-35.5 + 0.1 W (Region 6)	407	**407**
Seneca Falls Terminal	SEN-8.5 N (Region 2)	143	**143**
Seneca Lake State Park Marina	SEN-16.8 W (Region 2)	144	**144**
Seneca Marine Mart	SEN-16.8 E (Region 2)	145	**144**
Shady Harbor Marina	H-113.3 W (Region 1)	55	**55**
Shelburne Shipyard, Inc. (Shelburne Bay)	CH-37.0 + 10.4 E/S (Region 6)	381	**381**
Shumway Marine	AONT-67.6 + 0.8 (Region 4)	202	**202**
Sills Marina	AONT-95.2 + 1.6 (Region 4)	204	**203**
Skinners Harbour	E-128.7 N (Region 2)	91	**90**
Sloop Cove (Valcour Island East)	CH-26.5 + 2.3 E/S or CH-29.3 + 2.3 E/N (Region 6)	376	**376**
Smuggler Harbor (Valcour Island East)	CH-29.3 + 2.0 E/N (Region 6)	375	**375**
Snowshoe Bay Anchorage	AONT-140.0 + 18.2 (Region 4)	209	**208**
Snug Harbor Marina at Monty Bay	CH-12.1 + 1.5 W (Region 6)	362	**362**
Snug Harbor Marina at Valcour	CH-27.8 + 0.5 W (Region 6)	373	**373**
Sodus Bay Anchorages	AONT-95.2 + 1.2 (Region 4)	204	**203**
Sodus Bay Marina	AONT-95.2 + 1.2 (Region 4)	204	**203**
Spencerport Towpath Park	E-268.1 N (Region 2)	129	**129**
Spoon Bay (Valcour Island East)	CH-26.5 + 2.1 E/S (Region 6)	376	**376**
St. Albans Bay Anchorage	CH-18.0 + 14.5 E (Region 6)	370	**370**
St. Catherines Marina	WEL-0.0 + 1.4 E (Region 3)	184	**184**
St. Johnsville Municipal Marina	E-69.0 N (Region 2)	84	**84**
St-Antoine Public Dock	RC-17.6 W (Region 6)	339	**339**
St-Charles Docks	RC-23.2 E (Region 6)	339	**339**
St-Jean Public Dock	RC-49.5 W (Region 6)	345	**345**
St-Ours Lock	RC-12.1 E (Region 6)	338	**338**
St-Ours Public Dock	RC-10.7 E (Region 6)	338	**338**
State Ditch Cut South Anchorage	E-180.6 + 0.1 S (Region 2)	121	**121**
Stockport Middle Ground Anchorage	H-104.8 + 0.4 E (Region 1)	52	**51**
Stony Point Anchorage North	CH-1.8 W (Region 6)	361	**361**
Stony Point Anchorage South	CH-1.8 W (Region 6)	362	**361**
Sugerloaf Harbour Marina	WEL-23.0 + 0.4 W (Region 3)	182	**182**
Sugarloaf Marina Annex (Municipal Boat Docks)	WEL-21.9 (Region 3)	183	**183**
Sylvan Beach Terminal	E-128.8 N (Region 2)	91	**90**
Tarrytown Marina	H-23.5 + 0.6 E (Region 1)	31	**32**